Women in America

FROM COLONIAL TIMES TO THE 20TH CENTURY

Women in America

FROM COLONIAL TIMES TO THE 20TH CENTURY

Advisory Editors
LEON STEIN
ANNETTE K. BAXTER

A Note About This Volume

In this book, Ishbel Ross demolishes the idea that the city room of a newspaper is no place for a lady. In sweeping style it picks up the story of the newspaperwoman in colonial times and carries it with color and excitement through war and peace, in cities, towns, on frontiers and around the world into the times of woman's suffrage, the sob sister and the age of the metropolitan tabloid. "Miss Ross not only covers the various fields of news and news-feature writing but also introduces columnists, fashion experts and other specialists and concludes with chapters on the newspaper woven of different sections of the country," Katherine Woods wrote in *The New York Times*. "This is obviously encyclopedic and the product of the most amazing research. It is difficult to see how such a pioneer work as this, in so broad a subject, could have been done with more sustained interest and vitality."

LADIES OF
THE PRESS

ISHBEL ROSS

ARNO PRESS
A New York Times Company
NEW YORK – 1974

Reprint Edition 1974 by Arno Press Inc.

WOMEN IN AMERICA
From Colonial Times to the 20th Century
ISBN for complete set: 0-405-06070-X
See last pages of this volume for titles.

Manufactured in the United States of America

Library of Congress Cataloging in Publication Data

Ross, Ishbel, 1897-
  Ladies of the press.

  (Women in America: from colonial times to the 20th
century)
  Reprint of the ed. published by Harper, New York.
  1. Women journalists--United States. 2. Journalism
--United States. I. Title. II. Series.
PN4872.R7 1974   070.4'092'2   74-3972
ISBN 0-405-06120-X

LADIES OF THE PRESS

1. Margaret Fuller
2. Victoria Claflin Woodhull
3. Jane Swisshelm
   Courtesy of Minnesota Historical Society
4. Nancy Cummings Johnson
5. Kate Field
6. Grace Greenwood
7. Jenny June
8. Helen Rogers Reid
   Photograph by Ira L. Hill's Studio, New York City
9. Julia Harpman
   Courtesy of George Maillard Kesslere, B.P.
10. Anne O'Hare McCormick
    Courtesy of The New York Times Studio
11. Lorena Hickok
12. Elenore Kellogg
13. Eleanor Medill Patterson
    Photograph by Bachrach
14. Julia McCarthy
15. Genevieve Forbes Herrick
    Photograph by Bachrach
16. Grace Robinson
17. Ruth Finney
    Photograph by Harris & Ewing
18. Dorothy Thompson
    Courtesy of Eve Harrison, New York

19. Emma Bugbee
20. Imogene Stanley
    Photograph by Alfred Cheney Johnston
21. Geraldine Sartain
22. Alice Hughes
23. Mary Margaret McBride
24. Dorothy Ducas
25. Evelyn Seeley
26. Irene Kuhn
    Photograph by Hal Phyfe
27. Rachel K. McDowell
    Courtesy of The New York Times Studio
28. Dorothy Kilgallen
29. Helen Worden
    Photograph by Ray Lee Jackson, N.B.C. Studio
30. Dorothy Dix
    Courtesy of "International Newsreel"
31. Cora Rigby
32. Ada Patterson
    Portrait by Edward Thayer Monroe
33. Zoë Beckley
    Courtesy of "Foto Topics, inc."
34. Jane Dixon
35. Nixola Greeley-Smith
36. Helen Rowland
    Courtesy of Hal Phyfe
37. Winifred Black
38. Winona Wilcox Payne
39. Marguerite Mooers Marshall
40. Rheta Childe Dorr

For list of names see next page

For list of names see previous page

LADIES OF THE PRESS

"NELLIE · BLY."

The New York WORLD'S Correspondent,
who Placed a Girdle Round the Earth in 72 Days, 6 Hours, and 11 Minutes.

LADIES OF
THE PRESS

The Story of Women in Journalism by an Insider

ISHBEL ROSS

HARPER & BROTHERS *Publishers*

NEW YORK *and* LONDON 1936

To all the newspaper women who have contributed
so generously to this book

CONTENTS

PART ONE

I.	Front-Page Girl	1
II.	Stepping Out	14
III.	A Scold, a Siren and a Star	27
IV.	Hearts and Roses	39
V.	Nellie Bly	48
VI.	The First Sob Sisters	60
VII.	The Love Forum	74
VIII.	Horace Greeley's Granddaughter	86
IX.	The Ladies Travel	97
X.	The Crusading Spirit	109
XI.	War and Suffrage	119

PART TWO

XII.	In Command	135
XIII.	The New York Times	145
XIV.	Under the Gold Dome	165
XV.	Down by the River	180
XVI.	Two Aces	191
XVII.	Catching the Wire	203
XVIII.	The Earth Rocks	216
XIX.	The Ladies Have Adventures	225
XX.	Through Prison Walls	240
XXI.	On the Air	254
XXII.	Enter the Tabloids	261
XXIII.	The Tabloids Flourish	281

PART THREE

XXIV.	Covering the President's Wife	309
XXV.	Invading the Press Gallery	323
XXVI.	The Press Gallery Today	339

XXVII. *Debunking Capitol Hill*   350

XXVIII. *Foreign Correspondence*   360

XXIX. *The Woman Columnist*   379

XXX. *In the Field of Review*   399

XXXI. *In Black and White*   416

XXXII. *The Woman's Page*   425

XXXIII. *The Society Page*   441

XXXIV. *Country Journalism*   458

XXXV. *The Field Widens*   465

PART FOUR

XXXVI. *Boston*   481

XXXVII. *Baltimore*   493

XXXVIII. *Washington*   501

XXXIX. *Philadelphia*   511

XL. *Buffalo and Points North*   521

XLI. *Detroit*   532

XLII. *Chicago*   539

XLIII. *The Middle West*   552

XLIV. *Denver and Kansas City*   562

XLV. *California*   576

XLVI. *The South*   591

AUTHOR'S FOREWORD

IT WOULD be impossible to do full credit in the compass of one book to the history, efforts and accomplishments of all the newspaper women who have made their way on American newspapers, in face of opposition and prejudice. I have attempted to cover the field as broadly as possible, but regret the unavoidable omission of women whose names should be part of this history. I am deeply indebted to the scores of newspaper women in all parts of the country who have taken time to supply me with data which could only have been obtained through their coöperation. In addition to this original material I have freely used the newspaper files of the past and present, the magazines of five decades and such specialized publications as *Editor and Publisher* and *The Matrix*.

I am specially indebted to Stanley Walker, who suggested the book and the title; to Arthur J. Larsen, Minnesota Historical Society; Dr. Ralph D. Casey, University of Minnesota; Valta Parma, Library of Congress; Dorothy Dix, Genevieve Forbes Herrick, Ada Patterson, Mary Humphrey, Harry Payne Burton, Mrs. Fremont Older, Louise Dooly, Mary King, Frances Whiting, Mrs. Louis F. Geissler, Zoë Beckley, Marguerite Mooers Marshall, Bessie Marquis James, Julia McCarthy, Mrs. Marshall L. Darrach, Hettie F. Cattell, Marlen E. Pew, Fay King, Clare Shipman, Countess Morner, Winifred Mallon, Ruth Reynolds, Kathleen McLaughlin, Mildred Burke, Mary Weyer, Bess Furman, Helen Worden, Alice Hughes, Leland Stowe, Mary E. Prim, Kay Phelps, Grace Phelps, A. J. Montgomery, Mrs. Walter Huber, Dorothy Ducas, May Stanley, Zelda Branch, Emma Bugbee, May Schupack, Mary Dougherty, Joe Mulvaney, Adelaide Kerr, Frances Wayne, Clark Howell, Ward Morehouse, Mrs. Frances Parkinson Keyes, Mrs. Ralph Tennal, Geraldine Sartain, Evelyn Seeley, Josephine Lantz, Louise Malloy, Miriam Teichner, Alice Fox Pitts, Julia Harpman, Margaret Williamson and Robert Carse. No one was more helpful in the preparation of this book than the late Dr. Willard Grosvenor Bleyer, of the University of Wisconsin.

The books consulted were the *History of New England Woman's Press Association* by M. B. Lord, *Memoirs of Jane Cunningham Croly*, *The Boston Transcript* by Joseph Edgar Chamberlain, *Pio-*

neer Women Newspaper Writers in the United States, a thesis by Sarah Amelia Spensley, *Anne Royall* by Sarah Harvey Porter, *The Life and Times of Anne Royall, The Terrible Siren*, by Emanie Sachs, *Forgotten Ladies*, by Richardson Wright, *A Woman of Fifty* by Rheta Childe Dorr, *Red Heart of Russia* by Bessie Beatty, *Hawaiian Nei* by Mabel Craft Deering, *Main Currents in the History of American Journalism* by Willard Grosvenor Bleyer, *Around Manhattan's Rim* by Helen Worden, *Writing and Editing for Women* by Ethel M. Colson Brazelton, *Women in Journalism* by Mrs. Genevieve Boughner and *Timberline* by Gene Fowler.

I. R.

FOREWORD

by Stanley Walker

Author of "City Editor," "Mrs. Astor's Horse"
Former City Editor of The New York *Herald Tribune*

FROM the first, the woman who sought to make a place for herself in newspaper work has found editors prejudiced against her. Now, this prejudice is not so great as it was, but it still exists, and there are several reasons for it. Men are afraid of women, afraid and suspicious, for their dealings with this curious sex have taught them caution and skepticism. Another reason (there is no sense at this late day of putting on a bogus show of gallantry): A great many of the girls who have managed to get on newspaper payrolls have been slovenly, incompetent vixens, adepts at office politics, show-offs of the worst sort, and inclined to take advantage of their male colleagues. They have protested that they wanted to do a man's work, to be treated as men, but soon or later some situation would arise in which all these high-minded declarations of purpose were revealed as so much nonsense. These inferior members of an often admirable sex have done a great disservice to their sensible, straightforward sisters—the women who would be ornaments to journalism if they had only had a chance. By and large, it seems to me that the men in newspaper work have been uniformly friendly, sometimes extremely helpful, to their women co-workers, even to the point of changing typewriter ribbons for them—a simple task at which the female ingenuity appears invariably to bog down.

I suppose every newspaper man has his pet newspaper woman, one almost perfect practitioner of the lovely art of getting facts and writing about them. Of such a woman, the man will say: "Yes, I know it's true that, in general, women can be a good deal of a nuisance around a newspaper office, but this one was different." It is no secret that, around New York in the romantic 1920's, the particular favorite not only of myself but of many other newspaper men who admired unflustered competence was Miss Ishbel Ross, author of this friendly history of the ups and downs of women in journalism. True, there were many other good ones, but somehow

Miss Ross, with her lack of giddiness, her clear and forthright mind, her amazing and unfailing stamina on the toughest assignments, and her calm judgment, seemed to come closer than any of the others to the man's idea of what a newspaper woman should be. She could, as nearly as that can be said of anyone, handle any sort of assignment superbly. She was born in Scotland, worked in Canada for a time, and came to New York in 1919 to work for the old *Tribune*. For more than a decade, reporting for the *Tribune* and the combined flower, the *Herald Tribune*, she made a reputation for herself that many of us will still be mumbling about when, as ancient gaffers, we try to recall old times while sitting around spending our old age pensions and waiting for that evening sun to go down. She finally quit to write novels and have a baby, but when she was doing her stuff she was, in a word, good. A constant seeker for perfection in women, I could detect only two mild flaws in her during my entire association with her: (1) she was inclined to regard life as a fairly serious business, and never laughed enough, and (2) she was lacking in venom. But this, of course, is captious.

In this chronicle of the glories of newspaper women, Miss Ross deals with the life stories of some magnificent women, as well of some about whom the less said the better. God knows how many young women there are in America who would prefer, above everything else on earth, to get a chance on a newspaper. Probably the number runs into the tens of thousands. And very few of them, more's the pity, will ever get a chance. The field is crowded—perhaps more crowded than it ever was—and the preference somehow still seems to be for men. But if a young woman wants to find out what the work is like, and how many strange aspects it may have, and what a newspaper career really is, she can find the answers in this book. It will be pointed out that Miss Ross makes the life of a newspaper woman appear somewhat romantic and exciting. Well, what is wrong with that? For, say what you will, it is exciting, and the woman, or the man, who doesn't feel that way about it doesn't belong in the business. But the drudgery is there too, and the heartbreak, and there's no use trying to laugh that off either. I suppose, as in the case of a man, it all depends on the character and the equipment of the woman—that, and the breaks of the game.

PART ONE

Chapter 1

FRONT-PAGE GIRL

FIVE YEARS AFTER THE CIVIL WAR AN EIGHTEEN-YEAR-OLD GIRL named Sally Joy left the plush security of her home in Vermont and talked herself into a job on the Boston *Post*. It was only a matter of weeks until the men in the office were lining the floor with papers to keep her white satin ball gown from picking up the dust.

Sally did not need this newsprint carpet laid for her ambitious feet. It merely set the key for the befuddled dismay with which the normal newspaper man regards the unwelcome sight of a woman in the city room. Things have changed in the newspaper world since Sally's time. The typewriter has taken the place of the pen; the linotype has supplanted hand composition; there is little dust on the floor of the metropolitan city room; and the girl reporter rarely shows up during working hours in a white satin gown.

She must be free to leap nimbly through fire lines, dodge missiles at a strike, board a liner from a swaying ladder, write copy calmly in the heat of a Senate debate, or count the dead in a catastrophe. She never takes time to wonder why someone does not find her a chair, change the ribbon of her typewriter or hold smelling salts to her nose as she views a scene of horror.

"I want to be treated like a man," said Sally, who was a little ahead of her time. But she could not persuade her colleagues that she was anything but a helpless female. At first there was indignation about having "a woman on the sheet" and the youth assigned to escort her to all functions beginning after seven o'clock was the butt of the staff.

But the girl reporter hung on and got her reward. She was sent without masculine aid to cover a suffrage convention in Vermont, traveling with Lucy Stone and Julia Ward Howe. As the only woman at the press table, an admiring colleague chronicled her presence:

> Miss Sally Joy of Boston has a portfolio at the Reporters'
> table in the Convention for the *Post* of her native city. She is

pretty, piquante, and dresses charmingly. She has a high regard for Mrs. Bloomer, although she diverges from that good lady on the science of clothes. Miss Joy has made a reputation as a newspaper correspondent and reporter of which any man might well be proud. And this is saying a good deal for a woman. Miss Joy is as independent as she is self-supporting and she votes for Woman's Suffrage.

Sally was neither the first nor the best of the early women reporters. She was merely the symbol of a point of view that has changed surprisingly little in the last half century. She went from the Boston *Post* to the *Herald* to do a society column. She called herself Penelope Penfeather and sometimes wrote about fashions and the home. In due time she married and faded into the mists, but not until she had helped to found the General Federation of Women's Clubs and had served as the first president of the New England Women's Press Association.

Her demand to be treated as a man has echoed innumerable times in city rooms throughout the country. And all that she stood for is still regarded as a threat to the peace, honor and coziness of that sound haunt of masculinity—the city room, practically as sacred to men as a stag club or the pre-Volstead saloon.

To-day there are nearly twelve thousand women editors, feature writers and reporters in the country. They have found their way into all of the large newspaper offices and most of the small ones. They have invaded every branch of the business, but have not made much impression in the front-page field.

This does not mean that they have failed to make themselves felt in newspaper work; on the contrary, their success has been substantial. They hold executive posts. Two have dominant voices in important papers on the Eastern seaboard. Many of them edit small papers of their own. They run Sunday magazines and book supplements, write editorials, do politics, foreign correspondence, features, straight news, criticism, copy reading and sports writing, as well as the old standbys—the woman's page, clubs and social news.

They excel in the feature field and dominate the syndicates. They stop only at the political cartoon. They function in the advertising, business, art, promotion and mechanical departments, as well as in the editorial rooms. They have arrived, in a convincing way. But the fact remains that they have made surprisingly little progress on the front page, which is still the critical test. Not even a score of women take orders direct from the city desks in New York. The proportion is even less in other cities. They come singly or in pairs on a paper, rarely more. There are just as few on the general staff as there were at the turn of the century.

Whenever possible, they are steered into the quieter by-waters of the newspaper plant, away from the main current of life, news, excitement, curses and ticker machines. They are segregated where their voices will not be heard too audibly in the clatter. They get tucked away on the upper floors where the departments flourish. They lurk in the library, diligent girls wedded to the files.

Most of them would rather be where they are. The specialists increase in number and usefulness each year. They have better hours, fair pay, a more leisured existence. They get their own following. They don't have to beat the drums every day they live. They can make dinner engagements and keep them. They have time to buy their hats.

But out in the city room—where high-powered lights blaze on rows of desks, where copy readers bend like restless caterpillars over the reporter's work, where the city editor usually resembles a sedate professor rather than the Mad Hatter of the films, where phones jangle and tickers click—only two or three women can be found, working quietly at their typewriters in a fog of abstraction.

They are the front-page girls who somehow have weathered storms of prejudice—the odd creatures who have been pictured as doing things only slightly more impossible than they all have attempted at one time or another. They are on the inner newspaper track. They are there because they have felt the bewitchment of a compelling profession. There is little else they can do once they have tasted its elixir. Strange music sings in their ears. Visions haunt them as they walk the streets. They fall asleep with the sound of rumbling presses in their heads. They have seen too much and it hasn't been good for their health.

For the woman reporter goes beyond the news into the raw material from which it springs. She catches the rapt look of the genius and the furtive glance of the criminal. She detects the lies, the debauchery and the nobility of her fellow men. She watches the meek grow proud and the proud turn humble. She marvels only when people who have feared publicity get drunk with it, and strain for a place on the front page.

She walks unscathed through street riots, strikes, fires, catastrophes and revolution, her press card opening the way for her. She watches government in the making, sees Presidents inaugurated, Kings crowned, heroes acclaimed, champions launched on the world. She has a banquet seat with the mighty. She travels far and wide in search of news, and uses every vehicle known to man. She sees a murderer condemned to death and watches the raw agony of his wife while he dies.

Nine times out of ten her day's work takes her to the fringes of tragedy. News visits a home most often to annihilate it. The shadow of a reporter falling across the doorstep may presage the collapse of a lifetime of work. The woman reporter must face harsh facts without any qualms about her business. She must be ready for such hazards as may befall her. She must be calm and full of stamina. For she will savor strange bitters as well as alluring sweets; endure fatigue and disappointment beyond reason; withstand rebuffs that wither or exhilarate in turn; meet abuse with the equanimity born of self-control; and function with complete belief in what she is doing and loyalty to her paper.

She must have a sound sense of the values of life and great capacity to withstand the shocks of human emotion. She must see with clairvoyance, judgment or experience the salient points of any situation; be resourceful and good-natured; have initiative and enough perception to avoid being taken in. She must know how to get her facts, to weigh them with sagacity and, above all, how to write.

Where is this paragon to be found? No editor believes that she exists. She probably doesn't. And if she did, she would not have much chance to prove it, for although women have hit the sky in feature writing, they still have a long way to go to establish themselves as first-string news reporters. There have been no great women war correspondents. Few have written well on politics or economics, although Anne O'Hare McCormick, Dorothy Thompson and Ruth Finney are striking exceptions. But in the feature field they are hard to beat. They cover the town. They write with an interpretative touch. They put more emotion, more color, more animation into their work than the first-string girls. This is the special field for women. They get opportunities and they do it well. There were four at the Thaw trial in 1907. Dozens crowded the press rows at the Hauptmann trial twenty-eight years later. They have the excitement of going out on the big stories without the strain and responsibility of writing the news leads. They rarely have to bother with trivial events, but go from one major assignment to another. They are valued for their capacity to write.

With a smooth touch and a dramatic sense they often make names for themselves. Their salaries go up in proportion. The brightest and the most original step into the syndicate field. But the front-page girl is essentially an anonymous creature, a hard-working wretch who does not lightly exchange her job for the softer road.

She is in love with her work. She has the fantastic notion, shared by no one else, that an unsigned front-page story that passes through several thousand hands and soon lands in the gutter, most likely unread, is its own reward. The results are visible, immediate, alive—at least to her. A few hours earlier she watched the scene, talked to the people about whom she writes. There is speed and flavor to this rapid transfer of thought. In another twenty-four hours she will scarcely find the story readable, so soon does newsprint grow cold. But for the moment it possesses her imagination.

She cares little if she eats or sleeps until it is finished and the last fact is carefully checked and fitted into its niche. She moves in a trance. She forgets that she has a home, a husband, a child, a family. She hangs on by day and night, so physically exhausted that her head sings, waiting to get what she is after. In some respects she is almost as spectacular as the movies have made her; in others, she is a weary drudge, coping with minor obstacles.

But when things are running high, and her assignment is first rank, nothing stops her—neither storm, fire, frost, broken-down telegraph wires nor the rudeness of man. She is an implacable creature, bent on gaining her ends. When the story is in the paper, she rarely remembers what she has suffered in the pursuit of news. The excitement is its own anesthesia. Nothing is left but the afterglow.

So it never surprises her to hear an eager girl say, "How thrilling! I should love to do newspaper work." The girl is right. It is. The picture is not overdrawn. But good candidates for the job are rare. They are usually freaks who have landed head first at their goal, either by opportunity, hard work or luck—most often luck. Few women have what Mrs. Eleanor Medill Patterson, of the Washington *Herald*, calls flash in the handling of news. It's a gift that no school of journalism, no city editor, can impart.

The front-page girl has everything against her at the start. She may write quite well. She often does. But the most delicate test a reporter meets is in marshaling facts and assembling a big news story in perfect proportion, under pressure. This calls for lucid thinking, good judgment, and absolute clarity of style. The pace is like lightning. The most experienced men sometimes fumble among the countless intricate threads when hell is let loose too close to the deadline.

The woman reporter rarely gets the chance to try it. This is where she falls down flat in her editor's estimation, for it is the job that the star reporter is paid to do. It is his chief function for the paper. On the big story her vision is apt to be close and her factual grasp inadequate. The broad view is needed for a sound round-up. There is little time on a newspaper to cover up major mistakes in the construction of an important story.

The afternoon papers, which play their women feature writers to the limit, rarely trust them with the lead on a big running story. It has been done, but not often in metropolitan centers. Here the time element is of the utmost importance. If they fail, the paper is the loser. On the morning paper there is usually more time to pick up the stray ends when a woman has muffed her job. A crack rewrite desk is always waiting to iron out the imperfections of the reporters who go out on the street.

But city editors rarely take chances. They want complete reliability. They can't depend on the variable feminine mechanism. They might get a superb job. They might get a dud. No allowances are made for the failure of the woman reporter. She must stand on her own feet and prove her worth every day. When she draws a big story she is definitely on the spot. Nothing anywhere is going to help her, except her own intelligence and quick-trigger thinking. When a train has been wrecked, three hundred are dead, contradictory facts are pouring in on her and it is right on the deadline, all the copy-book rules melt away and she simply has to use her head.

There is no covering up as she sits before her typewriter with the lead story of the day at her mercy. The words must rip from her fingers in orderly procession. The facts behind them must be sharp and clear and the balance perfect. There are no excuses when the paper comes up and the lead story is feeble. The front page is exacting. The front-page girl had better know her stuff if she wants to function under the garish lights that burn down on the city room, revealing the flaws in her equipment with shocking candor.

This, definitely, is where women have made little headway and probably never will. It is the inadequacy that keeps them from ranking with the men stars. It has no bearing on their success in other newspaper departments, but it is the real reason why there is such a small percentage of women reporters on any large paper, in any part of the country.

Their second big hazard is in handling groups of men, which they must inevitably do on a first-string assignment. This is always a ticklish matter, although it has been done repeatedly with success. The best-natured newspaperman in the world—and they are an amiable and generous lot—is not apt to relish taking orders from a woman reporter. Yet back in the nineties Mabel Craft, of the San Francisco *Chronicle*, led a squad of men in a leaky launch through the Golden Gate to meet the ships returning from the Spanish-American War. The *Examiner* crew was already under way in a fine large tug. A storm was raging, they were warned that their launch would sink, but Miss Craft insisted on going ahead. She knew that her competitors were far out to sea and she feared that her paper might be beaten.

The men called a council and overruled her. Miss Craft took it with grace, conducted her expedition ashore, and hastily chartered a sea-worthy tug. They started off again and met the ships. They wrote their stories on the way in, with the tug lurching under them. Their editors were frantic by the time they showed up, waving their copy in their hands. It was the story of the year and they made it by a margin of minutes. They were not scooped by the *Examiner*. This was remarkable in the nineties. It would be remarkable to-day.

But here and there throughout the country there have always been girls who could meet the front-page test. Within recent years they have had more opportunity. The press services have given them golden chances. So have some of the conservative papers.

Lorena Hickok repeatedly wrote the news leads on stories of national importance for the Associated Press, which has gone in heavily for women after years of indifference to their merits. Genevieve Forbes Herrick brought distinction to her craft by her work for the Chicago *Tribune*. She outmatched her competitors time and again, doing the major stories of the day with grace, speed and accuracy. Marjorie Driscoll, of the Los Angeles *Examiner*, is another example of the finest type of news writer.

Grace Robinson has starred so often in the rôle of front-page girl that she has no competitor in the number of big stories she has covered within a given period of time. She did the Hall-Mills and the Snyder-Gray trials for the New York *Daily News*, and scores of other assignments that any man might envy. Elenore Kellogg, who died in the summer of 1935, led the *World* repeatedly with brilliantly handled news stories, and had the satisfaction of seeing her work under banner heads. Ruth Finney, a Scripps-Howard star, tops the field for Washington. She has achieved spectacular success in the political field and ranks with the best men in the Press Gallery.

These six are perfect examples of the successful front-page girl. They represent press services, conservative papers and tabloid journalism. They could handle any story from any given angle and walk away with the honors. They are the best refutation of all the criticism that has been leveled at the woman reporter. They have proved that a woman can cover a news story of prime importance as well as a man.

They have starred in the metropolitan field—the most severe test of all. Women get better front-page opportunities in smaller cities. A number throughout the country can point to front-page streamers, stories leading the paper, a heavy play on the big assignments of the day. But there are not enough of them to make much difference to the profession as a whole. They have merely established the fact, not revolutionized the status of their colleagues. They are remarkable only because they are the exceptions.

A newspaper woman's capacity, of course, should always be

measured by her opportunity. It is the conviction of every woman reporter of wide experience that she could match the best of the men if she had half a chance. The point is debatable. The city editor —chivalrous soul—keeps her down for two reasons: he doubts her capacity, and he hates to throw her to the wolves in the rough and tumble of big news events. He handles her with kid gloves when she wouldn't object to brass knuckles. He would rather she went home and never bothered him again.

However, if she has failed to make much headway with the city editor, she has attained some solid standing with her fellow workers in the city room. She can sit at adjoining desks with the reigning stars and neither be scorned nor pampered. No man needs to lay newsprint for her capable feet, or even spell a word for her. All that she ever asks him for is a match.

It is much more likely that the front-page girl will help her colleague with his story when he has been wooing the bottle, console him the night his sixth child is born, admire its picture a few weeks later, spur his ambition to write a great novel, or help him to buy a birthday present for his wife. She clucks over him like a mother hen. She nearly always likes him. It never occurs to her that he stands in her way and keeps her from the best assignments.

One of the more benign aspects of her job is the good fellowship of the men on the paper. They accept her as part of the newspaper picture. She sits with them through the mad hours of a political convention, writing quite sensible copy; she appears at the prize ring, unmoved by the noise and gore; she bobs up at a disaster and never lets her feelings get in her way. She isn't insensitive. Good reporters rarely are dead to what they see. They are objective first; but they must interpret the passions of their fellow men with some degree of insight. The apathetic man or woman does not make a fine reporter. The harp should twang a bit.

The woman reporter may be a paradoxical person, gentle in her private life, ruthless at her work. She may be of any age, type or race. She may be blonde, red-haired or brunette—a scholar who labors over polished phrases, or a rough and tumble slang expert who jollies the bailiff. Sometimes she is small, demure and savage; sometimes big, brassy and soft-hearted. One never can tell. She may wear pearls and orchids, be a débutante and sport a title, or shuffle along, a weary beldame with faded hair.

The outer shell has little to do with the value of a good reporter. The shrinking ones are often the lion-hearted; a feather may rock the Amazon. The best women reporters were once on the frowsy side. This is no longer true, although here and there a brainy girl may scorn the details of her costume. But the effect created by a group of women reporters to-day is one of good grooming, personability and poise. They have lost their distraught look somewhere along the years.

Forty years ago a few glamour girls got loose among the stringy-looking spinsters whose hair was always ruffled and whose shirt-waists bulged. But they were the exceptions. In the late nineties there was the general feeling that only a homely woman would barge out of the home and neglect her social life in order to write for the papers. But William Randolph Hearst took the stuffing out of this tradition by employing handsome girls with Lillian Russell figures and Harrison Fisher profiles; and Elizabeth Jordan, working for Joseph Pulitzer, so overawed Benjamin Harrison's butler with her elegant costume and ostrich feathers that she marched in and got a presidential interview at Cape May, when the door was closed to all other reporters.

To-day, the more smoothly they fit into the social scene the better their editors like it. If they must be eccentric and wear odd hats, their work should be good enough to justify it. An untidy woman is as out of date in the metropolitan newspaper office as papers on the floor, cigarette butts burning holes in the desks, or hats tossed blithely in the waste-paper baskets.

On the other hand, the girl reporter should not be too beguiling. When she dazzles the cubs and starts the copy boys writing poems, her stock begins to go down. Trouble, beauty and sex are threats in any city room, and the three can telescope remarkably quickly into one. Some gorgeous peonies have bloomed among the typewriters and ticker machines. The tabloids welcome them and encourage the ornamental touches. They argue that face, figure and clothes help to make the good woman reporter. They have proved the point repeatedly, but the rule is not infallible.

The most sensible usually make the best reporters. The women who have gone farthest in journalism are not those who have yipped most loudly about their rights. Unless aggressiveness is backed by real ability, as in Rheta Childe Dorr's case, it is only a boomerang. Nothing has done more to keep women reporters in the shade. Peace at any price is the city room philosophy.

It is absurd to maintain that a woman can do everything a man can do on a paper. She can't get into the Lotus Club in New York, or cross the Harvard Club threshold. She is denied the chummy barroom confidences of the politician, and cannot very well invade a Senator's room in Washington when he has no time to answer her questions except as he changes for dinner.

The rule does not work so conclusively the other way. The only obstacle the gentlemen of the press have encountered is Mrs. Roosevelt's Monday morning conferences. The youths who are picked for the pink tea assignments are welcomed with joy at the woman's meeting. It is a sad reflection for the woman reporter who swears by her sex that the most pampered scribe at feminine gatherings is usually a man—and a man who would rather not be there.

But admitting that there are a few places from which women reporters are debarred, this is scarcely an important argument against their usefulness. It has no more significance than the inability of a man to write a good fashion story without expert aid. The functions of the city staff are always interchangeable. A woman may cover a subway wreck and a man do a fashion show on the same afternoon, with excellent results in both cases. A good reporter can do telling work with almost any set of facts, short of relativity. He need not be a specialist. He need not even be initiated.

But the feeling is there and the seasoned newspaper woman has to recognize it. If she is wise she will go on her way, taking things in her stride. She will not fuss over periods of quiet. She will mind her own business, take the assignments handed out to her and never grouse unduly. She cannot always live in the news writer's seventh heaven. There are dull days with nothing but obits to write. But as sure as she lives, news will stir again. She will watch it rustle through the office. The city editor will come over to her, hand her a bulletin, and from this cryptic note may spring the story of the decade.

For news breaks with astonishing speed. It strikes a newspaper office like lightning. The front-page girl feels its impact from day to day. She never quite gets hardened to the sudden jolt when she sees a well-known name obviously bound for the gutter in a four-line bulletin, or hears a voice giving her the incredible news over the telephone: "Wall Street has just been bombed. Will you hurry down and see what's doing."

Not until a story is focused in black type does it have much reality for her, so absorbed is she in the mechanics of what she is doing. Yet this is the eternal fascination of her profession—to be in the thick of things; to move always where life is stirring; to have a grand-stand seat at the world events of the day, yet without responsibility for anything that may happen, beyond the task of turning out a good story on what she has seen and heard. She writes before the fever of the moment passes. Her best work is torn from her, take by take, under pressure. She lives herself through the news. If she is skilled at her job, she manages to convey the excitement to her readers.

For she must know how to write. There is practically no place in the modern newspaper office for the woman who is merely a news gatherer. There are men who work year after year for their papers and never actually write a line of copy. But the front-page girl must have a facile touch. The only way in which she can hope to prove her superiority is by the excellence of her style. She is rarely a wizard at getting facts.

The doubts raised by editors about her are legion. Can she write? Usually. Can she spell? At least as well as her masculine colleagues, often better. Is she lacking in a sense of humor? Probably, but only to the same degree as the rest of her sex. It doesn't make much difference to her paper. Is she emotional in her work? Rarely. Reporting now is largely realistic, except for the occasional word orgies at a sensational trial, and then it is an assumed frenzy, done with the tongue in the cheek. News writers have too much sense to beat their breasts in public now. Their editors no longer expect it. The public would laugh.

But the most serious charge brought against the newspaper woman is inaccuracy. This is the one real chink in her armor. Precision of thought is the first requisite of good reporting. As far back as 1898 Arnold Bennett seized on this weakness in the woman reporter. His criticism is much the same as the city editor's to-day. No amount of careful work has served to uproot it. Even the most unprejudiced editor shudders a little when a new woman walks through the city room. Will her sentences parse? Will she get the paper in a libel suit? Will she verify every fact? Will she know how to round up a story? Will she cause trouble in the office? He values the women who happen to have succeeded in his own organization, but he thinks of them always as the exceptions. He has not yet been able to accept the species without reservation.

Therefore, the newspaper woman has to be twice as careful as the newspaper man in order to make headway at all. The tradition of sloppy work dies hard. She has every reason to worry when the copy boy brings the wet paper fresh from the presses and lays it on her desk. There is something particularly appalling about the error in print. Her eye rushes to the head the copy reader has given her story. It isn't vanity that makes her read every line with care. She is desperately anxious to know if everything is right.

The layman who cherishes the foolish belief that only half of what he reads in a newspaper is true, never dreams of the conscientious work that lies behind the columns he hastily scans. No human being but a well-trained reporter would hunt through five books of reference to get a middle initial correct. No one else would find so many ways of checking a circumstance that the average person accepts at face value.

The reporter scourges himself to perfection. Yet the public still believes that he is slipshod, inaccurate, a deliberate falsifier. In actual fact, the conscientious news writer on a responsible paper is the most slavishly exact person in the world. He splits hairs and swears by books of reference. He has a passion for verification, an honest love for facts. The good woman reporter has the same exacting code. The crispness of her style, the keen viewpoint, the explicit phrase, the potent paragraph, are all nullified if she does not have the essential newspaper virtue of absolute accuracy.

Often her early training has a bearing on the exactitude of her mental processes. The newspaper women have arrived at their various goals by odd routes. They have taught and nursed and been stenographers. They have scrubbed floors and sold in shops and danced in the chorus. The present tendency is for them to break in fresh from college. Some have wandered into the profession by accident; others have battered their way in; a few have simply walked in the front door without knocking. But the same spirit of enterprise has propelled most of them into the exciting newspaper game.

In their off-moments they have unexpected tastes. There is no consistency in them. The girl who is most at home inside fire lines, checking up on casualties, is apt to spend her days off weeding her garden or reading Pater. She may worm her way into jail or sit without blinking as a jury condemns a man to death, but when she gets home she is likely to turn thoroughly feminine. She wants a quiet evening with her husband, an hour's play with her baby, a chance to mix a salad or knit a sweater.

She is often a little sharp of tongue, because she has listened to so much rot. She has seen strange things of which most women never dream. She is neither the terrible hard-boiled reporter who beats the town nor the angel-faced cutie who wins her way by guile. As a rule she is matter-of-fact. The code of her profession is an intangible one, not generally understood. She must be resourceful with honor, searching without being rude; she must not be put off easily by the lies constantly flung in her face; she must sense the important, discard the trivial, have a sense of proportion and the ability to make subtle decisions between right and wrong. She must build her own code as she moves, for the copy-book standards scarcely cover her profession.

On the whole, newspaper women make few demands on their city editors. They would gladly work for nothing, rather than be denied the city room. They scarcely ever fuss about their salaries, which range from $35 to $150 a week in the large cities, and from $7 to $50 in the smaller ones. They rarely ask for increases, or complain about their fate. They work hard and have a somewhat touching faith in what they are doing. They are seldom lazy. But the highest compliment to which the deluded creatures respond is the city editor's acknowledgment that their work is just like a man's. This automatically gives them a complacent glow, for they are all aware that no right-minded editor wants the so-called woman's touch in the news.

The fact remains that they never were thoroughly welcome in the city room and they are not quite welcome now. They are there on sufferance, although the departments could scarcely get along without them. But if the front-page girls were all to disappear to-morrow no searching party would go out looking for more, since it is the fixed conviction of nearly every newspaper executive that a man in the same spot would be exactly twice as good.

They may listen to smooth words and chivalrous sentiments, but what every city editor thinks in his black but honest heart is: "Girls, we like you well enough but we don't altogether trust you."

Chapter II

STEPPING OUT

NEWSPAPER WOMEN HAD TO GO IN FOR DIZZY SELF-EXPLOITATION before they could make themselves heard at all. The faint rustlings of the mid-Victorian era grew to a roar when the stunt age was launched by Nellie Bly. Up to that time their efforts had been desultory. But Nellie stormed Joseph Pulitzer, then the town, then the country, then the globe, which she circumnavigated faster than Phileas Fogg.

It was not an easy victory for the ladies of the press. Their sufferings were horrible. But they also had fun. And finally they got what they wanted. From stunts, crusades and coercing the woman's point of view in the news, a fallacious idea which they have abandoned long since, they have progressed to sound achievement on the plane of common sense. They no longer have to climb skyscrapers by rope or wear false faces to get their stuff in the papers. They do it on a workmanlike basis.

In four decades their interests and technique have changed. Broadly speaking, 1890-1900 was the stunt era; 1900-1910 the sob era; 1910-1920 the suffrage era; and 1920-1930 the tabloid era. They have followed the trend of the news and of their papers. The girl on the conservative paper has tempered her style to suit its frame; the tabloid girl has gingered hers up, however sober her tastes.

It was hard to get the woman idea across from any angle while antimacassars were still in vogue. Housewives did not read the papers before 1870 and there were no careerists. All attempts to snare their interest were coldly met until frills and cabinet pudding recipes were launched in occasional columns hopefully captioned "For the Ladies." The modern woman who reads her paper from the front page to the back does not inherit this taste from her grandmother.

But in 1834 Ann Oddbody launched a paper called *Woman* at a time when only a lady mattered. It died so quickly that no copies have survived. "There is a paper *Man* published, why shall not a paper *Woman* be also seen daily in the City of Gotham?" the editor demanded, not without reason.

Two years later, with the *Sun, Herald* and *Tribune* all doing well in New York, William Newell conceived the idea that there must be a feminine public lurking somewhere among the tidies and whatnots, if only he could reach it. He decided to go after it on deeply moral grounds. On April 30, 1836, the first issue of his paper appeared with this announcement:

> The *Ladies Morning Star* will sustain the character of a Literary, Moral Newspaper, which it shall be the endeavor of the proprietor to enrich with every variety that may improve and adorn the female mind, enlarge and strengthen the understanding, purify the soul, and refine the senses. . . .

However, it was not the most auspicious year for the moral tone. The first murder to attract public attention in America had occurred a month earlier, when Helen Jewett was found dead in a house of ill-fame at 41 Thomas Street, a copy of Lady Blessington's *Flowers of Loveliness* beside her.

James Gordon Bennett rushed at once to the scene, interviewed the buxom Mrs. Rosina Townsend who had found Helen's body, and wrote a lively first-page interview for the *Herald*. He followed this with an attack on civic complacency; he quoted fallen women and he badgered public officials. The circulation of his paper went up 3,000 in a single week, and some of the editions sold for a shilling instead of a penny. The population of New York was then nearly 200,000 and Broadway was lined with Lombardy poplars.

A young clerk named Richard P. Robinson was charged with the crime, had a cheering section at his trial, and went scot free. All the husbands in town were talking about Helen Jewett, and their wives heard the echoes. They were far from pleased when the *Ladies Morning Star* decided to ignore the case, except for pious editorials in which the editor pointed out the lessons to be drawn from the vicious lives of the principals.

There seemed to be nothing of distinctive interest for women in the reading matter of the *Star*. One of the early items was a lugubrious poem by Mrs. Sigourney on seeing an infant prepared for the grave. In the same issue the leading article was based on the "operative class of female," more commonly known now as the working girl.

The *Star* staggered along, keeping up the moral tone, but at the end of three months the circulation was only 2,000 and there was no advertising. The merchants objected vigorously to spending money on a paper aimed exclusively at women. The editor resisted their protests for six months, and then dropped *"Ladies"* from the title, with the following announcement:

Many mercantile gentlemen of high and honourable standing, have objected to inserting their ads in our paper, on account of what they consider the singularity of its name, and express their conviction that if its title were altered, and if it were called simply *The Morning Star* without the prefixture of the word *Ladies* it would not only obtain a much more extensive subscription, but also ten times the amount of advertising patronage, which they even promise to ensure us, if the change be made.

Although the name was changed, the lofty editorial tone was maintained. But the women of New York did not respond, the advertiser saw no hope, and the *Star* folded quietly. The noble experiment had failed. There is nothing to show that Mr. Newell consulted or employed a woman in getting out his paper.

Horace Greeley had a better idea soon after that. In the early forties he asked Margaret Fuller to write for the *Tribune*. She was the first really distinguished woman writer to contribute to an American paper. Mr. Greeley was a dominant figure in journalism at the time. He went about town in an old felt hat, his neckcloth awry, his trousers out of shape, his white coat bedraggled. He did not make the mistake of asking Miss Fuller to write for women. He employed her to write soundly for his flourishing journal. The idea spread. In 1850 Mrs. Jane Swisshelm invaded the Press Gallery and got the first foothold in the political field. She was followed by Grace Greenwood and Gail Hamilton, who did politics with a masculine touch.

In the fifties Jenny June and Fanny Fern launched a new school of journalism. They brought tears, fashions, recipes and women's problems out into the open. They went after the feminine public, from arrowroot to the new chignon. The languid heads swayed feebly on the antimacassars. There was a flicker of interest. From their early efforts sprang the woman's page of today, still the point of focus for the woman reporter. Jenny June took a desk in the city room, the first day-by-day reporter. Fanny cut fabulous didoes at $100 a column.

It was still the age of dilatory correspondence. The papers were swamped with charming letters in violet ink. They came from Washington, Hawaii, Europe—wherever the roaming correspondents happened to be. Editors were glad to print them. They didn't involve a woman underfoot in the office. Space rates were low. News was scarce. Essays were welcome to fill up the wide columns of hand-set agate that were read by gaslight. The newspaper world was very genteel, except for the stormy Mr. Bennett.

By 1880 every paper had its following of lady scribes who wandered about, picking up impressions and sending them in by mail.

It mattered little if the items had news interest. When the imagination failed a couplet would always work. Few of the correspondents had yet conceived the idea of getting on the staff of a paper. Only the female operatives bothered about jobs.

Ten years later Nellie Bly appeared, introducing the stunt age in journalism. She was followed by a wild outcropping of girls who freely risked their lives and reputations in order to crash the papers. Nothing stopped them. By this time they were more aggressive and were after jobs. They posed with equal nonchalance as beggars, balloonists, street women, servants, steel workers, lunatics, shop girls and Salvation Army lassies. They bothered the preachers and stampeded the town.

They had ample opportunity to use their ingenuity, for in 1895 Mr. Hearst invaded the New York field, taking the feeble *Journal* and building it up right under Mr. Pulitzer's nose. Both publishers went in for sensationalism. The competition was terrific. If the *World* had a stunt, the *Journal* went one better. Heavy streamers, such as New Yorkers never had seen, met them at every corner. Yellow journalism whetted the appetite of the public. Circulation figures leaped to extravagant heights. The town was amused, entertained, flabbergasted.

The hot competition was good for the working press. Arthur Brisbane, who had had great success with the *Sunday World*, joined Mr. Hearst and the battle raged more fiercely than ever. They invaded the afternoon field with the *Evening Journal*. In 1896 they got out a Sunday supplement with colored illustrations called the *Woman's Home Journal*. All the papers by now were making a play for women readers. The syndicate idea had been launched. Even in 1892 the *Herald* had characterized the *Recorder* as a woman's paper. And the *Recorder* flattered itself on having rounded up 100,000 women readers.

By the end of the golden nineties it was either clothes and the cookery book, or the stunt girl. The reader could take his choice. The one class had little respect for the other. Then, as now, there was a sharp division between the sober and the sensational press. The reactionaries were scornful of Nellie and her copyists, who went them one better, however, by being featured on posters and billboards. A frustrated colleague wrote self-righteously that Nellie had "prostituted her womanhood for the sake of a good story." The stunt girls earned from $50 to $100 a week. The conservatives drew down from $25 to $50, if they could get jobs at all.

Elizabeth L. Banks whipped up interest in the subject with her serial, *The Autobiography of a Newspaper Girl*. Elizabeth was a red-haired, freckle-faced girl from Wisconsin who hid under a desk in the local room when lightning filled her with fear. But later she learned to be brave in London. She worked as a servant, a flower girl, a crossing sweeper. She mingled with rag-pickers; she made artificial flowers; she worked in sweat shops. For the time being she was a minor sensation in the English press. She went to Hawarden Castle to interview Gladstone but could not batter her way past Mrs. Gladstone.

Then she returned to America and invaded Park Row in a new Knox hat and a tailor-made suit of the latest cut. She carried camphor and smelling salts, an alligator card case and an ivory-handled umbrella with which she waved office boys out of her way. But she refused to walk along Broadway and let herself be arrested— a stunt suggested by an editor who had become hardened to the self-immolation of the stunt girls. She made up for it by touring the sweat shops, crawling down the funnel of the comic little Holland Boat, and otherwise cutting capers in the approved manner of the sisterhood.

Then one day Mr. Hearst turned down a stunt suggestion. This was significant. The frenzy had passed. The public was tired of the daredevil girls. The space system was opening the way for the less nimble members of the profession. The reception rooms of newspaper offices always had a line of nervous spinsters in gored skirts, waiting patiently to see the editor. They came armed with ideas and scribbling pads. They got about town, nosed out events not regularly covered, and submitted their copy hopefully. If they hit the mark now and again they were grateful; if they kept it up, sometimes they landed steady jobs.

The amateur news hound was never ignored. Her offerings had potential value. Nowadays the news services have the field so completely covered in metropolitan centers that there is no use rushing to the fire without an executive order, unless, as sometimes happens, the tip is exclusive. But things were not like this in the nineties. The casual bearer of news was encouraged. There was none of the modern network that draws the strings of the world's news together, concentrates it on a few high-powered desks, then sprays it to papers everywhere.

The newspaper women worked without telephone, typewriter or taxi. The first of the telephones was installed in 1877, but the heroine of the day's story never seemed to have one in her house, and the papers made sparing use of this luxury. An important qualification was to write a legible hand. Good spelling was more of an asset than it is now, when some of the most learned reporters boast of their bad spelling and let the copy desk worry about the consequences. But in the candlelight era it was a shocking disgrace, a mark of ignorance, a social flaw of the worst order.

When something really serious was on foot for the woman reporter, an errand boy in blue ran up the stoop of her brownstone house with a message summoning her to the office post haste. She pinned on her sailor, gathered her skirts and rushed for the trolley to take her down to Park Row.

The life of the society reporter was particularly cruel. The elegant girls with hour-glass figures were sometimes allowed victorias in place of the trolley to take them from house to house, so that they could find out what the beau monde would wear at the party that night. If they preferred, they could always use their bicycles.

"What! You made only six calls today?" an editor shouted at one girl indignantly when she came in with meager scraps.

But their experiences with the party guests were much more harrowing.

"My gown! What impertinence!" a girl reporter heard the dowager say to the butler. "Tell the young person certainly not."

So she whirled away on her bicycle empty-handed, her lace petticoat brushing her black lisle stockings, her head seething with rage under a monster hat. But no matter how sharp the rebuff, Mrs. A's brocade and Mrs. B's point lace were properly chronicled in the paper. Society had not yet been put in its place. It was still firmly entrenched on the front page. The Bradley-Martin ball was the talk of the town for a year. So was the Marlborough-Vanderbilt wedding.

Next to society, the most important function of a woman on a conservative paper was to cover teas and clubs. The American woman was just becoming club-conscious. She was getting out of the home. She was beginning to think about suffrage. She was discovering that a club row was as stimulating as a spat with her husband. About this time city editors got into the habit of greeting their women reporters back from a club meeting with: "Were they funny or did they fight?" Otherwise, there was no story. It was not until after the vote had been won that women's meetings became straight news. Up to that time they supplied the city room with merriment.

The Spanish-American War cut the earnings of the newspaper girls, for the papers were filled with war news. But one of them staked a claim to momentary fame as Admiral Dewey's "tut tut" girl. She was Norah Donnelly, a beauty who wore white lace and magnificent large black hats with poppies. She was young, and inexperienced in newspaper technique.

When the Admiral was welcomed home she got aboard his ship. She waited until the other reporters had finished with him, then she dashed up and waved a small American flag in his face. Overcome with emotion, she burst into tears. The Admiral looked surprised. He patted her shoulder. "Tut, tut, little girl, don't cry," he implored her.

A colleague wrote the story for the *Journal*. It carried a handsome streamer in red: "*Tut, tut, Little Girl, Said the Admiral Kindly.*" Mr. Hearst saw it, was furious, ordered it killed. It lasted through one edition only. Soon afterwards Norah went on the stage. Then she married. She never went back to newspaper work.

By this time Dorothy Dix and Beatrice Fairfax were becoming household names through syndicate distribution. Winifred Black was roving over the country on first-string assignments for Mr. Hearst. Elizabeth Jordan was doing effective work for the *Sunday World*. Zona Gale was writing for the *Evening World* but was not showing any particular promise. Kate Field was getting out her journal in Washington. Margaret Sullivan and Mary Abbott were the reigning stars in Chicago. The Chicago *Tribune* had sixteen women in all its departments in 1896. It has more than four hundred now.

The woman's angle was being played hard. It was not the news event that mattered but the woman writer's reactions to it. She was allowed to sit at a desk in the city room, which a contemporary described as "the dirty, dingy, tobacco-polluted local room." The city editor shouted for her just as he did for the men. He told her to "rush it lively," in the brisk slang of the day. Her colleagues had abandoned the notion that they must leap to their feet at her appearance, put their pipes in their pockets, or take off their hats. They cursed and they drank as freely as if she were not anywhere about. But they never took her work seriously. There were as many as five women on some of the dailies. Others had one or two. But their status was ignominious, except for such stars as Mrs. Black, Miss Jordan and a few others.

However, the first big step had been taken. The syndicate idea was now established. Riches and journalistic fame were on the way for the smart woman writer. In 1884 S. S. McClure had started the syndication of 5,000 words a week, all fiction. A year later he enlarged this service to include general articles and the weekly output was 30,000 words. He landed the leading writers of the day, but he also remembered the housewife audience and launched the Patience Winthrop recipes, handled by himself. In 1892 he started a syndicated woman's page. But in the meantime Edward W. Bok had made a much more determined play for the woman reader through the syndicate service he organized with his brother, William J. Bok.

In studying the reading habits of women he was struck by the fact that they cared little about the newspapers. He came to the conclusion that this was because no positive attempt was made to interest them. He discussed the matter with several New York newspaper editors, all of whom agreed that they would like to get a feminine following for their papers. However, they told him frankly that they had no idea what women liked to read in a newspaper, or where suitable material was to be had.

Mr. Bok recognized it as an open field with great possibilities. He spotted a letter of gossip appearing in the *Star* called "Bab's Babble." He thought this might be syndicated as a woman's letter from New York. It was written by Mrs. Isabel A. Mallon. He made arrangements with her and the letter was sent to a group of papers. Jenny June had attempted the same thing on an amateur scale some time earlier.

The response was immediate. Ella Wheeler Wilcox was engaged to write a weekly letter on women's topics. This and "Bab's Babble" suggested an entire page of syndicated matter, which Mr. Bok launched in 1886. One of the earliest features was "Side Talks with Girls" which he wrote himself for a time. It was signed Ruth Ashmead and, later, Ruth Ashmore.

A syndicate of ninety papers was soon in full operation and the idea spread. He employed the best women writers of the day and asked well-known men to write on subjects of interest to women. Editors who were unable to get the Bok page launched their own to compete with his in the same territory. This was one of the significant steps for women in journalism, since it gave definite form to the woman's page and opened up great possibilities for women writers.

From isolated columns and stray fashion notes a page for women now began to take positive shape. In its fundamentals it was not unlike the woman's page of to-day, although any editor of that era would have shrunk in horror from the realism of some of the women commentators who now take sides boldly on anything from birth control to militarism.

It suited the woman in the home but was scorned by the girls who were beginning to stir about in the larger world. One writer protested bitterly in *The Club Woman* during 1900 that the woman's page in most newspapers was "principally mush and skimmed milk with a little cream and powdered sugar added upon occasion."

Although Mr. Bok had relinquished his syndicate work eleven years earlier to become editor of *The Ladies Home Journal*, he maintained his interest in the relationship of women to the newspapers. At the beginning of the century he wrote to fifty of the leading newspaper women of the country, asking them if they would like their own daughters to work in newspaper offices. Forty-two answered. Only three said yes. Then he wrote to the managing editors of the fifty leading papers in the country, all of whom employed women, asking them how they would feel about starting their own daughters in journalism. Horrors! The answer was overwhelmingly no. There wasn't one dissenting voice.

"I would rather see my daughter starve than that she should ever have heard or seen what the women on my staff have been compelled to hear and see," said an outraged father.

The editor of one of the largest dailies in the East wrote: "No, a million times no, and no words I can command can make my objections strong enough."

To-day the daughters and sisters of many newspaper men are working on papers throughout the country. In one case a father and daughter worked until recently in competition in the Hearst service. As a rule, newspaper fathers do not encourage their daughters to take this step, but the daughters themselves insist.

In 1901 Nixola Greeley-Smith joined the staff of the *Evening World* and a new page was turned in the history of women in journalism. She brought a rare and urbane touch to her work. Her interviews created a vogue. A group of women writers formed around her who cut the old-fashioned twaddle and wrote soundly about people and things. Nixola was their model. The fashion for interviews grew. Visiting celebrities were scarcely off the ship before the women reporters pounced on them. At last editors had found something that women seemed to do with a superior touch. They showed their gratitude by keeping them busy.

By 1903 more than three hundred women were regularly employed as reporters throughout the country. In the same year a girl breaking into newspaper work was asked on her first day to interview a ward politician, on her second to interview a monkey, on her third to tell how to trim an Easter bonnet. It was a comparatively short jump from this to Gertrude Stein, relativity and the New Deal.

In 1907 the Thaw trial gave them their first real taste of court work in the East. They showed great aptitude for this particular type of reporting. It is still the field in which they excel. The emotional and dramatic elements were heavily played. Nell Brinkley sketched Evelyn Nesbit Thaw in a dozen different poses. Winifred Black, Ada Patterson, Dorothy Dix and Nixola Greeley-Smith wrote impassioned paragraphs about her. This was the first of a long series of sensational murder trials at which women reporters had the opportunity to do effective work.

They now had a definite place in the city room. They took assignments. The space system was already passing. A few of them were getting jobs. Then the suffragists carried them along, lifting them unconsciously on the wings of their own ardent efforts to get the vote. Women reporters invaded the front pages of the most conservative papers with their stories on the feminists' doings. The general tone, however, was jocular. The war gave them further opportunities. Some went abroad and did foreign correspondence. Others took the places of men at home. They made the front page with increasing frequency. This give them experience, assurance, sound technique, and a number of good reporters were developed.

By now the feature writers were established on all afternoon papers throughout the country. The more sensational morning papers played them up with by-lines. The woman's page became a fixed feature in most papers. It leaned heavily on syndicate material. A lovelorn column was almost indispensable. At the same time, some attempt was made to catch the spirit of the contemporary woman and reflect her interests—whatever they happened to be at the moment.

By degrees the newspaper women stormed every department. They rose to executive office. They became specialists. They put themselves across by competence and push. Then in the summer of 1919 the *Daily News* was launched in New York and the tabloid era began, with new opportunities for women. Stunts came back into vogue. Composite pictures of frightful conception galvanized the town. There were more jobs for girls. They were welcomed with warmth in the city rooms of the tabloids. The pendulum swung to dizzy lengths and then things settled again. There is little personal exploitation now. Few crocodile tears are shed in the news columns. The standard has been leveled. The woman reporter is compelled to write with a degree of good sense, however highly her story is dramatized. And in spite of the front-page prejudice, every publisher has accepted the fact that he needs a few women on his paper.

"Who are these females? Fire them all," said James Gordon Bennett impatiently, as he walked through the editorial room of the *Herald* on one of his infrequent trips to America and saw a few hapless women sitting about. He was notoriously averse to pompadours in the city room, and the wise girls made themselves scarce when he came home. Both he and Frank A. Munsey were interested in social news and the club activities of smart women. They vaguely felt the need of one woman on the paper to cope with these matters, and Mr. Bennett liked precise descriptions of what women wore—particularly the President's wife.

There is no record that Mr. Munsey did much to help or hinder women in newspaper work, although occasionally he passed along a compliment to the city desk on a story by a woman that caught his eye. It was usually of the light and whimsical order.

Joseph Pulitzer had no aversion to women working for his paper if they showed enterprise. It was he who gave Nellie Bly her first big chance after she had pushed her way into his office and laid some stunt suggestions before him. The *World* had a fine succession of women writers from the days of Nellie Bly and Elizabeth Jordan down to the night the paper was sold, when Elenore Kellogg wrote a story for its last front page. The *World* women always had liberal opportunities to show what they could do.

Mr. Hearst, more than any other publisher, has helped to put newspaper women on the map. Hundreds of them have passed through his doorways, some to lose their jobs with staggering swiftness; others to build up big syndicate names and draw down the highest salaries in the profession. From the moment he entered newspaper work he dramatized them; got them to make news. They became the most spectacular, the most highly paid, the most dashing newspaper women in the country, if not necessarily the finest news writers. Wherever a woman has shown particular promise elsewhere an effort has been made to lure her into his service.

Mr. Hearst does not voice his opinion of women in newspaper work. He shows what he thinks by employing them in large numbers. Few of the women who work for him have ever seen him. Some of them have done sensational things for his papers without knowing in the least what he thought of their work. Yet he watches their progress closely and sometimes suggests the name of a newspaper woman to cover a story in which he happens to be interested.

More outspoken on the subject is Arthur Brisbane, who has found and fostered most of the women stars in the Hearst service. He is their best advocate. He believes they are essential to every paper. He has frequently said that he would like to see a paper published and run by women only. He has given them real opportunities and they have gone far with his backing.

Captain Joseph M. Patterson pursues a liberal policy with his women reporters. He believes that people like to read stories with a woman's by-line. He has had a succession of admirable women reporters on the staff of the *Daily News*, and has treated them handsomely. Often they have been starred above the men. He lets them know about it when he particularly likes their work.

The names of many clever women writers flash across the pages of the Scripps-Howard chain. Roy W. Howard has mental reservations about the accuracy of women reporters on straight news, but he has no doubt of their value in the feature field. Some of the best feature writers in the country are now working in his service. They get excellent opportunities. He is open-minded and flexible in his judgment, where they are concerned. Like Mr. Hearst, he is opening up new fields for them. However, the United Press still holds out against them, the last of the news services to ignore their uses. Only a few women have done U.P. work, either in America or abroad, and then only on a temporary basis. But they are firmly entrenched with the Associated Press, International News Service and Universal Service. The press services and the New York *Times* were the most stubborn points of invasion.

It was an understood, rather than an enunciated policy, that Adolph S. Ochs was opposed to having women on the general news staff of his paper. The *Times*, liberal in all other respects, stuck tenaciously to this policy for more than thirty years, although three women sat in the city room and took assignments of the departmental order from the city desk. The Sunday magazine and book review section meanwhile featured excellent work by women. In Anne O'Hare McCormick Mr. Ochs had as brilliant a woman correspondent as any publisher could hope to find. The feeling did not extend beyond the city staff.

Carr V. Van Anda turned all suppliants aside in a gentle manner but with an amused glitter in the eye, saying he could not possibly send them out for the *Times* after dark.

"If I had my way about it, all unmarried men would be taxed to support indigent women," he said to one woman reporter who tried to land on the *Times*. "Go back South, if you must work. New York is no place for any girl who must earn her living."

However, she believed that it was the ideal place for a newspaper career, so she stayed and became one of the ablest tabloid reporters in New York.

In 1934, before Mr. Ochs' death, the bars were let down a trifle on the *Times*. A girl landed a straight news job on the city staff, did well, but soon decided to move on to other fields. She was essentially a fiction writer. A few months later another capable candidate arrived and stayed to prove that a woman reporter can go out after dark and bring in her story, too.

Mr. and Mrs. Ogden Reid have shown confidence in newspaper women by giving them positions of the highest trust. The Sunday magazine and book review supplement of the New York *Herald Tribune* are managed solely by women. Throughout all departments of the paper the policy toward them is liberal. Mrs. Reid herself is one of the foremost newspaper women in the country. She is continually urging the women of her profession to show more enterprise and to seek opportunity in all departments of a paper, even the mechanical side. Few women have worked on the general staff of the *Herald Tribune*, but this has been left to the discretion of city editors and managing editors. It in no way reflects the policy of the owners of the paper.

Fremont Older, who gave newspaper women extraordinary opportunities on the San Francisco *Call* and *Bulletin,* and backed them in many original exploits, believed that editors did not employ enough women. He thought that in this they showed poor judgment, since he found that they worked harder than men, were enthusiastic and gave more faithful returns. He believed them to be natural writers, with greater facility of expression than men. However, although he cracked the whip over a brilliant group, in the long run his women reporters usually disappointed him.

"The ablest woman will always attach her elbow to some worthless man and let her work go," he mourned, as one after another foreswore his spirited tutelage.

As he grew older he came to the conclusion that few newspaper women were genuine careerists. They always wanted to mother someone—either a child or a man. This, he thought, was the one thing that kept them from being great reporters.

Chapter III

A SCOLD, A SIREN AND A STAR

ONE OF THE MORE EMBARRASSING INTERVIEWS OF HISTORY WAS obtained from a President of the United States by a termagant newspaper woman who sat on his clothes as he bathed in the Potomac and refused to budge until he had answered her questions.

The President was John Quincy Adams and his interviewer was Anne Royall, who used to rampage up and down the country under her own steam, a virago in a calico gown with mutton leg sleeves and a poke bonnet. Women covered themselves with veils as she hove in sight; men held their hats before their faces lest her demon blue eyes burn them up. Anne was a legend and a holy terror, convicted ultimately as a common scold.

Her immoderation made the nation laugh. There was something farcical about a cracked old woman belaboring the government of the country and pursuing a President to his morning plunge. Her *Paul Pry* was published from 1831 to 1836, one of the three personal journals launched by women during the nineteenth century. It was badly printed, fanatical and poorly edited, but while it lasted it had some interest as the mouthpiece of the fantastic Anne.

More destructive in its effects was *Woodhull and Claflin's Weekly*, issued from 1870-1876, a sensational publication backed by Victoria Woodhull and Tennessee Claflin, the sirens of Wall Street. *Kate Field's Washington*, the third of these ventures, caused scarcely a ripple by comparison. It blackguarded no one. It was written in a graceful and sprightly vein. Its pet causes, although odd, were abstract.

The three papers were short-lived. None of them lasted much more than five years. They all expressed the strong personalities of their editors, and lacked the steadying touch of common sense. The two muckrakers ran up heavy circulation by spectacular measures; but the Woodhull publication was too violent to attract the public for long and *Paul Pry* was a fanatical nightmare. If the editors of these two papers had not been raging in the public prints, they would have been smashing heads in other spheres, for they were born trouble-makers. Their papers were their platform, but their literary interests were thin.

Victoria had beauty and sex magnetism on her side. It was her ambition to be president of the United States. She moved in an aura of conquest and triumph. Anne was a prig, a hypocrite, a sectionalist, some thought a maniac. Kate was a dilettante. Each made herself felt on her generation but left no mark on journalism; they did nothing to advance the cause of women in the newspaper field.

Anne Royall turned to writing late in life. Her childhood was spent in Maryland, where she ran about wild, quite unlettered, knowing nothing except Indian lore. Her family moved from place to place, a vagrant mob, and finally settled in Virginia, attaching themselves to the eccentric household of William Royall, who had served as a general under Washington and Lafayette.

In 1797 Royall married Anne and she became mistress of a plantation with great acreage and many slaves. She was still a wild waif, ignorant and wilful. Her husband was a pedant as well as a soldier. He took her in hand, drilled her in the classics, made her read Voltaire and Jefferson, and stuffed her somewhat empty head with the abracadabra of Free Masonry.

In spite of differences in age, culture and taste, they lived together happily for sixteen years. Or, at least, if they squabbled, no one ever knew it. Then Royall died and Anne was left a widow. She took three of her slaves, hitched up her coach and started on a tour of the South, scribbling down her impressions as she traveled. Nothing escaped her. She became the national gossip. Her notes were tinged with malice; she beat the drum for her pet causes. Soon she became known as the "widow with the serpent's tongue."

Her wanderings continued for ten years. She pried with deadly insistence into the affairs of all kinds of people, writing maliciously about her discoveries. She marched on Washington in 1824, shortly after her husband's will had been broken, leaving her penniless. She applied for a pension as the widow of a prominent Revolutionary general, and this started a contest that went on for years. By crashing tactics she enlisted the aid of government heads from John Quincy Adams down. He found her a pest but liked her. He forgave her even the river interview and dubbed her the "virago errant in enchanted armor."

Having stormed Washington and dined at the White House, Anne set out on her second pilgrimage—this time to blackjack subscriptions for the book of impressions she had written on her first tour. She still found humanity weak and sinful. She raged and scolded, and waved her ragged banners. For seven years she stampeded up

and down the country, by coach and on foot, interviewing everyone who would speak to her, invading convents, smoking the pipe
of peace with Cherokee Indians, ransacking the garret of Thomas
Jefferson's house at Monticello.

This strange wayfarer was small and stout. Her eyes were an
astounding blue but no one liked their prying glitter. She had dazzling teeth, which were always visible, for she laughed even while
she raged. But it wasn't the laughter of good humor. She was persistent, ruthless, fussy and bad-tempered. She wrote in a chatty
style, venting her hates, condemning most of the places she visited
and the things she saw. Her local allusions brought trouble on her
head. Even children were warned to get out of the way when Anne
Royall came to town. Her shadow preceded her. And shutters went
up against her invasion. One of her victims whacked her on the
head; another knocked her down a flight of stairs. She was always
in the thick of battle and she loved it.

In 1829 she was arrested and charged with being a common
scold. Her trial caused thousands to roar with laughter. She was
found guilty, but because she was sixty, poor and thwarted, they
spared her the ducking stool and let her off with a $10 fine.

This failed to silence her. It merely gave her a new idea. In 1831
she brought out the first issue of *Paul Pry*, an oddity to be found
now in the Library of Congress and nowhere else. She bought a
second-hand ramshackle Ramage printing press, made room for it
by taking the sink out of the kitchen of a house she rented behind
the Capitol, hired a printer, took two small boys from a Catholic
orphan asylum to act as printer's devils, and launched her first issue.

It was a four-page paper, spiced with invective. The inside pages
carried editorials, political and local news. The front page was devoted chiefly to advertising. In her first issue Anne announced her
policy flatly: "No party, the welfare and happiness of our country
is our politics." Her obsessions were Free Masonry, which she advocated fiercely; Evangelicism, which she fought tooth and nail; her
pension, which she never got; and propagation, in which she had
an abstract interest.

Occasionally a gleam of common sense sifted through the thick
layers of fanatical upbraiding. Her criticism was sometimes acute;
her attacks on public corruption often valid. She pounced on public
grafters with witch-like intuition. She couldn't be bought, squelched
or intimidated. When offered a $2,000 bribe to hold her peace, she
promptly squealed her loudest. She hammered at corrupt officials,
sometimes to good effect. She campaigned for the complete disso-
ciation of church and state. She battled for sound money and waged
war on the Bank of the United States. This was the subject on which

she interviewed President Adams as he bathed in the river. She backed liberal immigration and tariff laws, the abolition of flogging in the Navy, better conditions for the wage-earner, and free thought, free speech and a free press.

She was liberal in her own interpretation of a free press, and sometimes confused candor with violent abuse. But in spite of its poor printing and proofreading, *Paul Pry* had a national circulation and was read with some degree of interest in Washington, the focal point of attack. Within a year she had agents all over the country handling her paper. She published the names of subscribers who failed to pay up. She stopped short at nothing.

Her venture into publishing was hard work. Snow sometimes covered the floor where her paper was printed and the ink froze before it could record her blistering phrases. Her attacks on public evils were leavened occasionally by chatty reports on the doings of Sarah, Mehitabel's earliest ancestor. Sarah was a column character based on Mrs. Sarah Stack, Anne Royall's alter ego, her companion and secretary, and the only person who sincerely mourned her when she died. She appeared often in Anne's writings as a rather likable figure, and gave occasional charm to the vindictive columns of the paper. In the middle of a spirited attack on Evangelicism, the reader might come on an odd little note telling what Sarah had done with the ink.

Anne stopped publishing *Paul Pry* in November, 1836, as suddenly as she had launched it, and at once got out a successor, *The Huntress*, which was less rancorous, better printed and more literate than its forerunner. This time she made some effort to keep up with the current style in journalism by printing stories, verse, anecdotes and some balanced editorial comment. She confined her own ramblings to her column, which always retained the flavor of her strong and eccentric personality.

She died on October 1, 1854, and was buried in the Congressional Cemetery. There was no money to mark her grave and to-day there is nothing to indicate the spot where she lies. Copies of her books and newspapers are rare. The other papers gave her little space when she died. She was a freak, who might have been born in any age. The laughter she had caused died quickly; there was little else by which to remember the virago of early journalism, except John Quincy Adams' epitaph and the interview on the banks of the Potomac.

More far-reaching was the commotion caused by Victoria Woodhull, who brought all her native dash to bear on journalism. It was in no mean manner that she crammed the columns of her paper with scandal. Her effects had some of the largeness of her own personality. She brought the Henry Ward Beecher case into court and did it with a flourish. Undoubtedly she would have gone further, had not Anthony Comstock clipped her wings by court injunction.

Victoria and her sister, Tennessee, were scarcely classifiable, either as journalists or human beings. They were magnetic, fascinating, eerie, raffish, triumphantly heralding the freedom of women, preaching free love, basking in the counsels of the great financiers, and using the honest craft of journalism for their own fell ends.

Victoria could have led an army or swayed a mob—as she sometimes did—but in actual fact she was an illiterate beauty, reacting to little beyond the emotional motives that drove her to dashing ventures. She never read a book, rarely looked at a paper, even her own. Neither she nor Tennessee did much for *Woodhull and Claflin's Weekly* except to inspire the wild plunges in policy which carried it along on its drunken course.

They had two smart ghosts in the background—Stephen Pearl Andrews and Colonel James H. Blood—who knew what to do with pen and ink and how to sail close to the wind. Colonel Blood was a scholar. He gave Victoria her halo of learning. But she needed little aid to put herself across. She was born for a headline rôle—one of the naturals of her generation.

She reached it in quick strides that took her from Homer, Ohio, to the heart of Wall Street with few stops by the way. An inconsequential marriage in her early teens to Dr. Canning Woodhull. Six weeks on the stage. Some lucky plunges in Western real estate and an intermission in Chicago, where she and Tennessee practiced clairvoyance. Tennessee communed happily with the spirits but Victoria could not bear such minor flights.

So she brought her sister with her to New York. They stormed the town in 1868. They looked up Commodore Vanderbilt, Jim Fiske, Jay Gould. They founded their own bank. They launched their own paper. While most of their sisters were sitting among the antimacassars waiting for blessed events, Victoria and Tennessee were hobnobbing with the big shots downtown. Tennie was the beauty; Victoria was supposed to have brains.

In the spring of 1870 the first issue of *Woodhull and Claflin's Weekly* was launched with the bold front-page announcement: *"Upward and Onward. Progress! Free Thought. Untrammeled Lives. Breaking the Way for Future Generations."* Striking a virtuous note, it deplored personalities in print, wilful misstatements or scurrility, and promised that all matters of vital interest to the people would be treated freely and without reservation in the new weekly. It would support Victoria C. Woodhull for President and would advocate suffrage without sex distinction.

Cunning Tennessee had already filled up the gaping chinks with juicy advertisements from her Wall Street friends. It was a five-cent weekly, printed on the finest paper. The other newspapers found it a "handsome and readable paper." But at first it was scarcely dashing enough to capture public attention. The editorials urged independence in woman. All manifestations of feminism were applauded.

Victoria rode about town in a carriage, handsomely turned out, the woman journalist of the hour. She billowed out of her home on Gramercy Park while the neighbors gaped at the lovely apparition on her way to Wall Street. Even at this early stage they were a little suspicious of the high jinks going on downtown.

However, the legend was growing that she was a clever writer. No one had a clue to the two verbose ghosts who pulled the strings in the background. She and Tennessee rode high as the Lady Brokers of Wall Street—a halo of gold around their handsome heads and money in their pockets. For the moment their newly founded bank was doing well.

But by September they saw that a dash of pepper was needed to keep their weekly going. Feminism and the campaign to make Victoria President were not strong enough drawing cards to build up circulation. So they plunged boldly into the muckraking field. There was no limit to their daring. All the banned topics of the day were flaunted in print—prostitution, free love, social disease, abortion. The very words were shocking to the prim readers of the day. Their circulation soared to 20,000.

The advanced women who had hailed the weekly as a fine gesture for freedom began to watch it with suspicion. Were Victoria and Tennessee working for the cause of women or for the glorification of their lambent selves? A woman compositor complained in another paper that she had found six male clerks at 44 Broad Street and no member of her own sex except Victoria, who had given her a bewitching welcome until she discovered that she wanted work and then had turned her away with the crushing observation: "We won't have our paper spoiled by women."

Harriet Beecher Stowe satirized her harshly in *The Christian Union*, little dreaming of the storm that was about to break for the Beecher family. Victoria had secret knowledge that Henry Ward Beecher was interested in Theodore Tilton's wife. She had heard it from Tilton himself, in one of his enamored moments, for he belonged to Victoria's circle of favored friends.

The evidence seemed convincing to Victoria, coming direct from the husband. She saw no moral obliquity in the fact itself, but deplored the pastor's hypocrisy. She preferred people to follow their instincts grandly, gloriously, in the candid Woodhull manner. She gibed the preacher constantly through the columns of her paper. It became so pointed that he had several interviews with her. She claimed once to have had him at her knees, begging for mercy. He refused to appear with her on a public platform, which was a pity for him. But the bomb had not yet exploded. The sirens had more immediate troubles. The Equal Rights Party had nominated Victoria for the presidency of the United States and the campaign was on. Two years earlier she had presented her famous petition to Congress demanding equal rights.

Her parents' choice of a name for her gave Victoria much cause for optimism while she was running for the presidency. But it developed that she had attached undue importance to its implications on this occasion. She and Horace Greeley took a bad beating from Ulysses S. Grant. The victor got 272 electoral votes, Mr. Greeley scraped up 66, but Victoria failed to draw one. She was less depressed than Mr. Greeley.

"I was the worst beaten man who ever ran for high office," he complained when the fight was over. "And I have been assailed so bitterly that I hardly knew whether I was running for President or for the Penitentiary. In fact, I am all used up."

But Victoria wasn't, although her prestige was now on the wane and her bank was on the rocks. Public suspicion of the Woodhull-Claflin motives was becoming rather strong. The suggestion of blackmail was in the air. Their journal announced that if certain women did not stop blackguarding Victoria Woodhull she would print their private histories. Some of them claimed they were offered immunity for $500.

Things went from bad to worse. The sisters were now notorious and unpopular. The ladies sitting behind the lace curtains who had watched them careering down to Wall Street went back to their knitting, sure that convention had won. The sirens could not rent a house. Soon they lost even their office and moved to a smaller one along the street. On June 22, 1872, they were forced to suspend publication.

But they were not yet finished. Victoria was doing well as a public speaker. She had been a sensation at the New York Academy of Music, lecturing on free love and the impending revolution. On the platform she was irresistible—a glowing figure in flounces and pannier, her hair streaming down to her shoulders, her face blazing with zeal. She was more convincing in person than in print.

In the autumn of that year she launched one of the major social scandals of New York history by spilling the entire Beecher-Tilton story in a long impassioned speech. She revived her journal for the express purpose of publishing eleven columns on this unusual triangle and getting every detail of it into the unbeatable clarity of print. The story had been dinner table conversation for months. But only Victoria Woodhull would have had the temerity to put it in black and white.

Her early threats were more than fulfilled. The lackadaisical Theodore decided he must do something about it, and brought suit against Dr. Beecher for alienation of affection. He had not minded so much until Victoria sprang the story in public. It caused a terrific sensation. The issue containing the charges sold on the streets for as much as $40 a copy. All social classes sat back and enjoyed the collection of fortifying facts that Victoria had assembled.

Anthony Comstock dashed to the rescue of Dr. Beecher. He found the sirens guilty of a "most abominable and unjust charge against one of the purest and best citizens of the United States." He rounded up evidence the day after their paper carried the story, and sought action against them through the district attorney and the federal authorities.

Victoria and Tennessee were discovered in a carriage on Broad Street, sitting haughtily on five hundred copies of their weekly. Not much surprised, Victoria shortly found herself in Ludlow Street Jail. She didn't really mind. She soon got out. And her journal was fully revived on the high winds of publicity. It resumed regular publication on December 28, 1872.

But Comstock would not let the matter rest. He trapped the sirens cunningly by mailing a letter from Greenwich, Connecticut, signed John Beardsley, and enclosing money for the Beecher issue. They were indicted and charged with sending obscene matter through the mails. This was a more serious affair. Colonel Blood was arrested first. He sent a warning to the sisters. Tennessee hid under a wash tub and Victoria dashed over to Jersey City with her bondsman. It was not that she objected to going to jail. She had been there before. But she was scheduled to make a speech at Cooper Institute and she wanted to keep her engagement.

It was January 9, 1873. The hall was packed with people who wanted to hear Victoria tell the Beecher story again. Marshals and policemen surrounded the building, determined to keep her from getting in. No one knew where she was.

An old woman hobbled down the aisle in a dress of Quaker gray and a coal-scuttle bonnet, and took her place in the front row. The chairman began to speak. She apologized for the absence of Mrs. Woodhull. "She can't appear to-night lest she be again thrown into an American Bastille," she said. "Though they may shut her out, they shall not prevent the delivery of the lecture, for she has deputized me to read to you 'The Naked Truth, or the Situation Reviewed.' "

Like a flash of lightning the old Quaker Lady bounded up on the platform in a whirl of petticoats, pulled off her bonnet with a triumphant gesture, dropped her outer robe at her feet and stood revealed as Victoria Woodhull. Peals of applause greeted her. She made a fiery speech. For an hour and a half a tempest of revelation swept the audience and kept them breathless.

The marshal with his writ for arrest was transfixed. The policemen listened with open mouths. At last one of them remembered his duty and moved toward the platform. Victoria was peremptorily escorted to Ludlow Street Jail. Her hour was ended. But she was found not guilty of sending obscene matter through the mails. The facts she had blithely published became a matter of court record. The Beecher case was now the talk of the town. Victoria aired it again in her journal in May.

But she was bored with journalism and its alarms. Her credit was no longer good. The suffragists cold-shouldered her and did not invite her to their convention. For the time being she conceded defeat. Her weekly ceased publication altogether, little regretted, even by its founders. The New York *Times* commented severely that "license never had been carried to such an extent as in the free love journal of Woodhull and Claflin, and the female name never had been more disgraced and degraded than by these women."

Eventually Victoria apologized to Dr. Beecher for having interfered in his private affairs. She made it quite clear that the only thing she objected to about his behavior was his hypocrisy. But New York was a little tired of her. So she traveled and lectured. When she felt she had exhausted America she went to England, taking Tennie with her. Again they moved like conquerors, their beauty and dash giving them a great advantage in this untilled field. They were the suffrage queens from across the sea.

Lecturing one night in St. James's Hall, Victoria made such an impression on John Biddulph Martin, banker and philanthropist, that he contrived to meet her afterwards and make her his wife. They lived happily together until his death in 1897.

So Victoria permanently joined her regal namesake in England and lived in great state. At last her name implied victory. With her sister's substantial backing Tennie became Lady Cook. Once or twice Tennie returned to New York and appeared at correct receptions, still beautiful, still full of spirit, harboring malice toward no one. When she died in 1923, her tenants mourned her and Victoria wept at her bier. She left more than $500,000 to her sister, whom she had always adored. Victoria scattered largesse, her generous spirit soaring with her fortune. She continued her work for the suffrage cause, helped to promote friendly relations between Great Britain and the United States, and was the moving spirit in the purchase of Sulgrave Manor. She died at her home in Tewksbury in 1927, at the age of eighty-nine.

. . . .

Kate Field also believed in the rights of women, but she brought a lighter touch to bear on journalism than her predecessors. Like Victoria, she created a dramatic effect, was handsome in appearance, dashing in style. She came of an accomplished English family whose roots were in Warwickshire. She was born in St. Louis in 1840, the daughter of Joseph M. Field, a man of varied interests. He studied law, abandoned it, was one of the founders of the New Orleans *Picayune* and contributed to the paper under the pseudonym "Straws." Kate's first story was signed "Straws Jr." and appeared when she was eight years old. Her mother, Eliza Riddle, was an actress.

At sixteen Kate was sent to a New England seminary, and three years later she took the first of many trips abroad. She traveled with an aunt and uncle from Boston and lived in Paris, Rome and Florence, meeting the celebrities of the time. Walter Savage Landor taught her Latin. Anthony Trollope referred to her in his autobiography as his "most chosen friend." She knew the Brownings and George Eliot.

Kate studied for opera but a fall from a horse in Italy impaired her health and her voice, so she turned to writing instead. She did a series of letters for the New York *Tribune*, the Chicago *Tribune* and other papers throughout the country during each of her trips abroad. Travel correspondence was in much demand at this time, and every paper ran flowery letters from traveling scribes.

After her return to America in 1874 she haunted the smart circles of Boston, Newport and New York, studied art, music and the drama, and knew everyone worth knowing. She was one of the quoted sophisticates of the day, much ahead of her time in many respects. Such was her versatility that she tackled the stage too, but with less success. She played Peg Woffington at Booth's Theatre in 1874. Her stage fright was so extreme that she could scarcely find her voice until the last act. She was rated a flop, but she toured later with John T. Raymond in *The Gilded Age*, and, as Mary Keemle, appeared on the British stage in a comedy written by herself.

The first time Queen Victoria picked up a telephone receiver, Kate Field sang to her over the wire. She was an astonishing person, with dozens of interests. She turned out books and comedies with great facility and it never ceased to surprise her that she could write better than she could act. In 1890 she moved to Washington and founded her weekly review, a novel experiment in journalism.

Most of *Kate Field's Washington* was written by Kate herself, with vigor, fearlessness and a vivid style. Her aim was to mirror the men and events of the time but she rode her own hobbies hard. She campaigned on Hawaiian annexation, international copyright, temperance, the prohibition of Mormon polygamy, and dress reform. On her return from one of her trips to Europe she decided that the dress of the American woman was ugly and overburdened. She established her own Cooperative Dress Association, but it made no dent in fashion and died a natural death within a year.

Although Kate Field sometimes mystified her friends by the causes she espoused, she never failed to charm them. Her journal was interesting and gracefully written but was not a great success. Her enthusiasms usually burst into vivid flame, then died quickly. In 1896 she suspended publication and went off to Hawaii. On a tour of the islands she rode through a hurricane and was blown off her horse's back. She died of an illness brought on by her exposure and the hardships of this ride. Kate had made a singular place for herself with her wit and ubiquity, and she was undoubtedly one of the more brilliant exponents of personal journalism.

But even before the nineteenth century women here and there in America were getting out their own papers. They were not spectacular personal journals like *Paul Pry*, *Woodhull and Claflin's Weekly* or *Kate Field's Washington*. The names of their owners suggest nothing today. But Rhode Island's first newspaper, published in 1732, was owned and edited by Anna Franklin. She and her two daughters did the printing and their servants worked the press. They were so adept that Mrs. Franklin was appointed printer for the colony and turned out all the official papers. They printed an edition of the Colonial laws filling 340 pages.

In 1772 Clementine Reid published a paper in Virginia, backing the Colonial cause. Two years later a rival paper was started by Mrs. H. Boyle in the interests of the Crown. Both papers were published in Williamsburg and were short-lived. In 1773 Elizabeth Timothy brought out a paper in Charleston, South Carolina. She was owner and editor and held the position of state printer for seventeen years. Another woman, Mary Crouch, published a paper in the same city contemporaneously. The chief motive for its existence was its opposition to the Stamp Act. She moved eventually to Salem, Massachusetts, but continued to publish her paper there. At about the same time Sarah Goddard was publishing a paper in Newport, Rhode

Island. But Sarah found she could not do it single-handed and was forced to bring in a man. Dozens of papers were launched by women during this period. They were all propagandist in tone and were correspondingly poor in the journalistic sense.

In different parts of the country to-day women may be found running their own papers, usually by inheritance from a husband or father. But none has essayed the intensely personal journalism of Anne Royall, Victoria Woodhull or Kate Field. These three were newspaper women only by chance. Essentially they were egotists grasping for the nearest medium of self-expression.

Chapter IV

HEARTS AND ROSES

FANNY FERN AND JENNY JUNE BOTH HELPED TO OPEN UP THE WAY for the newspaper women who came after them. They wrote so copiously that it was practically impossible for a confirmed newspaper reader to ignore the harmony of their alliterative names.

Fanny was the first to wail and sob and drag her widow's weeds through the public prints. She has often been called the grandmother of all the sob sisters. But Jenny was a sound pioneer, the first to make a business of going down to the office every day and writing at a newspaper desk.

The current fashion was leisurely correspondence paid for on space rates, written in the boudoir, on Timothy's mahogany desk or in a European pension. Jenny was a positive sensation when she ran around town, collected news and wrote it within sound of the presses. "Why, you go on so naturally and make so little fuss about your work that I sometimes forget you are a woman," said her grateful editor.

But Fanny Fern wanted all the world to know that she was a woman—and an oppressed one, too. Her paragraphs gushed forth with the freedom of an undisciplined mind. She exploited her own personality. She took up moral issues with a great hoopla and fastened on such piquant questions as drinking and smoking, the illicit practice of men walking through the ladies' cabin on the Brooklyn ferry, and the merits of gutta percha paddings for lantern jaws. Fanny was always on the side of law, order and the black wool stocking. Her style seems slightly anachronistic to-day. It had none of the dateless literary quality that makes Margaret Fuller, Grace Greenwood, Gail Hamilton and Kate Field as readable now as when they wrote for their papers more than half a century ago.

But none of her contemporaries could touch Fanny in popularity. The more thoroughly she was ignored by the literati, the better the public liked her. She was an early best seller. Her *Fern Leaves from Fanny's Portfolio* was a sensation and her sales ran up to 180,000. She was the talk of the town. Even her more genuinely talented sisters did not ignore her.

Fanny was blatant, sharp, and given to jocular buffoonery that passed for wit. Her style was cumulative. She rushed along with terrific outcroppings of dots, dashes and exclamation marks. She was breathless and breezy; loud but vapid. She belabored clergymen, lawyers and editors with strength and volubility. Her scorn for a man who could say "I can't" was appalling.

> "I can't." O, pshaw! I throw my glove in your face, if I *am* a woman! You are a disgrace to corduroys. What! A man lack courage? A man afraid to face anything on earth, save his Maker? Why! I have the most unmitigated contempt for you, you pusillanimous pussy cat! There is nothing manly about you except your whiskers!

This was more or less typical of Fanny on the rampage. She was at her best in a sea of pathos. Harps and muted violins were the obbligato of her staccato utterances.

She was forty before she turned to journalism. One life had already been lived. Two husbands had been lost along the way. Her own name was Sara Payson Willis. She was born in 1811 at Portland, Maine, and at six was taken by her parents to Boston, where her father edited the *Puritan Recorder* and *Youth's Companion.* Her upbringing was devout. She attended public schools in Boston and then did her finishing at Catherine Beecher's Seminary in Hartford, Connecticut.

At twenty-six she married Charles H. Eldridge, a Boston cashier. They had nine unremarkable years together, then he died, leaving her penniless and in debt. Her second venture was with a Boston merchant named Farrington. This was an unhappy marriage that ended in divorce. All that remains of Mr. Farrington in the records is the fact that he bolted to Chicago, leaving Fanny stranded. He did not even leave his first name behind.

The seven years that followed were lean ones. Fanny's father was unsympathetic. Her brother, Nathaniel P. Willis, editor and poet, was frigid. She lived in a furnished room. She sewed. She taught. She was wretched at both. At last her indignation with fate drove her to the point of action. She put the children to bed one night and then sat down to write a piece for the paper. Everyone in the family seemed to know what to do with a pen. Fanny thought she would try her luck. She marched in personally to the *Mother's Assistant* with the first of the fern leaves. It was accepted and her reward was fifty cents, but she had to dun the editor for her money. Her subject was a "model minister" and it was done in Fanny's best philosophical vein.

The members of her highbrow family were skeptical and paid no attention to her early gibberings. They could scarcely foresee that she was to become one of America's favorite authors. They thereby missed a chance to make a fortune but did not seem to care, for much later, when Fanny was highly successful and going along on her own momentum, her brother still scornfully refused to print any of her work.

But she caught on from the start. She had a natural instinct for the popular thing. She contributed regularly to the Boston *Olive Branch*, using the pen name Olivia Branch, and she did some sparklers at $2 a column for the Boston *True Flag*. The country was overrun at the time with jolly little publications that mopped up all the stray bits by the lady journalists. The religious papers were a lush field in themselves.

The editor of the *True Flag* was afraid the public might have a little too much of Fanny Fern, so he proposed the second pen name to spread the butter further. It worked very well. Fanny's stuff was liked under either name. She had the knack. The editor's comment on her style is illuminating:

> The manuscript was characteristic—decidedly Ferny—dashed all over with astonishing capitals and crazy italics—and stuck as full with staggering exclamation points, as a pin cushion with pins. In print, the italics were intended to resemble jolly words, leaning over and tumbling down with laughter, and the interjections were supposed to be tottering under the weight of double-entendre and puns. At first sight, the writing looked as if it might have been paced off by trained canary birds—driven first through puddles of ink, then marched into hieroglyphic drill on the sheet like a militia company on parade. All Fanny's manuscripts demanded a good deal of editorial care to prepare them for the press; her first productions, particularly, requiring as thorough weeding as so many beds of juvenile beets and carrots.

But Robert Bonner, who was her editor later on the *Ledger*, thought differently. Fanny's copy was sacred. She was treated with greater deference than Henry Ward Beecher, Alice Cary, or any of his other contributors. "We never think of cutting down, or even altering a word in Fanny Fern's articles," he wrote. For Fanny was a born circulation getter.

Soon the question was being asked on all sides: "Who is Fanny Fern?" The public wanted to know. A perspicacious publishing house heard the murmur, collected all the odds and ends she had written and published them in book form. When the scattered leaves were all assembled, the effect was overpowering. They launched the author as a public character in the year 1853. She now decided that the time had come to try New York.

Fanny was an elegant figure when she swept into the metropolis. She stepped high, had a florid complexion, an aquiline nose, an arrogant mouth and bold blue eyes. She moved in full sail. Her flounces took up the space of five uninflated human beings. She walked with a rustle and a swish. She ducked her head like a swan. She was lively, bad-tempered, gushing in her manners, trite in her style.

Fanny did not arrive empty-handed. She came with a novel in tow and offered it first to her brother for his *Home Journal*. The fastidious Nathaniel turned it down. He detested her "noisy rattling style." Fanny was furious. She stamped into his office and said he was jealous of her success. His publication was none too flourishing at the time. Nathaniel didn't care, even though it might mean more money in the till. He thought Fanny a humbug and preferred to stick to his literary standards.

But James Parton, his assistant editor, not only admired Fanny's work but loved her. He was an Englishman, a conscientious biographer who took her as seriously as he did his work. He had already written to her ecstatically without knowing that she was Nathaniel's sister. His defense of Fanny was so insistent that it cost him his job. Nathaniel was vindictive. But Parton married Fanny and continued to work on his biographies. She joined the staff of the *Ledger*. Within a year of her arrival in New York, Mr. Bonner was paying her $100 for a single weekly column of her exclamatory prose.

Fanny tempered some of her early extravagances, but her style did not change materially. However, she became so much of a household figure that the most dignified publications took note of her performances. *Harpers Magazine* saw her as the leader of a literary movement and published the following estimate of the passion flower of the press:

> She has won her way unmistakably to the hearts of the people; this we interpret as a triumph of natural feeling. It shows that the day for stilted rhetoric, scholastic refinements, and big dictionary words, the parade, pomp and pageantry of literature is declining.

This, probably, was the explanation of Fanny's phenomenal success. She was usually on the warpath. Mr. Bonner put it neatly when he said: "She is an embodiment of American womanhood, giving the world a piece of her mind, and the world is glad to get it." He exploited her handsomely, giving her full-page display advertisements in the other papers. Her work appeared exclusively in his paper, which had a large circulation at the time and was admittedly dedicated to "choice literature, romance, the news and commerce."

Fanny was eccentric, flippant, and masculine in her manners, but she had plenty of zip. She had her revenge on Nathaniel by caricaturing him in a novel she wrote called *Ruth Hall*. It was a poor book, scathingly reviewed, but there was so much talk about it that 50,000 copies were sold. She pictured the rather well-known Nathaniel as Hyacinth, a "mincing, conceited, tiptoeing, be-curled, be-perfumed popinjay" who paid $100 for a fine vase while his sister, the worthy Ruth, begged bread for her children in the streets. It was all most diverting for Nathaniel's sophisticated friends.

By this time Fanny was living a lavish life. Her marriage to the adoring Mr. Parton was a success. The family spent their summers in Newport. Each year her articles were collected and published in book form under such provocative titles as *Ginger Snaps* and *Caper Sauce*.

Her column ran in the *Ledger* until a week before her death in 1872. The *World* gave her a front-page obituary notice when she died, for she had become a really well-known figure. There was a big turn-out of literary celebrities at her funeral.

Of much more moment to the newspaper women who followed her was Jenny June, really the forerunner of the trained reporter of to-day. In the middle fifties there was no such thing as a woman's department in any of the papers. Why should there be? Women didn't read the papers. Jenny studied the field. She saw that there was nothing particularly stirring to record. Women were not yet interested in clubs; in fact she herself was to help found the first. They didn't go to business. They had no cravings for careers. They had not yet become eager for the vote. The only excitement they could supply was an occasional scandal or a gorgeous wedding, and a man was always on hand to act as official historian on these occasions. But parties, clothes and beauty were the topics that inevitably lit sparks at any feminine gathering, and Jenny wisely decided to concentrate on the vanities of woman.

As time went on she did editorials, book reviews and dramatic criticism, but her main preoccupation was with fashions. She also tackled the problems of the kitchen and the home. She had a fresh and breezy style; she went about the town; she knew people. She was amazed to find that her stuff was a success. So were her editors. They gave her more work to do. They liked having her around the office. She was bottled in a quiet corner, but there she was—"the female reporter, complete with quill and notebook." She had charming manners but was not openly aggressive. Jenny was small, vivacious, brown-haired, blue-eyed. "There is no sex in labor," she used to say, "and I want my work taken as the achievement of an individual, with no qualifications, no indulgence, no extenuations simply because I happen to be a woman, working along the same line with men." Her everyday conversation was on the oracular side but she was not a sentimentalist, like Fanny Fern.

She was the wife of David G. Croly, whom she married when he was making $14 a week as a reporter on the *Herald*. She was soon writing for the *World*, the *Tribune*, the *Times* and *Noah's Sunday Times*. When her husband was appointed managing editor of the *World* in 1862, Jenny took over the woman's department entirely, making a great success of it. She was known as one of the town's best reporters. In 1872 she went over to the *Daily Graphic* with her husband, syndicating her articles to papers in Boston, Chicago, New Orleans, Baltimore and other cities.

Jenny June's stories became a history of American fashion and the gradual changes in merchandising. In an article called "Returning to Town," which was published in September, 1873, she pictured the actual transition of trade from the small shop to the department store. She ran the first version of the now popular shopping column, for she named shops freely in her stories, pointing out that an excellent glove, fine, soft, well-fitting and extremely durable, had been introduced at Lord and Taylor's, or that Macy's was carrying "full samples of dolls, dolls' trousseaux and dolls' houses of every kind and degree, all the purchases being made in Europe under Mr. Macy's own supervision, so that ladies may rely on getting the best and the prettiest, as well as the cheapest, at this establishment."

Jenny campaigned vigorously against the slavery of custom in women's dress. She opposed foreign fashions, which were then beginning to flood the market, and maintained that women should wear only the becoming and the appropriate. She was withering about the pannier in 1865 and deplored the Grecian bend, saying sharply that she would like to give a good spanking to the "exhibitor of these doubtful airs and graces." She favored uniformity in dress and in 1873 campaigned for standard evening dress, but was no more successful than Kate Field a decade later. Women continued to dress as they pleased.

Jenny took stock of every fad in food and home decoration. She was always a little ahead of her time. In the rococo age she saw the virtue of simplicity. After the panic of the early seventies she advised her feminine readers to simplify their housekeeping.

In the autumn of 1873 Jenny, like the enterprising girl she was, went exploring the East Side for the *Graphic*, to study the condition of "female workers among the lowly and unfortunate." Her piece was entitled "What A Lady Saw." The hazards of the narrow overcrowded streets with their gesticulating peddlers were quite considerable for a lady like Jenny. She was shocked to discover the female workers living in unheated rooms without blankets or carpets. She found the lower East Side as "remote and strange to the eyes of New Yorkers as if it lay east of the Ganges or west of the Rocky Mountains."

To the newspaper girl of to-day, who dashes to the East Side at a moment's notice when a baby is kidnapped or an indignant wife polishes off her husband, Jenny June's reactions may seem slightly academic. But her copy was always sound and readable. She had a broad outlook on life. She knew most of the important figures of the day in journalism, art and politics. She conducted a salon, first on Grove Street, then uptown on Seventy-first Street. She found time to bring up five children and to run her home commendably. She was much ahead of her generation.

In 1868 Jenny helped to found the Sorosis Club, an idea that mushroomed amazingly throughout the United States. It was the result of feminine indignation because women were barred from the reception and banquet tendered to Charles Dickens by the Press Club. Jenny had applied for tickets, feeling that her position in journalism entitled her to an invitation. The men thought otherwise.

So she and a few other hardy souls founded the Sorosis Club. Alice Cary was appointed president. Kate Field and Fanny Fern were on the band wagon. They were heaped with ridicule. But Jenny brought the boys around in the end. The Press Club invited the Sorosis members to a breakfast, feeding them but not allowing them to talk or participate in the program. This was a great hardship for such eloquent women. They sat in frozen silence, being sung to and lectured, but they did not enjoy the occasion.

The Sorosis then gave a tea for the Press Club. The order was reversed. The men had to sit in silence while the women made speeches. They were not even allowed to respond to their own toast. The third exchange between the two groups was a Dutch Treat party, men and women paying their own way and sharing equally in the honors and responsibilities. This was one of the earliest occasions on which the two sexes sat down at a public dinner on approximately equal terms.

The Sorosis seemed to be the thing for which the women of America had been waiting. Clubs began to form everywhere. Nothing could stop them. Jenny June envisioned them all coming together, which they did in 1889, in the General Federation of Women's Clubs. She was the moving spirit in this consolidation. In the same year she organized the Woman's Press Club.

Indignant that her own craft did not give full recognition to newspaper women, Jenny invited forty women working for the New York papers to form their own organization. Eleven years later they had a permanent home and two hundred members. This was the reigning women's press club for many years, until it was superseded by the New York Newspaper Women's Club.

From newspaper work Jenny June branched out with Madame Demorest's *Mirror of Fashions*, a quarterly, writing it all herself for nearly four years. In 1887 she bought a half-interest in *Godey's Lady's Book* and soon afterwards launched *The Woman's Cycle*. This was consolidated with the *Home Magazine*, which she edited.

She began to write when she was seventeen years old. She took her pseudonym from a book of verse by Benjamin F. Taylor, given her when she was twelve years old by a clergyman who used to visit her family in Wappingers Falls. She was a social worker at heart as well as a newspaper woman, and before her death in 1901 she wrote her own epitaph: "I have never done anything that was not helpful to women, so far as it lay in my power." Jenny June often said that a "well-rounded club was an epitome of the world."

Of the same genre was Nancy Johnson, more widely known to the reading public as Minnie Myrtle. Nancy was a heroic and scholarly figure, crippled early in life, but pursuing her career with enterprise and talent. She was born in 1818 in Newbury, Vermont, and her first literary work was *Letters from a Sick Room*, done while she was convalescing from the amputation of one of her legs. She spent several years traveling with Catherine Beecher, acting as her secretary, and then settled in Saratoga Springs where she corresponded for the New York papers.

She was a friend of Henry J. Raymond, editor of the *Times*. He was interested in her work and in 1857 he sent her to Europe as a traveling correspondent. She moved from one country to another, described the vineyards and valleys of Germany, the weavers' cottages of Normandy, the castles of the Pyrenees, the Swiss mountains, the salons of Paris during the Napoleonic era, the plague of cholera that swept Europe, the oratory of Disraeli and John Bright in the House of Commons. She watched Queen Victoria pass in her gilded coach and the Empress Eugénie whispering and laughing with her husband while prayers were being chanted.

Nancy became a cosmopolitan. She was received all over Europe.

She went to receptions in broad-brimmed hats with streamers, and to balls in rose-colored silk. She had a perceptive eye for what went on around her, and readers of the *Times* got fresh and piquant impressions of the social life of Europe from her writings. She dedicated her book, *The Myrtle Wreath*, to Mr. Raymond.

It was not until Nancy was old that her wanderings ceased and she returned to the quiet New England village where she was born. There she spun marvelous tales of her adventures abroad for nieces, nephews and cousins. Many of them were handed down in the family and are best remembered to-day by Mrs. Frances Parkinson Keyes, her great-niece, herself a familiar figure in the Press Gallery and a well-known magazine editor and author.

Nancy was the author of several books, all of which sold well, and she kept on writing almost to the day of her death, which occurred at Haverhill in 1892.

Chapter V

NELLIE BLY

IT WAS NELLIE BLY WHO FIRST MADE AMERICA CONSCIOUS OF THE woman reporter. She burst like a comet on New York, a dynamic figure, five feet three, with mournful gray eyes and persistent manners. She dramatized herself in a new form of journalism, going down in a diving bell and up in a balloon, posing as a lunatic, a beggar, a factory hand, a shop girl and a Salvation Army lass.

But Nellie's great coup, which neither she nor any other newspaper woman equaled again, was her trip around the world in 72 days, 6 hours, 11 minutes, outdoing the dream of Jules Verne's Phileas Fogg and creating no end of an international stir.

She sailed from New York on November 14, 1889, and came home in triumph on January 25, 1890, the *World* bringing her across the country from San Francisco by special train and greeting her with the smash headline leading the paper, "Father Time Outdone!"

With two small satchels, two frocks, a toothbrush, some flannel underwear, a bank book, a ghillie cap and a sturdy plaid ulster, Nellie galloped and ran, roasted and froze, sped from ship to train, to burro, to jinrickshaw, to sampan, to barouche, until she reached the terrific climax of outdoing Father Time for Joseph Pulitzer. It was exhilarating journalism, good for the *World*, superb for Nellie, entertaining for the public, and it did no one any harm.

One had only to follow her career from its beginnings in Cochrane Mills, Pennsylvania, to know that Nellie was destined for front-page notice. She was born on May 5, 1867, in the small town founded by her father, who was a judge. Her name was Elizabeth Cochrane. She had enterprising blood in her veins. Her grand-uncle, Thomas Kennedy, went around the world before she was born but it took him three years and he came back with wrecked health. He intended to write the history of his trip but never did. However, Nellie carried on.

Her father, a scholarly man, took charge of her early education. She was an imaginative child, fond of books and given to scrawling fantastic fables on their fly-leaves. She went to a boarding school in Indiana at thirteen but was brought home within a year because of her delicate health. When her father died and his estate was settled there was no money, although he had been regarded as ·a man of wealth.

With the enterprise that was to mark her entire career, Nellie left home and sought her fortune in Pittsburgh. Almost at once she got in touch with the newspaper world by answering an article in the Pittsburgh *Dispatch* entitled "What Girls Are Good For." Her letter was not published but she was asked to write a piece for the Sunday paper on girls and their sphere in life. Without any hesitancy she put her views on paper, received a check for her efforts and was asked to write more.

Nellie's newspaper sense was alert from the start. Having landed on the springboard, she plunged boldly into the sea with a piece entitled "Divorce." She signed it Nellie Bly, a pseudonym suggested to her by George A. Madden, managing editor of the *Dispatch*. He had taken it from Stephen C. Foster's song, popular at the moment.

Nellie started her newspaper career with an original idea. She went through factories and workshops in Pittsburgh, her crusading spirit already in full flower. Her articles were emotional and spat their indignation. They all had the personal quality which gave her a steady and constant following in later years. At first she made $5 a week. Eventually she was to make $25,000 from her writings in a single year.

She covered society, the theater and art for her paper. She was young and looked it. She had only just put up her hair, and she seemed shy and sensitive. Her large gray eyes were honest and questing. Her manners were meek. This quality stayed with Nellie to the time of her death. It concealed some of the terrific driving force that made her dauntless in the pursuit of her object. It fooled many of her unwitting victims.

She set out on her travels early. She had not been in Pittsburgh long before she decided to see the world. She took her mother and they went to Mexico and journeyed everywhere that the train would take them. Nellie sent back rather trite letters to her paper. The smart newspaper girls who had preceded her had all done travel correspondence. Why not Nellie?

When she returned to Pittsburgh her salary was raised to $15 a week, but she had seen a larger world and she was no longer satisfied, so she decided to try New York. The walls of Jericho didn't crumble at the first blast of the trumpet. She tramped the hot streets in the summer of 1887 and wondered what she could do to make the metropolitan publishers know that she had arrived. Then, as now, they were singularly incredulous of the merits of a woman reporter.

Nellie reached her lowest ebb when she lost her purse with nearly $100, practically all the money she had in the world. Feeling desperate, she made another assault on the gold-domed *World* building. She had been beseeching Mr. Pulitzer by letter to allow her to go up in the balloon which he was sponsoring at St. Louis, but her pleas had been ignored.

She had no introductions but she was determined to crash the inner sanctum. She badgered the custodian of the gate for three hours until she got to John A. Cockerill and finally to Mr. Pulitzer himself. She was not particularly good-looking, nor was she smart. But she was a human dynamo and almost at once she enlisted the interest of her shrewd and experienced audience. She laid before the two editors a list of suggestions for stories—all of the stunt order. They looked them over and were favorably impressed.

Nellie then told them the tale of the lost purse. They felt sorry for the poor little creature in New York without a bean. In her soft, persistent way she could always wheedle people into doing what she wished. Mr. Pulitzer gave her $25 to keep her going until he and Mr. Cockerill had had time to come to some decision on her suggestions.

Nellie went back to her furnished room, sure that the battle was won. And indeed, from that moment on, all gates opened automatically for the small tornado, and nothing stayed her course. The *World* decided to let her work up one of her own ideas—that she should feign insanity and investigate the treatment of the insane on Blackwell's Island. There had been complaints about the way in which patients were treated there.

This was not the easiest assignment for a reporter on trial, but Nellie was a gifted actress. She practised her part before a mirror. She tore down her heavy brown hair and made faces at herself. She read ghost stories so as to create a morbid state of mind. She laughed wildly at her own reflection. Then, when she felt in the proper mood, she dressed in old clothes and went to a temporary home for women, where she feigned madness so successfully that she was committed to Blackwell's Island without any difficulty. Four physicians pronounced her insane. And to her horror she found that the more sanely she behaved, the crazier they believed her to be, with the exception of one doctor who apparently was not taken in by her histrionics.

As soon as she was out she wrote two sensational stories in which she described her experiences. This was her formal introduction to the New York public. The *World* was in its crusading heyday and was widely read, so that many thousands were aware that Nellie Bly had come to town. She told of the cold, the poor food and the cruelty to which the patients were exposed. She found the asylum a "human rat trap, easy to get into, impossible to get out of." She charged the nurses with goading their patients. She saw demented and gray-haired women dragged shrieking to hidden closets, their cries being stifled by force as they were hustled out of sight.

The headlines on Nellie's first-person stories announced that she had deceived judges, reporters and medical experts. The revelations created considerable stir in official circles. She was summoned to appear before the Grand Jury. She accompanied the jurors on a visit to Blackwell's Island. But, somehow, many of the abuses of which she had written so graphically seemed to have been toned down by the time they got there. Nellie ascribed this anticlimax to the fact that the official visit was expected. There had been time to clean up the halls, improve the look of the beds and move some of the patients to remote spots where their constant complaints could not be heard. Practically none of the patients she had described by name were to be found for questioning and the nurses contradicted Nellie on every point.

However, the Grand Jury sustained her findings, $3,000,000 was voted for improvements and changes were made in the management of the asylum. The *World* was pleased with Nellie and Nellie was pleased with herself. She was taken on the regular staff and was told to go to work on her ideas.

She went in for reform and one of her first attacks was leveled with deadly effect against Edward R. Phelps, whom she exposed as the lobby king of Albany. Her glee is apparent in her story which appeared on April 1, 1888:

> *For I'm a Pirate King!*
> *I'm in the Lobby Ring!*
> *Oh! what an uproarious,*
> *Jolly and glorious*
> *Biz for a Pirate King!*
>
> I was a lobbyist last week. I went up to Albany to catch a professional briber in the act. I did so. The briber, lobbyist and boodler whom I caught was Mr. Ed. Phelps. I pretended I wanted to have him help me kill a certain bill. Mr. Phelps was cautious at first and looked carefully into my record. He satisfied himself that I was honest and talked very freely for a king. . . .

From this point on, Nellie practically became the town reformer. Dr. Charles H. Parkhurst gave her credit for being of great aid to him. She visited the city prisons and turned out stories which resulted in the appointment of matrons to handle women prisoners.

In order to write authoritatively she had herself arrested and went through the regular procedure. She visited the free dispensaries as an invalid to see what sort of medical care the poor were getting from the city. She spent a day in a diet kitchen and visited old women's homes. She sought employment as a servant through a number of agencies. She worked behind the glove counter of a large shop. She made paper boxes in a factory and found that more men wanted to flirt with her at this job than at anything else she tried. She put on a campaign against the handsome bucks who sauntered through the park when the grass was verdant and the dogwood bloomed. She rounded up the scoundrels one by one but the master technician eluded her. He appeared only on Wednesdays, drove a dashing pair of bays at a smart clip through the park, ogled the girls and usually made off with a brace of beauties to an unknown destination.

It took Nellie half a dozen Wednesdays to snare him. She spotted him at last by his whiskers. They were a rippling bronze and swept his four-in-hand. At the first glitter of his percipient eye she stepped into his carriage, arranged a rendezvous, lured him on to his undoing, and then unmasked the villain, sparing him nothing. He was a bartender from downtown who attended to his business six days a week and on the seventh put on his cutaway, pomaded a curl over his forehead, waxed his whiskers, plunged a sparkling horseshoe deep into his tie and drove his equipage through the park, casting the glad eye on the bell-sleeved beauties.

Nellie went back to her desk under the gold dome of the *World* building and wrote her exposé in finicky longhand. She ran the masher off his beat. His magnificent whiskers were seen no more in Central Park. Meanwhile, she went complacently on her way, the darling of the reading public.

So pervasive was she that the officials of public institutions began to look at every beggar woman's face with the suspicion that the deadly Bly girl might be lurking behind some disguise. Readers of the *World* watched eagerly to see what Nellie would be up to next. Mr. Pulitzer was not blind to the value of her services. In the winter of 1889 he decided to sponsor her trip around the world. He had rejected the same idea a year before. She received four days' notice to start and all her transportation was bought for her in New York.

It was still a ladylike age. There was little talk of the vote. The woman's page in the *World* was headed "Fair Woman's World." It had flower garnitures, music notes, a lady with a fan and a bustle. *The Master of Ballantrae* was running serially when Nellie got her orders to run a race with Father Time.

Thousands had been entranced by the dream of Phileas Fogg,

who went around the world in eighty days. If the mythical Phileas could do it in a dream in eighty days, why not the enterprising Nellie in less?

She decided that luggage would hamper her movements, because of customs and porters, so she chose her wardrobe with care. She had a "blue plaid in ladies' cloth' made up in twelve hours at Ghormleys'. By noon the tailor had it boned and fitted, and at five o'clock on the same day it was ready for the final try-on. Miss Wheelwright, her own dressmaker, made her a tropical costume of camel's hair cloth. She selected a heavy Scotch plaid ulster and a gossamer waterproof for downpours. So enterprising was Nellie that she set off without an umbrella, a dashing piece of business for 1889. She had two satchels—one a substantial gripsack, sixteen by seven inches, the other a light contraption which she slung over her shoulder. She had a toothbrush, a bank book, a pair of "easy-fitting shoes" and some changes of flannel underwear. She wore a thumb ring on the left hand as a talisman. She had worn it the day she sought work on the *World* and so considered it lucky.

One of her masculine colleagues on the paper interviewed Nellie the day she sailed. "And what will you do for a medicine chest, Miss Bly?" he asked solicitously. Miss Bly laughed heartily. There would be chemists everywhere along the line in such a modern and well-ordered world, she pointed out.

Her send-off was quieter than her return. Her paper announced:

> On four days' notice Miss Bly starts out with a gripsack for the longest journey known to mankind—she knows no such word as fail, and will add another to her list of triumphs—circumnavigation of the globe. The *World* today undertakes the task of turning a dream into a reality.
>
> With all the millions now invested in methods and modes of communication, interstate and international, the story of Miss Bly will give a valuable pointer in enabling the reader to appreciate these avenues of intercourse at their full value, to see their merits and their defects and note the present advanced state of invention in these lines of human effort.

Nellie sailed on the *Augusta Victoria* and pushed on according to the itinerary which had been carefully prepared for her. She carried a twenty-four hour watch with her, so that she could keep track of the time in New York. She was to take her chance along the line. No chartered trains or extra fast ships were to speed her on her way.

Viewed at this distance, her feat scarcely seems as breathtaking as it did at the time, since all she had to do was to stick to her schedule and make her well-ordered connections. It was a bit difficult to keep the excitement going at first. Cable communication was not what it is today. However, the *World* staff worked hard. Attention was drawn to the hazards of fog, the monsoon and vagrant storms. A circular chart was published every day, showing Nellie's stops. The public followed the game with checkers or pennies or dice, betting when she would reach each point.

Her stories came through as often as possible. They bubbled over with gay comment on the odd ways of foreigners, the food she had to eat, the cold she suffered on sea and land. Nellie had her own particular way of making it seem cataclysmic if her coffee was cold. She managed to make even the carriage of an English train somewhat enthralling.

Her rapid survey of London forced her to the conclusion that it was a foggy city. She crossed to Boulogne and went to Amiens to visit Jules Verne. This was a romantic gesture she had thought of herself. She found him living a leisurely life in an old stone house where she made a breathless call. Jules looked with Gallic amazement at this enterprising girl who had grown so serious over a dream.

He wished her luck but told her frankly that he did not think she could do better than Phileas. She rejoined her ship and went on to Brindisi, sending her messages by special code. By November 27th she had reached Port Said. From there she proceeded to Aden and then to Colombo, where she had to wait five days for a ship. This gave her time to write about the elephants, the Cinnamon Gardens and the beauties of Kandy. Her travelogue was warming up. The stay-at-homes were beginning to feel that perhaps Nellie Bly had a good idea.

The ballyhoo was built up with cunning that would have done Barnum credit. When the cablegrams were sparse, columns were written by scornful whiskered scribes in the *World* office on "Some of the Queer Things Nellie Bly Will See During Her Stay in Japan." But never had the Japs seen anything more extraordinary than Nellie with her ghillie cap, her plaid ulster, her two knapsacks and her stop watch.

By this time the whole English-speaking world was more or less racing with Nellie, and reporters met her at every stop. She basked in this attention and wrote home graphically about it. A free trip to Europe was offered by the *World* for the person who most closely estimated the time she would take to complete her tour, down to seconds. It took considerable ingenuity on the part of the copy readers to think up new heads for the stories. "Nellie Bly's Rush" and "Nelly Bly on the Fly" were more or less typical. The excitement was intense.

Nellie sailed from Colombo on the *Oriental* and by December 18th was at Singapore. From there she went on to Hongkong, encountering a monsoon, the first genuine excitement of the trip. This gave her imagination full play. Nevertheless, she reached port two days ahead of her itinerary and had to wait five days before she could push on to Yokohama. These stops were trying to Nellie's ardent spirit. She preferred to be on the run.

She spent Christmas Day in Canton, eating her lunch in the Temple of the Dead. On December 28th she started for Yokohama on the *Oceanic* and spent New Year's Eve on shipboard. She had a stormy trip through the Yellow Sea and reached Yokohama on January 3rd. She went to Tokyo and saw the sights.

Four days later she set off again and had a rough trip across the Pacific. The *World* had a special train waiting to rush her across the country. Nellie traveled in state, flags flying along the route, crowds greeting her at every stop. It was a triumphal trip, although she didn't linger for welcoming speeches. Not until she reached New York did she learn that the train had nearly been derailed at one point along the route. Thus she was cheated of all the extravagant emotions that undoubtedly would have found their way into print had she known that danger lurked anywhere in her vicinity.

Ten guns boomed from the Battery and Brooklyn to welcome her home on January 25th. She had covered 24,899 miles. The *World* gave her its entire front page and most of the paper besides, the maximum publicity that any newspaper woman has ever received. An exclamatory two-column head led the paper.

FATHER TIME OUTDONE!

Even Imagination's Record Pales Before
the Performance of "The World's"
Globe-Circler

Her time: 72 days, 6 hrs. 11 mins.,-sec.

Thousands Cheer Themselves Hoarse
at Nellie Bly's Arrival

Welcome Salutes in New York and Brooklyn

The Whole Country Aglow with Intense Enthusiasm

Nellie Bly Tells Her Story

Nellie got off the train in Jersey City, bands playing, crowds cheering her. Again the unfortunate young man on the *World*, who had to see that Nellie's race was properly chronicled in her own paper, wrote—no doubt with the consciousness of Mr. Pulitzer's eye upon him:

> It is finished.
> Sullen echoes of cannon across the gray waters of the bay and over the roofs and spires of three cities.
> People look at their watches. It is only 4 o'clock. Those cannot be the sunset guns.
> Is some one dead?
> Only an old era. And the booming yonder at the Battery and Fort Greene tolls its passing away. The stage-coach days are ended, and the new age of lightning travel begun.
> And amid all the tumult walks the little lady, with just a foot of space between her and that madly joyous mob. She is carrying a little walking-stick in one hand and with the other waves her checkered little fore-and-aft travelling cap, and laughs merrily as her name is hoarsely shouted from innumerable throats. Tense faces stare from the long galleries that bend ominously beneath their awful load of humanity. The tops of passenger coaches lying upon the side tracks are black with men and boys. . . .
> But the little girl trips gaily along. The circuit of the globe is behind her. Time is put to blush. She has brushed away distance as if it were down. Oceans and continents she has traversed.

Cablegrams and telegrams poured in to the *World*. One of the first came from Jules Verne, who cabled handsomely: "I never doubted the success of Nellie Bly. She has proved her intrepidity and courage. Hurrah for her and for the director of the *World*. Hurrah! Hurrah!" The welcoming committee threw the final bouquet at her head: "Miss Bly has done for American journalism what Stanley did for it in 1873."

No wonder the little girl was set apart for the rest of her life and heard strange echoes of this welcome even to her dying day. After the tumult had died down she told her story in four detailed chapters, which were read by thousands of admirers. A race-horse was named after her. Her picture was distributed with the *Sunday World*. Games bore her name. Songs were sung about her.

Almost anything that happened to her after this was bound to be anticlimax. She lay low so as not to mitigate her triumph, and also because she needed a rest. After a breathing spell she returned to her desk and her racy stories again enlivened the newsstands.

Everything by Nellie was written in the first person. Her style had many airs and graces, comments and interpolations. Yet it was clear, readable and somewhat cunningly devised, although the sentiment often seemed forced and her desire to right the wrongs of the world was overpowering. She made an emotional play in a peculiar style that has not been duplicated by any woman in journalism. Much of it might seem like drivel in to-day's paper, yet it fitted the contemporary frame and no one could question her right to front-page attention. She thought up nearly all of her own stories, although her paper backed the crusades.

What Nellie's own opinions were no one ever knew, for she had stock sentiments which she trotted out to suit any occasion that might arise. She was strongly moralistic. Her stories evoked much money for charity, particularly her ten-column account in 1893 of the work of the Salvation Army after she had dressed as a Salvation Army lass and worked at the Front Street headquarters.

She interviewed murderers, passed a night in a haunted house hoping to meet a ghost, and described her own sensations in great detail. She wrote a biting piece about society women whom she discovered in pool rooms betting on the races. She exposed a famous woman mind-reader and described the misery of starving tenement dwellers. Little went on in the social order, in fact, that did not call for one of Nellie's smug sermons. The evil-doer had reason to draw the blinds when she was about. This was all good for the *World*, which was then riding high as an instrument of reform.

In 1895 she married Robert L. Seaman, a wealthy Brooklyn manufacturer whom she met at a banquet in Chicago. He was seventy-two. She was not quite thirty. Her more envious colleagues called her a gold digger. She lived in state at 15 West Thirty-seventh Street until her husband's death in 1910. She became slightly social for a time, having Sunday evening gatherings, but this was not the sort of thing for which she cared. She was one of Hetty Green's few intimates and used to go and visit her when the old lady of Wall Street felt she could tolerate company.

After her husband's death things went to pieces in remarkably short order. She was not so keen at business as at journalism, although her lawyers never were able to persuade her of this fact. She became involved in endless litigation. Her factory made steel barrels, tanks, cans and tubs. A series of forgeries by employees, disputes of various sorts, and a mass of vexatious squabbles swallowed up the millions that Nellie's husband had left her. She was reduced to a penniless state. When her company went bankrupt she formed another; when it, too, went bankrupt she formed a third. Meanwhile her creditors charged her with fraud.

Nellie packed up and went to Austria, but her troubles followed her. She transferred her property to an Austrian friend, which brought further complications during wartime under the Alien Custodians' Act. She came back bitter against her brother, charging him with having mishandled her affairs during her absence. In place of front-page stories signed by Nellie, obscure paragraphs now appeared in the papers dealing with Mrs. Seaman's battles in court.

She developed into a professional litigant. Her disposition had suffered and she had become shrewish, another Becky Sharp. It had always been Nellie's habit to win. She was stunned to find the world against her. She thought she was in the right. She was a bundle of contradictions. One moment she was tight-fisted; the next, generous to an excessive degree. She rarely referred to her brilliant past, so obsessed was she by her business troubles. She could not quite believe that her fortune had melted away so unreasonably.

Shortly after her return from Austria, Arthur Brisbane took her on the *Journal* and again Nellie Bly's name appeared above news stories. But in the meantime journalism had changed. It was no longer startling or even novel to do stunts. New Yorkers did not get excited when she started picking up stray children and finding homes for them—even taking them under her own wing in the two-roomed suite she shared with a woman friend at the Hotel McAlpin.

Nellie's last splash was a sensational one, yet it passed almost unnoticed. On January 30, 1920, she witnessed the execution of Gordon Hamby at Sing Sing, the first woman in twenty-nine years to see an execution in New York State.

Hamby was a spectacular young murderer, of the Gerald Chapman order. Just before he died he sent Nellie his ouija board with the note: "A slight remembrance (all I have at this time) for your infinite kindness and friendship."

Nellie saw the execution under the pretext of campaigning against capital punishment. She sat in the seat farthest away at her own request. Hamby smoked a cigarette she had given him as he walked jauntily to the chair. Nellie shut her eyes when the current was turned on. Her story in the *Journal* next day began:

> Horrible! Horrible! Horrible!
> Hamby is dead. The law has been carried out—presumably the law is satisfied.
> Thou Shalt Not Kill.
> Was that Commandment meant alone for Hamby? Or did it mean all of us?
> I only know that I kept repeating "Thou Shalt not Kill! Thou Shalt not Kill" . . .
> The horribleness of life and death. Through my mind flitted

the thought that one time this young boy going to the death chair had been welcomed by some fond mother. He had been a babe, lo, loved and cherished. And this is the end. . . .

But journalism had changed to such a degree that the new crop of women reporters scarcely noticed that Nellie had put over another tremendous scoop, and if they did, it no longer seemed to matter, for the day for such antics was over and newspaper work was on a different basis.

Nellie Bly was now little more than a legend. If this was bitter to her, no one knew it. She had never cared for the opinion of her colleagues. Her eyes had always been fastened on the larger audience. In any event, she was tired and ill, and her main preoccupation was with her abandoned children.

She had a private office at the *Journal*. Few of her fellow workers ever saw her. She had never lounged about the city room, or been one of them, for she was usually acting a part or was bent on secret missions. When she did appear, she wore a large hat and a veil with chenille dots. True to form, she carried herself with an air of mystery.

On January 28, 1922, the *World* ran a half column on an inside page announcing the death of Nellie Bly, the most spectacular star the paper had ever had. She had died of pneumonia on the previous day in St. Mark's Hospital at the age of fifty-six, lonely, friendless and worn out. Funeral services were held for her at The Little Church Around the Corner.

Those who knew Nellie Bly in her youth mistakenly recall her as a tall and rather stunning figure—one of the newspaper beauties, like Winifred Black, Polly Pry and "Pinky" Wayne. But this was an impression created largely by Nellie's own manner. Actually she was small and demure, with rather large ears, a courageous mouth and calculating eyes. As time went on she grew more massive and carried herself with dignity. She had occasional outbursts of temper but was never really aggressive. She was simply a woman of indomitable will.

Chapter VI

THE FIRST SOB SISTERS

HIGH UP ON RUSSIAN HILL IN SAN FRANCISCO, IN A SPANISH house that faces the Palace of Fine Arts which she saved from demolition, Winifred Black spent her last days, her sight fading, her memory choked with such events as come only singly to most human beings. She died in May, 1936, at the age of seventy-three.

The realistic women reporters of to-day were apt to think of her vaguely as Annie Laurie, a great syndicate name, having little relation to the active world they inhabit. Yet in actual fact she had one of the most breath-taking careers in newspaper history. She made news as well as wrote it.

For there is nothing they do to-day—politics, crime, catastrophes, uplift or interviews—that she did not do in a more spectacular way thirty years ago. She could have given them aces and spades on technique, as well as sound advice, and even in the last year of her life she was ready to rush out for the first good story that came along. One of her great disappointments was her daughter's failure to follow the career which for her meant everything in the way of human excitement.

Mrs. Black's life was packed with drama and adventure. She experienced all the gaudy moments of the yellow journalist—banner lines, personal exploitation, the crack assignments of the day, no matter where they took her. She never had the trivial things to do; only the cataclysmic. She covered the Galveston flood, the St. Louis cyclone, the San Francisco disaster. She crusaded, campaigned and made news. She belonged essentially to an era when the newspaper woman was exploited and dramatized. She set the pace, just as Nellie Bly had done a few years earlier. She became a personality as well as a reporter.

Such figures are rare to-day. They are scarcely possible in the highly-geared newspaper office where the paper counts and the individual doesn't. But Mrs. Black's sensational feats are only part of the picture. She was society editor, dramatic critic, city editor and managing editor. She worked for the Hearst bureau in London and went abroad many times as a syndicate writer.

She was known as Annie Laurie in the West, Winifred Black in the East. Actually she was Mrs. Charles A. Bonfils, although no one in San Francisco ever thought of her by her married name. She was one of the first of the Hearst stars and, in fact, was on the *Examiner* before Mr. Hearst left college. So she was identified with his beginnings in newspaper work. She was the one woman writer on his staff who was in his inner councils over the years and from time to time she brought talent to his attention. Their first encounter was not in the city room, but at a children's playground party, when he helped to quiet a yelping dog for her.

Mrs. Black strolled into the office of the *Examiner* straight from the chorus—a handsome girl with reddish hair and finely modeled features. She had been brought up by her sister, Ada C. Sweet, who was United States Pension Agent in Chicago. They were born in the deep woods of Wisconsin, the daughters of Colonel B. J. Sweet.

S. S. Chamberlain was managing editor of the *Examiner* at the time. Mrs. Black had never done any writing except for a letter published in the Chicago *Tribune* while she was touring with a theatrical company, but with some of the invincibility that followed her through life she managed to get on the staff. The first time she attracted official notice was when Elizabeth Bisland was starting off on her race around the world against Nellie Bly. This was in 1889. Mrs. Black was sent down to her ship to write the send-off story. It was her first big chance and she knew it.

She labored painfully over her piece. It was stilted and elaborate, and the adjectives were strewn like currants through a suet pudding. This was what she believed to be style. Mr. Chamberlain, one of the chief executives of the Hearst service for many years, called her into the inner room of the old newspaper office on Montgomery Street. The surroundings were dusty but he was a Beau Brummel of the nineties, with striped trousers and a gardenia in his coat.

There were no typewriters about, nor any ticker machines bringing in the small marvelous threads of news from all corners of the earth. It was slumbrous compared with the modern newspaper plant. All the energy was supplied by the human dynamos who dashed about, stirring things up. The mechanical note was absent.

Mr. Chamberlain looked at the new reporter and did not hesitate to tell her the truth.

"This is a bad story," he pointed out. "Very bad, indeed. We don't want fine writing in a newspaper. Remember that. There's a gripman on the Powell Street line—he takes his car out at three o'clock in the morning, and while he's waiting for the signals he opens the morning paper. It's still wet from the press and by the light of his grip he reads it. Think of him when you're writing a story. Don't write a single word he can't understand and wouldn't read."

As he spoke he was tearing her story into shreds. He made her do it over. And this was the last time she tried for an elaborate effect. She learned then that dramatic results were best achieved by simplicity; that short words in lucid sequence were the most potent form of expression.

Her next assignment of any consequence was a stunt. She was ordered to do an exposé of the receiving hospital in San Francisco. There were rumors that women were not being well treated there. She dressed in old clothes and worn shoes, cut a "Plain Sewing Wanted" ad from a paper and tucked it into her shabby purse, then went out in the street and practically threw herself under a truck, fainting as realistically as possible. She was carried into the receiving hospital, where she stayed for some time, taking mental note of what went on. The story she wrote resulted in the entire personnel being routed out. The method of handling women patients was improved.

This was the first of a long series of crusading stories. Soon afterwards she went to the Leper Settlement at Molokai with Sister Rose Gertrude, who was sent there after the death of Father Damien. The trip was more or less of a stunt. It did not involve any great personal hazard. But it was spectacular and created the desired effect at the moment.

By this time Mrs. Black had acquired the technique of vivid, personal writing. She knew how far to go with the emotional strain, how indignant to become and still stay within the bounds of news writing and common sense. Having abandoned the elaborate, she went in for startling effects—hard jolts in short paragraphs. She used adjectives, but not in such dizzy numbers. Her stories were highly charged with emotion.

This type of newspaper writing was in the ascendancy. The prosiness of the mid-Victorian era was passing, although the effects were still on the fanciful side. It was more usual to say "a conflagration has stricken our fair city, evidently the work of a fire fiend" than to go in for the sharp newspaper ellipsis of to-day and call it simply an incendiary fire. Mr. Hearst was against the roundabout and windy style. He ordered short sentences, short paragraphs and direct quotes whenever possible.

The staff of the *Examiner* thought nothing of putting in a sixteen-hour working day in the pursuit of news. There was no five-day week, and little leisure to pursue one's private interests. This was the period when the exclusive story was the keystone of journalism and the indispensable attribute of the reporter. It no longer is, unless other vital qualities accompany it. The ability to assemble news intelligently and to write it in effective and pointed prose is now rated more highly than the deft art of reaching the prisoner in his cell, finding the hidden diary or making the murderer confess. However, there is no editor alive who does not warm to the bearer of an exclusive story. The reporter who can write, and beat his rivals too, will always be the prize jewel in any newspaper office.

Mrs. Black functioned most effectively when the ability to be the only reporter on the spot was the thing that brought approbation. Whether by luck, strategy or some instinctive reportorial sense, she had singularly few failures. No other woman had a chance to work on the tidal wave disaster at Galveston in 1900. She was the first reporter from the outside world to get into the stricken city, although Richard J. Spillane, who was on the Galveston *News* at the time and was local correspondent for the New York *Herald*, was on the spot when it happened. He almost lost his life, and did valiant work while the storm was still raging.

A large part of the city was washed away. The death toll was 7,000. It was one of the major disasters of American history. Mrs. Black was rushed to the scene as soon as the first messages came through. She knew that no woman reporter would be allowed through the emergency lines by the heavy guard that surrounded the ruined city. She disguised herself as a boy, wearing a linen duster and carrying a package. She had to step over dead bodies piled high in the streets. Débris was scattered everywhere. Grief-stricken survivors ran helplessly in circles, looking for children, mothers, sweethearts. She walked the streets that were not inundated, and saw crazy and unforgettable sights. She talked to men and women too hysterical to recall even what had happened to them. She got her story and with much difficulty managed to get through the lines again to file it.

When she tried to get a little sleep, telegrams reached her announcing that four of the Hearst papers had relief trains on their way. She was asked to have a hospital ready when they arrived. She commandeered a building and eighty mattresses. Everything was organized by the time the trains got in. She directed the relief workers and distributed the $60,000 in cash that Mr. Hearst had sent to her personal account to be spent on relief. Altogether she helped to raise $350,000 for the survivors.

She was riding in a street car in Denver when she saw the head lines that announced the San Francisco disaster. In tears, she hurried to the office of the Denver *Post*. There a telegram from Mr. Hearst awaited her. It was one word long. It said "Go."

Mrs. Black always had a genius for organization. She could campaign, stunt or turn out a column with equal facility. This gave her work a strongly personal flavor and tinged her writings with the editorial note. It was not the news that mattered so much as what Winifred Black had to say about the news. Her own personality was largely responsible for this. She could cajole, be convincing, or turn autocratic. If feminine wiles didn't work, she simply smashed the door. When President Benjamin Harrison visited California, only one press representative was permitted to board his train. It wasn't Mrs. Black, but she managed to get on, nevertheless. The Governor of California, whom she knew, helped to secrete her on the train after the attendants had tried to keep her off. When they were under way, she was discovered hiding under a table and the President gave her an interview.

Once the stage hands were conquered, Mrs. Black never had any difficulty with the stars of the cast. She might arrive by way of the cellar, but she always left by the front door. She was openly aggressive. On one occasion she marched down a church aisle and beckoned to a minister as he was about to begin a prayer. His wife was expecting a baby, so he felt sure that the summons had come. When he found that it was the girl reporter, Winifred Black, dead set on questioning him about some unimportant matter that could have waited until the end of the service, he was angry; then she disarmed him and he thought it funny. But this was the direct method. Irreverent, perhaps, but effective. Mrs. Black found that she could get away with it.

She interviewed Henry Stanley, Henry Irving, Sarah Bernhardt and all the visiting celebrities of the era. She was swift and picturesque. There were no taxis to whir the reporter to his destination; no telephones for quick transmission. One had to be resourceful and meet competition halfway. It was not merely a question of being a good reporter, but also an effective person, able to bend others to one's will and make things happen. And at this Mrs. Black excelled. She could steam-roller opposition with amazing thoroughness. Her paper backed her up in everything she did. In the year of the Galveston disaster she found Governor William S. Taylor, who was in hiding after the assassination of Senator William Goebel, of Kentucky. While most of the papers were pronouncing him a suicide she turned him up in his hiding place.

She missed few important murder trials in forty years. One of her earliest court-room experiences was the trial of William Henry Theodore Durrant, the superintendent of a Baptist church, who was hanged at San Quentin in 1898.

One Easter morning some members of the congregation, decorating the church with lilies, opened a small closet off the library and discovered the body of a young girl named Minnie Williams. She had been violated and hacked with a knife from the kitchen of the church. They searched further. They broke down a door leading up to the steeple and there in the belfry they found another young girl, Blanche Lamont, strangled. She had been missing from her home for a week.

Durrant, brother of Maud Allen, the dancer, was arrested. He protested his innocence to the last. It was California's most notable murder trial, for it had all the surrounding elements of a startling crime among people of some social standing. It was the age when girls went whizzing along the highways on their bicycles and everyone sang "Dolly Grey." The spectacle of young women writing industriously at a press table about the odd vices of man was an astonishing sight. But Annie Laurie was calm under the shelter of her cartwheel hat. Beside her was Mabel Craft of the *Chronicle*, a handsome blonde girl and one of the reigning newspaper stars of the day. Somewhere else in the court room was the "sweet pea girl" whose quaint custom it was to come into court every day wearing a corsage of sweet peas, and to send a bouquet of the same flowers to the prisoner.

Durrant stole a page from the criminal history of the future. He acted like a tabloid hero. He insisted on having his father watch him hang. Just before he died he made a dramatic speech. He asked that the rope that hanged him should be burned after his death.

Nine years later the Thaw trial covered the front pages of the country's newspapers. Again Mrs. Black was summoned to write with tears and sobs of the unfortunate woman in the case. The tremolo stops were pulled. This time there were four women at the press table—Dorothy Dix, Ada Patterson, Nixola Greeley-Smith and Mrs. Black. The reporters covering the running story sat at tables in the center of the court room. The feature writers had a row of seats in a corner. This was known as the royal pew. Irvin Cobb was one of its occupants. A cynical colleague, looking a little wearily at the four fine-looking girls who spread their sympathy like jam, injected a scornful line into his copy about the "sob sisters." This was the origin of a phrase that in time became the hallmark of the girl reporter and only recently has worn thin from much abuse.

These four, then, were the first official sob sisters. Their function was to watch for the tear-filled eye, the widow's veil, the quivering lip, the lump in the throat, the trembling hand. They did it very well. Ada Patterson was the cynic in the row. She studied the face of beautiful Evelyn Nesbit Thaw under the lace ruching of her black velvet hat and concluded that her defense of Harry Thaw was all the bunk. However, her scepticism did not show in Miss Patterson's copy.

By this time Winifred Black was as well known in the East as in the West. She had no permanent resting place. She moved where the news broke. She went to England to write about the suffragettes when they were still horrifying creatures who poured acid into bright red letter boxes and kicked bobbies in the stomach. She investigated the Juvenile Court system in Chicago and pressed some needed reforms. In New York she launched an investigation of the Charity Organization Society. She went to El Paso to do a human interest story on the prize fight that was supposed to be the last one in America. A story she wrote on pigeon shooting at Del Monte brought an abrupt finish to this sport and resulted in her getting medals from the humane societies of Great Britain and America. She raised money to install a new ward each Christmas at the children's hospital in San Francisco. It is still known as the Little Jim endowment.

When Mr. Hearst's mother, Mrs. Phoebe Apperson Hearst, died in 1919 at the age of seventy-six, he insisted that Annie Laurie and no one else should write the story of her life. He gave orders that if she were not within reach, the straight news account was to stand until she could be found, and then she was to do a feature. It so happened that when the news came she was on a ferry boat on her way to Berkeley to attend a meeting. Her office made frantic attempts to reach her and finally succeeded. She had forty minutes to edition time, but she turned out three columns of copy. Later she wrote a biography of Mrs. Hearst, doing 54,000 words in twelve days, believing that it was coming out in pamphlet form. But the story was printed on parchment, the type was set by hand and the volumes cost $150 each.

Annie Laurie was always part of the life of San Francisco, right back to her girlhood days when, posing as a Salvation Army lass, like Nellie Bly, she went into the worst dives of the city to see how the Army functioned and then wrote a story that killed the criticism that had been growing up about the organization. Her power grew with the years. When the florists tried to do away with the San Francisco flower stands, she raised such a hullabaloo that they hurriedly backed down and let the vendors continue their picturesque business. After the exposition of 1915, the speculators tried to seize the site and tear down the Palace of Fine Arts, which Annie Laurie considered one of the most beautiful buildings in the world. She organized societies and clubs to fight this move, and every time there was a hint of demolition, she gave such loud shrieks of anguish in a public way that the matter was dropped cold.

She wore the gold star of the San Francisco police department. She was the Mother of the South O'Market boys' club and led the grand march at the policemen's ball. She helped to start many of the young in the newspaper game. When the novice climbed the hill and asked her for advice she told them: "The ideal newspaper woman has the keen zest for life of a child, the cool courage of a man and the subtlety of a woman. A woman has a distinct advantage over a man in reporting, if she has sense enough to balance her qualities. Men always are good to women. At least I have found them so, and I've been in some of the toughest places."

Mrs. Black chose Annie Laurie for a pen name because her mother was Scotch and had often sung her the song. When she rated her first by-line and was asked suddenly how the story should be signed, she thought of the old ballad. No reporter in those days would dream of using her own name. Her intimate friends called her Laurianna. She was married twice. Her first husband was Orlow Black of San Francisco. Her second was Charles A. Bonfils of Denver. For one brief period in her life she was away from the Hearst management and worked for the Denver *Post*. She had two sons, both of whom died. Her one book, *The Little Boy Who Lived on the Hill*, is the story of the eldest, who was drowned while bathing at Carmel in 1926. Her daughter, Mrs. Winifred Barker, has never shown any interest in writing.

Soon after her seventy-second birthday Mrs. Black flew over Mount Shasta, ten thousand feet up. Her love for speed and excitement would not die. To her each moment of living was personal, vivid, colossal. This was what made her a spectacular newspaper woman. She was a striking example of the fruits of personal exploitation.

Ada Patterson also went through the hoops of sensational journalism with the perfect touch for what she was doing. Her work on the Thaw case was penetrating and adroit, for Miss Patterson, under a mild manner, has a shrewd knowledge of human reactions in the light of fierce publicity.

She got her first New York newspaper job because she had seen a man hanged; in fact, had stood beside him on the scaffold while he died. He was Dr. Arthur Duestrow, the son of a St. Louis mining millionaire. One winter day he drove up to his home in a sleigh. He was in a drunken frenzy and could not understand why his wife should keep him waiting. He called her. She didn't hear. He jumped out of the sleigh and ran indoors. There was a row, a shot, a scream, a child's cry. He had shot his wife. The child went on crying. He seized her by the ankles and dashed out her brains against the wall.

The trial that followed was sensational. Charles B. Johnson, former governor of Missouri, was his counsel and he carried the case to the higher courts. The defense was insanity, but the verdict of guilty was always affirmed. "You are demanding the life of a maniac unaccountable for his deeds," Mr. Johnson flung at his opponents in court time and again. This was more than a legal gesture. He believed it with all his heart and fought hard to prove his point. The prisoner's actions strongly bore him out. But on a snowy day in 1897 he was hanged at Union, Missouri.

When the time for his execution drew near Miss Patterson, who was then working on the St. Louis *Republic*, was assigned to take the place of a fellow worker who had gone on a bender. As she had interviewed Dr. Duestrow several times in jail, her city editor thought her a logical enough selection for the gruesome task.

She went into his cell to talk to the youth shortly before he was led to the scaffold. They could hear the nails being hammered in the gallows outside.

"Do you know what is going on, Dr. Duestrow?" she demanded.

"I have a pretty good idea," he told her calmly.

"Have you seen Governor Johnson lately?" she asked.

"Have you?" he retorted. "I wrote to him that you and I were going to be married."

His delusions were many. A little earlier he had insisted that he was going to marry Queen Wilhelmina. He raved continually about marching armies and mythical war gods. When the hour of his death approached the crowds swarmed so thickly around the scaffold that Miss Patterson was hoisted up on the platform. The wretched man noticed her as he mounted the steps.

"Good morning, miss," he said in a clear tone.

"What do you want to say?" she prompted him.

"There is going to be a war," he remarked irrelevantly.

As the black cap was put over his head he turned toward Miss Patterson and gestured with a thin brown hand: "I didn't kill my wife. There she stands."

The arm of another reporter steadied the stupefied girl. To this day she wonders whether he died shamming insanity. Her story about the execution was a testament of shivering horrors. Bradford Merrill, then with the *World*, later with the *American*—the editor whose much advertised slogan was vigilance, enterprise and accuracy —saw the story and summoned her to New York.

But when she arrived he was away on vacation and no one else knew about Miss Patterson. She was short of funds and had the dismayed feeling that many girl reporters have had when they tried to crash the New York newspaper field and found that the gates wouldn't budge; that even the office boys looked at them with chilly eyes.

By chance she met a man she had known in the West. "Doing anything?" he asked.

"No," said Miss Patterson.

"Come over to our shop. An editor wants a woman's job done in a hurry."

"Our shop" was the *American*. The editor in question did not waste words. "I want someone to go down in the caisson of the bridge being built across the East River," he said. "The men who work in the caisson are having the bends. The air pressure is apt to cause deafness. Want to take the risk?"

"Gladly," said Miss Patterson.

In this way she made her début in New York. She went down in the caisson; it wasn't such a bad experience. She wrote the story. Her paper, feeling sure that it was exclusive, held it out for several days. In the meantime the *World* had got wind of the fact that a girl had pulled a new stunt under the East River. The rival editors worked fast and had one of their own young ladies explore the regions of the sand hog. The result was that both papers appeared simultaneously with a caisson story. This was a bitter pill for Miss Patterson, but these were cut-throat days. She took it out many times on her rivals later, for she garnered a rare crop of exclusive stories for her paper.

Some of her best work was done on the trial of Charles Becker, the police lieutenant who was electrocuted for the murder of Herman Rosenthal. On the October night in 1912 that the verdict was brought in, Miss Patterson happened by chance to take the seat that Mrs. Becker had occupied throughout the trial. The wife was not in the court room that night, because word had already leaked out that the verdict was death.

As the jury filed in, Becker weakened for a moment and looked helplessly in the direction of the chair, expecting to see his wife. He stared straight into Ada Patterson's observant eyes. She could read the fright in his. A moment later the verdict was announced. He took it like a man in bronze, without moving, but she saw him swallow, detected the straining muscles of his neck. She had seen many men condemned to death but had never witnessed such outward composure.

Miss Patterson was the first reporter to interview Mrs. Lillian Rosenthal after the murder took place. While the house was being guarded by members of her craft, she got in and talked to her by getting a letter from Charles S. Whitman, district attorney at the time and later Governor of New York State.

"I spend my days praying that Becker will be punished for his coward's crime," she told Miss Patterson.

The case moved slowly. There were the usual appeals. The fight went on for three years. At last the date of execution drew near. Miss Patterson went to Mrs. Rosenthal.

"Where are you going to be on the night of the execution?" she asked.

"I think the only thing to do is to hide."

"Well, come and hide with me."

So for two days and nights, while reporters hunted high and low for Mrs. Rosenthal, she was hidden in Miss Patterson's apartment in the Forties. On the night of Becker's death they kept vigil together, receiving bulletins from hour to hour.

"Governor Whitman has received Mrs. Becker," came a flash, "but as she has no new evidence to offer he has declined to interfere." . . . "Becker is calm." . . . "A clergyman has been praying with him." . . .

Mrs. Rosenthal was bitter. She poured out her wrath in Miss Patterson's ears.

At last the final flash came from the *American* city room. It was early morning. They had talked all night. Becker had died at 5:53 A.M. It had taken three shocks to kill him.

Mrs. Rosenthal fell back across the bed, exhausted.

"Now he has atoned," she exclaimed. "God save his soul."

When Nan Patterson became the pet murder defendant of 1904, Ada had to testify to an interview she had had with her in jail. She had sent her a note hidden in a basket of fruit, asking for a few minutes' talk, and the prisoner, struck by the similarity in their names, had seen her.

Nan Patterson was the Floradora girl who was charged with murdering Caesar Young, her bookmaker lover. The killing was rather public—in a hansom. There were witnesses who thought they saw her pull the trigger, but it made little difference in court. She was soft-voiced, beautiful. She had a patient air, and was an excellent witness in her own behalf. By the time she got off the stand the jury was quite persuaded that Caesar had shot himself. Ada Patterson, not at all gullible, always believed that he had.

The trial was a sensation. The Earl of Suffolk, who was engaged to Margaret H. Leiter, sat on the bench beside the judge, absorbing local color. Women battered at the doors. They were told sternly that a murder trial was no place for the weaker sex, but by main force they got in and the *Times* reporter was so shocked that he made this invasion part of his lead next morning.

Nan celebrated riotously the night she got off. She was quite a public darling while her vogue was on, but after the acquittal she was soon forgotten. More than one trial had been needed to make her freedom final. Less popular with the public was the dreary Mrs. Annie M. Bradley, who was charged two years later with the murder of Senator Arthur Brown, of Utah, in a Washington hotel. The motive was clear. He intended to throw her over to marry Mrs. Annie Adams, the mother of Maude Adams, the actress.

There was no doubt of her guilt, but Miss Patterson unwittingly got the evidence that would have proved premeditation, had she chosen to use it in her paper. Mrs. Bradley had two children which she said were the Senator's. He always denied they were his. But her married life had been broken up on his account. When he left to join Mrs. Adams in Washington she pursued him from Salt Lake City. She told Miss Patterson about it later in jail.

"I swore over the bodies of our children out West that if he did not marry me I would kill him," she said, tears streaming down her face. "I came East to find him. The clerk gave me the key to his room. I found some letters that turned my suspicion to certainty. He was deserting me. He did intend to marry the other woman."

Miss Patterson stared at the hysterical prisoner, half on her knees in the cell. Clearly, she did not know that she had established a perfect case of premeditation. Miss Patterson left her, confronted with a problem that now and again invades the reporter's conscience. She knew that if she held her tongue the woman would get off. She was a pitiable creature and her official story was the usual threadbare tale of a struggle, the mind going blank, the gun going off—which was somewhat different from the deliberate trip from Salt Lake City, bringing a revolver with her.

When she got back to New York Miss Patterson's mind was made up. She wrote the story of the interview in three instalments. It was all interesting reading. She left out the vital line that established premeditation. Six months later Mrs. Bradley told her lawyer the same story.

"Have you ever mentioned this to anyone?" he asked.

"Yes, to Ada Patterson," she said.

"My God, a newspaper woman! She's saving it for the trial. She'll spring it on us then."

Miss Patterson went to Washington to cover the trial. The day before it began, Mrs. Bradley sent for her. She was greatly agitated.

"I said a good deal to you the day you were here," she said. "I spoke of many things that I shouldn't have mentioned."

Miss Patterson set her mind at rest. She seemed to her one of the most pathetic women defendants she had ever seen. "You did tell me a lot," she agreed. "I published everything that I could remember."

The woman went on the stand and swore that Senator Brown had come into the room, had knocked her about in his rage at finding her there, and that then the revolver had gone off. In her letters to the Senator she had always been his "little mint julep." But Ada Patterson wrote of her as his "bond woman." The lawyers picked up the phrase and cemented it into the testimony of the trial. Mrs. Bradley was acquitted with flying colors in 1907.

Miss Patterson took an active hand also in a famous triangle case revolving around Claudia Libbey Hains, the beautiful wife of Major Peter C. Hains, who shot and killed W. E. Annis, her lover. The major was in the Philippines when he got word from his brother, Thornton Jenkins Hains, that his wife was constantly in the company of Annis, a magazine publisher.

The husband hurried home and confronted his wife. She confessed and he brought suit for divorce. Two months elapsed, then she decided on a counter-suit. A few days later loungers and bathers at the Bayside Yacht Club were horrified to see Major Hains pump several bullets into Annis as he emerged from the water.

Mrs. Hains fled to her mother's home in a suburb of Boston. Ada Patterson went in pursuit. By using the name of a friend of the murdered man she got in to see Mrs. Hains—the only reporter to interview her. The conversation that followed was remarkably revealing. Although intelligent, Mrs. Hains was totally lacking in a sense of self-preservation. She seemed unconscious that she had a yellow journalist sitting across from her in the drawing-room, taking mental notes. She condemned her husband, stood by her lover, talked bitterly of love and marriage. Everyone in the case was prominent. It was a front-page beat for Miss Patterson, as well as a startling human document. The disclosures had been drawn from Mrs. Hains by a highly skilled interviewer, for it is in this field that Miss Patterson has always excelled. Though her reportorial work was usually of the sensational order she ranks high among the better interviewers— a distinct branch of the newspaper profession. She brought a vigorous intellect to bear on what she was doing, and was adept at all the skullduggery of the profession.

She saw Martha Place—the last woman to be electrocuted in New York State before Ruth Snyder—well on her way to the chair. She went into a lions' den at Dreamland, Coney Island, for a story. She drove a locomotive from St. Louis to Chicago, went down in a submarine, and walked ninety feet on a plank above the City Hall in St. Louis while it was being built, to see what the view was like.

Once she combed the lower East Side, picked out the most miserable child she could find and took her to call on Hetty Green. This was one of Arthur Brisbane's ideas—that it would be interesting for the richest woman in the world to tell the poorest child in the world what she should do to get rich. The child's parents were drunk when Miss Patterson arrived, so they let her go without a qualm. Hetty sat at her desk in the bank, her gimlet eyes fastened on the little girl. Although she had been coached, the child was too frightened to speak, so Miss Patterson sprang the key questions. Hetty put her formula in a nutshell, with rusty glee.

"Save your money and when you get a little ahead, don't put all your eggs in one basket," she said.

The little girl agreed readily enough. She was bewildered by her surroundings. The sharp eyes of the strange old woman frightened her. Hetty didn't start a savings account for her. But she posed for a photograph with the child.

This was a comparatively quiet day in Miss Patterson's spectacular newspaper life. She was more often on the trail of violence or scandal. For a time she did dramatic criticism and she now has a wide acquaintance among the people of the stage. In 1923 she resigned to devote her time to magazine work. She entered journalism by way of a pupil teacher's desk and long before she found the open door on Park Row, she was known as the Nellie Bly of the West.

Chapter VII

THE LOVE FORUM

When Mrs. Frances Noel Hall mounted the witness stand on a dull November day in 1926 and scornfully denied the murder of Mrs. Eleanor Mills, she was watched with sage eyes from the press row by a tiny figure, housewifely and plump, who looked like somebody's grandmother who had strayed by accident onto a scene of horror.

Few knew that she was Dorothy Dix, billed with ample justification by her syndicate as America's Mother Confessor, the most highly paid newspaper woman in the world. She looked too mild for such grim surroundings. Her smile was kind, her silver hair reassuring under the cluster of cherries that bobbed from the brim of her hat.

Yet no one who witnessed the melodramatic happenings in the courtroom at Somerville, New Jersey, was any better fitted to estimate the motives of the eccentric human beings who made the Hall-Mills trial one of the remarkable news events of the period. The story of the choir singer who stole the rector's love and died a violent death with him under the crab apple tree in de Russey's Lane held no surprises for her. For nearly thirty years she had been watching the murder defendants who made newspaper history. As far back as 1904 she saw Nan Patterson's cunning performance on the witness stand. Three years later she listened to Evelyn Nesbit Thaw weeping and baring her love secrets to save the life of Harry Thaw. Dorothy Dix has covered many trials since then but she still regards this as the perfect murder story from the newspaper point of view.

The last time she stepped out in response to an editor's summons was for the Hall-Mills case. When it was over and the defendants went free, it was generally conceded that her stories were the best analytical writing done on the trial. It is one of her few boasts that no defendant whom she believes to be innocent ever has been convicted. Her stories were sympathetic to Mrs. Hall, the rector's widow who went through the trial with a show of fortitude and pride that baffled the hostile forces crowding her on all sides.

In all her experience, Dorothy Dix never had seen a woman charged with murder show such a granite surface. Nor had anyone else. Mrs. Hall stared with amused disdain at the wax bust of her rival, Mrs. Mills, ghoulishly introduced by the prosecution—a childish trick designed to unnerve her. The same mockery was apparent when Jane Gibson, the pig woman, dragged into court on her bed in a dying condition, screamed her identification of Mrs. Hall as the woman she saw weeping by the light of the moon beside the dead bodies in de Russey's Lane, when her mule carried her close to the crab apple tree.

Dorothy Dix was covering the story for the New York *Post*, but the headlines played her up in the strictly personal manner to which she had become accustomed on the *Journal*—"Hall Defendants Amaze Miss Dix." She was not anxious to cover the Hall-Mills trial. She never has cared for the undisciplined rush of human emotions inseparable from a great murder mystery. To most reporters the Thaw, Hall-Mills, Leopold-Loeb or Hauptmann trials, terrible in fact, would be memorable peaks in their careers. Newspaper women have done their best work on murder trials, when their pictorial sense and emotional reactions have helped them to write convincingly.

But Dorothy Dix took the assignment without question, left her home in New Orleans for a furnished room in Somerville, sweated over her copy every night like any novice and did a workmanlike job. She was nearing sixty at the time. She had listened to more than her share of the world's grief and had been a spectator at the dazzling news events of nearly three decades.

Now she prefers the peace of her fireside, or the mild stimulus of travel. She lives in an apartment in New Orleans, surrounded by old carved furniture from French châteaux. She dines at a table taken from the palace of a Bonaparte, under a chandelier that has dropped wax on the dandies of the Empire. She has traveled around the world a number of times and has collected bronzes, mosaics, embroideries—all the loot of the Orient. For week-ends she flees from the telephone and her mail to a long white house set among oaks eighty miles out of New Orleans. There she gardens, sees her most intimate friends, lives an animated and inquiring life. It is absolutely necessary for her to escape now and again from her mail, for she is credited with an audience of 35,000,000 readers and receives from 100 to 1,000 letters a day. Her column syndicates in 200 papers in America, Canada, England, the Philippines, Japan, China, South Africa and Australia, and is translated into Japanese and Spanish.

Nothing amuses her more than to be asked if she makes up the letters on which she bases her columns. There is little need for such stuffing. A visitor from Mars would find her correspondence an illuminating commentary on the American people. It has a bit of everything. At times she may smooth out the sequences or correct the grammar in order to meet newspaper standards, but beyond that, the cries of pain and distress are apparently genuine outpourings of the human heart. Each letter receives serious consideration. Her style in handling them is mellow and sometimes profound. Even the changing tempo of the woman's page has not shunted Dorothy Dix's smoothly written philosophy from a leading place, for she has kept step with the times. The problems may have changed to some extent, but the essential constituents are nonvariable.

She can be sharp with her correspondents when the occasion seems to demand some stiffening of the spine. Her advice has the fluidity of all such columns. The viewpoint is never constant. The mother-in-law may be right to-day and wrong to-morrow. Miss Dix has to deal with the ridiculous as well as the poignant. People ask her questions they would never fling at their friends. "Many of the problems are so intricate that only Almighty Wisdom itself can solve them, but to all I give understanding, and the best advice I have in the shop," she says.

The response she gets might overwhelm anyone less balanced. Physicians tell her that they give her articles to their neurotic feminine patients instead of pills and potions. Girls write to inform her that she has turned their feet from dangerous paths. Discouraged housewives bless her for the assurance she gives them that the kitchen can be the shrine of noble effort. She is effective at persuading the hesitant man or woman that the double life leads to grief. On a few occasions she has had the assurance that her advice prevented suicide.

Dorothy Dix is known as Mrs. Elizabeth Meriwether Gilmer in New Orleans, where she had her newspaper start and now makes her permanent home. She was born on November 18, 1870, on a race-horse farm that lay on the border line of Kentucky and Tennessee. She grew up in great isolation, so far as the outside world was concerned. Up to the time she was twenty she had not traveled beyond Nashville, had rarely ridden on a train, had never seen a play. When she told this to a well-known editor in the early days of her success, he said, "Now, by Jove, I understand you and your work! To a matured mind you bring the keenness of interest of a child. Everything is new and wonderful to you, and that is why you can give a fresh viewpoint to what you write."

But her life on the breeding farm was exciting enough in itself.

She used to gallop at breakneck speed with the other children across the countryside, yelping dogs behind them. An old thoroughbred, once the pride of her grandmother's stable, frequently raked her off his back as she passed under the bough of a tree or a clothesline. Her family were the new poor after the Civil War, living a life of oddly mingled poverty and luxury. They still owned their house and acres. Their silver had been saved by a faithful servant who had hidden it in a graveyard so that the "hants" would guard it. Their grandmother was an epicure and they had sumptuous fare, peacock often being served for dinner. But there was little ready cash, and whatever was available went for the upkeep of the farm. The children wore copper-toed shoes and linsey frocks made of wool from their own sheep and woven into cloth at a neighboring mill. They were taught to fear God, speak the truth, and never whine. Their mother instilled some orthodoxy into them; their black mammy taught them manners with her knuckles. "Mind yo' manners," she would say. "Anybody would think yo' was po' white."

Elizabeth, as she then was known, was educated chiefly in her grandfather's library where a demented old man, like Mr. Dick in *David Copperfield*, taught her to read and to enjoy good fare. However, she went eventually to a female academy, and if she failed to learn much there, at least she was handsomely graduated in a white organdy frock and was launched on the world in true Southern fashion.

At eighteen she married George O. Gilmer and expected to settle down to a conventional domestic round for the rest of her life. But after a few years he had a severe nervous breakdown which clouded their lives and forced her to go out and find some way of earning a living for herself and for him. She didn't know which way to turn, became ill from worry and finally went to the Mississippi Gulf Coast to recuperate. This move proved to be fate, for it propelled her into newspaper work. By chance she stayed next door to Mrs. E. J. Nicholson, who owned and edited the New Orleans *Picayune*. She showed her neighbor a story she had written and it was bought for $3. Then she went to work on the *Picayune* and almost at once showed the instincts of a newspaper woman.

Mrs. Gilmer was zealous in her study of newspaper technique. She buried herself in books of synonyms and the dictionary. She memorized editorials that she liked and followed newspapers from all parts of the country to see how they played the same stories, an excellent idea for any aspirant to journalism. She sopped up all the knowledge that she could about newsprint and the weird and fascinating goings-on in any newspaper office, large or small.

Soon she was doing a weekly article for women, which was really the forerunner of her present column. She decided to write realistically about the relationship of men and women and avoid the romantic vaporing of the era. She called her columns the "Dorothy Dix Talks." Women liked them, men read them and the Dorothy Dix tradition spread.

She was on the *Picayune* from 1896-1901. Then Mr. Hearst, who was scouting for talent for his new acquisition, the *Journal*, invited her to join his staff. Her first big assignment was to go to Nebraska with Carrie Nation, who had just embarked on her saloon-smashing career. This gave Dorothy Dix a rare insight into the psychology of termagants and humbugs. She found Carrie a "queer, frowzy, fat, unromantic Joan of Arc who heard voices and saw visions, and who made no move unless she was spiritually guided." One night scores of women came to her headquarters, each with a brand new hatchet concealed in the folds of her skirt. Carrie spent hours on her knees praying for a sign, but it didn't come, and so the foiled reformers went home quietly, their battle-axes still unstained with liquor.

Dorothy Dix worked under Arthur Brisbane and Foster Coates during the period when efforts were being made to achieve sensational results. She was rushed from one major story to another, covering murder trials, vice investigations, political conventions and events of broad general interest. Her news stories were suavely written and emotional. She was usually sympathetic to the woman in the case, a Hearst tradition, but one which accorded perfectly with her own outlook. Right through her reporting days she maintained her column, although the strain sometimes was heavy. She joined the Wheeler Syndicate in 1917 and the Philadelphia *Ledger* Syndicate in 1923. When the New York *Post* was bought by J. David Stern in 1933 her column began to appear again in its old setting, the *Journal*.

Dorothy Dix is calm, gentle, truly beloved by those who know her. But she is also shrewd and wise. Her earnings are extraordinarily high for a newspaper feature. She is a completely free agent, beyond the exigencies of getting copy delivered in time, and she is so experienced at this that she keeps well in advance of her schedule.

She is scarcely five feet tall, even when she wears high heels. She has black eyes that twinkle and search and miss very little. Her vitality is tremendous. She rises with enthusiasm at seven every morning, does a daily dozen, drinks a small cup of black coffee, has a slice of toast, then settles down to her mail with her secretary. This is a staggering job, but she has grown so adept over the years that she can absorb the contents of a letter almost at a glance and make up her mind quickly on the issues raised. She has a heavy sense of responsibility about her work, based on the conviction that at the moment they write to her, her correspondents are undergoing genuine emotional upheaval. Therefore, their letters are not to be taken too lightly, however absurd the problems may seem by the time they reach the fireside in New Orleans.

During all the years that Dorothy Dix's column has been before the public another one, equally well known, has been featured in the Hearst press. At the turn of the century, when the young dashed about on bicycles built for two, they first learned to write to Beatrice Fairfax. They do it even today. From a mere name she has become an institution, a catchword, a national pet.

> *Just write to Beatrice Fairfax*
> *Whenever you are in doubt*
> *Just write to Beatrice Fairfax*
> *And she will help you out.*

The old song is dead, but the column goes on, in spite of many ups and downs. But who is Beatrice Fairfax? Does anyone really know? The dark suspicion that a pipe-smoking, cursing male takes the love confessions of harassed youth and wisecracks at their expense has provided many a newspaper joke.

The fact is that the Beatrice Fairfax column has been written for most of its thirty-seven years by two women who have taken the job seriously and now and again have played a hand in destiny. The true Beatrice Fairfax, however, is more or less of a metropolitan character. Strange ghosts handle the local letters in certain parts of the country, so that there is good ground for the suspicion that Beatrice Fairfax is often in masquerade. Arthur Brisbane has batted for her at a pinch in New York. He supervised the inception of the column, and has followed it closely from its start to the present time. When it has shown signs of ailing, he has always taken a hand and doctored it up.

Whatever the reason, it has survived the years and changing newspaper tastes with singular tenacity. It got a strong hold on the public when newspaper features were comparatively rare. The name caught on at once; there were songs and jokes about it, and all the automatic ballyhoo of a public response. It got over without much pushing.

One day in the summer of 1898, Mr. Brisbane, who was then managing editor of the *Journal*, called in the two young women who got out the household page and handed them two letters that had just come in to the contributors' column. One was from a woman who wrote that her husband was being lured away from her by a siren who met him daily for luncheon. Another girl confessed that she had been basely deserted by a young man who had every reason to give her his support.

These were not the usual *pro bono publico* letters to the editor. The current topics were the high cost of living, the burning question of woman suffrage and the right of the citizen to spit in trolleys.

"Can you use letters like these?" Mr. Brisbane asked.

"Why not have a column along the same lines?" suggested Marie Manning, one of the girls he addressed.

"That's a great idea, if you can carry it out," Mr. Brisbane agreed enthusiastically.

Miss Manning got the job. She had a place in Fairfax County, Virginia. She had been reading Dante, so she selected her name by the simple process of combining Beatrice with Fairfax, thereby giving herself a pseudonym that became nationally known with astonishing speed. An idealized pen and ink portrait of Miss Manning appeared at the head of her first column. She pasted the picture inside her desk but could scarcely foresee what she had started. On the same page that day was a picture of the future King Edward VIII at the age of four, dressed in a reefer and carrying a toy musket.

At first the column needed a little coercion. Miss Fairfax had to dash off a few notes to herself, which was a simple matter, because she knew all the answers to her own questions. But she didn't have to keep this up for long. Hearst readers became crazed on the subject of putting all their problems up to Beatrice Fairfax. New readers joined the family circle and the letters poured in.

Park Row never had seen so much mail addressed to one individual as to the mysterious Beatrice Fairfax. The *Journal* offices were then in the *Tribune* building. Office boys went across the street to the post office and staggered back laden with sacks of mail for her. A grim spinster, secretary to one of the editors, helped sort the letters. Miss Manning called her Atropos. She scorned romance, and sniffed and muttered under her breath as she slit the horrid notes—many of them on lavender paper with spidery scrawlings in purple ink. She couldn't understand the rank emotionalism of the Fairfax devotees.

But Miss Manning and her assistant loved it. They were both young and romantic. They felt that this was getting them in touch with the larger world. It excited them to see the mail pouring in to their department. Beauty and fashions seemed tame by comparison with these intimate documents that touched life in the raw.

Miss Manning was always practical and specific. She avoided the emotional response. Her general plan of advice was: "Dry your eyes, roll up your sleeves, and dig for a solution." The favorite question was: "What can I do to be more popular?" In the nineties no youth worried on this score, but most of the girls did. Now it is usually the other way around among the Beatrice Fairfax correspondents. One of the most pressing questions of the day was: "Is it ladylike to permit a young man to hold and kiss my hand, when I'm engaged to someone else?" Beatrice Fairfax always said no.

The problems she had to meet were legion. She was the Emily Post of love. Should the young man go down on his knees while proposing? Should he get the consent of the girl's parents first? Should he have the engagement ring ready in his pocket in case the girl should say yes? The chaperon was another pressing problem of the period. What should they do about her when they went out on a bicycle built for two? Was it all right to go for an outing with their beaux after church, and was ten o'clock at night too late to get home?

Divorce problems, which make up the bulk of the Beatrice Fairfax letters now, were rarely mentioned in those days. Nor did the question of a girl keeping her job after marriage ever arise. All her yearnings were toward the ladylike, and the public conception of a lady didn't involve tearing down to the office and mixing in the public fray.

As time went on Beatrice Fairfax was quoted with facetious affection in vaudeville skits. She had gone over in a big way. The young and the old sought her advice. Miss Manning had become the oracle of love. Imitators sprang up everywhere. But she gave up her column to marry Herman Gasch. She retired to private life, leaving Beatrice Fairfax behind her. For a decade she was busy bringing up a family. In the meantime the column fluttered from one pair of hands to another.

When war broke out she took on the job again. Then she retired for a time, but when the depression came along she resumed direction of the popular column she had created. She now conducts a regionalized Beatrice Fairfax column from Washington, where she also covers Mrs. Roosevelt for the International News Service. The questions she answers are broader in scope than they were at the beginning of the century. Love is still the dominant note, but she also gives advice on education, vocational training, and the economic problems of the day.

The original Beatrice Fairfax is six feet tall, lively, witty, an adroit speaker at women's clubs. Her home is in Washington. She has a farm twelve miles out in Virginia where she grows delphiniums nearly as tall as herself and leads an animated family life. She writes books and magazine articles and has traveled extensively.

As Marie Manning she started her newspaper career on the *World* when she was twenty. She was one of the girls who worked their way in through the space system. She was pursuing elusive facts from Harlem to the Battery when her managing editor called her in one day and told her he was going to send her out on an assignment that had stumped the most experienced reporters. "Of course, you won't succeed," he told her bluntly, "but Mr. Pulitzer has sent word from Bar Harbor that if all the good reporters on the paper have tried and failed, then we are to send some of the bad ones."

Her task was to get to Grover Cleveland and ask him what he would do about going to war with Spain if he were still President of the United States. All the other reporters who had gone to his home in Princeton had been thrown off the steps. But Miss Manning stepped blithely off the train on a lovely spring morning, nothing but hope in her heart. She was so green that she did not know what she was up against. Her card did not indicate that she represented the *World*. It gave her address as the Hotel Judson, on Washington Square, where she was living at the time, a few rooms away from Mrs. R. L. Stevenson and her son and daughter.

It so happened that she had the same name as the daughter of Daniel Manning, who had been Mr. Cleveland's Secretary of the Treasury. She was admitted without question. The former President came in, his face lighted with an anticipatory smile, which froze suddenly when he saw a huge girl rise to her feet and announce that she represented the *World*. She was almost speechless with terror, now that she had reached her quarry. She couldn't think of anything to ask him.

He let her know at once that he had turned down everyone else. But she began to detect signs of compassion in his face when she told him that this was her first important assignment.

"And what happens if you go back without your story?" he asked.

"Oh, we're fired, if not boiled in oil," said Miss Manning, her spirits beginning to pick up.

He asked her if she had a pencil. Her hopes skyrocketed as she hunted through her purse for one. He dictated a statement. It was short, but under the circumstances it was important. He said that nothing was easier than to criticize a President; that the difficulties which beset the office of chief executive could not be imagined by anyone who had not held it. He urged patience on the part of the people and said he hoped they would not attempt to rush the President into war by unthinking clamor.

Miss Manning went back to her office and was received with amazement by her more seasoned colleagues. She told them at once about the mistake in identity, and then they understood. Mr. Hearst was putting the Spanish-American War across. Mr. Pulitzer was delighted to run the Cleveland statement in the *World*. He sent her $50 in gold for a smart, if inadvertent, piece of work.

From the *World* Miss Manning went to the *Herald*, lured by the idea of doing music criticism and attending all the best concerts. She found the owl-encrusted building on Herald Square haunted by the ghost of its strange proprietor, James Gordon Bennett, who visited America at intervals of ten years or more, yet kept so closely in touch with his office that the legend was he knew when the wastebaskets were emptied.

It was a short step from the *Herald* to the *Journal* and the Beatrice Fairfax column. The success of the feature amazed its originator. As time went on it became a gold mine for Hearst, selling to 200 papers and sometimes bringing in as many as 1,400 letters in a day. The column has changed slightly in character from time to time as different writers have handled it, but aside from the founder, the person who carried it for the longest period was Lilian Lauferty, who joined the staff of the *Journal* during the war and wrote the Beatrice Fairfax column until 1924, when she married James Wolfe, the Metropolitan opera star.

Miss Lauferty is the daughter of Minnie Eliel, who was a social worker and a cousin of Felix Adler. She was born in Fort Wayne, Indiana, and was brought up in an atmosphere of public benefaction. She met Mr. Brisbane at the home of Nathan Straus. He said to her, "Your mother's daughter ought to be able to big sister the world." Soon she was Beatrice Fairfax, the recipient of more than one million letters during the years that she ran the department. They reached her from such distant points as Harbin, the Philippines and Alaska.

Before the war 75 per cent of the Beatrice Fairfax letters were from women. After the war 45 per cent were from men. From 1914 to 1918 half of the letters were from girls between sixteen and nineteen years of age. More recently 66 per cent of the mail has been from men and women between twenty-five and forty-five. Thus the column no longer caters to giddy youth as it did in the valentine age. There is more real tragedy behind it now. The mail is full of letters about homes that are breaking up, the forays of the love pirate, the ennui of the restless wife and the problem of the children of divorced parents. In the nineties when a girl got married, that practically ended all correspondence with Beatrice Fairfax. Now marriage is only the beginning of the widespread traffic with the love oracle.

One of Miss Lauferty's strangest experiences as Beatrice Fairfax was the twenty-page letter she received from a woman who wrote that she was in love with her employer but could not bear to steal him from his wife and children. He was in love with her, too. Miss Lauferty recognized the genuine note of agony in the letter. Much practice had accustomed her to the emotional variations of her correspondents, so that it was easy to detect an authentic plea for aid. She felt it was a case for personal action but she did not know how to reach the writer. The girl had given her name but no address. She put a note in her column but there was no response. A few days later the front pages of the papers carried the story of the double suicide of the girl and her employer in a public park.

Futility and tragedy underlie many of the Beatrice Fairfax letters. They often come from weaklings who are afraid of the machinery they have set in motion and do not know how to cope with it. Fear is apparent in their self-abasing scrawls as they turn to a symbolic figure and shrive themselves for the time being. Few of them are self-conscious about attaching their true names and addresses, even to the most revealing documents. Such is their trust in the detachment of the love forum.

To meet this craving, which had its first journalistic expression in the Beatrice Fairfax column, papers all over the country feature their own confessionals, on the theory that one section of the public yearns to see its woes in print. They buy them as syndicate features or employ women to run them locally. The most remarkable example at the present time, outside of the syndicate field, is Nancy Brown of the Detroit *News*, although she is averse to having her department carry the lovelorn label.

When Malvina Lindsay took over the woman's page of the Washington *Post* she decided on a column that would skirt the sentimental issues and be of practical aid to those who needed help. Her assistant, Mrs. Elizabeth Reardon Young, a newspaper woman from Ohio, was assigned to carry out her plan. The column now appears as "This Business of Living" under the pen name of Mary Haworth.

Mrs. Young answers questions on dress, etiquette, ethics, philosophy, psychology and religion, as well as love. She tackles each letter much as a reporter goes into action to get the facts on a story. She ferrets out the proper sources to supply the answers, instead of functioning as the oracle herself. She has the coöperation of the social, medical and educational associations in Washington, and is able to give her correspondents tangible aid from time to time.

Dorothy Dix was succeeded on the New York *Post* by Anne Hirst, who does an excellent job of her syndicated column and also edits the woman's page. She is a Baltimore girl, the daughter of a physician and the granddaughter of a Methodist minister. She entered newspaper work by way of advertising. First she did department store, then national advertising, and was war correspondent in France for the magazine of the Suffrage Unit. On her return she ran her own advertising agency in Cleveland. Then she joined the staff of the Cleveland *Times*, doing a shopping page of her own, and a daily radio program which she sold, wrote and broadcast.

After she married Leslie Peat, a newspaper editor, she moved with him to Philadelphia and tried the stay-at-home life, but didn't like it. So in 1930 she became woman's editor of the Philadelphia *Record*. The paper wanted a "heart" column, and she launched her own. For three days she wrote letters to herself and answered them. On the fourth day three letters arrived. Then they came in showers. In a remarkably short space of time her mail reached impressive proportions. Unlike most women running columns of this kind, she uses part of her own baptismal name, which is Anne Hirst Curry.

One-third of her mail is from men, mostly of the professional class. An analysis of a thousand of her letters, taken at random just as they were opened, showed that only 17 per cent were from adolescent readers. This included a number from mere children, smitten with calf-love. It also included the unmarried girls who would rather tell Anne Hirst than their mothers when they are going to have babies.

Why do men and women write about their most intimate problems to a stranger—and to one who can answer them only through a newspaper? Anne Hirst's answer is because they have nowhere else to turn. Often she hears the sequel, when her advice has been followed, for she belongs to the small but extremely potent group of newspaper women who get closer to the public than any other class of newspaper writer. Their mail is a revelation of human grief and weakness.

The lovelorn editor is working against heavy odds when she sits down to advise the baffled, the hopeless, the desperate. She rarely hears from the successful or contented newspaper reader. She holds the grab bag for the woes of the reading public.

Chapter VIII

HORACE GREELEY'S GRANDDAUGHTER

WHEN MRS. ASTOR MADE THE GRAVE MISTAKE OF SENDING $2 by way of a maid to Horace Greeley's granddaughter, she got one of the few snubs of her buffered life. "Tell Mrs. Astor," said Nixola Greeley-Smith to the horrified maid, "that she not only forgets who I am, but she forgets who she is. Give her back the $2 with my compliments and tell her that when John Jacob Astor was skinning rabbits, my grandfather was getting out the *Tribune* and was one of the foremost citizens of New York."

This interchange took place at the turn of the century when Nixola was doing a series of interviews with social leaders for the *Sunday World*. Mrs. Astor, known then and thereafter as *the* Mrs. Astor, had never talked to a reporter, but Nixola went to her with a letter of introduction from Chauncey M. Depew. Mrs. Astor received her and talked quite frankly. She gave her views on all sorts of things after her clever interviewer had persuaded her that what Queen Victoria was to England and the Empress Eugénie was to France, she was to the United States. This cut ice with the un-crowned queen of New York society.

Nixola was not altogether prepared for an interview. She thought that it was to be a social chat during which she could make arrangements for the story that she hoped to get. But Mrs. Astor did not even connect her with the *World*. She cataloged her in the rather general terms of a magazine writer. Nixola won her completely and before she left she had an excellent interview. Few reporters would have dreamed at that time of walking in on Mrs. Astor and getting her to talk for publication. Her inaccessibility was a newspaper tradition.

Nixola went back to her office, her mind made up that she would see Mrs. Astor again and get her permission before using the story in the *World*, so that there could be no possible misunderstanding about it. Her Sunday editor saw no reason for this scrupulous consideration of Mrs. Astor's feelings. However, Nixola returned to 842

Fifth Avenue and sent up her name. There was a long delay and then a maid appeared with the message that Mrs. Astor was sorry but she could not see her. She held out a $2 bill.

"Mrs. Astor sends you this because she knows that you work for a living and that you have been put to some trouble coming here," said the maid.

Nixola stared at the $2 bill, and then at the maid. Her hauteur could equal Mrs. Astor's.

"Will you deliver a message exactly as I give it to you?" she asked.

"Certainly, madam," said the maid.

It was then that Horace Greeley's granddaughter shot her annihilating bolt at Mrs. Astor, but she never knew if the message reached its mark. She went back to the *World*, burning with fury.

"You can print the Astor interview any time you like," she told her editor.

"Did the dowager actually say yes?" he demanded.

Then Nixola told him what the dowager had said.

"Oh, you mustn't mind a little thing like that," he told her soothingly. "Look at the check for $250 that Mary Baker Eddy once sent me. It tickled me so much I had it framed."

It was hanging on the wall in his office. But Nixola was not appeased. Raging, she sat down and put the caustic finishing touches to her story. Posters announced Mrs. Astor's one and only interview. Her son stormed into the *World* office and threatened action if the story were run. He insisted that his mother had not given an interview to Nixola Greeley-Smith. But the *World* would not be intimidated.

Mrs. Stuyvesant Fish was another of the social leaders interviewed as part of the series. She treated Nixola quite differently, and for the first time gave her views on society for publication. The stories created a stir. The subjects were all women of prominence who had practically never lent themselves to publicity before.

Annie Leary, Mrs. George Keppel, Mrs. Richard Croker and Mrs. Charles H. Parkhurst all talked illuminatingly to Nixola at different times and she did an amusing telepathic interview with Harry Lehr through a medium. She soon proved herself a newspaper woman of exceptional capacity and great personal fascination. She started to write for the *World* at a time when silly newspaper stunts had reached their peak. There was immediate interest in her along Park Row because of her lineage. The Greeley tradition was fresh in the minds of publishers and editors when she wrote to

Joseph Pulitzer, saying that she would like to enter newspaper work. He invited her at once to work for his paper.

At that time a woman's club meeting was about the only alternative to a stunt, and the women writers on Park Row had thin fare. The Home Page, as it was called in the *World*, was edited by Harriet Hubbard Ayer. Among the subjects for comment were: "The Dangers of Getting Off and On Cable Cars the Wrong Way," "The Awkward Way to Pick up a Book" and "How to Singe Hair."

The magazine section, on the other hand, struck the sensational note. Club women were interviewed on the provocative question: "Is the Moral or the Immoral Woman the Greater Power in the World?" Marie Corelli was busy "lashing society," according to the current headlines. Queen Wilhelmina of Holland, surprisingly enough, was billed as the "worst flirt in Europe," and columns were devoted to such rhetorical questions as: "Is Fashionable Society Corrupt and Wicked?" and "Is the Millionaire a Blessing?"

Kate Carew was doing her clever interviews and caricatures with such celebrities as Mark Twain, Coquelin, and Sarah Bernhardt; Lavinia Hart was covering the local girls with a touch of humor; Ella Wheeler Wilcox and Margherita Arlina Hamm were assigned to King Edward's coronation by different papers; and Emily Crawford was keeping *World* readers posted on the Paris Exposition. The social world was heavily played in every Sunday issue.

The quality of Nixola's work was apparent almost at once. She brought a sophisticated touch to bear on the most commonplace assignment. She had great dignity and finesse, got entrée everywhere and inspired confidence. She inherited her grandfather's instinct for newspaper work. Her style was vivid, scholarly, revealing. She had more personality than most of the celebrities she interviewed. Frequently they recognized her special gifts. Lord Northcliffe was so impressed by her that he tried to lure her away from the *World* to one of his papers. Mrs. Taft and the first Mrs. Woodrow Wilson, both publicity shy, talked freely to her. General Joffre gave her a personal statement during his visit to America.

Her triumphs were endless. She had the knack, to a remarkable degree, of getting the best out of any subject. She shot her own epigrams at the tongue-tied and they came back at her with double force. On one occasion she analyzed herself at a reception given by the Entertainment Club in the old Waldorf-Astoria:

> I describe myself as a cream-colored journalist because I prefer the rich cream of fancy to the skimmed cream of the baldest fact. Some people I know don't like cream in their journalism any more than they do in their tea and I have no quarrel with them if they prefer lemon in both. . . . A cream-

colored journalist is one who interviews a distinguished clergyman in the morning, stops by the Tombs to obtain the views
of a condemned murderer, gets a pen picture of a big Wall
Street man, and then goes out of town and gets the opinion of
a prima donna about some vital subject and telegraphs it in for
the first edition the following morning. . . . If a man you are
interviewing hasn't a personality, it is the correct thing to give
him one, and if he hasn't sense or tact enough to express an
opinion, you should branch out with a brilliant epigram or some
other pearl of thought and wind up with the question "Don't
you think so?"

This, to some degree, was Nixola's own technique. She could
take the most unpromising person and mold him into a figure of
substance, without distorting the picture in the least. When she encountered a fruitful mind, she stripped it bare and turned out an
interview of depth and subtlety. Her questions were intelligent,
amusing, surprising and sometimes impertinent, so that people were
blown off guard. But they found her irresistible. At times she was
sharp, both in her personal relations and her work. In a dozen
damning words she could impale the person who annoyed her, but
she was infinitely gracious to those she liked.

"I pity the unwary who are interviewed by Nixola Greeley-
Smith," said Mary Heaton Vorse on one occasion to Theodora Bean,
another New York newspaper woman. "She has the smile of a
happy child, the inscrutability of a sphinx; she has wisdom and
philosophy, yet behind the sweetest smile she hides a disdain and a
bitterness that in point and scope can surpass anything I have ever
known."

It was she who popularized the better type of interview for newspaper women and made it one of their most useful functions on a
paper. Every visiting celebrity for nearly two decades was done by
Nixola Greeley-Smith. She went after people that no one had
dreamed of interviewing before. She was not afraid to take an academic subject and make it good newspaper reading. Her style was
disarmingly simple; she was flowery only under stress of obviously
emotional situations and even then she was restrained for the period.
She was analytical and editorial, and used the capital I, but without
egotism.

Nixola was essentially a woman's writer but she was not in any
sense of the word a sob sister. However, she happened to be one of
the four women covering the Thaw trial in 1907, and thereby automatically came under the blanket indictment leveled at the women
of the press on that occasion.

She followed the case with characteristic absorption. Her point of view seemed to change as the trial went on. She was critical of Evelyn at the start, then became more sympathetic. In one of her first stories she wrote:

> I have no illusions about Evelyn Thaw. I think merely that she was sold to one man and later sold herself to another, and that most of her troubles were due to the fact that the White benevolence was a family affair while the Thaw golden shower was not so inclusive but fell on Evelyn alone. . . .

But Nixola's tone soon changed. She was completely won over to Evelyn's side. This was how she pictured her on the witness stand on February 7, 1907, after the white veil that had covered her features during the trial had been removed:

> But the taking off of her white veil this morning revealed the fact that another white veil—the filmy fabric of lauded child-hood, still wraps her, despite all the sins and shame she has been through. Looking at her I almost fancied myself in the children's court. It did not seem possible that this pale child could be the grown-up cause of Stanford White's alleged drugging of her, with such genuine and terrible shame that sitting there listening to this baring of her besmirched child's soul I felt myself almost as great a criminal as she made him appear. . . . When, broken and trembling, still less moved than those before her, she ceased to talk of White and began the story of her life in Pittsburgh, the tension relaxed. The horror had been too great even for strangers to endure, and they found relief in hearing her tell of days when they had only biscuits to eat. . . .

Nixola and one or two of the other newspaper women fled as William Travers Jerome drew from Evelyn with savage cross-examination the details of her rape by Stanford White. She and her colleagues "writhed and bowed their heads before this hideousness" but "fled in vain, for the horrors followed them." Next day she took issue with Mr. Jerome, although acknowledging that he was doing his duty in his cross-examination. "I am offering no criticism of his methods," she wrote. "I simply feel that compared with the ordeal to which this frail young woman is subjected, a prize fight must be an elevating spectacle, and a day at the Chicago stockyards a pastoral delight."

Delphin Delmas, counsel for Thaw, was delighted with the sob sisters. "What strikes me most forcibly in the accounts of the Thaw trial," he said, "is the power of analysis and description displayed by the women writers. . . . I would say that the writing of Miss Nixola Greeley-Smith is a most remarkable illustration of feminine intuition brought to a logical conclusion."

But Nixola was not at her best on the emotional story. Her mind was essentially sharp and creative. She was an intellectual, for the moment writing down to what the occasion seemed to demand. She did not often veer in this direction.

Sitting at the press table with her was Andrew W. Ford, whom she later married. They had met in the *World* office and their romance developed during the Thaw trial. Mr. Ford was one of the editors of the *Telegram* for years and is now on the *Sun.*

Nixola was handsome and memorable, although there was nothing striking about her features and she gave little thought to the way she dressed. She was short and inclined to be stout, but she had the grand manner and was always quite impressive. She had dark hair, waved and parted in the middle, and candid brown eyes. Her face was full but the nose and chin had a certain piquancy. Her manner was soft and wistful and she flushed easily.

Some time before the war she left the *World* and went to work for NEA. Harry Payne Burton, now editor of *Cosmopolitan* and then on the staff of NEA, had watched her work for years and admired it. When he was asked to recommend names to strengthen the service he suggested Nixola Greeley-Smith, Franklin P. Adams and Walter Lippmann. He had run across Mr. Lippmann while working on a story involving the Rev. George R. Lunn, who was Socialist Mayor of Schenectady from 1912 to 1914 and later became Lieutenant Governor of the State. Mr. Lippmann was working then as secretary to Mr. Lunn and Mr. Burton was much impressed by him.

Nixola was making $80 a week at the time. She was offered $7,000 a year and a two-year contract. She moved from the *World* editorial rooms down to the third floor in the same building and went to work for NEA. Roy Howard and William W. Hawkins, now chairman of the Scripps-Howard board, shared one office at this time. There was another large room for the rest of the staff and the telegraph instruments. A third room completed their quarters. This was the nucleus of the large organization that now functions under the direction of Mr. Howard.

Nixola did not care for her new job. Frank I. Cobb and her other friends from the *World* editorial rooms were constantly stopping in to see her. They thought that she should not have made the change. She herself was soon persuaded that she had made a mistake. She wanted to write sophisticated interviews and essays on women's rights. She disliked the jazzed-up assignments she got. One day she quoted Wordsworth in one of her stories and her copy went over the wire "as the *poet* Wordsworth says," This was disconcerting to Nixola. She made up her mind then that she would resign.

But the final straw was her assignment to work as a salesgirl in Woolworth's one Christmas Eve to write a first-hand story on the Christmas shopping rush. She gave it consideration for one evening. Next day she walked into the office and mentioned her dead grandfather, to whom she rarely alluded. "Last night I talked to my grandfather," she announced, "and he said, 'You and I have always reached such peaks as we have attained in newspaper work by our intelligence, our true journalistic sense and good writing. We never have had to stoop to cheap tricks and we won't now.' And Sam Hughes can take my resignation."

Nixola's contract was about to expire in any event. She left and went back to the *World*. But while she was with NEA she did excellent work and got practically any assignment she wanted. She suggested many of her own stories. It was much the same on the *World*. She could be quite independent in her actions, for her editors were hypnotized by her skill at her job. They felt it was an honor to have her work for them. She received extravagant offers from Mr. Hearst, which she always rejected.

Although her specialty was the interview, she did good work on straight news assignments. She wrote survivor stories on the *General Slocum* disaster and was assigned with Mr. Burton to the *Empress of Ireland* wreck in 1914, when 954 lives were lost. She was a swift, careful reporter. She mapped out her stories, typed them awkwardly, but they were always effective, and often sparkling. Her picture appeared practically every day on page three of the *Evening World*.

It was Nixola who gave Theda Bara her professional name. The actress was christened Dora Goodman and appeared in the *Quaker Girl* as Theodosia de Coppet. When she went into pictures she decided that she must have a new name. Nixola gave the matter some thought, then picked Theda Bara as suiting her exotic type. The Bara is Arab spelled backwards.

Nixola was a suffragist long before suffrage became fashionable, but she was always quite balanced on the subject and retained her sense of humor about it. When Mrs. Oliver H. P. Belmont launched her "no vote, no husband" campaign, Nixola wrote: "Possessing the established supremacy in the realm of emotion, why experiment with it at the risk of failure? . . . The slogan will win no votes, and possibly lose a great many husbands . . . a good thing for suffragettes to have, since it guarantees to them at least an audience of one." She was in a theater when she heard that the vote had been won for women in New York State. She wept with joy. "This is the greatest day of my life," she said.

Nixola was ailing for at least two years before her death. She had a thyroid condition and lost weight rapidly. When she felt she could no longer do the running around required for interviews and general news, Zoë Beckley took on this work and Nixola did her writing at home, turning out three columns a week on modern marriage and the problems of the day. They expressed many of her own theories on life and love.

Her education and upbringing were liberal and unusual. She was born in 1880 at Chappaqua, the old Greeley homestead. Her mother was Ida Greeley, the eldest daughter of the famous publisher, and her father was Colonel Nicholas Smith of Kentucky, a typical Southern gentleman with a goatee and courtly manners. Nixola adored him. He lived in a midtown hotel in New York in his later years and passed much of his time with her and his other daughter, now Mrs. Louis F. Geissler, of Northport, Long Island.

Nixola attended the Sacred Heart Convent in New York, spent some time in Canada with her father and from there went to Belgium, where he was stationed as American consul. Her education was completed at Liége. She spoke French fluently and one of the best interviews she ever did for the *World* was with Sarah Bernhardt, who was much impressed by her and appreciated the fact that she was interviewed in perfect French.

At twelve Nixola wrote a short play which was published in the *World*. At sixteen, just after her return from Belgium, she did an article on the labor movement in that country. Her first mature writing was a short story published in *Harpers Magazine*. At eighteen years of age she began writing regularly for the Sunday magazine section of the *World*. She went over to the *Evening World* in 1901. As the years went on she became increasingly enthusiastic about her profession. She often spoke in public, and on one occasion said:

> I now believe, as I certainly did not when I adopted it, that journalism is the best paid and most self-respecting profession open to any woman with a brain to sell. It needs strong health, perseverance, good nerves and mental poise. For the woman with a good head and a healthy body and no nonsense about her, newspaper work presents splendid opportunities.

Nixola devoted herself heart and soul to her work. She had many friends and they all adored her. Her home was in West Orange, New Jersey, and there she kept her dogs. This was her one recreation outside of her reading, which was extensive and scholarly. She preferred the French classics to anything else. She admired Thackeray and considered *Vanity Fair* the finest book in the English language. From time to time she wrote verse, short stories and essays for the magazines.

Nixola Greeley-Smith died in the spring of 1919 at the age of thirty-eight. Marguerite Mooers Marshall, who knew her well, gave her impression of her in the following verses published in *Ainslees*:

Mona Moderna

Like that great lady of the Renaissance
  Who's sent her sighing poet and lovers away,
  To watch, bright-eyed and lonely, the gold day
Blur into dark—you in your beauty glance
From out your portrait—all that may enhance
  Your magic—velvet, lace, the white array
  Of hand and arm and shoulder, interplay
Of eye and lip and witty brows askance.

If, debonair, you smile—yet never face
  More questions asked, more happy faiths put by;
You've dreamed with love and challenged life a space,
  Found love—a fragrance, life—a tired cry;
Fastidious, frank, ironic in your grace
  And bloom, you smile. . . . I think you wonder why.

Miss Marshall is another newspaper woman who has shown rare skill at the interview and the woman's column. Like Nixola Greeley-Smith, she brings her own vivid intelligence to bear on the person she is questioning. She is shy, hesitant, comes armed with highly probing questions, ignores the absurdities of a mass interview and sticks to her own line of questioning until she develops a cumulative train of thought.

The mob interview is a development of recent years. It is the lazy reporter's delight but is usually a careless and disorderly proceeding with so many conflicting questions being hurled at the victim that he is likely to shut up in disgust or dismay. The solo interview calls for more careful technique and keener mental processes. Both Nixola Greeley-Smith and Marguerite Mooers Marshall stand out among all their colleagues in this particular phase of newspaper work. Fundamentally there is no better outlet for the newspaper woman's skill. She can demonstrate good technique, real intelligence, humor—if she has any—insight into human nature, knowledge and writing ability in the well-planned interview. She can get away from the restraints of the copy desk more readily in this type of story than any other. And it is the one job that the city editor does not necessarily think a man can do better.

After the shipboard amenities were over, Miss Marshall got the first thoroughgoing interview with Margot Asquith when she came to New York, including her unexpurgated, off-the-record opinion of Lady Astor, which was not flattering. When H. G. Wells came over to attend the Disarmament Conference he gave her one of the frankest and most intelligent talks she ever had with anyone. In his book about the United States Sir Philip Gibbs said that she was the best interviewer he encountered in this country. Sir Gilbert Parker shared this view. Miss Marshall has interviewed hundreds of celebrities from all parts of the world, as well as the headliners of America. And she has always managed to keep her work on a high plane.

She is tall, rather slim, has an absent-minded manner, dresses mostly in tweeds, cares little for appearances, is creative in her work. She is a native of Kingston, New Hampshire. Her family has lived in New England since early Colonial days. She was educated at Sanborn Seminary and was graduated from Tufts College, taking honors in English and Latin, doing four years' work in three, and earning her Phi Beta Kappa key.

Fresh from college, she headed the Department of English at Westbrook Seminary in Portland, Maine, but she wanted to write, not teach, so she began almost at once to work without pay in her spare time for the Portland *Press* in order to get experience. Then she wrote Sunday stories for the Boston *Herald* and managed to get on the staff of the paper after a few months of teaching. In a year her salary was doubled. Next she moved to New York with $15.86 in her pocketbook, free-lanced for a few weeks and landed on the *Sunday World* in May, 1909.

Like Nixola Greeley-Smith, she soon moved over to the *Evening World*, where for twelve years she did feature stories, most of them interviews with celebrities. In 1922 she started her column "The Woman of It." This was a free and novel column in which she could write about anything that appealed to her at the moment. She took the stand that she was a "middle-of-the-road-feminist, pro-woman but not anti-man." She commented philosophically on women in public affairs, marriage, love, motherhood, books, home life and any topic suggested by the news of the day. She believes that women are more interested in these matters than in patterns, recipes and the usual woman's page fodder.

When the *World* was sold, Miss Marshall was offered a post in the Hearst organization and she joined the staff of the *Journal*, changing the title of her column to "Just Like a Woman." She still writes editorial comment in her chosen vein, contributes to the regular editorial page, and does feature articles, such as her running comment on the Hauptmann trial. She worked on the Halls-Mills and Snyder-Gray trials, and covered the curious witchcraft murder trial in Buffalo of Lila M. Jimerson, the Indian girl. She has visited the Dionne quintuplets practically every month since their birth, watching their progress and interviewing Dr. Allan Roy Dafoe regularly.

Miss Marshall has contributed verse and prose to the magazines and has had several novels published. Her first was *The Drift*. Her other three are stories of young love written against a New Hampshire background—*None But the Brave, Salt of the Earth,* and *The Golden Height*. She corrected proofs of the last one while covering the Hauptmann trial.

All of her writings have a strong philosophical tinge. She is a thinker, rather than a superficial reporter, and her work has rich texture. She receives hundreds of letters from women of widely differing ages and interests, who write to her for counsel on their problems. Those she values most are the letters from women who share her own conviction that marriage for love is the best and most permanent feminine destiny.

She has been felicitous in her own marriage after stormy beginnings. She is the wife of Sidney Walter Dean, the editor who gave her her first job in Boston. They live deep in the country with the three stepchildren she has brought up. Miss Marshall swims, reads, writes constantly. They have the ocean lapping at their front porch and pines and wild flowers at their back door. But she hankers after the food, the flowers, the salty Yankees of southeastern New Hampshire where she grew up. Some day she and her husband intend to go back there, buy an island, sail about in a cabin cruiser and let the days slip by.

Chapter IX

THE LADIES TRAVEL

Now that isn't the way to do it," roared H. G. Wells to Zoë Beckley when she called on him in his London home to get him to write a history of women for a magazine. "Let me show you. Come back here and I'll teach you how to approach me.

"Bang, bang, bang. That's you knocking on the door. I open it and say, 'Why, how do you do?' Then you say, 'I'm well, how are you, Mr. Wells, and what are you working on?' Then I say, 'I have just finished a fantastic Utopian romance—would you like to see it?' Then you say, 'Yes, indeed, I would, and I should like to buy it for my magazine.' "

Mr. Wells threw himself on the sofa and roared with laughter. He explained that he never wrote to order and that therefore Miss Beckley must let him dictate a cablegram to her magazine. It began: "Mr. Wells absolutely refuses to write at any price the work you suggest, but he has at present for your consideration . . ." The message ran to fifty words. Miss Beckley urged him to omit the Mister, the absolutely and the but, and thereby save money.

"No!" he shouted. "The Mister is for respect, the absolutely is to avoid argument, and the rest of it is my philanthropic willingness to give them the first chance to use my latest story. Change nothing."

Mr. Wells then made tea for Miss Beckley and showed her how that should be done, too. They chatted for hours. She found him a great wag. No newspaper woman ever has left Mr. Wells empty-handed. He makes copy as he breathes and enjoys talking about himself and the universe.

Authors frequently furnish newspaper women with good copy. John Galsworthy was the exception. He was so tongue-tied when he came to America that Elizabeth Eskey, of the *World*, wrote an amusing story based solely on his "ah's" and "hm's."

Miss Beckley managed to get to George Bernard Shaw once at his home in Adelphi Terrace and found him in an amiable mood. After that she tried for an interview every time she was in London.

She framed the last postcard she got from him. It read: "I am, as you see, out of reach in the country, so cannot see you. But here is your postcard. Bon voyage. G.B.S."

Miss Beckley was already a seasoned interviewer when she called on Mr. Wells. She had crossed the Atlantic on the trail of news a number of times, and had tackled the great, the near-great, the absurd, the pathetic, the brave and the ignoble. It was she who launched both Queen Marie and Coué on America. Few newspaper women have had careers as exciting as Miss Beckley's. She has always been in the thick of things, for she is both clever and lucky at her work.

"You had better get out of newspaper work before your impertinence gets you into difficulties," Anne Morgan once told her, when Miss Beckley asked her why she had never married. Ida M. Tarbell, a former newspaper woman herself, thanked her for asking the same question, saying she had always vaguely wondered why she had not married, and welcomed the chance to think it through to a conclusion. May Sinclair told her: "I have never married because an intellectual woman is always a lonely woman. Only inferior men care for a woman such as I—and I don't like inferior men. So I have to remain single."

Miss Beckley is one of the few newspaper women who are native New Yorkers. She was born in an old house on West Eighth Street. Her New England mother had had spirit enough to break away from the family fold and teach French in a Young Ladies Seminary in Richmond, Virginia. There she met Zoë's father, who sang in the same church choir and was a handsome member of the old Richmond Blues, a real Southerner at heart—couldn't make money, couldn't think of his daughters doing anything to earn a pair of party gloves or help buy the beef for Sunday's dinner.

He had lost everything after the Civil War and so he moved to New York, where Zoë was born. Her layette consisted of two print dresses and two pairs of worsted bootees her mother had knitted. Her aunt Molly named her Zoë after a child she had met once in a Pullman. She impressed the fact on Zoë that her name was Greek for life, and that she must never forget to put the dots over the "e," so as to keep people from pronouncing it Zo. Zoë always remembered about the dots but few others did.

Aunt Molly, who was a crack stenographer at a time when the mere sight of a woman worker in the Wall Street district nearly caused a riot, taught Zoë to typewrite. Propped on Webster's dictionary and two pillows, she punched out letters to her dear Mamma and dear Papa at the age of four. A dozen years later she capitalized this accomplishment by snatching at a job in a mail order house, unknown to her father. She could type fast and spell. Her salary was $7 a week. But her father soon found out and was deeply hurt. He took her into his own office as a compromise, but after the rent was paid there was nothing left for Zoë. So she struck out again. She worked in factories and offices of every sort. She batted the typewriter for an employment agency, a detective, a public stenographer, an editor, a wholesale butcher, a broker and a deaf old gentleman who was writing a book on finance.

Her Aunt Molly made her go to a night school and add shorthand to typewriting. After this her pay check fattened. She earned and saved, lived at home and went three times to Europe on a shoestring, for she was born with a mania for travel. She married the man who lived next door, but he died seventeen months later of typhoid-pneumonia. Later she married Joseph Gollomb, the author.

She worked at anything and everything. She painted dinner cards, photographs, frames and book-plates in the knickknack days. She copied manuscripts. She took stenographic jobs and finally she met Helen Rowland, who laughed heartily at what she told her about her occupations. One day Miss Rowland urged her to try newspaper work. Such a mad thought never had entered Zoë's head. But the columnist insisted that she should try a few paragraphs. She gave her a letter to Richard J. Spillane, then Sunday editor of the venerable and now forgotten *Press*. After his spectacular work on the Galveston flood he had come north and entered the New York field. He bought three of Miss Beckley's pieces for fillers and her first newspaper earnings amounted to $2.65. She kept on doing her work as secretary to James R. Sheffield, then a prominent attorney and later ambassador to Mexico. She earned $22 a week and used all her spare time doing elegantly typed pieces for the *Press*.

Mr. Spillane assigned her to interview the circus people one Saturday afternoon but she had a row with the Sheffield office clerk, who objected to her taking the half-holiday. So she blithely handed in her resignation and bolted for Madison Square Garden. On Monday she sought Mr. Spillane and asked him for a job.

"I can't hire you," he said. "Got no money. You couldn't make a living writing anyhow. Go back to your job and don't be a damn fool."

But Miss Beckley now knew what she wanted and wouldn't be put off. She hired a typewriter, got the copy boy to rig up an electric light and sat in the back of the city room where dirt from the stereotyping room sifted all over her. She beat out stories as if her life depended on it. Mr. Spillane took all he could and was kind to her. He was the most gifted profanity-slinger Miss Beckley ever came across in a newspaper office. Her space earnings brought her

in from $26 to $50 a week. The paper had a double page featuring
"Little Stories of Manhattan" and she wrote practically all of these
after the first few attempts.

Then Mr. Spillane fell ill and was away from the office. Miss
Beckley did not fare so well with the assistant editor. Walking up
and down Broadway and wondering what she should do she stopped
at Fulton Street and stared at the *Mail and Express* building. "That's
a paper," she thought. "I'll go in and ask."

"Where do I find the editor?" she asked the elevator boy.

"Which one?" he demanded, logically enough.

"The biggest one," said Miss Beckley.

"Aw, Mr. Stoddard's the biggest. He's over six feet. Try him."

So Miss Beckley got in to see Henry L. Stoddard, the publisher.
Her zeal seemed to amuse him. He turned her over to T. E. Niles, the
managing editor, who handed her a clipping and said, "Do a feature
on that." Not having the remotest idea what a feature might be, and
fearing to ask Mr. Niles, Miss Beckley stopped a red-headed youth on
her way out and asked him. He turned out to be Fred Knowles.
His face was a picture as he said, "A feature, my poor woman, is a
story that isn't news but is based on news. Keep it short, make it
interesting and don't begin with 'the.'"

The interview was with Mrs. Martin Littleton, who had made a
speech in place of her husband when he became ill suddenly. This
was during the suffrage period. After telling Miss Beckley how she
had come to substitute for her husband, she added, "But don't put
anything about all this in the paper." Miss Beckley felt completely
sunk. This was her first assignment and things seemed to be going
wrong. Then Mr. Littleton marched in and sized up the situation.

"Go on, Peggy, do some shopping," he said. "I'll attend to this
girl. I know what a newspaper wants."

He gave Miss Beckley a fine story. From that time on she was
always lucky about getting stories and landing in places at the right
moment. It's a special gift in the reporter that the wise editor
should see a mile away and cherish.

She worked hard, had good health, contributed an enormous
amount of energy and enthusiasm to what she was doing, had initiative and resource, was facile with words. Robert E. MacAlarney,
who was then on the *Mail*, urged her not to stay too long in newspaper work. A year's enough, he told her. But she stayed and never
was sorry. Her days were filled with variety, excitement, achievement.

Her first big assignment came to her quite by accident. Mr.
Stoddard was passing her desk one day. "Well, young lady, what are
you doing?" he asked.

"I'm writing a dull piece for your paper while you are about to board a special train with a picked crew of writers bound for the Bull Moose Convention in Chicago," she said a little querulously. "It must be great to be a Political Power."

Mr. Stoddard went into his office and twenty minutes later came back. "It's ten minutes past one. Could you be at Grand Central by 2.30 to get aboard that special?"

Miss Beckley was alarmed over the outcome of her levity. In spite of all the difficult things she has done, she is not yet panic proof. She can still get bumpy knees at a difficult moment. But George Henry Payne, political feature writer for the *Mail*, came to her rescue. He dragged her into one of the Pullman rooms, where a type-writer and a pile of copy paper rested on the table, and gave her a lecture. "Think of these delegates you're so concerned about," he said, "as being utterly dependent upon you. You're their vehicle of expression and without you they'd be sunk. Ask the old dames a question—any question—and they'll talk their heads off. Get the one best idea for your lead, then throw in a little palaver of your own for color, then elaborate on what they say, if anything, and pull the whole thing together at the end. And there you are. Now write 800 words and I'll show you how to put it on the wire at Buffalo."

Miss Beckley's convention stories came through without a hitch. She had her first taste of real newspaper excitement. When she got back she dug in at $30 a week. She turned out four and five stories for one issue, some signed, others not. But she got many raises and survived five city editors. By 1917 she was tired of doing war stories and she asked Dr. Edward A. Rumely, editor of the *Mail*, to let her go on a tour of the country. She wanted nothing but her railroad fare. V. V. McNitt, who later founded the McNaught Syndicate, for which she now writes a daily column, was then with the *Mail*. He routed her through thirty-seven cities from New York to San Francisco, and she interviewed everybody along the way who seemed to be worth while.

When she got back, she found the *Mail* greatly changed. The old staff had melted away. There were new faces everywhere. Miss Beckley learned that $20 had been lopped off her $80 a week salary. She decided to leave and work on her own. She did syndicate work for NEA and NANA and some magazine features. Then the *Evening World* offered her a three-day-a-week job to alternate with Nixola Greeley-Smith. This went on up to the time of Nixola's death. Miss Beckley stayed with the *World* for some time longer, then out of a clear sky she got an assignment from a magazine to interview Sir Oliver Lodge. That was in the summer of 1919.

She stayed in Europe for ten months, writing a serial and doing syndicate stories from Central Europe on the relief work for children. She traveled all over the Continent, saw annihilating things, and cared less for this than for anything she ever did. She was in Paris when she got a cablegram from NEA asking her to find the Kaiser in Holland and interview him. She showed the message to Henry Howe and asked him what she should do. He gave her a letter to Jan Bruna, editor of the *Nieuwe Courant* of The Hague, and thither she posted. Bruna laughed his head off and she was leaving his office in a depressed state of mind when he called her back.

"Look here, have you got any money to spend?" he asked.

"My message said to spare no expense."

So she hired a car and on Sunday they both went to Amerongen where the Kaiser then was, in the castle of the Bentincks. The guards brushed them off and threatened to take away Miss Beckley's camera. They prowled about but failed to pick up anything on the Kaiser. They went to an inn for coffee and liqueurs and Bruna talked to everyone in sight. The waiter pointed to the houses opposite, where the crack reporters of Europe and America had put up for three months, hunting the All-Highest in vain, and finally had gone their ways.

"Why doesn't the lady go to Doorn where the Emperor is remodeling his castle and soon will live?" he asked. "She might chance on something."

So they drove to Doorn and found the lovely old castle, the chapel, the moat, the wooded grounds, the ancient bridge, but no Kaiser. Her friend Bruna spied a good burgher and his *vrouw* having coffee in their little garden adjoining the royal grounds.

"Oh, yes," said Vrouw Van Zetten casually, "the journalist lady can see the Emperor if she cares to . . ."

She proceeded to give minute instructions as to where Miss Beckley should stand and wait any fine morning for the Emperor to show up at ten o'clock. She was to watch for the green car. She was to be sure to stand on the highway, not on private ground.

Miss Beckley sent Bruna back to The Hague and returned alone to the famous little Pabst Hotel at Doorn. She carried out the *vrouw's* directions precisely, not dreaming that she would actually get a sight of Wilhelm or have a chance to take his picture. But everything happened as the Dutch woman had predicted. She got three pictures—including a fine close-up of the Kaiser with his first wife, Empress Augusta Victoria. Then the state police, riding on bicycles, pounced on her. The chief of police called later on Miss Beckley at the little inn, scrutinized her passport, asked her numerous questions and ran her out of town. But not until she had seen the Kaiser twice again. Vrouw Van Zetten told her that if she bowed to him as he passed in his car he would lift his hat. Next day she tried it and he did. His hair was thick, white and wavy. She thought that he looked like a tired old wolf in a cage at the Zoo.

Miss Beckley was detained at The Hague until her ten-day visa had expired. The officials refused to renew it and they made her skip straight back to Paris. The chief of police was courteous but said she had "disturbed the Emperor and blown a lot of dust down the road" and must not stay in Holland any longer. So, although she did not get her interview with the Kaiser, she got excellent pictures and such an entertaining story about him that NEA offered her a job. This was in 1920. A year later, when Mr. Stoddard resumed ownership of the *Mail*, he urged her to return. She had been so fond of the paper that she did not hesitate. She was to work only three days a week and receive $125 for her labors, the same salary that she was getting from NEA.

When she noticed a paragraph on an obscure chemist in France named Coué who was curing people of their ills by auto-suggestion she showed it to Mr. Niles, who was interested at once and sent her to Nancy to watch Coué at work in his clinic there. She followed him to Paris and accompanied him back to America. She sent stories daily by wireless from the *Majestic* and stuck with him throughout his American tour.

One night in the spring of 1922, Mr. Stoddard thought of sending her to England to come back with Lady Astor on her first trip to America after taking her seat in the House of Commons. He telephoned Miss Beckley's home but she was out of town. It was not until the following Monday, when she came into the office for her half-week, that he casually mentioned the assignment. "But of course it's too late now," he added.

Miss Beckley was disappointed. She dragged uptown to interview Dame Clara Butt and found her surrounded by luggage, all piled up for sailing. It was labeled S.S. *Mauretania*. The ship was due to leave next day at noon. Miss Beckley rushed from the suite, telephoned to Mr. Stoddard, begged him to let her try to make the *Mauretania*, which was sailing eastward as an oil-burner for the first time and would no doubt break her own record. She got a renewal visa for her old passport by telephoning to Washington, snatched her laundry from the hands of the ironer, packed a bag, and had Harry Acton, who was then on the *Mail*, get her accommodations. She finally made the gangplank with only eight minutes to spare.

Lady Astor made no attempt to avoid publicity. Miss Beckley was able to wireless exclusive stories every day, which gave her a considerable start on the newspaper women who swarmed aboard at

Quarantine. She watched her do her gym work-out and talked to her at length. By the time the ship docked Lady Astor's opinions on all sorts of topics had appeared in the *Mail*. It was a bright piece of journalism.

Miss Beckley went over to the *Telegram* with the sale' of the *Mail* but left soon afterwards to join Famous Features Syndicate, which was new and wanted something for an opening splash. She suggested Marie of Rumania, who had not yet become the publicity queen. The suggestion was made in a facetious vein but she was taken up seriously. She composed an urgent cablegram and got a leisurely answer, suggesting that she come to Rumania and see the Queen. The date set was for eleven days ahead. In no time at all Miss Beckley was on the *Mauretania* again, tapping out her regular column with one hand and holding on to a rocking berth with the other. For she is adept at writing under strange conditions. She has turned out copy in Pullmans, on ships, in airplanes, in borrowed offices, in homes where she was a guest, in royal palaces, in a hospital bed, in odd inns all over Europe—everywhere, in fact, except on a curbstone with her feet in the gutter.

She stopped off in England and got a letter from Lady Astor to pave the way with Queen Marie. But no introductions were needed. The Queen received her enthusiastically. Before being ushered in to her presence she got precise instructions about her behavior. She was not to wear a coat or hat, she was not to turn her back and she was to kiss the Queen's hand. Miss Beckley promptly forgot all the royal etiquette and she and Queen Marie hit it off at once.

She was not there for an interview. She wanted to get a series of articles signed by the Queen for her syndicate. Miss Beckley had a bad moment when she was asked how much she would pay for the stories. She had no idea what to offer. She did not want to run her syndicate into an extravagant figure. On the other hand, she was afraid the Queen might sheer off if the price named were not sufficiently high. So she added up her own and Helen Rowland's weekly salary, divided the total into two and offered the Queen this sum for each article.

It was a ticklish moment. She had no idea how Marie would take it. The Queen went on placidly knitting a red cap for the gardener's child.

"You know, I think that is rather decent," she said.

After this Miss Beckley was more or less in constant attendance while the Queen wrote the articles. She strolled with her in her rose garden and sat with her in her boudoir—a picturesque room with rough rafters into which gold powder had been rubbed, some of it by the Queen herself. Miss Beckley traveled in state with her to

Belgrade. Marie turned out to be a human gold mine of copy, spilling her confidences with startling abandon. But she wrote her own articles, except for a little help on English. Three times Miss Beckley crossed the Atlantic to visit her. She regards these trips as the most interesting part of her newspaper career. To this day she hears from the Queen. Although it was she who started the publicity that rolled up to such proportions on her visit to this country in 1926, she never thought that Marie should have made the expedition, and was not surprised when it turned into something of a circus.

Calvin Coolidge was the least responsive subject Miss Beckley ever tackled. After she had given him up completely, frozen out by his persistent silence, he turned hospitable and he told her a funny story. She discovered then that he was afraid of women reporters. When she stayed as a guest at his house, he was almost genial with her.

Miss Beckley figured once that she had written between four and five thousand interviews with every sort of human being during her years on the *Mail* alone. She has had as varied experience as any newspaper woman could hope for, and has traveled more than most of them ever get a chance to do in their professional capacity. She is of medium height, dark and vivacious. She lives deep in Connecticut, writes her column at home, enjoys her work to the full, has seen an extraordinary number of places, persons and things. She has a lively sense of humor, an optimistic outlook on life.

Another newspaper woman who has crossed the Atlantic more than once in quest of news is Miriam Teichner, who sailed from Hoboken on the Peace Ship on December 4, 1915, and thereafter lived through Alice in Wonderland days of nonsense, bravado and downright lunacy. There were more than sixty reporters aboard and almost as many students, taken along to be educated in the ways of peace. There were a few sincere men and women who went because they had faith in Mr. Ford's idea. The rest of the passengers were assorted cranks of one kind or another.

It all made good copy for Miss Teichner, who was covering the story for the *Globe* in New York and the *News* in Detroit. There were ructions and alarms from the moment the *Oscar Second* sailed. The Peace Party split wide open and divided into two warring factions before they had been aboard twenty-four hours. The reporters were unpopular with everyone, because they insisted on knowing and writing the truth. Rosika Schwimmer charged them with being in the pay of armament manufacturers and said in a speech that they were "serpents in the bosom of the expedition." This inspired a verse which the correspondents chanted lugubriously to the tune of Beethoven's Funeral March when they made merry at their New Year's party in Copenhagen:

> *We have come from Sweden,*
> *Snakes in Schwimmer's Eden.*
> *On to the morgue,*
> *That's the only place for us.*

Miss Teichner saw little of Henry Ford, nor did anyone else. He never received the press and he gave every appearance of regretting the expedition before it was well under way. When he appeared among the fanatical crowd on board he seemed diffident, withdrawn, his face half shrewd, half badgered. He left the ship before they reached Stockholm. The announcement that he and Dean S. S. Marquis, the Detroit clergyman who had accompanied him, were on their way home, was made to the reporters by Louis Lochner at a press conference called some time after midnight on a freezing train in the heart of Sweden.

Miss Teichner found that everything about the expedition was half mad, badly thought out, doomed to failure from the start, but she believed the dark, thick-spectacled Rosika to be sincere. They made crazy progress from Hoboken to Christiania, from Christiania to Stockholm, from Stockholm to Copenhagen, from Copenhagen across the Baltic and then, carefully guarded by German soldiers, across war-time Germany to The Hague, and home from Rotterdam.

The entire expedition had a fantastic quality for the press. There were entertainments, public meetings and innumerable speeches in every place they visited. But few of the important officials of any country visited turned out for them. Nothing but ridicule ever came of the *Oscar Second*. The only passengers who got anything out of it were the press, and they got good copy and merry laughter. Soon after Miss Teichner returned she was sent on a second quixotic expedition—this time the Hughes train.

These were lively newspaper days. Zest and excitement were in the air. She moved rapidly from one story to another. She made a study of conditions among the immigrants on Ellis Island. Europeans were still pouring into the country and the shawl and sabot line was long and picturesque. Miss Teichner investigated New York's flop-houses and breadlines. She spent a night in the warden's office at Sing Sing with a family group that had come to say good-by to a man who was due to be electrocuted in the morning. His sentence was commuted just before dawn.

She went behind the scenes at the Metropolitan with Bill Guard to interview Caruso, glittering in the golden robes and bronze beard of Meyerbeer's "Prophet." In a spangled gown of peacock velvet and a gold crown she sat in a howdah and rode an elephant in the circus at Madison Square Garden because her city editor had said to her, "Go get a job with the circus for a day." Dexter Fellows had arranged it.

She interviewed most of the stage, screen and opera stars of the period. She talked to criminals in the Tombs and Anzac soldiers on their way to war. She held the tail of a Hippodrome lion while he was being operated on—well roped—for an abscessed tooth. She interviewed celebrities of all kinds, and down-and-outers. For several years she did the verses that appeared on the editorial page of the *Globe.* Then Miss Teichner took a leave of absence from her paper for a few months to do publicity for the New York State Woman's Suffrage party in its campaign for the state amendment. She was offered the job on the strength of a satirical story she wrote about anti-suffrage headquarters.

When the armistice came she wanted to go abroad again. By the spring of 1919 she was working in a Jewish Welfare Board hut at Camp Covington, an embarkation camp outside Marseilles. The climate was trying. It was never cool. The blue satin sky was cloudless. The sirocco blew in a burning blast from Africa; the food was bad; she had no regular hours. She came down with rheumatic fever and was taken back to Paris. When she got home she still had a crippled arm. She went back to Detroit to convalesce, and before long she was back on the staff of the *News,* the paper on which she started.

In 1921 she was sent to Germany and she stayed for eighteen months. She traveled all over the country and was in Berlin during a general strike in mid-winter, when for a week there was no light, no heat, and the German housemaids stood for hours in the freezing streets, waiting for their turn at the hydrant to get buckets of water to drag up innumerable flights of stairs. Miss Teichner wrote human interest stories about post-war conditions as they affected the man in the street and his wife and children. She went to Oberammergau for the first production of the Passion Play after the war, and interviewed Anton Lang and the other members of the cast. Before returning home she visited Vienna, Budapest, Switzerland and France.

Then came a break in her newspaper career. She was very ill after she returned to America. She has never been entirely well since. During the years of invalidism she did publicity, fiction, interviews and verse. Then she went to work on the *Evening World.* Again Miriam Teichner's intelligent reporting appeared regularly in the columns of a New York daily and she thought she was settled for life under the Pulitzer gold dome. But the paper was sold. Nearly three thousand men and women were thrown out of work. The *Globe*, too, had died of sale and amalgamation.

Miss Teichner's newspaper career started in Detroit, where she did verse, paragraphs and editorial comment for the *News* before being taken on the city staff. E. G. Pipp, her managing editor, initiated her with two pieces of advice. One was: "To learn to write, you need only four things—the Bible, Shakespeare, the *Saturday Evening Post* and the *News*." The other was: "Get things *right*. Walk a mile, if you have to, to find out a man's middle initial, but get it, and get it right."

Miss Teichner had intended to be a nurse but newspaper work suited her so well that she was never able to understand why she should be paid for her efforts. Every day seemed to her to be high adventure. She never walked into the noisy city room without an actual physical quickening. She is one of the many infatuated newspaper women who think their profession the most dazzling in the world. She hopes that when she dies the words "*She was a good newspaper woman*" will be written on her tomb.

Chapter X

THE CRUSADING SPIRIT

RHETA CHILDE DORR WALKED INTO THE CITY ROOM OF THE NEW York *Mail* one day in 1917 and found the men on the staff hovering over the ticker tape. At once she detected the suppressed excitement that to the initiated implies news. She leaned over to see for herself what was stirring. The Czar had abdicated. Russia was a republic.

Mrs. Dorr clutched the arm of the city editor. "I'm going to Russia," she exclaimed.

No one looked surprised. No one said she couldn't go, as someone undoubtedly would have done when she first struggled into journalism in the late nineties, fighting her way by inches. In 1898 she was told by a baby-faced young man at the *Sun* office that his paper had no women on the staff and never expected to have any. At the *Post* an editor assured her that he would rather die than help a woman to get a job in such an accursed business. Park Row was then practically a masculine monopoly.

But by 1917 no one questioned Mrs. Dorr's right to go to Russia and report the Revolution if that was what she wanted to do. She had shown that she could handle any sort of news story and open doors often closed to men. So she sailed for Russia in a Swedish steamer, with eleven bearded Norwegian captains whose vessels had been sunk by U boats. She had been in Russia twice before. She was a student of the French Revolution and she thought that nothing could be more thrilling than to write about a nation in the throes of revolt.

Mrs. Dorr first ran into excitement in Finland, where she was held up while all her medicines and toilet articles were examined. She was forced to demonstrate the harmlessness of her belongings, at the expense of her stomach. She took aspirin, soda mints, quinine, bromide, epsom salts, strychnine tablets, aromatic spirits of ammonia and wound up with a swig of cologne. She compromised on the iodine by smearing some on her wrist.

"There," she said. "Satisfied?"

The officials were practically persuaded that she was not carrying explosives and she went on her way with her medicine kit. When she arrived at her destination she employed a young Russian girl to act as interpreter. She wandered through the streets, parks and factories and watched the councils of the Soviet. To her the Communists seemed lunatics. She saw the Paris of 1792 all over again—on one side of the legislative chamber the Lafayettes and Mirabeaus; on the other the Dantons, Marats and Robespierres, the red zealots ablaze with the frenzy of destruction.

She visited the Battalion of Death and struck up a friendship with Marie Skridlova, a slim girl in her twenties who was adjutant of the regiment.

"If you girls ever go to the front I am going with you," said Mrs. Dorr.

Before Botchkereva, the big peasant woman who commanded the Battalion of Death and had previously fought in a men's regiment, had time to get a permit for her, they moved off to war without giving her warning. Mrs. Dorr saw their crimson-tipped lances go by; heard the clatter of a thousand Cossacks escorting them on their way.

She rushed from one official to another but got no aid. So she started off without a permit, two dollars in her pocket, a briefcase under her arm. At the station in Warsaw she found the regiment in a preliminary mêlée with Bolshevik soldiers bent on keeping them from leaving. Her friend, Skridlova, gave her a nurse's coif and labeled her a *sestra*. She became part of the regiment. It took them two days and nights to reach the Dvinsk front. Then they marched into a camp where 100,000 soldiers were stationed. Mrs. Dorr slept on a rough plank bed without blankets. For nine days she watched them drill and lived with them under camp rules.

At the end of that time they were ordered to the front. She returned to Petrograd and was soon in the thick of the July Revolution. The Battalion of Death went into action at once. Half the women were killed or wounded. She never heard of Skridlova again, but she saw Botchkereva when she passed through the United States a year or two later.

Mrs. Dorr went to the Convent of Mary and Martha in Moscow to talk to the Grand Duchess Serge, sister of the Czarina. She found her in an old-world setting of lilac bushes and mignonette, with calm-faced nuns in pale gray habits raking up leaves while the revolution raged nearby. They talked for an hour. The Grand Duchess wanted to know about the Battalion of Death. Mrs. Dorr carried away with her an impression of peace and beauty. She was to remember it vividly when she read later of her death—thrown down an abandoned mine shaft in Siberia, bombs flung on her for flowers.

She also met Anna Alexandrovna Virubova, for years the intimate of the Czar and Czarina and a member of Rasputin's innermost circle. Later Mrs. Dorr was to write a striking story about the Russian summer night on which she listened to this pale woman on crutches, her face dim with peril and grief, her blue eyes that had seen so much evil washed pure as those of a child, telling of her life with the Imperial family, the chaos of the Revolution, the death of Rasputin. Years later they met again and Mrs. Dorr helped Mme. Virubova write her memoirs. They worked together in a small German hotel, the Czar's letters strewn around them, Virubova talking and talking, recreating the atmosphere of vice, cruelty and superstition in which she had moved.

Mrs. Dorr left Russia in September, 1917. On her return she sat at her typewriter in a small office in the *Mail* and wrote for five weeks, turning out thousands of words, all from memory. She had come out of Russia without a single note. She lost herself in her surroundings and when she finished for the day, she was always astonished to see from the windows the New York skyline instead of the roofs of Petrograd. She lived in a dream until she had translated her experiences into copy. Her stories ran on the front page of the *Mail* for weeks. They were published later in a book called *Inside the Russian Revolution*. The Reds pounced on her at once. Louise Bryant, another able correspondent, challenged her to debate. But Mrs. Dorr refused to take up the challenge. She lectured and wrote, and appeared at times in the *Mail* office in riding breeches and military coat, the war correspondent's uniform.

She went abroad again in December and toured the munitions factories of Britain. She interviewed Lord Northcliffe and carried away an unforgettable picture of his massive head outlined against a background of yellow narcissi. On that occasion he accurately predicted for her the appointment of Foch to the supreme command.

Like all the other women who tried to do war correspondence in France, Mrs. Dorr found herself tangled and defeated by red tape. General Pershing allowed her to go through the lines as far as the tiny village where the Americans were taking over their first sector. Her son, Julian, who later entered the diplomatic service, was wounded twice. Years later, when he was a consul in Italy and Mussolini arrived in Naples on his conquering way to Rome, Mrs. Dorr told her son that she would have to see hostilities through. Julian threw up his hands and exclaimed, "My God! If there's a war Mother joins it."

For Mrs. Dorr's whole life has been patterned in excitement, dat-

ing back to the day she sneaked out of her home in Lincoln, Nebraska, at the age of twelve, to listen to Elizabeth Cady Stanton and
Susan B. Anthony lecture on women's rights after her father had
forbidden her to attend the meeting. During her adolescence she
spent long hours in the library, lapping up history and romance. She
went to Nebraska State University but was unpopular with her classmates, for she was a strong individualist. Later she worked in a post
office and watched life flow by at the general delivery window. She
knew Walt Mason, who was then on the editorial staff of the *Nebraska State Journal*. He asked to see some of her writings. He called
her Sappho and said she had a literary future ahead of her. But all
she wanted was to play Nora of the *Doll's House*.

In 1890 she traveled East and first saw the New York skyline
from the forward deck of a Jersey City ferry boat. It was lower
then and less brilliantly lighted, but it seemed an enchanted scene
to the eager girl from the West. She lived at the Art Students'
League and discovered a new world. But this time she had not come
to stay. Two years later she married John Pixley Dorr, twenty
years her senior, and in the spring of 1893 they moved to Seattle,
where the first years of their married life were spent and their
son Julian was born.

Mrs. Dorr's mind was foraging now for fresh material. She was
filled with the consuming fires of discontent. She scrapped Jane
Austen; read the moderns. She argued endlessly with her husband,
for she believed that men and women should live on absolutely equal
terms. She interviewed the prospectors who sailed into Seattle with
treasure from the North, and sent her stories to New York. She
went as far as the White Pass and watched the dog teams start on
their journey into the wilds.

Her husband could not understand her strange interests. He
thought that women should not budge from the nursery and fireside.
So she left him and returned to New York in 1898 with $500, a two-
year-old child, a marriage adrift. The *Sun* printed some of her work
but she could not get steady employment. For three years she ped-
dled her wares on space. She never received a word of praise or
encouragement, nor was she able to see anyone in authority. She got
tired of supercilious young men who came out to snub her, representing the poobah inside, for she felt, with absolute justice, that she
could write.

At last the American Press Association, one of the earliest syndicates, took a weekly column of fashion notes for boiler plate. And
a photographic concern, seeing that she had fresh ideas, gave her a
photographer to go about with her. Together they filled an occasional Sunday page. In the meantime Mrs. Dorr pawned everything

that she had—down to the last of her silver spoons and even her engagement ring. Things did not look up for her until she was assigned to get pictures of Theodore Roosevelt at Oyster Bay, when he was officially notified of his appointment as vice-president.

Colonel Roosevelt was in an ill humor at the time. He was annoyed because his wife and children had been pestered by camera men, so he gave orders that none was to be allowed on the premises on the day of the notification. Mrs. Dorr was promised a bonus of $25 if she could persuade the Colonel to pose. She went to Sagamore Hill, wearing her last good linen dress. She got to Colonel Roosevelt, but as soon as she mentioned photographs, the bulldog look flashed. She stood her ground and argued with him for ten minutes. Then he said:

"Well, Mrs. Dorr, if you will boss the job, and see that not a man points his camera except at me and the notification committee, I will let them in. Is that fair?"

"It's fair," Mrs. Dorr conceded. "And I shall be responsible."

So a score of camera men were admitted on the strength of this pact, the pictures were taken, and the family was let alone, although the children overran the porch and grounds. By the time it was all over, Colonel Roosevelt was in high good humor. He invited the photographers to stay for luncheon and led Mrs. Dorr into the dining-room on his arm.

After this she sold copy regularly to the woman's page of the *Tribune* and to the *Post*. One day Hammond Lamont, managing editor of the *Post*, invited her to join the staff to cover women's activities. The business office had been complaining bitterly that women did not read the paper and that the advertisers were aware of this significant fact. But before committing himself, Mr. Lamont questioned Mrs. Dorr about her educational qualifications and degrees.

"I haven't any," she told him candidly.

The *Post* at the time was overrun with scholars. They lurked in every corner. *Post* reporters, Mr. Lamont explained, should be of good breeding and education because often they got in where the garden variety of reporter was barred. And they had to be of impeccable character.

Mrs. Dorr noticed a picture of Alexander Hamilton hanging over Mr. Lamont's desk.

"It gives me a certain sense of superiority to think that I am to have a job that Alexander Hamilton couldn't possibly have aspired to," she remarked impudently.

Mr. Lamont looked slightly dazed but the transaction went through. She got $25 a week and Oswald Garrison Villard told her later on that he never would pay her more, for the simple reason that she was a "female," and he could employ all the females he wanted for $25 or less. By this time a girl had chiseled her way onto the *Sun* staff but she was not permitted to enter the city room. She got her assignments and wrote her copy in an office boy's nook.

Mrs. Dorr now plunged into journalism with a vengeance. She did women's clubs, fashions and housekeeping in a sophisticated way. She wrote editorial paragraphs and columns of interest to women. She took on book reviewing but her salary was not increased.

When the New York State Federation of Women's Clubs assembled in Brooklyn, she offered the city desk a daily story on this event, which seemed to her to have general news interest.

The city editor looked at her coldly.

"You can do me one funny piece," he said.

"I can't do that," Mrs. Dorr protested. "This isn't funny. These women are organizing. Women all over the country are organizing. And it isn't funny. It is serious. Perhaps it's the most serious thing you and I are facing in our lives. I simply won't ridicule it."

"Young woman," said the editor sternly, "the first lesson a cub reporter has to learn is that he has no opinions. He writes what his superiors tell him to write and he writes it in their way."

But all the other papers treated the Federation seriously next morning. The editor was forced to haul down the flag. "I see, after all, that they are reporting this damned nonsense over in Brooklyn," he said. "You'd better telephone in a short story at 11.30."

So Mrs. Dorr delivered the story and it wasn't funny. She never saw anything amusing in the struggle of women for equality. She was more than a mere reporter where their early strivings were concerned. She was one of the belligerents herself. In the years that followed she watched their progress with a sympathetic eye. She began to worry about the harassed faces she saw in the streets and subways. She took two rooms on the East Side, had them cleaned and fumigated, and lived there for two years while she was on the *Post*, studying her neighbors' lives, talking to them, taking courses at the University Settlement in Rivington Street.

But she failed to find the rebellious woman in this environment. Marriage was still the solitary goal. So she sought for discontent among the sporadic strikers. Still she couldn't find the fighting spirit. It was not until she went abroad in 1912, talked to Ellen Key in Stockholm, saw the women of Norway and Finland striking out for freedom, that the suffrage cause caught her with full force. Then William F. Bigelow bought Mrs. Emmeline Pankhurst's story for *Good Housekeeping* and Mrs. Dorr was assigned to collaborate on it. She met the suffrage leader in Europe and sailed with her for America. Mrs. Pankhurst was held at Ellis Island, but Mrs. Dorr was allowed to walk off the ship. She felt indignant, for she longed to be a martyr to a cause which she had passionately espoused. But the immigration authorities saw no reason for penalizing her.

When Mrs. Pankhurst returned to England, Mrs. Dorr went with her, with the $20,000 that had been raised in America sewn into her corsets. The feminist leader was arrested on landing in England, but again Mrs. Dorr was obliged to go free.

She was in Christabel Pankhurst's flat in London when the news came that the fight had been won.

"You must stand for Parliament," said Mrs. Dorr to Mrs. Pankhurst.

"No, no! Christabel is the one," said her mother.

Mrs. Dorr was baffled by the complete femininity of the suffrage leader. She found her a "Victorian lady who had a Pomeranian to which she loved to talk baby-talk, and she adored sitting with her feet on a hassock sewing yards of lace on dainty muslin underwear."

Fired with the Pankhurst spirit, Mrs. Dorr went to Washington in 1914 with Alice Paul and the other leaders of the Woman's Party. She was the most militant of the group that pitched into President Wilson on the suffrage question. He stiffened under her interrogation. At last he turned on her and said, "I think it is not proper for me to stand here and be cross-examined by you."

All through the years that she fought for the suffrage cause, Mrs. Dorr was a newspaper correspondent of no mean order. For a time she ran a school page for the *Mail* and backed John Purroy Mitchel in his fight for better schools. She ran a syndicated daily editorial column called "As a Woman Sees It." She got first-class assignments from the *Mail* and was paid as much as any man on the staff.

She refused to go on the Peace Ship, but she traveled on the Hughes train, filed a thousand-word story every night, wrote her daily editorial and made speeches, too. She was in the *Mail* office when Dr. Rumely was arrested on a charge of buying the paper with German money. She resigned after that and free-lanced. She did a series of articles on the Dawes committee for the *Herald Tribune* and worked on the Dawes plan.

One day a motorcycle ran her down in New York and she had a nervous breakdown, which kept her out of the writing game for many months. She went to Czecho-Slovakia to convalesce and again began to pound her typewriter. She was in Italy during the early days of Mussolini's rise, and she wrote illuminatingly about Fascist doings, but did not sign her work, for her son was in the consular service. She told how Mussolini dosed the opposition with castor oil so that he could march through the gates of the Caesars unimpeded. In 1925 she was in Bulgaria during the Communist outbreaks. She got to Sofia just after the Cathedral had been mined and blown up. Afterwards she wrote a number of articles on Bulgaria and Rumania for the *Herald Tribune* and other papers. She was handsomely treated in both countries.

Since 1925 Mrs. Dorr has done little newspaper work, but she still writes and lectures. In 1928 her biography of Susan B. Anthony was published. In the following year she wrote *Drink: Coercion or Control?* Her autobiography, *A Woman of Fifty*, is a fascinating account of the life of a woman reporter who overcame the obstacles of the nineties and rode high on Park Row during the war period. She is a woman of fiery courage and strong convictions. Now and again among newspaper women a crusader arises. Rheta Childe Dorr is one of these. She went after news with intense purpose and wrote with power and finish. She was never a negligible figure in a newspaper office. She loved her profession but was not insensitive to its drawbacks.

The most realistic critic of women's status in journalism, however, is Catherine Brody, whose experience is an antidote to the glamour stories that invest the girl reporter. She found prejudice and niggling injustice rather than adventure on Park Row—another side of the picture, and true in many cases. After watching the women in the city rooms of several New York papers, Miss Brody came to the conclusion that they were the victims of every kind of discrimination. Certainly no one made things easy for her, and she had to fight for recognition. Yet she was an able and conscientious reporter.

Miss Brody took a course in journalism at New York University at night, chiefly because one of the classes met in the city room of the *Globe*, and she thought that this would give her an opportunity to see what a city room was like. She had another job at the time, but she conceived the idea of writing a series of stories signed by different types of girls, telling how they felt about their work, their prospects and their daily round. She did realistic portraits of a dressmaker, a stenographer, a manicurist and others.

George T. Hughes, city editor of the *Globe*, read the first, liked it and offered her a post. She was on the paper for two years—first as a special feature writer, then on general assignments. She got stiff jobs to do, for she had shown her capacity to get at facts. She worked on the copy desk but felt all the time that she was interfering with her colleagues' freedom and that they resented her.

She left the *Globe* to go abroad, having first made an arrangement to send back two features a week. She steered clear of straight news but got sharp slants on many of the social problems of the day. The proceeds from her work supported her in France for six months. Then she came back to find that all the city editors of all the New York papers—including her own—had filled their quotas of girl reporters, which she estimated was one-half of one per cent of the male staff. Eventually she got on the *World.*

It was then that Miss Brody thought up for herself the assignment which brought her a reputation as a newspaper woman of enterprise and courage. She did a cross-country tour, working in factories, doing odd jobs under all sorts of difficult conditions, and writing the results in a series called "What Happens When a Girl Goes Job-Hunting." It was widely syndicated and provoked much discussion. Miss Brody worked for a week each in twenty cities and industrial towns. It took her six months to complete her trip. She traveled with a portable typewriter and an overnight bag and umbrella. She landed in a town on Monday morning, checked her things and rustled up a job that suited her requirements. She had to vary the industries as much as she could. She usually chose work associated with the city—an automobile factory in Detroit, a packing factory in Chicago. She arranged her living conditions to suit her pay, which ranged from $8 to $13 a week. She kept up her notes every night and at the end of a week took a day off to pound out a five-thousand-word story. Then she caught a train for the next town.

When she got back she found that a *World* staff man who had been doing a traveling series under much more comfortable and remunerative conditions—his expenses paid by the office—was back on the staff again, whereas there seemed to be no place for her. So she decided to try free-lancing. She wrote several excellent books—one of them, *Nobody Starves*, getting critical recognition. But to Miss Brody the glamour stories of Park Row are so much ectoplasm. She remembers the long hours she worked, the poor pay she got, the editorial distaste for a woman on the staff, the general badgering about that sums up her impressions of newspaper life.

Another crusader who used the news columns of her paper for social causes was Sophie Irene Loeb, who pushed through various legislative reforms in New York State. She was on the staff of the *Evening World* from 1910 until her death in 1929. Few newspaper women have been able to effect so much in the way of concrete legislation. She was the social worker first, the newspaper woman second; but she managed to combine both phases of her career to the benefit of her paper. The *Evening World* backed her in her campaigns, played up her stories, many of which had the propagandist note, and helped her materially to put her reforms across. It was an arrangement of mutual benefit.

Miss Loeb was born in Russia in 1876 and was brought to the United States when she was six years old. She embarked on child welfare in 1910, when she made a study of the plight of widows in the congested parts of the city. She got her facts at first hand. She learned from the workers' widows how she could best aid them. Her dominating idea was to keep children out of orphanages. At her insistence the New York State Commission for the Relief of Widowed Mothers was appointed in 1913.

Miss Loeb went to Europe, studied parallel conditions there, and laid her report before the legislature in 1914. She became well known in the lobbies of Albany and before long the pension system for widows became legislative fact. For years Miss Loeb served as president of the State Board of Child Welfare. During her tenure the annual appropriation to aid widows was increased from $100,000 to $5,000,000. She fought to have the word illegitimate expunged from the legal terminology of the state; she sponsored penny lunches in the public schools, housing relief, public play streets for children, maternity service for mothers, sanitary and fireproof buildings and the bonding of taxicab drivers.

She was an authority on traffic and was asked to mediate in the walk-out of taxi chauffeurs in 1917. She not only acted as mediator but settled the strike in record time. She helped to frame the taxicab rates of Manhattan. Miss Loeb never received pay for any of her public work, and she always declined to run for office. Her history as a journalist is the record of a humanitarian and reformer, for her stories from day to day were almost invariably tinged with propaganda. Although other newspaper women have gone in for public service, they have done it in a secondary way or to sponsor campaigns for their papers, but Miss Loeb's energies were devoted first and foremost to the cause of reform, and for this she was well known both here and abroad. Her newspaper work was merely the expression of her strong social interests.

Chapter XI

WAR AND SUFFRAGE

WHEN THE SOUTH AMBOY EXPLOSION OCCURRED ON October 4, 1918, Eleanor Booth Simmons was assigned by the
New York *Sun* to cover the relief and refugee angle of
the disaster. She belonged to the Frank Ward O'Malley era and her
own work shone, even in this competitive setting.

The explosion, followed by fire, had laid waste the largest shell-
loading plant in the world. The death list was 64 and 150 more were
badly injured. All that night and most of the following day the
fire raged and firemen fought to keep it from reaching 8,000,000
pounds of TNT stored in the vicinity.

When Miss Simmons got to South Amboy she found Mr.
O'Malley and Russell Owen, of South Pole fame, in charge of the
story. All of the men on the spot were wondering how they were
to get permission from the military police to go into South Amboy
and Morgan, the banned district where the fire still raged.

Miss Simmons knew that if the men were having trouble there
was little hope for her, so she hung about Red Cross headquarters,
picking up human interest copy. By chance she heard one of the
gray-uniformed girls of the Motor Corps tell another that she was
going to try to get into South Amboy. Miss Simmons begged for a
lift. She was thrust into the back seat of the car, with the warning
that she would have to look out for herself if the soldiers on the
bridge stopped them. The area was under heavy military guard.
Their car was stopped repeatedly, but the driver was good-looking,
she jollied the guards effectively, and roared right through. Miss
Simmons shrank low in the back seat and was not noticed.

In a few minutes they were in the wrecked district, surrounded
by black ruin. The bewildered survivors wandered about, still dazed
from what had happened. Miss Simmons worked quickly, going
from one to another and getting their experiences. She rode back
to South Amboy with the last load of refugees. The men's faces
were studies when she appeared. They had not yet succeeded in
crashing through.

"How in the world did you get over there?" they demanded.

"I asked a woman to take me," said Miss Simmons.

She was told to get to the office as fast as she could and write her story. She had some sprinting to do before she could find a conveyance. The street cars were not running, the trains were late, but at last she found a taxi that took her to Jersey City for $15. She wrote seven columns of admirable eye-witness copy, as fine a clean-up as any newspaper woman ever put across on a major catastrophe.

Miss Simmons started work on the *Sun* in 1915, moving over from the *Tribune*, where she had done women's assignments. Kenneth Lord gave her news stories to do almost at once. He even let her cover a fire, which was enterprising for that period. Then one day she asked him to assign her to the Willard-Moran prize fight in Madison Square Garden. This was long before newspaper women dreamed of invading the press rows around the prize ring. Mr. Lord was astonished by the strange request. He took half an hour to think it over; then he called Miss Simmons and said, "The idea of a prize fight story from a woman's angle appeals to me; better do it." She turned in a story that justified his decision.

Miss Simmons had many good assignments during the war days. This was a period when newspaper women got an excellent play. The staffs were short of men. There were a number of women reporters about. They got their innings. War and suffrage landed them effectively on the front page. Then came the parades. Flags on Fifth Avenue. Tramping feet. Gleaming bayonets. Repeatedly she wrote of the marching men on their way to France. When President Wilson headed the Red Cross parade a policeman lifted her right out of the ranks by the back of her neck, spurning her police card. Sarah Addington, of the *Tribune*, another excellent woman reporter who has since had success in the short story field, was yanked out with the other hand.

In January, 1924, Miss Simmons went out one afternoon to interview Rebecca West by appointment. Miss West was not in an amiable mood. She yawned. She was bored. "I have had a wild, wild day," she told Miss Simmons and yawned again. New York wore her out. It kept her from sleep. She turned her back on the reporter and read letters. "Did I tell you to come this evening at six, really?" she asked at last.

"You did," said Miss Simmons firmly. "But of course if you want to dine ——"

"I shall not dine for hours yet," said Miss West mournfully.

Miss Simmons asked her for her views on newspaper work. Miss West gave them readily:

It is very different in England. It is nearly all routine work there. In America you seem to make an adventure of it. You are so restless. But I cannot understand this idea of newspaper work being a good preparation for fiction writing. Turning out such endless columns must exhaust the mind. Now I—I blazed a trail for myself very early. I would write only what I wanted to write and I would sign everything. I do very little newspaper work except now and then an important trial for the human interest of it.

Then Miss West decided to take a bath. The interview went on by reluctant stages, above the splashing of the water, then to the accompaniment of swishing silk. Miss Simmons got more and more annoyed. All efforts to penetrate the author's indifference were unsuccessful. At last Miss West smoothed her hair demurely and said, "By the way, what time is it? And do you mind letting yourself out?"

Miss Simmons let herself out gladly and went back to her office. She wrote a piece of devastating satire. Next day Heywood Broun said in his column that if he had $1,000,000 to give away for the best story of the year, it would go to Miss Simmons for her interview with Miss West. Alexander Woollcott called it an "artful, convincing and delicately murderous" piece of work, but he thought she had not been fair to Miss West, whom he greatly admires. The story was widely quoted. It was a scathing piece of writing. Miss West was annoyed. In an article in *Harpers Magazine* she said that the reporter had come to her with hatred in her heart—an odd mistake, Miss Simmons thought, for another journalist to make.

No stories were signed during Miss Simmons' days on the *Sun*, although the columns of the paper sparkled constantly with witty and sophisticated writing. Her own stories were clever, humorous, often very sharp. She could take a single fact and spin it into an entertaining column. It was not the kind of reporting that flourishes to-day, but it was part of the old *Sun* tradition.

Miss Simmons broke into newspaper work quite by accident. She began writing poems, stories and essays as a girl in Wisconsin. She sent them out and some were accepted. When her parents died she moved to New York, thinking that her mission in life was nursing. She entered a hospital to train but defied the head nurse, and that ended her career as a probationer.

While she was still in the hospital she met one of the first of the Henry Street visiting nurses. In those days Lillian D. Wald frowned on publicity, but this nurse took Miss Simmons with her secretly on her rounds. Miss Simmons wrote a story on what she saw and sent it to the *Tribune*. This got her a job. She did Sunday specials for a time and then was transferred to the woman's department, which was secluded on an upper floor. Madeline Pierce, the editor, sent all the copy downstairs to the city room by boy so that no one would suffer from the obnoxious sight of a female in the city room. George Burdick, the city editor, was dubious of the strange beings who inhabited the upper regions.

But gradually the scope of the woman reporter's work widened. The suffrage movement began to get interesting about 1911. The feminists captured plenty of front-page space. The high point was the suffrage parade to Washington on March 3, 1913, when mobs of hoodlums defied the police and broke up the orderly line of 9,000 marchers, knocking down women, spitting in their faces, yelling epithets at them. Miss Simmons saw old Mrs. Henry Villard picking herself up from the mud, Inez Milholland riding straight at the rioters on her white horse, and the cavalry arriving on the dead run from Fort Myer. She was knocked down herself, but she got to Continental Hall in time to hear Dr. Anna Howard Shaw's denunciation of the Washington police.

Miss Simmons has retired from newspaper work. She lives in Demarest, New Jersey, and does publicity. Her hobby is cats. Her book *Cats* is the last word on the subject. She reads the papers with the detached interest of one who has shared in many great stories and is now content to watch the parade go by. Few women have written more brilliantly for the New York papers; none more wittily.

Soon after Miss Simmons got established on the *Tribune*, a shy girl with candid blue eyes and a New England conscience walked into the office and got a job. She was fresh from Barnard and a year's teaching in Methuen High School. This was Emma Bugbee, who for a quarter of a century has been writing for the one paper. She has seen reporters come and go, be spectacular, write stirring stories and fade out of the picture. Meanwhile, she has gone along at a level pace, recording every advance made by women in public life.

Miss Bugbee does political writing in the straight news style that suits her paper. She is a specialist in this field, although she can cover any type of assignment from a flower show to a murder. She was on the front page during the war with her suffrage stories. She is on the front page to-day with the doings of Mrs. Roosevelt.

She is the only women reporter on the *Herald Tribune*, a paper where the entire outlook on women's activities is broad. This means that she is constantly in demand for assignments involving the progress of women in public life, which suits her perfectly, for she is a feminist by conviction. She has nursed the suffrage cause from its infancy. She has been on hand for every innovation—the first woman judge, the first woman governor, the first woman registrar. When they fail or turn corrupt she is incredulous. When they do a good job she is quietly triumphant.

In the busiest years of the suffrage campaign Miss Bugbee and Miss Simmons did little else. There were several different headquarters to be covered every day. There were no press agents, no hand-outs. They had to go personally to see Dr. Shaw, Mrs. Carrie Chapman Catt or Mrs. Belmont. They had to dig out letters from their mail that might make news. Things were particularly lively during the days of the Bull Moose campaign. New women's political organizations were forming overnight. The reporters were run off their feet. One summer day when Miss Simmons and Miss Bugbee were away on vacation, Evangeline Cole (now Mrs. Martin H. Wehncke) wrote virtually a complete page of the paper.

The women were allowed to work up a story, but when it became front-page stuff they were snatched off it and a man was put on the job. One striking example was Mrs. Emmeline Pankhurst's detention at Ellis Island, when she came to America in the heat of the suffrage campaign. A man was assigned to the story. It was apt to be the same with the suffrage parades.

However, on the eve of the last big parade, Miss Cole was deputized to ask Ogden Reid if the women could handle the entire story themselves. Mr. Reid, who later became one of the most liberal editors to his women reporters, hesitated at first but said finally that if Milton Snyder, the night managing editor, consented, it would be all right with him. The battle was won, because Mr. Snyder liked the work of the women reporters. Mr. Burdick surrendered and helped to map out the day's schedule. Miss Simmons wrote the lead, a double column story on the front page. Miss Bugbee did the straight news story. Ethel Peyser, who specialized in domestic science news for the *Tribune*, helped her. Miss Cole and Christine Valleau, the department secretary, took the side stories. They filled nine columns between them. Not a word of their copy was changed. This was a great triumph for the suffrage reporters.

Thereafter they marched side by side with the militants and shared in the brickbats and cheers. In the winter of 1914 General Rosalie Jones announced that she would hike to Albany, carrying a petition to Governor Martin H. Glynn, urging suffrage measures before the New York State Legislature. It began to look like a story. The managing editor said to Miss Bugbee:

"I think we ought to be covered on this. Could you get one of the women to keep in touch with us every night and tell us what happens?"

"I supposed I should go along with them," said Miss Bugbee.

But editors in those days felt that women reporters should not get their feet wet, if it could be avoided. Some of them still do.

"Oh, we wouldn't want you to do a thing like that," he said, a little shocked. "It would be so cold."

"But I want to," Miss Bugbee insisted hardily.

"Well, it would be fine if you feel that way about it."

So she was allowed to march, and the editor's worst expectations were fulfilled. She rode in a police patrol to Yonkers. She got cold and wet. She invaded her first saloon and startled the bartender by demanding coffee. The trek was 150 miles. She had good companionship along the way—Dorothy Dix, Ada Patterson, Viola Rodgers, the silver-haired beauty from the *American*; Zoë Beckley, Sophie Treadwell, Martha Coman, Ethel Lloyd Patterson (now Mrs. Liston L. Lewis), Virginia Hudson and several others.

They were en route on Christmas day. The local women arranged meetings along the way. There were many human interest stories about this motley army, tramping through the snow in the burdensome costumes of the period. They arrived in Albany led by a police escort and fife and drum corps. General Jones carried a lighted lantern. The camp followers and "war correspondents" had to struggle with the spectators on the sidewalk to keep them from breaking through the line to shake hands with the little general.

Governor Glynn received them cordially.

"Are you Diogenes?" he asked the leader as he noticed her lighted lantern.

"I'm looking for an honest statesman," said the General, extending her hand.

"I feel honored that you called," Governor Glynn assured her.

The purpose of the march was to make people talk and think about suffrage. Miss Bugbee's stories made the front page. They were done in a jocular vein. No one took suffrage seriously at this stage, except the suffragists themselves. However, the trip to Albany incited them to further efforts. They decided to storm Washington. This time they wore pilgrim capes and brown hoods for identification. The same group of newspaper girls accompanied them. Miss Bugbee took them as far as Philadelphia. Miss Simmons marched them into Washington. The *Tribune* was thoroughly covered all along the route of march.

On another occasion Miss Bugbee found herself in the thick of a suffrage brawl when Alice Paul, of the Woman's Party, tried to crash the Metropolitan Opera House with her followers and banners, while Woodrow Wilson was speaking there. They wanted to badger him on the suffrage question. But the police got rough with them instead. One minute they were walking on the sidewalk; the next the police had pounced on them and the street was filled with tumult.

All these stories helped the status of the women reporters in New York. In 1915 the *Tribune* girls were brought downstairs to the city room. Women's news had now officially become part of the general schedule. Bessie Breuer was the last person to shepherd the flock as a separate body. One of her understudies was Doris E. Fleischman, who now functions as a public relations counsel with her husband, Edward L. Bernays. She was graduated from Barnard in 1913, worked for the *Tribune* for two years, and later became associated with Mr. Bernays.

Soon after this women ceased to be a novelty in the city room of the *Tribune*. For a time they swarmed within call of the city desk. Ernestine Evans, Marie Montalvo, Hannah Mitchell, Blanche Brace, Solita Solano, Sarah Addington, Hilda Jackson, Natalie Mc-Closkey (now Mrs. Leon Gordon), Rebecca Drucker, Selma Robinson, all came and went, finding their ultimate fortunes in other fields.

Miss Bugbee celebrated with the suffrage workers when the vote was won in 1917, and continued to cover their activities. Women candidates became her job on election night as well as candidates' wives. She has watched them in triumph and defeat, and has hurried back to the city room, strung with wires, desks jammed together, the air vibrant with excitement, to write fast copy to catch an edition.

She went to her first political convention in 1924 and has covered them all since then. At Houston Mrs. Al Smith was her particular care. When the nomination was made someone gave the candidate's wife a baby donkey, which she held in her lap like a baby. She did not want to give an interview. She never has cared for publicity, leaving all that to Al. Her box was high above the floor. Two policemen lifted Miss Bugbee until she was on a level with Mrs. Smith and could talk to her.

"This is the proudest day of my life," said Mrs. Smith, with tears in her eyes.

Miss Bugbee has followed Mrs. Roosevelt's activities closely. The high point of her newspaper career was her flight with her to Puerto Rico. She has done more than 10,000 miles with her altogether. The Puerto Rican trip alone was more than 6,000; the return from the West in the summer of 1934 was 3,000, and she has been back and forth to Washington by airplane and train with Mrs. Roosevelt (a distance of 239 miles) more than half a dozen times.

One of Miss Bugbee's early assignments was a trip in an armored plane, a stunt suggested by Mr. MacAlarney. Her newspaper experience has been extraordinarily varied and has covered more than two decades of changing social customs. She followed Lady Astor and Madame Curie on their trips to America. She spent an eerie night at Roosevelt Field with Mrs. Bert Acosta and the other flyers' wives, waiting for Commander Richard E. Byrd to take off on his trans-Atlantic flight.

Miss Bugbee has certain annual stories which she has not missed in more years than most women reporters have held jobs. She covers all the women's conventions of any importance, and sometimes crosses the continent on an assignment of this sort. All the club women know her. In spring her desk is buried under flowers when the annual flower show comes along. She does the cat show and she is one of the first reporters hunted up by the amiable Dexter Fellows when he comes to town with the circus.

Miss Bugbee's position on the *Tribune* is unique. She has outlasted many city editors and has watched scores of reporters, men and women, come and go. She writes editorials on women in the news and does graceful nature pieces from time to time, in addition to her work for the city desk. The political writers like to talk things over with her, for she is sagacious and shrewd, and she has seen a great deal of the devious ways of politicians. She is a calm and restrained reporter, but when she gets the chance she can write gay and dashing stuff, for she has a keen sense of humor, a light touch. Miss Bugbee is never run off her feet, no matter how hectic things are around her. It is characteristic of her to stroll in on a story, neither breathless nor expectant. She makes a neat speech, writes an occasional outside article and has many friends both in and outside the newspaper world.

She has been president several times of the New York Newspaper Women's Club, which was founded by Martha Coman in the early twenties to take the place of the gatherings the women reporters had when they covered suffrage headquarters. They used to have tea together almost every day to talk over the news they had picked up. Because they felt lost without this regular daily meeting it occurred to Miss Coman that it might be a good idea to form a club. She invited eight of them to tea one Sunday afternoon to talk it over. This was the beginning of the club, which is now a flourishing organization. It is clear of debt, has club rooms in the Savoy-Plaza, and counts among its members the leading newspaper women of the city. Each year its members give a smart ball. They try to find employment for newspaper women out of work, have many social gatherings and have helped to raise the status of the newspaper woman in New York.

It was Miss Coman who boldly tackled Frank A. Munsey on the subject of men smoking in the city room soon after he bought the *Herald*. Her letter to the ogre of Park Row caused laughter among her colleagues. He thought that a city room should be large, light and clean. He hated to see paper strewn on the floor and, above all, he could not bear to have anyone smoke. This was a' hardship to the men who had recently been puffing their pipes and cigarettes in the more liberal atmosphere of the *Herald*. The lack of tobacco interfered with their thinking processes. It made them all despondent.

As they were aware that Miss Coman knew Mr. Munsey personally, they asked her to take their case to headquarters. They intimated—somewhat facetiously—that it was because of her presence in the city room that they were not permitted to smoke. She happened to be the only woman on the staff.

Miss Coman, always a good sport, wrote to Mr. Munsey. She took the precaution first of asking all the women secretaries if they objected to smoking. She showed her letter to some of the editors. She pointed out in it that she had been brought up in an atmosphere of *Herald* smoke. Mr. Munsey took the matter quite seriously. He told her solemnly that he would rather give up his magazines and papers than let the men smoke. After that there were no two ways about it. They had to sneak their smokes in corridors and vacant offices.

Miss Coman entered newspaper work by chance. She lived on the Pacific coast, went to college in California, and came East only because her sister had preceded her and she was suddenly fired with the ambition to follow her and get a job. She was not trained for anything specific. But through her sister, who was on the Munsey staff, she got a clerical post, and with her aid started selling photographs to newspapers and magazines.

One day, when she went in to show the Sunday editor of the *Herald* some photographs, he bought a batch of them, then offered her a job at a guarantee of $25 a week, having just fired most of his staff. She stayed with the paper until it was bought by Mr. Munsey. The suffrage movement was in full swing, so that she found her opportunity almost at once. Mrs. O. H. P. Belmont and Mrs. Clarence Mackay opened up decorative headquarters and the women reporters stopped in daily for news. Miss Coman fared well from the start. She was calm, poised, workmanlike, could do any job in a competent way, had dignity, good looks, and in every respect was the ideal choice for a newspaper office not friendly to women. She seemed the sober blend of all the desirable qualities. She understood women's interests, was mildly sympathetic to the suffrage cause, but had a twinkle in her forthright eye that suggested she was not being taken in by their silly antics. She never felt the slightest discrimination, and for years she covered straight news stories just like the men with whom she worked.

The nearest she ever came to suffering injustice from an editor was on the old *Herald*. She had sent out three suffrage stories by the copy boy, one of which Mrs. Belmont was particularly anxious to have printed. For some reason the others appeared but not the pet story. Mrs. Belmont raised a terrific row and threatened to cable to Mr. Bennett and have Miss Coman discharged. The city editor promptly sent a cablegram to Mr. Bennett saying, "The woman reporter says she wrote the story and gave it to a copy boy." He was evading responsibility because the story evidently had been spiked. Mrs. Mackay heard about the incident, was most concerned, and said she would get in touch with Mr. Bennett at once, protesting any action against Miss Coman. The row raged for a few days. Then it blew over. Mr. Bennett was somewhere in the Mediterranean on his yacht and in those days wireless had not been perfected, so that news could not reach him as quickly as now.

The only time Miss Coman ever encountered Mr. Bennett personally was in the West Indies, where he had sent her to stay for the winter. He had an idea that this region should be developed into an American Riviera. She was assigned to do social affairs, cover the islands and boost the resorts. Mr. Bennett arrived one day on his yacht and they had a chat together. She had heard many tales of her stormy employer but she found him peaceable enough face to face.

Miss Coman was one of the reporters on the famous Hughes train that toured the country in an effort to back up Charles Evans Hughes for President, because he had declared himself in favor of the national suffrage amendment. Other newspaper women on the expedition were Ernestine Evans, Miriam Teichner, Fanny Butcher, Mary Ross, and Rheta Childe Dorr, who did a double job, writing the news of the trip for her paper and making speeches for Mr. Hughes at every stop.

There were parades, luncheons, teas, dinners and mass meetings. The train got many fancy appellations such as "The Diamond Special" and "Golden Limited." It had some of the absurd elements of the Ford Peace Ship about it. The country's most active suffrage workers were on board. Miss Coman's orders from her city editor were to spoof the expedition. She did this without any difficulty at the start. But when she began to send more serious stories she soon got a telegram from the *Herald* reminding her of her orders. From then on one nonsensical episode followed another, so that it was not at all difficult to maintain the jesting touch.

The women who ran the train were bitterly disappointed that the important papers should have seen fit to send women reporters instead of men. The *Times* was the only exception. Feminists though they were, they felt they were not being taken seriously enough because the star political reporters were not on board. Yet some of the most intelligent and experienced newspaper· women of New York were on the train.

On the morning after they left, the reporters made their way back to the observation car to get the day's program. They were rudely ushered out and told not to return. The suffrage leaders refused to give them an itinerary or information of any sort, so they had to get their news by the grapevine route. This was so much the worse for the Hughesettes, as they were called. The stories that went sizzling back to New York made fun of the whole expedition. Ridicule met them at every point. The legend of sables and diamonds spread like wildfire and made no hit with the public.

In one manufacturing city where they stayed over so that they could speak at noon outside one of the big factories, the men coming out for lunch jeered at them, calling them millionaires and idlers. One of the organizers answered these gibes. She made a stump speech in which she said that the women on the train were not a wealthy group. In fact, she added, not one of them had more than $100,000. The hoots of the workers drowned all further efforts to speak. In another place they lunched at the smartest club in town with all their diamonds showing. In the afternoon they made a slum expedition and turned their rings around. "Diamonds In, Diamonds Out" was the headline on a story written by one of the facetious scribes on the train about this false gesture.

The women campaigners did not show the deft political touch. Before they reached San Francisco the reporters had word that funds were giving out. One of the organizers had to dash back to New York for cash. It was about this time that a telegram reached Miss Coman's paper asking that she be recalled, as the passengers thought she was treating them with too much levity. Next day the *Herald*, delighted that her satire had been so successful, sent Miss Coman a copy of the message without comment.

Their magnificence dwindled as the expedition came to a close. They returned to New York with much less elegance than they had started out. They had dusted the country with noise, fuss and feathers but had done Mr. Hughes little good.

Miss Coman left the *Herald* a year before it was bought by the *Tribune*. Since then she has edited a weekly newspaper, done publicity for Harpers, directed Smith College publicity for four years and is now with the Phoenix News Publicity Bureau.

In nearly every small town in the country, and at many cross-roads, are women who have seen Marjorie Shuler, of the *Christian Science Monitor*, or heard her speak. She is one of the ablest members of the profession, and has covered more ground in the last decade than almost any of her colleagues. In 1934 she flew 22,000 miles in South America, going completely around the continent and into the interior of the Brazilian jungle.

Like Dorothy Thompson, Miss Shuler was identified with the suffrage movement, did publicity for it, campaigned for women's rights, covered all conventions of importance, no matter where they were held, and frequently helped to draft resolutions as well as to report the event for her paper.

Her life has all the glamour of the foreign correspondent's. She has a roving commission and goes wherever constructive news is in the making. She has been sent to Europe half a dozen times to report international conventions. They have not all been women's gatherings, but have embraced law, education, science and banking. She was in Budapest when orders came for her to interview Alexandra Kollontai, the newly appointed Soviet Minister. She hurried across Europe but through mistaken information given her by an English official she went to Sweden instead of Norway. She reached Stockholm at noon one Saturday. In short order she had to get a railroad ticket, a Norwegian visa and change her passage back to England, meanwhile wondering if she were not being misinformed again. It was difficult to get accurate information because of language complications.

No sleepers were available on the train to Norway. She sat up all night and had to go without breakfast in the morning. She arrived in Oslo exhausted and hungry but there her bad luck stopped. She found Kollontai, talked to her for two hours, and brought back the first interview with her for publication in America.

When she was abroad in 1926 she had an interview with the King of Spain, obtained through the intervention of a non-English speaking aide, after it had been denied through the usual diplomatic channels. Miss Shuler began by telling the King an amusing story and he talked to her frankly after that.

On the day that Queen Marie landed in America she had a ship ladder adventure that nearly landed her in the ocean off Quarantine. It was a rough day. The long wooden ladder was covered with sleet. She climbed up it from the tug on her hands and knees, but it was worse getting back. Most of the other newspaper women stayed on the ship and sailed into port with the Queen. But Miss Shuler had a deadline to catch. She insisted on leaving the ship, although she was advised that it would be dangerous.

Three times after she had started she was pulled back because the swell of the sea had carried the tug beyond reach of the ladder. On her last try she heard a yell and looked down to see that the ladder had swung out so far that the men holding it had to link their feet around the rail of the tug and slant their bodies outward over the sea. She finally got to safety. Boarding an incoming liner is not always such a perilous business.

When she was on her way to Mexico for a vacation Miss Shuler stopped off in Havana and instinctively got on the trail of a good story. She decided that there must be some human interest angles on the Cuban officers who were imprisoned in the National Hotel within sight of their own homes, while they were waiting to be shot. She hired a badly frightened taxi driver to take her close to the hotel and she hung over the side of the car, smiling at the soldiers. They were bored after so many days on guard, so they talked. They rested their rifles on the running board and told her what they meant to do—how they would kill some of the officers and let others go free. Meanwhile the officers watched them as they talked, peering through the doors and windows of their sumptuous jail.

Miss Shuler borrowed the purser's typewriter on her ship, batted out a good human interest story, and sent it by airmail from Yucatan. It arrived in the nick of time and ran under a four-column head on the front page of the *Monitor* the day the hotel was fired on.

In addition to her extensive newspaper and club work Miss Shuler has written four books and contributed to the national magazines. She won a *Bookman* award for the best newspaper story taken from any paper in the world. It was a short piece about Mrs. Lindbergh, ripped out paragraph by paragraph from her machine, right on the deadline—which is the way that some of the best news stories have been written.

Miss Shuler started newspaper work at the age of sixteen, when she was fresh from high school. She worked on the Buffalo *Courier* for two months for nothing, then joined the *Express* staff at $8 a week. On the *Monitor* she has achieved a national reputation as one of the leading newspaper women in the country.

PART TWO

Chapter XII

IN COMMAND

AT FIVE O'CLOCK IN THE AFTERNOON, JUST WHEN THE LIFE IN THE city room of the New York *Herald Tribune* is beginning to quicken, a small figure, exquisitely groomed, may often be seen walking past the reporters' desks on her way to the office of the managing editor. This is Mrs. Ogden Reid, a quiet but potent force in New York journalism.

Her glance travels slowly from face to face in the city room. It is a wise, perceiving look of singular concentration. She knows the history of all the writers and desk men within sight. She has an accurate idea of their capacity and usefulness to the paper.

Mrs. Reid's position in journalism is unique. Technically, she is vice-president and advertising director of the paper, but she has more power than these positions ordinarily would convey. For she is the wife of the owner and works on a partnership basis. All important decisions are made by Mr. and Mrs. Reid together. Her influence is subtly wielded. She never issues blanket orders. Brief memoranda signed H.R.R. find their way to the heads of every department of the paper, but they rarely contain anything stronger than a gracefully worded suggestion. However, that is enough. They are instantly accepted as law.

Mrs. Reid interferes little with the editorial department except in major matters of policy. She rarely passes judgment on a story or volunteers an opinion on the way in which it has been played. But where advertising interests are at stake, a big syndicate feature is about to be bought, or a new department is being started, she gives the most careful and tireless interest to nursing along the project.

She did not rest until she got the papers of Colonel E. M. House in the winter of 1926. She and Mr. Reid were first on the trail, stuck to it and offered the highest figure. They bought the newspaper rights for a substantial sum. In the end the feature cost the paper little, for the letters syndicated so well throughout the country that the original outlay was virtually covered. Three years later Mrs. Reid went after the serial rights of Ray Stannard Baker's *Life and Letters of Woodrow Wilson* with equal enterprise. The *Times* and the *World* were in competition. She telephoned to Doubleday, Page for a four-day option, as Mr. Reid was duck shooting at "Flyway," his place in North Carolina. The publishers refused politely to hold things up. The time element was of vital importance, with competitive bidding imperiling their chances of getting the serial rights. She did not want to sign on her own responsibility without consulting Mr. Reid, so she took the first train south, hired a car and bumped over a rough road that the Negro chauffeur thought was impassable. Mr. Reid agreed with her that they should pay top price. She had the publishers on the telephone by seven o'clock that evening and closed for the New York rights at a formidable figure.

The purchase of these two features was part of a general liberalizing plan for the paper. Although the editorial page remains a model of what the well-disciplined Republican might like to read with his coffee, the news columns have shown some revolutionary tendencies within the last few years. Mrs. Reid is an ardent Republican but she has always been interested in La Follette liberalism, a taste carried over from her Wisconsin days. She was born in Appleton, Wisconsin, the youngest of a large family. She was educated at a boarding school in Fond du Lac, and at Barnard, which she entered when she was sixteen. She majored in Greek but soon discovered in herself a deep interest in science. To this day popular science is one of her hobbies.

She was graduated when she was twenty and became social secretary to Mrs. Whitelaw Reid. She held this post for eight years, spending most of her time in London where Whitelaw Reid was Ambassador at the Court of St. James's. In 1911 she was married to Ogden Reid in Racine, Wisconsin. He had then been on the paper for three years, training as a reporter, copy reader and editorial writer, before becoming editor.

For the next seven years Mrs. Reid devoted herself to her home and the suffrage campaign. In 1917 she was appointed treasurer of the New York State Woman's Suffrage party and she helped to raise $500,000 for the cause. When the vote was won she decided to go into newspaper work. In the autumn of 1918 she became an advertising solicitor for the *Tribune*. Three months later she headed the department and in 1922 she became vice-president of the paper.

At first the heads of large firms welcomed Mrs. Ogden Reid on the strength of her name when she called to see them. Doors opened automatically. But those who thought it a mere whim on her part soon had their eyes opened. They saw that she meant business. She talked convincingly. She showed close knowledge of the field. She drew in accounts. Although she had entered the newspaper world in the most unostentatious way, it soon became known along Park Row that Helen Rogers Reid was becoming a power on the paper.

The *Tribune* was not the flourishing organization then that it is to-day. The city room downtown was old and cluttered, a contrast to the shining efficiency of the new plant uptown. The desks were battered, the typewriters were jittery, but the atmosphere was warm and friendly. It was the newspaper man's idea of a city room. But the paper lagged in advertising. Mrs. Reid set out to build up this department. In five years' time the advertising went up from 4,170,-812 to 11,203,082 lines. She lured in errant accounts and put over a particularly smart stroke in getting Gimbel's advertising back, after it had been lost during the *Tribune's* campaign against dubious advertising. In 1918 the circulation of the paper was 95,000. It increased substantially with the purchase of the *Herald*, and went on from that point. Now it is 320,000 on weekdays and 450,000 on Sundays.

Her success was so conspicuous that Mrs. Reid became an important figure in advertising before she had been at it for any length of time. To-day she has the respect of her competitors and the admiration of the advertisers with whom she deals. She goes right after business with a direct and conclusive touch. When she sees an advertisement in another paper that she thinks the *Herald Tribune* ought to have, she gets on the telephone or makes a personal call and argues the matter out with the advertiser. She does not always get the business but she invariably has a hearing.

This is the side of newspaper work that interests her most. She believes that people read advertising as they do news. But she is alive to the other aspects of newspaper work, thinks it the most fascinating profession in the world, and cannot understand why women do not branch out more than they do in the different departments. Discussing their place in journalism in a speech, she said:

> There are still a lot of prejudices against newspaper women and the future is not a rosy one, but newspapers are an all round institution and need the woman's point of view. On the business side there are very great opportunities because eighty per cent of all the advertising is calculated to appeal to women. Even the mechanical side offers some very real chances with its need for proofreaders and linotypers. . . .
>
> One real trouble with women is that they haven't projected their imaginations toward higher positions. Of course they feel a certain satisfaction in helping others but they should acquire more self-confidence and take more pleasure in what they themselves can do.
>
> Ability is still rated as a natural masculine characteristic and is considered the exception among women. A woman should

work harder to establish the idea that a good piece of work is only a normal piece of work. . . .

Mrs. Reid is a genuine and consistent feminist, both in theory and in fact. She believes in the minor manifestations as well as the major ones. No post is too big for a capable woman, in her opinion. She advocates the modern trinity of a job, a husband and children. She asks no special favors from the moment she steps into the office. She prefers the men on the staff not to take off their hats when they ride in elevators with her. She does not like them to get up when she appears. She wants to work with them on an absolutely even basis.

Mrs. Reid does not attend the editorial conferences, but she is in close touch with everything that pertains to the news and when a big story is breaking she haunts the city room. She is interested in stories that record the advance of women in any field. She has an eye for scientific news and anything relating to medicine or nursing. But she is much more likely to suggest an editorial than a story for the news columns. She watches the society page closely. The personal column of the *Herald Tribune* is the hardest to crash in the country. None but a Social Register name ever appears in it.

Mrs. Reid is progressive, yet sticks to the family and political traditions of the paper. She has a sure touch for details as well as a broad grasp of the larger issues. She never asks anyone to do anything that she wouldn't do herself. She works laboriously over matters that interest her, returning to the office and pitching in until all hours of the night. When the *Tribune* bought the *Herald* in 1924 she did much of the detailed work connected with the negotiations. Mr. Munsey set out to buy the *Tribune* but she opposed this from the start. Mrs. Whitelaw Reid, who wielded great power in the paper for many years and was happy to see her daughter-in-law occupying an executive post, was not completely convinced of the wisdom of buying the *Herald* but Mrs. Ogden Reid was never in any doubt about it. She usually favors the bold and daring course, for she is a liberal at heart.

Mrs. Reid's office in the advertising department closely resembles Mr. Reid's on the editorial floor. A picture of Mrs. Whitelaw Reid, whom she greatly loved and admired, hangs above her desk. There are no fancy touches about her surroundings and she is always accessible to her staff. At her right hand is Mrs. Helen Leavitt, a sagacious campaigner of the suffrage days, who is assistant advertising director of the paper and has considerable influence. She is authorized to make decisions after six o'clock if Mrs. Reid has left for the day, so that many of the advertising problems are put up to her when the deadline is near at hand. Mrs. Leavitt understands the business end of the paper and works with great discretion. Mrs. Reid has complete confidence in her judgment and gives her plenty of leeway. Mrs. Leavitt's daughter, Martha, does features for the Sunday paper.

Mr. and Mrs. Reid give women an even chance throughout the organization. No Sunday magazine editor in the country has more power than Mrs. William Brown Meloney, and the talented Irita Van Doren is left in absolute charge of "Books." Elsa Lang functions with skill in the promotion department and there are a number of women advertising solicitors working under Mrs. Reid's own direction. The crossword puzzle department is admirably handled by a woman, Mrs. Dorothy Kiggins.

The paper has real fascination for Mrs. Reid. She carries its problems home with her at night, and she and Mr. Reid reach most of their important decisions away from the office. But she is modest about her accomplishments. She never gives an interview. She rarely talks about herself, always about the paper. In recent years she has made a number of speeches but she avoids publicity whenever possible. She prefers to remain anonymous.

She has some of Mr. Munsey's passion for a clean and tidy newspaper office, although it does not extend to a ban on smoking. When the new plant was opened uptown, the editorial room had all the air of a large business office. Every desk had an ash tray and a wastebasket. These were alarming manifestations at first to the untidy scribes from Park Row, but soon they got used to knocking off ashes in the proper place, instead of letting their cigarettes burn holes in their desks. They also got into the habit of hanging up their coats and hats, leaving the office looking rather prim.

Mrs. Reid is ready to challenge the judgment of the men executives on anything in which she thoroughly believes. She was largely responsible for Walter Lippmann being brought into the organization. She backed F.P.A. when he refused to take the salary cut imposed on him. She doesn't believe in letting the talented slip away.

One of her chief interests in the paper is the domestic science institute, which has grown from women's page beginnings into a housekeeping organization of no mean order. Its tested recipes are models of their kind. Another of her pet interests is the Fresh Air Fund, which sends 16,000 children to the country every summer. She believes that the ideal newspaper reaches the whole family; therefore she has favored the re-introduction of features long dropped from the metropolitan morning paper. Food news, fashions and bedtime stories all appear in the daily issues. She maintains that since women do eighty per cent of the nation's buying, the newspapers should encourage their patronage.

Mrs. Reid is proud of the *Herald Tribune* and all its functionings as a newspaper. She and Mr. Reid frequently bring guests in after the theater or dinner to show them the paper being run off the presses. King Edward VIII, then Prince of Wales, made one of these tours; so did the King and Queen of Siam when they stayed at Ophir Hall. Like her husband, Mrs. Reid understands every step of the mechanical processes, knows most of the linotypers by their first names and never forgets those who have been in the organization for a long time.

In November, 1935, she received the American Woman's Association award for eminent achievement and a month later Mrs. Carrie Chapman Catt included her in her annual list of the nation's ten outstanding women. She has been the recipient of honorary degrees at various universities.

In spite of her preoccupation with the paper, Mrs. Reid manages to live the life of a woman without business responsibilities. She goes in moderately for social interchange but is more interested in people who do things than in those who simply live for the social round. She has two sons, Whitelaw, now about to get his first taste of journalism, and Ogden Rogers Reid, commonly known as "Brownie." Her only daughter, Betty, died in 1925 at the age of nine.

The Reid family have several homes and they take brief holidays but never leave the paper for long. In town they live in the former Doherty house at 15 East Eighty-fourth Street. Part of the year they spend at Ophir Farm, their country home at the gates of Ophir Hall, which was Mrs. Whitelaw Reid's estate. They pass a month every year at their camp in the Adirondacks and a month in Florida in winter, but Mrs. Reid hurries to New York at a moment's notice if anything comes up at the office that requires her attention.

She manages to spend a good deal of time with her children and follows all their interests with the most intense curiosity and delight. She plays tennis, swims, rides, skates and helps to take her canoe over the "seven carries" at their camp in the Adirondacks, just like her sons. She has enormous vitality and likes the same quality in other people. She cannot understand a lack of ambition. She goes to the theater often, and occasionally occupies the family box at the Metropolitan. In recent years she has attended most of the big prize fights and she sits in at the Republican conventions with Mr. Reid, but she is not fond of talk. She is essentially a woman of action. She is quite small, her features are piquant, her eyes have an extraordinarily penetrating quality. They are a clear gray with a flicker of fire in the pupils. She is always beautifully turned out and is not so engrossed in business that she cannot give time to her clothes. But no social engagement is ever allowed to impinge on her work. She follows it like a religion.

Her voice is soft and slow. It has a subtly persuasive quality. She never raises it to make a point. But she speaks gracefully in public. In dealing with people she is thoughtful, perceptive and intensely curious about their motives. She likes to see what makes the wheels go round.

When she and Mrs. Meloney stand together on the platform at the *Herald Tribune's* Forum on Current Problems, they represent plenty of dynamic force between them. They are breath-taking ladies of the press, somewhat akin in quality, which may explain the deep friendship that exists between them. Sometimes they disagree. Both are strong-minded, and passionate in their convictions. But each respects the other.

Mrs. Meloney is one of the more remarkable newspaper women of her generation. She has a wide acquaintance among all sorts of citizens—Presidents, scientists, statesmen, writers and artists. She brought Madame Curie to America and raised the fund for her radium. Owen D. Young is one of her closest friends. She was a favored guest at the White House during the Hoover term. She called on Mussolini during a trip abroad in the summer of 1935 and the interview she had with him made the front page of her paper.

She worships names. She makes forays on Europe and rounds up manuscripts of august authorship. When the United Newspaper Magazine Corporation was formed to launch *This Week*, which first came out in February, 1935, with a string of twenty-one metropolitan papers, Mrs. Meloney was the person selected to edit the magazine. Mary Day Winn, another capable newspaper woman, is her chief assistant.

While Mrs. Meloney was editing the *Delineator* she followed the work of newspaper writers closely, searching for fresh creative talent. She came to the conclusion then that the Sunday papers were on the wrong track in running stories in their magazine sections turned out by staff men to augment their salaries. She saw no reason why Sunday editors should not enlist the services of writers and artists of big reputation.

Mrs. Meloney was challenged to demonstrate her views when she joined the staff of the *Herald Tribune*. She went after acknowledged talent with swiftness and success. She turned out a new kind of newspaper magazine. Executives looked a little dazed when the bills came in, but the magazine flourished and so did Mrs. Meloney. She got G. K. Chesterton, P. G. Wodehouse, Arnold Bennett and other stars of the same magnitude to write for her magazine, until it sometimes suggested an international gathering of the celestials. It was not always their finest stuff but their names carried it along.

Science, politics, economics, dogs, cats, babies, nature, literature, all had their run. Balancing the intellectual fare was a thoroughly sound domestic science section that won the approbation of housewives. Her experience with women's magazines had taught her that food was a subject of primary interest to the reader. She estimated that more than 7,000,000 persons had to be fed in New York every day and that therefore food news was important news. So she concentrated on the institute, extended its functions, appointed a committee of important names to back it up, and made its kitchens and laboratory show-rooms for visitors to the *Herald Tribune* building. She devoted plenty of space to fashions, beauty, home furnishings, gardening, etiquette, cooking and antiques. She went in for specialists of all kinds and had a daily check kept on the trends of the food market.

In 1930 Mrs. Meloney launched her annual forum which mushroomed at once to astonishing proportions. With impartiality she got Herbert Hoover to open one of the annual conferences and Mrs. Franklin D. Roosevelt to speak at another. She went after celebrities of the first rank. Crowds now storm the forum. It is one of the brightest stunts a newspaper has put across. Monica Walsh, who did promotional work on the women's clubs, had much to do with initiating the idea. Mrs. Meloney directs it with good generalship. She is tiny, sprightly, full of humor and dash. Her entire career has been one of battles and triumphs. She can fight to a finish, and she sometimes has to, in order to get her way.

Although she was in the magazine field for years before she joined the staff of the *Herald Tribune*, she was doing newspaper work at the beginning of the century. As Marie Mattingly, she fared forth to find a newspaper job in Washington at the age of seventeen. She got the position but lost it at once. She was assigned to meet a Senator in the Congressional Library for an interview, but she became so absorbed in a collection of rare music that she forgot her appointment, and when she came out of her stupor she couldn't find him.

Scott Bone, of the *Post*, fired her. "If you love music that much," he told her, "you will never make a good reporter. Your heart isn't in it."

But Admiral Dewey unwittingly restored her to favor one November day in 1899. She was in St. Paul's, where she sang in the choir, when she was asked if she wanted to be present at an historical event. The Admiral was being married quietly in the rectory that day. She hurried to the *Post*.

"I've got a good story for you," she said to Mr. Bone.

"Yes?" said Mr. Bone skeptically. "What is it?"

"Tell me first—do I get my job back?"

She covered the wedding and was taken back on the staff. Miss Mattingly also acted as correspondent for the Denver *Post* while she was in Washington and did some work for the New York *World*. She wrote bright sketches of political celebrities and was an animated figure in the Press Gallery when the sight of a woman there was still astonishing. She did feature stories on the national conventions, and got so exhausted with her activities for the three papers that she had to go to Arizona for a rest.

When she returned she tried New York. The *World* assigned her to interview Mark Twain. He was a friend of her father's and he talked to her freely. Her next assignment was a stunt and one which she disliked, so she resigned. Then she landed on the *Herald* and worked for the paper for three months. Her next move was to the *Sun*, which was notoriously averse to women. She submitted all kinds of stories on space. The first one accepted was an interview with an astronomer who had returned with a new chart of the southern skies. Still she did not get on the staff.

Then she offered to substitute for *Sun* reporters on church news. Alexander Dowie, the evangelist from Zion City, was preaching at Madison Square Garden. She wrote stories about him which were accepted, but the *Sun* promptly sent out a star man to follow up the assignment. One night he got drunk and she wrote his piece for him. At last the city editor was persuaded that she not only was a good reporter but a good scout into the bargain and he put her on salary.

This was in 1901. After four years on the *Sun* she married William B. Meloney and was out of newspaper work for nine years, bringing up a son. She returned to the writing world in 1914 as editor of *Woman's Magazine*. She puffed life into it when it seemed to be dying. Even then her gift for lassoing celebrities was apparent. She got Theodore Roosevelt to write for the magazine in his characteristically frank vein. From 1917-1920 she was associate editor of *Everybody's*. In 1920 she became editor of the *Delineator*. In the following year she organized the Better Homes movement which later spread far and wide. Herbert Hoover was the first president when it was launched.

Mrs. Meloney is almost as well known in Europe as in this country. She has been decorated both by the French and Belgian Governments. She backed the Junior Red Cross and did relief work for European children during the war. She has a hundred different interests and gets about where things are stirring. She knows celebrities of all kinds and her Kentucky eggnog parties in her penthouse at the Hotel des Artistes are famous.

Mrs. Meloney often gives an excellent news tip to the city desk, for her reportorial instincts are strong. But her newspaper work is only one part of her dynamic existence. To her colleagues she is known as "Missie." She has a slightly elfin air, as if she were always laughing up her sleeve. The chances are that she is.

Chapter XIII

THE NEW YORK *TIMES*

URING THE BRIEF PERIOD THAT JOHN BIGELOW WAS EDITOR-IN-chief of the New York *Times* he was astonished to see a huge girl in Irish tweeds glowering down at him over his desk one day. She had a letter of introduction in her hand and she wanted a job.

"The only vacant post we have is livestock reporter," he told her.

"I can fill it," said the odd apparition. "Why not?"

"All right, try," said Mr. Bigelow, after she had talked him down with a persuasive Irish tongue.

She was Midy Morgan, one of the most extraordinary figures that ever strode through a newspaper office. She became New York's one woman livestock reporter and was on the *Times* from 1869 until her death in 1892.

Midy was a rare girl, eccentric in appearance, sound at her work. She soon became well known at the cattle yards, horse shows and race courses. She was six feet two, and swung along with tremendous momentum, knocking down anything that got in her way. She wore high-laced boots for ordinary jobs and hip-length rubber waders on stormy days. She walked with a limp which she got when her foot was crushed by a horse. Her hair was bunched in a waterfall and she carried a six-shooter. She went in for rough tweeds and her hats were terrific.

Her handwriting was so bad that her copy was always sent to the same compositors—men who had become accustomed to its peculiarities. But what Midy had to say was worth the trouble. No one excelled her in her own department. All the horse breeders got to know her and valued her advice, which she usually gave them in harsh phrases uttered in a melodious voice. General Ulysses S. Grant sought her opinion on horses. King Victor Emmanuel of Italy commissioned her to buy Irish mares for his stables. She was the friend of Commodore Vanderbilt, Chauncey M. Depew and many of the better known men about town. They respected Midy as a person and an expert. She was stalwart, honest and plodding. Her passion for accuracy exceeded all bounds. Often she rose before dawn to count the cattle cars as they lay in railway sidings at Hoboken and was perturbed for a week if she found herself one figure out.

She adopted the name Midy for newspaper purposes. Her own name was Maria Morgan and she was born in 1828 on an estate near Cork, the daughter of Anthony Morgan, a landed proprietor. She grew up with horses around her and hunted almost as soon as she could read. Before she was fourteen she knew all about farming and breeding. She was as expert at languages as at taking a jump on a hunter.

When her father died in 1865 nearly all of the family property went to the eldest son, and Midy left for Italy with her mother and sister. For the next two years she lived in Rome, fox hunting on the *campágna*, and reading Byron, who was then the rage. She went on to Florence in the spring of 1867 and there met Baron Ricasoli, Prime Minister of Italy, who arranged that she should be presented to the King. "I am rather more than three parts crazed on the subject of horseflesh, and I naturally wished to be presented to King Victor Emmanuel, who is doubtless the most sporting crowned head in Europe," said Midy at the time.

The King was impressed with her knowledge of horses. He showed her his stables and commissioned her to go to Ireland to make purchases for him. She left at once for her native land and did some careful buying. Then she started out with her six mares, which she called her countrywomen, for the return trip to Italy. This became something of a pilgrimage.

> I knew we had thirty-two changes to make, from rail to steamer, from steamer to rail, and so on, diversified by having to cross Mount Cenis on foot, then rail again until we reached the city of Flowers. I thought if these doings are to continue, even if I get clear out of the United Kingdom without being indicted for manslaughter, how in the name of everything that is sporting am I to get these wild beasts through France, where not a mortal being knows a horse's head from his tail, or which side or end of him ought to be uppermost? I then recollected that Hannibal had crossed the Alps, as also in later days had Alfieri; that both had had horses in their train, though the Italian bitterly complained how his English thoroughbreds suffered, and I cheered up.

The mountain trip was trying, however, and as they neared Florence the box cars were partially burned. But Midy turned up with all the mares in good condition and delivered them to the King. He approved of her choice and gave her a double-case hunting watch with his initials encrusted in diamonds, a token of his gratitude.

After she came to America she kept it in a safe deposit vault, but when the King died Midy got it out, had a mourning chain made to match and wore it for a year. Then she put it back in the bank.

She landed in this country on June 30, 1869, with letters of introduction from American friends in Italy to Henry J. Raymond of the *Times*, and Horace Greeley. Mr. Raymond had died shortly before her arrival and she and Mr. Greeley did not hit it off. Midy undoubtedly was a strange spectacle for any editor to take to on sight. Later the *Tribune*, as well as the *Times*, was to run some of her excellent work, but at the moment the door was not open to her.

Midy thought America a hostile country. People stared at her in the streets. It was a change from Italy, where her mission for the King had made her a social pet. However, she wasn't dismayed. She went to work as a chambermaid in the Stevens House in Boston, while she looked about for something that would suit her rather specialized talents. In July Leonard Jerome gave her a letter of introduction to Manton Marble of the *World*, who thought Midy a comic figure, but sent her to Saratoga as special correspondent to cover the races.

Her first story was a thundering blast about the poor hotel accommodations at Saratoga. Having basked in the splendors of France and Italy, she didn't think well of the racing quarters of America. But before the races were over, she had demonstrated that she knew horses. On her return she went to the *Times*, able now to show some of her work. It was then that she stampeded Mr. Bigelow into giving her the unpromising livestock job.

She soon showed that she could cope with it, and in no mean way. She got to know every cattle breeder of prominence in the country and qualified personally as a sound judge of cattle. She was expert on the fine points of a dog and at a pinch would cover a cat show, although the cat was the only quadruped in which she had no faith. Few could match her on horses. Midy sat on fences with the experts and brought her trained eye to bear on the animals parading past. She preferred horse races to market reports, but was as careful of her lists as the statisticians are to-day of their Stock Exchange tables. It was all original research, without any of the ready aids of later years. No one thought of having lists prepared for the use of a reporter. Midy tramped miles over the marshes to get her facts and check on her figures. She got up at unearthly hours and spared herself nothing.

At first the breeders looked with amazement at this huge awkward girl who went about chewing straws, but after watching her work they doffed their hats to her. It was much the same in her office. When she showed up she stamped through the city room like a tornado, wrote her horrible-looking copy and had little to say. She was never communicative with her colleagues. Most of them thought that Midy lived in the cattle yards. They could not imagine her in a home. But she had some thwarted domestic impulses. Soon after coming to America she adopted a German youth. When he decided to marry, Midy, in a great rage, cast him off and never saw him again.

She had a tidy fortune tucked away in the bank but she didn't believe in splash. Although she bet moderately, she was cautious about her finances. Soon after she landed in America Commodore Vanderbilt invested such money as she had in New York Central securities. She opened deposits with various savings banks around New York, bought some property on Staten Island, and, as time went on, rolled up a substantial sum for her old age.

During the last seven years of her life she was having a fine house built for herself on this piece of land. But she would have nothing to do with builders or architects, so the work dragged on year after year and she did not live long enough to occupy it. She had her own idea of what a house should be like, and was sure she could direct things herself. This led to trouble with workmen and a strange hodgepodge of operations. Midy soon saw that some of her plans were impractical, but she had a vision of the perfect house and nothing could shake her in her determination to go on with it in her own way. It was quite as much of a spectacle as Midy herself. People traveled distances to stare at her lopsided citadel. It was three stories high and each floor was a huge room. The ground floor was paneled in California redwood. The second floor was finished in fine woods brought from different parts of the world. The upper floor was done in ash. The walls and ceiling of the extension dining-room were covered entirely with thousands of tinted sea-shells. Her sister, Jane, who had studied art in Florence, did the decoration. The house was fire-proof, the bathroom equipment was much ahead of the time, and every window had iron bars.

It was Midy's plan to retire to this home when she could no longer get up at dawn and scramble through the cattle yards. She had assembled furniture from different parts of Europe to fill the four rooms and create the atmosphere that she fancied for her old age. But she always put off the day of leisure, and it came too late. While all this was going on, she lived in a barren room in the railway station at Robinvale, New Jersey, where she worked as station agent, selling tickets intermittently and employing a woman to substitute for her while she did her newspaper work. Thus she had free rent and passes on the railroad and that meant much to the thrifty Midy.

But the house on Staten Island was never finished and her only home until her death was the dreary station. She left $100,000 and willed some fine jewelry to the Metropolitan Museum, one of the pieces being King Victor's watch, which she had treasured above all her possessions.

Her death was the indirect result of a fall she had on the icy stockyards in Jersey City in the spring of 1891. She went back to work but was never wholly well again. In less than a year she was taken to a hospital with dropsy and had two operations in quick succession. She died on June 1, 1892, and was buried from the Little Church Around the Corner.

During the last eighteen years of her life she had made three trips to Europe. The first time, she traveled on a cattle boat. She was outraged over the treatment the animals received and on her return wrote a series of articles that resulted in improved methods of handling cattle at sea. She campaigned against various stockyard abuses and was always on the lookout for the interests of the animals.

There never has been another newspaper woman quite like Midy Morgan. She is so little remembered in New York newspaper circles that her name falls on the ear with unfamiliarity. Yet in her way she was one of the distinctive newspaper women of the century.

In Midy's day the columns of the *Times* were as open to the space contributions of the woman correspondent as any paper in town. But after her death no disposition was shown to welcome a successor. Mr. Ochs felt about women on the staff as he did about features. They were not part of his conception of the perfect paper. Yet Mary Taft found her way into the city room in the late nineties.

Years later when a young woman, bitten with the desire to write for a paper, approached Mr. Ochs and asked him for a job, he told her at once that the *Times* did not take women on the city staff.

"You have Miss Taft," the suppliant pointed out.

"Oh, yes," Mr. Ochs admitted. "But Miss Taft was practically born here."

The legend that the *Times* would have no women in the city room has always been widespread in journalistic circles. Job seekers knowing the ropes felt it was hopeless to try their luck at the gates of the leading paper in the country. It was the last citadel. Long after the Associated Press had welcomed women, the *Times* still regarded them with suspicion. Yet in actual fact, the paper had three women over a period of years within call of the city desk—Mary Taft, Jane Grant and Rachel K. McDowell. And Mr. Van Anda's night secretary, Ethel Walton Everett, also contributed to the news columns at times. But their work was more or less departmentalized.

They never went out on murders or fires, although on isolated occasions they landed on the front page.

It was not until the summer of 1934 that the barriers were openly let down and Nancy Hale, the gifted short story writer and descendant of Nathan Hale, was welcomed into the city room. By this time Miss Taft and Miss Grant had retired from active newspaper work, and Miss McDowell had a private office, away from the stir of the city room. Miss Hale stayed for a few months only, then went back to writing fiction. She was followed by Kathleen McLaughlin, an experienced newspaper woman from Chicago, who arrived at a propitious moment and got the much-coveted job of being the only woman reporter on the general news staff. But the crowning touch for women, so far as the *Times* is concerned, was reached in the summer of 1936 when Anne O'Hare McCormick was appointed a member of the editorial council—a real landmark for women in journalism.

Miss Taft landed on the paper in the lavender age chiefly by her own enterprise. Her shy manner concealed a hardy spirit. She was one of the members of the Rainy Daisy Club, which boldly launched short skirts for wet days at a time when braided hems trailing in the dirt were the hallmark of that mysterious creature known as a lady. The Rainy Daisy girls thought it was nonsense to pick up the dust. By the time she had allied herself with this brigade and shied from the stones thrown by little boys and the jeers of street loafers, Miss Taft thought nothing of storming the *Times*. She submitted some paragraphs to Mrs. Philip Welch, who ran a discreet column on women's doings in an obscure part of the paper. Mrs. Welch accepted them but assured her that she was a foolish girl to have any serious ambitions about the *Times*, for it was a journal that never would take a woman on the staff.

But Miss Taft, a handsome girl with plenty of spirit, continued to sit about in the waiting room, looking patient and biding her time. She got her first innings when the Professional Women's League was formed. Having a theatrical membership, it was much less averse to publicity than the Sorosis Club, which abhorred being mentioned in the press. Miss Taft joined the livelier organization and proceeded to pepper the *Times* and the *Tribune* with newsy paragraphs which, much to her surprise, they seemed to welcome.

She wrote her items on elevated trains, in the public parks or at home. She had no competition and did quite well. When her work for the two papers began to conflict, she devoted herself exclusively to the *Times*. The day dawned when she could walk right into the city room and be welcomed by the city editor. He beamed on her and actually gave her assignments. He even let her sit at a desk. But his smiles faded when her space began to run up to more than $30 a week. The day came when his assistant took her aside and said that the paper would have to dispense with her expensive services, unless she would join the regular staff at $19 a week.

A staff post on the *Times*? Miss Taft almost swooned with joy. She would have said yes at any price. For the next two decades she did good work for the paper. She followed women's activities, did art criticism and made herself generally useful. But she felt the binding strings of prejudice against the woman reporter. She covered the suffrage activities until they became front-page news. Then a man was assigned to take over—the usual fate of the woman reporter until recent years. The suffrage leaders were so annoyed by this discrimination and the anti-feminist attitude of the *Times* that they threatened to boycott the paper. But in the end they accepted a policy that seemed to be the publisher's business rather than theirs.

Soon after her retirement from the paper Miss Taft married Robert Welch, a colleague who had worked with her for many years on the *Times*. They settled at first on the Riviera, then returned to America. She is now a widow and lives at Marblehead, Massachusetts.

Shortly before the war Jane Grant, fresh from Kansas, landed on the staff with little difficulty. She had no thought of being a reporter. She was studying singing and wanted something to do on the side. Florence Williams, for years Mr. Van Anda's secretary, introduced Miss Grant to her employer. He said that he would give her a post in the society department as a stenographer, but he made the point that she must not expect advancement. He knew that the bright girls who get into the departments of a newspaper are apt to cast longing eyes on the city staff. Some of the foremost newspaper women in the country have started in this way.

Miss Grant made the transfer with astonishing speed. Her knowledge of stenography was meager, but she saw the exciting possibilities of covering news. The society editor sent her out on a few assignments. The first was to cover a dinner of the Salmagundi Club. When she arrived she found that it was a stag costume affair. However, the hosts were cordial to her and sent her back to the office laden down with flowers. She soon persuaded Ralph Graves, who was then city editor, to give her a chance as hotel reporter. This meant interviews, conventions, club meetings, fashion shows and anything that goes on under the spreading roofs of the New York hotel world.

When America entered the war she took a leave of absence to go to France with the Y.M.C.A. to sing for the soldiers. On her return she was taken back on the staff as a general reporter, and the sphere of her work widened. Like Miss Taft, she pioneered on the feminist side. She was one of the founders of the Lucy Stone League.

Miss Grant had an active hand in launching *The New Yorker.* The magazine grew out of endless talk, dating back to the war days when she sat in cafés in Paris with Harold Ross, Alexander Woollcott, F.P.A., Adolph Ochs, 2d, and John T. Winterich, and they all discussed what they would do when the war was over. At that time they were preoccupied with the *Stars and Stripes.*

After her marriage to Harold Ross, Miss Grant and he worked on several ideas, which found their final fusion in *The New Yorker.* Although they are now divorced, she is still a stockholder in the magazine. Few newspaper women have a wider acquaintance among the town's celebrities than Miss Grant. She and her husband shared a house for a time with Mr. Woollcott, where the sparkling wits used to gather. Since retiring from the *Times* because of ill health, she has traveled extensively and done magazine and radio work.

This left Miss McDowell the sole remaining member of the old feminine guard on the paper. It is a legend in New York newspaper circles that a City News man, when assigned to cover a religious story of any kind, always leaves his office with the warning: "If you see Rachel McDowell there, take everything, even the Bishop's hat." There is justice in this, for Miss McDowell cannot be touched in her field. She knows the clergy of every denomination—their ritual, their private and public tastes, what they are likely to do, what they never would do. No churchman would deny that she has a wider acquaintance among the clergy than any other person in New York.

Her black-garbed figure, large and cheerful, is usually in evidence at any religious gathering of consequence. Time and again she has brought in exclusive stories of real importance to her paper. Although religious herself, and the founder of an anti-profanity society in the *Times* office, she never lets her convictions sway her honest news sense. She is wary of propaganda and the blandishments of churchmen too eager to get their oratory into print when it has no news value. She understands to the full that editors—and many of them, the Godless wretches, set ministers high among the liars—print religious stories only when they are news. Sometimes she has ructions with the churchmen, for she is always alert where the interests of her paper are concerned. Her work is her life. She makes her home in a lively hotel near Times Square because it is only a step from her office, and she finds it as easy to speak to her ecclesiastical friends on the telephone from this worldly paradise as anywhere else.

She goes to church to enjoy the sermons as well as to report them, and she plays no favorites. In the summer of 1935 she went to Rome and had a special audience with the Pope at his summer residence, Castel Gandolfo, receiving his blessing. On her return she wrote an enthusiastic story about her pilgrimage for the *Catholic News*. She was deluged with letters. *Time* took up her story and a lively controversy raged over such uncommon devotion for the Pope on the part of an acknowledged Presbyterian. Some of her own flock condemned her for her adoration. Others applauded her fervor. Miss McDowell found to her surprise that she had stirred up quite an ecclesiastical tempest.

It was her own idea to do religious news and she has been responsible for all the New York papers giving more space to the churches. She started on the *Herald*, where she built up such an excellent department that when Mr. Munsey bought the paper, both the *Times* and the *Sun* sought her services. When she first began writing for Mr. Bennett's vivacious journal it was emerging from the long litigation over its so-called red light columns, Dr. Charles H. Parkhurst having led the fight against them.

Mr. Bennett had a hard and fast rule that Dr. Parkhurst's name was not to be mentioned in his paper. As he was the most distinguished minister in New York at the time, Miss McDowell had to run her religious department with Hamlet left out of the play. Mr. Bennett had so many don'ts for *Herald* employees that it was difficult for his editors to get out the paper without omitting news or inciting his ire.

In view of his attitude, it was considered quite an innovation when Miss McDowell was allowed to launch a weekly page of church news. She came from Newark and had no direct knowledge of the field. Her first move was to study the list of clergymen in the Brooklyn *Eagle* Almanac. The *Herald* sent out a form letter announcing her connection with the paper and asking for weekly bulletins of church news. The clergy leaped at this open door. News poured in. Every reporter knows that the preacher ranks next to the actor in courting publicity, and often outstrips him.

Miss McDowell set out to round up the leading clergymen. She was struck at once by the fact that New York had 2,000,000 Catholics, so she tackled St. Patrick's Cathedral first. She was received by Monsignor Michael J. Lavelle, now one of her staunchest friends. But he regarded her with suspicion twenty-seven years ago.

He looked at her card and then at her. "Are you a Catholic?" he asked.

"No, sir," said Miss McDowell meekly.

"Then it's utterly useless for you to try to report Catholic news," he told her.

He waved his hand in dismissal but Miss McDowell stood her ground long enough to ask him how she should know what was going on in the Catholic Church.

"You can buy the *Catholic News* at any general newsstand every week," he said.

This frosty reception was salutary. Miss McDowell made up her mind that she would prove him wrong. As time went on he conceded his mistake. She went out and bought the *Catholic News*. She became an authority on Catholic as well as Protestant church news. Her editors gave her all the latitude she wanted. It was easy enough to fill her page with routine news, but when she had this in hand, Miss McDowell did not confine herself to the offerings of the clergy. Like all good departmental reporters, she went to original sources and dug up real news. She made contacts that became invaluable in after years.

One of her earliest church friends was Bishop David H. Greer. She soon found that he sincerely disliked publicity. He said to her once: "I could eat my breakfast better on a Monday morning if I knew I was not in the newspaper."

The Bishop concerned himself with Miss McDowell's soul. On one occasion he sent for her after a service in the Cathedral of St. John the Divine.

"Did you receive Holy Communion?" he asked her bluntly.

"No," said Miss McDowell.

"Why not? You are a child of God and you have no business to sit coldly by and not participate."

"Well, Bishop, I did not feel in the proper mood," said the conscientious Miss McDowell. "I was late and I was nervous and my mind was set on getting the news."

"After this, whenever you are anywhere that I celebrate Holy Communion, you get down on your knees and ask God to forgive your sins, and then come to the chancel rail and receive Holy Communion," he said.

Cardinal Farley also was concerned over Miss McDowell's spiritual well-being. He used to plead with her to become a Catholic. Once, in the reception room at the archepiscopal residence on Madison Avenue, he brought down his fist on the table with a bang and declared, "You are a Catholic in spirit and you should become a Catholic in reality. And when you do, I shall baptize you."

Miss McDowell got many exclusive stories from 452 Madison Avenue, both for the *Herald* and the *Times*. One of the best of these was an interview with Cardinal Farley after Charles W. Fairbanks, vice-president of the United States, had his embarrassing interchange with the Pope. The vice-president was in Rome and he had an appointment for an audience with the Pope. But he went first to the Methodist Mission, which was considered such a breach of etiquette at the Vatican that his audience was canceled.

Every paper in the United States carried the story on the front page. The New York papers sent reporters to get comment from Cardinal Farley. But no interview was forthcoming. The following afternoon, as Miss McDowell walked into the *Herald* city room, Mrs. Elizabeth Cody, the head telephone operator, opened the door of her booth and called, "Cardinal Farley wants to see you at once."

Since Cardinals rarely call the press, Miss McDowell sped to the official residence. John, the butler, opened the door and ushered her in—not to the reception room where she usually waited, but to the drawing-room. To her surprise the Cardinal was there, waiting for her with a long typewritten manuscript in his hands.

"Read that carefully and then ask me any questions you want," he said.

He had noticed an item in one of the dispatches from Rome which seemed to him incorrect. This had caused him to break his silence and Miss McDowell was the person who profited. Her editors on the *Herald*, knowing that the story was exclusive, held it out until the last edition so that none of the other papers could pick it up. It got a heavy play. Next day reporters from all the papers camped on the Cardinal's doorstep, but he had nothing further to say.

Shortly afterwards she got a second exclusive story that stirred up the town. It was Cardinal Farley's ban on the tango. She went to the official residence on another matter. As Cardinal Hayes, then a monsignor and chancellor of the Archdiocese, was ushering her out, he happened to mention how disturbed Cardinal Farley was over the tango dancing which was then the rage. He disclosed that the Cardinal was about to issue a pastoral letter forbidding all Catholics to indulge in the dance. He put no restriction on the information, and again Miss McDowell walked off with a front-page beat of no mean order.

She caused a sensation in church circles when she disclosed that Bishop Henry Codman Potter's body had been disinterred at the Cathedral of St. John the Divine, years after his death. It was taken across the river to Fresh Pond Crematory and the ashes were returned and placed in the vault in the Potter Memorial Chapel at the cathedral. The disinterment was done at night so as to avoid publicity. It was a necessary measure because the recumbent tomb was too small for the coffin.

One of her most disconcerting experiences while she was on the *Herald* was her anxious pursuit of President Wilson and his wife when they visited New York on one of the gasless Sundays of wartime. They stayed at the Waldorf. No one knew which church they would attend. Miss McDowell hung about and watched until an attendant informed her that they had slipped out the back entrance and were on their way to the "little brick church."

This was a strong enough clue. She hurried up Fifth Avenue and caught the Wilsons as they approached Brick Presbyterian Church. An usher who knew her seated her two pews behind the President. Miss McDowell craned and fidgeted. She watched every move he made. As she wanted to let her office know that she was on his trail, she went out during the service to telephone from the parish house. When she returned she saw that the secret service men were watching her. There was no doubt that she had been acting suspiciously. Some time later she learned that they thought her a German spy and that Mrs. Merrill, wife of Dr. William P. Merrill, minister of the church, had saved her from ejection by telling who she was.

On the day that the *Herald* was sold, Miss McDowell, like everyone else, was caught unawares, although there had been much speculation after Mr. Bennett's death as to the fate of the paper. The news came on a Saturday night. She had just been robbed of her life savings by a woman she had met at one of the Billy Sunday tent meetings, so she was not in a cheerful frame of mind. Outside, the snow was so deep that the Broadway street cars were not running. Miss McDowell walked through it for ten blocks to her office. When she started up the golden stairs of the *Herald*, Sullivan, the old porter, called down to her, "Oh, Miss McDowell, have you heard the news? The paper has been sold to Frank Munsey and the plant will be closed down in a week."

She hurried into the city room. It was in a state of confusion. Her colleagues were standing on their desks, or sitting about in dejection. Sullivan had spoken the truth. Nearly a thousand men and women would be jobless.

Miss McDowell went to her home in Newark and wept all next day. The death of a paper is like the death of a human being. It did not occur to her to rush out and look for another job. When she went again to the *Herald* office she found a blue slip in an envelope buried at the bottom of her mail. It read:

> Mr. Munsey would like you, Miss McDowell, to continue as the Religious Editor of the *Sun-Herald*.

It was signed by William C. Reick, who was managing editor of the *Sun*. She looked around the office. She could see nothing but disconsolate men with families and no jobs. She decided not to mention her good fortune. An hour later Osmond Phillips, city editor of the *Times*, got her on the telephone and asked her to call and see him. In the interview that followed, she was invited to join his staff.

Immediately she did more general news than had come her way on the *Herald*. She covered assemblies and conventions, wherever they happened to meet. Her assignments took her all over the country. In her twenty-seven years in New York she has reported twenty-five of the annual conventions of the Episcopal Diocese of New York. She has missed only four meetings of the Presbytery and it assembles six times a year. In addition to the local gatherings, she has taken in the general meetings of all denominations.

When Bishop Manning launched his $10,000,000 campaign for the completion of the Cathedral of St. John the Divine, he sent word to the newspaper offices that he would see reporters at five o'clock one afternoon to make an announcement. Miss McDowell took the wrong subway train and was late. She found a group of twenty reporters gathered around the Bishop, who looked at her rather reproachfully and said, "Miss McDowell, we have been waiting for you for fifty minutes."

Over at one side of the room was Franklin D. Roosevelt, who headed the New York campaign committee. He looked up with a smile and said quietly, "Well, the New York *Times* is worth waiting fifty minutes for."

For some years Miss McDowell was assigned regularly to the men's Bible Class of what is now Riverside Baptist Church, whenever John D. Rockefeller, Jr., was scheduled to speak. This was usually about twice a year. She also attended the annual dinners of the class and she had the ranking of an associate member. But one year a speaker told a smoking-room story at the dinner. Mr. Rockefeller and Dr. Cornelius Woelfkin, the pastor, both expressed their regret to Miss McDowell, but nothing would appease her and she never went to another of the class dinners.

She did impartial and thorough work on the long drawn-out controversy in the Presbyterian Church when Dr. Harry Emerson Fosdick was retained as special preacher in the First Presbyterian Church. This story carried over from her *Herald* to her *Times* days and paralleled in popular interest Dr. Percy Stickney Grant's row with Bishop Manning.

She was the only reporter to catch the implications of the story when it broke. City News sent out a routine announcement that Dr. Fosdick had been called to the church. He was described as a professor at Union Theological Seminary. But she happened to know that he was pastor of the First Baptist Church in Montclair, New Jersey. She wrote a story pointing out that it was most unusual for a Presbyterian congregation to invite a Baptist to fill its pulpit.

She began attending the First Church, and soon the Fosdick controversy was raging. She chronicled every move and frequently got inside information on what was going on. When Dr. Fosdick preached his last sermon in the church, having been ousted finally by mandate of the General Assembly, she was down in front as usual, taking notes on what he said. The church was packed. Hundreds stood outside. After the service Miss McDowell saw Mr. Ochs walk up the middle aisle behind Dr. John H. Finley.

Always alert to a good story, Mr. Ochs said to her, "Have you the complete text of that sermon? I want to publish every word of it to-morrow morning."

Miss McDowell had rough notes. At this time Dr. Fosdick never prepared a manuscript for publication. Mr. Ochs spoke to Dr. Fosdick and told him what he wanted to do. Immediately Miss McDowell pounced on the pastor, feeling that her publisher, who rarely interfered directly with the work of his staff, had asked for something and it must be done.

"If you never did anything for me in your life before, Dr. Fosdick, you have got to help me now," she pleaded.

He told her frankly that what Mr. Ochs wanted could not be done, as he had no manuscript and the sermon had not been taken down by a stenographer.

"Can't you preach your sermon over again if I send up stenographers to your home?" Miss McDowell demanded in desperation.

Dr. Fosdick weighed the problem. "To-morrow morning?" he inquired.

"No, this afternoon," she insisted, "and the sooner the better."

Dr. Finley added his persuasion. Finally Dr. Fosdick agreed to repeat his sermon to a stenographic audience. Meanwhile, other reporters, seeing Mr. Ochs there and hearing of his request, informed their papers, with the result that all the papers carried the complete text of his farewell sermon next morning.

Dr. Fosdick is a Modernist of the first rank. All of Miss McDowell's sympathies are with the Fundamentalists. But when he had preached his last sermon in the First Presbyterian Church he wrote to her saying that although they were poles apart in conviction, she had never written a line which indicated her own leanings, and he thanked her for the fairness of her work—a rare compliment from a churchman to a reporter who has had to use the good and the bad in a bitter controversy.

Again she beat the town with the story that Bishop Manning had directed the New York Churchmen's Association to cancel its invitation to Judge Ben B. Lindsey, of Denver, who was to have spoken on companionate marriage. This started another church row of consequence. And when Dean Howard Chandler Robbins resigned his diocesan post because of a disagreement with Bishop Manning, she was the first reporter to hear of it. She carried this rumpus through its various stages and was still good friends with both sides when it was all over.

Miss McDowell was the first to reveal that Cardinal Mercier would visit America. Another of her beats was the announcement that Dr. Selden P. Delany had resigned as rector of the Church of St. Mary the Virgin to adopt the Catholic faith—a development in church circles that had been hatching for some years. Miss McDowell has hit the front page an astonishing number of times with exclusive stories. She has never been blind to the fact that harmony in the fold is only departmental news, but that a good row rates the front page.

One of the more unhappy days of her newspaper life was when she was assigned to cover the funeral of Princess Anastasia of Greece, the former Mrs. William B. Leeds. The Princess died in England. Her body was brought back to America for burial, but the funeral plans were kept secret. The report was that a service would be held at St. Thomas's. Dr. Ernest M. Stires, an old friend of Miss McDowell's, was away on vacation and she could not reach him for confirmation. Officials at the church denied all knowledge of the plans.

Then T. Walter Williams, the indefatigable ship news reporter of the *Times*, found out that the body was to be taken direct to Woodlawn for burial. When Miss McDowell arrived there, the functionaries at the cemetery were mysterious.

"Are you a reporter?" the gatekeepers demanded.

"Yes, I'm from the *Times*."

"Well, you can't come in. I just received a telephone call from the family and they said they didn't want any reporters present."

"A cemetery is a semi-public place and they can't exclude me so long as I don't disturb the peace," Miss McDowell protested.

By standing her ground, she got past the man. With the aid of gardeners and gravediggers she finally found the family mausoleum, reaching it just as an automobile from Thorley's arrived filled with flowers. The head gravedigger told her she could stay if she made herself inconspicuous. She stood to one side as the cortège drove up. She saw an undertaker whom she knew quite well. Then came Dr. Stires. He gave her a kindly look and whispered, "Rachel, I will help you later."

Prince Christopher of Greece appeared; then William B. Leeds and the Princess Xenia. The service was quickly over. Soon only the undertaker and Miss McDowell were left. He suggested that she step into the vault. This she did without a moment's hesitation. She noticed, with interest, that the Princess had been buried, not in the Leeds mausoleum but in her father's. She began copying the epitaphs on the other tombs.

When she came out of her absorption she saw to her horror that she was locked in. The undertaker had disappeared. There wasn't a soul in sight. By standing on tiptoe, she could just see through the glass over the iron grill. No one but the undertaker could possibly know where she was. Not even the *Times* would be aware that the Princess had been buried in her father's mausoleum. There were no other reporters present to record the fact.

Miss McDowell pictured herself slowly starving to death at Woodlawn. Who would suspect that she was in a mausoleum? Her reflections were getting dreary when suddenly the big doors opened and the prankish undertaker walked in. Miss McDowell did not tell him what she thought of him. She bounded for the open air. This was twelve years ago and she still does not know whether he locked her in by accident or intent. She sees him occasionally but never mentions it. The subject is too painful.

Miss McDowell, like so many other newspaper women, intended to be a teacher. She was born in Newark, attended private schools there and went to normal school for a time. She soon decided that she had no taste for teaching so she went to work as a clerk in an insurance office, and devoutly prayed every night for something to do that she could really enjoy. On the day of Queen Victoria's death she produced a sonnet. Her father, Dr. William O. McDowell, submitted it to one of the Hearst papers and it was printed. John L. O'Toole, then city editor of the Newark *News* and now vice-president of the Public Service Corporation of New Jersey, gave her her first newspaper job at $10 a week. She stayed on the Newark paper for more than six years and did society, clubs, a school column, women's and missionary activities and general assignments. She became religious editor of the *Herald* through doing occasional stories for the Sunday edition.

All of Miss McDowell's ancestors were churchmen. They had a share in founding Princeton University. Her great grandfather, the

Rev. Dr. William Anderson McDowell, was Moderator of the General Assembly in 1833.

Kathleen McLaughlin, the newspaper woman who finally overcame the prevailing prejudice against women in the city room, came to the *Times* fresh from the swift-paced Chicago *Tribune*. Although born in Greenleaf, Kansas, she moved so early in life to Atchison that she has always considered it her native town. Ever since she was old enough to read a paper she had the idea that she wanted to be a reporter.

She worked for a year and a half under Eugene Howe, on the Atchison *Daily Globe*, then went to Chicago on vacation, taking some clippings with her. She went to the *Tribune* on a gamble. She didn't dream she would land a job. But it happened that Maurine Watkins had left a month before. It was a strategic moment. She was the girl on the spot. She had a capable manner, a persuasive tongue. The city editor studied her clippings and told her she could go to work in the morning.

Miss McLaughlin first made an impression when she landed an interview with Olgivanna Milanoff, the Montenegrin beauty who had been arrested under the Mann Act with Frank Lloyd Wright and their illegitimate daughter, Iovanna, when they crossed the Mississippi River one September day and drove into Minneapolis. Olgivanna had held her tongue until Miss McLaughlin got to her, except for a chat with Lorena Hickok when she was first brought into jail. Up to that time she had been a mystery. But she talked illuminatingly to Miss McLaughlin, and as all Chicago was interested in the adventures of the brilliant architect, it made a good story.

From this Miss McLaughlin was swept into the whirlpool of crime reporting. It was the era when machine guns rattled through the streets of Chicago with astonishing frequency and the overlords ran the town. When Big Tim Murphy finished his jail term for his share in the Dearborn mail robbery, she was sent to Leavenworth to travel back with him. Jake Lingle, the *Tribune* staff man who later was murdered, introduced her to Florence Murphy, Tim's wife. She and Mrs. Murphy traveled to Leavenworth together and established friendly communication. Miss McLaughlin found her quarry genial and candid. He was more than six feet three, a hearty soul, graduated from swimmin' school—a natural who could spin a lively tale. Some of the best stories Miss McLaughlin ever wrote were done on Big Tim. They were written with Irish wit and sparkle.

After that she always looked after the Murphys when they got into hot water, which was quite frequently. When Big Tim was wiped out with machine guns on the front lawn of his Morse Avenue bungalow, she wrote the funeral story. It was one of the spontaneous carnivals of gangdom, for Big Tim had been popular.

She had a clean scoop a year later when Florence married handsome John ("Dingbat") Oberta, gangster and politician. The bride and groom obligingly posed for a *Tribune* picture, looking calm and happy. But Dingbat went on his way too, his life rudely ended by three associates in a liquor deal. Again there was a fine funeral with hearts of roses and crosses of lilies, which Miss McLaughlin covered from force of habit.

That night the widow broke down and told her who had done it, but the story was too dangerous to use. There was one dramatic moment at the wake when the watchful bruisers turned everyone out of the house except the widow and Miss McLaughlin, closed the front door, opened the back door and secretively admitted Polack Joe Saltis and his bodyguard. At the moment he was one of the big shots of gangdom. He had been Oberta's chief in the beer racket, and Miss McLaughlin watched him somewhat cynically as he stood in the light of the flickering candles, staring down at the corpse. The slain man was handsome as a movie hero, young and incredibly vicious. Saltis was beetle-browed, huge, coarse, revolting. He is now a farmer in Wisconsin, raising potatoes.

Miss McLaughlin reached the home of Tony Lombardo, head of the Unione Sicilione, before his wife had received the news of his murder. He had just died from a volley of bullets that caught him as he stood at Dearborn and Madison Streets watching an airplane being hoisted into a top window at the Boston Store. His wife, a plump young woman with dark bobbed hair, flung open the door when Miss McLaughlin arrived, expecting to see her husband. As a rule bad news reaches an Italian family like wildfire, and their mouths are shut tight by the time the police and press arrive. But Miss McLaughlin had to tell her that Tony was dead.

The woman threw herself on the floor, tore her hair, rent her pink housedress, and shrieked insanely for her two children, who added their howls to hers. Just as Miss McLaughlin and her photographer were about to hurry her to the scene in the *Tribune* car, the gang arrived and cleared them out. After that no one got in—not even the State's Attorney.

The flowers next day overflowed the house and yard. The largest was a heart of red roses, seven feet high, inset with "My Pal" in carnations. The card read "Al Brown." This was from Capone himself. Lombardo was one of the many heads of the liquor syndicate snuffed out during Capone's mad reign. Supposedly he was one of his friends.

Miss McLaughlin interviewed the crime czar, chased Prince

Nicholas of Rumania through the streets of Chicago, found Lady Diana Manners modest and Peggy Hopkins Joyce high-hat. She met the celebrities, freaks and criminals of the period. She did a series on maids by going out herself to apply for jobs. When she went to Europe for a holiday she sent back a series of articles on good eating abroad. For eighteen months she edited the woman's page of the Chicago *Tribune* and launched an annual conference patterned after the New York *Herald Tribune's* Forum on Current Problems. In February, 1934, she started a woman's page column called "Through the Looking Glass," which is now conducted by Eleanor Nangle. It is written with a light, adroit touch, sells commodities without using trade names, and gets a response of more than two thousand telephone calls a day.

Miss McLaughlin walked into the New York *Times* office at as apt a moment as she had tried her luck on the Chicago *Tribune*. The paper was about to start a woman's club page. She now edits this page, covers women's conventions and does general news assignments, for she is a versatile and experienced reporter. Her stories on the political conventions of 1936 made the front page day after day. She is accepted in the city room on exactly the same basis as the men—a triumph in the eyes of her colleagues, who have long regarded the *Times* as the last post to capture.

However inhospitable the city staff has been to newspaper women, the Sunday magazine section has made free use of their talents. The work of Anne O'Hare McCormick and Mildred Adams is feature writing at its highest level. Miss Adams is a reporter of mature talent with a sound background in history, economics and languages—invaluable assets for the feature writer to-day. She prefers politics and economic subjects, and likes the interview as a form of reporting, but she is endowed with a graceful pictorial style which enables her to write fluently on anything from fashions to a bullfight. On a visit to Spain she became interested in the experiments being made in modern education there; but a message from her London office urged her to cover a bullfight, which resulted in a graphic story on the Spaniard's favorite sport.

Miss Adams has witnessed some of the dramatic spectacles of recent years on both sides of the Atlantic. She watched Spain making its constitution in 1931. She was on the sidelines at Geneva when Russia joined the League of Nations. She found correspondence abroad more complicated than reporting in America, because of the difficulty of assessing the relative importance of crowding details in an unfamiliar country.

Only twice has she been aware of sex limitations in her work. When she attempted to interview a Maharajah, his secretary solemnly assured her that if the news got back to the nabob's province that he had talked to an unveiled woman, he would be laughed out of countenance. On another occasion, when she was seeking realistic copy on the barge life of the river, she found so many obstacles put in her way that she finally realized a newspaper woman was not really welcome in this hard-boiled domain.

Whenever possible Miss Adams does interviews. Once she made Calvin Coolidge talk for an hour and a half. He refused to discuss politics but he unbent to an unexpected degree and grew almost loquacious over the depth of the lake near his summer home and other matters that interested him at the moment. On another occasion she caught Huey Long on a train, talked to him for an entire day and assembled a convincing picture of him at a time when his shouts were first being heard outside his own state.

Miss Adams majored in economics at the University of California. For two years she had a social service job, but did not care for the future it offered. Until she moved East she had never written anything; in fact, she modestly thought that the literary world was beyond her aspirations. But when her family gave her the chance to try her own wings in New York, she felt as if she had received the key to heaven.

Her aunt was managing editor of the *Woman's Journal*, a publication which needed copy but had little money to spend for it at that time. So Miss Adams gladly contributed to its columns. Then one day she went to the *Saturday Review of Literature* and William Rose Benét gave her an armful of the worst novels she had ever read. This gave her heart. If such stuff could be published, she thought that there might be hope for her. Soon afterwards she made a connection with the *Times*. That was ten years ago. To-day her articles appear with regularity in the Sunday paper. They cover a wide range of subject and are always written with an informed touch. Miss Adams also contributes to magazines.

Chapter XIV

UNDER THE GOLD DOME

THE CITY ROOM OF THE NEW YORK *World* WAS JAMMED WITH an anxious crowd as midnight approached on the night of February 26, 1931. Reporters, desk men, editors, copy boys went about their tasks. The paper had to come out. It was not yet quite dead.

Vivian Gordon's body had just been identified. That was a three-column head. In Washington President Hoover had been overridden by the House on the veterans' bonus. That was front-page news too. But the question remained—was the sale of the *World* or Vivian Gordon to lead the paper? Surrogate James J. Foley alone could give the answer.

At 11.56 P.M. the City News bulletin ticked into the *World* office with the sentence of death: SURROGATE FOLEY APPROVES SALE OF WORLD. A few minutes later a staff man came tumbling in with the text of the decision. Ben A. Franklin, night city editor, grabbed the pages from him, tore the meat from them, tossed off paragraphs for Lindsay Parrott to digest and rewrite as he sat at his typewriter, containedly batting out the requiem of a great paper.

Allen Norton seized the copy, take by take, rushed it to Mr. Franklin for fast editing, then saw it on its way to the composing room. It was the last important story written for a paper that had vigorously and brilliantly served the public from the day Joseph Pulitzer took it over in 1883—a paper singularly beloved by the craft.

Then the presses began to roar and the staff to let off steam. The men and women gathered around the night city desk burst into "Hail, hail, the gang's all here," ending with the defiant note: "What the hell do we care now?" Upstairs compositors who had been with the paper for forty years sang "Auld Lang Syne" more gravely.

In the group that watched each move as the last issue went to press was Elenore Kellogg, one of the genuinely first-rate women news writers of the country. She had written her last front-page story for the *World* that night—a murderer confessing a killing in

Jersey. She was one of the chief mourners for a paper that her style peculiarly suited, for it was witty, penetrating and unafraid.

Miss Kellogg died after an operation in 1935. At the time of her illness she was with the Associated Press, but her career reached its peak during her days on the *World*, when she contributed an assured and sparkling touch to the news columns. She was a feminist and deplored anything in the way of a feminine assignment or the woman's angle on a news story. Like Lorena Hickok, she did straight politics or any major assignment that came along. Her best work was done on trials and her stories frequently led the *World*.

When Judge Ben B. Lindsey jumped up in his seat to call Bishop Manning a liar in the Cathedral of St. John the Divine on December 7, 1930, he nearly bowled over Miss Kellogg in his excitement. He was sitting next to her.

"Bishop Manning, you have lied to me," he shouted.

The judge was hastily ejected. The service went on. Miss Kellogg's story led the *World* next morning with a two-column head. It was a dramatic account of a disturbing moment in the life of a Bishop.

Miss Kellogg was in the thick of a rumpus again when she was assigned to cover a gathering of Communists and Socialists in Madison Square Garden. The rioters jumped on the press tables, threw chairs and struck out in all directions. The battle raged for two hours. More than a hundred persons were injured before things quieted down. This was a story that suited Miss Kellogg's style. Like any born reporter, she liked a good row. She went through many of the Communist riots and saw the mounted police charge the marchers in Union Square when Grover A. Whalen led his handsome blue-coated police regiment into action.

She followed Dwight W. Morrow's successful Senatorial campaign in New Jersey in 1930 and trailed Al Smith on his swing through New England in the presidential campaign of 1928. When she went to the Democratic headquarters in Boston, the politicians were flabbergasted to see a girl show up. They turned her over to a woman so that she could get the feminine angle on the story. They would not give her a press ticket for Al's big meeting, but told her that she could sit in the spectators' gallery. Her protestations that she was writing the lead did not move them.

Miss Kellogg immediately telephoned to Western Union.

"You get me a typewriter and have it in the press section at that meeting," she said.

When she arrived the typewriter was there. She marched in, took a seat and remained to cover the meeting. Her work had the firm touch of the seasoned political writer.

One of the most difficult stories she ever did was the first clash in court between Isidore Kresel and Max Steuer during the Bank of United States investigation. It was a complicated financial story. She was sent to write a special feature on the two enemies face to face. She took sketchy notes for a color story. But at the last moment the night desk decided that she was to write the lead. This was a task calling for the quick assimilation of involved testimony, perfect balance and fast work on the typewriter. She turned out a finished job in jig time—a real test of a newspaper woman's skill on the type of story which she is not supposed to handle well.

She showed another facet when Texas Guinan and Helen Morgan were battling prohibition charges in court. Her stories were models of satire. She had the dramatic touch on court work and saw many murderers on their way to the chair. The *World* stories on Earle Peacox and Colin Campbell, the two torch murderers, were all written by Miss Kellogg.

She often did the tiresome holiday and weather round-ups, which are an essential part of every paper's front page, but which, for the reporter, involve hours in stuffy telephone booths while the rest of the world is on holiday, listening to correspondents babbling the myriad details of crowds and drownings at Coney Island, packed highways, automobile accidents, thunderstorms and all the vagaries of nature and the holiday maker.

Occasionally she filled the column left vacant by Heywood Broun when he went over to the *Telegram*. Here she was at her best, her literary and imaginative qualities in full flower. Her travel pieces were choice. It was her custom to go abroad in freighters, stopping off at obscure ports and turning out contemplative pieces on what she saw, thought and ate. She was an epicure and wrote intelligently of food.

When the *World* was sold, Miss Kellogg was on the list of reporters invited to join the *Herald Tribune* staff. Her vivid style flashed again on the front page in a different setting. This was a period when the Reds were marching and shouting around Union Square and she wrote with gusto of their activities. She did a smart round-up that led the paper when a package of bombs was sent through the post office in 1932. She followed this with a witty succession of stories on a nudist colony near Poughkeepsie. Her victims liked her satire. They invited her back as a guest. They assured her she could wear clothes if she liked; it wouldn't debar her from their colony. So she went, taking pyjamas and a bathing suit, so as not to be too much out of the picture in the nudists' paradise.

From the *Herald Tribune* Miss Kellogg went to the *Post* to conduct the woman's column in the absence of Marion Clyde Mac-

Carroll. She turned out a sharp and sophisticated column, refusing to cater to the traditional feminine interests. She did not believe in the separation of men's and women's activities in the daily paper.

She joined the staff of the A.P. in 1934 and here again she was in her element. She did ship news and an art column as well as general assignments. In her interviews she projected the personality of her subject in sharp focus. This was a trick she first learned on the *World*, where the staff were allowed great freedom of expression. They could write realistically and reproduce eccentricities of dialect, manner or grammar to a degree not permitted in the more conservative papers. This gave their work a racy quality and permitted Miss Kellogg to use her gift of caricature. She had a vigorous intellect and an unobtrusive manner. There was no need for her to lean on any of her colleagues, for she was entirely capable of getting her own facts and presenting them in a sound and entertaining way.

Elenore was a true Bohemian. She knew the poets, artists and radicals of Greenwich Village, liked evenings of talk, had discriminating taste in books and art, was always sympathetic to radical causes, sought out odd restaurants to indulge her epicurean tastes, had a pampered Persian cat named Hubert, once owned an island in the Bronx, and had a passion for the sea.

She was born in Chicago, attended normal school there, then switched to a course in journalism at the University of Wisconsin. She came to New York in 1918, went the rounds of the newspaper offices, got the cold shoulder everywhere. She did not even succeed in seeing the city editor of the *World*, where she was later to shine. Once she got a pointed message from him: "We have one woman on the staff and we have had her for twenty-five years."

She landed on the *Call*, covered labor meetings, joined the Socialist party. Then her paper blew up. The staff walked out and that was the end of it. She went over to the *Globe*. Catherine Brody was on the staff at the time and romance was blooming in the city room between Henry Pringle, who later became a fine biographer of the debunking school, and Helena Huntington Smith, an attractive young newspaper woman who soon went on to domesticity and the magazine field.

But after six months on the *Globe*, Mr. Munsey stepped in and again Miss Kellogg knew what the sale of a newspaper meant in human values. For the next three years she worked on the *News*, but never liked it. When she left she was told: "You are too calm and critical to work on a tabloid. You would be all right on the *Times*." Her next move was to the *World*, where she was perfectly adjusted and turned out copy that was alive, biting and intelligent. But for the third time her paper was snuffed out. This time more drama and public mourning attended the event, for the death of the *World* was unlike the death of any other paper.

Miss Kellogg was forty-one when she died. Ann Cutler, an old colleague from the *World* days, gave a blood transfusion to save her life, but it was no use.

Miss Cutler got her job under the gold dome in 1928 by putting over a beggar girl series at a time when the streets were filled with panhandlers. She found a ragged outfit at the Salvation Army headquarters, made herself up like a hag, got a license for $2 and walked the streets selling pencils and holding out a battered cup.

She learned that Wall Street in the pre-depression era was one of the softest spots in New York for the beggar, and there she garnered in from $5 to $10 an hour. She found stenographers more generous than women buyers in the shopping region. The subways were lush picking. If one person reached for a coin when she entered a car, the other passengers followed suit. Broadway after the theater was best of all. Up to that time few panhandlers had tried it, but when her story appeared beggars swarmed into the theatrical district.

The summer before the *World* was sold Miss Cutler was sent to South America with Vinnie Sullivan, the marble champion of the United States by default. Vinnie gave performances before all the presidents of South America and provided his press representative with plenty of copy.

Miss Cutler was an enterprising reporter who knew how to put a stunt across. She had herself arrested on a technical charge of disturbing the peace of Pennsylvania, so that she could spend three days in the county jail of Reading, where there had been a riot. For a time she worked on the *Sunday American*, writing weird stories about prehistoric man, ghosts who came to life, scandals in high society and pseudo-scientific copy. Now she does publicity. She is a graduate of Marshall College, Huntington, West Virginia. She played for a time in stock and worked on the Charleston *Daily Mail* and Cincinnati *Enquirer* before reaching Park Row.

Of all the newspaper women who have worked for the *World*, no name is more closely identified with its history than that of Mazie Clemens, who was on the staff for twenty-five years and was well known to politicians, churchmen, judges and jailers. She was one of the more adventurous reporters, famous for crashing prisons and reaching the principals in a story when no one else could get near them.

Miss Clemens is small and dark, has an animated manner, plenty of nerve and a sound knowledge of New York's complex political machinery. She has strong Catholic connections and is the only reporter who can compete with Rachel McDowell on a story centering on St. Patrick's Cathedral. She gave the *World* many exclusive stories but she always made a mystery of her successful technique. In order to get into a jail she has been known to dress in flowing black as a sorrowing relative and so beguile the guards. But more often Mazie has won her way by blarney. She has a smooth tongue, a shrewd eye, and a wary knowledge of the devious ways of politicians and crooks.

She joined the staff in 1906 and worked until 1914 as a statistician and assistant editor on the staff of the *World* Almanac. Occasionally the city desk borrowed her to do a story and in time she was transferred to the general staff. Nothing in the way of a snub ever daunted her in the pursuit of her duty—an immunity which makes life easier for the reporter.

When Bonaventura Cardinal Cerretti was sent on a tour of the world by the Pope and passed through New York, she got a signed interview from him for her paper. When Cardinal Logue, primate of Ireland, was here on a visit in 1908, she had a talk with him. She and Miss McDowell invariably made it a point of pride to interview visiting Cardinals.

She went abroad in 1919 and rounded up a number of celebrities. She talked to General Pershing, was received by Cardinal Mercier and got an anti-German outburst from Foch. She was presented to Clemenceau and interviewed Queen Elizabeth of Belgium. Then she went to Rome, where she had both public and private audiences with Pope Benedict. When d'Annunzio declared a blockade on Fiume, she dressed as a peasant, went in, made a survey of conditions and left before the authorities could catch her. Her vivid dark eyes and black hair made the deception a simple matter so far as appearances went, but the language was more of a problem. One of her greatest triumphs was an interview with the Archbishop of Canterbury at Lambeth Palace.

In her earlier newspaper days Miss Clemens did a number of stunts. She walked across Manhattan Bridge on the footpath before the cables were laid. The *World* gave her a bonus of $100 for this feat, and splashed the story on the front page.

She and her dog Freckles figured in the Hall-Mills trial. The morning after the bodies of Dr. Hall and Mrs. Mills were discovered, Mazie drove up to the Hall home with her small dog, in time to see Henry Carpender come out of the house and burn some papers on the lawn. When he went on trial four years later she was called to the witness stand by Senator Alexander Simpson to testify to this incident. During the months that the case was brewing she and her dog became familiar to all the residents of Somerville.

After the sale of the *World* Miss Clemens worked in the Department of Correction. In private life she is Mrs. Louis Caldwell.

Another veteran of the *World* who worked alongside Miss Clemens was Emma de Zouche, who covered women's activities. For a time the talented Mary Ross was on the general staff. She followed the suffrage struggle, was on the Hughes train and saw Margaret Sanger through her early difficulties. Miss Ross, the former wife of Lewis Gannett, is now associate editor of the *Survey*, a free lance writer and book reviewer.

One of the last of a string of young college girls to join the staff was Louisa Wilson, who invaded Park Row fresh from college. Her upbringing was unusual. She was born in an inland missionary summer resort in China and attended a Chinese school until she was eleven, when she went to a boarding school in Shanghai. At the age of fifteen she was brought back to America and her education was completed at Wellesley.

She went to the *World* office with a letter to Mr. Swope from the father of one of her classmates. She spent three anxious days on the bench outside the editorial rooms, full of hope and anxiety. Then Mr. Swope saw her and did his best to discourage her. Louisa was tall, fair, delicate and obviously unhardened to life's bumps. Mr. Swope told her that she could not last, and that she had no conception of a newspaper woman's life. It was rough and tough and hard, he said. Bad hours. Difficult tasks. All sorts of obstacles.

Fearing that her collegiate appearance was giving him the wrong impression of her background, she told him earnestly that she had to work for a living and that she was staying in a $5 a week room. Her total capital was $100, and she was desperately anxious to land on the *World*.

Mr. Swope was less implacable about women reporters than most newspaper executives, although he always began by frightening them out of their wits. If they survived the barrage he gave them real opportunities and praised their work. He engaged Miss Wilson temporarily at a small salary.

"I'll raise you or fire you at the end of a month," he told her candidly.

He was gambling on her persistence and nerve. She soon showed that she didn't lack either. Her work had a sensitive touch, but she was hardy at getting news. Although she looked like a schoolgirl let loose in a grim world, she showed good sense and skill at her job. She also had beginners' luck. When Old Glory crashed she was assigned to interview the widows of the aviators. They were in seclusion at a hotel and refused to see anyone from the papers. Miss Wilson was still running around New York in campus sweaters and flat sport shoes and looked as young as she was. She told the hotel elevator man who was guarding the aviators' wives from intrusion that she had to get an interview or be fired. There could be no question about the sincerity of her statement. It was written in her face. He let her in, although her competitors were barred. The result was an exclusive story for her paper.

Soon afterwards the city editor gave her another stiff assignment. "Find Henry Ford," he said. "He's somewhere in town, registered under his own or an assumed name. Have a good talk with him."

Until recent years Mr. Ford was one of the genuine inaccessibles, and was so catalogued in every newspaper office. It was a sensation when Wilbur Forrest, of the *Herald Tribune*, first got to him, and he saw him only because he thought Mr. Forrest looked as if he might make a good mechanic.

Miss Wilson went from one hotel to another trying to find the automobile king. On her way into the Ritz, she spotted his lean figure coming through the door. For a moment she was paralyzed with surprise. Then she hurried after him.

"You are Henry Ford?" she said excitedly.

"I am," he told her, "and what do you want?"

Miss Wilson said she was from the *World* and that all she wanted was an interview. To her astonishment he smiled and nodded his assent. Then, as she sat down beside him in a quiet corner of the lobby, she realized that in her anxiety to find him, she had given no thought to preparing herself for the interview. What should she ask him? She didn't know. She had a rare opportunity, but at the moment was too inexperienced to make the best use of it. They talked on but she felt later that she had wasted a golden chance. Her questions evoked nothing of interest. Several years later, on Mr. Ford's sixty-seventh birthday, she talked to him again. This time she was prepared. The result was a rich and absorbing interview. She could have kept him busy for hours answering questions, for in the interval she had learned how to strike flint.

Her first out-of-town assignment was to write about Mrs. Al Smith when her husband was nominated for the Presidency in 1928. Charles Michelson, then head of the Washington bureau of the *World* and now publicity director for the Democratic National Committee, was writing the lead. He, Louisa and William Woodford, of the *World's* political staff, had breakfast together on the morning of the nomination.

Miss Wilson told Mr. Michelson with some alarm that she had a stomach ache, brought on, she was sure, from excitement over such an important story. Mr. Michelson looked at her over his orange juice and observed:

"When a reporter doesn't have a stomach ache or other symptoms of excitement over a big assignment, then it's time for him to become an editor."

On two occasions Miss Wilson was assigned to interview youthful heirs to family fame—John D. Rockefeller, 3d, and Gloria Caruso. When young Rockefeller had finished his education and his travels, and was about to take his place in the business world, Ivy Lee notified the newspaper offices that there would be an interview. He asked that a "high class" reporter be assigned. Since nothing irritates a city desk so much as being dictated to, and particularly by a press agent, there was general annoyance in the *World* office, and Miss Wilson got a scoffing send-off from her colleagues. High class, indeed!

The elder Rockefeller introduced his offspring with considerable pride. "My son, John," he said. "I really needn't talk for him. He can take care of himself."

One brash reporter turned to young John and asked him if he had to live with his family, or if it would be possible for him to branch out and make a home of his own. Mr. Rockefeller's face was a study as he smiled at John and answered for him:

"No trouble so far, have you?"

Gloria Caruso was nine years old when Miss Wilson interviewed her. By a court decision she had just been awarded two-thirds, instead of the expected one-half, of her father's fortune. She was brown-haired, thickset, a sturdy miniature of her famous father. She disliked reporters, she confessed to Louisa, because they and the photographers always kept her from getting a clear view of the Statue of Liberty when she came in from Europe.

She was polite to Miss Wilson but begged one favor. "I hope you won't put in the paper that I can't roller skate," she said, "because some children read the papers and I don't want them to know that I can't roller skate."

But Louisa, the heartless wretch, gave Gloria away, and next morning any child who dipped into the *World* as he ate his cereal might read the sad truth about Caruso's daughter.

Miss Wilson and John Chamberlain, of the *Times*, tried to outdo each other one season with their fabulous circus stories. They were encouraged in this by Dexter Fellows, the genial impresario who fed out items about his entourage—the madder the better. But the best joke was on Miss Wilson herself. Mr. Fellows had been building up a terrific ballyhoo on the importation of Goliath, the Sea Elephant. At last Goliath arrived and Louisa was sent to give the big boy the once over. She first beheld the monstrous creature in a wooden crate. She wanted to be thorough in assembling her facts about him.

"Does he swim?" she asked, absent-mindedly.

This furnished a story for the other papers next day—the deflation of Goliath's ego when a girl reporter asked if he could swim.

Miss Wilson did considerable court work during her years on the *World* and for one period had the Supreme Court beat. The part a reporter may inadvertently play in court-room procedure was illustrated for her one day when a justice walked with her from the Supreme Court Building to the *World*. He had been presiding in a case where a woman was suing a prominent hotel manager for giving her a black eye.

"I couldn't tell from your face *to-day*," he said, "whether you thought the woman was lying or not."

When an aunt of Miss Wilson's died and left her some money, she decided to use it for travel. She went to China. She lived in Shanghai and made extended trips into the interior. She interviewed Madame Chiang Kai Shek, wife of the head of the Chinese government, and other outstanding Chinese women who had broken their shackles.

The *World* was sold while she was in the Orient. She got the news in Shanghai. It gave her an astonishing feeling of grief, even at that distance. When she got back she worked on the *World-Telegram* for a time. She now does publicity and is the author of a novel about China called *Broken Journey*, a delicately told story of the child of a Chinese missionary. By a coincidence she heard that it was accepted on the day of her marriage to Read Hager, whom she first met as a child in a school in Shanghai.

Soon after the war Elizabeth Eskey landed on the *World*, a girl from the Middle West who quickly learned the ropes, although she could scarcely type and did not know what a stick of copy was when she joined the staff. She was told by the city editor when he gave her a job: "A cub reporter is a liability to a paper, not an asset. And I've never had a woman cub. God knows what I'll do with you."

Her first court story was libelous and had to be rewritten from City News, but later she did excellent work. In the end she found newspaper work wearing, and she left it to run a tea-room. Two other girls who worked on the *World* during the same period were Helen Mockler, a capable newspaper woman who could handle any sort of assignment, and Elizabeth Houghton, a sensitive college girl who wrote well but suffered acutely in the hard-boiled atmosphere of Park Row. Miss Houghton's first important story was the trial of young Francis Kluxen for the murder of Janette Lawrence, an eleven-year-old girl who was killed in the woods near Madison, New Jersey, in 1921. Although only sixteen Francis was an amazing witness in his own behalf. He baffled everyone, in spite of the strong evidence against him. He was acquitted and went on to further trouble. He changed his name, went West and has been accused of murder again.

When Dempsey knocked out Firpo, a blue-eyed, fair-haired girl watched the contest from the press row and wrote a story that got her a by-line in the *World* next day. This was Margaret Pratt, a Vassar girl who had been broken in on the Boston *Traveller* and the Albany *Evening News* before reaching Park Row. She attended the Sacco-Vanzetti trial, but at the time it seemed less important in Boston than the case of an impeached district attorney and two local murders then in the news.

Although exceptionally competent at her work, Miss Pratt did not stay on the *World* for long, because working at a desk nearby was C. B. Allen, flyer and aviation writer. Theirs was another of the swift newspaper romances. Soon Miss Pratt handed in her resignation and married Mr. Allen, who is now aviation expert for the *Herald Tribune*.

She was followed by Isabel Boyd, who was taken on the staff by Mr. Swope and soon was doing the features that teach the young reporter how to find her way around New York. Miss Boyd interviewed a woman in New Jersey who had not spoken to her husband for twenty years. The hold-out threw a pail of water at her for her pains. She investigated the bathing suit situation at Bayville. She followed Mary Pickford to a Boy Scout camp, and wrote features about immigrants caught in red tape snarls at Ellis Island. When a deer broke loose in Central Park Zoo and ran down Fifth Avenue in the thick of the traffic, her story landed on the front page, for the *World* never missed a trick on a human interest story. After getting some general experience Miss Boyd free-lanced abroad, then returned and did features for the *Sunday World* magazine. She is the author of a child's life of Hans Andersen. She has done short stories and book reviewing and for a time she did publicity for the Women's City Club.

The next to come along of the capable group of newspaper women who worked for the *World* during the early twenties was Gertrude Lynahan, a handsome girl whose work was rated with the best that Park Row produced at that time. Her first newspaper experience was on the Springfield *Union*. She had a level-headed approach to any story and was equally adept at straight news and features. After working for two years on the city staff she moved over to the sports department in 1927—an innovation at the time.

Later she did fashions for the *Times*. Miss Lynahan is the wife of Joel Sayre, of *Rackety Rax* fame, one of Park Row's favorite graduates, now turning out motion picture scripts in Hollywood.

While Miss Lynahan was still on the paper, Mabel Abbott was also doing good work for the *World*. She used her shorthand to advantage on trials. Born in Iowa, she got her first newspaper job in the State of Washington and then worked her way from coast to coast on large and small newspapers.

The morning, evening and Sunday editions of the *World* were always hospitable to women, from Nellie Bly's time until the day the paper was sold. Marie Manning (the original Beatrice Fairfax), Zona Gale, Anne O'Hagan and Josephine Robb followed Elizabeth Jordan. Then came Nixola Greeley-Smith, Marguerite Mooers Marshall, Sophie Irene Loeb, Ruth Millard, Fay Stevenson and Bella Cohen, all of whom wrote for the *Evening World*.

Miss Cohen, who started her newspaper career on the *Call*, worked on both sides of the Atlantic, sending correspondence from Germany, Russia, Bulgaria and Hungary. It was she who first sprang the story of the Princess Anastasia who claims to be the daughter of the Czar. The Russian girl was lying ill in a hospital when Miss Cohen first heard of her. She got to her nurse, armed with roses, and bit by bit dug out the story which became part of the curious history of the Russian emigrées.

Miss Cohen married Sam Spewack, a *World* star, who did foreign correspondence for several years, after covering the Stillman divorce and other celebrated stories in New York. They are now successful playwrights. One of their joint plays, *Clear All Wires*, dealt with the foreign correspondent in Russia—a subject with which they both were familiar.

When Allene Talmey, fresh from Vassar, rushed away from a prom to get to New York to keep an appointment with Mr. Swope about a job, she did not know that there was no need to hurry. She waited a whole day for him to show up. When he arrived he kept half a dozen telephones busy at once, calling up Bernard Baruch, John J. Raskob and four or five more of his intimates— all names that caused reverberations in Miss Talmey's head.

"You don't want to be a reporter," he shot at her suddenly, banging down one of the receivers.

"But I do," Miss Talmey insisted.

"Do you know what a reporter's life is like? Just listen to me," barked Mr. Swope and then he detailed the horrors.

However, she was taken on the staff and continued to work for the *World* from 1924 to 1927. While she was still quite green Mr. Swope came striding into the city room one day, shouted for her, and raged on, while she stood frozen among the typewriters. When the furore had died down, and the onlookers in the city room were beginning to relax, it became apparent that he was merely praising a story she had written, but it had taken volleys of spirited words to get the idea across. Miss Talmey practically fainted from stage fright over Mr. Swope's dynamic commendation. After leaving the *World* she did motion picture and magazine work and is now an associate editor of *Vogue*.

From 1926 to 1930 Beatrice Blackmar Gould was assistant editor of the *Sunday World* while Louis Weitzenkorn was running it. She launched the women's section, wrote feature articles, edited pages and got a variety of executive experience. Helen Worden, Gretta Palmer, Phil Stong and Paul Sifton were all doing staff work for the Sunday section at the time.

Mrs. Gould comes from Iowa. She edited the *Daily Iowan* at the University of Iowa and she and her husband, Bruce Gould, both did reportorial work on the Des Moines *Tribune* before moving East. While Mrs. Gould worked on the *World* her husband was on the *Evening Post*. They have collaborated successfully on short stories and plays—one of which was produced by the Theatre Guild in 1929. They now edit the *Ladies Home Journal*—a unique magazine appointment for husband and wife.

Thirty years before Mrs. Gould became assistant Sunday editor of the *World*, Elizabeth Jordan was filling precisely the same post with Arthur Brisbane. It was not so sensational for a woman to hold an executive post of this sort in 1926, but it was in 1892, when Miss Jordan used to bedazzle the compositors by showing up in immaculate shirt-waists and slinging type with an experienced hand. When everyone else was sweating and in a state of collapse from heat and overwork, Miss Jordan would look completely self-possessed. At the end of a particularly frenzied night one of the editors exclaimed ferociously as he waited for the elevator: "Good God! What a job. Can you imagine anything worse?"

"Oh, yes," laughed Miss Jordan, waving her dummy pages. "To lose it."

Miss Jordan was born in Milwaukee in 1867. Her mother was Spanish and Elizabeth was convent bred. She contributed to the Milwaukee, St. Paul and Chicago papers, and worked on the Chatsworth disaster for the Chicago *Tribune*. She went to the scene of the accident, and stayed for several days, helping to care for the injured.

Miss Jordan came East in 1890 at the invitation of John A. Cockerill. She made an impression from the first moment. She had an elaborate wardrobe and was dashing in appearance, and she managed to get into the most inaccessible places. She was never bothered with minor women's page assignments, but combined the best features of the stunt age with sound writing. She tested the accommodations of jails and asylums, rode an engine cab, interviewed social leaders, and covered the news of the town. She traveled through the mountains of Virginia and Tennessee on horseback, fording rivers, climbing gorges, forcing her way through thick forest, her only companion a Negro guide. She visited a lonely mining camp in the mountains, in which no woman had ever set foot. Armed with a Spanish stiletto she explored the camps of the moonshiners and did a series for the *Sunday World* that was copied widely.

When the Koch lymph treatment was first exploited she spent a night on Blackwell's Island at the deathbed of a consumptive, so that she might write the story of the woman's final struggle. The patient died at 3 A.M., holding on to Miss Jordan's hand. Three hours later the story was written and turned in to the *World*.

Miss Jordan had the balanced temperament invaluable in journalism. She was calm, sure in her judgment, humorous in her outlook. Ballard Smith, brilliant and irascible, gave her severe training. He taught her the importance of concentration and the value of terse language. At six o'clock one evening he threw a stack of papers on her desk and said, "Have this story ready for me when I come back."

Miss Jordan dug into the documents. It was the opening move in the long-drawn out prosecution of Carlyle Harris, the medical student accused in 1891 of poisoning Helen Potts, a girl whom he had secretly married while she was still in boarding school. There had been preliminary investigation and suspicion but no arrest. The youth had walked boldly into the office of De Lancey Nicoll, then District Attorney, to demand an inquiry so as to still the buzz of talk. But that night the *World* had the exclusive story that Harris was about to be arrested. The documents Mr. Smith threw on Miss Jordan's desk were the affidavits of physicians and teachers, on the strength of which he was to be charged with murder.

Miss Jordan went to work on the papers. She quickly got to the core of the subject and turned out columns in longhand. When Mr. Smith returned from dinner the story that astonished New York next morning was ready for his inspection. Harris was ultimately convicted.

In the early nineties the *World* ran "True Stories of the News" every day, a feature which was revived again in its declining years. Miss Jordan wrote most of these, finding her material in hospitals, morgues, police courts and tenements. She embodied some of them later in her book, *Tales from the City Room*. As time went on Mr.

Smith took her on his staff of editorial writers and in April, 1892, she was appointed assistant Sunday editor, to work with Mr. Brisbane. She remained with the *World* until 1899, when she was appointed editor of *Harper's Bazaar*. From 1912 to 1917 she was literary adviser for Harper and Brothers. She resigned to work for Goldwyn Pictures. She has written a number of books, short stories and plays.

Miss Jordan was one of the really notable newspaper women of the country, at a time when merit and recognition were a combination not readily found among the women who had gained a foothold in Park Row.

Chapter XV

DOWN BY THE RIVER

IT WAS GETTING CLOSE TO THE DEADLINE. THE FIRST EDITION OF THE New York *American* would soon be in. The rewrite men were busy over their typewriters, green eye-shades concealing the mockery of their faces. The city room was bright, noisy and cluttered. Typewriters tinkled. There were explosive shouts of "Boy."

A blonde girl reporter sat at her desk, unconscious of the bedlam, anxiously waiting for copy from T. P. O'Connor. Ruth Byers had been to see Tay Pay that afternoon. She had arrived before the reporters from the other papers, and had had a chance to talk to him alone. She told him frankly that she knew nothing about Irish politics. He laughed and said, "Young lady, I don't know anything about Irish politics either, but I'll try to help you out. When these other reporters come in, you just sit here and wait, and I shall write out something for you."

Miss Byers felt relieved. She had not been a reporter long. She was still at the trustful stage. When her competitors put solemn and knowing questions to Mr. O'Connor about the turbulent state of affairs in Ireland, she sat back calmly and viewed their efforts with the assurance that all would be well.

She returned to her office. Evening fell. At eight o'clock there still was no word from Tay Pay. Just as she was beginning to give up hope a messenger arrived with six sheets of hotel stationery in handwriting that no one in the office could read. After a frantic effort to decipher even one line of it, Miss Byers got his secretary on the telephone. He taxied down to the *American* and glibly translated Tay Pay's views. Next morning she could not find a trace of her story in the paper. She went down to the office feeling crestfallen. Her city editor greeted her with congratulations and told her she was getting a raise.

"Great story. You beat the town," he said.

She was quite bewildered until he showed her the banner head on the story leading the paper. It had never occurred to her to look for one of her stories on the front page. Later that day Mr. O'Connor telephoned and asked her to meet him at Grand Central Terminal. He arrived in a long flowing cape and kissed her hand in gallant farewell before an audience of commuters rushing for their trains.

Soon after this Miss Byers was sent to Queens on an assignment and found herself locked in a room with a woman suddenly gone mad with grief over her domestic troubles. She greeted the reporter pleasantly enough and ushered her into her library. Once inside, she changed into a demon. She locked the door, put the key in her pocket and faced Miss Byers with blazing eyes.

"I have been shadowed and trailed for months," she cried. "I know you are a detective posing as a newspaper woman, but you will never get back to report anything on me."

She picked up a bronze lamp and hurled it at her visitor. The lamp cord spoiled her aim. But for the next two hours Miss Byers had to work frantically, trying to pacify the woman and dodge the things she threw. She thought she would never get out of the room alive. But the demented creature suddenly calmed down and collapsed. Miss Byers escaped, brought assistance and stayed long enough to see her regain consciousness. Before she left she had the interview she wanted.

Then came the day when she was sent out to Sheepshead Bay Speedway to ride with "Gil" Anderson, just before the Astor Cup Races were run. She rode in an automobile at 101 miles a minute—the thrill of a lifetime. Next day Anderson won the cup race. Ten miles in six minutes was fast work for pre-war days.

Another of her stunts was to walk on the bottom of the sea without a diving suit, and still keep dry. Captain Simon Lake had invented a tube device which made this possible. Miss Byers made the experiment off Bridgeport, Connecticut, picked up a horseshoe crab and came out quite dry to pose for her photographer.

She covered Richard Harding Davis's funeral, interviewed women when their sons and fathers were on the way to the electric chair, attended political conventions, gave advice to girls, wrote recipes, and acted as a handwriting expert, receiving 15,000 letters in one week from a public that thought her opinion of their handwriting mattered.

She got her job through Talcott Williams, first dean of the Columbia School of Journalism. He gave her a personal letter of introduction to the city editor of the *American*. Her first signed story was an interview with Jess Willard on his return to New York after winning the heavyweight championship of the world.

Miss Byers left the Hearst papers to do war work. She was appointed director of publicity for the Y.W.C.A. and later launched the Phoenix News Publicity Bureau, the oldest women's publicity organization in the country. She is now Mrs. Thomas D. Heed and lives in Chicago.

War-time brought real opportunities to women reporters, as Grace Phelps soon found when she went to work for the *American*. On the night that Becker died in the electric chair she was assigned to cover his wife. Mrs. Becker set out for Sing Sing by car. Miss Phelps pursued her and lost her in the traffic. She caught the first available train but found that it did not stop at Ossining.

"It has *got* to stop," she told the conductor. She explained her urgency. Everyone in the country knew that Becker was to die that night. His trial had been one of the sensations of the decade. Officials on the train finally agreed that under the circumstances they would slow down for long enough to let her get off.

When she left the train she was mobbed by reporters. They knew that Mrs. Becker was expected and they were sure that the train would stop for no one else. But Mrs. Becker's car had broken down on the way. She arrived at about 2 A.M. and stayed with her husband until it was time for him to go to the chair.

Miss Phelps wrote her story that night under great emotional stress. She hunched her elbows on her typewriter and could not think of a word to write. She was too upset. At last to her astonishment she found she was turning out verse, not prose. The theme was "Waiting, Waiting." It was used next morning in her paper.

Some time later she was sent to Westbury, Long Island, to interview Jacques Lebaudy, the millionaire son of a French sugar king. He was quite mad and thought himself Napoleon. She found him drilling a company of telegraph boys. This was his army. Meanwhile his wife and daughter were starving in their house of fifty rooms known as "The Lodge." Soon after this his wife shot the eccentric "Emperor of the Sahara," as he was generally known, in defense of their thirteen-year-old daughter, Jacqueline. The murder took place on the night of January 11, 1919, and she was acquitted early in 1920.

Miss Phelps staged a number of campaigns for the *American*. One was conducted on behalf of a young girl who was sent to the reformatory just before her baby was due to be born. Her mother wrote to Mr. Hearst, pleading for newspaper backing so that her daughter could get married and thereby legitimatize the child. Miss Phelps was assigned to the case. She had three weeks in which to get the girl out of jail and married. She interested the women's clubs. She badgered officials. She got committees working on it. The girl was released. The marriage was rushed before the child was born. The paper set her up in housekeeping. It was one of the gestures that newspapers make now and again, when they step aside from the usual business of purveying straightaway news.

Again, when a poor Italian woman in the Bronx was convicted of murdering her husband, orders came down that Miss Phelps was "to save her from the electric chair." She was the first woman in many years to be in actual danger of going to the chair in New York State. Miss Phelps summoned her club backing. She got enough women together to fill a special car for Albany. They presented the case to Governor Whitman. The woman's sentence was commuted to life imprisonment.

Miss Phelps investigated the flower-making industry and conducted a vice crusade, which led to threats against her life and general intimidation. A letter was sent to Robert McCabe, her city editor, ordering him to call her off the investigation or "she would get hers." She continued to write the stories but her by-line was dropped for her own protection.

Miss Phelps started newspaper work in Philadelphia on the *North American* and the old Philadelphia *Press*. After leaving the *American* she did syndicate fiction and publicity. She now free-lances in Washington. Her husband, Edmond McKenna, is a newspaper man.

On the night that Lebaudy was killed, Anne Dunlap of the *American*, and Gene Fowler, one of the rarer souls of Park Row and now a successful author and screen writer, were sent out on the story. Gene got through a window and into the Emperor's room. His collaborator wrote a number of stories about Mrs. Lebaudy, for whom there was much sympathy.

Miss Dunlap was one of the more decorative members of the profession, in addition to being extremely competent. Her manner was so impressive that she frequently got in where others failed. In March, 1919, she married John K. Winkler, a star on her own paper and now the author of several biographies. For several years she worked in the same city room as her husband, and sometimes on the same story.

One of her stiffest assignments came soon after she joined the staff. In January, 1918, the American troop transport *Northern Pacific* went aground off Fire Island with 3,000 persons aboard, most of them soldiers, sailors and marines. Many of the passengers were sick and wounded. Miss Dunlap had been out on New Year's Eve covering an elopement for her paper. When she got back to her office she was rushed to Bay Shore, Long Island, without so much as a toothbrush. She was to assist Martin Green, who was in charge of the story. There was only one wire to the mainland and the A.P. had it sewed up. Miss Dunlap stayed at a tiny hotel at Bay Shore, and went out in an oyster boat at six o'clock in freezing weather for two mornings to watch the rescue work going on. The fog was dense. Most of the passengers were taken off in lifeboats. The sea was so rough that the surf boats of the life guards were constantly in danger of capsizing. The hospital ship *Solace* stood by and the passengers were transferred to it, but it was a slow and painful process. The weather was bitterly cold, with lashing blasts of sleet. The reporters worked under difficulties, and with real physical hardship. Miss Dunlap was soaked to the skin repeatedly, half frozen and caked with icicles. Her work on this occasion was so good that inquiries were made about her at the *Herald*, and Victor Watson, her managing editor, immediately offered her a three-year contract.

She soon learned what it was to stay up all night in court; to go without food or sleep; to wait for hours outside jails and homes visited by trouble. In the spring of 1922 she was sent to Mount Holly, New Jersey, to cover a circus murder. "Honest John" Brunen had been killed by a shotgun fired through the window of his home as he sat in his kitchen reading a paper. He was a wealthy circus owner. His wife and her brother, Harry C. Mohr, were tried for the murder. Mrs. Brunen was acquitted. Mohr was convicted.

The witnesses were a strange parade of circus figures—clowns, lion tamers, tight rope walkers. The gold wheels of the circus caravan rattled through the the testimony. Miss Dunlap, Julia Harpman and a third woman reporter wired ahead for their rooms to the one hotel in town. When they arrived they were all ushered into one vast chamber with honeycomb bedspreads and scrim curtains.

"As you were all newspaper ladies, we thought you would like to be together," said the proprietor. "Anyway, we haven't another room."

They happened to be friends, so they bunked together. They had dinner close to midnight every night in the dark dining-room after they had filed thousands of words to their papers. One night the wires came down in a snowstorm and one of the girls had to tramp miles through the snow along the railroad track to file her story from a signal tower. Her copy was interrupted every few minutes for train signals.

When Mrs. Stillman took baby Guy and fled to Lakewood, New Jersey, immediately after her husband filed his sensational charges against her, Miss Dunlap was assigned to follow her and get an interview. For a month she and her colleagues stood guard at Laurel-in-the-Pines, waiting for a glimpse of Mrs. Stillman. She ignored their notes, refused flatly to see them, and never emerged from her room lest the photographers spot her. Guy was only permitted to get an airing under heavy guard.

Early one morning she ditched them completely. She motored away from Lakewood before dawn and went to Poughkeepsie, where John E. Mack, her counsel and guardian ad litem for Guy, arranged an interview for the men who had been waiting there, while the newspaper women had been trailing her at Lakewood. This was a bad moment for the ladies of the press. Mrs. Stillman soon realized what she had done, and invited them up to Poughkeepsie for tea. But the cream had been skimmed from the story. The first interview had made the front pages without their assistance. However, by this time she was talking freely. Mr. Mack had advised her that she could help her cause by getting sympathetic publicity. So she went amiably to the daisy fields in gypsy costume and posed for the photographers from any angle they suggested, and even with her arm around a cow's neck. She never shunned the headlines again, although often they must have made her wince.

This was one of the last big stories that Miss Dunlap covered before leaving newspaper work. She was launched in Birmingham, Alabama, in 1915. She had taught for three years in a county high school. Her pupils were older than she, for she was only sixteen when she started. Their chief interest was the rotation of the crops. Her own tastes were urban. So she determined to change her profession. She worked for seven months on the Birmingham *Ledger* and then attended the Columbia School of Journalism as a summer student. She edited Teachers College Record for $25 a week and continued her studies at the same time. Then Franklin P. Glass, who was editor-in-chief of the Birmingham *News* from 1910 to 1920, offered her a job on his paper. He was a friend of her father's.

She went back and worked there for a year and a half. America had entered the war. The staff men were all leaving for army service. Miss Dunlap was doing relief operator duty one day when she heard a man's voice mumbling a strange story over the telephone. He had just left the state penitentiary after serving nineteen years of a twenty-year sentence for the murder of his wife. A little late to do him much good, his wife had turned up alive in Alaska, with another husband and a child. Miss Dunlap called the head of the composing room and told him what was coming. Then she got the warden of the penitentiary on the telephone and found that a man bearing the name of her unknown informant had been a prisoner there. She was sure the story was true. She rushed it for the bulldog edition, wrote the headlines herself, and beat the town with the story. It was a skilful piece of work.

Not long afterwards she came to New York, because her mother was ill and needed her. She decided she would try her luck on Park Row. She landed on the *American*, where she soon became the ranking woman star and one of the best women reporters of the period. Ultimately she left journalism and is now a senior in the interior decorating department of Macy's. She is remarried to W. Wallace Clements.

Working with her at the same time was Ruth Dayton, an attractive girl whose first big assignment was the trial of Olivia Stone. She left newspaper work to go on the stage. Another contemporary of Miss Dunlap's was Geraldine Fitch, who survived innumerable shake-ups in her office and covered more types of story than most girls ever get a chance to tackle. She is now Countess Morner, having married Count Gösta Morner, whom she met on a story. One day early in 1930 her city editor handed her a letter and clipping. The letter said that Count Felix von Luckner, the "Sea-Devil," would tell reporters about a trip he proposed making, if they went that afternoon to his yacht, the *Mopelia*. The clipping said that Count Morner of Sweden was visiting Count von Luckner aboard his yacht.

"See what Luckner has to say," said her city editor to Miss Fitch, "and ask Count Morner why neither he nor Peggy Hopkins Joyce has married again since they were divorced years ago."

Count Morner told Miss Fitch that he had every reason to dislike newspaper people, but that if she would wait for a week he would give her a good story. They met often after that. He did not give her the promised story until she wrote up her own engagement to him to make a feature for a dull Labor Day. Late in September, 1930, she became the Countess Gösta Morner av Morlanda in the Municipal Building. They observed the Swedish custom—two gold rings for the bride, one for the groom, who also has a gold chain soldered around his left wrist. Some of her friends from the *American* office were to attend the ceremony, but as they were leaving, a story broke, and they went back again. In this way it was a typical newspaper wedding.

Miss Fitch was thoroughly versed in all the ins and outs, whims and sacred cows of the Hearst organization. She loved the speakeasy hours of happy companionship, the stimulus of working among the unconventional and talented men of the press. She had listened to Joe Mulvaney, one of the ablest of the lot, offer his sage advice to each new girl coming into the office. For Mr. Mulvaney has been father confessor to many girl reporters, advising them, fixing up their copy, annihilating them with his criticism. Like Robert B. Peck, of the *Herald Tribune*, he can write circles around any of them on a genuine sob story.

Miss Fitch took it all in when she first landed on the *American* after studying music in Chicago and appearing in the opera chorus with Mary Garden as director. Her first assignment had been a free-lance piece for the *Globe* on opera from behind the scenes. She was told that if she were patient she might get a job on the staff, but her funds ran out and she joined the musical comedy, *Two Little Girls in Blue*, as a show girl. Jack Donahue was the star. She went on the road with it and came back in 1922. She badgered Victor Watson for a job for eight weeks and soon found herself working for Mr. Mulvaney, who was getting out the tabloid section enclosed in each issue of the *American*. Her salary was $50 a week.

For a year she wrote special columns and fillers. In that hall of wonders, the composing room, she learned about make-up and editing—how to cut chunks out of a famous author's serial and still have it make sense; how to read copy and write heads. Finally Martin Dunn took her over on the city staff and she soon learned how sharp and bitter life can be for people touched by the news. The usual number of doors were slammed in her face. She tramped dark and lonely roads at night, to visit houses stamped by tragedy. She cultivated lawyers handling big divorce cases. She comforted a demented Russian princess and a less demented chambermaid, both of whom eventually wound up in Bellevue psychopathic ward, calling for her. She interviewed every sort of celebrity; rushed out on fires; covered murder trials eagerly; worked on Christmas Day and holidays; tossed verbal roses at political friends of the paper and stepped on the toes of its enemies; stole the wrong picture and had a damage suit slapped on the paper when it was published. She withstood all manner of shake-ups in a temperamental organization.

Once she climbed tenement stairs to tell a mother that her lost little boy had been found—dead in a dank cellar. The woman was young and pretty and she had five other children. She clung to Miss Fitch, asking her what she would do if it had happened to her.

When she went to get a story on a bootleg king in Rockaway, his wife turned three police dogs loose on her and Josephine Higgins, a photographer from her paper. Before they reached their taxi their clothes were partially torn off. They were clawed and chewed and the camera was smashed. But they protected the plates.

When she interviewed Dr. Raymond L. Ditmars in the Bronx Zoo Reptile House he put the snakes through their hisses and strikes for her benefit. Then he quietly wrapped a slithery black snake around her neck. It looped harmlessly, while her photographer took a picture of the petrified girl reporter embraced by a snake.

On Easter Sunday, 1930, she was assigned to get a piece of the dress from a young woman's body, just found in the East River, on the chance that the pattern, if photographed, might lead to her identification. She made her way through a line of bodies in the morgue, young and old, male and female; heard a voice singing "Love, thy magic spell is everywhere" and found the singer—a blonde, cheery attendant singing at her work on the body Miss Fitch sought.

She made notes on what she saw. She cut a piece from the dress lying nearby. It was a rusty black. She carried it away. The body turned out to be that of Anna Urbas—garroted and drowned by gangsters. She was the friend of Eugene Moran, a bodyguard of Arnold Rothstein. She had been sunk with a necklace of iron weights. Moran had been murdered some months earlier and the theory was that the slayers feared she might squeal.

By the end of four years Miss Fitch had had broad and varied experience. In between staff assignments she did dramatic and motion picture criticism. When the Christmas Fund was being built up into a large charity, she publicized it. And she was always requisitioned for art. During her years on the *American* the art market was at its height. The Anderson Galleries had brilliant nights and the American Art Association held sales of magnificent art collections from all over the world, surpassed only by Christy's. Mr. Hearst insisted that these sales should be covered in a certain way. Catalog numbers, articles, buyers and prices were all listed. Different reporters had muffed the job and he made many complaints. As he followed the subject closely, nothing could evoke panic in the city desk like an art auction. From the time she went on the *American* until she left Miss Fitch covered these auctions, and even when she had a chance to do a big story, she was held in reserve if an art sale loomed. The sales were exciting in themselves. The auditorium was packed with millionaires. Bids rose to a quarter of a million dollars. The peak was reached with the Reifsnyder sale of early American furniture. When she saw the name W. W. Wood, she always knew that Mr. Hearst was buying. He did not care at all for modern or Oriental art, but bought rare Italian and Spanish pieces at any price. And he acquired some magnificent books.

Like all of her colleagues at one time or another, Miss Fitch went through the torture of having an assignment she had hoped to get handed to someone else; of seeing her own story being quietly rewritten by the third man on the rewrite desk; of being recalled from a front-page story to take over a stupid feature; of being scooped cold. But she also did her share of scooping. She, too, rewrote someone else's story; learned the delights of praise, of a by-line in large type, of the good story pasted on the bulletin board, followed by a raise.

Miss Fitch left the *American* in the spring of 1931. Her next assignment was to cover the Lenz-Culbertson Bridge tournament for Clyde West of Universal Service. She did not tell Mr. West she knew nothing about bridge. Her husband is an expert. He provided her with precise data throughout the tournament, which she sent in a continuous flow over the telegraph wire. She now writes advertising commercials and radio continuity.

Miss Fitch is tall, exotic-looking, red-haired, with the reposeful manner of a figure in an Italian primitive. She was followed on the staff by Helen Nolan, small, dark and pretty, who met her husband, Edward J. Neil of the Associated Press, while they were both covering the first Lake George marathon swim. She scooped him on the story and then they fell in love. Miss Nolan was working for the Albany *Evening News* at the time. Mr. Neil had come over from Saratoga with Jack Dempsey, who was then in training for a ring come-back.

The marathon involved a mad newspaper scramble for telephones along the shores of the lake, which went on for a day and a night. Thunderstorms wrecked the wires. Swimmers kept getting lost. The reporters had no time for rest or food. They worked with the fine frenzy which besets the press on an occasion of this sort. It was not the perfect moment for romance. But Miss Nolan, less wistfully helpless than she looked, beat the seasoned Mr. Neil and the A.P. with a flash on the finish of the race as dawn broke. Then she went to breakfast with Mr. Neil and love bloomed in its mysterious way. Six months later, after she had come to New York and gone to work on the *Mirror*, Miss Nolan married her newspaper competitor.

On another occasion she swam a mile in the Hudson River with Lottie Schoemmell in bitter December weather. Lottie wore a coat of grease instead of a bathing suit. Miss Nolan just escaped pneumonia. She is an expert swimmer, a graduate of the Sargent School for Physical Education. She intended to teach swimming in Nassau for a season when by chance she found herself covering society for an Albany paper at $15 a week.

When she came to New York she free-lanced for the *Post*, worked for two years on the *Mirror* and then moved over to the *American*, where she still is. When Frances St. John Smith disappeared from Smith College she spent six weeks haunting the campus, disguised as a student in a rented coonskin coat and bandana. Reporters were kept off the premises but Miss Nolan looked the perfect student type as she rattled around in her open galoshes and sickened herself with chocolate fudge, cementing her news sources over the teacups.

When Justice Joseph F. Crater disappeared, she followed clues all over northern New York State and into Canada. She wound up at Belgrade Lakes, Maine, where she and Mrs. Crater were the only summer survivors for a period of six weeks.

She went to Hollywood to chaperon Miss New York, who had won a Mary Pickford jaunt as a typical girl. She proved to be typical in everything except her appetite. She gorged her way across the continent, and arrived in California ten pounds overweight. At nearly every stop Miss Nolan had to drag her away from the station lunch counter. Finally she got her back to New York, plump and frustrated. Miss New York had not landed in the movies.

Miss Nolan worked on the Lindbergh kidnapping and the Hauptmann trial. She also did angles on the Morro Castle disaster, the murder of Jack Diamond and the O'Connell kidnapping. She is a clever digger and investigator as well as a good reporter. Her beguiling looks open many doors for her, and she knows how to follow a clue to a dead end.

Newspaper girls come and go with astonishing frequency in the Hearst offices, shine or fade, marry or go into some other kind of work. Pearl Gross, who did capable work for the paper in the early twenties, is in Hollywood. The glamorous Anne S. Kinsolving is now Mrs. John Nicholas Brown and lives in Providence, Rhode Island. Viola Rodgers, no less stunning, lives in a villa in France. Ann Carr, a Follies beauty, Helena Fox, and Antoinette Spitzer, are all married and out of the newspaper game. Belle Kanter is doing publicity. Helen Morgan, who came from California and worked on the Hauptmann trial, has returned to her native state. Mignon Bushel, daughter of Hyman Bushel, the lawyer, is still doing exposés and crusades for the paper. Florence Wessels, a graduate of the San Francisco *Examiner*, is learning to know the town as only a reporter knows it.

The girls of yesterday are soon forgotten but the flow of news goes on to the same tune. Murders, trials, kidnappings, lost babies, Easter parades, love triangles. When nightfall comes the girls sit at their desks, smoke cigarettes, discuss the story of the day. Through the waterfront windows the river looks soft, the lights are blurred. Over the two bridges crossing the East River slip the rush-hour trains —like illuminated link bracelets, like water mocassins. By and by the presses roar. An ephemeral world, an exciting world, known only to the ladies of the press and the men with whom they work.

Chapter XVI

TWO ACES

WHEN COLONEL LINDBERGH CIRCLED OVER LE BOURGET after his trans-Atlantic flight Jane Dixon was swept the entire length of the landing field on the crest of a howling human wave. A moment earlier she had been standing with John O'Brien of the United Press and her husband, Major W. H. Wells.

All three were separated when the mob rushed the iron fence as though it were papier-mâché. A few minutes later they found themselves together again, under the landed plane. Miss Dixon had fought her way through many mobs in the course of a long and spectacular newspaper career, but she had never seen anything like this. All the cyclists of France seemed to be underfoot, adding wire spokes to the general confusion.

She lost her stockings, a shoe and a new hat, just bought on the rue de la Paix. She was scratched with bicycle spokes and pulled to pieces. Somehow or other she struggled back to the U.P. headquarters and wrote her story. It was an historic moment and the reporters worked with the savage intensity that besets them when an action story is at its height. Then they are at their best—quick, ingenious, clear-headed and fluent.

Miss Dixon had been waiting for hours in the Aviation Club at Le Bourget, sharing the general belief that Lindbergh must be lost. Then came the flash that his plane had been sighted over Ireland. When it was reported nearing the field the reporters went down into the enclosure inside the huge iron fence which kept the mob back. They heard the motor—a faint roar in the night sky—then saw the lights. The plane circled like a bird and swooped. The crowd murmured, then surged forward with Gallic shouts of welcome. Miss Dixon remembered little else until she was under the plane and looking for the young man who had just announced: "I am Charles Lindbergh."

A decade later she sat in a stuffy court room in Flemington, New Jersey, watching the same young man, older, more grave, sitting with folded arms listening to the testimony that edged Hauptmann, his son's slayer, closer to the electric chair. Again she was covering for the United Press, this time beside Sydney Whipple, Harry Ferguson and James Austin. As her copy flowed in, Earl Johnson, at the New York end, kept sending her such messages over the teletype as: "Good work, Jane. Keep your foot on the gas."

Miss Dixon has always known how to keep her foot on the gas. Few have equaled her at the job. Her experience might well make any newspaper novice gnash her teeth with envy. For years she has had a front seat at every story that mattered. She worked for the old *Telegram*, under Andy Ford, who is still her favorite editor. She did trials, interviews, prize fights, conventions, spectacles of every sort. She did them with dash and a highly dramatized style. Her tolerance, good nature and sound approach endeared her to the men and women of her profession. Nowadays she goes out only on the really sensational story when the United Press, which does not employ a woman in New York, assigns her, as they did on the Lindbergh case.

When the baby was kidnapped Miss Dixon was rushed out to Hopewell, where reporters were converging from everywhere. This time she was covering for NANA. She managed to wheedle Paul Gebhart, whose hotel became the gathering place of the press forces, into letting her have the hired girl's room, second floor rear. But the telephone company's minions moved in while she was out on her first scouting trip. They knocked down partitions and installed a double row of telephones, twelve on each side, just outside her door. In the furious days that followed, news writers screamed and babbled over these phones at all hours of the day and night. But this did not dismay Miss Dixon. She can turn out her copy with plaster falling on her head, voices roaring in her ear, typewriters jingling on all sides, and still her sentences parse and the picture is authentic. For she is probably the calmest practitioner of her craft. She has never been known to rush or turn frantic under stress. She goes along with a fine sense of balance that is more effective than the do or die technique.

Fifty-four hours after her arrival in Hopewell she washed her face for the first time since leaving home and got a little sleep. Meantime she had been in the side cars of motorcycles, on sound movie trucks, bumping over the trails of Sourland Mountain in vintage automobiles, and had even taken a short airplane hop to Hartford, Connecticut, and back. The weeks that followed the disappearance of the Lindbergh baby have rarely been equalled in newspaper tension.

Miss Dixon married Major Wells, affectionately known to the

press as "Cappy" Wells, on the Saturday preceding the opening of the Snyder-Gray trial. Next day she did her advance story for Monday's paper. She almost missed her honeymoon altogether as a result of this case. Her paper assured her that it would be over in two weeks at the most. But it took as long as that to fill the jury box. She and Major Wells missed half a dozen ships to Europe.

She saw Ruth Snyder convicted, and finished her work on the case at four o'clock one Thursday morning. They sailed at ten. Her colleagues from the trial went down to the ship to see them off. They were bedraggled, half hysterical from weariness, lack of sleep and relief that the job was finally over. The French Line gave the bride and bridegroom a sailing party. The ship was delayed fifteen minutes while frantic Frenchmen tried to persuade the boys and girls of the press to leave the gangplank.

One of Miss Dixon's most unusual newspaper experiences was when she was attached as correspondent to Pancho Villa's Army in northern Mexico. Floyd Gibbons was a member of the party of writers, artists and officials on the Villa private car attached to various troop trains. They were traveling through the desert when the train jerked to a stop. A bridge ahead of them had just been blown up. They had to wait until repairs were made.

Miss Dixon liked Pancho. He was the only General she ever met who could wear as official uniform an old pair of wrinkled cotton trousers, a boiled shirt without a collar, a large diamond button in his neckband, an African sun-helmet, and still get away with it. And Miss Dixon knows the army. She now lives at Fort Hamilton, right in the thick of it.

She was one of the first newspaper women to cover the big prize fights, and she always wrote exciting stories about them. She saw Dempsey win his championship from Willard in Toledo and lose it to Gene Tunney at Philadelphia in torrents of rain. She covered every Dempsey bout except the one in Shelby. When Firpo knocked him out of the ring Dempsey was headed for Miss Dixon's typewriter but Jack Lawrence caught him first.

She covered tennis at Forest Hills, racing at Kentucky, Saratoga and the New York tracks, Sir Thomas Lipton's yacht races, the football games and the World Series. In short, everything that went on around the town was graphically chronicled by Miss Dixon. She did hundreds of interviews of every sort. She went down the Bay as regularly as celebrities arrived. She learned to turn out her copy under every conceivable set of circumstances. She juggled adjectives with an experienced touch.

It was her early ambition to be a trained nurse. Her mother wanted her to stay at home. There was no compromise so Jane became a newspaper woman. Mrs. Warren G. Harding started her on her way. Miss Dixon comes from Ohio. When she was just beginning, Mrs. Harding was business manager of her husband's paper, the Marion *Daily Star*. She helped and sponsored Jane, when the towns-people frowned on her for being unwomanly enough to write pieces for the paper. A girl reporter was something new in Marion. Years later, when Warren Harding became President, Miss Dixon caused consternation among her colleagues by getting exclusive stories from the President's wife.

After several months on the Marion paper, she worked on the Poughkeepsie *Star*. She traveled to New York one day and dropped in at the *Telegram* office. She knew no one there, but she was told to take the woman's page and write her opinion of every story on it. She was to send in the result at her leisure. She sat down in the outer office and did the job on the spot. That was on a Thursday. On the following Saturday she got a wire asking her to report for work on Monday. She went in on Sunday, fearing her benefactor might change his mind over the week-end.

Miss Dixon was a success from the start. Soon she became one of the ranking women feature writers of the country. She had a fluent, easy touch. It was as natural for her to write as to breathe. She went to the political conventions. She saw Harding nominated in Chicago and heard Franklin D. Roosevelt make the nominating speech for Alfred E. Smith in old Madison Square Garden. She did running copy and interviews at the Disarmament Conference in Washington along with Mary Roberts Rinehart. She has written six newspaper fiction serials and she now does a column for the Bell Syndicate.

During the Hall-Mills trial in Somerville Miss Dixon lived with Julia McCarthy, then of the *Journal*, now of the *News*, in a one-room cold water apartment over Charles K. Levy's clothing store on Main Street. A dog in the backyard bayed at the moon most of the night. It was then time for the baby in the adjoining flat to start yelling. The two exhausted newspaper women who wrote without a break from four in the afternoon until one o'clock in the morning, rolled over wearily and prepared to face another day in court. In addition to covering for their own papers, they were filing special stories to half a dozen out-of-town papers.

But in spite of the exhaustion and physical hardship of the game, excitement keeps the newspaper woman going during a story of this kind. Time and again Miss McCarthy has worked the round of the clock and still turned in sparkling copy for her paper. Like Miss Dixon, she is one of the personalities of the profession. For years she has been in the front row on the major news stories. In some respects she resembles Rusty McGowan, Paul Gallico's newspaper heroine.

She is big, courageous, sharp at repartee, warm-hearted, always over the fire lines when there is trouble. She can handle the dowager or the policeman, and has often proved the point that the intelligent reporter can talk down opposition. She prefers the front door method but has also been known to use the fire escape and she is one of the best fact-getters in the business. Her record of exclusive stories is impressive. She isn't one of the meek who take easy snubbing. The doorman and butler are usually forced to surrender in a battle of wits. If they don't, she is apt to out-smart them.

At the funeral of Mrs. Alice Gwynne Vanderbilt the press was barred. But Miss McCarthy and Lady Terrington, of the *Mirror*, marched with complete assurance into the house. They went up to the second floor ballroom, without stopping to reconnoiter.

"I am slightly hard of hearing," Miss McCarthy confided to a footman. "Please put me well forward. I wish to hear dear Bishop Stires."

The two reporters were placed immediately behind the family. They bowed their heads and wisely refrained from producing copy paper. Miss McCarthy followed the funeral party to New Dorp Cemetery on Staten Island, where the Vanderbilts are buried. She had a camera man with her and they were after pictures.

They wandered about among the graves until they came on a gardener, raking up leaves.

"Oh, just to think that Staten Islanders like us never saw where the Vanderbilts are buried!" said Miss McCarthy artfully.

The gardener showed them the way. The flowers were being taken out of the mausoleum. He ushered them in. The photographer took his flashlights with speed. Then he and Miss McCarthy vanished among the tombstones.

Her most spectacular work was done in the summer of 1935 on the suit involving the same Mrs. Vanderbilt's daughter-in-law, Mrs. Gloria Morgan Vanderbilt, over the custody of her child. She got one beat after another for her paper on what might be called the perfect tabloid story. Reduced to its simplest form it had all the elements that fitted the frame. Big names. Mother love. Wealth. Gay doings in high society. Actually it was a grim and nauseating struggle.

Mrs. Vanderbilt's eye first lighted with interest on Miss McCarthy when Julia walked up to her after Emma S. Keislich, little Gloria's nurse, had told of her spying operations in her employer's home.

"Where did you find her?" she demanded of Mrs. Vanderbilt. "If you had searched the whole world over, you couldn't have found a worse biddy."

Mrs. Vanderbilt smiled vaguely and made no response. But two nights later Miss McCarthy got word that she wanted to see her.

"You endeared yourself to me for life by what you said in court," she announced.

From that time on Miss McCarthy had the inside trail on the story. She was able to get hold of Mrs. Vanderbilt at any hour of the day or night. She went to her house practically every evening. Often she anticipated the news. She was the first to spring the story that a cash payment had been offered for little Gloria. She learned in advance that the child was going to take the stand and be the key witness. When Gloria paid her first visit to her mother after the suit was brought into court, Miss McCarthy was allowed to talk to the little girl, and her cameraman took pictures of her in her home. Week after week the *News* ran stunning and intimate poses of the child, obtained by Miss McCarthy, who was allowed to select all she wanted from Mrs. Vanderbilt's own stock of photographs taken at all ages. She carried them to her office in their jade, silver and leather frames. This was priceless for a picture paper.

She had two exclusive interviews with Mrs. Laura K. Morgan, mother of Mrs. Vanderbilt and Lady Furness, in which she spoke slightingly of her daughters. Then her paper scooped the town with the transcript of the testimony taken secretly in the case. This rounded out a sensationally good job of covering a big scandal story.

Miss McCarthy is at her best on an assignment of this kind. She is smart at making and keeping contacts. She knows how to outwit her rivals. She works with the energy of ten and spills a clever line of satire when the story lends itself to caustic treatment.

She was sent to Pottsville, Pennsylvania, on a hex murder in 1934, to write about a boy who was jailed for murdering a reputed witch. She learned that he had a girl named Selanie, who lived deep in the fog of the slate-colored valley. She went to see her, for she wanted a picture of the girl. She also wanted to outdo the reports in the *Journal* that the witch had crucified cats on the side of a barn.

She had no difficulty on this score. The hex-conscious neighbors outdid themselves in telling her lurid tales. They insisted that the witch had left her coffin before the burial and was roaming the hills at that moment in the guise of a black cat, leaving three toads in the coffin for burial. But it was no joke getting Selanie's picture.

The girl said she couldn't pose unless Paw and Maw agreed. Julia and Selanie then set out to find Maw. And when they found her she said they would still have to see Paw. They traveled around until they met Paw, but he had a big shotgun on his shoulder. When told what Miss McCarthy was after, he glowered and said, "Get out—I'm gonna shoot yo' hat off."

"Ho, don't do that," said blue-eyed Miss McCarthy, looking very bold, although her knees were bumping. "It's the only one I've got."

Paw compromised. "All right," he agreed. "Then I'm gonna shoot yo' head off."

"Don't do that, either."

Miss McCarthy used her persuasive Celtic tongue. Maw talked to Paw, too. Finally Maw thought of the solution. She turned to her visitor and said, "There's one way you can get that picture. Selanie needs a new Easter outfit. If you fix her up you can take her picture."

Miss McCarthy looked at her photographer and he looked at her. An Easter outfit! Could it be done? Would the office stand for all this expense?

"Well," said Miss McCarthy, "how much will it be?"

Paw and Maw put their heads together and began figuring. Julia and the photographer found that they had $80 between them, but they were supposed to make that last for several days. If the Easter outfit came to more than that, they were sunk.

Maw turned to Julia at last. "Wal," she said, "she'll need a hat and some shoes and a dress and some stockings and a slip."

"Yes," said Miss McCarthy urgently, "and how much will that be?"

"Wal," said Maw triumphantly, "it'll be all of five dollars."

Julia successfully concealed her relief. "It's a go," she said.

Paw dropped the shotgun, the picture was taken, Selanie got her Easter wardrobe and there was rejoicing all around.

But Miss McCarthy has wriggled out of tighter spots than this. During the Snyder-Gray case she, Irene Kuhn and Oliver H. P. Garrett were all arrested in a Connecticut town for the somewhat obscure crime of bunching.

Judd Gray's wife had gone to South Norwalk to stay with her sister, whose husband was a local official. The three reporters followed her. They drove to the house and saw her standing in the yard. They decided to dismiss their car and form some sort of plan for approaching her. They walked along the sidewalk three abreast. They had not gone near her or even rung the doorbell when a policeman walked up and said he was going to arrest them.

"Arrest me?" said Miss McCarthy indignantly. "I dare you to."

"Don't be foolish," said Mr. Garrett soothingly, but Julia still seethed.

However, they were taken into custody and were charged with bunching in the street, under an old Connecticut law which forbids blocking the sidewalk. They were run out of town and were told that they must never under any circumstances appear there again.

"Positively not," said Julia, fit to be tied.

They were escorted to the train by a bodyguard.

"You will never come back," their guard insisted as he pushed the savages from New York onto the train.

"Sir, we will never come back," Julia assured him, swinging into the carriage and dusting herself off.

On the night that Ruth Snyder died, Miss McCarthy, who was then on the *Journal*, was one of the newspaper women who waited outside the prison while a huge crowd made shocking whoopee at the gates. It might have been a carnival instead of an execution. There was a screaming mob of more than 2,000. There were cars with licenses from five different states. Boys in raccoon coats with bottles of gin in their pockets sat in parked roadsters. This was still the hip flask era. There were children and Boy Scouts. Vendors sold hot dogs and popcorn. It was like a Roman holiday. The crowd waited for the lights to flicker, but the electric chair is on a separate current. The lights outside do not flicker when someone dies at Sing Sing.

The most seasoned reporters were startled by the antics of this ghoulish crowd. Brick Terrett, a tall red-headed youth from Montana and one of the abler members of his profession, came out after it was over. He had seen Ruth die in the chair.

"Julia, for God's sake, take a walk with me," he said to Miss McCarthy. "Talk to me about anything. My God, she looked so little."

Another man who had come out with him from witnessing the same scene vomited on the spot.

Miss McCarthy was on the *Journal* for ten years—from 1918 to 1928. She was Margery Rex, a busy girl who did news, features, dramatic criticism and, in the beginning, illustrated her own work. She got liberal experience during the gaudy days of crime, gangsters, night clubs, visiting celebrities, cults and other manifestations of the boom era.

She comes from Chicago, where she studied at the Chicago Art Institute. In 1917, when she was a full-fledged commercial artist with a studio, she dined one night with a group of Chicago newspaper men who were going to war. They happened to remark on the striking appearance of a waitress in the place.

"Look at her hands, she must be somebody," said one of the men.

"She is," said Julia and told them her story.

She had noticed the distinguished looking man who came to the restaurant every night to take the girl home. The pair engaged her interest to such an extent that she followed them one night, learned who they were, where they lived, and something about their history.

"That rates a job on a paper," said one of the reporters. "If you would do that for fun, just think what you would do on a story."

He saw to it that she got a newspaper job. In this way she entered journalism. She had her baptism in a fiercely competitive field. She worked sixteen hours a day on a Chicago paper, covering children's court and domestic relations during the day, then chasing stories and pictures of war heroes from dinnertime until midnight. Many of the families lived in the foreign quarter of Chicago. Miss McCarthy soon gave up trying words and gestures to get what she wanted. She simply took the elegant crayon enlargements, frames and all, off the walls, and galloped for the car lines with enraged families in pursuit.

After a few months of this delirious handwork, she came to New York with a letter to Tom Dibble, city editor of the *Journal*, in which her Chicago city editor described her as the most industrious woman he had ever known. This was early in the summer of 1918. Mr. Dibble was on vacation. Miss McCarthy had her sketches under her arm. She insisted on seeing someone in authority and she talked herself into a job. At first she illustrated her stories. Then this became too strenuous because of the rush of getting her copy in on time. She used three by-lines—her own name, Margery Rex and Julia West, which appeared over her dramatic reviews.

One of her first assignments in New York took her to the Park Avenue apartment of a woman whose indiscretions had landed her on the front page. She talked freely and Miss McCarthy listened. Julia casually brought back to her office a handsome picture of the girl, frame and all. It had become a habit. And right away she learned that her early technique needed some modification. She was told to wrap it up at once and send it back by messenger. But as it was vanishing from view the desk man looked at it anxiously and exploded: "Wait till we copy it, for God's sake."

When the Liberty Loan drives were on Miss McCarthy did sketches of the Foreign Legion—dashing figures with bayonets gleaming. She tried to crash the Bankers Club when they were entertained there but was told, "No ladies allowed here."

"I'm not a lady," said Julia indignantly.

But the bankers insisted that she was. They wouldn't let her in.

Her sketches of Eddie Rickenbacker were syndicated over the country. She covered parades and harbor greetings, talked to war heroes and their wives. Then the post-war celebrities began to pour into New York—generals, royalty, psychoanalysts, authors, actors, seeresses and cranks.

She covered the Prince of Wales. She listened to Arthur Conan Doyle-Sherlock Holmes turned spiritualist. She sat in dark parlors with greasy mediums seeking for communication with the other world, and nearly jumped out of her skin when Dr. Walter Prince, the investigator of all such phenomena, had a book leap out at her from his library shelves—a little trick to disconcert and entertain the visitor.

She interviewed Isadora Duncan in a scarlet nightgown and Ibáñez when he was wearing a union suit. He cursed her freely in Spanish and closed the door in her face. James Stephens talked to her for hours and walked down the hotel lobby singing songs for her. He looked like a leprechaun—a small man with a big head and an eerie expression. He sent her a copy of his *Crock of Gold* with the song he had sung to her written in the flyleaf. She refused to give up an English first edition of *The Green Hat* to its author, Michael Arlen, who wanted it badly. Instead, she got him to autograph it for her.

Then one day she went to the Biltmore Hotel to see Sir Thomas Lipton, who was nearly always amiable to the press. But at the moment he was out of sorts and he refused to see reporters—until he caught Julia's name.

"McCarthy? Come right up, my lass," he said.

The old sod did it.

When Olivia Stone, a middle-aged nurse, killed Ellis Guy Kinkead in a Brooklyn street one summer day in 1921, Miss McCarthy was instantly assigned to the story. Olivia shot him down near his home, pumping bullets viciously into his body even after he was dead.

Edward G. Reilly, who was later to defend Hauptmann, put on a cunning and histrionic defense for Olivia and got her acquitted. She wore a flowing black veil and took the stand with a meek and injured air, fainting at strategic moments. She was tried in Brooklyn in the spring of 1922 and was acquitted on an April day. She tried to resume nursing but could not make a go of it.

Just before Christmas she telephoned to Miss McCarthy, whom she had come to know rather well during the trial.

"I'm wretched," she said. "I've got a bottle of poison with me and I'm going to drink it."

"Hold on a minute," said Julia urgently. "Wait for me. I'll be right up with a photographer."

Olivia was angry and only half succeeded. She took a little poison and regretted it next day. This was the golden age for murderesses. They all got off, except Mrs. Lillian S. Raizen, who was found guilty of second degree murder in the spring of 1923. Again Miss McCarthy covered every phase of the story, writing analytical pieces on the bride who shot Dr. Abraham Glickstein because his memory clouded her new life.

By this time the Stillman divorce was the leading story of the day. For two years it held the front pages, a scandal of unprecedented proportions in a divorce-addicted nation. Miss McCarthy wrote one piece after another on the spectacular Fifi Stillman. When the case was at its height and the revelations in the papers were searing, Julia asked her one day how she felt about it all.

"It's like standing in the middle of Fifth Avenue in one's nightgown," said Mrs. Stillman.

She was present when Mr. and Mrs. Stillman met at their daughter's wedding and exchanged civilities—their first encounter after the bitter exchanges of the suit and counter-suit. No one who followed the case would have believed that they could have borne to be under the same roof again. The meeting took place at Mondanne, their Pleasantville estate, when their daughter Anne became the wife of Henry P. Davison.

Miss McCarthy was standing beside Mrs. Stillman when Fifi's eye lighted on her husband.

"What are you going to do?" Julia asked.

"Watch and see," said Mrs. Stillman.

She walked gracefully across the hall toward her husband, a decorative figure wearing a tan velvet dress and a hat with an aigrette. She smiled up at him. "Won't you have a glass of champagne?" she asked.

The bitterness seemed washed away. He responded. Later that day he patted the blond head of little Guy, whose legitimacy he had impugned. The story made the front pages of papers all over the country. It was a case with an extraordinary number of twists— the Indian guide and Flo Leeds allegations, the secret hearings, the failure of both sides to prove their cases, the sudden and startling reconciliation, the second split and Mrs. Stillman's subsequent marriage to young Fowler McCormick.

When Miss McCarthy was assigned one Christmas to interview Daddy Browning, he was in the gift-giving frame of mind. It was his custom to ply reporters with expensive presents—a most unusual and unwelcome habit for the working press. On this occasion he thrust into Julia's arms a huge teddy bear of turquoise plush with a purple bow around its neck and a victrola in its inside. She didn't want it. She told him so. But he insisted on her taking it, so she said she would give it to some deserving child.

Julia did not know what to do with her teddy bear when she reached the street. Passersby stared. She ducked hastily into a taxi. All the way down to her office policemen peered into the cab at traffic stops to see what monster she had beside her on the seat.

"It's from Daddy Browning," she explained patiently.

Everyone seemed to understand.

In 1928 Miss McCarthy moved from the *Journal* to the *World*, where she did features for a year and a half. She turned out profiles of Al Smith, John J. Raskob, and other political figures. She investigated conditions at Auburn Prison and found abuses of various kinds. She did a clever piece of writing for the *Sunday World* on Frankie Yale's funeral. She talked to some of his companions and wrote her story in the argot of the underworld. Herbert Bayard Swope, of the red-gold curls and Roman Emperor profile, who always appreciated a story of zestful quality, sent her a characteristic note on this occasion. "Superb. Swope."

Chapter XVII

CATCHING THE WIRE

ON MARCH 7, 1932, BEFORE THE NAME BRUNO R. HAUPTMANN was known to any but the small circle of his friends, the Associated Press received a tip that Colonel Lindbergh's missing baby had been returned alive. The child's body was then lying in the woods but only the murderer knew it.

Lorena Hickok, A.P. star and a newspaper woman of the first rank, started up Sourland Mountain toward the Lindbergh home with Edward O'Haire, a camera man whose usual beat was the White House. She knew that nothing would satisfy her office but a personal report from the spot. The Lindbergh home was incommunicado at the time. All news was being handed out through Colonel Norman H. Schwartzkopf. The chances of getting an authenic report from the house were practically nil. Police barred the main entrance, but Miss Hickok had learned of a path through the woods at the other side of the house.

There had been a blizzard. It was a stormy night. The country was coated with ice. The wind whistled through the stripped trees. Miss Hickok wore her taxi driver's overshoes and kept tripping at every step. She and Eddie expected momentarily to be caught and thrown off the premises. It took them forty-five minutes to get to the edge of the clearing. Lorena's legs were slashed by the underbrush. O'Haire set up his camera and took a six-minute time exposure of the house. Then he slipped back into the woods, so that he could make a quick getaway if they were detected.

Miss Hickok went down on her hands and knees in the snow and crawled as close to the house as she dared. She saw that the family was still keeping vigil. There were no signs that the child was back. The ill-fated nursery was in darkness. The baby had then been missing for five days.

She crawled back and rejoined her companion. They got lost in the woods and wandered about for hours. They both took flu and it was weeks before Miss Hickok recovered her voice. However, as the story was a dud, she got little credit for her enterprise. Only results matter in the exacting newspaper world.

But this had little effect on a front-page girl like Lorena, who was used to coping with all sorts of emergencies, to exposing herself to hazards and rebuffs in the pursuit of news, to working at top speed under pressure. For the tempo of the newspaper reporter is magnified three times over in press service work. There is no let-up. Every minute is a deadline if the news is hot. The reporter working for one paper can relax when her last edition has gone, but the wire service girls go on and on. They file leads and new leads, lead alls, precede leads and bulletins until their heads jingle. They have complicated mechanical symbolism to master in addition to getting and writing their stories. They must be quick, clear-headed, ingenious and accurate. Their mistakes, when they make any, are repeated in scores of papers, thereby spreading the damage.

Miss Hickok achieved standing with the A.P. that no other woman has matched. And she did it on sheer capability. She covered straight politics, which is considered the most difficult and unsuitable work for newspaper women. She reported the Walker-Seabury hearings before the Governor. She traveled on campaign trains, often the only woman reporter with dozens of men. None of her competitors ever needed to give her a helping hand. She was much more likely to be first with the facts. She was hard-boiled and soft-hearted at the same time—a big girl in a casual raincoat with a wide tailored hat, translucent blue eyes and a mouth vivid with lipstick.

The path to stardom was one of adventure and grim work for Lorena. She was born in East Troy, Wisconsin, over a creamery. Her father was an itinerant butter maker who roved about, so that before she was thirteen she had moved fifteen times through Wisconsin, Illinois and South Dakota. Then her mother died and her father remarried. She went to work to take care of herself. One of her first jobs was as a slavey in a boarding house in Aberdeen, South Dakota, which was frequented by railroad men. The Milwaukee Railroad was then being built through to the Missouri River.

Until she was sixteen Lorena knocked about, working as a domestic, but she had no gift in this direction and was constantly getting fired. While she was in the employ of a saloonkeeper's wife in Bowdle, South Dakota, she decided she would try teaching in a country school. She passed the necessary examinations, but when her age was discovered, she was turned down. Too young, by a couple of years. Her employer, somewhat concerned about her, wrote to one of Lorena's cousins in Chicago. The result was that she was dragged from domestic service, dressed up in fine clothes and sent posthaste to Battle Creek, Michigan, to live with relatives and attend high school.

She did well until she was sent to a small denominational college in Wisconsin, but she was not happy there. Dr. M. L. Spencer, who later became president of the University of Washington, called her in. He had been a newspaper man. On his advice she returned to Battle Creek and got on the staff of the Battle Creek *Evening News*, then owned by C. W. Post, of cereal fame. This was in 1913. Her salary was $7 a week and she collected personals. She made the rounds of the shops and office buildings and soon learned that quantity rather than quality counted in the personals for a small paper.

An extra dollar a week lured her over to a rival paper, the Battle Creek *Journal*. Her publisher was an eccentric creature known as "Wild Bill" Thomson. In the winter of that year she first learned that some of the metropolitan papers had characters known as copy readers. So she sold "Wild Bill" the idea and became the *Journal's* first copy reader, at $10 a week. Every afternoon the rest of the staff went to the composing room, got hold of the proofreader's hooks, saw what she had done with their copy and promptly raised hell.

Then came the World War. Inspired by Karl Von Wiegand's stories, which ran in her paper, Miss Hickok decided that she wanted to be a war correspondent. She thought that perhaps if she tried college again she might achieve her aim. So she went to Lawrence College, in Appleton, Wisconsin, where Edna Ferber had worked, as a reporter, meanwhile getting a job as correspondent for the Milwaukee *Sentinel*.

She soon abandoned the academic life and worked regularly for the *Sentinel* at $15 a week. She read Miss Ferber's newspaper story of Milwaukee, *Dawn O'Hara*, got the habit of drinking chocolate in a fine old German coffee house and steadily put on weight. By this time she had learned a good deal about newspaper work. She was society and woman's editor. Her paper carried the work of Sophie Irene Loeb, Nixola Greeley-Smith and Marguerite Mooers Marshall. Lorena read them and thought how dazzling it would be to work in New York. Dreams sometimes come true.

After her own work was finished she hung about the shop in the evening, hoping to get news stories to cover. One night she was told that Geraldine Farrar was coming to town and that she might interview her. For days she brooded happily over this great opportunity.

Miss Farrar arrived late one November afternoon. It was cold and rainy. Lorena was wearing a hat with a feather, which disintegrated shockingly in the rain and smelled of glue. She found the singer's private car in the railroad yards close to Lake Michigan. Miss

Farrar refused to see her and her Boston bull terrier chewed most of the fur off Lorena's best suit. Finally she went back to the office, cold, wet and angry, and wrote what she thought was a stinger on haughty prima donnas. Next day it appeared under her first by-line. It was a witty story and brought her commendation. It got her out of the woman's department.

Miss Farrar's manager came round with an autographed photograph of the star. He said she would be glad to see Miss Hickok if she would go back stage between numbers at her concert. But Lorena retorted that she was too busy to interview Miss Farrar. Years later she met her in New York when the singer first went on the air, but she did not mention the incident. It was not Miss Farrar's practice to be rude to the press. She was usually one of the more amiable subjects for interviews.

By-lines now became a matter of course in Miss Hickok's life. She did general assignments and features. In the late summer of 1916 she got itching feet and decided to try Chicago. Every week, on her day off, she badgered Chicago editors and finally concentrated on Teddy Beck, of the Chicago *Tribune*, but without success. She gave up at last, press-agented a Belgian actress, and landed in Minneapolis on her birthday, March 7, 1917, completely broke. In less than a week she had a job on the *Tribune* at $20 a week. Most of the men had gone to war. She became an experienced and trusted member of the staff, but she had heard of the Battalion of Death and she wanted badly to go to war.

On January 1, 1918, she started off for New York. Her real objective was Russia. She was caught in Chicago in the worst blizzard in years. She was too short of funds to go to a hotel. So she spent three days and three nights in the old Michigan Central station, on the Lake Front. She reached New York in a daze and sought the inhospitable benches of Park Row. However, Garet Garrett, then managing editor of the *Tribune*, gave her a chance. He was one of the few New York newspaper executives who have really believed in having women on the staff, and he offered them generous opportunities. But Miss Hickok was bewildered, shy and worn-out by her hard experiences. New York appalled her. In six weeks she was let out and she felt as if the sky had fallen.

Russia seemed far away. She tried to be a yeomanette. She went after all sorts of jobs, from trolley car conductor to acting as secretary to Chapin, of the *World*. Finally she got work with the Commission on Training Camp Activities. When she was assigned to do a moral survey of all the parks of Greater New York, she decided to return to the Minneapolis *Tribune*. She started in on the night side at $25 a week and just missed being appointed night city editor, because the publisher did not think that the post should go to a woman. That year large tracts of northern Minnesota were burned up in forest fires. She did brilliant rewrite on this succession of stories. Her keenest disappointment came the night that the fire swept down to Duluth. A staff man was sent out to cover the story. Her editors would not send Lorena, good as she was, because she was a woman. There was black murder in her heart.

Later she learned that the reporter who got the assignment had to climb a pole and tap a telephone wire to get his story out. Could she have done it? At least at the time she thought she could. She rewrote the story, but she wanted the greater excitement of being on the spot. She has never cared for desk work.

In the autumn of 1918 she went to the University of Minnesota, starting all over again as a freshman. Her rhetoric instructor called her up after class one day and said, "You write well. I thought you might be interested in knowing that the *Tribune* wants to get some campus reporters on space."

This made Miss Hickok laugh. At the time she was writing half of the front page of the *Tribune* every day. She had an 8 A.M. class five mornings a week, finished at the university at 1 P.M., slept all afternoon, went to the office at 7 P.M. and, if it was a quiet night, managed to do some studying between midnight and 3 A.M.

In the early summer, when the university closed, she was appointed Sunday editor of her paper. And that ended her uncontrollable habit of going after higher education. She did not really care for her new desk job but she learned how to make up a paper. After a year of it, Thomas J. Dillon, managing editor of the *Tribune*, took her out of the Sunday department, gave her a by-line and made her his number one reporter. For the next six years Miss Hickok did consistently good work and got a heavy play. Her story on the passage of the Harding funeral train through Honey Creek was included in a collection of the best news stories of 1923.

She found Tom Dillon a sympathetic editor and a good newspaper man in every way. She was treated exactly like a man, which is what every newspaper woman hankers for when she joins a city staff. She covered straight politics and wrote football for four years, touring the Big Ten conference with the Minnesota team. These were the days of Red Grange, Knute Rockne and Benny Friedman. Miss Hickok picked up a fine line of slang and a sound knowledge of how to work with large groups of men reporters. The legend was that she smoked a pipe in the city room. One summer Mr. Dillon gave her a chance to write editorials for the paper. It was during this period that she developed into the fine reporter she now is.

In the late autumn of 1926 she was ill and went to California for her health. A year later she returned to New York and landed on the *Mirror*. She was the last reporter hired by Phil Payne before he started off on his fatal flight in Old Glory. She stayed on the paper for a year, then went to the Associated Press, where she was the first woman to be trusted with straight news leads on big stories. She could tackle anything and she wrote with color, finish, a keen news sense and good judgment.

She grew familiar with the Tammany spectacle before the frost set in. She watched girls in white strewing roses, provided by a Greek florist, in Jimmy Walker's path when he returned from the Seabury hearing in Albany to the strains of a band playing "Happy Days Are Here Again." She was a spectator at John R. Voorhees' funeral. The 102-year-old Grand Sachem was almost forgotten that day in the fuss over Al Smith and Franklin D. Roosevelt, because Mr. Smith had announced the day before that he would accept the nomination in Chicago if it were offered to him.

Miss Hickok did outstanding work on the *Vestris* disaster. Her by-line appeared on page one of the New York *Times*, which rarely happens to the local press service reporter, man or woman. When Starr Faithfull, lovely and wild, was found drowned on the sands of Long Beach, she was one of the first reporters on the job. She covered every twist of the investigation, sprayed the secrets of Starr's fantastic and tortured life to the press all over the country, and finally let it rest, another unsolved mystery.

In Martin A. White, then of the A.P., now head of Universal Service, she found a rare and understanding editor. He never hesitated to give her the best story that came along. Like Tom Dillon, he was her preceptor and friend. He first impressed her because he was the one newspaper executive in New York who offered her a chair when she went in to ask for a job.

After the Roosevelts entered the White House Miss Hickok was put in an embarrassing position at her office because of her friendship with the President's wife. She was disinclined to use this link to get news. She had first met Mrs. Roosevelt in 1928, while she was covering Democratic National Headquarters. This was another occasion when she was doing a man's work, to the horror of John J. Raskob, who looked alarmed the first time he saw a woman stamping into one of his press conferences.

She had also had contact with Mrs. Roosevelt off and on while her husband was Governor. Miss Hickok thought her excellent copy and suggested that she should be closely watched during the Presidential campaign. The result was that she was the one reporter assigned to cover her regularly. She and Mrs. Roosevelt were thrown together on train trips and became good friends.

The assumption was that Miss Hickok could have ready access to the President's wife on news. As time went on this became a problem. She resigned late in June but stayed on longer than she intended, in order to finish reporting the trial of Charles E. Mitchell, a story so complicated that it needed a special background in Mitchell finances.

Since the summer of 1933 Miss Hickok has been confidential observer for Harry L. Hopkins, Federal Relief Administrator, traveling over the country and making exhaustive reports. Occasionally she travels with Mrs. Roosevelt. She accompanied her on her air trip to Puerto Rico, in her capacity of relief investigator.

Miss Hickok was followed on the A.P. by Mary Elizabeth Plummer, who walked in one summer day and got an excellent job after three years on the *Courier-Journal* in Louisville, Kentucky. When Lincoln Steffens, on a lecture tour, read a piece she did about Blackstone, the magician, he wrote from Nashville: "If I were still with a New York magazine I would wire the editor that I had found one."

However, Miss Plummer found her own way to New York and since then her name has appeared with increasing frequency throughout the country on A.P. stories. She worked on Hauptmann's trial and managed to crash the guard that the *Journal* had set up around Mrs. Hauptmann. The wretched woman let her in one cold night toward the end of the trial, talked to her for an hour in German, showed her a bureau drawer full of letters that she had received, and told her something of the misery she was enduring in the court room at Flemington.

Miss Plummer was the first person to identify the Rev. Vincent G. Burns, the pastor who disturbed the trial by shouting from a windowsill. She also recognized Ford Madox Ford in the crowd swarming around the doors and got him to write a signed article for her press service. She covered John Jacob Astor's somewhat sensational wedding at Newport and was with James J. Braddock's family in New Jersey while they listened to the broadcast the night he won the world title.

Miss Plummer comes from Bedford, Indiana, a stone mill town with a population of 15,000. After leaving college she became Indiana's first girl sports columnist, writing for the local paper. At the same time she taught English in a junior high school and often got up at 5 A.M. to do her column, while the milk wagons rattled along and the early shift passed on their way to the mills.

After three years of this, she tried Chicago, but failed to land a newspaper job, so she worked in a settlement house until an offer reached her from the *Courier-Journal* that sent her speeding south.

There she had a whirl at everything—straight reporting, feature writing, editing special sections, doing book reviews, society and rewrite. She worked until nearly midnight every night while the dance bands played.

Since moving to New York Miss Plummer has married Davidson Taylor, of the Columbia Broadcasting System, whom she met in Louisville, Kentucky, when he was radio editor of the *Courier-Journal*.

Another of the younger press service girls who has soared to the top is Dorothy Ducas, star woman graduate of the Columbia School of Journalism. She has worked for the *Herald Tribune*, the *Post*, *McCall's* and I.N.S.

Miss Ducas was in a theater with her husband, James Herzog, on the afternoon that the Lindbergh baby was found dead in the woods. Between the acts she saw an afternoon paper with the ultimate in banner lines. She dashed out of the theater and called her office.

"Where on earth have you been?" she was asked. "We've been looking for you everywhere. Hop the train at once for Hopewell."

Going down in the train Miss Ducas began to think about Mrs. Lindbergh. She had a little boy herself, almost the same age. He had been ill and had caused her much anxiety. Without waiting to get to Hopewell, she took out her pencil and copy paper and began to write. "The story is ended so far as Anne Lindbergh is concerned," she began. Every line of the story was personalized. It was one of the few sob stories Miss Ducas has written, since she prides herself on being a straight news reporter, but the occasion seemed to warrant it. Coming from the heart, it had a moving quality and was a good piece of work. She had covered the news lead on the Lindbergh wedding three years earlier—a three-column head leading the *Evening Post*. She had worked on the kidnapping during the anxious days of the quest.

When Dr. Elisha Kent Kane, professor of Romance languages at the University of Tennessee, was charged with drowning his wife in Chesapeake Bay in 1931, Miss Ducas was sent to cover the trial. She made efforts to see Dr. Kane, but his lawyer assured her that the professor would have nothing to say for publication. His defense was that his wife, subject to heart attacks, had died of heart failure while swimming. Miss Ducas walked across the street to a restaurant for a meal. Almost at once she spotted Dr. Kane at a table. He was an unmistakable figure, extremely tall, with a beak-like nose, receding gray hair and burning eyes. Although charged with murder, he was free on his own recognizance. Miss Ducas sauntered over to where he sat.

"Please don't think me forward," she said, "but I have come from

New York ahead of the other reporters in order to get an interview with you."

"Sit down and have some lunch," said the professor amiably.

He talked freely and she was able to file an interview. The professor was acquitted, but during the days of the trial he paced his hotel room like a madman all night long. Miss Ducas had the next room. It got on her nerves to such a degree that she moved to another room. On this case she wrote the straight news lead and the features, too, which is a stiff grind for a news service. It involves filing thousands of words of running copy all day long, then doing a picturesque piece on the side. Miss Ducas has done this repeatedly for I.N.S. It is the real test of the news service girl. But the feature, not the news lead, carries the by-line, although the other is often the more exacting job.

When young Edward H. B. Allen shot Francis A. Donaldson in Overbrook, Pennsylvania, in 1931 to avenge his sister, Miss Ducas again was rushed out to cover a story that had unusual elements. Local feeling was high. The families were well known. It was the sort of tragedy that might have occurred in any middle-class home.

She had a four-minute beat on the verdict, which was acquittal for young Allen. The scramble over a murder verdict is always intense. A half-minute is a substantial beat on a news service. Four minutes is a sensation. Miss Ducas arranged with someone to stand at the exit, catch her signal and get out before the court-room door was shut. Her collaborator rushed to the wire room, handed the flash to Visconti, veteran Western Union man who has handled all the big news round-ups of recent years, and scored a clean beat. This makes little difference to the public, but it is closely watched by the craft. The most elaborate arrangements were made to catch the Hauptmann verdict—blind raising, signals across the room, and other abracadabra, but the result was a disastrous mix-up that led the A.P. to flash the wrong verdict over the country.

When the unexpected bulletin that Calvin Coolidge was dead hit the I.N.S. offices, thirteen large teletypes all stopped simultaneously. Verdicts are expected; but this was a bolt from the blue and a story of prime importance in any newspaper office.

Miss Ducas was sent to Northampton to write about the funeral. She mopped up color and anecdotes from friends of the family. She went with the cortège to Plymouth and saw the ex-President laid to rest in the driving rain. Spectators lined the roadside. The country was grim and gray, coated with ice. It was much like the dreary day on which Woodrow Wilson was buried.

Miss Ducas got her newspaper experience early and fast. She moved quickly from one point to another. She won the Pulitzer traveling scholarship when she was twenty years of age. Her family wanted her to go in for advertising but she was determined that nothing should stop her from being a newspaper star. She fastened her attention on the *Herald Tribune*. She wanted to be the Columbia correspondent, knowing that this was an entering wedge.

Dwight S. Perrin, now with the St. Louis *Post-Dispatch*, was city editor at the time. Mr. Perrin was a fair-minded and able city editor but he thought that any city staff could get along without a woman, an undeniable fact. Miss Ducas knew she would have to get in on wings to sell herself to the city desk of the *Herald Tribune*. She bombarded Mr. Perrin with requests for a job.

"But supposing there was a fire in one of the dormitory buildings— what good would you be?" Mr. Perrin asked her on one occasion.

"Well, supposing there was a fire in Barnard, what good would a man be?" Miss Ducas countered.

"Why don't you work on your home town paper?" Mr. Perrin demanded.

"This is my home town," said Miss Ducas stoutly.

"Well, go out and adopt one."

So she went to Hackensack and worked for a summer on the Bergen *Evening Record*. She was then taken on as Columbia correspondent for the *Herald Tribune*. She was married secretly five days before she went abroad on her traveling scholarship. She worked on the *Express* in London and sent back features by mail to the *Herald Tribune*. When she came back in March, 1927, she got the coveted staff job.

When she went out on her first three-alarm fire and tried to get through the fire lines, a policeman pushed her back.

"But I've got to get through," said Miss Ducas. "I'm a reporter."

"Oh, go on," he said, "they don't send women to cover fires."

"Oh, yes, they do and she belongs in here," said Whitney Bolton, a colleague whose wife, Frances Schiff, is another graduate of the School of Journalism who did capable work on the *Herald Tribune* before her marriage.

Miss Ducas soon distinguished herself on the *Post*, to which she moved in October, 1927. She was almost the first reporter to rush the field and get under the Graf Zeppelin when it ended its historic round-the-world flight at Lakehurst. She was shouting up at Lady Drummond Hay before the huge dirigible had settled into place. This was another of the confused mob scenes where the press went slightly haywire.

She covered Ishbel Macdonald when she came to the United States with her father on his official visit. She went to Canada with her, watched her getting her first impression of Niagara Falls, and persuaded Miss Macdonald to write three signed pieces for the *Post*.

During the three years that Miss Ducas spent on the paper, Vincent G. Byers, her city editor, thought up a number of original stunts for her. One day she was hoisted to the top of a pole in Madison Square Garden to talk to Flag Pole Kelly. She wore trousers, scaled the rafters and was suspended in the air while she got his views on mundane matters. Again she was sent out with Richard Montague, who carried his coat on his arm, to see how many of the smart restaurants in town they could crash, in spite of the informal touch. This was one of the summer sillies that editors think up for the dog days. They were turned down flat at two out of six places but went nonchalantly on their way.

She got to know Dr. John Roach Straton by falling head first into the lake at his doorstep when she was assigned to cover him at Greenwood Lake, New York, while he was having his widely publicized dispute with Al Smith. She was fished out of the lake and was taken in to the Straton fireside to dry. Mrs. Straton kept her for dinner and from that time on Miss Ducas got a number of exclusive stories from the fire-and-damnation Baptist divine. It was she who first launched the story of his challenge to Al to stage a debate with him, if they could get St. Patrick's Cathedral for the purpose. She followed up his faith healing meetings and covered Uldine Utley, the child evangelist who flapped her angel wings for a time in Calvary Church. Dr. Straton sometimes shook his head over Miss Ducas's worldly approach to the doings at his church. She found him a fanatic of terrible sincerity.

A profile of Ishbel Macdonald, which she did for *McCall's*, led Otto Wiese to offer her a post as associate editor. She deserted newspaper work for a short time but returned to it in 1931, joining the staff of I.N.S. Exciting assignments came thick and fast. She moved from one trial to another and began to take in wide territory, as the press service girl does. She and Margaret Lane went to Chicago for the political conventions of 1932. Miss Lane was an English girl who tried her hand at American journalism for I.N.S. and made a success of it. She did interviews and special features, which were heavily played by her service. During the Kentucky strikes of 1931 she went South and registered at a hotel as Mrs. Campbell. Reporters were being run out of town at gun-point, but Miss Lane, carrying a tiny pocket camera, was able to move about freely, take pictures and write readable copy. She is back in England now, is married, and writes for the *Daily Mail*. Her first novel, *Faith, Hope, No Charity*, was a great success in England.

The Hearst wire services have been fortunate in the capable newspaper girls they have picked. Corinne Rich and Winifred Van Duzer did excellent work for them in the twenties. Miss Rich, who was married to William Haggard, then on the *World*, died some time after giving up her newspaper work. Miss Van Duzer turned to newspaper serials and fiction writing. None was more spectacular than Mildred Morris, red-haired, erratic star of I.N.S., who started on the old *Republican* in Denver, moved East and soon made a name for herself as she pulled off one scoop after another, including an interview with John D. Rockefeller. She was generous, brilliant, indifferent to money and her own interests, but gifted and alert in her profession.

Dorothy Roe is now the leading woman star with Universal Service, a poised dark girl of real capability, usually on hand for the big stories of the day. Miss Roe is another of the School of Journalism girls to achieve standing in her profession. She was one of Dean Walter Williams' students at the University of Missouri, her native state. She got her first job on the *Daily News* of El Dorado, Arkansas.

Her parents had settled there at the time of the oil boom, and when she arrived the town had all the characteristics of the Klondike. There was a murder in front of the principal hotel practically every day. There were dope rings and "barrel houses," as the dance halls in the oil field were known, all of which she proceeded to expose for her paper with enthusiasm. She did practically everything, from police reporting to a Sunday shopping page. She handled make-up, ad-writing, selling and lay-outs on the side, and wrote a daily column, illustrated with chalk-plate cuts which she also made for good measure.

She worked for a time on the Los Angeles *Examiner*, then on the *Herald Examiner* in Chicago, and finally landed in New York with a comic strip which was sold several times but never released. She did Sunday features for the *World* during its last days, worked on the Brooklyn *Times*, and did a Wall Street column for the *Daily Investment News* before landing a job with Universal Service, where she now writes a little of everything.

In addition to doing general news, features and rewrite, she has turned out a daily fashion column for the last four years. Sometimes it has been difficult to keep it going, as for instance during the death watch for Thomas A. Edison, when she was on guard night and day in the Edison garage, waiting for his life to flicker out, and at the same time had to produce fashion notes. The same situation confronted her at Flemington, where she filed daily news features on the Hauptmann case and in addition had to dash off flim-flam about the clothes worn by the women who swarmed into the court house.

Miss Roe has traveled about on assignments and has had many adventures. Once, when she was at home in Arkansas for her Christmas vacation, she got a wire from her office to leave immediately for Springfield, Missouri, where a gang, led by "Pretty Boy" Floyd, had killed the sheriff and five of his deputies.

The last train had left El Dorado for the night when the message arrived. There would not be another until the next afternoon. So she set out with her father in a car, leaving half an hour after the train. They made a mad dash and overtook it, motion picture fashion, at a junction ninety miles away. Miss Roe got aboard and covered the story. The newspaper woman usually gets there, if she has a fast car and half a chance.

Chapter XVIII

THE EARTH ROCKS

EVELYN SEELEY WAS DRIVING INTO LOS ANGELES ON A MARCH night in 1933 when her car began to wabble as she came to a halt at a traffic stop on Sunset Boulevard. She was returning from Pasadena where she had been interviewing Dr. Albert Einstein.

Models in spring costumes did grotesque gyrations and tumbled to the floor in shop windows. Oranges rolled madly from fruit stands. She drove on to the office of the *Illustrated Daily News* where she was going to write her Einstein story for the New York *World-Telegram*. But first she sent a wire to New York: "There seems to be an earthquake. Do you want a story?"

As she sat at her typewriter there was another temblor, this time a light one. The building swayed. The floor rocked beneath her feet. She felt slightly dizzy. There was a menacing rumble. The lights blinked and dimmed. The rewrite men sat tight at their desks, ready for anything.

"Five hundred to one thousand dead in Long Beach," came the first report over the wire.

Miss Seeley decided to set out for Long Beach.

The earthquake had made dizzy inroads on the countryside. A grocery store was flattened out beside a roadside mission that stood intact. Small fires burned through the fog. Miss Seeley got past the lines and saw what looked like a caricature of Long Beach. Houses gaped, the front façades ripped off. Bricks and débris lay scattered in the streets. Distracted residents ran about, looking for friends and relatives.

She went to American Legion Hall, where the dead were taken. She counted the still figures under gunny sack. The total death list was less than the first report—5,000 injured, 116 dead—but at the moment it seemed like thousands more. Rheba Crawford Splivaloo, the Angel of Broadway, was directing relief. Ambulances clanged back and forth. Shivering residents lined up for coffee, still shocked by the upheaval. Miss Seeley stayed at the scene all night, gathering graphic copy for I.N.S. and the *World-Telegram*. In the morning she rode home through the dense fog, emerging from a grim disjointed world to the sunshine and bustle of Los Angeles.

Again she was on the spot for the general strike in San Francisco in July, 1934. Her husband, Kenneth Stewart, was an instructor at Leland Stanford University at the time. At the first hint of excitement Miss Seeley was out in the thick of things. She saw the pedestrians trudging in two lines along Market Street, bound for work; she watched roller skates and bicycles blossoming all over town. Her vivid first-hand stories were flashed to the *World-Telegram*.

Miss Seeley is a reporter with the knack of being on the spot when news breaks dramatically. By chance she was in Santiago when the Chilean government was overthrown in 1930. She saw the crowd gather, watched the mounted soldiers charge with their lances. One of them missed her by a hair's breadth. Isaac Marcosson and his wife were in a doorway nearby at the time.

Miss Seeley is equally at home in newspaper work in San Francisco, where she started, or in New York, where she now makes her home. She was born in Illinois, went to school in Montana, attended the Montana State College of Agriculture and Mechanical Arts, and landed in San Francisco one Good Friday bent on getting a newspaper job. She went to see the editor of the San Francisco *News*. She had done some secretarial work in college but otherwise had no training for journalism.

"Have you a clean mirror in the back of your mind so that you can reflect news honestly?" he asked her.

"Yes."

"How old are you?"

"Twenty-one."

He told her that it was important for a reporter to be without prejudices and that it was good to have the emotional imagination to feel, and yet to write with detachment. The *News* seemed like a madhouse to the shy girl who got occasional assignments from the city desk. Milly Bennett Mitchell, who had started reporting at an absurdly early age and who thought nothing of kicking up her heels and roaring at the city editor, gave her some advice. "What you have to do is hang around," she told the bewildered novice.

The hanging around was painful. Evelyn did neighborhood features and at last was taken regularly on the staff, chiefly because she knew stenography, and Fred V. Williams, the star feature writer, liked to dictate his stories over the telephone.

Her city editor was the old-fashioned sort who snorted and roared at the staff.

"What do you mean by this, Seeley?" he would yell. "Do you call this a story?"

He badgered her until she wept. Then he sat down and wrote the story himself. After this it took her years to get over her dread of city editors.

As she moved around and saw the variability of the social system, Miss Seeley developed a strong social conscience. She went to live in the Cuneo flats which the family of Amadeo Peter Giannini's wife had built for the fishermen. Hordes of Sicilians occupied them. They were shocking fire traps. Miss Seeley posed as a factory girl, borrowed a mackinaw from her father, found a room for $7 a month and had some furniture moved in. An office boy went along with her for protection. He posed as her husband.

She did a graphic exposé of conditions at the flats. The club women were stirred up and a few bathtubs and other comforts were installed under pressure. But coal was soon to be found in the tubs. It was the usual flash in the pan of municipal activity that follows a newspaper crusade, before things settle back into their habitual state of indifference.

Miss Seeley soon set out to see the country. She worked in Santa Fe for the New Mexico *State Tribune* and was at Albuquerque when the evidence against Albert B. Fall was being dug up. She went on to the El Paso *Times*, where she learned about mining and heard rumors of revolution. She returned to California and sailed for New York. But she left the ship at Havana and worked on the *Telegram* there. She learned to paste up cables, write heads and edit copy.

Miss Seeley arrived in New York in 1925, went the rounds of the newspaper offices, heard the usual story of full staffs, with no place for a woman. She went to work in Alfred A. Knopf's office, then moved north to Montreal and landed a job on the *Herald*. She was on the spot when Mrs. James A. Stillman started a commotion at her son's wedding in the summer of 1927 by throwing china at the photographers. Miss Seeley and Morris Tracy, of the United Press, landed in La Tuque while all their competitors were miles away at Grand Anse, lulled by a message from the Stillman home that there was no use going to the scene until the wedding day, as news would not be forthcoming. But Miss Seeley and Mr. Tracy talked to the mother of Lena Viola Wilson, Bud Stillman's bride-to-be, and then drove to the Stillman home. The result was thousands of words of advance copy on the wedding. They telephoned to their rivals and gave them what they could, but it was practically a clean sweep.

Next day, when the marriage service was over and the bride had sunk a silver knife into a four-foot wedding cake, Mrs. Stillman boxed the ears of a motion picture cameraman when she saw him grinding out a picture on the lawn.

"Out you go, get out of here," she exclaimed.

Seven other cameramen went on with their work. Mrs. Stillman pushed one over, then picked up a plate and hurled it at the remaining offenders. It landed on a pile of small punch glasses with crashing effect. The photographers ducked, but Mrs. Stillman pursued them, slinging plates with the skill of a discus thrower. One broke a window. Another landed on the head of a Fox News man.

It was not according to Emily Post but it made good front-page reading next day. The pipe band, the smart guests from New York, the *habitants* in their Sunday best, even the bride and groom became secondary in interest to Mrs. Stillman's plate-throwing orgy. Miss Seeley did full justice to the story.

By 1929 she was working for the *Telegram*. Her first task was to interview Frances Perkins. Soon her underscored and revealing interviews became a regular feature of the paper. She avoided the trite, tossed overboard all the stock bromides of the newspaper interviewer, and got her effects by economy of expression and the restrained use of detail. In the mob interviews of the day, she made it a point to peg away at her subjects until they had worn out their publicity chatter and were ready to give her something spontaneous and revealing. The result was quite effective.

One of the most difficult subjects the New York newspaper girls ever had to handle was Marion Talley, from the time the child wonder first brought the mounted police galloping to subdue the crowds that swarmed around the Metropolitan on her opening night until she decided to retire to the farm.

When she announced her withdrawal from opera she received the press to the extent of letting them into her drawing-room but there the rapport ended. All she would say was yes, no, or perhaps. She refused to let herself go. By degrees the newspaper girls grew annoyed. They began to batter her with senseless questions.

"Do you like cows, Miss Talley?" said the bronze-haired Miss Seeley gently.

Miss Talley looked blank.

"Do you like chickens?" said another.

Miss Talley looked frosty.

"Do you like horses?"

Miss Talley turned her head away.

"Do you like PIGS?" shouted an annoyed flapper, for it was still the flapper age.

Miss Talley's nostrils flickered. She weighed her words, then sprang a surprise. "No," she responded at last. "They smell."

Everyone sighed with relief. At last an expression of opinion. Her canary kept trilling.

"Well, *he* won't stop singing," said Miss Seeley.

"But I'm not like that," said Miss Talley complacently.

Miss Seeley wrote about Lindbergh's welcome home, Ella Wendel's death, the annual Easter parade—scores of the town's events. She interviewed actors, authors, scientists, cranks, cultists and visiting royalties. She found Dr. Einstein wandering about in his garden, not sure whether it was yesterday or to-day. She met Amelia Earhart down the Bay, and drove through Long Island in an open car, sirens screeching, while she took a bow in the wake of Charles Kingsford-Smith. She was with Christie R. Bohnsack, the rubicund stage master of the best parades and the friend of the press. The renowned city welcomes of the twenties were all in Mr. Bohnsack's capable hands.

On the Sunday before the Lindbergh baby was kidnapped, a group of newspaper people were gathered at the Seeley-Stewart home, when someone launched the favorite newspaper question: "What would be the biggest news story that could break?"

"If a dirigible should hit the Empire State Building and explode," said one.

"If someone should kidnap the Lindbergh baby," said another.

Everyone scoffed. Impossible. That never could happen.

But news is frequently more terrible than the mature mind, disciplined to restraint, can credit.

Three nights later George F. Lyon, then city editor of the *World-Telegram* and now managing editor of the Buffalo *Times*, called Miss Seeley at 1.30 A.M.

"Have you any money?" he asked.

"No," she said. "But I can get some."

"Well, hurry up and come down here as soon as you can. The Lindbergh baby has been kidnapped."

Miss Seeley hung up the receiver, incredulous. She called her husband who was then working on the copy desk of the *Herald Tribune*.

"George must be dreaming," she said.

"He isn't," said Mr. Stewart. "It's true."

Miss Seeley hurried to Hopewell, where she found the press assembling from all points. Reporters are usually impersonal about their work, but this was a story that penetrated the thickest skin, as clues were followed, hopes were raised, then dashed, over a period of four months, until the quest ended abruptly when the baby's dead body was found in the woods.

Miss Seeley now free-lances. Her husband is on the editorial staff of the *Literary Digest*. Both are active workers in the Newspaper Guild—a well-known and popular newspaper couple.

Another Californian starred in the *World-Telegram* is Geraldine

Sartain, a capable member of the profession who has turned out copy in all parts of the world. She attended the University of California, took a six weeks' summer course in journalism, and then began to batter at the doors of the *Chronicle*. A fatherly city editor pointed out all the traditional pitfalls supposed to strew the girl reporter's path—long hours, bad food, drunkenness, a flighty approach to life, indigestion, misanthropy. But Miss Sartain laughed them off and was back again when the conservative city editor moved on to the Sunday department and a successor was appointed.

To show her good-will she worked for three months for nothing, earning her living by day, writing for the *Chronicle* from five o'clock until midnight. Then she landed on the staff at $30 a week and was sent out to cover a Rotary luncheon. Her first by-line appeared on an interview with Mrs. Worthington Hubbard, wife of a San Francisco lawyer, and the woman who hung the first Fatty Arbuckle jury when the comedian was tried for the death of Virginia Rappe, the actress. Mrs. Hubbard was a personal friend of Miss Sartain's and she gave her the inside story of the way in which a local politician had attempted to coerce, intimidate and bribe her.

Miss Sartain did courts, crime and anything that came along in the months that followed. She wrote about the '49 celebration in Sacramento and was one of the six *Chronicle* reporters who worked under Marjorie Driscoll in a suite in the Palace Hotel adjoining the room where President Harding lay dying. This was one of the more spectacular stories in Californian history, and a harassing assignment for the press, because of the mysterious rumors that spread over the country like wildfire when the President died.

In the autumn of 1924 Miss Sartain went to Honolulu as the business partner of George Nellist, a newspaper colleague. Together they turned out a history of the Hawaiian Isles backed by the *Star-Bulletin*. When this task was finished Miss Sartain joined the staff of the paper, covered police and City Hall and sopped up sunshine.

The City Hall beat in Honolulu was an uproarious one. The administration was in a frenzy all year. The Democratic mayor and his supervisors were at loggerheads with the Republican appointees. Impeachment proceedings were brought against the mayor, and he in turn tried to have his political enemies removed from office. This meant that the police had to attend the board of supervisors' meetings to prevent bloodshed. Miss Sartain frequently had to duck chairs and fists. But there was little crime in the islands at the time. The police moved at the leisurely gait indicated by Charlie Chan. There was the usual amount of minor graft and now and again the papers grew indignant over some civic abuse.

But on the whole the reportorial round in Honolulu was singularly pleasant. By comparison with the metropolitan whirl, it was a lotos-eaters' paradise. Flowers bloomed at all seasons. The sky was ceaselessly blue. There were no chilly mornings down the bay or snowdrifts in Jersey. Miss Sartain and her colleague, Louise Johansen, went to work in the morning in summer dresses and hats, and kept Japanese oil-paper parasols in their desks for the gay afternoon showers known as liquid sunshine.

The competition was not keen. They started work at 7.30 in the morning; finished at 3 P.M. Then they went home and slept until five, when they emerged for drinks and a swim at Waikiki. After that they were ready for dinner, dancing and the moonlit tropical night. Miss Sartain toured all the large islands—Oahu, Hawaii, Maui, Kauai and Molokai—with an official mission and at last regretfully cast her ginger blossom and frangipanni leis into the iridescent waters off Diamond Head while the Royal Hawaiian Band played "Aloha Oe."

That phase of her newspaper career was ended. She landed in Shanghai on Easter Sunday, 1926. Next morning she went job-hunting. On the second day Charles Laval, known from Colombo to Yokohama, took her on his staff. He was the editor of the Shanghai *China Press*, which was owned by the Sopher brothers, two Bagdad Jews who had been educated at the University of Bombay. It was published primarily for the American colony in Shanghai.

By a coincidence, when she was a cub in Shanghai, her eyes fixed longingly on the Orient, Miss Sartain had written to Mr. Laval asking about prospects. He had advised her to get more experience in America before tackling China. She saved his letter. When she called to see him in Shanghai she sent it in with the pencilled notation: "I did what you said. Now here I am. What are you going to do about it?"

Mr. Laval did the obvious thing and gave her the job she wanted. The first person she heard about on the paper was Elsie McCormick, who had worked there, married and then sailed away. Time and again their paths crossed, but it was not until they both landed on the New York *World* that they met and discovered how often they had been within range of each other at the outposts of the earth.

Miss Sartain soon found that the newspaper conventions in Shanghai give the reporter plenty of time to herself. After being hired— a somewhat formal matter—she went home and waited for four days until her "contract" arrived, the usual custom. She signed and returned it and then started work the following week.

The *China Press* office was small, friendly and cluttered. The city editor was Anthony Hope, also a Jew from the University of

Bombay. He always stood up when a girl reporter approached him —an appalling gesture for a hardened lady of the press. There never was any hurry about the news. Today, tomorrow, it didn't matter. When he handed out an assignment he would apologize. "I know you're very busy, and I don't like to ask you to do this, but if you have time, will you go to this place today? But if you haven't time, don't give it a thought. Tomorrow will do."

The rival paper was the *North China Daily News*, which catered to the English colony. It presented the news inside and the advertisements on the front page in the approved British manner. Miss Sartain did the United States Court for China, and found it singularly like an American court, except that the witnesses were frequently Orientals. The British Court was like Old Bailey. She went the rounds of the important hotels by rickshaw, seeking interviews. She sailed down the Whangpoo River to meet incoming celebrities. She did reviews of cinema openings and amateur theatricals. But the climate of Shanghai ruined Miss Sartain's health, so she went on her way, taking a three months' trip around the world by way of Hongkong, Manila, Singapore, Sumatra, Colombo, Port Said, Cairo and across Europe to Paris.

By moving so much she sometimes caught up again with celebrities she had previously interviewed. She saw Yehudi Menuhin when he made his début in San Francisco at the age of four—a fat, golden-haired child; she interviewed him again in Paris when he was eight; and caught up with him in New York years later. She found Robert Dollar (Cappy Ricks) in San Francisco, Honolulu, Shanghai and Paris. She talked to John McCormack at various ports of call.

She worked on the Paris *Times*, when it was owned by Courtland Bishop and edited by Gaston Archambeau. Among her colleagues were Vincent Sheean and Hillel Bernstein. During 1927 she wrote fresh, entertaining copy on celebrities passing through Paris. It was a period when they came in droves.

Miss Sartain first appeared on Park Row in 1927 on her return from France. She sold some features to Louis Weitzenkorn of the *Sunday World* and landed on the city staff of the *World* in the spring of 1929, doing excellent work up to the time it was sold. Then she went over to the *World-Telegram* and her by-line appeared with increasing frequency over spirited pieces of satire. One of her smartest feats was getting inside the Wendel mansion after Ella's death, for even when the spinster was no longer there to hate intrusion, the doors of the gloomy house were tightly closed to the press. But Miss Sartain was taken through the fantastic rooms by Isabel Koss, Ella's only friend and one of the chief beneficiaries of her will.

Miss Sartain is a warm-hearted, witty and impulsive member of the craft, but she has a caustic touch when she sits down at her typewriter. Few women reporters can surpass her at puncturing the arrogance, stupidity or egotism of the strange human beings who flit through the news columns. She spears her victims with a bland touch, and is a reliable reporter on straight news. Her own interests run to politics, economics and the social sciences. She is an ardent worker for the Newspaper Guild. Her husband is Carl Baumhart, an advertising and publicity man.

A third newspaper woman, equally at home on the Atlantic and Pacific coasts, is Florabel Muir, who started her newspaper career in Salt Lake City, moved to the San Francisco *Chronicle* and worked as the sole woman copy reader in town, then ran a paper in Long Beach. After moving East she was on the *Daily News* and the *Post* in New York, with intervals in Hollywood. She now does publicity for Fox Films.

Miss Muir is an enterprising reporter, trained in the dare-devil school. She was broken in sharply by getting an execution to cover for the Salt Lake *Tribune*. When the paper had gone to press, Ed Holden, her managing editor, walked over to her and said, "That was a good story you did. I was afraid of it. Thought you'd slop over, but you handled it just like a man. It was all right."

These words were her accolade. She was no longer a cub. She was not a sob sister but a regular reporter. She had many adventures after that, but none more weird than her vigil at the execution of a Rumanian, shot one bitter winter morning by a firing squad in Salt Lake City for the murder of the girl he loved.

Chapter XIX

THE LADIES HAVE ADVENTURES

DOROTHY DAYTON CLUBBED BY POLICE" RAN A HEADLINE IN THE *World* on a March morning in 1926. This was once where the girl reporter's press card did not save her skin. The policemen of Passaic, some on foot, others in sidecars, had just routed 3,000 strikers outside the Botany Worsted Mills, where a fire hose had been used for the same purpose the day before.

Miss Dayton had been assigned by the *Sun* to write a special feature story on the family life of the strikers. She stopped at a police station in Passaic for directions and ran into C. B. Allen of the *World*. He was just coming out.

"Come on," he said. "There's trouble. The police have been breaking cameras."

They taxied to the spot. As soon as they got out, the police surrounded them. Miss Dayton began taking notes. She was whacked over the arm with a nightstick and her copy paper was seized. Six photographers were beaten and fourteen cameras were wrecked. One photographer jumped into a kitchen, threw his camera under the sink and persuaded the housewife to let him stay instead of calling in the police. The man from the *American* leaped fifteen feet off a fire escape to elude arrest and save his film. The $2,500 motion picture camera owned by the Fox newsreel man was reduced to débris when the police seized the tripod and banged the camera against the pavement.

Miss Dayton thought nothing of the incident. It was all part of the day's work. But the *World* played up her share in the riot next morning and she was asked to write her own experiences for her paper. It is rarely that the newspaper woman encounters physical violence, however hazardous the spot in which she may find herself. But Miss Dayton's entire newspaper career has been one of adventure and enterprise. Years earlier she spent two weeks in the State Penitentiary at McAlester, Oklahoma, in a small cell with more than twenty other girls. The series she wrote caused local repercussions. Not even the warden or matron had suspected her identity. She was working for the *Daily Oklahoman* at the time.

Her experiences were written in fourteen newspaper instalments. She told how the girls slept in bunks in the walls and how dreadful the sanitary conditions were. She described the flagrant evils of the institution. The circulation of her paper went up by 10,000. An investigation followed which led to the erection of new quarters for the women prisoners. Miss Dayton became famous in the district. She was invited to speak at an evangelical meeting. A minister turned to her as a martyr and said, "This poor little girl. Her soul is seared by the terrible experiences she has gone through."

This was a little more than the girl reporter had bargained for. Next day her paper made her write a reply to the over-zealous churchman. She did not feel that her soul had been seared in the least. She had merely done a good job of reporting. But she could not quell the solicitude of the reformers. They named the Dorothy Dayton chapel for her. After this she did a dance hall exposé at Cromwell. She explored the gaudy dives, talked to the girls, walked unguarded through the streets where torch flames blew weirdly in the Oklahoman winds. Again she turned out startling pieces for her paper.

Miss Dayton wrote her first short story when she was eleven and kept a diary from her thirteenth birthday until she was twenty-one. She ran a newspaper in her boarding school and wrote and destroyed a novel before she was graduated. She lived in a little country town near San Antonio, Texas, and made her first plunge into the competitive world as a stenographer for a mechanical supply company.

She picked up the San Antonio *Express* one afternoon, read an item in it and then announced to her colleagues: "I bet I could have written that. I'm going to get a job there, because I know I can do it."

Her instinct was curiously sound, for Miss Dayton today is one of the best women reporters in New York. At the moment she contented herself with addressing a heartfelt letter to the editor of the *Express*. He wrote back and said he would give her a job. But she didn't snap at the chance. She insisted that he must pay her at least as much as she was getting as a stenographer. He agreed to that, too. She has always been lucky with letters.

But it took time to mount the precarious newspaper ladder. She worked as assistant in the society department and wrote Sunday leads. Then the flu epidemic came along. The paper was shorthanded. She got all sorts of assignments from the city desk. One of the first was to interview Caruso. She was told he would not see anyone, but she heard him snoring in his private car. She wrote a humorous story about the discordant snoring of the great tenor and so got her first by-line.

After a year on the *Express* she was offered a fancy publicity job. She traveled around Texas but was soon left high and dry, and once again turned her thoughts to newspaper work. This time she landed on a paper at Wichita Falls, Texas, the hottest place she was ever in. Cockroaches ran over her typewriter. So she sent out letters here and there, fishing for offers, until Walter Harrison, of the *Daily Oklahoman*, gave her the job in which she was to make a name for herself.

She studied the police blotter and wrote crime and state politics. There was nothing temperate about the political feeling of the moment. Eggs and tomatoes were freely thrown at meetings. After her prison series Miss Dayton began to think of more distant fields. She took French leave from her office one day, saying she was ill, and went off into the Ozarks with some friends on a fishing expedition. As they were driving along they heard screams and came on an overturned car. Under it was the leading judge of the district, his neck broken. He had been talked of as candidate for Governor and was extremely well known.

Miss Dayton and her friends drove to the nearest farm and got help. She was supposed to be at home ill, so her office was somewhat astonished when she telephoned in from many miles away with one of the scoops of the year. She had recognized the judge at once. The story carried a seven-column streamer. Under the circumstances everything was forgiven.

But Miss Dayton's heart was set on New York. Two of her friends were traveling north by road. She joined them and they got as far as Washington, where they sold their car for $18. They came the rest of the way by train and arrived at Grand Central with knapsacks and Indian blankets. Miss Dayton tried the various newspaper offices. She soon saw that the going was stiff. She had been assigned by her Oklahoman editor to cover a beauty contest in Atlantic City. So she wrote a story on that, which she sold to the *Telegraph*, and another on hunting a job in New York, which she sold to the *Evening World*.

When she called at the *Sun* office Edmond P. Bartnett, the city editor, was interested in her prison stories and suggested that she free-lance for the woman's page. Eleanor Stanton, another capable newspaper woman, edited the page at the time. She gave Miss Dayton good assignments, praised her work, and backed her up in every way. Within a week Mr. Bartnett took her over on the city staff. Soon she was assigned to cover a Japanese princess who was staying at the Waldorf-Astoria. There were hand-outs from the press agent, Albert Crockett, but it was understood that no one could interview a princess. Miss Dayton, not knowing any of her colleagues, kept talking to a Japanese who was sitting in the group. When the others left he said, "I am going in to make a picture of the Princess. You can come as my assistant."

So Miss Dayton carried in his plates and talked to the Princess. She got enough material for a good story. Mr. Crockett called up Mr. Bartnett and said that she had been the only reporter to get in. Soon afterwards she trailed Queen Marie on her American sojourn. The press arrangements were particularly messed up in Philadelphia. The officials of the hotel where the Queen was staying high-hatted the reporters. Because his luggage was lost, the Prince was late for a dinner given in their honor. He had to sneak in through the servants' entrance. A policeman told Miss Dayton that the Prince had lost his pants with the missing luggage, so she wrote a facetious story about this royal mishap.

On the day that Colonel Lindbergh arrived in Washington on a cruiser after his trans-Atlantic flight Miss Dayton did the news lead on the story for the *Sun*—the sort of assignment that her paper rarely entrusts to a woman. It was a gorgeous summer day. Crowds saw the ship come in and Lindbergh's blond head on the bridge. He was still the bachelor flyer, almost a symbolic figure. Miss Dayton had a taxi waiting around the corner to rush her to her bureau. But a navy guard with bayonets blocked her way.

"You can't get through here," they told her.

"But I *must*," said Miss Dayton, her afternoon deadline in mind, and before they could stop her she had crawled under a bayonet and was fleeing hot-footed toward her taxi. This was an important story for a girl to write single-handed and she did an excellent job of it.

Like most of her contemporaries, Miss Dayton sat in at the Hall-Mills, Snyder-Gray and Browning trials, doing features for her paper. She covered the King of Siam and the other visiting royalties of the last decade. In spite of all her adventures she is far from being the hard-boiled girl reporter. She holds liberal views on social and political questions. She is dark, attractive, a good thinker, a skilled writer, and undoubtedly she is one of the more enterprising members of her profession.

Sitting often at the same press table with Miss Dayton is another reporter who has adventured here and there and always knows what to do when a story breaks. She is Irene Corbally Kuhn, of the *World-Telegram* until her appointment as managing editor of the *New York Woman* in the summer of 1936. She was born in Greenwich Village when it really was a village, with backyard gardens, trees in the streets, band concerts in the parks and May parties in Central Park on Saturdays, reached by chartered trolley cars with ribbons flying from their poles. The horse cars used to jog and jingle through West Houston Street, where she was born, a stone's throw from her maternal grandfather's cooperage shop, established by him around Civil War time. Her father was a Dublin man. Her maternal grandparents were Irish, too.

Miss Kuhn had the writing craze when she was still in school. At sixteen she got her first job—as a stenographer making $9 a week. Then she took classes at Columbia and soon learned that the way to land on a New York paper was to get out-of-town experience. In 1919 she went to work on the Syracuse *Herald* at $18 a week. She was frightened out of her wits. It was the first time she had been away from home. Her family made her send her laundry back each week and she lived in a house with two prim maiden ladies.

Her paper ran the Inquiring Reporter box which had been launched some time earlier in the New York *Globe*. When her city editor handed her a slip with the question on it: "Do you wear pyjamas or a night shirt, suspenders or a belt? Why?" she went out into the street to get ten answers. She spent fifteen minutes screwing up courage; then, on the principle that the worst should come first, she asked a traffic policeman. He looked at her as if she were crazy. She explained who she was and why she was so interested in his haberdashery. He laughed heartily, gave her the answers and a pat on the back, and called on some of his friends to help her out. She stayed on the job all morning, got ten answers and returned in high fettle.

"And where the hell have you been?" her city editor demanded. She showed him the results of her morning's work.

"For God's sake," he said, "you weren't supposed to get all that. Everyone on the staff asks one person. The answers are compiled at the end of the day."

Ten days later Miss Kuhn scooped the town with a picture and spread on the daughters of Nathan L. Miller, who was then candidate for Governor. She was raised to $25 a week.

While still in Syracuse she flew with Tex McLaughlin for a story. The egg crate he was piloting was a remodeled war plane. She was strapped into the open cockpit, given a pair of goggles and off they went. He gave her a thorough initiation. They looped, did Immerman turns, the falling leaf and every trick known to airmen at the time. When she came down thirty minutes later Miss Kuhn confessed that she had never been up in an airplane before. She was one of the first women reporters to fly for a story. Next day McLaughlin, whose special stunt was changing from one plane to another, was the victim of an air pocket that held the two planes in position a fraction of an instant too long. He was swung into the propellor of one and his back was slashed to ribbons. He died two days later.

At the end of six months Miss Kuhn arrived in New York with a letter of introduction and Mr. Payne took her on the *Mirror*. These were the days when tabloids were regarded with great suspicion and every citizen felt it was his duty to kick the tabloid reporter who came to his door right into the street. Miss Kuhn learned during this period that a tough hide is useful equipment for a reporter.

Nearly a year later she had a chance to go to Europe on an advertising job. She took a letter from Mr. Payne to Floyd Gibbons, then European director of the Chicago *Tribune* bureaus and editor of the Paris edition of his paper. She soon had occasion to use it, for her other work blew up. She walked into the *Tribune* office just when Rosemary Carr had given notice. She was returning to America to marry Stephen Vincent Benét. Miss Kuhn was employed to take her place. She became fashion editor, feature writer and general reporter. She did a series of stories on the American Army of Occupation in Germany; chased Grover Bergdoll all over Switzerland; and covered Deauville and the resorts in clothes borrowed from the *couturiers* for show-off purposes.

Peggy Hull, war correspondent on three fronts—Mexico, France and Siberia—and now the wife of Harvey Deuell, managing editor of the *News*, was in Paris preparing to go to Shanghai. It was suggested laughingly at her farewell party that Miss Kuhn should go along. The idea appealed to her. Braced with two goblets of champagne she hurried over to the *Tribune* office and handed in her resignation. She left Paris with just enough money to buy passage on the 4,200 ton Japanese freighter that was taking Miss Hull to Shanghai. Once aboard they were suspected of being spies. Miss Hull had pictures of herself in uniform on display in her cabin. They were never out of quizzing range of the ship's officers.

Miss Hull left the ship at Hongkong. Miss Kuhn went on to Shanghai. The night she sailed north, a general strike was declared at Hongkong. Not a wheel turned. Not a ship moved out of the harbor after theirs. The paralysis lasted for six weeks. She got to Shanghai in the middle of the New Year holidays, with everything closed down tight. She had approximately $50 in gold. Her hotel bill at the end of three days was $36. Just as the shutters were taken down from the shop windows and business began again she met Herbert Webb, editor of the *China Press*, and he gave her a job on the *Evening Star*, an American paper owned by the same publisher. The staffs were interchangeable.

The first day she went to work she attended a newspaper wedding, caught the bridal bouquet and there met her future husband, Bert L. Kuhn, a Chicago newspaper man who had been city editor of the *Bulletin* in Manila and had responded to a good cable offer from Mr. Webb to become news editor of the *China Press.* They were married four months later and after a time moved to Honolulu where their daughter was born. Mr. Kuhn worked there on the *Star-Bulletin.* His wife was correspondent for I.N.S. For the first time in her life she also kept house and cooked. Ten days before her baby was born she scooped the A.P. and the U.P. with the story of a tidal wave. The I.N.S. bonus virtually paid for the baby.

When the child, Rene Leilani Kuhn, was five months old they went back to Shanghai at Webb's request. They started off with the infant in a cradle made out of a slat-sided box, covered with mosquito netting and fitted between the bunks on board ship. One day out of Honolulu they ran into a storm that tore down the wireless, caused many mishaps and kept them out of communication for three days. They arrived in Yokohama without scenting trouble and some hours later sailed for Kobe, where at noon the next day, while they were lunching in the Oriental Hotel, they were suddenly pitched out of their seats by the first shock of the great Japanese earthquake.

The second shock came almost immediately. Chandeliers were swaying, dishes clattering on the floor as they ran into the streets. There was the eerie feeling of being suspended in mid-air while they waited. It passed and they dismissed it as just another Japanese earthquake. But that night the ship's radio brought news of the terrific damage done.

In Shanghai new adventures overtook them. They shared in the excitement of the riots of the summer of 1925. Miss Kuhn helped to organize the Women's Volunteer Motor Canteen Corps which took food and drink to the volunteers and the marines of all nations doing outpost duty around the settlement. They set out at midnight each night and returned at six in the morning.

Then the paper changed hands. Attempts were made to break their contract. They had to take alternate four-hour shifts. While one of them worked the other stayed at home, watched the baby and guarded the house with a gun. There were no servants. Their nurse vanished one night and came back in the morning badly beaten up. They cooked on toasters and grills, plugged in on the stairs or wherever they could put them.

Miss Kuhn was one of the first women to broadcast in the Orient. When the station was established in 1925 parts were bootlegged in and set up, until eventually there was a sending station as well as several radios around town. This was the only means of communication and was used as a warning to isolated sectors when the internecine wars began boiling after the Communist trouble in 1925.

In the late autumn of that year Miss Kuhn sailed for America with her baby. At Vancouver, an hour before her ship was due to sail, she had word that her husband had died from unknown causes. She free-lanced for six months in Chicago, then moved to New York and went to work for Mr. Payne on the *Mirror* in July, 1926. Almost at once she was assigned to the Hall-Mills case and was told to find a woman, deaf from birth, who could read lips, but this fell plan of Mr. Payne's did not lead to any startling results. She worked on the Lindbergh flight and covered the trial of Leonard Cline, the talented newspaper man who shot a friend in a drunken argument and some time later killed himself.

Miss Kuhn did the Snyder-Gray case from beginning to end and chaperoned some of the trained seals employed by her paper on this occasion. She wrote Peggy Hopkins Joyce's stories so that they fooled even Peggy herself. She did an interview with Ruth Snyder on behalf of her colleagues. A rival paper tried to circumvent her, but some of the newspaper men carried Irene through the hall so that her feet never touched the ground, and pushed her through the door to foil her competitors. She took in Evelyn Boone, of the *American*, for confirmation.

Evelyn was another of the smart newspaper women of the period. She did excellent work while she was on the *American* and was the first reporter to get an interview with the hostile Mrs. Hall during the exciting days of the Halls-Mills trial.

From the *Mirror* Miss Kuhn moved to the *News*, where she covered the usual assortment of murders, scandals and lively doings. She was sent to Washington to chronicle the social snarl created by Dolly Gann and Alice Longworth. She was assigned to the test dinner, which was to establish Mrs. Gann's status beyond question. She had no card, but Carlos Davila, the Ambassador from Chile, got her in and provided her with an escort. Later she had an excellent interview with Mrs. Gann, in which the vice-president's sister launched some homely back fence philosophy.

Miss Kuhn worked for *Liberty* for a time and took six months' leave of absence to revisit Hawaii, where she did a beach column and police news for the Honolulu *Star-Bulletin*, and an investigation of juvenile delinquency in the islands. She returned to the *News* and did rewrite. Then she went to Hollywood in 1931 to work for Fox Films. Two years later she returned and joined the staff of the *World-Telegram*, where she did features of all kinds.

One of her best jobs was a series from London on the rise of motion pictures in England.

Miss Kuhn is one of the more capable members of her profession. Her experience has been broad and exciting. She knows how to get news and what to do with it. She is not easily diverted from her purpose, but has the strong will and sturdy spirit that make the good reporter. She is the wife of Gerald Breitigam, feature editor of the *World-Telegram.*

A beauty contest indirectly propelled Mabel Greene, of the *Sun*, into newspaper work. She was born in Avoca, Iowa, attended high school there and later taught school near her birthplace, walking five miles morning and evening to a country district where she had sixteen boys to manage. They did all the work, built the fires, swept the floors and washed the blackboards, so that she had time to read the Omaha *World-Herald* during the noon recess periods. One day the paper announced a beauty contest for the best-looking blonde and brunette, to be selected from six of each type in Iowa and Nebraska. Miss Greene showed the paper to a friend who, without her knowledge, entered two photographs taken when Mabel was graduated from high school.

The following Friday the appalling news came over the telephone that she had been chosen as one of the six brunette beauties. Her mother received the message and before she hung up the receiver Mabel had summarily withdrawn from the contest. But her retirement from the lists came too late for the editors of the *World-Herald* to kill the cut of her which already had gone to press. When her mother saw the Sunday paper there were serious reverberations.

After this Miss Greene did summer work for the *World-Herald*, then drifted into War Savings and Liberty Loan campaign work in Missouri. On Armistice Day she arrived in St. Louis with $50, no acquaintances and no job. By some miracle she landed on the *Post-Dispatch*, which is usually a closed shop to the newspaper woman. She was soon launched on special drives and campaigns. Shortly after joining the staff she won a prize of $100 offered by the publisher, Joseph Pulitzer, Jr., in an annual competition for suggested improvements in the paper. She told him that the woman's page was terrible. During the next seven years she had a chance to put some of her ideas into effect. She made up the woman's page for more than three years, working under the direction of Harry Niemeyer, the feature editor. She ran a daily food column and did all sorts of odd jobs. Meanwhile she hounded the managing editor for city staff assignments—until at last he sent her out on the story of a club woman who had been sued by another woman for alienating her husband's affections.

"Mrs. X. disappeared with her elderly, semi-invalid father just half an hour before process servers arrived at her home to serve her in the suit," he told Miss Greene. "The best reporters in town have been hunting for her for a week without success. If you can locate her and get a statement I'll see about giving you a chance on the staff."

Miss Greene went out and found the woman, after deciding what she would have done under similar circumstances. It was midwinter and she learned from friends that the love pirate had talked of taking her elderly father to a warmer climate. Miss Greene checked the hour of her departure from her home through a taxi driver and neighbors, traced her to Union Station, and then, armed with a photograph of the woman which she borrowed from the *Post-Dispatch* morgue, she interviewed Pullman porters until she found one who remembered seeing her in his car on her way to Jacksonville, Florida. He recognized her picture and remembered that her father had needed a wheel chair to leave the train. With that information she went to the woman's lawyer and pulled a bluff.

"I'm off to Jacksonville to see Mrs. X.—" she began.

The attorney capitulated. He said he would get his client's side of the story for Miss Greene. She made him telegraph for it, and when the letter came the opening sentence made a good lead. It read: "Nine Wives had faith in Mrs. X. when she worked in the business and professional world with their husbands ——"

Miss Greene was sent to Louisville to cover the Kentucky Derby from a fashion and social angle. She saw a black two-year-old win a race and decided she would bet on him, if he were entered in the next year's Derby. She put $15 across the board in the winter books the following January, and Flying Ebony galloped home with $500 for her. So she resigned from the *Post-Dispatch*, went to California, and by this roundabout way landed in New York in January, 1926, with $12 and no job. She spent nearly a year as fiction editor of the McClure Newspaper Syndicate, writing newspaper serials in her spare time. She earned $1,000 for one story written during the evenings over a period of six weeks, so she began to free-lance and learned about markets during the next two years.

Then for six months she toured the country as personal road representative for Mr. and Mrs. Martin Johnson and the American Museum of Natural History, publicizing the lion picture "Simba." When she was offered a job on the *Sun* in 1929 after putting up a constant bombardment, she left the Johnsons and their lions flat in Birmingham, Alabama, and hurried to New York.

In the next six and a half years Miss Greene covered many of the exciting stories of the day. She did the news lead on the Starr Faithfull case. After four months' close investigation, she brought about the doom of *Town Topics*, the scandal magazine started by Colonel William Dalton Mann, and also its companion publication, the *Tatler and American Sketch*, which rated debutantes according to the stock-buying abilities of their parents. She brought the stock-selling rackets of the publishers to the attention of the Attorney-General, with the result that permanent injunctions were finally issued against the owners and editors.

She was the only newspaper reporter to get into Hauptmann's home for five days after his arrest as the kidnapper of the Lindbergh baby. In spite of the triple guard of New York police, New Jersey State troopers and federal officers, she had a story describing in detail the interior of the house, particularly the nursery furnished by Hauptmann for his own baby from the proceeds of the Lindbergh ransom money.

Miss Greene's toughest assignment was rewriting the Bible. In March, 1933, the *Sun* discovered one of the few known copies of the only book that gives a complete chronological story of the Bible in pictures—Matthew Merian's *Icones Biblicae*, a series of nearly 250 etchings. She wrote the captions for the series, which the *Sun* printed over a period of nearly eight months. She condensed the text of the Bible into a running story. It entailed two months' hard work.

Miss Greene is the wife of Edgar R. Bean, news editor of the *News*. Her sister, Elinor Greene, is also a newspaper woman, who worked on the Detroit *Mirror*, the Boston *American* and Boston *Sunday Advertiser*. She free-lanced her way around the world, doing feature articles for English and American papers. After several months in the Far East she returned to New York and now does publicity and advertising for Elizabeth Arden.

Working on Park Row in the booming twenties was Elisabeth Smith, who wrote for the *Telegram* for six years and survived three of Mr. Munsey's mergers. She first became interested in newspaper work through Florence Davies, of the Detroit *News*, whom she met while taking her master's degree at Columbia. Armed with a Phi Beta Kappa key, but unable to distinguish agate from ten-point century, she offered her literary wares in Herald Square. She would have acted as charwoman to James Gordon Bennett's famous staircase, if necessary, in order to get on the paper.

Frank Sullivan, Cornelius Vanderbilt, Jr., and Miss Smith all started their newspaper careers together in the same week and the same city room. At first she did a school column, then moved on to murders and other front-page news. She became familiar with the murderess of respectable mien, who invariably wore black kid gloves at her trial and looked as if she could make the best watermelon preserves in the county town.

Alice Paul did her best to persuade her that she was oppressed by her employers because she was a woman.

"But I earn more than a great many of the men," Miss Smith remonstrated. "Any intelligent newspaper woman gets as good a break as a man."

Miss Paul glared at her. "But you can't be an editor," she said triumphantly.

"But I don't want to be an editor," said Miss Smith.

On one of her first assignments she got a helping hand from a quiet newspaper man who chatted with her for a couple of hours while the story they were covering unfolded in Central Park.

"Who was that?" she asked a colleague later.

"Why, don't you know? That was Frank Ward O'Malley," he said, with a touch of reverence.

Miss Smith, who is a cousin of Charles Brackett, is now out of the newspaper game and is married to Andy Ford, who was her managing editor on the *Telegram*. She and Elizabeth Custer, the sister-in-law of Scott Nearing, both worked on the paper with Jane Dixon.

It is a rare circumstance for the girls who work on the Brooklyn papers to cross the bridge and seek jobs in Manhattan. But Grace Cutler, now Mrs. Beverly Smith, is one of the exceptions. She moved from the *Eagle* to the *Daily News* and then to the *Journal*. Working with her on the *Eagle* was Marjorie Dorman, the enterprising reporter who once invaded the White House kitchen, wrote thousands of words on Nathalia Crane, Brooklyn's child poet, and did bold work on most of the big stories of the period. Miss Dorman was an experienced reporter who let nothing in the way of obstacles stop her.

She was followed by Isabelle Keating, who took a course in journalism at the University of Colorado and moved to New York after preliminary newspaper experience in Denver and in Boulder, Colorado. She worked briefly for the Associated Press and then got practical experience editing the Nyack *Evening Journal*, a six-column four-page paper with two pages of boiler plate inside, hand set heads and almost illegible type on the front and back pages. It was run off on an old flat bed press that groaned and trembled over each copy. It threw them out, unfolded, across the composing room floor. As it started to roll, all hands were needed to catch and subdue the leaping papers.

When a new management transferred the publication to a better building, a make-up stone rolled off its carriage and was found to be a tombstone. The underside, chipped but still legible, was inscribed to Ezra, a four-year-old child who died in the early 1800's. In the new plant the *Journal* was published in standard size. With two local newspaper women to help her, Miss Keating did an energetic job getting out the paper, while the townspeople watched with wonder and interest.

Within a year she tried New York again and went to work on the *Eagle*, where she remained for eight years. During that period she had ample experience and became a first-class craftsman. It was she who discovered that Anne Sullivan Macy, Helen Keller's teacher, had become totally blind, and that the pupil had turned teacher. There was a scramble for the story once she had broken it in the *Eagle*. It was one of the human interest tales in which all city desks take satisfaction.

Efforts were made to get her into the death house at Sing Sing for the execution of Mrs. Anna Antonio, the wretched woman who hired two men to kill her husband for his insurance and who paid the price in August, 1934. She was twenty-eight years old, the mother of three, and the more sensational papers worked up considerable feeling on her behalf. Warden Lawes informed the *Eagle* that the last woman to witness an execution had been Nellie Bly and that it had upset her greatly. So the city desk sent a man to the execution, but he fainted, just as any sob sister might have been expected to do.

Miss Keating organized the *Eagle* unit of the Newspaper Guild and was elected twice to the Guild's executive board. She stirred up a flurry of praise and criticism with an article she did on the Guild for *Harpers Magazine*, and became recognized as an authority on the subject. She was persuaded during her early days on the *Eagle* that reporters were shockingly underpaid and that their hours were long beyond all reason. Her paper had a space assignment system which netted them $1 a story, no matter how many hours they worked. She was on call twenty-four hours a day seven days a week; but the assignments handed out to her often brought her no more than $5 or $10 a week. At the best, working eighteen or twenty hours a day, she might make $15. Remembering the unremunerative grind of her early days on the paper, she became a sincere advocate of the Guild, to which nearly all the newspaper women of New York now lend support, some passively, others with fervor.

Miss Keating met her husband, Morton Savell, when he was Sunday editor of the *Eagle*. He is now managing editor of the *Literary Digest*. They have an infant son, Michael.

The other girl reporter from Brooklyn most often seen on big assignments is red-haired Alice Cogan, born of a newspaper family. She has divided her sixteen years of reporting between the *Eagle* and the *Times Union*. She started newspaper work at the age of seventeen, green from high school. She wrote the lead on the Hall-Mills trial and did feature stories on the Snyder-Gray and Hauptmann trials. Once, when she was sent to interview the president of a reptile society, she sat in the dusk chatting to the woman for fifteen minutes before the lights were turned on. Then Miss Cogan jumped to her feet. The room was full of snakes. They were curled on the buffet, victrola, chairs and tables. She got out as fast as she could. She found this the most terrifying of her newspaper experiences.

Miss Cogan's parents met forty years ago when they were both working for the *Eagle*. Her mother, Anne Luxton, was a proofreader, and the only person on the paper who could read Joseph Cogan's handwriting. He has done newspaper work for fifty years and is still writing editorials for the *Times Union*. Her sister, Constance, works for the Brooklyn section of the *American*.

In the autumn of 1888 a Brooklyn newspaper woman, Mrs. Eliza Putnam Heaton, took passage from Liverpool to New York in the steerage of the *Aurania* to study life among the immigrants, much as Genevieve Forbes Herrick did thirty years later. She landed at Castle Garden and accompanied her fellow passengers to Chicago on an immigrant train. Her stories were written for the Brooklyn *Times*. Her husband, John L. Heaton, was associate editor of the paper at the time. When the New York *Recorder* was launched in 1891, Mrs. Heaton started the woman's page and made a success of it. When her husband established the Providence *News* she went with him, and Mrs. Christine Terhune Herrick, daughter of Marion Harland, succeeded her on the *Recorder*.

Today New York has one woman managing editor, Peggy Foldes, who runs the *North Side News* and is so well known in her borough that when someone cut her picture out of a paper, pasted it on a postcard and addressed it to Peggy, the Bronx, it went straight to her desk.

Miss Foldes does local editorials, makes up the front page, writes the streamers, does theatrical reviews and turns out a gossip column about Bronx politicians which she calls "Peggy's Diary." She has ten reporters on her staff and has to spend considerable time interviewing the journalism graduates who are looking for a start on a smaller paper and consider the *North Side News* a good jumping-off place.

She made her own newspaper start this way on the advice of the talented Lester Markel, now Sunday magazine editor of the *Times*. For two years he held the post that she now has on the *North Side News*. George W. Markey, publisher of the paper, told her that she could hang around the office and do odd jobs for her luncheons and carfare. During her first week in the city room she was assigned to an automobile accident in which a family of seven was wiped out. She wept as she wrote her story. It made the front page with a by-line. She was taken on the staff at $10 a week, and soon learned the ropes, from proofreading to covering murder trials.

She was editing the *National Centre*, a weekly published in Washington, when Mr. Markey wired her to return to the *North Side News* as quickly as possible to pinch-hit for the managing editor. She was twenty-four and looked young and flapperish. She was told the post would not be permanent, but she still holds it, after nine years. At first the men in the composing room resented dictation from a woman. Miss Foldes stopped the presses oftener than was necessary, chiefly because it gave her a feeling of power to think that the roaring machines would halt for her. But she soon learned better.

Her paper is Democratic. She attends conventions, political banquets and all local functions of any consequence. Everyone knows her as Peggy. She was born in Budapest, came to the United States for a visit before the war, settled down, attended high school, then the Columbia School of Journalism, got married, had a baby, was divorced and is now married again, to Lou Joffe, an attorney whom she met while doing newspaper work in Washington.

Miss Foldes has no trouble keeping her staff in order. It's an old story now to have a woman managing editor on the *North Side News*.

Chapter XX

THROUGH PRISON WALLS

OUTSIDE THE IRON GATES OF CHARLESTOWN PRISON, MASSA-chusetts, a crowd of 5,000 men and women shouted and roared with the atavism of those who take odd comfort from watching gray walls while criminals die inside. Now and again a voice rose sharply above the din with "Let them die!"

It was June 7, 1935, and the men due to go in quick succession to the electric chair were Murton Millen, Irving Millen and Abe Faber, killers and bank robbers.

At the gates a slim, dark girl was trying to push her way past the guards.

"But I'm Dorothy Kilgallen, of the New York *Journal*. I'm assigned to cover the execution for my paper. I *must* get in."

"Quit kidding us," they told her for the tenth time. "You're no reporter. What would you be doing at an execution, anyway?"

Dorothy is the daughter of James Kilgallen, one of the ablest reporters in America and for years star man on I.N.S. until he became assistant to Joseph V. Connolly, of King Features.

She was bursting with indignation. She couldn't cajole or force her way past the guards. She knew that she had to be there. She was in despair when a batch of her colleagues drove up.

"What's wrong, Dorothy?" they demanded.

"They don't believe that I've got to get in," she said. "You tell them."

"Say, what's wrong with you, anyway?" said one of the peremptory gentlemen of the press to an abashed guard. "Don't you know she's one of us? You can't keep her out. She's a swell reporter. She's got as much right here as anyone."

Miss Kilgallen got in. In Massachusetts it is customary to allow only one reporter to witness an execution. He then describes it to all the others, who wait for him in the warden's office. This rule was followed in the Sacco-Vanzetti case. Three representatives of the news services, however, were admitted to the Millen-Faber execution. Miss Kilgallen, being a girl, was barred. The death chamber is one of the few spots that the girl reporter cannot enter, the cinema notwithstanding, except in certain states or under unusual conditions.

At midnight eight witnesses entered the buff-colored room. There were three chairs but no one sat. One dim electric light hung from the ceiling. Gas flickered blue in jets on the wall. The yellow door to the left opened and Murton Millen walked in.

During the three executions Miss Kilgallen stayed in a bleak little room near the death chamber, listening to a deputy warden report, over a prison telephone: "Irving's in the chair now . . . . the first shock, 2,000" . . . . pause . . . . "second shock, 1,500" . . . . pause . . . "third shock" . . . . "fourth shock" . . . . "He's dead."

She listened to the same story with slight variations three times over. A few minutes later she heard the report of her colleagues who had witnessed what happened. She sat down at her typewriter, shaken. She wrote a story that crackled and stang. It was different from the sentimental style of Nellie Bly when she covered the Hamby execution for the same paper fifteen years earlier.

Like their colleagues of the other sex, girl reporters turn sick when they are assigned to do any work on an execution. It is scarcely their job, but they do it, for death and catastrophe are the daily lot of any reporter on a metropolitan paper. Miss Kilgallen was only twenty-one when she came face to face with her first execution. She had an early baptism in lurid journalism. At seventeen she was out on the street, sometimes working on the same story as her father. In four years' time she achieved the ranking of a star, for she quickly displayed a real gift for her work.

When the trial of Hauptmann was in progress at Flemington she neatly scooped her father. She got an advance interview with Bruno through his lawyers, indicating what he would say on the witness stand. I.N.S. picked up the story and sent it over the wires. It led the Hearst afternoon papers throughout the country. Dorothy had stolen the lead from her father. But Mr. Kilgallen has never put anything over on his bright young daughter, notwithstanding the fact that there is no such thing as family solidarity around the press table. When husband and wife, or father and daughter, work together on a story, the competition is cutthroat. The paper comes first.

Mr. Kilgallen never intended that his daughter should be a newspaper woman. He had seen too many of them worked to death, and sitting through murky court testimony that would turn the stoutest stomach. He felt a bit like the editors who were queried by Mr. Bok at the turn of the century as to whether they would like their daughters to become newspaper women. Dorothy had no particular longings in this direction herself. It never struck her that newspaper work would be fascinating. Few members of a newspaper family do. She knew that her father had odd hours and was always out of town.

She was at the end of her freshman year at the College of New Rochelle when she went to a party with her parents and there met Amster Spiro, city editor of the *Journal*. Mr. Spiro is the only city editor left in New York who approximates the motion picture conception of a frenzied gent with five telephones working simultaneously while he bawls out the staff.

"I suppose you're going to make a reporter out of her," he said, looking at the dark graceful girl, convent bred.

"Not if I know it," said Mr. Kilgallen emphatically.

"Well, if you decide to put her to work, I'll give her a job," said Mr. Spiro.

She went back to college with this suggestion vaguely implanted in her head. When she told her friends about it they thought it a dazzling idea. They were all cinema fans. Oh, to be a girl reporter, save the innocent lad from the chair, stop the presses (that nonsensical touch that has practically no reality in the authentic newspaper world), beat the town, and marry the hateful star on the rival paper!

Miss Kilgallen caught some of the excitement. She went home and insisted that her father let her go to see Mr. Spiro. He consented, after much persuasion. On her way to a prep school prom she stopped in at the *Journal*, told Mr. Spiro she had an hour in which to make a train, and asked him to give her a job.

It was a casual way of going about the desperately difficult task of getting on a New York paper, but her father's fine reputation was sufficient guarantee for any editor. Mr. Spiro said he would give her two weeks' trial. That was in June, 1931. When she got back from the dance she started work and she never went back to college.

She looked the part of the sweet girl graduate as she stepped out on her first assignment. Her professional ducking was swift and thorough. For the first summer she practically lived in police stations, court houses, hospitals and the morgue. It wasn't easy. Newspaper work was exciting enough, but more of a struggle than she had imagined. But she stuck it out and became an excellent reporter. No one tried to make things easy for her because she was Jimmie Kilgallen's daughter. When an assistant city editor on her paper discovered one day that she had never seen a dead body, he set out to correct this inexperience. She was assigned repeatedly to the morgue. She wrote a succession of stories about unidentified suicides, described their clothes and urged their relatives to come forward and claim them. She interviewed every sort of freak and celebrity.

The infantile paralysis epidemic was raging that summer, and she spent hours talking to children in respirators. She gave all the children names so that they could be identified in the stories—"Angel Face Tommy," "Sunshine Sally" and "Smiling Ben." Nobody wanted to go near her while she was engaged on this dangerous task.

Then for the first time she met her father on a story, proving that she had made the grade as a star. They were both working on the Collings mystery. In September, 1931, newspaper readers first became aware of the existence of Mrs. Lillian Collings, a sad-faced woman who told of an elderly man and a youth boarding her husband's cabin cruiser in Long Island Sound, beating him, trussing him and throwing him overboard. They forced her into a canoe, leaving her daughter Barbara in the cruiser. Next morning she was found by some boatmen to whom she told her weird tale of attack and murder. She was held for questioning but was soon released when her story stood up at every point. Her husband's body was washed ashore, battered and bound with rope, as she had described it. It was a particularly savage and seemingly motiveless crime.

While Mrs. Collings was being questioned she ferried over every day from Stamford to Mineola for conferences with District Attorney Elvin I. Edwards and Inspector Harold King, both veterans of a number of mysteries, including the Starr Faithfull case. Miss Kilgallen usually accompanied her. One afternoon, as the ferry pulled in at the Long Island side, she saw a familiar-looking figure, copy paper in hand, waiting on the dock to greet them.

The other reporters were astonished to see a girl in an Empress Eugénie hat run off the boat and kiss "Kil."

"Why, hello, dad," she cried. "What are you doing here?"

After this, father and daughter met repeatedly on stories. They were both in court on the day that Mayor Walker testified at the Seabury hearing. They worked together on the Morro Castle disaster and the investigation that followed it. When the ferry boat *Observation* was blown to smithereens in the East River with a boiler explosion on the morning of September 9, 1932, Dorothy was counting up the long row of dead lying in a shed on the wharf when she bumped into another reporter who proved to be her father. He had started at one end of the row, she at the other, and they met in the middle. The men had been tossed into the air, blown on rooftops or into the water. Seventy-two were killed; sixty-three were injured.

As is customary on the more sensational papers, Miss Kilgallen did features at first on the big stories of the day, but as time went on and she grew more experienced, she was trusted with the lead on a number of important assignments. The first trial she covered single-handed was that of Jessie Costello, the capricious belle who was tried at Salem, Massachusetts, in August, 1933, for feeding her husband cyanide.

The trial lasted for five weeks and Miss Kilgallen wrote 250,000 words of copy. The jurors sent flowers to her hotel room every day. She never could understand why. Jurors are a strange species who sometimes entertain themselves watching the antics of the press when the witnesses bore them. They picked the flowers during their morning walks, and one of the local papers carried a story about it. There was no doubt that they were unconventional jurors. They sent a box of candy to black-eyed Jessie while the trial was going on, and acquitted her triumphantly when it was over. They wanted her to know how completely they were on her side.

Edward J. McMahon, the kiss-and-tell policeman who figured prominently in the story as Jessie's lover, was the star witness against her. The papers rode him so hard that he detested the sight of a reporter. But Miss Kilgallen scooped all her rivals by interviewing him and getting the exclusive story of his love life with Jessie. No one could understand how she did it, because it was well known that he would not even open the door to reporters.

But, as a matter of fact, her technique was based on simple psychology. She wore a white dress, low-heeled shoes, an innocent expression, and tried to look youthfully dumb. McMahon let her in at once, thinking she was one of the neighborhood children. And before he had a chance to throw her out she convinced him that he owed it to the *Journal* readers to tell his story. It ran in three copyrighted instalments and was a blistering tale.

After the Costello trial Miss Kilgallen went from one good story to another. She saw Eva Coo convicted at Cooperstown, New York, and she turned out more words on the American Tragedy trial in Wilkes-Barre than any of the other correspondents there, even Theodore Dreiser, who sat in the press row, watching his own story more or less retold. Her output was 65,000 words in six days. She soon developed a surprising acquaintance among the gentry quick on the trigger. In 1934 no fewer than five men and women whose trials she had covered went to the chair.

Miss Kilgallen has had a taste of the other side of newspaper work, too. She goes down the bay to meet the celebrities who come in on ships. And when the *Journal* gets one of its periodical series attacks, she devotes herself for a week or two to commercial models, international marriages, beautiful shop girls or whatever the whim of the moment happens to be. Or else she crusades. When her paper was exposing the marriage rackets in New Jersey in 1933 she assisted, and narrowly escaped getting rushed to the altar with Sid Boehm, a fellow reporter on her own paper. She has done some mad things for the *Journal*, but she drew the line at Lohengrin.

Miss Kilgallen is not the only newspaper daughter in New York to follow her father's profession. Dixie Tighe, of the flaming locks, who has not missed many important stories in the last ten years, has inherited her newspaper instincts from both sides of the house. Her father, Colonel Matthew F. Tighe, was dean of the White House correspondents for years and was nationally known for his scoop on the blowing up of the *Maine*. Her mother, Josephine Tighe, does special feature work in Washington today. She was one of the early newspaper women there, and was on the Washington *Times* when she met Colonel Tighe. One of her more spectacular assignments was the trial in the West Virginia hills that climaxed the Allen feud. She was present when the prisoner shot up the court room, including the judge. Dixie's brother, Matt, is also in newspaper work and at one time was city editor of the Washington *Herald*. Her uncle is Charles G. Hambidge, for years a political reporter for the New York *Times*.

Miss Tighe got her newspaper initiation on the Washington *Herald* in 1925. Her first big story was the aviation inquiry involving Brigadier General William Mitchell. Her next move was to the Philadelphia *News*, where her city editor soon assigned her to cover the Hall-Mills trial single-handed, a stiff job. She appeared soon afterwards on the Palm Beach *Post* where she did interviews and got a taste for aviation. She flew to Havana to invite Colonel Lindbergh to visit Palm Beach, and was lost on the way for three hours. The Colonel declined to make the trip.

When she interviewed Paul Block he offered her a job on his chain of papers. Soon she became a familiar figure on all the big stories of the day. She covered the conventions, was assigned to the Snook trial in Columbus and saw Mae West, Texas Guinan and a variety of celebrities through their court troubles.

Arrangements were made for Miss Tighe to travel on the Graf Zeppelin when Lady Drummond Hay decided not to make the return Atlantic crossing after her first flight to America. Dixie was taken to the hangar at Lakehurst by Grover Whalen, representing Mayor Walker, and was on board the dirigible when Mr. Hearst changed his mind about letting a Block representative in on his exclusive contract. She was put off the ship, although it took two marines to get Dixie down to earth again. Mr. Block sent her to Hollywood to ease the disappointment. On her return trip she visited the Block papers in the West, and for the time being became a stunt reporter. She went through steel mills, walked on the bottom of a river in a diver's suit, shot the rapids, made a parachute jump, did stunt flying and explored numerous mines.

Miss Tighe was a war correspondent during the Cuban Revolution, flying to Havana for I.N.S. She worked on the Lindbergh kidnapping and was the only newspaper girl besides Evelyn Shuler, of the Philadelphia *Ledger*, to write the news lead on the Hauptmann trial. One day she was assigned to meet the *Majestic* for a ship news story and there she ran into C. V. R. Thompson, arriving to represent the Beaverbrook papers in New York. Miss Tighe is now Mrs. Thompson and, like her husband, corresponds for the London *Daily Express*. She is also on the staff of the New York *Post*, a paper which has had a long succession of capable women reporters since the time of Rheta Childe Dorr—Louise T. Nicholl, who wrote excellent verse; Clara Savage, who is now Mrs. Walter Littledale and edits *Parents' Magazine*; Mary Lee, who was co-winner of the Houghton Mifflin and American Legion $25,000 prize for the best war novel by an American; Laura Mount, who left the paper to do advertising and later married Thayer Hobson; Dorothy Ducas, and Ruth McKenney, who is now a colleague of Miss Tighe's.

While she was with the Block chain of papers Miss Tighe, like most of her contemporaries in New York, chronicled the night club and speakeasy era, when the gangsters were busy and crime filled the front pages incessantly. There were night club raids, speakeasy killings, and hold-ups of staggering proportions. The *crime passionel*, on the other hand, is likely to occur in or out of season. It has little bearing on the current trend in social manners. In this class was the murder of Elizabeth Mowry by Colin Close, otherwise known as Colin Campbell, the torch murderer of New Jersey.

He was an elderly man who had built up a substantial reputation for himself and had lived the double life so successfully that even his wife had been completely fooled and had believed him to be the perfect husband. Although convinced ultimately of his guilt, she still found extenuating circumstances for him.

When the story broke, Mildred Gilman, of the *Journal*, was one of the first reporters on the job. When her competitors were out of earshot she persuaded Mrs. Close to let her into her apartment. She told her that it would be good for her husband to have the public know of their happy married life. She promised to protect her from the other reporters.

At first her rivals did not know that Miss Gilman was inside. When at last they began to suspect that she had outwitted them, they sent in a policeman to investigate, but Mrs. Close persuaded him that Mildred was a nurse. Meanwhile, the unfortunate woman was able to get some rest. The apartment was on the ground floor and, therefore, was quite vulnerable. Miss Gilman stayed overnight. At midnight Ray Jaurez, of the *Graphic*, pounded on the door, claiming she had turned up another wife and child of the murderer. She demanded immediate entrance. It took some time to quiet her. Finally Miss Gilman telephoned for a police guard. He cleared the reporters off the premises and let her slip out, ostensibly to a drug store. Actually she rushed to the wire and filed a story. When no one was in sight he helped her to get back surreptitiously. He was staggered a day later at the court house to discover her identity.

Meanwhile, she had collected enough material from Mrs. Close for a series of stories, and by the time she left, the unhappy wife had a lawyer who could protect her from further invasion. After-wards Mrs. Close worked under a pseudonym on the *Journal*, to earn enough money to keep herself and her children alive. She hated it, but she did not know how else to raise any money. She was a courageous and loyal figure but circumstances were too much for her.

Miss Gilman is the author of *Sob Sister*, a book which gives a veracious picture of the life of a girl on a sensational paper. The incidents in it are only slightly more spectacular than some of those in which the author actually has participated, as well as her *Journal* colleagues—Janette Smits, Jean Vernon and Isabel Johnston. The first episode in the book, in fact, is based on Miss Gilman's own performance on the Earle Peacox story, another torch murder. She climbed the back fence of his wife's home in Westchester while the other reporters were all gathered in front. She marched in through the back door behind Earle himself. She had no idea then that he was the murderer. Nor had anyone else. He had not yet confessed and little suspicion attached to him. She thought he was a local reporter putting something over on her.

She stayed in the house for twenty minutes before anyone even noticed her. She heard all that Earle had to say to the relatives of the wife he had killed and burned with gasoline. They suspected nothing where he was concerned, but they advised him to go to the White Plains court house to be questioned, since the police had been looking for him. He was a handsome young man, literate and seem-ingly well-behaved. The murder was incomprehensible to those who knew him best.

Finally someone noticed Miss Gilman sitting in at the family councils. They asked her who she was. She said she was a friend of Dolly's. Dolly was the wife Earle had murdered. She hastened to add that she had come to offer condolences. Each thought that the other had let her in. She was promptly ushered out. She was telephoning the story to her office just as Peacox was confessing the murder. He quickly broke down under interrogation. She was a lap ahead of all her competitors in rounding up a dramatic story.

Another time Miss Gilman was asked to sit at College Point in a parked car with a photographer while the 3-X murders of Queens were on the front pages. The murderer in this case, still at large, had the quaint idea of writing advance letters to the *Journal* telling whom he would kill, when, and the approximate place. His particular eccentricity was to murder men in parked cars and attack the girls with them, or else let them off with a lecture on morality.

On the night he was due to commit his second murder, Miss Gilman's orders were to park near the home of the girl who had been his first victim. She and her escort waited for hours but the 3-X terror was not abroad that night. Marion Carter, another *Journal* girl, parked near the home of his last victim at the same time. It was a foggy night, but her only fear was that she might be missing the real story.

Another time Miss Gilman was submerged thirty feet in a diving suit in January, near the coffer dam of the Turnpike Bridge being built over the Hackensack River. The idea was to record the dying impressions of Peter Trans, who had drowned in a diving suit a few days earlier in the icy waters of the Rivière des Outardes, near Montreal. This was in January, 1930.

One of Miss Gilman's strangest experiences was with Gladys Mae Parkes, the middle-aged woman who adopted two children from a relative and was arrested subsequently in Camden, New Jersey, for their deaths. One died from slapping; the other fell downstairs and was killed. She put them in a suitcase; then buried the little four-year-old girl in a cellar, and the twenty-months-old boy in the woods under leaves.

She was a former cinema house pianist and cabaret performer. She was treated throughout her trial as a sane woman; but all the evidence pointed to insanity, and after she had been in jail for seven months, serving her sentence, she was transferred to the Trenton State Hospital for the Insane.

She showed extraordinary resistance to the fierce grilling of the police. After three or four days of it, the reporters were worn out, but not the demented woman. Relays of detectives kept up the barrage, but she seemed made of stone. Miss Gilman was on the job night and day. On the fourth day she got back to her hotel at about 1 P.M., dead tired, and found that her husband, Robert

Wohlforth, had been trying to get her on the telephone. Exhausted and slightly hysterical, she called him back.

"Haven't they found out anything yet?" he demanded.

"No more than they've known all along, that she killed the babies, put their bodies in a suitcase, and buried them," said Miss Gilman. "Really, I can't stand this place much longer. It's driving me crazy. I want to get home."

"Why don't you leave everything and come on home?" Mr. Wohlforth responded.

An hour later, after Mildred had sunk into the deep sleep of fatigue, there was a knock at the door and the manager appeared with two men. Her first thought was that Gladys had confessed and that some of her colleagues were protecting her, for in spite of the deadly competition there is an unwritten code in the newspaper profession to cover the absent member.

Mildred wrapped herself in her fur coat, while her visitors planted themselves unceremoniously on the bed and began to question her roughly.

"What did you say to your husband this evening over the phone?" they demanded. "Who is in with you on this? You can't hide anything. We know what you said. Why don't you admit you killed someone?"

It dawned quickly on Miss Gilman that she herself was suspected of having committed a crime. She was shivering and in a state of collapse from fatigue. She could not find her police card. They would not believe that she was a reporter. They searched her belongings. Finally they were persuaded to call the *Journal*. Her identity was established at once and they retired, much embarrassed.

The New York telephone operator had overheard her conversation with her husband, had telephoned to the West Thirtieth Street police station that she had heard Miss Gilman say something about putting a body in a suitcase. Two Camden detectives, less than bright, were immediately set on her trail. It is frequently true that reporters incite suspicion by the very nature of their work, when they overrun a town and cudgel their brains for ingenious ways of getting at the news. They have been known to wear disguises but this is not a general practice. However, on the more sensational papers they sometimes pose as being the chambermaid or the duchess. But usually they do it with a humorous touch that takes the curse off their duplicity.

In the spring of 1929 Miss Gilman was rushed to Wilton, Connecticut, when a railroad clerk named Edwin J. Melhuish poisoned himself after shooting Mary Yates, a senior in Norwalk High School and the friend of his daughter, Elaine. The crime took place on

George Middlebrook's place, Melhuish was seen driving along with the girl. The car zigzagged and hit a tree. A shot was heard. Then Melhuish got out and sat on a wall, eating an orange. Suddenly he fell backwards. At the same moment there was a second shot.

When Miss Gilman arrived to cover the story, she learned that he had added a trifle to the annals of crime by devising a new mode of death. A fat book, *The History of Scotland*, was found in the car beside the dead girl. He had cut out a deep nest in the book to hold a revolver and a bottle of cyanide of potassium. His organs were filled with the poison. He had eaten it out of the orange. Either he had used the revolver too, or it had gone off as he fell, for he was shot as well as poisoned. He had been in love with Mary and had lost his job for inattention to his work.

During a trip to Germany Miss Gilman did an interview with General Goering for Universal Service. He wore a blue velvet dressing gown and sat like Caesar at a massive desk, with a nine-months-old lioness beside him. The light from the window over his head suggested a Belasco setting. He answered all the questions she put to him on the Reichstag trial then in progress, his attitude to Jews, and other topical matters.

"Germany considers her priests and her women too sacred for politics," said the General to the surprised feminist from America.

Miss Gilman is tall, blonde, with Nordic blue eyes touched with ice. She is an energetic, fast-moving reporter who has had more adventures than most. She is hard-boiled at her work, but not in her manner. She landed on the *Journal* at $100 a week, although she had never had a day's experience as a reporter. She was born in Chicago and was educated in St. Louis, Grand Rapids and at the University of Wisconsin. She spent six weeks writing lengthy leads in the School of Journalism there, a technique which she promptly abandoned when she embarked on sensational journalism. She did nothing about being a reporter until she had written three books, *Fig Leaves*, *Count Ten* and *Headlines*. Then Howard Cushman, a fellow reporter, told her that she had a natural newspaper style and that anyone reading *Headlines* would think she had worked on papers all her life.

He got her a letter of recommendation from a local city editor, intended for the *American*, but she got off on the wrong floor and thereby became a *Journal* employee. Her first good assignment was to go down the Bay in the cutter to meet the *American Shipper*, which was bringing in the *Vestris* survivors. She was fired three months after she got her job, and during the two weeks that she had notice, one of the staff members took her in hand and drilled her so thoroughly that she was reinstated without any lapse of time. From then on she did assignments of the first rank.

Almost immediately after she resigned from the *Journal* she wrote *Sob Sister* and followed it up with another book and magazine work. She lives in Ridgefield, Connecticut. Her first husband was James Gilman, head of the Publishers Guild. Mr. Wohlforth, her present husband, is the author of *Tin Soldiers*, a book based on his personal knowledge of West Point. Miss Gilman has two sons of her own and a third whom she has adopted.

When the *Journal* wants something spectacular in the way of coverage, Adela Rogers St. Johns is called in. Her name is nationally known, both in the magazine and newspaper field. When the Hauptmann trial was running its uncanny course, she sat in the press row turning out thousands of words for the Hearst publication. They were blazing words, for Miss St. Johns' prose, like her face, smolders with feeling, and nowhere is she more at home than at a trial. She was nurtured on court-room drama—the daughter of Earl Rogers, famous criminal lawyer of the West who defended and cleared Clarence Darrow when he was indicted for jury bribery in Los Angeles many years ago.

She traveled about with her father as a girl, getting liberal glimpses of life's grim by-ways through his legal practice. She detested school and flunked consistently in mathematics. She failed to graduate from grammar school but went to high school. She failed to graduate from high school but went to college. Then she plunged headlong into newspaper work. She had seen the press swarm around her father; she had listened to the glamour tales that invest the city room. While she was still in her teens Charles E. Van Loan, an intimate friend of her father's, got her a job on the Los Angeles *Herald*. Her salary was $7 a week and the paper was pleased to have her, as a link with Earl Rogers' office.

Adela, fairish-haired, her eyes an intense blue-gray, her face singularly expressive of her highly geared emotions, batted out her first half-column with an instinctive sense of how to do it. She became irreconcilably a newspaper woman. Today she lives on Long Island, turns out short stories that command high prices, works prodigiously, sells scenarios when she feels like it, but ditched Hollywood and a $2,000 a week contract to pursue the life she prefers. This involves turning on steam now and again for the Hearst papers, which she does with great aptitude. Her name is a guarantee of vivid, breathless writing. Her newspaper work is less calm than her fiction, which is compressed and highly dramatic. Her short stories are often taken from the raw material she encounters in news-

second husband was Dick Hyland, the Stanford half-back, but this marriage went up in smoke. She is now the wife of Francis T. O'Toole, an air line executive. She is the mother of three children.

Miss St. Johns mulls over her stories for weeks; then sits down and writes them with a burst of speed. She gets up at eight o'clock every morning, no matter how late she has worked the night before. She is a vivid figure in any press section and a good craftsman. She has never missed a deadline and is not easily fooled on news. Miss St. Johns need never do anything but fiction. However, a big court-room drama always draws her in, and she reports it with the enthusiasm of a cub on her first assignment.

Chapter XXI

ON THE AIR

WHEN MARTHA DEANE'S BEGUILING VOICE COMES OVER THE air in the early afternoon with a casual stream of information for the woman in the home, all her hearers do not know that the person behind it is Mary Margaret McBride, as smart a newspaper girl as ever scaled a ship ladder before dawn to listen to the babblings of a visiting celebrity. Her folksy manner is a natural gift, for she understands the heart throbs of the less cynical part of the population, in spite of the fact that she went through the realistic newspaper school herself.

Miss McBride has had varied journalistic training. She has chased royalty all over Europe and comforted East Side mothers when their babies have been found dead in cellars. She is also one of the more successful ghost writers and has functioned in this capacity for Paul Whiteman, Anne Morgan, Prince Christopher of Greece, David Sarnoff, Owen D. Young and Marion Talley, among others.

She has been turning out copy of one sort or another ever since her first poem was printed in the *Drover's Journal* of Chicago when she was six years old. Her family wanted her to do this and that—play the piano, do charcoal drawings, recite with expression or teach school, but Mary Margaret had only one idea and they couldn't shake it out of her. She wanted to write for the papers.

She was born on a prairie farm near Paris, Missouri, in the same county as Mark Twain. She still likes the smell of earth, honeysuckle and clover. Her forebears came from Virginia and Kentucky, which accounts for the slight Southern twist to her tongue. Her paternal grandfather was a substantial settler who had owned a white-pillared house, but it passed from the family hands when Mary Margaret was a little girl. She used to ride past it in the spring wagon and share her grandfather's resentment over the severance. He was a scholar who tried to teach her Latin and Greek almost as soon as she could speak. It was he who first put the idea into her head that she must be a writer.

Her maternal grandfather was a Baptist minister, known to every-

one as B. Craig. He, too, set his mark on Mary Margaret's life, for she used to ride with him behind a small white horse while he declaimed whole chapters of the Bible for her benefit. From that time on she had no ambition to swing on a trapeze, dazzle Broadway or study art in the Latin quarter. She merely wanted to write. She read everything she could find about newspaper people. Her days in a country school were mere stepping stones along the way.

When she was eleven she was taken over by her aunt, Mrs. William Woods, who founded William Woods College at Fulton, Missouri. She was sent to a boarding school, where she tried piano and gave it up, picked on the mandolin, but to no good purpose, and finally found in herself a gift for elocution. She became a pupil teacher and from that went on to the State University at Columbia, Missouri, determined to take a course in journalism. But her aunt disapproved. She was sent home and landed at her objective without another pause, through Tom Bodine, who was getting out a weekly paper at the time—the Paris *Mercury*—hand-set, with wide sheets. His editorial page was called The Scrap Bag, and he wrote it from beginning to end. He gave Miss McBride a place on his staff and let her write news. Then he took most of her items and did them over in his own fine style, signing her name to them. The result was that soon she was being quoted in the Missouri notes of the Kansas City *Star* and elsewhere.

Her next step was to cover society for a paper in Columbia. She had never seen a social column done in the gossipy vein, but she launched her own on this plan. Often she got her social notes by the simple device of calling up the dairies to ask who was ordering extra ice cream. Then she astonished hostesses by telling them she knew they were having guests. It was a Southern college town, quiet and leisurely. Mary Margaret wandered about the streets, hatless, inquiring. Residents called her into their homes as she passed—fed her and gave her news. She was soon doing courts as well as society. She called herself managing editor of the paper and no one disputed the point. Her pay was $10 a week and it wasn't always forthcoming. But Mary Margaret's eyes were persistently fixed on the East. She moved steadily in that direction until she landed in Washington as a folder in the United States Senate. There she typed gas bills and learned the costs of senators' funerals.

One day she received a message from Victor Morgan, of the Cleveland *Press*, offering her a job. Mrs. Ernest Hemingway, a former classmate, had recommended her to Mr. Morgan. She started at $35 a week but soon traveled East again, this time to cover a religious convention. As she was one of the few reporters who stayed sober on the job, she was asked to do publicity for the Interchurch World movement in New York. And, as luck would have it, when this petered out Miss McBride went to work for the *Mail*, where she soon made a substantial reputation for herself. She announced dramatically on her first day that she wanted to cover fires. The city desk took her at her word and sent her out on a fire. It was a good one and she landed smack on the front page with a byline. This does not often happen with fires.

From 1921-1924 her name appeared constantly in the *Mail*. She did interviews, spectacles, features on crime, parades, welcomes and cat shows. She went after celebrities abroad. The *Mail* never hesitated to send its women reporters to distant parts in quest of news. Like Zöe Beckley, she hunted royalty in Europe. Her paper had a weakness for crowned heads, and these were the days when the few remaining thrones were tottering on their bases. She found ex-King Manuel of Portugal raising geese at Twickenham, and the Princess Zita in the Basque country, somewhere near Zuloaga's home. George of Greece was absorbed in mechanical marvels when she talked to him. Ferdinand of Bulgaria eluded her because he was chasing butterflies in Sweden when she was on his trail.

Miss BcBride always chose her own assignments and they were never dull. She was under contract and made $100 a week, until Mr. Munsey's chilly hand swept the paper out of existence. She was asked to edit the religious page of the *Telegram*, which had absorbed part of the *Mail* staff. It was then that she decided to write for the magazines. Almost at once she landed in the *Saturday Evening Post* with the story of Paul Whiteman's life.

For the next few years she isolated herself and worked night and day on her protracted ghosting jobs. Then she and Helen Josephy, who got her newspaper training on the *Globe* and *Mail*, did a series of books together. It was the boom time for tourists. Miss Josephy went to Paris, worked on the *Herald*, lived in pensions, explored the shops, restaurants, churches, race tracks and odd corners, and dug up an amazing amount of useful data for the tourist, which she and Miss McBride put together in *Paris is a Woman's Town*. They followed this with similar books on London, Berlin and New York. Miss Josephy is now associated with *Mademoiselle*, which features the work of members of her craft.

Miss McBride was widely known in her profession, even before she began to broadcast. Her success on the air was instantaneous. She continues to be a reporter when she gives her daily talks. She knows the value of facts, and presents them in a soft, insidious way.

Long before she turned to radio, another newspaper woman, known to nearly every city editor in the country, was on the air. This was Nellie Revell, whose copy had been appearing for thirty years in the papers of Chicago, Denver, San Francisco and New York. Miss Revell got her first chance as a reporter when she was sixteen. Her father owned the Springfield *Journal*. He would not employ her, so she went over to the opposition and scooped the family paper on her first assignment. Then he relented and gave her a job.

She worked for the Chicago *Times* and covered her first murder trial for the Chicago *Chronicle*. She was present at the coronation of the Czar and Queen Victoria's funeral. She was one of the first women to appear at prize fights and write about them. She broke the inside story of a series of fur robberies in Chicago.

Four generations of newspaper people preceded her on one side of the family tree and five generations of show people on the other. In the end she followed both careers. When she went to see a small circus at Morris, Illinois, she was so carried away with enthusiasm that she threw up her newspaper job and went in for circus exploitation. This was the beginning of a long and spectacular career in press agentry. Like Dexter Fellows, whose annual appearance is hailed with real warmth by the leading city editors of the country, Miss Revell became the herald of the big tent show. When she first joined the circus she used to watch a youth who sold lemonade, danced, sang, acted and made himself generally useful. His name was Fred Stone.

Within a few years she was press agenting six circuses, and as her career ripened, she did publicity for Mrs. Patrick Campbell, Al Jolson, Frank Tinney, Lily Langtry, Norah Bayes, Lillian Russell, Elsie Janis, Eva Tanguay, Will Rogers and scores of others. But in 1919, when her professional reputation was at its height, she had an accident and her spine was fractured. For years afterwards she lay in a plaster cast in a hospital. Her doctors thought she would never get up again. Actors and writers flocked to her bedside. When it was learned that she was penniless her theatrical friends gave her a testimonial dinner. Her book, *Right off the Chest*, written while she was flat on her back, was Nellie Revell in profile.

Soon she began to get about in a wheel chair. Her indomitable will had conquered her invalidism. Then she went on the air. Her fortunes rose again. Miss Revell is a pet of the show world. She is dynamic, spirited, full of good stories. She knows the lingo of the tanbark, can put it across when she is in the mood, and is one of the town's characters.

A newspaper woman of a different type, whose work also was closely allied to the theater, was Theodora Bean, who died in 1926. She was handsome, imperious, and abhorred sentiment. She had executive qualities that made her as good in an editorial post as on the street—a rare combination in the woman reporter.

She was a Minnesota girl who left Carleton College at nineteen years of age to seek a newspaper job in Chicago. Charles H. Davis, of the Chicago *Daily News*, gave her her first assignment. It was to write an advance on a society bicycle race. Her story made the front page and was illustrated by John T. McCutcheon. Her style was so adroit and original that she was taken on the staff at once. She did club news, worked in the sports department, took general assignments and was coached in rewrite by George Ade, a member of the staff at the time.

When Carrie Nation descended on Chicago, determined to clean up the saloons, Miss Bean was assigned to interview her. She pulled a fast trick on her rivals by persuading Carrie to spend the night at a Turkish bath. Naturally no one could find her and Miss Bean scored with an exclusive interview.

After free-lancing from Europe for a time Miss Bean joined the staff of the New York *Telegraph* as a feature writer. All her work had a witty, sophisticated touch. Her interviews were penetrating. Even her news stories had an amusing turn. She attracted the attention of James Gordon Bennett with the pieces she did on the gatherings of suffragists at the Newport home of Mrs. O. H. P. Belmont, and he asked her to write for him.

After a third trip to Europe Miss Bean returned to the *Telegraph* as Sunday editor. The old barn-like building was a friendly spot after the theater. The Sunday section of the paper was large and sprawling. It involved a great deal of careful management. Miss Bean was well equipped to cope with the technical problems. She had decision and firmness of character, and a masculine outlook on her work. She could manage printers, handle make-up and see that everyone did his job. Louella Parsons worked for her during this period and was one of her close friends.

Miss Bean had a keen sense of fun and knew how to ridicule the mealy-mouthed; she could never stand bores or stupid people. But she was intensely loyal to her friends and to her profession. She followed the advances made by newspaper women during her time with an appreciative eye. Her own characteristics were distinctive. She smoked cigars, carried a walking stick and had a passion for detective stories. She was a familiar figure at first nights, and in her spare moments went in for painting furniture. Cooking was one of her hobbies. She could plank a steak like a chef. She detested cats, liked dogs and always predicted that eventually she would retire to the country and breed them.

But she was still pursuing her profession when she died. She resigned from the *Telegraph* in 1924 and founded the T-Bean syndicate which she ran for two years. Her strong personality was missed from the newspaper scene, for she had rare qualities that made her a memorable figure in journalism.

Another newspaper woman whose work was closely interlocked with the theater was the gifted Ruth Hale, reporter, critic and ardent feminist. She was the wife of Heywood Broun and the founder of the Lucy Stone League. A native of Tennessee, she attended Hollins Institute, and studied painting and sculpture at the Drexel Academy of Fine Arts in Philadelphia. At eighteen she was working for the Hearst bureau in Washington, one of her earliest stories being her account of the marriage of Alice Roosevelt to Nicholas Longworth.

For a time Miss Hale was dramatic critic of the Philadelphia *Ledger* and she was one of the first women in the country to cover sports. During 1915 and 1916 she wrote for the Sunday edition of the New York *Times*. Then she went into magazine and press theatrical work. It was during this period that she met and married Mr. Broun. When he was sent to France as a war correspondent she went with him and worked on the Paris edition of the Chicago *Tribune*.

Miss Hale was essentially the intellectual type of reporter. Her interests lay much deeper than the superficial turn of event. She took up causes with the intensity of a crusader and backed anything that involved woman's rights. She put up a successful fight on the passport issue and was the first woman to go abroad under her maiden name. Like Mr. Broun, she was vocal on the Sacco-Vanzetti case and always lent her support to the liberal and humanitarian cause. She was the daughter of Annie Riley Hale, who sought the Democratic Senatorial nomination in California in 1932. She had one son, Heywood 3d.

Back in 1909 Anna Marble sat in a busy little office in the Hippodrome building day after day, directing a spectacular publicity campaign. Before then she had worked for the Brooklyn *Eagle* and the New York *Telegram*. She left newspaper work to press agent *Floradora*. Subsequently she was business manager for Elsie de Wolfe, Nazimova and other stage celebrities. She knew the theater from all angles and wrote one-act plays, stories, verse and fairy tales. Anna Marble is now Mrs. Channing Pollock and the mother of an excellent newspaper man, Warren Irvin.

Marian Spitzer is another of the newspaper women to link her fortunes with the theater and cinema industry. Handsome, talented and enterprising, Miss Spitzer worked effectively for the Brooklyn *Times* and the New York *Globe*, then did theatrical press work and went on to Hollywood, where she is now an assistant producer for

Paramount. She writes for the leading magazines, has a novel to her credit, is the mother of a small son and the wife of Harlan Thompson, the playwright.

Nearly a quarter of a century ago Dorothy Richardson, who is now with Paramount, was a star on the *Herald*. She employed Ann Grosvenor Ayres to do a questions and answers column. Miss Ayres was soon assigned to full-page Sunday features on Broadway figures, and from this she went on to theatrical press work and producing. Newspaper work for women is apt to lead in any direction—but most often toward publicity or creative writing.

Chapter XXII

ENTER THE TABLOIDS

IN JUNE, 1920, FOUR MONTHS AFTER HER ARRIVAL IN NEW YORK
from Tennessee, Julia Harpman went to the doorstep of Joseph
Bowne Elwell, the bridge expert who had been found dead that
morning in his house in West Seventieth Street, a block away from
where she lived.

There she bumped into a tall young man who turned out to
be Westbrook Pegler. He was not then the famous columnist that
he is today, but he was the same able reporter. Newspaper romances flourish in odd spots. Several great murder cases have ended
in newspaper marriages. Julia and Peg, as they are best known to
their colleagues, are a notable case in point.

At the moment of their meeting nothing was further from their
thoughts. They were both intent on rounding up the details of a
startling new crime. They had the impersonal approach of two good
reporters out on a big assignment. They were experienced enough to
know that the Elwell murder had the quality that keeps a crime on
the front pages week after week, while the public debates it endlessly
from a thousand different angles. They did not yet know that it was
to become one of the baffling mysteries of the era.

It had a liberal assortment of provocative elements—intrigue,
wealth and beautiful women; gamblers, bootleggers, wronged husbands and race track touts; a dancer, a manicurist, a countess, an
Egyptian princess, a South American publisher. And for the central
figure the mysterious Elwell, found dead as he sat in a chair, bare-
footed, blood flowing from a hole in the middle of his forehead.

For weeks Miss Harpman wrung the last bit of drama from this
story for her paper. To this day she and Westbrook Pegler debate
the possible solution over the fireside of their Bavarian home in
Connecticut. It is only one of many murders, solved and unsolved,
which haunt Julia's memory from her newspaper days. The interest
of a reporter in the solution of a crime is intense, by the very nature
of her work. After she has devoted herself to it night and day for
weeks and months, followed up futile clues that seemed at the

moment to point to a solution, talked to suspects, and come to know at first hand the weird human parade that gets the spotlight with every major crime, she would be curiously indifferent to her job if she failed to take a scientific interest in any sequel that fate may provide.

Miss Harpman covered crime with such thoroughness and skill that she left her competitors trailing far behind. She pioneered in the tabloid field in this country. The New York *Daily News* was launched on June 26, 1919, and eight months later she joined the staff. This was a significant step in the history of women in American journalism. It gave them a new place in the city room. It provided more jobs. In June, 1924, Mr. Hearst started the *Daily Mirror*. Three months later Bernarr Macfadden flooded the newsstands with the *Evening Graphic*, which far outdid its rivals in monstrosities of make-up, composite pictures and sensationalism.

The whole idea was experimental. The tabloids could not compete with the established papers on their own ground. They had to astonish, bemuse, dazzle or horrify the reader. Their editors did handsprings to startle the town. Their reporters had to follow suit. A group of clever girls adopted the new technique with success. Miss Harpman led the procession. By the end of 1925 the approximate circulation of the three tabloids was 1,350,000. The *Graphic* was unsound and it failed. It made the cardinal newspaper error of ignoring truth. But the *News* and the *Mirror* flourished and the tabloid idea spread.

There was a heavy crop of sensational murder cases in the early twenties. Miss Harpman took them all in. Her paper played these stories hard; then dropped them overnight and went on to the next, when another beautiful woman shot another dastardly man in some remote corner of New Jersey. One winter night she slept in a filthy shack while a man suspected of a famous murder stirred restlessly in the next room. On another occasion she trudged eight miles through snow above her knees to get the story of a woman who had been thrown into jail as a spy. She watched a murdered man's body being grappled out of a quicksand swamp and the bones of a baby being scraped from forest soil eight years after his disappearance. She saw men convicted and women faint with joy over their acquittal on charges of murder. She accompanied Gertrude Ederle in her swim across the Channel, egging her on from a launch. She crashed a thousand feet into the ocean at dusk in a crippled seaplane on her way to cover an assignment. She was threatened with death repeatedly. She talked to gangsters in their haunts and listened to the ravings of their molls.

Miss Harpman was broken in to tabloid journalism by Philip A.

Payne, as distinct a personality in his way as Charles E. Chapin or Walter Howey, both of whom justly earned the title of being hard-boiled city editors—one in a ruthless manner, the other with a more whimsical touch. Miss Harpman liked the extraordinary Payne, as did most of the reporters who worked for him. He was half deaf and near sighted. He had bristly, untidy hair which matched his mad ideas. He had been a preliminary boy in a cheap fight club earning $8 a week as a minor league reporter before invading Park Row. He lacked any literary instincts but he did know news. And his ideas brought quick returns in circulation—first for the *News*, then the *Mirror*. He died as spectacularly as he had lived—trying to fly the Atlantic in Old Glory.

Mr. Payne gave the girl reporters a heavy play. He believed in their work. He spurred them on to daring feats. He was a hard driver—sincere, quick-tempered, inconsistent. He was quick to spot a good story and he whipped his reporters into pursuing every clue to a dead end. This was excellent training, if somewhat hard on the staff. He would have been staggered had any of his girls dared to say she would not gladly go out and die for the *News*. Miss Harpman worked for him night and day. She moved from place to place without much sleep or time for meals. She froze and got soaked to the skin and survived feats of endurance that seem incredible in retrospect.

She grew familiar with the pitcher and bowl existence of the traveling salesman, for it is a newspaper platitude that the great crimes take place in the most obscure spots. The result is that the importunate press must commandeer the local inn and rent all the available houses in the district. Lunch counters mushroom overnight; taxis fill the town; a premium is put on telephones when this lunatic invasion hits the town, turning it upside down, putting it on the front page, disturbing the somnolent peace of Main Street.

Miss Harpman was not a newspaper novice when she started out on her first murder in New York. For two years she had been covering courts in Knoxville, Tennessee. But she knew nothing of tabloid journalism. Her entire fortune consisted of a bundle of newspaper clippings, a borrowed squirrel coat, $63 in cash and a letter from Bishop Thomas F. Gailor of Tennessee. She got to town on the day that the *Sun* and *Herald* were combined, an inauspicious time to seek a job. The second city editor who turned her down suggested that there might be something for her on the new tabloid. It was then known as *The Illustrated News* and was published in the grimy old building occupied by the *Mail*.

"I'll give you a trial assignment—not a job," said Mr. Payne. "Take a run up to the Church of the Ascension on Fifth Avenue and see what the vestrymen decided at their secret session this afternoon. There's been a fight between Dr. Percy Stickney Grant, the rector, and Bishop Manning. The vestrymen are meeting today to see whether they will stick with Grant or split the church. You find out what they did."

This was a stiff assignment for a reporter new to the city. The diocese was in a turmoil over Dr. Grant's defiance of the Bishop. He had threatened to deny the Virgin Birth, then had sidestepped the issue. Underlying was the bad feeling over the Bishop's refusal to let him marry Mrs. Rita de Acosta Lydig and still retain his parish.

When Miss Harpman asked for Dr. Grant at the rectory, a butler slammed the door in her face. This wasn't much of a blow. Butlers and reporters are sworn enemies. The custodians of the door are invariably more rude to the press than their masters. Next Miss Harpman went into the dimly lit hallway of the silent vestry house. She went upstairs and on the top floor discovered a singular figure like a gnome, cutting out choir vestments. He held his scissors in mid-air when he saw her.

"What do you want?" he demanded.

"I want to know what's going on at that meeting," said Miss Harpman authoritatively.

"You won't tell who told you," he cautioned her, "but I heard the vestrymen vote to support Dr. Grant. And there's some kind of Bolshevik meeting going on now on the second floor. Go in and sit down as if you belonged there and you can find out what it is all about."

Miss Harpman discovered an assorted group listening to a speaker with wild red hair. He was advocating the abolition of the Supreme Court and the abrogation of the Senate. His face seemed familiar.

"Isn't that ex-Governor Sulzer speaking?" she asked the woman sitting next to her.

"Certainly, that's the Governor," she was told.

Miss Harpman left the hall quietly. She got hold of one of the vestrymen and confirmed the tailor's tip that the church was supporting Dr. Grant against the Bishop. She went back to her office.

"Did you get the story?" Mr. Payne asked.

"I did, and also another."

Miss Harpman told him what she had.

"You've got a job," said Mr. Payne, who had not really expected any success, for he had sent out two other reporters who had failed to get the Grant story. Every move was being kept secret from the press. Next day the *News* appeared on the street with this and the story of the ousted Governor's insurrectionary words under an Episcopalian church roof.

Mr. Payne was never to regret his decision to take Miss Harpman on the staff. She proved to be one of the finest reporters, men or women, that New York has produced. She soon had the star men on the most conservative papers trying to keep up with her. She had a great gift for nosing out unexpected facts and was an indefatigable worker. Her record on the Halls-Mills case was impressive. She was one of the first reporters on the scene after the rector and choir singer were found dead under the crab apple tree in New Jersey. From that point on she was a step ahead of everyone else in rounding up the witnesses in the case. Sometimes she reached them before the police. Like the other reporters working on the early investigation, she was well aware of the muddle-headed operations of the rival prosecutors who were supposedly trying to solve the case. She and Boyden Sparkes, of the *Tribune*, badgered them relentlessly, and forced them to some sort of activity when they seemed to be going to sleep at the switch.

Night and day she motored about the country, rounding up people whose lives had been oddly threaded in with the crime, finding gravediggers and village gossips, seamstresses and farmers who heard shots, habitués of de Russey's Lane and firemen friends of Willie Stevens. She was the first person to get a coherent story out of Mrs. Jane Gibson, the pig woman who accused Mrs. Hall. When Miss Harpman called on this fantastic creature in her shack in the country, she was greeted with a shotgun.

"Get off my land, you so-and-so," Mrs. Gibson yelled at her.

The dogs were turned loose. The rifle was brandished dangerously. Julia held her ground. She has a gentle, persuasive manner. In time she got around Mrs. Gibson, although it took persistence to wear down her hostility.

In one of the great murder cases of the period, still unsolved, Mr. Payne was convinced that the person least under suspicion had committed the crime. As an amateur ball-player Mr. Payne fancied the terminology of the diamond.

"Let's pitch to this guy's weakness, if he has one," he told Miss Harpman.

She happened to know that the man in question was interested in spiritualism. So Mr. Payne decided that he would frighten him into confession at a séance. He had the art department prepare a letterhead designed for a mythical Madame Astra. It had hoot-owls, cobras, bats, black tomcats and toads surrounding a line-drawing of a veiled brunette with curtain rings in her ears.

Bernadine Szold, an exotic-looking girl reporter then working on the *News*, was assigned to go the rounds of the New York mystics to pick up atmosphere. She was to be Madame Astra. Bernadine might have been born for the rôle. She went to Cain's warehouse, where the scenery of Broadway's forgotten shows is stored, and dug out a black velvet backdrop that had been used in the *Follies*, a plaster pedestal with a green snake coiled around the column, a large brass Buddha and a mock throne. She borrowed a crystal ball from an optician, and a scene-shifter set up the magic props in her apartment.

Madame Astra then wrote to the suspect, saying that her spirit control had news for him. The day after the letter arrived, Miss Harpman talked to him in his kitchen. He was used to hourly invasions by the press and it was quite natural for him to chat about the letters he received. He was an odd character—seemingly as simple as a child; actually very cunning. He asked Miss Harpman's advice about the letter from the seeress.

"Well," she said, "I don't believe in spirits, but if you do, I don't want to advise you against seeing this woman. But watch out for a trick."

"I was afraid of that," he said. "I won't go unless you go with me."

So they went together to Madame Astra's. They were welcomed at the door by a swarthy young man masquerading as a snake-charmer.

"You stay out," he told Miss Harpman. "The gentleman must come in alone to see Madame."

Behind the velvet curtain sat two stenographers, the prosecutor, two detectives and Mr. Payne. Every effort was made to crack the seemingly feeble mentality of the victim. All sorts of abracadabra was sprung on him. The legend on Park Row at the time was that his wife's ghost appeared with clanking chains but failed to make him turn a hair. Bernadine tried to break him down by subtle and obvious methods. She evoked strange images from the crystal. She recalled the looks and gestures of his wife. But the suspect rambled along in his characteristic vein and showed no signs of alarm.

By this time he was used to all sorts of inquisitions. For weeks some of the toughest tykes and brightest wits of the newspaper profession had been badgering him unmercifully in his kitchen and his invariable reaction had been to lift the stove-lid with its holder and spit thoughtfully into the flames. They were just as unsuccessful as the police.

So the séance was a flop. The suspect didn't confess. He didn't even bat an eyelash. He was never charged with the crime.

Shortly before Gerald Chapman, the bandit who was shockingly over-touted in the Robin Hood rôle, was due to hang at Wethersfield Prison in Connecticut, Miss Harpman was conducted to a curious hideaway in Newark to meet an Italian gambler who thought she was a friend of the bank robber and murderer. She found her host playing a Sunday School organ. He welcomed her and reminisced for two hours on the days when Chapman posed in New York as the English owner of oil wells in Oklahoma and frequented his gambling house in the West Nineties. At that time there was a reward of $100,000, alive or dead, on his head. Dutch Anderson was always with him, passing as his secretary.

The Italian told Miss Harpman that the police had had both men in their hands one night while every station house in the country was placarded with their pictures, and had let them get away. They were in his gambling house at the time. A raid was pulled. A woman gave the tip. She stood at an open window, fanning herself with a handkerchief. This was the signal for the detectives to rush the place. Chapman sat down hurriedly on a couch and stuffed a pistol under a cushion. Then he thrust a roll of money into a detective's hand and slipped away. Anderson was taken into custody but was not identified.

"Chapman," said the Italian, "had the nerve to drive down to West Side Court in a limousine behind a chauffeur next morning and wait for Anderson and me to get through with our hearing. When we were released he drove us away. Dutch posed for a picture in court but even when it was printed, nobody recognized it."

Miss Harpman looked up the picture in her paper and found that the Italian was telling her the truth. It was unmistakably Dutch's somber countenance that had appeared in connection with a cheap shake-down complaint. On the day that Chapman went coolly to the chair, the *News* circulation went up by 110,000. Only a world championship fight boosts the circulation of a tabloid more than an execution. The picture of Ruth Snyder, snapped by stealth while she was dying in the electric chair, augmented the press run by 120,000 copies. The Sacco-Vanzetti execution sold 185,000 extra copies. The subway disaster at Times Square in 1928 resulted in additional sales of 180,000 papers. Major prize fights usually run the circulation up by at least 100,000 copies. The Tunney-Dempsey fight in Philadelphia touched the top with the sale of 240,000 extra copies. The Dempsey-Sharkey fight ran to 200,000; the Sharkey-Schmeling bout to 193,000. The Tunney-Heeney fight sold 187,000 extra copies of the *News*. Election returns also bring phenomenal jumps in circulation. But spectacular crime is a sure and sustained circulation builder in the tabloid field.

Miss Harpman wrote vivid pieces about the murder of Dot King, who was found dead in her apartment in the spring of 1923, chloroformed, and with tape around her mouth. This was the "Broadway Butterfly" crime that involved a well-known banker and enriched the new tabloid vocabulary. About this time the succinct terminology of the tabs began to gain ground and get into general currency—love nests, gin mills, torch murders, cry-baby bandits, bobbed-hair bandits, sugar daddies, on the spot, trigger men, crooners, gang slayings, muscling in, death pacts, heart balm, wonder girl, dream babies, tiger woman, and torso murders. The blondes were always svelte; the brunettes were vivacious. Each new crime launched its own phrase.

After Dot King's death a murder of almost identical characteristics repeated the Broadway butterfly theme, and again Miss Harpman chronicled it with all the graphic touches of the full-blown tabloid story. This time the victim was Louise Lawson, a music student from Texas who was found smothered to death in her apartment. Neither crime has yet been solved.

Miss Harpman was on the job a few minutes after her city editor received the dramatic bulletin that there had been an explosion in Wall Street. This was in the autumn of 1920. She was in time to witness the first confusion, before anyone knew what had happened. She covered the Ku Klux forays in Georgia and the last of Harry K. Thaw's sanity hearings in Philadelphia. She went to prize fights and World Series games. It was while she was flying to Atlantic City to do a feature on Luis Firpo training for his fight with Dempsey that she fell a thousand feet into the ocean and miraculously survived. She had just returned from a mountain hamlet, where she had been covering a murder, when Morrow Krum offered to fly her down the Jersey Coast to Atlantic City.

When they were over Sandy Hook, engine trouble developed. The airplane made straight for the sea. Mr. Krum kept his head, tried to right the plane, and at the same time reached over and batted Miss Harpman severely on the neck to get her head into the lee of the windshield. Next minute they struck the water violently. The sea roared into the cockpit. Miss Harpman thought she was dead, but strangely enough she wasn't. She and Morrow Krum poked out their heads simultaneously. They didn't feel like laughing. No land was visible. Half a mile to seaward they spotted a tug with a lumber barge in tow. It was dusk and they did not have flares or signal lamps. The pilot stepped out on the bow, waved his arms and shouted for help. All sounds were lost in the wind.

But they had been spotted. The tug hove toward them, although the barge resisted stubbornly. At last their rescuers were close enough to form a lee and give the airplane a chance to steady a trifle. Sixteen sailors stood by while Miss Harpman clambered out on the wing of the plane. A rope was passed. The plane rose on a swell and she jumped for the tug.

At the critical moment, she turned to look for her companion. There was a shout of warning. Two sailors grabbed her by the arms. Another caught her by the ankles and swung her up in the air in time to escape the lash of a tow-line that had suddenly pulled taut as the tug rode the waves. One sailor was tossed into the sea but when the hawser slackened he caught it and climbed back to safety. Morrow Krum stuck to his airplane and it was put in tow astern the barge. They all set out for Brooklyn, but ten minutes later the hawser snapped and the barge and seaplane went adrift. By the time they were taken into tow again, the unhappy pilot was glad enough to board the barge.

On August 6, 1926, Trudy Ederle swam the English Channel in 14 hours and 31 minutes, setting a record. Miss Harpman accompanied her in a launch on her historic marathon from Gris Nez to Kingsdown. It was an exciting day in the life of a reporter. The Chicago *Tribune* and the *News* had bought the exclusive rights to the girl's own story of her training, and the big day itself. Miss Harpman had gone abroad with her and knew all Trudy's emotions before, during and after the swim. She was thoroughly sympathetic to the unsophisticated girl who was deluged with fabulous offers after swimming the Channel, then was soon forgotten.

Her welcome home was second only to Lindbergh's. Miss Harpman followed her every step of the way. It was one of the old gala days of ticker tape and delirious crowds downtown, while James J. Walker was still riding high, the speakeasy flourished, the depression had not set in, and citizens liked to line the streets and cheer for an incoming celebrity. But Trudy's day passed swiftly. She flashed through the news columns, made the headlines, tasted the heady wine of extravagant publicity; then went out of sight with the speed of an expiring rocket.

This was one of the last important stories that Miss Harpman covered. She retired to live in the country. Her health was not good. She had rounded out a remarkable newspaper career. She is still cited on Park Row as the ideal woman reporter. All the men and women with whom she worked admired her. They called her gentle Julia. She was that paradoxical creature—the feminine reporter with the masculine touch on news. She had great driving force behind a mellow manner. She could translate deeds of violence into vivid prose, and write withering copy. She faced danger many times in the course of her work, and for a long period was desperately ill. The assignment that took her to Elwell's door was one of the lucky moments of her life. Her newspaper marriage has been singularly happy. She travels far and wide now with Peg. She is still a party to many of the news stories of the day. But she can watch them as a spectator. She no longer has to worry about deadlines, beats or the lead story for page three.

She was followed on the *News* by Grace Robinson, who is always to be found in the front row at any great murder trial, rubbing elbows with Damon Runyon, and pushing a pencil with speed and competence. She is small, slim, frail in build but tenacious of purpose, sturdy of will. Grace is so reserved that she is a mystery even to her closest colleagues, who uniformly admire her. Her record of big stories is one that any man might envy. Sometimes her copy seems astonishingly sharp, coming from so mild a person. She does not euphemize, and knows to a dot how far a tabloid can go and still not incur a libel suit. She is calm in the middle of a hysterical scene. She responds to good court-room drama like any born reporter, but one never would suspect it. Her tilted eyes conceal their awareness. Her manner is restrained. She has been in plenty of tight spots but rarely talks about her experiences. She has been jailed on one or two occasions in the pursuit of news.

Miss Robinson knows, as few women reporters do, what it means day after day to have the lead play on the big news story of the day. But in her spare time she flees to a two-hundred-year-old house in Weston, Connecticut, where she has her meals on a terrace, surrounded by bird houses and flowers. There she indulges in quiet contemplation away from the fever of her work. She can cook as well as she can turn out a pyrotechnic picture of the criminal world. Of such contradictory elements is the good newspaper woman made.

Jack Diamond sent for Miss Robinson when he was on trial in Federal Court on a liquor charge. He had read some earlier stories she had written about him. Then, when he saw that she was covering the federal trial, he sent a message by an indirect route that he would like to be interviewed by her.

"Don't let anyone know who I am, for I will be thrown out," he warned her. "Come to this hotel and ask for Mr. Jones."

Miss Robinson went to a well-known commercial hotel in midtown New York. She found him looking ill and nervous. He presented his bodyguards to her, mumbling the names of the strange assortment of thugs who filled the small hotel room. They were all deferential to her. Diamond ordered them out of the room. Then his wife, Alice, came in. She fussed about, rouging her cheeks and doing her hair.

"Go on up to the roof where it's cool, honey," he suggested. And she went.

Miss Robinson was now left alone with him. He locked the door and took careful observations out of the one window. He seemed to be in constant fear. The waiter came. Supper was served. They ate and drank. He was anxious to propitiate Grace. He held up a copy of her paper. It carried a banner line about him.

"See," he said indignantly. "These jurors walking through the lobby see just that. I want you to know that I'm not a bad fellow."

"Mr. Diamond, you say you are not a gangster," said Miss Robinson boldly. "Just what do you do for a living?"

"Well, that's a little difficult to explain," said Diamond evasively. "I can't describe how I make my living. I couldn't now, anyway, because I'm afraid the government is going to investigate income taxes."

Miss Robinson could get nothing out of him. So she fell back on the stock tintype questions—what size shoes he wore, what food he preferred, what he read, how he passed the time. Jack worked hard to make a good impression on her. He fancied himself as a smart and scholarly fellow. He was far from being either. The interview made an entertaining Sunday story.

In 1932 Captain Patterson, who is deeply interested in motion pictures, assigned Miss Robinson to accompany Greta Garbo to Sweden. She got visas for a number of European countries, not knowing where the star might get off. She boarded the *Gripsholm* quietly. Her cue was to travel as a passenger until she got access to the publicity-shy Garbo. But she was soon detected as a reporter. The secret code that had been worked out in the *News* office was transparent to the wireless operators. They told her to save herself the trouble of translating her messages into symbolism. She had been working laboriously in her stateroom from a large chart.

The Captain conspired to protect the hallowed Garbo. A special stewardess was assigned to guard her. Miss Robinson deluged her with notes, all of which were returned unread. Her deck chair was moved from the top deck so that Garbo could play games undisturbed. If she saw Miss Robinson approaching, she ran like mad, leaving the game flat. She appeared in the dining-room only three times and refused to meet any of the passengers except three or four who sat at the Captain's table. Finally Miss Robinson sent her a letter through the post office, believing that no one would dare to interfere with the mails. On the night before they were due to land in Gothenburg, she found the star's door unguarded for a moment and knocked on it. She heard the famous throaty gurgle: "Who *is* it?"

"It's Miss Robinson, the reporter," said Grace, somewhat desperate by now. "I'm very anxious to interview you. Did you get my message?"

"Tomorrow morning at ten o'clock in the smoking room," Garbo announced in the dramatic tones that have thrilled movie fans from Alaska to Timbuctoo.

Next morning Miss Robinson faced her, bitter over her treatment. By now the Swedish reporters were swarming on board.

"Oh-h-h. . . . It was you who ruined my night," said Garbo reproachfully. "I wasn't able to get back to sleep."

She had taken a sleeping draught to prepare herself for meeting the reporters, it developed. Miss Robinson came to the conclusion that she was genuinely timid and thought a newspaper interview an ordeal.

After this trying experience Grace went to Finland and Russia, then to Berlin, where she got a cablegram from Frank Hause, of the *News*, saying that Mayor Walker was about to sail from Italy and that she was to accompany him home. He wanted to get back in time for the Democratic rally at which a mayor was to be nominated. Miss Robinson boarded the *Rex*, but the ship, which was on its maiden trip, broke down at Gibraltar. The Mayor was burned up with impatience and decided to get off. She had spent all her money and she couldn't use the radio while the ship was in port. It was a tight spot for her to be in. The Italian Line refused to cash a check for her. It was a week-end, so that she knew she could not raise any money on shore. There was only one train a day to Paris. The plane from Africa to Paris had been discontinued a few days before.

She saw Mr. Walker saunter off the ship. She would have asked him for money but her paper had attacked him consistently, and she knew that it would not be the thing to do. She had the desperate feeling that the reporter gets when circumstances seem hopelessly against him, coupled with the compelling instinct not to let the paper down. At last some money came through from her office with the order: "Must follow Walker." It wasn't nearly enough, but it would take her to Paris. The Mayor was already on his way north in an express. Some of her competitors were with him. It was Sunday. At the very best, by catching the next train out of Algeciras, she would arrive in Paris only forty minutes before the boat train left for Cherbourg, assuming that her train was on time.

Miss Robinson traveled north through Spain and France, sweating with anxiety all the way. She had eight pieces of luggage, which added to her embarrassment. They contained Swedish glass and pewter, Spanish shawls, several bottles of vodka which she was determined to get through, glasses from Russia with the Czar's coat of arms, as well as several cameras. The customs officials regarded her with suspicion.

She had telegraphed to the Chicago *Tribune* office in Paris, explaining her plight. Her colleagues scrambled about and collected all the francs they could obtain on a Sunday, but still the sum was not enough. Miss Robinson's train was on time. She joyfully hailed her rescuer, rushed to the steamship office with her francs but was told it was too late to buy a ticket there. She got to the station just as the boat train was about to pull out. The Mayor was having last-minute flashlights taken. Although he had never seen her except for a few moments on the *Rex*, his infallible gift for faces did not fail him. He saw her pushing through the crowd that surrounded him.

"My dear child, how did you get here?" he demanded.

"If you only knew!" muttered Miss Robinson, immensely relieved to be on the right track at last.

She boarded the *Europa* but she was still short of money and was forced to buy a second-class ticket, until the purser took her check and transferred her to first class. Four men from rival New York papers and press services were covering the Mayor on his anxious dash across the Atlantic. On the night of the political gathering he told them all he would have a statement for them at 8.30 P.M. It was to be read at the same time from the convention floor. He did not want to release it to them until it was public property in New York.

When the time came the five reporters surrounded him in the smoking room. There Mr. Walker announced his retirement from politics. He did it somewhat dramatically and seemed to be very much moved. The race had taken it out of him. He had been desperately anxious to get to New York in time but the odds were against him.

The reporters rushed upstairs to cable their stories. Miss Robinson stumbled over her long dress in her haste and fell head first. Evening dress is apt to get in the way of the girl reporter. She batted out her story at top speed. Hers hit New York first. It reached her office before the announcement of the Mayor's retirement had been read at the convention, and was on the street a few minutes afterwards, a neat piece of work for her paper.

King Edward VIII, then the Prince of Wales, was staying at the Burden estate on Long Island when Grace circumvented his guards and got into conversation with him at a polo field. He has always been one of the more difficult celebrities to cover and he led the press a dizzy chase during his visits to America. No information was given out about his movements. Yet the reporters had to feed their papers authentic details about him. This meant camping on his trail; chasing across the countryside in pursuit of him; using all their ingenuity to get wind of anything he might do.

State troopers and Department of Justice agents guarded the Burden estate. The Prince arrived on a Friday. He spent Saturday in Washington, paying his official call at the White House. Sunday was his first free day, and he was scheduled to play polo somewhere on Long Island, but none of the reporters knew where. Oliver Garrett, of the *World*, joined forces with Miss Robinson and one or two other reporters. There were four entrances to the estate. She was assigned to guard two that were close together. They were the back gates and seemed to be the least likely points of exit. Whichever one spotted the Prince was to follow him and then join his colleagues later on and share what he had. In spite of the competitive spirit in newspaper work, there is always collaboration when the mechanical odds are heavily against the press.

Miss Robinson's car was driven by an East Side sharper. The *Daily News* was placarded in large letters on the side. When she took her stand at one of the gates it struck her that this was being rather obvious, so she had her driver take off the sign, leaving them an anonymous pair.

"The Prince of Wales may come out by this entrance," she told her companion, "and if he does, don't let anything stop you. Not anything, mind you."

"Sure, Miss," said the delighted chauffeur.

A Rolls Royce purred smoothly through the gates. Miss Robinson was not altogether sure that it was the Prince. But her driver was.

"There ain't no doubt of it," he said. "I seen the ring."

They kept close on his trail all the way to the polo field. They rolled up so importantly behind him when they reached the barriers that they were assumed to be part of the entourage. Miss Robinson told her driver to park the car and she walked on to the field, conspicuous in an orange knitted suit. She did not know what she should do, now that she was on the spot. She stood about and watched the Prince. There were not many persons in sight—only the grooms and one or two society women who had heard that he was going to be there. There were fewer than a dozen spectators altogether.

Miss Robinson saw that Burt, his Scotland Yard man, had left his side for a moment while the horses were being changed. Now, she thought, I shall have to go through with this. She walked straight up to him and flung questions at him. He was so surprised that he answered them instinctively. She wanted to know if he would play in the International matches. She pressed him about his plans.

"Are you from the press?" he shot at her shrewdly.

"Yes," said Miss Robinson.

He was quite pleasant about it and went on with his polo. He stopped playing a few minutes later. As Grace was walking away,

Burt came running after her and said, "The Prince wants to see you."

This time he was the inquisitor. He wanted to know what press arrangements had been made to cover him. He said that he wished to be free to have a quiet time. He had not counted on being pursued by reporters. How could things be managed so that he would be left alone? he asked Miss Robinson.

This was a fine opportunity for a reporter to tell a Prince what he should do about the publicity he inevitably incurred. "It may be a little disagreeable to you," she said, "but you probably don't know how many millions of people like to read about you, and perhaps you don't realize how utterly friendly their interest in you is."

She told him that the arrangements for covering him were most inadequate. "We get merely what your secretary wishes to hand out and what you are actually doing we don't know," she explained. "Therefore, we are forced to the expedient of following you."

The Prince said that he would rather have the news given out more generously than that he should be trailed. He asked Miss Robinson for her card, but the careless girl didn't have one. So she borrowed one from a spectator and wrote down her name and the address of the little hotel where she was staying. As the Prince left the polo field he waved a friendly good-by. Her enterprise had not offended him in the least. Next day a call came through for her from one of his staff who wanted to arrange a better way of distributing the news.

But in spite of the Prince's wishes, things went from bad to worse and communication was virtually cut off altogether. This meant wild flurries of activity every time a car rolled out from the estate; mad dashes after anyone who looked like the Prince; frantic telephone calls to New York; lurking figures in the bushes, waiting for pictures; and all the horrifying mystery that surrounds the celebrity whose press relations are not on a completely frank and open basis.

But Miss Robinson had not yet played her last card. On the night that Clarence H. Mackay staged his party for the Prince at Harbor Hill she and Shannon Cormack, then on the *Times*, decided that they would be present if they had to crash the gates. Grace was staying in a Syosset railroad lodging house, as there were no hotels within reach. Her roommate was Lucy Doyle, widely known in Canada as Cornelia, of the Toronto *Telegram*. Grace attired herself dashingly for the party in a coral frock and turquoise evening wrap. The Ford company had put a Lincoln car and a chauffeur named Jimmie at the disposal of the reporters. She and her escort commandeered it and set off on their somewhat daring expedition.

"The thing to do," said Shannon, a war veteran with a fine row of decorations and an enterprising spirit, "is to be bold."

Mr. Cormack has never been less than bold and Miss Robinson, under a retiring exterior, can always hold her own with the most hard-boiled members of the profession, when the interests of her paper are at stake. She marches in quietly where the blustering might falter.

They rode up the avenue through a border of pine trees strung with colored lights. Mr. Cormack leaned forward and advised Jimmie to throw away his cigar. He switched on all the lights. His war decorations blazed against his black suit. Miss Robinson bared her shoulder and looked as casual in the back seat as one of the ladies in a cigarette advertisement. They went triumphantly past all the guards. Whenever they were stopped Mr. Cormack, who is an Australian, leaned forward and spilled a few words in an accent that linked him convincingly with the British Empire. A great many Britons were arriving as guests. Then, as they neared the door, he spotted a tan car with a General inside. It was General Robert Lee Bullard, whom he happened to know. This was a lucky circumstance.

As the butler's eye fell on the arriving pair, Mr. Cormack was deep in conversation with General Bullard at the front door. The Department of Justice agents knew the two arrivals by sight, but such was their ease that it never occurred to them that the reporters had crashed the gate right under their noses. Frank L. Baker, society editor of the *Times*, was there by invitation. It seemed logical enough that the others might have arrived by the same conventional route. But Ellin Mackay wasn't fooled. As Miss Robinson approached her in the receiving line, her face froze up. She spotted her at once as a crasher. However, she made no move to have her put out. All night long Miss Robinson expected someone to come and whisper in her ear that she had better move on. But soon she was dancing with one of the Prince's aides and enjoying herself thoroughly. She and Cormack stayed much longer than the Prince. He danced four times, then went on to a smaller party. He was repeating history in dancing with his hostess, now Mrs. Irving Berlin. His grandfather, King Edward VII, had danced many times in London to the Victorian measure with Ellin's grandmother, Mrs. John W. Mackay. She had been one of his favorites and he had frequently been a guest at her home in Carlton House Terrace.

Before the evening was ended Burt had given Miss Robinson an exclusive story on the sale of the Prince's polo ponies and the fact that he was going to visit South America. She shared with her colleagues all that she had picked up at the party.

When Captain Patterson evolved the scheme of building a swimming pool for the White House, Miss Robinson was assigned to broach the matter to President Roosevelt. She first introduced the subject at one of Mrs. Roosevelt's press conferences. Stephen Early regarded the suggestion favorably. The bank holiday was on and the President was extremely busy. A number of complications arose. But he received her and drew plans himself for the type of pool he wanted. The original plan was to make it an elaborate $40,000 pool. But he said that he wanted a simpler one, costing about $25,000. In sketching it for Miss Robinson he explained the symmetrical needs that accorded best with the architecture of the White House.

When Mr. Payne, who had moved over to the *Mirror* in the interim, engineered the reopening of the Hall-Mills case in 1926, four years after the murder, there was no more diligent worker on the story than Miss Robinson. Like Julia Harpman before her, she worked night and day on this difficult assignment. She was doubly harassed by the knowledge that the *Mirror* had the inside trail on the story.

When Mrs. Hall was released from jail and her brother, Willie Stevens, was about to be taken into custody along with Henry Carpender, Miss Robinson, Edward Hall, of the *Times*, and Robert Conway, of the *American*, were all arrested for loitering in the vicinity of the Hall home in New Brunswick, New Jersey. A thunderstorm was raging. Miss Robinson, in a light summer dress, was standing dripping between Mrs. Hall's paved walk and the curbstone. She was not actually on her property. The rector's widow, behind the curtains of her home, was furious to see reporters within range of the house. At all times she resented any attempt to photograph or talk to her. She was particularly solicitous where Willie was concerned, because of his mental deficiency. And she knew that he was about to be taken into custody. So she telephoned to the police, demanding action. An officer appeared and told them that they were all under arrest.

"And on what charge, may we ask?" they chorused.

"There is a city charge against loitering," said the policeman.

Miss Robinson stood her ground. "I can't move," she insisted. "There is going to be an arrest in a few minutes, and I've got to have the story."

This was unanswerable logic to a reporter but not to a policeman. Mr. Hall began to argue and Mr. Conway high-hatted the officer of the law. "Never fight with a vulgarian," said Bob. It is one of his newspaper principles.

It was getting close to Miss Robinson's deadline. The arrest of Willie Stevens, after the suspense that had been worked up in the case, was obviously a story of impressive proportions. She knew that her rivals were ambushed around the block. But she was marched off to the police station, protesting bitterly all the way. The situation was worse for her than for her companions. The *News* and the *Mirror* were in hot rivalry and working on the same deadline. Obviously Phil Payne's crew were not going to be slow about announcing the arrest of Willie Stevens. The one piece of new evidence that had been dug up hung directly on Willie—the fingerprints alleged to be his which were on the card that rested fantastically against Dr. Hall's shoe when his body was found in de Russey's Lane. Willie had not yet had his chance to give his impressive performance on the witness stand, thereby demolishing all his critics with his dignity, candor and clear-headedness.

Her reflections on the importance of the story did not add to Miss Robinson's peace of mind when she got to the police station and found that she could not even telephone to her office. She and her companions were treated like ordinary criminals. Finally they were released on $20 bonds and were told to report in court that evening. As soon as they could escape they leaped into a taxi and got back to the Hall home a few minutes after the arrests had taken place. Miss Robinson got her office on the telephone. A man was already on the job. That night the judge reprimanded the three reporters for loitering. It seemed farcical to veterans who had been bivouacking for years outside homes where tragedies were being played out.

During this period Miss Robinson worked eighteen hours a day, dashing about in taxis, pursuing fantastic leads. Every murder investigation brings the same mysterious round of tips, some of which hold up, most of which end in smoke. But they all seem vital at the time to the reporter working on the story. They have to be checked to the last ditch.

She did brilliant work on the trial, writing the lead day after day, turning out thousands of words, giving graphic pictures of one of the most remarkable court-room dramas of the century. She is one of the few successful women reporters who make free use of shorthand. It has aided her greatly in her trial work, since her paper runs voluminous question and answer testimony. Her most exciting day in court—and she has had a few—was when Mrs. Gibson was carried in dying on her hospital cot, to denounce Mrs. Hall; and her mother, an old crone, hobbled down the aisle in turn to denounce her.

Again Miss Robinson turned out volumes of words on the Snyder-Gray trial, saw Ruth take her sentence, watched her daughter Lorraine mount the stand, an innocent figure in a blue cape and tailored hat. That day she wanted to make Lorraine the lead of her story, but it was also Judd Gray's day on the witness stand, and her news sense overruled her sympathetic reaction to the child's appearance in this grisly case. Attempts were made to have Miss Robinson cover the actual execution of Ruth Snyder, but Warden Lawes, who is always averse to the presence of women on these occasions, would not hear of it.

Miss Robinson is not a sentimentalist. She has listened to too much sordid court testimony to be swayed much by the attitudes of witnesses. She got her court baptism at the Rhinelander divorce trial, as stiff a dose of realism as any girl reporter would encounter in a lifetime of work. Most of the testimony was unprintable and Justice Joseph L. Morchauser cleared the court room of women when Kip Rhinelander's letters to Alice, his mulatto sweetheart, were read. Three women reporters were allowed to stay. She was one of them.

Miss Robinson was born in Beatrice, Nebraska, and went to the University of Nebraska but did not graduate. She had planned to teach English literature and rhetoric. But her father died when she was finishing her junior year in college. So she set out to earn a living. She worked on the Omaha *Bee*, starting at $10 a week. She is now one of the most highly paid women reporters in the country, and with good reason.

When she first came East she worked for six months on the Newark *Ledger*, most of the time as city editor. Then she moved to New York, where she knew no one. She had her first cocktail at the Brevoort, her first cigarette at the Port Arthur tea-room in Chinatown. She found a room for $3 a week and set out to capture a newspaper job. Her first venture was the *Times*. She saw Mr. Van Anda time and again. He was amiable but discouraging. She tried all the other papers in town. Then she went to work as a typist for the League to Enforce Peace, which was sponsored by William Howard Taft. She got $22 a week and enjoyed the job. Next she did make-up for a weekly paper run by John Walker Harrington. When this expired she sold stories on space to the *Sun*. For one period she worked in the magazine bureau of the Red Cross. Then a friend on the *Mail* told her that the woman's page editor had just been fired. She knew make-up and headlines, so she went after the job and got it at once.

Miss Robinson wanted to modernize the woman's page of the *Mail*. But she was up against tradition. She loved the composing room but felt cramped in her editorial capacity. She heard of an opening on the *American*, which was starting a magazine section of tabloid size to go inside the paper. Florence McCarthy hired her at once. She worked for him for two months and then received an offer from the *News*. The new tabloid was beginning to be a success but was still regarded with some doubt by the conservatives. The paper was set up in the *Mail* composing room and she had been spotted there by executives of the *News*. They wanted a society editor. They offered her $20 a week more than she was getting, and also a contract. But it took her some time to make up her mind as to what she should do. They explained that they wanted a girl who had a good news sense and a flair for feature stories rather than one who knew society.

She took the job and luck was with her from the start. She was covering society at Palm Beach and was lingering on the sands late one afternoon, wondering what on earth she would file that evening, when she saw flames leaping from the roof of the Breakers Hotel. She had never covered a fire in her life. The Fire Department had not yet been called. She put in the alarm and she and a companion ran to meet the guests who were beginning to pour out of their rooms.

She had a mental record of the well-known people who were staying there. It was the height of the social season. She rounded up what she could get on the spot, then left her friend to cover for her and raced across the golf links through clouds of smoke to the nearest Western Union office. The fire was swift and spectacular. She got a leased wire and hung on to it while she batted out her story. Her friend came in an hour later and fed her with additional details. She beat the Associated Press and all her rivals. By the time they arrived no wires were available.

The sparks from the Breakers set fire to the awning of her hotel. The lights went out. Miss Robinson rushed upstairs to her room for a bag containing some important papers and kept it beside her, afraid that the hotel would burn down while she wrote her story. She dictated direct to the operator in the darkness. She finished with a fine round-up on an important news story.

Soon after this she ceased to cover society as "Débutante." Her news stories appeared under her own by-line. Her reputation grew rapidly as she did one capable job after another. She left the city staff for a time to work for *Liberty*. She went on a cross-country tour with her sister, writing up the adventures of the Gasoline Gypsies. But she was glad to get back to the city room, where she is singularly at home; to hurry out of the office with a bulletin launching a brand new story; to sit in court during the tense moments when a jury files in with the verdict "Guilty" or "Not Guilty." Miss Robinson can give the entire sisterhood lessons in the dramatics of her profession.

Chapter XXIII

THE TABLOIDS FLOURISH

THE MUSIC WAS SOFT, THE LIGHTS SUBDUED, ALL THE DÉBUTANTES of old Quebec were gathered in the dining-room of the Château Frontenac. A slim youth sat at a table, his nervous glance flickering over the room. No one needed to look at him twice to know that he was Edward, Prince of Wales. This time he happened to be traveling incognito as Baron Renfrew.

Across the room was a girl in green, her blonde beauty luminous against the dark paneling of the walls. In her hand was a glass of sparkling Burgundy. Two pairs of light blue eyes met for a moment. She waved her glass delicately in an implied toast and drank. That night she danced again and again with the Prince of Wales, rained questions on him, got candid answers.

But twelve o'clock struck. The moonbeams broke, the dancing ended and the modern Cinderella had to dash in her silver slippers to the Western Union office to tap out copy for her paper on a typewriter. She had a pencil in her purse and a story that any tabloid city editor might dream about in his more delirious moments. She was the one newspaper woman who had danced with the Prince of Wales, broken down his guard, seen behind the polite mask he turns to the public.

But she never wrote the story she might have written or the story her paper wanted. She wouldn't use the capital I which gave it its primary interest. She remained the mystery girl in green who was starred on the front pages of newspapers from Alaska to Australia next morning as having bewitched the Prince on a dance floor. Only her own paper seemed to be short of the facts.

Miss Stanley suffered when the dance was over and the evening's glamour had turned to ashes. The Prince had thought her a New York débutante under the wing of a chaperon. He had talked to her freely, had given her his views on many things, from ties to official pomp. But she was a newspaper girl. She knew the tradition of her craft—always the paper first, and the Prince could not be quoted. No girl reporter was ever in a more embarrassing spot.

She wrote a story and made it completely impersonal, then three others in the same vague vein. They were done in the fairy-tale style of the girl's dream prince. Any girl dancing with any prince. Not Imogene Stanley, dancing with the Prince of Wales. Her editors were disappointed. Her more hard-boiled colleagues condemned her for letting her personal reactions interfere with her news sense. The articles were brought to the attention of the Prince. He regretted that they had been written. Discreet inquiries through official sources were started from Buckingham Palace about the "girl in green" who had emerged full-blown into a tabloid reporter.

The dream faded. Imogene went back to her desk. She covered police court, murder trials, kidnappings—all the grist of the day's news. Soon afterwards she left newspaper work altogether. Today she lives with her sister on a lonely hacienda in the middle of the thorny Mexican brush—an orchid strangely lost in the desert.

Yet she was generally regarded as the loveliest reporter who ever set foot in a New York newspaper office. She would have shone in any setting; in a city room she was a sensation. No one knew much about her except that she came from Texas. She made her first appearance in the early twenties—her fragile beauty giving her a winged air in the dingy court rooms to which her work took her. Pale gold hair framed an arresting face. She was slim, tall, eager. She had grace and an ardent spirit. Lawyers slowed up in their summations and fumbled for words when she walked in and took her seat at the press table. Judges beamed on her and jurors were a little bedazzled. Only her skeptical colleagues looked at her with equanimity, wondering vaguely how so delicate a piece of humanity had got loose among them, and what she could possibly be doing that was useful.

Soon she surprised them by proving that she was also a good reporter. She had brains as well as a perfect profile. She could write. There was little she couldn't get in the way of news. Doors opened automatically for her. Lawyers gave her secret tips on stories. Butlers thought twice before banging the door in her face. Her paper was the *Daily News* and she was manna from heaven for a tabloid. So Philip Payne thought the night he ordered her to leave at once for Canada to cover the Prince of Wales and "get an interview." He believed that nothing was impossible for the ingenious tabloid reporter. Practically nothing is.

Imogene packed her best evening dress. It was to identify her later among the Prince's dancing partners as the girl in green. She took the train in an anxious state of mind, sure she was setting out on an impossible assignment. She lay awake all night as she journeyed north, considering ways and means to attain her object.

She did not really believe for a moment that she could crash the Prince's guard. She knew that he had never said more than "How do you do?" or "It's warm, isn't it?" to a girl reporter before, and always in a formal way in a receiving line. He had danced at different times with all sorts of girls but had avoided those who wrote for the papers. The dangers were too obvious. His aides were doubly careful on his trips to America to protect him from such hazards. They particularly feared the merry antics of the tabloids.

It was the autumn of 1923. Royalty was still more or less divine. Queen Marie had not yet got chummy with the press. Nor had quite so many princes visited American shores. Imogene knew that it was lèse-majesté to quote a prince, more particularly the heir to the British throne. She made her first attempt to get near him at the Quebec Golf Club but all she saw of him was a fast moving figure through the blurred September haze. She was one of a group of scribes who watched his movements from a distance. As the day wore on she went to the telegraph office and filed a routine story on what he had done, how he had looked, the clothes he had worn.

He was leaving for the West on the following day. She knew that she had little time to try for an exclusive story. The evening was her only chance. She returned to the Château Frontenac and donned her spectacular green gown. She had heard that he might appear in the public dining-room that night.

By chance, as she stepped from the elevator, she encountered a New York woman and her daughter, both old friends. They exchanged greetings and went in to dine together. Imogene now had the conventional backing of a chaperon. The Prince of Wales and his party were already seated. The newcomers were placed at a table almost directly opposite the royal group, but some distance away. Imogene faced the Prince. There were masses of autumn flowers. Every table was taken. The dining-room was festive with gay colors and the rustling silks of the débutantes of Quebec and their mothers. Everyone in the room was concentrating politely on the table where the young Prince sat.

His blue eyes flickered wearily over the familiar scene. Crowds everywhere. The attention of too many people. He smoked and took it all in. Imogene watched him closely. She saw every move that he made. She was taking mental notes for her paper. What he wore. What he ate. Her glance strayed around the room. She wondered which of the buds of Quebec he would choose for dancing partners. That was where her story would lie, since everyone knew that he usually picked a partner who danced well, and went on and on until he felt like stopping the band.

It was then that she saw that his glance was resting on her. She waited until she was quite sure before she raised her glass in a bold bid for his attention. Then she sat back and wondered what she had done. She thought of Phil Payne, of her paper, of the beat she would score if the Prince consented to talk to her, even for a few moments. She drank her coffee, her hands shaking with excitement. The dancing began. It was the era of screeching jazz, before the crooning vogue. There were snatches of laughter, voices rising and falling in erratic waves. The sense of excitement in the dining-room was intense. It revolved around the fair-headed youth who seemed more nervous than anyone present.

Which girl would he single out as a dancing partner? It was not a private party. He was there incognito. There was no obligation on his part to dance with anyone in particular—no hostess or hostess's daughter to be shepherded around the floor. He could take his pick. The barrage of invitation was terrific. He ignored it all and chose Phyllis Burstall, a Quebec girl, for the first dance. Immediately the floor was filled with swaying couples. The dance was on.

Imogene sat and watched, her chin cupped in her hands. Her glance followed the Prince's steps with interest. She was mentally taking notes. She must have something to write when the dance was over. It might not be much but it would make a livelier story than his game of golf. The public was always interested in the dancing partners of the Prince of Wales. She was still abstracted when General Gerald F. Trotter, the Prince's groom-in-waiting, approached with a military stride and asked her for a dance. As they whirled around the room he told her he wished to present her to Baron Renfrew. The fox trot ended. She found herself shaking hands with the Prince, looking directly at a boyish countenance. He gave a quick bow.

"May I have the next dance?" he asked.

Every eye in the room was fastened on the girl in green as her steps fell into tune with those of her royal partner. They made a stunning pair. Two blond heads of the same shade. Two pairs of eyes of the same light blue. Her face was not known in Quebec. Whence had she come? Dowagers exchanged questioning glances; the débutantes were a little staggered. They couldn't deny her beauty. They saw that she was chic.

Imogene knew that the dance would soon be over. She swayed thoughtfully in the Prince's arms, her mind on the alert. Questions bubbled to her lips. But at first she said nothing. She remembered royal etiquette—that he must be the first to speak. He had just sent word to the band to play with a little less gusto. He told Imogene why—that he didn't like fast time. "Dancing is work when they play so fast," he explained.

He saw at once that she was an American. He tactfully recalled that he had danced to Paul Whiteman's orchestra in London and thought it good, the time quite perfect. He pounced on a new slang phrase that she used and asked her what it meant. She explained that the sports writers of New York were threading it into the English language. He laughed at that. He liked American slang. She found that the Prince didn't care for the one-step, but could forgive the swiftness of rhythm if the tune were good. He preferred the drum beaten slowly and the saxophone not jazzed up in the Ted Lewis manner. He seemed to her a good dancer, because he liked what he was doing. He paid no attention to the vigilant glances following them around the room. It was nothing new for him. But Imogene found it an embarrassing experience. He talked little at the start. When the floor was jammed he showed adroitness in weaving his way through the dancing couples.

The Prince found her an engaging partner. He had no suspicions when her questions began to come thick and fast. She remembered his flair for setting new fashions; she knew that her paper would expect some comment on his dress, so she ventured a remark on the unusual width of his black tie. "Don't you like it?" he shot at her quickly. She said that of course she did. By degrees she asked him all the things that occur to a reporter who has little time in which to get information. He was candid, responsive, charming to her. At last he gave the signal, the music stopped and he took her back to his table where General Trotter and Sir Godfrey Thomas, his secretary, sat. They drank champagne and chatted of inconsequential things. He danced with her again—and then again. The orchestra played the numbers he liked. Imogene followed his intricate steps with accuracy.

The evening wore on. The air became quite electric. She was conscious of the suppressed fury that surrounded her. None of the other beauties in the room had a clue to the girl who was usurping the Prince's attention so completely. He seemed to see no one else. He became more articulate. She learned that he suffered under the restraints of his position, that he could not understand the insatiable curiosity that surrounded him, that he hated snobs but would rather fall in with their plans than hurt their feelings, that he was sensitive to the world's conception of him as a pleasure-loving Prince. He spoke of his travels, his speech-making, handshaking, visiting. "I call it work," he said, "if the world doesn't."

Imogene caught a fleeting impression of his likes and dislikes. She learned that his life was a constant compromise between diplomacy and the exercise of his own free will. She concluded that the laborer or cab driver was more fortunate than the so-called happy Prince.

But she was conscious throughout her conversation with him of his sense of responsibility for his office.

She noticed personal details as she sat beside him at his table—the cigarettes made from a special blend of Virginian tobacco which he smokes incessantly and carries in a plain silver case, the gift of his father; the plain gold ring on the little finger of his right hand; his habit of saying "How amusing" or "Very funny."

There were other reporters present. One or two from New York knew who Imogene was and flashed the story to their papers. They were the only persons in the room aware of her identity. Others who did not recognize her sent out press service dispatches about the "mystery girl in green" who had danced continuously with the Prince. This was the first inkling her editors had that their girl reporter had achieved the incredible. While she was still out on the dance floor they knew it. Phil Payne's assignment had been a success. They hoped for a thrilling story that night. It did not come.

Cinderella, in her silver slippers, fresh from dancing with the Prince, filed a routine add to her earlier story that made the night men gnash their teeth. They were disappointed in her. To have talked to the Prince and not delivered the story was incomprehensible to the exacting newspaper mind. But she had an appointment to see him next day. She knew that she must tell him who she was. She would beg him then for facts that she could use. Having gained his confidence and enlisted his interest, she felt sure that he would give her something for publication. Her office had sent her a list of questions to ask him. They knew that she was to see him again before he left for the West.

Next day the Prince received her in his suite. She told him at once that she represented a New York tabloid paper. It was an embarrassing moment. He looked at her with dismay, then turned to General Trotter, who was appalled, since it was his particular duty to protect the heir to the British throne from a situation such as this. But after he had taken it in, it made no difference to the Prince. His manner did not change, but he was wary when the questions were sprung. They were not the questions usually asked a Prince. In the cold light of morning, away from the roseate glow of ballroom lights, they seemed a little brash. They went right to the mark on the ticklish subject of a royal marriage. This was the period when one European princess after another was being named as the possible bride of the Prince of Wales. He refused to be serious on the subject, however. When a fiancée was mentioned he shook his smoothly brushed blond hair and exclaimed: "Great heavens, I've had eight already. I'm not engaged. And marriage is something to be considered in the far future. I have no intention of marrying soon."

The Prince caught his train for the West, en route to his ranch. Imogene hurried again to the Western Union office to get her story on the wire. First she sent a flash to Phil Payne announcing that she had her interview. Then the trouble began. Although he had sent her to Quebec on the odd chance of getting a few words with the Prince, his keen news sense convinced him that he now had a different kind of story on his hands. He no longer cared about the straight interview. He wanted the story of Cinderella's romantic evening, written by Cinderella herself. He wanted to know what she had thought while dancing with the Prince; what he had said to her; what her reactions had been in the crowded ballroom with hundreds of curious eyes upon her.

Imogene had been frank with him, but she would not write the story along the personal lines he laid out. She tried to show him how difficult her situation was. The wires burned with hectic repartee. Finally, after hundreds of words had been exchanged by telegraph, she flatly refused to do what he wanted. But she filed a story describing the evening in a detached way, not using the personal pronoun. Only the initiated newspaper reader would gather from it that Imogene herself had danced with the Prince of Wales. A picture ran beside it identifying her as the mystery woman in green. From that time on she became known in newspaper circles as the girl who danced with the Prince.

She had traveled far and fast in a short space of time. Only a few years earlier she had dreamed of a newspaper career as she sat at a desk in a high school in Dallas. When chosen class prophet in her senior year, she saw herself as a successful newspaper woman in the prophecy she wrote. But she did not foresee that she would become a New York newspaper star and dance with the future King of Great Britain.

She entered the profession, like many others, by the stenographic route. After high school she took a business course and moved to Washington, where by chance she became stenographer to the free-lance political correspondent of a string of Western papers. He dictated his dispatches to her and from them she got her first ideas of newspaper style. When he could no longer afford to employ her, he gave her a letter of introduction to Lowell Mellett, city editor of the Washington *Daily News*, who promptly gave her a trial assignment. Soon after she joined the staff, the roof of the Knickerbocker Theater collapsed. It was a Sunday night, January 28, 1922. Washington had been swept for twenty-eight hours by a heavy snowstorm. Twenty-nine inches of snow had fallen and the roof, strained beyond capacity, collapsed suddenly, bringing down the balconies. The dead numbered ninety-five. It was one of the worst disasters in the history of the capital.

Imogene was tobogganing with friends in a park nearby and heard the crash of the falling roof. The *News* was an afternoon paper and there were no editions to catch at that time of night, but, glowing with youthful zeal, she rushed to the telephone and reported to the man on dog watch what had happened. Then she went back to the scene and found that it really was a major disaster.

By this time Mr. Mellett had routed reporters out of bed and a crew had arrived. But Imogene had been first on the spot and she brought in a generous amount of color and eyewitness material. In the general confusion two stories appeared in one issue with her by-line. This was only two weeks after she made her newspaper début—heady fare for a young reporter.

Some time later she decided to try New York. She arrived with letters of introduction. The second one, together with some sample clippings, landed her a job on the *Daily News*. She was motion picture critic at first, then was transferred to the city staff. Her first murder case was at Toms River, New Jersey, where Mrs. Ivy Giberson was being tried for sliding an army pistol along the pillow beside her sleeping husband's head and pulling the trigger. This was in the summer of 1922.

Imogene walked into court with her fair hair cut like a page's, and her light blue eyes slightly touched with wonder. The testimony was sordid and cruel. To her it seemed like a Grand Guignol performance. She had never encountered anything like it before. She wrote excellent stories on a typewriter borrowed from a lawyer, her paper illumined by an old-fashioned coal-oil lamp. The woman was convicted and sentenced to life imprisonment. She was a plump, middle-aged harridan who took the jury's findings without blinking. It was a strong dose of court-room drama for an ingénue. From this time on Imogene drew one murder trial after another. She saw women convicted, men sentenced to death. The most notable of these was Gerald Chapman. He was handsome, debonair—scoffed at the fate that had overtaken him.

While Ruth Snyder's jury was deliberating on a May day in 1927, Imogene was assigned to stay with her mother, Mrs. Josephine Brown, and convey the verdict to the unfortunate woman when the city desk gave her a flash. No one doubted what the verdict would be. Ruth's ten-year-old daughter was there, unconscious of the dreadful position her mother was in. There was a long wait. They sat in the living-room and Imogene and Lorraine played with a puzzle of twisted metal rings. Mrs. Brown sat in silence, except for an occasional sigh. The neighbors stayed away from the tragic household. At last Lorraine went out to play with some friends.

The jury came in at 6.58 P.M. A few minutes later Imogene got the verdict by telephone from her city desk. Mrs. Brown rose silently and walked toward the foot of the staircase. Then she was told that her daughter had been sentenced to death. Mrs. Brown made no outcry but dropped in a spreading heap. The detective who had been guarding the door had disappeared. So Imogene half carried, half dragged the unconscious woman upstairs and got her into bed.

When she came downstairs again Lorraine had come in. Her cheeks were flushed. Her eyes were bright from play. In her hand was a bunch of violets she had plucked. Imogene had received orders from her paper to explain "tactfully" to the child about her mother's fate. She couldn't do it. She never did.

When Jack Dempsey was still champion (shortly after the Firpo fight) she was assigned to interview him. The meeting was friendly and Jack asked her if she would dine with him some night when she was free. He said he would telephone to her at her paper. A few days later, when she returned from an assignment that had kept her out of the office all day, Colonel Hause, her city editor, came over just as she was about to write her day's story. He leaned over her desk and said:

"Say, is it possible that Jack Dempsey might telephone you here?"

"Why, yes, it's possible," said Imogene. "In fact, it's probable. I'm expecting a telephone call from him."

The Colonel turned red, then white. He explained that a call for her had been switched to the city desk. He had taken it. He had heard a high-pitched voice ask for Miss Stanley and add, "This is Jack Dempsey speaking." The Colonel had never heard that Dempsey's voice did not match his physique. Nobody was going to pull his leg.

"Oh, yeah, how do you get that way?" he demanded.

Said Dempsey, again in a fine soprano, "What do you mean? This is *Jack Dempsey* speaking."

The Colonel sneered. "Yes, I heard you the first time. Well, if you're Jack Dempsey, I'm Firpo."

Jack got mad. "Why, you so-and-so, I'll come down and *teach* you I'm Jack Dempsey." He then hung up.

"It was Dempsey all right," said Imogene.

"Whew! I'm going to pack a gun for a few days," said Colonel Hause.

When she dined later with Jack, she told him the story and he was amused. He had calmed down by then and thought it funny.

One of the best jobs Imogene did, from the news point of view, was the way in which she covered the collapse of an elevated structure in Brooklyn in June, 1923. A two-car Bay Ridge elevated train jumped the rails and plunged with a grinding roar and a flash of electric short circuits thirty-five feet to the street. Seven persons were killed and seventy injured. She was at the scene before the injured had been taken away. Looking an utterly frivolous object in high-heeled slippers, with a wad of copy paper in one hand and a pencil in the other, she picked her way through the confusion and horror, counting the dead, making accurate notes on what she saw. She did a calm and well-planned round-up for which any man would have been commended. It was reminiscent of the theater catastrophe in Washington and was not the sort of story on which women often write the news lead.

The last big story Imogene covered was the visit of Queen Marie of Rumania. This was after the Prince of Wales episode. Her nerves were shattered and her chase after the Queen through the snows of a Canadian winter did not improve her health. She was assigned at the last moment and was unable to get on the Queen's train. The result was that she had to keep up with the royal party by means of the regular railway schedules and hired automobiles—a killing race. She felt worn-out, ill and crushed. She decided to give up newspaper work altogether. So she walked into her office one day and quietly resigned. Since then she has never written a newspaper story.

She went to Hollywood for a time to write for the films. Then she joined her sister on her Mexican hacienda. The new highway connecting Mexico City and the United States passes within eight miles of it, but the road between is dusty, rutted, gouged with holes, crowded on either side with thorny slashing brush. A house, a stable, a windmill and a gasoline engine are grouped on a walled plot of tamed ground. There are a few cultivated fields and a cluster of tumbling adobe houses in which the employees of the hacienda live. And here Imogene, still a beauty, lives in solitude, with memories of gala days. Her newspaper career was brief, vivid, highly keyed. She touched the high spots in a dramatic way.

"Once upon a time just an ordinary girl danced with a prince of royal blood, and, not unexpectedly, found him to be just a nice boy," she wrote on one occasion. "Most certainly, when at play, he is an unassuming gay companion. Quite full of spontaneous, wholesome fun. . . .

"She had floated across a polished floor in the arms of the world's most exalted dancer. To each girl it will remain the most thrilling hour of her life. . . ."

The *Daily News* has employed a number of able newspaper

women, both on the Sunday and daily editions. In the early days of its existence Roberta Yates did a capable job editing the Sunday paper. She came to New York in 1921 from the Cincinnati *Post*, worked for the *News* staff for two years and in 1923 was appointed Sunday editor.

Today Ama Barker assists Richard Clarke in getting out the Sunday paper, which has a circulation of nearly 3,000,000. On his days off she takes complete charge. Miss Barker's newspaper career started concurrently with Julia Harpman's in Knoxville. When these two bright girls were assigned to cover a star chamber session of the Daughters of the Confederacy, involving the honor of some of the members, they climbed into a large empty box beside a thin partition at the rear of the hall where the cup-cake contretemps was under way. When judgment was pronounced on the errant daughters, Ama climbed out of the box, bolted down the back stairs, and telephoned her scoop to the *Sentinel*.

But for once such zeal was greeted icily in a newspaper office. The managing editor sent for the eager cub. He was related by marriage to one of the Daughters of the Confederacy; he knew their ruling had not been made public. He was angry with his enterprising reporter. The result was that Miss Harpman's paper got a clean beat. In time Miss Barker went on to Chicago, where she worked for the *Herald Examiner*, when it was trying out an illustrated tabloid section. In 1922 she came to New York and free-lanced successfully until 1925, when she joined the staff of the *News*.

When she was called on to impersonate a relative of the family in the Peacox torch murder, Miss Barker bought herself a gray switch with three strands. With two she arranged a demure hair part; the third was used for a bun. She set forth, thoroughly disguised as a faded spinster, to join Grace Robinson, who was covering the story. The switch is kept in a locker in the *News* office, ready for further sleuthing.

Miss Barker's functions now are mostly executive, although she writes frequently for the Sunday paper. She reads copy, does make-up, writes heads, arranges for pictures and superintends the manifold details involved in getting out the pup, the pup replate and the Saturday afternoon edition—the three phases of supplying the *Sunday News* readers with their favorite paper.

The weekly features are expanded news stories with the facts brought up to date. They represent an astonishing amount of research in different parts of the world. Ruth Reynolds, another member of the Sunday staff, assembles most of them. She first goes through the morgue for every available fact on the persons involved in the story. Then she works out a series of questions which will bring the chronology up to date. For instance, she used dozens of correspondents in cities all over the world to trace the survivors of the *Titanic*, *Lusitania* and *General Slocum* disasters, and find out what had happened to them in the intervening years. She followed the same technique for the Iroquois Theater fire in Chicago, the *Morro Castle* disaster, the Chester Gillette murder of 1904, and dozens of other stories. Sometimes she telegraphs or cables direct to the persons involved. Her lines are cast out all over the globe. She weaves the old and the new material together in full-bodied stories that make illuminating reading.

Miss Reynolds is a Milwaukee girl who worked her way through Marquette University and took a course in journalism. She functioned for a time as secretary in a coal office, and then managed to get on the staff of the *Wisconsin News*. It was January 2, 1926, when she started newspaper work. Everyone in the office but Miss Reynolds had a hangover. She was twenty-two years old and was wearing a new homemade dress. After working for half a day she discovered that in the excitement of a brand new job she had forgotten to remove the bastings after pressing. Her salary was $15 and she found life exciting.

Then she met Harry Richard Zander, to whom she is now married. He introduced her to Genevieve Forbes Herrick, and through her indirectly she came to New York and landed on the *News* at $40 a week. She didn't know Astoria from Jersey, but she supplied herself with nickels, rode subways, street cars, elevated trains and ferries until she was dizzy, and when she started work on a July day in 1928, she knew more about the city than most born New Yorkers. But she skipped her lunch that day. She dashed into Woolworth's for a ring; hurried over to the Municipal Building to get a license and promptly married Mr. Zander, without mentioning to anyone at her office how she had spent her lunch hour.

She now lives on Long Island, has two children, and manages to do an extremely smart job on Park Row, like her colleague, Miss Barker, who also combines matrimony with newspaper work, as the wife of Edward Bailey, of Pacific and Atlantic Pictures.

Another girl with important executive functions in the same organization is Molly Slott, assistant manager of the Chicago *Tribune-New York News* Syndicate, Inc. She started on the *Tribune* as secretary to the circulation manager and has been assistant to Arthur Crawford, general manager of the syndicate, for the last fifteen years. She helps to select the comic strips and other syndicated features for more than five hundred papers throughout the country. There are ninety releases in the comic strip department alone.

Miss Slott watches color and make-up in the Sunday pages and keeps in touch with the salesmen on the road. She has negotiated a number of contracts with cartoonists, contributors and publishers, and made fast offers on the life stories of Will Rogers, Wiley Post and Huey Long, when news of their deaths was flashed into her office. Miss Slott sent the first successful wire photograph to a syndicate list of newspapers as far back as the knock-out blow in the Dempsey-Carpentier fight.

The grim mansion at Thirty-ninth Street and Fifth Avenue, where the six Wendel sisters led their curious ingrown lives, was not opened to a reporter from 1896 until the day more than thirty years later that the Lady Lon Chaney of the New York press bluffed her way in, posing as the employee of a restoring company.

The stray bits of news that floated to the outside world from this frugal family of vast wealth provoked endless speculation in newspaper offices. It was known that Ella lived in a gas-lit world, wore Victorian frocks of rusty black, starved herself and doted on her poodle Toby, for whose benefit she jealously maintained a valuable corner lot on Fifth Avenue.

Edna Ferguson, the parachute jumper who evolved into New York's chameleon sob sister, was called up to the city desk of the *News* one day.

"See if you can get into the Wendel house and have a look around," she was told.

"O.K.," said Miss Ferguson unhesitatingly.

This was a stiff assignment. To get into the Wendel house was reputedly as difficult as breaking into the Tombs. Miss Ferguson surveyed the ground carefully. She talked to the doorman of a nearby Fifth Avenue shop and learned that Ella, the last of the sisters to survive, was in the country and that all house repairs were handled by a carpenter who lived along the street.

She telephoned to the caretaker of the Wendel home and told him that the carpenter was sending her to look things over for repairs. He let her in but was plainly suspicious. When she crossed the threshold she found herself in incredible surroundings. Time seemed to have stopped. Through the gloom of the hall she saw the old grandfather clock with wooden works, and the carved oak stairway. Gas brackets were still in evidence everywhere. First the caretaker showed her the rooms that were seldom used. At last she got to the dining-room. The legend on Park Row was that there were two tables—one for Ella to dine on, one for her dog. She found that this was correct.

She had to talk fast to allay the man's suspicions. He had been trained in the Wendel tradition. She went into a description of a new patented process for the restoration of old ceilings. She took measurements and made notes. She noticed the cracks and the falling plaster. But her real interest was centered on the Victorian furnishings and the old tin bathtubs—an anachronistic touch on Fifth Avenue. She insisted on seeing Miss Wendel's bedroom. The caretaker demurred.

"But I have special instructions for this room," she said.

"All right, then." Begrudgingly he opened the door. It was a faded old room, barren of any note of comfort.

"Two beds," commented Miss Ferguson, as she looked into the dim corners.

"Yes," said the caretaker. "One is for the dog."

Miss Ferguson went back to her office and turned in the first circumstantial story of the interior of the house that had found its way into print in thirty-five years. Remsen Crawford was the last reporter to have seen the Wendel home—undoubtedly one of the curiosities of America.

Before she took up newspaper work Miss Ferguson hung around Roosevelt Field, parachute jumping when she got the chance. There she met someone with influence on the *News* who gave her the proper introductions. She was taken on for two weeks' trial. She had never done newspaper work before. She had two children at home and she had no idea how one went about covering a story. She was underfoot for the first ten days. Then suddenly she was assigned to interview Larry Fay, who was in the news at the time in connection with the milk probe. It was then she thought of the first of the tricks that later earned her the title of the Lady Lon Chaney.

Larry Fay always avoided reporters. Miss Ferguson decided to approach him as a gangster girl. She slapped on rouge and mascara with a heavy hand, arranged her ash-blonde hair in spit-curls around her face and tilted her hat over one eye. Miss Ferguson is tall and slim, with brown eyes. With a few deft touches she achieved the hard-boiled effect. She minced into Fay's office, looking mysterious and tough. She said that she had an important message for him but she would not identify herself further. She was allowed to wait in his private office until he telephoned in. She caught his call and interviewed him over the telephone before his assistants knew who she was. Finally they realized what she was doing and cut her off.

Miss Ferguson laughed and went back to her office. Her city editor was delighted. "You'll do," he said. After that she got a desk, a locker and a mail box, and was treated as a member of the staff. Since then she has done dozens of impersonations. She is acting a part nine times out of ten. She is really quite alone in her field, and is successful at it. When the *News* was conducting a drive against tax-free private property, she was assigned to get into Gramercy Park, if she could. She had already barged into the sacrosanct Morgan Library by wearing a smart new hat and an excessively haughty manner. The invasion of Gramercy Park called for some ingenuity. It was absolutely essential to have a key, or else to climb the fence. Carl Warren, a fellow reporter, had scaled the fence the day before. It was up to Miss Ferguson to devise something new.

She watched people coming and going and then she hit on an idea. She got her camera man to hide behind one tree in the street while she concealed herself behind another. She waited until two mild-looking women sitting on benches started toward the gate. Then she nonchalantly strolled to the entrance, reaching it at the exact moment that they did. As they came out she nipped in, smiling gaily and waving a bunch of keys. The rule is that all members with keys must close the gates after them and let no one in who does not have a key. But they assumed in this case that things were all right.

Miss Ferguson moved smartly toward a sunny bench. In due time the custodian of the park escorted her out. Her camera man recorded every stage of the ejection. The caption ran, "Getting In, Coming Out." They also took pictures, or pix, as the tabloids puckishly call them, of street gamins looking wistfully in, while the presumptively well-off children romped among the trees. The photographer and Miss Ferguson combed Third Avenue for the most ragged children they could find. But they had to be bribed with nickels before they would wear an envious air over their smartly dressed contemporaries. The nickels, however, brought them in mobs. Miss Ferguson and her companion had to brandish their police-cards to persuade passersby that they were not a pair of fiends with a pied piper complex.

Another time Miss Ferguson impersonated a health inspector in order to expose the careless kitchen habits of a smart club in Westchester. She learned that a number of guests had been ill after eating broccoli with hollandaise. Knowing that it would be futile to question the manager about the episode, she tackled the house physician.

"I'm from Dr. Shirley Wynne's office," she told him sternly. "I was sent down to inspect the food here. I understand you have been using an inferior brand of sauce, not up to the local food laws at all."

The doctor was alarmed and assured her that it was not the fault of the food at all, but carelessness on the part of the cook, who had failed to wash the broccoli thoroughly. She used the same approach again when there was a similar occurrence at one of the leading hotels in New York. This time the house doctor told her that a maniac was at large in the hotel, poisoning the food. His handiwork had been detected several times. The culprit was caught finally. He was a demented bus boy, with a fancied grudge against the management. Like Edna Ferguson, Rosaleen Doherty is also a stunt girl on the *News*, ready to tackle skiing, wear shorts where they are banned, or do other monkey shines at the behest of her city editor.

Another of the newspaper women who add adventure to the mere coverage of the news is Lady Terrington, who did hardy work on the *Morro Castle* disaster. She drove down to Asbury Park in the storm and helped all night in the rescue work. She managed to get on the ship while it was still burning after the wreck. She was hauled aboard in the breeches buoy. Her hands, feet and hair were badly burned. She helped to rescue a photographer, and she got a good first-hand picture for the *Mirror* of what things were like on board the smoldering ship. When she was back on shore again her feet were so badly burned that she could not wear her shoes. She had to get a friend to drive her car back to New York. On the way she spotted a blaze at South Amboy, and went to cover that too. The old fire-engine urge. The reporter feels it even more than the public.

Working for Emile Gauvreau, Lady Terrington covered all sorts of assignments. She joined the *Mirror* staff in 1932, first as a guest columnist, then as a regular reporter. One of her first assignments was to spend the night in a woman's flop house. She dressed the part and carried it off, in spite of her smooth British tongue. Lady Terrington is the daughter of Colonel William S. Swiney, who commanded the 2nd battalion of the Black Watch and was aide-de-camp to the Duke of Edinburgh. She married Lord Terrington in 1927. She has done newspaper work on both sides of the Atlantic, has traveled everywhere, written for magazines and played the lead in one of the first talking pictures made in England. She now free-lances and is special correspondent for the *Empire News*.

The tabloids open the doors to different types of women reporters. Their editors have fewer prejudices against the species. A girl has much more hope of walking in and landing a job than she has on the conservative paper. Stunt girls and beauties are welcome. It isn't essential for them to know how to write if they are exceptionally good at getting facts, or have the knack of finding their way in where other reporters are barred. But there are always a few who can turn in a workmanlike job under any circumstances; who know how to write and get a sound grip on a story. Norma Abrams, of the *News*, falls in this class. She works on absolutely even terms with the men on her paper and most of the time covers a steady court beat. She is married to Jack Miley, one of the stars of the *News*. For twenty years she has been gathering up the straws of experience that made the seasoned reporter.

Originally she made her newspaper début in Bellingham, Washington, a small town on Puget Sound. She was teaching at the time and hated it. An uncle who had pull with the local editor got her a newspaper job. She was assigned to make a census of the church membership of the city. The Puget Sound region teems with Scandinavian churches. For weeks she plodded about, getting her statistics. Her editor was surprised when finally she confronted him with the figures. They represented an incredible amount of effort. Actually he had cared little about getting them. It was just one of the tryout dodges an editor can apply to the ever unwelcome woman reporter.

Since she had delivered the story there was nothing for him to do but give her a job. She got $6 a week and worked for him for two years until she moved on to a larger paper in Seattle. She interrupted that to do a year's war service in France with the Red Cross and shortly afterwards she went on to the San Francisco *Chronicle*. In 1929 she joined the staff of the *News* in New York, after several years of newspaper work in San Francisco, two in the Hollywood studio publicity departments and some free-lancing.

One of Miss Abrams' best scoops was obtaining exclusive pictures of Jack Diamond and his wife in an Albany hospital after he had been shot at the Aratoga Inn in the spring preceding his murder. Pictures, to the tabloids, are as precious as an exclusive story. Diamond demanded a large sum of money to pose and he wanted it in advance. Miss Abrams was in Albany. She called her city desk in New York, but the money was not available and could not be had until the bank opened next morning. Diamond was too temperamental for her to feel sure that he would stick to his word. It had taken a week to get his consent.

Finally, in desperation, Miss Abrams went to the manager of the De Witt Clinton Hotel. She could not tell him why she wanted the money but she insisted that she had to have it. She was in the hotel without luggage and he had never seen her before, but he took a chance and gave her the sum she wanted. The camera man proceeded to the hospital, while Miss Abrams stayed at the hotel beside a telephone in case further difficulties arose. And they did. The hospital authorities refused to let the camera man in and, finally, at the door of Diamond's room the state troopers on guard brought everything to a standstill.

For an hour Miss Abrams telephoned frantically to state officials, trying to break down this opposition, and fearing that Diamond would change his mind or that the other papers would learn what was up and block the whole business. Finally it was accomplished and the plates were on their way to New York.

Another of the more difficult moments in Miss Abrams' career was when she and Helen Nolan, of the *American*, waited at the gates of Dwight W. Morrow's home in Englewood, knowing that the wedding of Colonel Lindbergh and Anne Morrow was pending. They had been on guard duty for six weary weeks.

When they learned that the wedding had taken place they rushed to telephones and gave their news in great excitement, but they were coldly informed by their offices that Colonel Lindbergh had released the story two hours before through the Associated Press. They were in deep disgrace until the facts were cleared up the next day. No blame attached to them. The wedding had taken place practically under their noses and they had watched the bridal pair drive away with no idea that it was all over. But this was the Colonel's ruse to fool the reporters, whose presence at the gates he greatly resented. After the kidnapping of his child Miss Abrams was assigned again to the Morrow home at Englewood during the days of false alarms and twenty-four-hour vigils.

When Eugene Van Clief, ostensibly the second husband of Mrs. Frances Kirkwood, who had disposed of her first husband with a knife, began to be apprehensive of a similar fate, he sought the aid of the *News*. He was a quavering person in the last stages of tuberculosis. Miss Abrams was assigned to deal with him. He told her that he was not actually the husband of Mrs. Kirkwood and that he was mortally afraid of her. He insisted on making an affidavit, so sure was he that something was going to happen to him. Miss Abrams kept him in tow for several days, trying to get Mrs. Kirkwood put under bond to keep the peace. Then he disappeared. Two nights later, on August 27, 1930, a call came from her office asking for the affidavit. It was in a lawyer's office and was not available. Van Clief had been found dead with a bullet wound in his heart. Mrs. Kirkwood was beside him, shot through the head.

Miss Abrams rushed to her office and reconstructed the affidavit from memory. On the strength of this the *News* maintained for three editions that Mrs. Kirkwood had killed Van Clief. Actually, the maddened creature had finally gained peace by killing the woman and then himself. Miss Abrams often wondered afterwards if she might not have prevented this tragedy in some way. But every sort of crank invades a newspaper office, and the tendency is to discount the lurid quality of their thoughts.

On the other side of the fence from her often is Jane Franklin, a blonde energetic reporter who covers many of the lead stories for the *Mirror*. She is one of the more successful graduates of the Columbia School of Journalism. She got her job by the somewhat simple device of walking in to see George McDonald, then city editor of the *Mirror*, and demanding two weeks' free trial. She had it and he was satisfied. He gave her the salary she asked for and she landed head first on the street of adventure.

She virtually broke up the Atlantic City Beauty Pageant in 1933 after the *Mirror* had entered its own contest winner in the finals as "Miss New York." The beauty telephoned to Miss Franklin that everything was not as it ought to be along the boardwalk. With a camera man Miss Franklin hurried down the next morning and dug around until she uncovered information indicating that the sponsor and co-judge of the contest had already signed up one of the beauties for a long period. The *Mirror* withdrew its entry and splashed the story. Miss Franklin got affidavits from several of the beauties, charging mismanagement. They played the story hard, together with a first-person narrative from one of the girls whom Miss Franklin had brought back to New York with her. There was no contest the following year, and that year's winner, Marion Bergeron, did not reap the usual rewards of being chosen Miss America.

One of the first lessons Miss Franklin learned on the *Mirror* was the importance of getting pictures. A few weeks after she started she was sent to Coney Island with another reporter when Frankie Marlowe, the gangster, was killed. A dancer and her sweetheart had been arrested by the police as material witnesses. Miss Franklin and her companion went to see the girl's mother. While the more seasoned reporters were in the kitchen begging her to tell all, Miss Franklin noticed a picture of a handsome youth on a small table in the parlor. This, she decided, must be the man under arrest whose picture her city editor wanted so badly.

She expected lightning to flash and the voice of Jehovah to talk to her as she put the photograph under her coat and walked out. She was wildly excited and much frightened by her own legerdemain. When her colleague came out he was full of congratulations until they discovered that the man behind the frame was George Raft, then a dancer on Broadway. It was one of the standardized theatrical photographs that adorn the parlors of bewitched fans.

Three years later Miss Franklin went to Elizabeth, New Jersey, one Sunday afternoon on the story of an Italian girl who had been shot by an ex-suitor, along with the man she was going to marry that day. After the routine interviews with the police and priest, Miss Franklin went to the girl's home to talk to the family and to get a photograph. She met a *News* reporter outside the place, which was a tough roadside saloon. He advised her not to go in, as the family were a hard-boiled crowd. Miss Franklin went up the back stairs, meeting no one. There were two rooms. She could not see any photographs in the first she entered. She crossed the hall to the other room, thinking it was the dead girl's, and was rummaging about when she heard a fuss on the stairs. Not finding any picture, she walked out and saw the father of the murdered girl—a saloon owner—coming up toward her.

"I get you, you thief, I kill you," he yelled, brandishing a knife. Miss Franklin thought of doing a Douglas Fairbanks and swinging down over his head. There was no other exit. But she knew that this was ridiculous. So she tried to soothe the infuriated father. Finally, he made such a racket cursing and screaming that some of his beery customers heard him and came to the rescue. But as they held him back, they agreed that they were silly to save her.

She managed to get downstairs and out to the *News* car. Her rivals had considerately waited for her, expecting trouble. She was shaking all over. She had a somewhat similar experience in 1934 in Flushing over a woman who had shot her lover and killed herself. She walked into the house and was received by a man whom she could not identify. Obviously he thought her a friend of the family and he talked over the entire tragedy with her.

Eventually an old woman emerged from another room. She asked who Miss Franklin was, and the man said he supposed she was a friend of the dead girl's.

"Well," said the old lady, "I've lived with my daughter for years but I've never met you. Who are you, anyway?"

"I'm Jane Franklin, of the *Mirror*."

She set at the girl reporter with fury and tried to push her downstairs. Jane quickly broke her grasp. Then she picked up all the loose vases and started throwing them. Her aim was bad. Jane telephoned to her desk and George Clarke, city editor, said to her, "She can't do that to you. Get a cop and go back and tell her so."

This was much like Chapin's observation to the reporter who had just been thrown downstairs. Miss Franklin didn't bother to go back.

One of her less hazardous jobs was chaperoning the fine wood-chopping girls of Idaho brought on to New York by Arthur Brisbane to shame the metropolitan girls who smoke cigarettes and drink highballs instead of milk.

Ruth Hoershgen and June de Graff, the prospective mothers of American Charlemagnes, did not quite live up to their billing. No sooner did Jane get them on the ferry, bringing them into New York, than they pulled out cigarettes and offered them around. But the climax came at a dinner given in their honor at the Hotel Warwick. The camera man forgetfully invited the wood-choppers to have drinks. June rushed at hers. Miss Franklin pleaded with her to reject it under the circumstances. But she lost the battle. And so, while the two fine American girls sat at the table with their drinks in front of them, the dissolute New York reporter was jazzing up her nerves with pure cow's milk when Mr. Brisbane arrived.

Miss Franklin had much to do with the anti-alienation of affections law now in effect in New York, modeled after the Nicholson bill of Indiana. The girls on the tabloids frequently have to drum up campaigns for their papers. Hettie F. Cattell, also on the *Mirror*, put across the idea of installing radios in the city hospitals and she crusaded to do away with some of the evils of the workmen's compensation administration.

She is the living embodiment of versatility in a newspaper woman and has done virtually everything on a paper except set type. She started in Denver under the redoubtable Josiah Ward, who broke in his reporters with a fabulous technique of mock terrorism. When she sought a job from him after six months of teaching he peered at her over his glasses and said, "You won't be here two weeks but I'll try you for one."

After two years of the *Post* she packed up her things and boarded a train for California. She found a position in Pasadena and worked there for nine months as hotel reporter. She put over a daily scoop on her rival. She haunted artists' studios. She lived with the mother of an aviator and picked up technical knowledge of aerial navigation. She wrote "Happy Hester's Hunches" for the editorial page.

Miss Cattell had $30 in the bank when she got a call from the Fort Worth *Record* and she started at once for Texas. There she did the police run, hung around City Hall, rode on the police patrol, and lounged in the sergeant's office watching for news. After six months of this she returned to Denver and went to work on the *Rocky Mountain News*. She was doing a full page of book reviews and covering the theater when John C. Shaffer, owner of the Chicago *Post*, bought the *News* and *Times* of Denver. At the same time he invited her to take charge of a paper in Evanston, to be edited and managed solely by women. It was called the *Review*. This was one of the few experiments of the kind that has been tried and it was not a success. In the first place, there was no money to spend. Miss Cattell was constantly battling against odds. She was supposed to do editorials, edit all the copy and write the heads. She was office boy, too, because the paper was printed on the Chicago *Post* presses and every scrap of copy had to be carried over to the *Post*, where she had a desk. Not a line could be squeezed into the paper after Thursday night and the subscribers received their papers Saturday morning. She was told to ballyhoo the Progressive Party.

Miss Cattell had plenty of laughs out of the experience of a paper with an all feminine cast. She also had much mental torture. Her staff was rent by envy and bickering. Mr. Shaffer's loss when the paper folded up, a year after it was launched, was $10,000. He had thought that a paper run by women would get the town's following. But he found that the newspaper is a curiously sexless institution.

When Miss Cattell moved East with her husband, Gilman Parker, a well-known newspaper man of nomadic instincts, she joined the staff of the *American* to do a psychoanalytical feature called "Your Dreams." Then she went over to the *Mirror*. She is one of the most industrious women reporters in New York, with great capacity for digging out facts.

The first woman reporter on the *Mirror* was Helen Hadakin, who had previously worked as Gil Boag's secretary in his night club, the Rendez-vous. She had come from a farm in Maine and was the daughter of two preachers. When the club went bankrupt she determined to get on a paper. She had written a few stories and they had been accepted. She walked into the *Mirror* office one hot June afternoon. There was no one to stop her; the place was a jumble of workmen and editors in shirt sleeves. Mr. Howey was pointed out to her and she asked him for a job as a reporter. He read a piece she had written.

"O.K.," he said. "If you don't make good as a reporter, you can be my secretary."

Miss Hadakin was anxious to do well, because she knew little shorthand. But she was left sitting around. No one would give her an assignment. So she decided to assign herself. She cut out a paragraph from an afternoon paper concerning a woman held on Ellis Island, and asked the editor to let her go out on it. He did, but neglected to add that Commissioner Henry Curran never let reporters interview people detained there. She soon discovered this when she got over to the Island. She was on her way down the clanking stairs, ready to weep, when she ran into an indignant man coming up. He spied the clipping in her hand and said, "Isn't it a shame?" Miss Hadakin agreed with him. Then she told him that she had been denied an interview with the woman.

"Come with me," he said at once. "You can pretend you're my daughter. I have a pass."

It developed that the woman was his wife. So she got into the grilled detention room where the unhappy immigrants swarm about, voicing their complaints in a score of different languages. The woman said she would jump into the river if she were sent back. Miss Hadakin, having got the one story, wandered about, trying to pick up something else. As luck would have it, one of the men to whom she talked revealed that he had $100,000 worth of statuary lying on the docks. He had an order for a statue in Minneapolis, but for some reason he was being detained for investigation. He had photographs of all the marble nudes he had brought to America and he gave them to Miss Hadakin for her paper.

Her editors cared nothing about the detained woman, but they were vastly interested in the statuary story. They used the pictures all over the back page. After that Miss Hadakin was assigned regularly to Ellis Island, one of the most difficult beats that any reporter could have, for publicity is frowned on there, and red tape meets the press at every turn. She worked at it furiously for six months. And she brought in many stories. She found a gold star mother who was held on the Island, and had an interview with the girl Firpo brought to America, only to be detained on the moral turpitude charge made famous by Lady Cathcart. Eventually Miss Hadakin was barred from the Island. Mr. Curran disliked her sob stories. But by that time she was carrying around her own camera and doing double duty all over town as photographer and reporter.

When Mr. Payne became managing editor of the *Mirror*, one of his first notions was to have a woman reporter go through the Holland tunnel, which was then being built. Miss Hadakin got the assignment. The engineers dressed her in overalls so that the sandhogs would not know she was a woman, because of their superstition about bad luck. Her photographer balked at going into the compression chamber, so she went down alone and saw them break through beneath the river from the New York to the Jersey side.

When Mr. Howey returned to the *Mirror* after Mr. Payne's death Miss Hadakin was assigned to the task of selecting fiction for serialization. She recommended Ursula Parrott's *Ex-Wife* and Viña Delmar's *Bad Girl*. When Mr. Gauvreau took over the managing editor's desk, he gave her the title of feature editor, for she was then writing a page feature every day, as well as editing and making up all the features. She now selects the serials and short stories, and reads more than thirty books a month. There was much apprehension when she took on *The Postman Always Rings Twice* and *February Hill*. This was strong fare for newspaper consumption. But both stories proved to be good circulation getters.

For a time she was the only woman make-up editor in the composing room and was regarded with professional suspicion. Her orders had to be relayed through the foreman to the make-up man on the feature page. But times have changed. The features are no longer the stepchildren of the newspapers. The wagons carry posters on the new serials as well as the latest murder confessions.

Many of the lead stories in the *Mirror* from day to day are done on rewrite by Ruth Phillips, who has also found time to write three novels in the last few years. Miss Phillips comes from northern New York, was educated in Buffalo, ran away from school at the age of thirteen, piled her hair in a majestic mound and became state editor of the Buffalo *Enquirer* at $7 a week. After a whirl on most of the Buffalo papers she returned to school, went to college and earned $25 a week writing two pages of fiction for the *Sunday Express*. Then she became paralyzed and during her two years at home she earned $80 a week writing features for the *Express*.

After a trip abroad she settled in New York. Walking up Fifth Avenue one afternoon she came face to face with a chimpanzee out for a stroll by itself. She followed it home, wrote the story and sent it to the *Telegraph*, which was then going through its *New Yorker* phase under the editorship of Gene Fowler. Next morning she was asked to do a daily column at a good salary. Ring Lardner and Lois Long were two of her co-workers. She wrote "Along Came Ruth" until she was fired one day with fourteen others. Then Walter Howey hired her to work for the *Mirror*, where she has been for the last seven years.

When Mr. Payne bought the second serial rights to a novel called *Fame*, he was sufficiently interested in the talent of the bright young author, Micheline Keating, to give her a job on his staff. Micheline was one of the more dazzling members of the profession. She was on the stage when she turned to newspaper work. During her school years she had studied dancing and dramatics. Her mother, Mrs. Pearl Keating, was in the theater and it had never occurred to Micheline that there was any other career for her. She had just appeared in Lionel Barrymore's *Laugh Clown Laugh* when she tried Park Row. She was soon in the thick of big news stories. She covered the Dwyer bootleg trial and the raising of the submarine S51. She interviewed "Little Augie" the week before he was betrayed by Legs Diamond and murdered. Then in rapid succession she worked on the Snyder-Gray trial, the Peaches Browning farce, the Cry Baby Bandits trials, Queen Marie's visit to America, Lindbergh's trans-Atlantic flight, and the Valentino funeral, one of the mob scenes of America. She was present at the two Dempsey-Tunney fights and was assigned to the International Polo Games in 1927 and 1930. Dan Parker borrowed her from the city department to cover the matches, as she was familiar with the game, the horses and the players. She arrived at the polo field at Westbury, Long Island, in high spirits and made her way to her press seat. She had been there only a few minutes when Lynn Farnol, who was handling the publicity for the Polo Writers' Association, walked up to her and said that she would have to leave, as the polo writers had agreed that no women were to be allowed in the press section.

Miss Keating insisted that she was working press and not a spectator. He told her politely but firmly that this made no difference. She was a female, and females were not allowed in the press section for any reason whatever. She was indignant and appealed to Harry Cross of the *Herald Tribune*, who at the time was president of the Polo Writers' Association. He went into consultation with several of his colleagues and they came to the conclusion that it would be a bad breach of etiquette to allow her to sit with them after making so positive a ruling.

Miss Keating stormed and raged and said that she had to get her story in for a 7 P.M. deadline. They went into another huddle and returned with the suggestion that although she could not sit with them, there was nothing to prevent her from parking herself in the spectators' section next to the press. They got her a ticket for a seat and she wrote her story balancing her typewriter on her knees and handing it across a two-foot-wide aisle to where her telegraph operator sat comfortably with the working press.

After two years on the *Mirror* Miss Keating switched to King Features, where she turned out copy for the Saturday *Journal* and the Hearst Sunday editions throughout the country. It was inside work and less exciting than being on the street. So she turned her thoughts to fiction again, and when her second book, *City Wise*, was published and she had sold some short stories, she decided to give up newspaper writing altogether.

PART THREE

Chapter XXIV

COVERING THE PRESIDENT'S WIFE

WHEN MRS. HOOVER INVITED THE WASHINGTON NEWSPAPER women to tea at her house on R Street after the nomination of her husband, they found a photograph of Mrs. Coolidge displayed on a table. By chance, each reporter's glance seemed to light on it with unmistakable affection.

Mrs. Hoover watched them with interest. "If, four years from now," she observed at last, "even one of you looks at my picture as you all seem to look at Mrs. Coolidge's, I shall feel I haven't lived in vain."

Sooner or later every President's wife has to make up her mind what to do about the women of the press, and they must abide by her decision. She cannot escape them altogether, but they are singularly dependent on her good graces in getting their news. Until Mrs. Roosevelt entered the White House, the going was extremely thin. They were forced to admire the President's wife from a distance, describe her clothes, take note of her flowers, have a last-minute glance at her dinner table before a state function, see her always as a smiling shadow at her husband's side. They never got anything that even approximated news, or penetrated beyond the outer fringes of her official reserve. It was neither vanity nor curiosity that drove them to ask for more. They were simply doing their job.

From this desolation they entered the fat lands of Canaan in 1932. The transition was so swift that the old guard could not cope with it. Mrs. George F Richards, a veteran political writer who had known a number of Presidential wives, went to Mrs. Roosevelt's first press conference, took a look at the incense burners seated on the floor and decided that she never would attend another. She was the last woman in the Press Gallery to sport a tippet, jet beads and a Victorian bonnet. She wrote a sound column signed "Richards" for a string of New England papers. Had she lived a little longer the chances are she would have been won over, like the other Republican reporters.

For the scoffers changed their tune; the enemy surrendered with astonishing speed. Mrs. Roosevelt bowled over reporters of all persuasions—those who liked dignity and the slow tempo; and those who could stand a bit of dash. She stepped into the White House with a fully developed knowledge of newspaper needs. She did not have to grope or fumble in putting her press relations on a sound basis. She shunned halfway measures and made a dramatic move that was not a sop to their vanity so much as a sensible plan for the dissemination of news.

She established her own press corps; treated its members as honorable human beings; encouraged a barrage of questions; and answered them all with candor, while reserving the same off-the-record rule as the President. In so far as she could, she put them on the same footing as the men who covered her husband. The only thing she could not do for them was to give them much front-page news, although here, too, she went one better than any of her predecessors.

The change in technique was overwhelming to writers who had been frozen out from one administration to another; who had had to fight over such petty matters as dinner table lists, flower decorations and the kind of gown the President's wife would wear at a state function. Mrs. Roosevelt showed how simple, how direct, how effective, the other method could be. Only newspaper people understand that she does not assemble her correspondents to publicize herself. She does it as a convenience for them. The general effect is to create good-will, but the actual benefits to her are negligible. Time and again the newspaper women have come away from her conferences without a line for publication. Few good stories have originated at these gatherings. The only important beats were on the decisions to use beer and wines at the White House table. Some of the busier women in the Press Gallery do not take time to attend them, feeling that they are not a vital source of news.

Yet the access is there. They always know that if there is any question they want to put to the President's wife, they can walk in on Monday morning and get a straightforward answer. This makes for sound and honest relations with the press. Mrs. Roosevelt realized from the start that it was better to see the reporters in person than to turn them over to secretaries and housekeepers for harmless details on the functioning of the nation's chief household. She saw them as a valid link with the public, and she believes that the public has a right to know what is going on in the White House. Fundamentally her approach is based on her own absence of fear where publicity is concerned. All of her predecessors felt that shocking things would ensue if they talked frankly to reporters. They had an exaggerated view of the dangers of candor. When Mrs. Roosevelt swept into the White House like a strong April breeze, she blew the cobwebs of tradition out the window, invited the press upstairs, showed them where the President slept, let them look at him having his tea, and generally made them feel that they were welcome.

She did more than give them news; she made news for them. They traveled with her by plane, motor car and train. They talked to her in coal mines and swimming pools and on Puerto Rican hillsides and by her own somewhat movable hearth. She invited them into her car and drove about with them in taxis. She telephoned to them when she was in inaccessible spots, so that they could get their stories on the wire; she kept one from scooping another; and she took excellent care not to scoop them herself in any of her writings. They not only knew what she did but what she thought. They dined at her table and sometimes gave her advice on matters affecting their craft. At a pinch they could call up the White House and get her on the telephone—an unprecedented means of access to a President's wife. She took an interest in their families, their ambitions, their work, their clothes.

And the bonanza still goes on. Never was there such a gift from heaven for the working press. When the New Deal ends and another President's wife takes over, will the newspaper women ever again be content with mere crumbs from the White House table? Won't they hanker after the abundant days when they were on chummy terms with the President's family? Or will Mrs. Roosevelt's successors see that she had a good idea and follow suit?

In the nineties they took notes on the handsome Mrs. Grover Cleveland shopping for gloves. By the turn of the century society editors were clamoring for some sort of aid on state functions. The days when they dashed about from house to house in victorias, asking the guests what they would wear, were passing. From the moment Theodore Roosevelt took office the White House bubbled with life. Newspaper correspondents were called in at the whim of the President. A sparkling daughter made news by the day, but the women reporters got no innings then. Even the wedding of Alice to Nicholas Longworth in 1906 was a job for men to cover, with few exceptions.

However, the bars were let down an inch. Mrs. Roosevelt employed the first of the social secretaries. She sent out dinner lists, so that at least the society editors were appeased. At the bottom of each list there usually appeared an item about the flowers, and a brief note saying that the President's wife would wear black satin and pearls, and Alice would wear blue, or whatever the costume of the evening happened to be.

James Gordon Bennett believed that the attire of the President's wife was a matter of absorbing interest to the women of America. In his opinion, one of the few good reasons for having a woman on a paper was so that she could be on hand every four years to write something about the wardrobe of an incoming President's wife. The idea has given newspaper women many bad moments.

Mrs. Taft continued to send out dinner lists but dropped the items about flowers and dress. She was a lavish hostess. Her salads were as famous in their way as Mrs. Franklin D. Roosevelt's Sunday night scrambled eggs, but news about the White House was scanty during her time. She made no overtures to the writing women of the capital. Yet there were many gorgeous functions during the Taft administration. The gala event was the last of the pre-war New Year's Day receptions, when the diplomats of the old régime turned out in full fig with the gleam and clank of a dying era. The Russian Ambassador galloped up to the White House door behind two horses and a fur-turbaned Cossack footman. The diplomats of Germany and Austria wore swinging capes, high boots, helmets with eagles and flashing silver and gold. None of them knew it at the time but the days of pomp and circumstance were over.

During the Wilson era there was practically no entertaining, after the first flurry of double functions for the representatives of the Allied nations and their enemies. Neither Woodrow Wilson nor either of his wives had much contact with the press.

Then came Mrs. Harding, who tried for some rapprochement but feared its consequences and did not carry it far. She talked freely at first to Jane Dixon, of the New York *Telegram*, whom she had known in Ohio. But she sooned learned that she could not single out one reporter for her confidence. She was the first of the President's wives to receive groups of women, and after a serious illness she invited some of the reporters upstairs to her private quarters for an informal tea, receiving them in a rose velvet negligée. This was the first time that most of them had been upstairs in the White House or had seen the President's wife in informal attire.

When Mrs. Harding visited New York to buy her inauguration gown, a score of women reporters were led a merry chase, trying to cover her on a shopping expedition. She was staying at the Ritz-Carlton Hotel. They had no clue to her movements. She refused to see them for a moment. None of her staff would divulge a word of information. By mere chance they learned at the end of the day the bare fact that she had chosen a blue dress to wear on March 4th, and the information came from commercial sources. This trivial bit of news was the best that could be collected about the woman who was about to step into the White House. It was played up on the front pages of the most conservative papers, illustrating their eagerness to have something about her, and the trifling results. Yet Mrs. Harding had no intention of harassing anyone. She was simply carrying on a tradition. The wives of the Presidents had always understood that it was better to bow and smile, surround themselves with flowers and beware of the least civility to a reporter.

On the night Mrs. Coolidge arrived in Washington from New England, she was met at the station by a score of women reporters. She made an instantaneous hit. She was vivid, glowing, natural and responsive. She seemed to be genuinely glad that she was on her way to the White House.

The question of clothes came to the fore the day before inauguration, when the women reporters asked Mrs. Frank Stearns, her closest friend, what Mrs. Coolidge's wardrobe was like.

"I'll show you," said Mrs. Stearns, without a moment's hesitation. "It's all here."

She went to a clothes closet and pulled out five or six dresses—a red homespun, four or five simple day frocks and one evening gown. They were busy taking notes when Mrs. Coolidge appeared at the door of the suite. She saw her clothes spread out on the bed, with a mob of strangers hanging over them. For a moment her face was the picture of dismay. Then she laughed and joined the group. "Goodness!" she said. "What's going on?"

She was getting her first taste of what it meant to be the President's wife.

"Do you like entertaining?" she was asked.

"We haven't entertained much," she replied. "We never could afford it, but I'm sure I shall enjoy it."

But even before she entered the White House Mrs. Coolidge began to feel the binding strings. She was spontaneous by nature and, like Mrs. Roosevelt, believed in doing the kind and impulsive thing. A magazine sent a newspaper woman to get a brief statement from her under her own name. She received the proposal with favor. She was on the point of agreeing when Mr. Coolidge walked into the room, heard what was going on, and put his foot down. After that, Mrs. Coolidge conformed to all the traditional customs and although she was beloved by the newspaper women, her relations with them were as conventional as those of her predecessors.

She worked always through a social secretary. Dinner lists were sent by messenger in good time. She invited the press to tea occasionally, she took some of them down the Potomac in the *May-*

flower, she gave a garden party for them. But until Mrs. Franklin D. Roosevelt's time the newspaper teas at the White House were merely a social courtesy—a recognition of the existence of a group of newspaper women in the capital. There was little consciousness of the women reporters as individuals. They were merely the symbol of a powerful force in public life. If Mrs. Coolidge had a favorite, it was Cora Rigby of the *Christian Science Monitor*. But they always came away from contact with Mrs. Coolidge warmed by her presence. She had a genius for avoiding the pitfalls of social life and she left Washington with nothing but good-will on all sides. This extended to the press, although as a source of news she was negative.

Mrs. Hoover looked unhappy the day she entered the White House and relieved the day she left it. She was a tactful hostess but a problem for the press. It was difficult to get a dinner list in time from the Hoover household, as they frequently invited guests at the last minute and the lists could not be sent out until they were complete. Mrs. Hoover figured little in the news except in connection with her Girl Scout activities, and on the few occasions that group interviews were arranged, the reporters were primed on the questions they might ask and were specifically warned against branching out in any direction except scouting.

It was scarcely possible for Mrs. Hoover to steer clear of the limelight entirely, for she had several important guests from abroad while she was in the White House. She entertained Ramsay MacDonald and his daughter Ishbel. And she had the ticklish problem of the King and Queen of Siam, involving many worries over Eastern etiquette. They did not stay at the White House, but Princess Svasti, the Queen's mother, went whirling along in her car for her official call, smoking a fine cheroot. Mrs. Hoover took her over Mount Vernon, but the royal feet hurt and early American history was boring to the Oriental mind. She sat on a Colonial sofa and would not budge. All these problems were met by Mrs. Hoover with tact and subtlety.

But she always seemed at a loss with the press. A reporter out after news got short shrift from her. While crossing the country on a campaign trip, she might invite the one woman reporter on the train to have tea with her in her private car, but there never was a line of news, beyond a paragraph on the flowers received at the last stop. However, when her guard was broken down, she could be frank and entertaining with the press. At a tea she gave for them in the Oval Room of the White House shortly before the President's term ended, she spoke quite thrillingly of her days in China, of the Boxer siege, of some of the adventures she and Herbert Hoover had

had. She was also at her best when she entertained them at Rapidan, because of her passion for the outdoors. They tramped through the woods, lunched under the trees and almost felt that they were welcome.

Mrs. Franklin D. Roosevelt's press relations were a success from the start, because they were founded on mutual trust.

"I was brought up under a very wise newspaper man—Louis Howe," she told the newspaper women. "He has always assured me that there are no higher ethics than those of newspaper people. My confidence has been betrayed only once in my life, and I never saw the reporter again."

Two nights before inauguration Mrs. Roosevelt met the women reporters in a flower-filled suite in the Mayflower Hotel. It was the usual scene on these occasions—a mob interview, with some sage questions being asked and others equally daffy, and in the middle of it all, a smiling figure who might turn into any sort of news possibility.

She was better known to reporters than most of the women who had preceded her in the White House, for she had figured actively in club work in New York. The general impression was one of great frankness and affability. Mrs. Roosevelt spotted old friends, registered new names and faces, and gave a little more information than they had come to expect on these occasions. But they had no conception of what was coming. They were in the usual skeptical frame of mind. The wives of other Presidents had shaken hands with them cordially before inauguration, then had mounted the stairs of the White House to their private quarters and closed the doors behind them sharply. It was a legend that a Brooklyn newspaper woman, by some unknown strategy, had got into the kitchen of the White House once and had tried to count the pots and pans.

On the afternoon of inauguration Mrs. Roosevelt invited them all to tea, although in the past the first afternoon had always been anticlimactic, devoted to relatives and new adjustments. The newspaper women gathered in the East Room. As they filed in, Mrs. Roosevelt said to one after another, "How nice to see a familiar face." The next meeting was held in the Red Room. There were still some skeptics who thought that it could not keep up. The die-hard Republicans did not feel that they could warm to the Democratic invasion. But Emma Bugbee, of the New York *Herald Tribune*, although a Republican, did not belong to either class. She had known Mrs. Roosevelt's activities in New York and admired her.

Emma lingered after the conference to say good-by. She had covered inauguration; now she was due back at her desk in New York.

"I've always been crazy to know what things were like upstairs," said Miss Bugbee, without any special guile.

A good New Englander, fond of the institutions of her country, she had great interest in the White House. She had picketed it during suffrage days, attended diplomatic receptions, seen the Easter eggs rolled on the lawn.

"Oh, I'll show you upstairs any time," said Mrs. Roosevelt cordially. "Come and have lunch with me some day."

"That would be wonderful," said Miss Bugbee, "but my office has called me in. I'm leaving to-morrow."

"Well, come to lunch to-morrow and bring all the New York newspaper girls with you."

That was the beginning of the new order. After they had lunched, Mrs. Roosevelt took them on a tour of the White House. "Now, this is Franklin's room," she said, "and here is where Anna sleeps."

They went from room to room. They inspected pictures, chintzes, hangings, favorite books, bibelots, antiques, rugs, photographs; they got an accurate picture of the home life of the President's family.

"May we write about this?" demanded Dorothy Ducas, of International News Service.

"Oh, yes, why not?" said Mrs. Roosevelt. "Anything you see is all right to write about."

So the sacred precincts, never so thoroughly invaded by the press before, were described in a personal, chatty way next day and there was no repercussion from any quarter. Instead, the Monday morning eleven o'clock press conferences became a firmly established institution.

Newspaper women of all types assembled to cope with this new aspect of political life in Washington. The first-string news girls came on the run. The feature writers took leisurely notes. The society editors, from the Cave Dwellers' monoliths to the gossip columnists, saw that things were going to be cozy. All the writing women with any suitable link of communication were admitted. They made a gathering of nearly seventy-five. There were not enough chairs to go round. The surplus squatted on the floor. This became a subject of jest. A few of the Fundamentalists didn't like it. They saw the dignity of the White House tottering. A gibing cartoon appeared in one of the papers. The President made a jesting remark about the newspaper women sitting at his wife's feet.

More chairs were installed, but great informality still prevails. If someone wants to sit on the arm of a chair, squat on the floor, or take a seat beside Mrs. Roosevelt on the sofa, there is never the slightest objection, although the reporters are a little sensitive now about the ridicule they have incurred. The conferences get smaller as time goes on. The group now numbers from twenty to thirty. The curiosity has worn off. The girls who do straight politics cannot spend an hour and a half in chit-chat when there is no story in prospect. But there is always the possibility that Mrs. Roosevelt may stun them with something sensational.

They are all quite at home in the White House now. They wait confidently in the Green Room, knowing that the usher will open the iron gates to the formal stairway and let them march upstairs. At the west end of the second floor corridor they walk around a screen and enter the region where Mrs. Roosevelt breakfasts, has informal teas and holds her press conferences. During the Hoover term it was filled with potted palms. Now it is much like anybody's living-room, with comfortable sofas and large easy chairs, plenty of low tables and such cheerful signs of life as the family knitting, the current magazines, a toy or two and masses of flowers.

Mrs. Roosevelt comes in after everyone has arrived, Mrs. Malvina Scheider with her. She is usually glowing with life and vitality and the conference takes on animation from her mere presence. When she rides at nine o'clock she comes in wearing jodhpurs, a sweater or white silk shirt, and the blue bandeau she prefers to a hat. Other days she is likely to be wearing a printed silk or a dark blue frock with a white collar. She often brings candy and on sizzling days she may order lemonade for her guests.

There is no such thing as crashing one of Mrs. Roosevelt's conferences, although it is never difficult for a properly accredited correspondent to get entrée. The one taboo is on men. This was a facer for the pampered gentlemen of the press who cover Washington. Women reporters have equal rating with men at the President's conferences, but no man may invade Mrs. Roosevelt's gatherings— a strong gesture on behalf of the women writers, who have had few privileges in Washington. Her idea has borne fruit. She has raised their status and their pay; she has created new jobs for them. But some of the extreme feminists protested the point. They argued that they had fought for years to be received on a footing with men. Why, then, should men be barred from their conferences? However, the rule stands, and has not been violated.

It meant that the United Press, which is averse to women, had to look around and find a woman correspondent. The choice was Ruby Black, one of the group of five newspaper women who are nearest to Mrs. Roosevelt. The others are Lorena Hickok, formerly of the Associated Press; Miss Bugbee, Mrs. Genevieve Forbes Herrick, magazine writer and former star reporter of the *Chicago Tribune*, and Bess Furman, of the Associated Press.

Mrs. Roosevelt is quite impartial in the distribution of news, however. She may address some of the reporters by their first names and have them to luncheon, tea or dinner more often than others, but she has handled the entire group with such tact and trust that there have been no complaints in any quarter. The general understanding is that she will not discuss politics in any shape or form, but her alert mind, ranging from one subject to another, often throws off a dart on political problems. In this way her conferences are valuable as background for the women writers, as well as for spot news. They sometimes fancy that they get an inkling of the President's mind through hers. They know that she constantly clips out pieces from papers and magazines which she thinks he ought to see, and puts them on his bedside table, along with selected letters from her correspondence.

Her own interests are broad. There is no telling which way the interview may veer. The President's taste in reading at one moment; decentralization of industry at another. She freely discusses education, pensions, minimum wages, good housing, recreation, subsistence farms, factory projects and all kinds of labor problems. She likes to introduce a woman engaged in some useful public work and let her speak for herself. Frances Perkins was one of the first to be launched in this way at the press conference.

Mrs. Roosevelt talks more freely now than she did in the beginning but she says less for quotation. She has had a few lessons in the dangers of speaking as the President's wife. One was her comment on the Hauptmann verdict. This remark was made while she was away from her Washington corps. Otherwise, the chances are it never would have got into print. The off-the-record idea barricades her at every turn. She was warned by a prominent publisher that she should not hold these press conferences. She was told that they would be full of dynamite. But she went ahead and nothing has happened to prove her wrong. There have been few tactical blunders, although she has discussed practically every subject under the sun with reporters.

This is partly because a protective system has grown up around her that keeps the wrong sort of information from getting out. This may have damaged her news value materially but probably has saved her embarrassment. However, no woman needs this sheltering touch less than Mrs. Roosevelt. She is an experienced politician and rarely says anything she needs to regret. She is candid without being indiscreet.

On one subject only has she drawn the line, even off the record, and that is the difficulties of her children. She made every effort to shield Anna Dahl from publicity at the time of her divorce and subsequent marriage to John Boettiger. This was one of the more delicate moments in White House history, and Mrs. Roosevelt recognized it as such.

There are times when she would be more frank than she is permitted to be and not worry about it, but the moment she grows spontaneous, a vigilant newspaper woman is sure to interrupt and say, "That is off the record, isn't it?" Mrs. Roosevelt, never slow to apprehend, immediately catches on and says yes. She is not supposed to be quoted without permission. If there is any doubt about anything she has said, Mrs. Scheider reads back her notes. Once, when Stephen Early wanted to bar one of the newspaper girls because she had used something which presumably was said in confidence, Mrs. Roosevelt studied the transcript herself, decided that she had not made it clear that her statement was off the record, and upheld the girl.

But she was definitely annoyed when a story was published giving a false impression of her interest in the Val Kill furniture factory. The inference was that it was profit-making for her, which was far from being the truth. Aside from these two breaks, there have been singularly few ill results from her absolute honesty with the press. She never grows irritable, as the President has done a few times in handling the correspondents.

The newspaper men were apt to scoff at these all-feminine gatherings in the beginning. They were glad "the girls" were having a good time. Poor things, they needed it. There was precious little else for them to do in Washington. But one day the girls staggered them by springing a story that they all would like to have had. It was the announcement on April 3, 1933, that beer would be served at the White House.

This was a nice front-page beat for the feminine contingent. It caused a ripple among their White House colleagues. Carlyle Bargeron, who was then on the Washington *Herald*, pointed out that the girls seemed to be getting the news and that smart editors should do something about it. This was followed by another coup when the question of wines and hard liquor came up in January, 1934.

Again they stole a march on the men. As they walked in to the Monday conference, Raymond Muir, chief usher, handed them all a five-line statement, announcing that wines—preferably American brands—would appear on the White House table. They were told to hold this announcement until the conference was ended, but one newspaper woman misunderstood. She went off in a rush to telephone the news to her paper. There was consternation when the others discovered what had happened. Instantly Mrs. Roosevelt grasped the situation. She sent Bess Furman, Ruby Black, and Mrs. Marie Manning Gasch, who represents International News Service, to her private telephones. As they all represented press services, it would mean most to them in loss of time. She held up the conference until they had time to relay the news to their offices.

This is more or less typical of her thoughtful attitude to the press, and she does not let a bit of formality stand in the way if the newspaper women are pressed for time. The policy of a reporter's paper makes no difference to her, and the doorman of the *Herald Tribune* has witnessed the astonishing spectacle of the First Lady delivering Miss Bugbee at the door in a taxi. Such dizzy doings had never before been seen at the threshold of this Republican stronghold.

The second Sunday Mrs. Roosevelt was in the White House she called on Cornelia Jane, Ruby Black's baby daughter. She telephoned the night before to ask if she might stop in when she was out motoring next day. When she arrived, she promptly got down on the floor and played with the baby. Later Cornelia was invited to Sistie Dahl's birthday party at the White House. No newspaper woman's baby daughter ever had a more dashing début at her first party, with the President of the United States popping crackers for her.

Mrs. Roosevelt is interested in the pleasures and sorrows of her corps of correspondents. She is the first to sympathize with them when anything goes wrong; the first to rejoice when they get raises, or the baby cuts a tooth, or they put over a neat piece of writing. She has been known to send an exhausted reporter to Campobello or Warm Springs to recuperate. When her Scottie "Meggie" bit Bess Furman while she was giving her a lift in her car, Mrs. Roosevelt took her to the hospital for treatment and banished the pet dog.

But the big adventure for five of them was her trip to Puerto Rico and the Virgin Islands in 1933. Miss Hickok, Miss Bugbee, Miss Furman, Miss Black and Miss Ducas were her fellow adventurers and it was something new in the way of a newspaper assignment. The flying corps moved fast, covered more than 6,000 miles, picnicked on tropical hillsides, circled in fog, went from one reception to another, and were heavily fêted. Miss Black is the Washington correspondent of *La Democracia*, a Puerto Rican paper, and her name is as well known there as Mrs. Roosevelt's. She speaks some Spanish, which was useful for the rest of the party.

It was a hectic as well as a festive jaunt. They got little or no sleep, but Mrs. Roosevelt was never tired. After two weeks of it, the correspondents, nerves on edge, engaged in an argument at an airport early one morning with officials who wanted to charge them excess on their baggage. They were exhausted and irritated.

It was pitch dark outside. The local officials were bidding Mrs. Roosevelt a formal farewell. They were laden down with flowers, and elegant speeches in Spanish poured from their lips.

Through all the din Mrs. Roosevelt saw that her press following was in difficulty. Without a moment's hesitation she detached herself from the local potentates, walked over to where they were arguing fiercely with the officials, and offered her help.

"Is there any trouble?" she demanded. "If any of you needs any money, I can let you have any amount you want."

They explained that they were merely arguing over principle.

The worst hour for the correspondents was when they ran into fog between Santo Domingo and Port-au-Prince. They flew in circles for an hour. It began to look like a story. First Lady Lost in Fog. They begged to be allowed to send a bulletin by the airplane's radio. But they were told that no commercial messages could be accepted. Bess Furman wrote bulletins feverishly, feeling that if they crashed, the entire story of their last moments would be found clutched in her hand.

"Why do you write so much?" asked Mrs. Roosevelt, interestedly watching her.

Miss Furman could not think of a reason, except that it was force of habit for an A.P. reporter to feed bulletins to the wire. They turned back to San Pedro. By the time they got there the suspense was over, but there was still a story to file on Mrs. Roosevelt circling blindly in the fog, the plane in danger, and all the accompanying details. But when they settled down in the harbor, the sea was so choppy that they could not get near the wharf. Bill, the steward, was surrounded by three shrieking reporters, determined to get their copy off, demanding that they get ashore. Miss Bugbee, having plenty of time to catch her deadline, did not share in the frenzy of her colleagues, all working for rival press services.

Bill rose to the occasion. He climbed out on a bobbing pontoon, yelled for the skipper of a small rowboat, and handed him the press dispatches, with minute instructions as to what he was to do with them. They were to go to the cable man, pronto! After so much furore, the story seemed tame in print, but it was exciting enough for the reporters covering the President's wife.

When they got home from the trip they were all in a state of exhaustion, except Mrs. Roosevelt, who was still in the pink of condition. None of them can match her on physical vitality. When they followed her to Reedsville, Virginia, to see her homestead project, they traveled all night, rose at six o'clock the next morning, motored more than 300 miles and heard her make fourteen speeches. At the end of the day they were desperately tired, but she wanted to chat with them on the train. So they all went on talking until eleven o'clock. Then she got up to go. They told her they were not surprised that she should want to get some rest at last. "Oh," she said blithely, "Malvina and I will do a magazine piece before I go to sleep. I'm not tired."

Covering Mrs. Roosevelt, then, requires health, strength and lively footwork. She is never tired, never bored. The reporters sometimes are. The nearest she has ever come to showing fatigue was at a dull spelling bee between newspaper women and congressional wives. She was seen to yawn. It was so unusual that everyone noticed it.

There is no formality about the way Mrs. Roosevelt invites her press following to break bread with her at the White House; she does not feel that because she invites one she must invite all the others. This would be a worry to most hostesses in her position, but she never gives it a thought. She simply follows her impulses. It is true that the invitations fall more thickly in some quarters than in others. This is based largely on personal friendship. Newspaper husbands often accompany their wives to the informal Sunday night suppers at which the eggs are scrambled personally by Mrs. Roosevelt and the conversation is good.

The newspaper women have profited enormously by her attitude toward them. They have gained prestige, and their usefulness to their papers and press services has increased, not to mention the personal satisfaction they feel at having fireside standing in the White House. To have such a large body of newspaper women consistently on one's side takes a somewhat subtle combination of tact, intelligence and what is commonly known as having the goods. Some admire Mrs. Roosevelt more than others, but without exception they find her generous, fair and open-minded.

They may be a little flattered. They may like to think that the President's wife calls them by their first names, invites them to luncheon, seeks their advice, and lets them in on weighty secrets. They have had so many years of neglect at the White House that they welcome a little warmth. But at bottom, the answer lies in her own integrity. And they know, as reporters, that her technique is enough to make them shout hosannas, from the professional standpoint alone.

Chapter XXV

INVADING THE PRESS GALLERY

J ANE GREY SWISSHELM, AN INVINCIBLE DAMSEL WHO STARTED LIFE
as a child prodigy, quoted the New Testament at the age of
three, badgered Daniel Webster, helped to drive Governor Lowrie of Minnesota out of his mind, and caused havoc in the hospitals during the Civil War, was the pioneer who first opened the
Press Gallery to the woman correspondent.

Mrs. Swisshelm had no intention of lingering in the halls of government. She merely wanted to open the door to show that it could
be done. One day was sufficient for her purpose. She was in the
capital on a junket, having persuaded Horace Greeley to buy her
Washington letters at $5 a column. After seeing the town she felt
the urge to do something spectacular before returning to Pittsburgh:

> There was yet one innovation I wanted to make, although
> my stay in Washington would necessarily be short. No woman
> had ever had a place in the Congressional reporters' gallery.
> This door I wanted to open to them, so I called on Vice-Presi-
> dent Fillmore and asked him to assign me a seat in the Senate
> Gallery. He was much surprised and tried to dissuade me. The
> place would be very unpleasant for a lady, would attract atten-
> tion, I would not like it; but he gave me the seat. I occupied it
> one day, greatly to the surprise of the Senators, the reporters,
> and others on the floor and in the Galleries; but felt that the
> novelty would soon wear off, and that women would work
> there and win bread without annoyance.

Mrs. Swisshelm's prophecy was correct. That was in 1850. Today
the newspaper women sit on terms of comparative equality with the
men in the Press Gallery. They are few in number but they happen
to be good workmen. The result is that they have overcome most,
although not all, of the moss-grown prejudice.

Jane was thirty-five when she stormed Washington—an abolitionist, a feminist, a woman bored with her husband. Her invasion
of the Press Gallery was a side issue. The big event of her trip to

Washington was her attack on Daniel Webster through the columns of her paper, the Pittsburgh *Saturday Visiter*. Scouting for news, she unearthed a dark secret about him. "Then I knew why I had come to Washington," she confessed. "I gathered the principal facts of his life at the Capitol and submitted them to a correspondent who advised me to keep quiet, as others had done."

Mrs. Swisshelm knew that her exposé would not be applauded by Mr. Greeley, and she liked to bask in the "social distinction and the courtesy" which her connection with the *Tribune* commanded. So she wrestled with her Calvinist conscience but finally decided to expose Mr. Webster in her own paper. She walked the streets of Washington hesitating to post the letter that she knew would cause a sensation. She had not misjudged her facts. A storm of denunciation broke loose. The *Tribune* condemned her. The religious press was shocked by her indelicacy. But the damaging paragraph was copied everywhere. "It was so short and pointed that in no other way could its wickedness be so well depicted as by making it a witness against itself," Mrs. Swisshelm declared.

Mr. Webster was a candidate for the Presidency at the time. In her autobiography the redoubtable Jane takes credit for having killed his prospects. When the national convention met in Pittsburgh in 1852 to form the Free Democratic party, she attended the executive branch. The chairman rushed up to her to say: "I want to take the hand that killed Daniel Webster."

But Mr. Greeley forgave her and she continued to write occasionally for the *Tribune*. She had some of the ruthless frenzy of Anne Royall and made trouble wherever she went. Her husband was not literary, and she considered herself his mental superior. He, too, had his eccentricities. He kept a panther and bears. One day the panther nearly swallowed Jane whole while she was loping about on crutches after an accident. But this did not still her tongue or arrest her pen.

She started her newspaper career by writing for the Pittsburgh *Commercial Journal*. She knew what to do with words. Even today her style seems sharp and lucid. Soon she announced she was going to start the *Saturday Visiter* as an abolitionist organ. Her financial backer begged her to spell visitor in the usual way.

"Johnson is my authority," said Mrs. Swisshelm, and stuck to her point for years.

The paper was a six-column weekly. Horace Greeley and the haughty N. P. Willis both gave it recognition. All the hobbies and reforms of the day were dealt with realistically—Fourierism, spiritualism, vegetarianism, phonetics, pneumonics, criminal caudling and

Magdalenism. Jane advocated coeducation of the young. After a railroad wreck she took credit for proposing the red light signal for the tail-end of trains, which later came into general use. She left the paper in 1857 and walked out on her husband soon afterwards, having just given birth to her first child at the age of forty. In a final flourish she announced:

> I had lived over twenty years without the legal right to be alone an hour—to have the exclusive use of one foot of space—to receive an unopened letter, or to preserve a line of mss. from sharp and sly inspection.

Plainly Jane was fed up. So she took her baby and went to St. Paul. For years afterwards she was involved with her husband in litigation over property and other matters. But his spirit seems to have been more generous than hers, for he said of her on one occasion: "I believe she was the best woman God ever made and we would have had no trouble except for her friends."

She proceeded to St. Cloud, Minnesota, and there began the campaign which drove Governor Lowrie into a sanitarium. It took some time to accomplish his ruin, but Jane persisted. He lived in what she considered semi-barbaric splendor on the banks of the Mississippi surrounded by slaves. He was a handsome man, mesmeric and entertaining. Again Jane had a weapon of attack. She launched the St. Cloud *Visiter* and did occasional printing. This gave her a public. She badgered and hounded the Governor and went to extravagant lengths in running down his anti-abolition tendencies. Soldiers were brought out, her home was stoned, she was the center of a continual uproar. At last the Governor was committed to a sanitarium, worn out by the struggle, and Jane went on to fresh forays in the hospitals of Washington.

Years later she and her victim met for the first time, after his release. He said to her sadly:

> I am the only person who ever understood you. People now think you go into hospitals from a sense of duty; from benevolence, like those good people who expect to get to heaven by doing disagreeable things on earth; but I know you go because you must; go for your own pleasure. You take care of the sick and wounded, go into all those dreadful places just as I used to drink brandy—for the sake of the exhilaration it brings you.

Jane rampaged through the wards, insisted on taking over nursing duties, had rows with the staff but finally made herself useful by rounding up lemons to cure gangrene. She made her appeals through the columns of the *Tribune*:

Hospital gangrene has broken out in Washington and we want lemons! *lemons!* lemons! *LEMONS*. No man or woman in health has a right to a glass of lemonade until these men have all they need; send us lemons.

For a time Jane held a government job, making $60 a month. She continued to correspond for newspapers and became a regular contributor to the *Southern Monthly*, published in New Orleans. She wrote fiction, essays and straight news, but the propagandist note was ever present in her work.

After her solitary day in the Press Gallery, a few feminine scribes slunk in to do gossipy letters under assumed names. They were usually clerks recruited from government offices. Then came Mary J. Windle, the author of several books. She was at her best during Buchanan's administration; at her worst during Lincoln's. He had her imprisoned as a Confederate spy, and when he was assassinated she tore down the crêpe which soldiers nailed all over the house. Then she was imprisoned again.

The next woman to make any sort of impression in the Gallery was Mrs. Emily Edson Briggs, the author of the Olivia letters. She arrived in Washington from Iowa in 1861. She wrote for the Washington *Chronicle* and then for the Philadelphia *Press*. For more than forty years she was in and out of the Gallery, and saw government in the making. It was a big day in her life when she first began sending off "telegraphic dispatches to the press of other cities, giving details of legislation as it was being enacted." This was an advance on the leisurely feuilleton, but it was some time before women used the telegraph regularly to send their dispatches. There was no thought of covering spot news. The correspondents were essayists or commentators. They wrote frankly and often in an unflattering vein. They shared the general abusive tenor of the press of that period. And, whenever possible, they broke into original verse.

Olivia was a founder of the Woman's National Press Association, which was organized in 1882. She died in 1910. One of her contemporaries was Mary Clemmer Ames, who wrote for Henry Ward Beecher's *Standard*, which later became the *Independent*. Mrs. Ames' output was stupendous. One of her books was a gossipy story of life at the capital which stirred up talk at the time.

The number of women in the Press Gallery began to creep up in the early seventies. The 1874 directory of the Forty-third Congress carried the following list:

Mrs. Emily Edson Briggs (Olivia), Philadelphia *Press*
Mrs. H. M. Barnard

Mrs. Mary Clemmer Ames, New York *Independent*
Mrs. Mary Fuller, St. Louis *Times*
Grace Greenwood, New York *Times*
Mrs. Mary E. Nealy, New York *Home Journal*
Mrs. F. C. Snead, Louisville *Courier Journal*
Austine Snead, New York *Graphic*
Mrs. E. D. Wallace, Philadelphia *Evening Telegraph*
Eva McDonald Valesh, St. Paul *Globe*
Mrs. E. S. Cogswell, North Carolina *New Era*

When Grace Greenwood and Gail Hamilton came along they set a high standard for the others to match. They were cosmopolitans and women of wit—much sought after by government figures, to the envy of some of their colleagues, none of whom managed to cut so wide a swathe. Like most of her contemporaries Grace Greenwood did leisurely correspondence, but, unlike the others, she infused a lively charm into her work and skipped the hurdles to avoid being trite. Her style was fresh and spirited. She had none of the intellectual incandescence that consumed Margaret Fuller, but she was better adapted to the urgent needs of newspaper work.

Grace Greenwood was one of the assumed alliterative names of the period. She was born Sara Jane Clarke, the daughter of a theologian, and her early days were spent in Pompey, New York, and Rochester. Her first literary attempts were lugubrious verses which dwelt lovingly on death. The vaporings of seventeen made acceptable newspaper reading in those sad days. "First the undertaker, then the minister, then Sara," her brother gibed.

At nineteen she was spending her winters in Philadelphia and contributing to the newspapers and to *Godey's Lady's Book*. In 1850 her sketches and letters were collected and published as *Greenwood Leaves*, three years before *Fanny Fern's Leaves* came out with stupefying success. Grace was inclined to be literary, so she could not hope to keep step with Fanny in popularity. But Dr. Gamaliel Bailey, editor of the *National Era*, asked her to write for his paper, which was published in Washington. This she did, at the same time corresponding for the New York *Mirror*. In 1852 she went abroad and sent back a series of vivacious letters to the American newspapers.

The public was not yet surfeited with the travelogue idea. Few Americans had been abroad. Transportation was slow and expensive. To see Europe and some of its celebrities through the eyes of the observant and witty Grace Greenwood was a treat for the stay-at-homes. Thousands got vicarious enjoyment from her travels. She could make a trip to Newgate a thrilling event at the fireside. She wrote illuminatingly on Mr. and Mrs. Charles Dickens after dining at their home. Dickens was the victim of many of these chatty visits on the part of lady correspondents from America. England was rich in literary celebrities, and as there were no syndicates to usurp their names and get their own output, they made fair pickings for the visiting correspondents.

Grace Greenwood stayed in this fertile area for a year, rounding up Thackeray, Browning and a dozen others. She went up Mount Vesuvius; she was presented to the Pope. She explored churches and picture galleries. She was an indefatigable traveler and an abundant writer, filling many columns in the New York papers. At this time rival papers amicably printed correspondence from the same person. It might run concurrently without the slightest concern in either office—a practice that would be unthinkable today.

On her return to America, she married Leander K. Lippincott, of Philadelphia, but went on writing for the papers and magazines. She read and lectured to soldiers in camps and hospitals during the Civil War, and made herself so generally useful that President Lincoln called her "Grace Greenwood, the Patriot." Her Washington sketches were published first in the New York *Tribune*. They were a smooth blend of the personal and political, written in a light and sometimes satirical vein. Occasionally she took a whack at the politicians:

> I have for some time abstained from chronicling Congressional doings, leaving the not very agreeable duty to your other and abler correspondents. I have been waiting for "our honorable body" to return to a decent equanimity of temper and Christian-like behavior. These saucy serving-men of ours are really becoming disagreeably and uncomfortably quarrelsome. They "take the wall" to each other and "frown and bite their thumbs" on every occasion. We are told that a Congress of women would be shockingly unruly, passionate and slanderous; but it would take women of forty Billingsgate power to surpass the late displays of honorable gentlemen of both honorable houses. Scenes there have been in the stately chambers which in their rise and progress remind one of the memorable tea-fight between Sairey Gamp and Betsy Prigg; scenes that half-inclined one to think there might be, as in the case of that little unpleasantness, something a little stronger than tea in the pot.
>
> Really, these eternal Republican family quarrels and bickerings are getting rather tiresome—especially as, rough and rancorous though they seem, we know they are but words, words, words, mere passion-poisoned breath—safe insults, bloodless duels. One almost wishes the wordy combatants would have a regular stand-up fight, after the old-fashioned, chivalrous style, and have done with it.

Later she contributed "Occasional Washington Notes" to the New York *Times*, commenting on people and events. When she made a trip through the West in 1871 she sent back letters written intermittently as she traveled, lectured and went sightseeing. They all had the flavor of an alert intelligence. She did not strike the reforming note, like most of her contemporaries, or beat the bass drum. She was content to record what she saw.

She returned to Europe later in the seventies, and her sparkling letters came from London, Paris, Milan or wherever her wandering feet took her. She came home in 1887 and lived in Washington until 1900. Four years later she died at the home of her playwright son-in-law, Henry Field Winslow, in New Rochelle, New York.

More satirical than Grace Greenwood, and a really potent force in Washington, was Gail Hamilton, one of the sharpest writers on political topics of the nineteenth century. She was a cousin of Mrs. James G. Blaine and was in the inner councils of her husband. She lived in their home and wrote Mr. Blaine's life history shortly before her death. Journalism was only one of her interests. She wrote verse, biography, juvenilia, essays, history and sermons. Fanny Fern's estimate of her gives some idea of the vigor of Gail Hamilton's pen:

> A lady, at whose mention stalwart men have been known to tremble, and hide in corners; who "keeps a private graveyard" for the burial of those whom she has mercilessly slain; who respects neither the spectacles of the judge, nor the surplice of the priest; who holds the mirror of men's failings till they hate their wives merely because they belong to her sex.

Gail was a spinster, a Calvinist, a farmer's daughter. Her name was Mary Abigail Dodge and she took the Gail from her middle name and Hamilton from the town in Massachusetts where she was born in 1833. She grew up in New England, the youngest of seven children. She was educated at Ipswich Female Seminary and was graduated in 1850, turning to teaching, first at Ipswich, then at Hartford. Dr. Bailey, who first published Grace Greenwood's work, also gave Gail Hamilton a platform, not suspecting the political power she was to wield as the years went on.

She moved to Washington in 1858 to become the governess in his home. There she met the celebrities of the capital and her social sphere widened considerably. She got to know Whittier, Mrs. Harriet Beecher Stowe and Nathaniel Hawthorne. Soon she developed the habit of writing constantly and voluminously. She was at the height of her power while Mr. Blaine was Secretary of State, and was credited with influencing his judgments and aiding him with his speeches. Political leaders and literary celebrities all courted her favor and listened to what she had to say. She haunted Congress, as Alice Longworth does today, and her work appeared in the *Tribune*, the *World* and the leading magazines of the day. Her words were barbed. Her witticisms were quoted far and wide. She understood statecraft better than most politicians. Her political articles were informed, if somewhat intemperate in tone. She interviewed all the men of the hour and wormed secrets out of close-mouthed officials.

Her point of view was rarely constant. She attacked Horace Greeley savagely when he ran for the Presidency. Five years later she was tirading against civil service reform in the *Tribune*, which by that time was edited by Whitelaw Reid. Her first article on this subject appeared in 1877. It was followed by eight more instalments of dubious prose and cockeyed reasoning. Gail was a stand-pat politician in some respects; advanced in others. She backed abolition and was an early suffragist. She campaigned on behalf of the Armenians and worked frantically for the liberation of Mrs. Maybrick, an American woman imprisoned in London on the charge of murdering her husband. She always maintained that "woman was born into the whole world."

In 1878 her name appeared in the *Tribune* again with seven articles on "Politics in the Pulpit—the Need of Pulpit Reform." They were based on the Fast Day sermons preached throughout the country, and they were free and abusive in tone. The clergymen quailed before Gail's onslaught. She called them liars, ignoramuses and threw brickbats freely at their reverend heads. The public enjoyed the inkslinging until she tired of the church and turned her satire into other channels. Today, such stories in all probability would be killed for their excessive rancor. However, personal abuse was the order of the times. Publishers set the example on their editorial pages; reporters followed suit. It was a merry free-for-all. But even in the Press Gallery Gail Hamilton's pen was felt to be sharp. She was the best informed of the correspondents and sometimes the most astute but she did nothing to prove that a woman was capable of unbiased reporting.

Gail was a homely figure but magnetic. She dressed plainly in the Press Gallery but went in for all the luxury of the era on her evening forays. Her head was excessively large and her features were heavy and masculine. She had a high forehead and bulbous steel-blue eyes. But her conversation was delightful, informed and witty, and the cleverest men were glad to sit beside her at dinner. Her writings always had background. She demonstrated that a woman political writer could wield real power, although how much of this was due to her own efforts and how much to the Blaine connection, it would be difficult to determine. Unquestionably she was a formidable political reporter and critic, and she wrote with a sting that is unequaled in the Press Gallery today. Her ear was always to the ground, and even if her conclusions seem debatable now, they must have been potent at the time.

But all the women correspondents were in the same predicament by 1877. They were kicked out of the Gallery. For fourteen years it was again a masculine monopoly. However, the ban was not confined to them. It was a general tightening up of the rules of admission. A number of men were barred at the same time. Today only correspondents who send their dispatches by telegraph are regularly admitted to the Press Gallery. And not more than a dozen women make steady use of the privilege.

After the ban went into effect it was not until the early nineties that a woman appeared again in the Press Gallery. This time it was Mrs. Isabel Worrell Ball, a Westerner born in a log cabin and as handy with a gun as a pen. She preferred a group of squabbling politicians to a roomful of women at tea. She was not a suffragist, unlike most of the early women writers, who used their press outlet to campaign for women's rights.

Mrs. Ball was born in 1855 near Hennepin, Illinois, and at thirteen years of age began to read law with her father. When she was eighteen the family moved to Kansas. She roved the prairies, helped to herd her father's stock, learned to throw a lasso like a cowboy and to swing a gun. She taught in the first public school in Pawnee County, Kansas, and spent a year clerking in a shop three miles from her home, galloping back and forth on her pony. After her marriage she lived an adventurous life in New Mexico and Arizona.

Her newspaper work began in 1881 on the Albuquerque *Journal*. The Atlantic and Pacific Railroad was then being built from Albuquerque to the Needles. Her husband was a member of the construction gang and was away from home most of the time. If there was a washout, an Indian outbreak or a wreck, he was expected to be on hand. Mrs. Ball's life was filled with hazard. Once wolves tore her clothes as she outrode a ravening pack. Both Navajo and Apache Indians were constantly skirmishing around her home. Again, a train on which she rode was surrounded by Indians and escape was cut off by a washout. The box car in which she hid was riddled with bullets and two men were killed, but she escaped unhurt.

Her experiences gave color to her work. After two years in these wild surroundings, seeing no woman's face but a squaw's, she became editor of the *Chronoscope*, a Republican paper in western Kansas. Her next move was to Topeka to do editorial work for the *Daily Commonwealth*. Two years later she became literary critic of the

Times in Kansas City and a year later she moved over to the *Star*. In that same year she called together the better known writers of the West and founded the Western Authors and Artists Club. She left the Kansas City *Star* in 1891 and moved to Washington. Soon afterwards she took her place in the Press Gallery.

The pen name Howard Glyndon which appeared frequently in the New York and St. Louis papers during the sixties and seventies belonged to Laura Catherine Redden, a Maryland girl who became deaf and dumb after an attack of spinal meningitis, yet managed to correspond from the Press Gallery during the Civil War. She adopted her pen name for its masculine sound. This was the period when the Fanny Fern, Jenny June and Grace Greenwood alliterations were in vogue. Miss Redden wrote for the St. Louis *Republican*. Like Grace Greenwood, she did travel correspondence for the *Times* from Europe and on her return in 1868 joined the staff of the *Mail*. During the next few years she studied articulation with Alexander Graham Bell and learned to speak again. In 1876 she married Edward W. Searing, a lawyer, and when her health failed she and her husband went to live in California.

Long before Marguerite Young appeared in the Press Gallery espousing the labor cause, Mrs. Eva McDonald Valesh, the daughter of a Minneapolis carpenter and labor agitator, was sending fiery pieces to the St. Paul *Globe*. She had worked in stores and factories and had written a series of letters for her paper on the working girl of that era. She had mounted soap boxes before she was twenty-one, and was one of the first correspondents in Washington, man or woman, to view government from the workingman's point of view.

Another of the pioneers in the Gallery was Fanny B. Ward, who represented the New Orleans *Picayune*. She was an itinerant reporter, sending letters from wherever she happened to roam. She was one of the first American correspondents to enter Cuba in 1898 and was there when the *Maine* was destroyed.

At the turn of the century Marie Mattingly, small, vivid and enterprising, was in and out of the Press Gallery doing political sketches. Mrs. Frank Leslie, wife of the owner of *Leslie's Weekly*, also liked to watch the legislators from the Press Gallery. But the woman who did more than any other to break down prejudice against newspaper women in Washington was Cora Rigby, for many years head of the *Christian Science Monitor* bureau and as able a correspondent as any man. At first the newspaper men resented her presence. It was something new to have a woman head a bureau which employed men. But she was so unobtrusive in her manner, so sound in her work, that she soon won their admiration. Her style was nervous, compact, forceful. There was nothing about her copy to indicate that it was written by a woman. Her mind was excellently geared for political work and she was sometimes uncanny in her divinations. She did straight reporting and could cover anything, from melodrama to an international incident.

At one time she was threatened with tuberculosis. She was told as she lay in a hospital bed that she must leave at once for New Mexico to remain there permanently, if she were to live for more than two years. When the specialists left, she calmly got out of bed, dressed herself, walked out of the hospital and fainted on the way home. Next morning she was at work and she never went to New Mexico. Toward the end of her life she insisted on going to the political conventions, although she knew that she had only a short time to live.

Miss Rigby was appointed Washington correspondent of the *Monitor* in 1918 and headed the bureau for more than seven years. She had the confidence of all the politicians. Presidents and ambassadors treated her as a friend. She knew the Hoovers during the war days in London, and she was a special favorite of Mrs. Coolidge's. She often had precedence in official quarters. Once she went to get a statement from a Cabinet officer on some current issue. He was not in when she arrived, but his secretary suggested that Miss Rigby sit down and write the statement herself. She did. Then she was asked to return in an hour, so as to give him time to study it and see if it had his approval.

When she returned, the Cabinet officer handed Miss Rigby two sheets of paper with the remark: "I'm sorry I had to dictate this in such a hurry. I am not sure that it is exactly what you want. Will you read it?"

He handed her her own copy, word for word, without a comma missing.

"Just exactly what I wanted, Mr. Secretary," said Miss Rigby, and bowed herself out.

Her earliest connection with a newspaper was political. She was born in Lancaster, Ohio, and was educated at Western Seminary, Ohio State University and Boston University. After her graduation she went home to Columbus, Ohio, to live. Her father was Judge William L. Rigby, and she heard plenty of political gossip under the family rooftree. Before she had been home long she conceived the idea of writing a daily column for one of the local papers. The editor was scandalized. When she showed up in the local room he told her that a newspaper office was no place for a nice girl. He knew that her father was an important figure in town. So he put on his hat and escorted her home. Then he told her mother to keep her there. But next day Cora showed up with another column of comment.

He told her he would not think of using it. But he looked it over and was interested. It appeared in the paper next day, but without a by-line. Cora returned with another. Every time she appeared he tried to discourage her, but he kept on using her work. Finally he paid her for it. Meanwhile, the column became so authoritative that the townspeople believed the Governor's secretary was writing it. Miss Rigby encouraged this gossip and laughed up her sleeve. One day she asked for a desk in the office.

"Of course not," said the obstinate editor. "Besides, we haven't a spare desk."

Miss Rigby went over to a dusty desk in a corner. She opened the drawers and found them empty. She sat down and wrote her column on the spot. It was only a matter of days until she was sent out to cover a woman's meeting. After that she did all the news of this sort in the city, until her job became too easy and she decided to try Boston. There she did assignments on space for a time and then moved to New York, where she worked for the *Mail* and then for the *Herald*. She ran contests. She covered general news. She edited the Sunday magazine. A Scot in the composing room taught her make-up. To run the magazine and please James Gordon Bennett was no light task. To begin with, he disapproved of women in positions of trust. She was in England working for the *Herald* when war broke out. On her return to America Mr. Bennett gave her a Pekinese pup as a present—a special sign of his favor. Miss Rigby was with the *Herald* for fifteen years. When Mr. Munsey bought it she moved over to the *Christian Science Monitor*, where she remained until her death in 1930 at the age of sixty-four.

In her off-hours Miss Rigby liked to wander about the countryside, studying flowers, birds and old houses. She had a generous spirit and was an easy mark for schemers and promoters. Anyone out of a job, anyone hard up, sought Miss Rigby and usually got aid. She liked to see young newspaper women progress in their field. She served seven terms as president of the Women's National Press Club and in her will left the club women money to aid impoverished members of the craft. Her closest friend was Margaret Williamson, who knew her intimately for twenty years, lived with her in New York and in Washington and went abroad with her twice.

Miss Williamson is another newspaper woman who has worked on the *Monitor* for years. At one time or another in the twenty years she has been with the paper she has edited five of its feature pages, done essays, special articles and book reviews. She now edits the Home Forum.

It was Miss Rigby who launched Mary F. Hornaday, who does capable work in the Press Gallery for the *Monitor*. Miss Hornaday was fresh from Swarthmore when Miss Rigby, short-handed in the bureau, took her on in 1927. It was natural for Mary to gravitate to journalism. She comes from a newspaper family. Her father, James P. Hornaday, has been Washington correspondent of the Indianapolis *News* for thirty-four years. A brother, Hilton P. Hornaday, is financial editor of the Buffalo *Evening News*. An uncle, William D. Hornaday, is professor of journalism at the University of Texas.

There wasn't much else for her to do but get christened in news print. She was launched directly into the Press Gallery without any slow or painful apprenticeship. She knew most of the correspondents through her father, and they did not attempt to freeze her out, in spite of her youth and inexperience. Miss Hornaday took readily to political work. She is quiet, modest, competent. Covering the President's wife is only one aspect of her work, for she is regular in her attendance in the Press Gallery. She did the Senate lobby and munitions investigations and during the days of the NRA covered many of the alphabetical agencies. Occasionally she does features for the New York *Herald Tribune*.

One of the familiar figures of the Press Gallery for many years was Mary Osborne Carpenter, who was in charge of the Washington news bureau of *La Prensa*. She was frequently consulted by her colleagues because of her knowledge of Spanish and Latin American affairs. For three years she acted as special correspondent of the United Press at the Institute of Public Affairs in Charlottesville, Virginia, where her advice was sought in planning the Latin-American round tables. Miss Carpenter was a native of Tennessee. She learned Spanish when she went to Puerto Rico as secretary to Governor Regis Post. Later she held official posts in Argentina, Chile and Peru. She worked for the Creel committee during the war and toured most of the countries of South America.

A woman correspondent who writes for a string of papers and inherited her connection through her husband is Mrs. Elisabeth May Craig, who has papers in Maine, Montana and North Carolina. For the last twelve years Mrs. Craig has written a lively column for the Portland *Press-Herald*. She has a shrewd political sense and understands the men with whom she deals better than most of the correspondents who flit in and out of the Gallery. She can give the low-down on the clay feet of the political buddhas.

Her column frequently conflicts with everything else on the editorial page of her Maine paper. She says what she likes. It may be philosophical comment; it may be a stinging attack. When delegations arrive from Maine, she shepherds them about and sees that their Representatives give them a proper reception. She is known in the Gallery as "Quoddy," so carefully has she nursed along the Passamaquoddy power project. As a result of her patient work over months and years she got a clean scoop when the Government abandoned the loan idea and decided to make it a federal project.

Mrs. Craig's husband, Donald A. Craig, a descendent of Kate Field, headed the Washington bureau of the New York *Herald* for years. He was in the press car that plunged over an embankment near Denver in 1922 while he was following President Harding. Mr. Craig was injured. His companion in the car, Thomas F. Dawson, was killed.

Mrs. Craig helped her husband with some of his out-of-town correspondence and occasionally she wrote an item for the *Sunday World*. Then one day she was asked by the *World* bureau in Washington to get a story on how Calvin Coolidge dictated. One of the stenographers at the White House happened to be from Maine. It was a simple matter for the quick-witted Mrs. Craig to find out from her how Cal did his work. The story was picked up and quoted all over the country. It netted her only $1.27 at the time but after that she did more work for the *World*.

Today Mrs. Craig is the most conscientious conference-goer in the Gallery. She misses nothing. She likes to pick up background even when she is not looking for spot news. She is interested in people and has a quick sense for the trivia that illumine human character. Her eyes are wide open to political bunk and she can give any political aspirant tips on how to take the hurdles. She was born in South Carolina but has lived in Washington since she was ten years old. She is small, animated, with a sparkling glance that rests shrewdly on the passing parade. Her son, Don Craig, is motion picture critic of the Washington *News*.

The State of Maine is ably served in the Press Gallery by two of the brightest members of the corps—Ruby Black and Mrs. Craig. They are also the champions of women's rights in their sphere. Jane Swisshelm probably would be disappointed could she come back today and find that women have made so little real headway in the political field. Only a handful pass regularly through the doors she blithely opened. And most of the correspondents are still doing features rather than news, or they are covering for papers which get their main political correspondence from the press services. Ruth Finney is the exception. She has gone farther than anyone else. She has quietly hurdled every barrier and ranks with the best men in the Gallery. She is the only woman to write lead political stories for a national string of papers.

With only one or two exceptions the women who haunt the

Gallery are on the trail of local angles. Frequently they are as close to the states they represent as their congressmen. They study special problems—farming, fisheries, canning or mining, according to their geographical interests. So weak is the editorial faith in their judgment, however, that occasionally, when they get important beats through their local connections, their own papers await confirmation from the press services. This has happened repeatedly, to the chagrin of experienced and careful newspaper women.

The correspondent in Washington is beset with news. She works in a rich field. But she must be wary of propaganda. It overflows her desk each day, sometimes in the most insidious form. She is forced to exercise care and judgment, for she has to interpret and appraise her facts with a shrewdness not required in any other branch of reporting.

The politicians treat the women correspondents exactly as they do the men, although they are frequently squeezed out of smoking-room confidences. As a rule legislators weigh the importance of the paper behind the girl, but they rarely ignore her because her connection is inconsequential. One senator will refuse news to a correspondent whose paper opposes him politically; another will hand it out with candor to a girl who writes for half a dozen papers that attack him regularly.

The woman correspondent is accepted more generally by the legislative body than by her own colleagues in the Press Gallery. She has not yet been accepted into the brotherhood on free and equal terms, although the prejudice is dying fast, largely because a few capable members of the craft have helped to raise the professional standing of the women in the Press Gallery. But the girls share little in the black-sheet system of Washington. This does not worry them, since they are energetic and would just as soon rustle up their own news. But it bothers the more ardent feminists that they are not admitted to membership in the National Press Club. The nearest they get to it is the virgin solitude of their private dining-room next door to the chamber where the master minds discuss the government of the country. Another bitter pill is the failure of the White House Correspondents' Association to invite its feminine members to the annual dinner, at which the President is always the guest of honor. When they made an issue of this and applied for reservations in a routine way, they were coldly turned down on a pretext that did not fool them for a minute.

But Mrs. Roosevelt has raised their stock and made amends by launching her own masquerade for the ladies of the press and legislators' wives on Gridiron night. And she is the guest of honor at their annual stunt party. Invitations for this affair are eagerly sought by the official set.

The Women's National Press Club is a progressive and cohesive unit with a membership of 133 newspaper women. It meets for luncheon every Tuesday, gets speakers of distinction and has annual parties of some account. The Newspaper Women's Club of Washington also functions smoothly, with a membership of 92 writing women.

Chapter XXVI

THE PRESS GALLERY TODAY

A SLIM GIRL WITH REDDISH HAIR AND A SELF-CONTAINED MANNER stood in a dusty sawmill talking into the one telephone in sight. Nearby forty-seven men lay entombed in a gold mine. It was September 18, 1922, and the girl was Ruth Finney, covering the Argonaut Mine disaster at Jackson, California. Her office was on the telephone, calling her to ask what was doing. She had the one incoming wire in the sawmill, where most of her competitors were quartered. Suddenly she saw a reporter, who had gone scouting to the mouth of the mine, break into a run.

"Hold on, something is happening," she exclaimed.

She held the receiver, caught the quick flash, gave the story over the wire while the A.P. man stood listening with a ghastly face. She was covering for the U.P. and her paper, the Sacramento *Star*.

After two weeks the rescuers had broken through. The whole country had been waiting to learn the fate of the entombed men. Help came too late. They were dead. Miss Finney's flash carried the news to every outpost. It was a thrilling beat. She had worked against heavy odds, with only two assistants to match the hordes from rival papers.

A fire in the Argonaut Mine had trapped the men. In order to reach them the rescue party had dug down to another mine two miles away and had then done a cross-cut. More than a hundred reporters were on the spot. They had to stay up night and day, not knowing when the rescuers might break through.

The Hearst papers had a leased wire at the mouth of the tunnel. The other reporters were cooped up in the sawmill, which was private property. The owners were hostile to the press and everything was made as difficult for them as possible. They had only the one wire and they had to send their copy in to Jackson by courier, or get along as best they could. It was the usual mad scramble that any sort of catastrophe means for the press. Nothing Miss Finney has done since then has seemed to her as exciting as sending through the flash on the entombed miners, although for years she has been a national headliner.

Today she ranks as the leading woman political writer working in Washington. She is a recognized authority on power, oil, labor and federal budgeting. Her work centers chiefly on constitutional questions but she knows the newspaper game from every angle—its alarms, its speed, its drama. She is a Scripps-Howard star and has never worked for anyone else. She is the wife of Robert S. Allen, co-author of *Merry-Go-Round*. Their romance began in the Press Gallery and developed while they were covering the Presidential campaign of 1928.

Miss Finney has fiery personal convictions but is objective in her work. Her stories are lucid and terse. She can cut through masses of figures, clarify the most obscure technicality, give point to the hidden implications of a story. She abhors bunk, knows it when she see it, and has a smart way of knocking it into a cocked hat. Frank J. Hogan, raging over her stories on the oil scandals in 1926, called her "Poison Ivy." As chief counsel for Edward L. Doheny, he didn't like her explicit reporting. When the jury box was being filled at the trial, one venireman admitted that he had formed an opinion on the merits of the case from reading Miss Finney's stories. After that any candidate who admitted knowledge of her work was rejected by the defense. Again, she was in the thick of the Scripps-Howard fight to have the oil territory at Elk Hills and Teapot Dome returned to the United States.

Like many another good newspaper woman Miss Finney comes from California. She started on the Sacramento *Star*. She had been teaching for thirty days when she got her chance to enter newspaper work, and she did not hesitate for a moment. Within a week she was doing the City Hall beat. This gave her a taste for politics. Her paper ran a successful city charter campaign which the Sacramento *Bee* opposed. The contest was stimulating to a young reporter. It gave her the first whiff of battle, an instinct which was to carry her through many subsequent campaigns.

When the flu epidemic laid the staff low, she covered state and city politics wearing a mask. During this period she learned to do make-up, desk work and copy reading. From 1922 to 1923 she was city editor of the paper, with a staff of men working for her. When her paper was sold, she went to the San Francisco *News*. In 1924 she was transferred to Washington as correspondent for the Scripps-Howard papers in California and New Mexico. She was also assigned to write features and editorials. But in 1930 she was relieved of her regional work to concentrate on the national field. She still does editorials on subjects in which she specializes.

When she arrived in Washington she saw at once that the Press Gallery was a man's world. Most of the important subjects were already preëmpted by someone or other in her organization. So she decided to concentrate on a neglected department. And she hit on power. While the Public Utility Holding bill was pending, she studied it from every angle. This was not by any means the ABC of journalism. Men much more experienced than she shied off it and gave it superficial treatment. But Miss Finney devoted time and thought to the bill. She studied the whole subject of power. She mopped up the most abstruse facts, sifted them through the clear channels of good reasoning and wrote stories that were informed and alive. She became one of the few political writers who could throw light on the intricacies of the power question. Coupled with this, she was fearless and independent. She campaigned hard for the bill providing for the construction of Boulder Dam. It was a slow fight. It took eight years to go through and her stories were a clear and forceful record of every step along the way. When the bill was in its final stages in the Senate, the other correspondents swarmed around Miss Finney for information. She was more interviewed than Senator Hiram Johnson, its author. No one was in a better position to tell them what it was all about.

She has applied the same thorough technique to her other work in Washington—covering the oil scandals, the Federal Trade Commission, bankruptcy, the budget and relief. When the NRA was created, she followed its whirlwind course and the papers of the Scripps-Howard chain carried her crisp stories on America's gigantic experiment in autocratic legislation. This was a night and day job for the first six months, one big story cracking after another. Immediately after the NRA was organized she and Turner Catledge, of the New York *Times*, had the jump on their competitors by getting first news on the blanket code and what the terms would be. The various advisory boards were in session most of the night, and no one else knew precisely what was going on.

Miss Finney's power lobby stories during 1935 were much discussed. Her expert reporting on this subject excited interest, regardless of the reader's point of view. Late in June, 1935, she conducted a stunt for the Scripps-Howard papers, when she directed a corps of reporters in a check-up on the teller vote taken by the House on the Utility Holding Company bill. They came close to the correct line-up. As soon as they had assembled their figures, they gave them to their colleagues, and the public learned just what had happened behind the screen of the teller vote.

Miss Finney's assignments are never of the pink tea order. She sat in jail writing an impressionistic story while Sacco and Vanzetti were being executed. She has written a number of labor stories and did the Communist trials in Atlanta. When she went to Europe with her husband in 1930 she sent back stories on the new American tariff schedule and unemployment in the chief cities of Europe. During 1934 she wrote a sparkling editorial column called "The National Round-up" but gave it up for lack of time.

Miss Finney can take a budget story and make it simple reading for the average man. But behind this clarity lies the rare reportorial knack of being able to synthesize the most complicated facts and turn them into readable copy. She has simplified her style to the last degree. She never writes a superfluous word but manages to convey in a half column what most political writers take two columns to tell.

Miss Finney and her husband live in an old house in Georgetown, furnished with pieces brought from Mexico and South America. She gardens and puts in domestic touches when she is not wrestling with the intricacies of government or studying desiccated tracts on power. Her intellectual vigor is masked behind a quiet feminine manner. She is retiring and contemplative by habit, but dauntless in her work. Her vague expression turns to intense concentration when she is interested. She pounds out her stories in the Press Gallery with the assurance that comes from having complete grasp of her subject. Her co-workers do not all agree with her in some of her views, but they have the utmost respect for her work. She is that rare and practically undiscoverable creature—the perfect woman reporter.

A senior colleague of hers, Winifred Mallon, has the distinction of having led the New York *Times* on different occasions with her Washington stories—the only woman to have achieved this prominence in the conservative *Times*. She is a sound and experienced reporter and has been watching history on Capitol Hill for long enough to know its implications.

Miss Mallon can cover a social function or write straight news with equal facility. She has handled practically every type of story at one time or another and in her busy life has managed to crowd in time for fiction and magazine articles, as well as her newspaper work. She began sending news dispatches from Washington in 1902, and in 1918 was admitted to the Press Gallery. For twenty years she wrote for the Chicago *Tribune*, before joining the staff of the *Times*.

Miss Mallon came originally from North Evans, New York, and lived in Washington for ten years before leaving school to begin the business of earning a living. She learned about newspaper work from such experienced men as Raymond A. Patterson, Arthur Sears Henning and Grafton Wilcox. Mr. Patterson headed the bureau when she started. His by-line "By Raymond" was one of the best known coming out of Washington. Miss Mallon's first paragraph, contributed to the Raymond column, was an item about Mrs. Theodore Roosevelt's selection of books for the White House Library. The date was December 26, 1902, and it revealed that Mayne Reid was the favorite author of the White House children.

When Admiral Sims was recalled from London in 1921 and was reprimanded by Secretary of the Navy Edwin Denby for a political observation made in a speech, he was received by President Harding at the moment that Mr. Denby was telling the press about the rebuke. Miss Mallon covered the Secretary's press conference for her bureau and it was she who brought out the fact that official disapproval of the Admiral's reference to pro-Irish republican "resolutions forced by jackass votes" was departmental and not presidential —unlike the incident in 1911 when Sims, then a captain, was reprimanded by President Taft for predicting in a speech delivered in London that if seriously menaced by a European coalition, the British Empire could "count on every man, every dollar, every drop of blood of your kindred across the sea."

Miss Mallon went from the press conference to Admiral Sims' hotel to see what he had to say about the case. She was having tea with Mrs. Sims when the Admiral came in from the White House. They exchanged notes on his reception and reprimand. He was undismayed, even cheerful. He said that his call at the White House had been a pleasant one and that so far as the official reprimand was concerned he had "got what was coming to him for having spilled the beans."

"I'm sorry to have caused the administration any embarrassment," he said. "The fact is, I didn't know it was loaded—at least so much." All of which went to the making of a neat story on an episode of national interest. A month later Miss Mallon wrote the story of the Admiral's vindication and commendation by the Senate Naval Affairs sub-committee which investigated the controversy.

The day after Mrs. Terence MacSwiney appeared before the American Commission on Conditions in Ireland in 1920 and told the story of her husband's last days, a telegram reached Miss Mallon's bureau from Chicago: "Whoever wrote the story about Mrs. Mac-Swiney this morning did an excellent piece of work and a bonus of $25 is awarded to him. Who did write it?"

Mr. Henning, who was then head of the bureau, wired back: "Miss Winifred Mallon wrote the story. We are proud of her."

The two features—"Side Lights on Congress" and "Lest We Forget"—which ran on the editorial page of the Chicago *Tribune* during 1918 and 1919, were written by Miss Mallon. When Ellis Island was like the Tower of Babel, swamped with multitudes from Europe, she interpreted the immigration and passport snarls that developed in Washington. She had specialized knowledge to bring to bear on this subject, for she had worked for a time in the government service on Ellis Island. She wrote a series of articles on passport legislation and the plans to amend the laws.

When the Soviet leaders tried to enlist the support of Senators and other politicians in the name of the American Red Cross, Miss Mallon first broke the story from a tip turned over to her by Mr. Henning. This exposé led to a rumpus between the American agents of the Soviet and Herbert Hoover, then Secretary of Commerce.

From 1925 to 1929 Miss Mallon free-lanced, and during this period she worked up such a sound connection with the New York *Times* that she was taken regularly on the staff—a distinct innovation for the Washington bureau of this paper. While still on an assignment basis she was sent with the *Times* crew to the Republican and Democratic national conventions in 1928 and in the autumn of that year did a solo campaign swing through five states to report what women were thinking of Al Smith and Herbert Hoover. She dug underneath the surface and assembled an illuminating mass of material. She talked to women in kitchens and in drawing-rooms, on the street, in restaurants, on doorsteps, wherever she found them. Her stories made good reading. In July, 1929, she was accepted as a member in full standing on Richard V. Oulahan's staff, and was assigned regularly to cover political stories for the *Times*—a landmark for women in journalism.

Miss Mallon reported the hearings held in 1929 and 1930 by the Interstate Commerce committee of the Senate on the Couzens communications bill, which resulted in the reorganization of the Radio Commission and its rebirth as the Federal Communications Commission. This was a technical and important assignment. Her stories got a heavy play in the *Times*. When the hearings were over the committee counsel complimented her on the accuracy, clarity and general excellence of her reports. Her next assignment was to cover the lively lobby committee hearings conducted by Senator Thaddeus H. Caraway during the spring of 1930. Sparks flew every day as the witty Senator clashed with the witnesses drawn into the inquiry.

Annually since 1919 Miss Mallon has reported the two-week sessions of the Institute of Public Affairs at the University of Virginia. She has covered all manner of gatherings, ranging from the Institute of Law and the American Bar Association to the Anti-Saloon League and the D.A.R. Most impressive of all her assignments was the return of the Unknown Soldier, brought back through the early dusk of a cold and rainy November day to lie in state for a night in the Capitol on the catafalque which had borne the remains of Lincoln, Garfield and McKinley. She wrote a simple and moving story on this event.

In the following week she attended the most brilliant of the social functions she has witnessed in Washington—the reception held at the Pan-American Union by the Secretary of State and Mrs. Charles Evans Hughes for the delegates to the Conference on Limitation of Armaments in 1921.

She saw war missions and visiting royalty come and go, assisted in reporting both visits of the Prince of Wales and attended the reception given for him at the Library of Congress during the Wilson administration. She watched Ishbel MacDonald, José Laval, Madame Curie and the King of Siam face the social barrage in Washington. During the Hoover administration she followed the laughable twists and turns of the involved social comedy known as the Dolly Gann-Alice Longworth incident. Her work has been extraordinarily diversified. Better than most, she could draw a picture of the Washington of yesterday and today, for her memory is stocked with passing faces, stories, pageants and events.

Wherever news is breaking in a lively way in Washington red-haired Bess Furman may be found, digging up the last detail with the zeal of the born reporter. For Bess was literally cradled in a newspaper plant in Nebraska. She has dashed about a lot since then, written millions of words, caught the wire in unlikely places, and listened to a fearsome amount of political speech-making. She is a reporter who catches the drama of what she is doing long before it achieves the aura of retrospect. Her profession will never grow stale for her. She finds it a daily adventure. Nothing escapes her, and she builds up her stories for the Associated Press with a fine mosaic of detail.

Miss Furman was born on Main Street, Danbury, Nebraska. A sign on her home read the Danbury *News*. But this was only half the story. Behind the editorial front her father functioned as a barber. On Saturday night the townsmen came in to be shaved. They told him how many bushels to the acre the wheat was running—all grist for the editorial mill. On alternate Saturdays a "scene" was rolled down from the ceiling and the dining-room became a photograph gallery. There a visiting photographer from Oberlin, Kansas, took pictures of the bride-to-be, while Bess's father showed the samples of the wedding invitations and garnered facts for his paper. There was always a tramp printer about to spout Shakespeare and tell tall stories, and usually a printer's devil was in the offing, working for his board while he went through high school. Bess hung around the print shop, doing typesetting, inking, paper folding and writing up the children's birthday parties of the neighborhood. At the age of ten she was accepted as a bona fide member of the staff. At fifteen she stayed out of school for a year to help her father run his paper. Behind the scenes her mother managed the house, brought up five children and performed editorial functions in her spare moments.

As a result of her practical experience, Bess was chosen to run the *Antelope* of the State Normal School at Kearney. She pitched in at her editorial duties during summer terms and taught in winter. From the age of sixteen until she was twenty-two she haunted schoolrooms and was nearly lost to journalism altogether. But when making up the *Antelope* in the office of the Kearney *Daily Hub*, she was offered a staff job. It was war-time and the paper was short-handed. A veteran Nebraska editor taught her some lessons she never forgot. When the news of the Armistice set the country on fire he said, "Get out into this and sop it up."

Miss Furman went into the streets, found a huge auto hearse carrying a placard "The Kaiser." Small boys, their faces raddled with mud, kicked up their heels all over it, and small girls clung to the fenders. Bess sopped things up. She wrote a vivid piece. To this day she plunges deep into the feeling of any story and writes with animation. She detests stories of a set pattern and is wary of the hand-out.

After her baptism on Armistice Day, she worked off and on for the *Hub*, teaching at intervals. Then she left Kearney to join the staff of the Omaha *Daily News* at $35 a week. For the next ten years she had the time of her life. Every day there was something doing—red-blooded tales of Fred Brown the Manacle Man; the deadly Sniper; the thrice-terrible Axe Murderer; the *crime passionnel* in Little Italy; Louise, the Bootleg Queen; Margaret, the Cigarette Heiress; and countless other ups and downs in the social scene. She talked to all the visiting celebrities, did rewrite on police-court stories, and took a whack at fashions. She was sent to the Black Hills to do special features not covered by the press associations when President Coolidge established his summer home there.

In 1929 she landed in Washington with the Associated Press and for two years covered the House of Representatives. There another of the Press Gallery romances developed. Working on the same beat was Robert A. Armstrong, Jr., of the San Francisco *Chronicle*, and they soon were married.

Miss Furman is the newspaper girl who has most closely tagged the wives of Presidents during recent years and is always on hand for political conventions. She went with Mrs. Hoover on four campaign trips and had a hard time wringing any news out of her doings.

It was another story when Mrs. Roosevelt entered the White House. Miss Furman was able to write with a lavish hand. She went with her on her Puerto Rican flying trip. She followed her up White Top Mountain one summer day, forgot the time while she was writing her story and suddenly realized that she had to get back to file her copy. It was late Saturday afternoon. They were off in another world. The Sunday papers go to press early on Saturday night. And Mrs. Roosevelt was about to leave for another call.

So she and Corinne R. Frazier, one of her colleagues who was in the same plight, hopped out of place in the official procession and appealed to the state troopers for aid. They were thrust into a car and were rushed down the mountain, siren shrieking. It was a forty-mile drive downgrade over a dusty road. Miss Furman clutched her hat and her copy. They cut corners at dizzy speed and broke all traffic rules. They were in a daze when they came to a stop at last at the telegraph office.

Many times Miss Furman has written her copy in large letters going over a bumpy road in a swaying car, or has dashed off bulletins against the side of a train or on somebody's back. This is a trick the press service girls learn, for they file copy day and night on an exciting story. Miss Furman has been known to carry on an argument with a town marshal and two committee chairmen, all insisting she could not be present at a meeting, while she calmly batted out her story under their eyes on a portable machine.

When she is not in the thick of national drama, she enjoys the quiet of her home. She likes folk dancing, swimming, tennis, parties, her husband's amateur movies, and she vows she can tat. But when the telephone rings and her office is on the wire, Miss Furman charges to answer it. She is a newspaper girl who gets the full measure of fun out of her work.

While Bess Furman chronicles Mrs. Roosevelt's doings for the A.P., Ruby Black does the same job for the U.P. In addition, she runs her own bureau which furnishes news to papers in Maine, Wisconsin, Western New York and Puerto Rico. This means that Miss Black catches the Washington scene from every angle—downtown and up on the hill. She is a staunch and able member of the Press Gallery corps, believes firmly in the rights of her sex and writes with clarity and good judgment.

A congressman asked her once as they rode up in one of the Capitol elevators, "Is everything you are writing today the truth?"

"Everything not enclosed in quotation marks," said Miss Black smartly.

She can stand her own ground, both with the politicians and her colleagues in the Press Gallery. An acknowledged Lucy Stoner, she was the first woman to get a passport under her own name. The Woman's Party made hers a test case. She never used it, but it was a moral victory.

She comes from a Texas farm, and had a vague urge to write while she was in high school. She went to the University of Texas, taught for four years in her native state, then went on to the University of Colorado, where she took a summer course in journalism. Her first newspaper job was on a weekly, the Thornton *Hustler*. She made $6 a week, set type by hand, addressed and folded wrappers. She got practically all the news, wrote editorials and sold advertising. She developed an interest in politics when Jim Ferguson, who had been impeached, ran against Lieutenant Governor William P. Hobby, who had succeeded him. It was a bitter fight and Hobby won. Miss Black's editor was a Ferguson man. She was local chairman for Mr. Hobby. She wrote and set up the news and editorials for her candidate. Her editor did the same for Ferguson. Thus all the news on both sides appeared in the paper.

By 1921 Miss Black was in Chicago running the Woman's National Journalistic Register, a Theta Sigma Phi placement bureau. After five months of this she taught journalism for two years at the University of Wisconsin, writing for syndicates and trade journals on the side. During this period she met Herbert Little, whom she married in the autumn of 1922. When he was transferred to St. Louis, she accompanied him there and worked on the St. Louis *Times*. After the 1924 election Mr. Little was transferred to Washington by the Scripps-Howard Alliance and she followed him to the capital.

But she found that Washington was the hardest place in the world to get a job; the easiest place to get news. She spent a year looking for a berth of some sort. She went to every paper in town and most of the bureaus. She got tired of being told to come back next week, or that girl reporters were not wanted. Miss Black has passionate convictions about a woman's capacity to do any job as well as a man.

At last she got into a bureau owned by George H. Manning, with a string of forty papers and trade journals, including *Editor and Publisher*. She worked there until 1928 and then formed her own bureau around the Portland *Evening News*, a liberal paper which had been going for a year. She now has ten papers. Two girls assist her. Dorothea Lewis takes over her duties when she is out of town. At other times she covers the downtown run and the government departments. Gertrude Lee covers the House. Miss Black has demonstrated that a woman can run a successful news bureau out of Washington, although it is always a precarious venture. Another successful experiment of the kind is the Griffin News Bureau, run by

Isabel Kinnear and her husband, Bulkley S. Griffin. They feed a string of ten New England papers.

Miss Black has to watch the local interests of half a dozen states, as well as the broad sweep of the news. She has been asked by local editors to do everything from digging up a Washington telephone directory to persuading the army to send airplanes to participate in the dedication of a municipal airport. She is a level-headed reporter, with a good news sense, and is always in the forefront of any group of women reporters in Washington, for her personality is dominating and decisive, and she is absolutely fearless.

She and Herbert Little and their small daughter, Cornelia Jane, live in a house in Alexandria built in 1780. While she was ransacking the attic Miss Black stumbled on the way bills of the old stage coach lines that used to pass near the spot where her home stands. Among them was a contract to carry mail between Alexandria and Warrentown. The engraving of a coach and six at the top of the bill was a fascinating spectacle for modern eyes. When Miss Black found a passenger list that included the name of Robert E. Lee, she decided that this was something for the President to own, so she made him a present of it. Seven more of these curiosa are mounted and hanging in her home.

Chapter XXVII

DEBUNKING CAPITOL HILL

WHEN PRESIDENT ROOSEVELT REVIEWS THE FLEET OR SETS off on a speech-making trip with his corps of correspondents, Doris Fleeson goes along—often the only girl in the pack. Next day her paper, the New York *Daily News*, carries thundering banner lines over her name.

In addition, she and her husband, John O'Donnell, do a joint Washington column called "Capital Stuff," written in the tabloid manner with all excess baggage thrown overboard. If there is anything to be uncovered, that is the angle they play. They make it bright and readable. Sometimes it has an impudent note that riles the politician. Miss Fleeson steers a free and independent course. She asks the most searching questions with a bland air, and is not easily hoodwinked by the scheming politician. The joint family column made its first appearance in August, 1933. They divide the work, worries and perquisites of the job, but Miss Fleeson has one advantage over her husband. She can cover the President, but he is barred from Mrs. Roosevelt's conferences.

Early in her newspaper career in New York Miss Fleeson concentrated on a specialty. She covered the city scandals from beginning to end. She showed a ready knack for this sort of work, and was accepted into the smoking-room fellowship which is an aid to the political writer. She landed on the *Daily News* one November night in 1927. Up to that moment her newspaper career had been slow getting started. But once under way she leaped ahead like a whirlwind. She comes from Sterling, Kansas, and was graduated from the University of Kansas in 1923. Her first intention was to be a doctor; then she majored in journalism and economics.

In the summer of her junior year in college she worked for the Pittsburg *Sun*, Kansas, covering a school board fight, a strike in the coal mines and Phil Campbell's contest for reëlection to Congress. After her graduation she traveled East to New Haven, where her sister was taking her Ph. D. in the graduate school of Yale. She tried to get a newspaper job but the New Haven papers spurned her; so she worked in a wire factory making up production schedules and pushing them through. Then, in 1925, she tried Chicago, but the newspaper doors banged shut in her face. So she lived at the Theta Sigma Phi house for $15 a week, which gave her room, breakfast and dinner. And in the meantime she worked for a holding company to raise the necessary $15.

In the spring of 1926 she went to work on the Evanston *News-Index*, which has been hospitable to a number of newspaper women who later were heard from on metropolitan papers. She was society editor and occasionally landed a story on the front page. In the following December she turned up at Great Neck, Long Island, where she became city editor, reporter, copy reader, picture editor, make-up man, proofreader and office boy for the Great Neck *News*. Her next move was to New York's most flourishing tabloid.

There Miss Fleeson soon emerged as an enterprising and talented reporter. She went through all the hoopla of the city room during that period. Gun girls, cry baby bandits, magistrates' courts, and breach of promise suits. She chaperoned Bridget Farry during the trial of George A. McManus for the murder of Arnold Rothstein. Wild Bridget was the scrubwoman from the Park Central Hotel who refused to aid the state against her "friend" McManus, whom she had never met but whose Irish name sounded like a bit of all right to her. She threw a monkey wrench into the trial, baffled the judge and was sent to jail as a non-coöperative witness. As soon as she was free again, she celebrated by buying herself a new spring hat. Bridget made the town laugh.

Miss Fleeson did La Guardia's first campaign for the mayoralty when he made charges which were then ignored by a public that still worshipped Jimmy Walker and reëlected him by a conclusive majority. During the first Seabury investigation she did some unofficial sleuthing for Chief Magistrate Corrigan, decking herself out as Daisy Smith of Broadway, a gaudy girl. She did an effective job, single-handed, on the trials of Magistrate Jean Norris, who was found unfit for judicial office, Magistrate Louis B. Brodsky, who kept his place on the bench, and Magistrate Jesse Silbermann, who was removed from office. The murder of Vivian Gordon, a side issue of the investigation, fell to Miss Fleeson and was heavily played in her paper.

By this time she had inherited virtually all the stories linked with the city investigation. Her daughter, Doris, was born in March, 1932, while she was doing the Seabury hearings, but she worked almost to the last day, and was back in time for Mayor Walker's dramatic day in court. The *Daily News* philanthropically gives its girl reporters six weeks' leave on pay while they are having their babies.

Three months after her daughter was born Miss Fleeson was writing copy at the conventions in Chicago, and was doing committee meetings and women's features on the side. Next she followed Joseph V. McKee and J. P. O'Brien through the mayoralty contest. She was at the Democratic State Convention when John F. Curry tried to block the nomination of Herbert Lehmann to succeed Franklin D. Roosevelt. By this time Miss Fleeson had had a good taste of politics at its hottest. She had an alert eye for the dramatic, and wrote with vigor. She did the banking crisis of 1933, a difficult story to handle. Then she nursed the beer bill through the State Legislature and before long was turned loose on the complicated trial of Charles E. Mitchell.

She put over a neat piece of work when Huey Long was biffed on the nose by an unknown assailant at Sands Point, Long Island. Having lived in the vicinity Doris had enough contacts at the Casino to get inside facts, and so missed none of the high points of the battle.

Another girl in the Press Gallery who does not tamely accept whatever is handed out to her at its face value is Marguerite Young, who did a right-about-face from the conservative haunts of journalism to run the Washington bureau of the *Daily Worker* with her husband, Seymour Waldman. Miss Young is a girl of courage and conviction. She has done a good job, although perhaps all her hopes have not come to pass. The millennium is no more to be found on the *Daily Worker* than the Scripps-Howard chain, for which she previously worked. But she and her husband have helped to raise the general level of reporting on their paper.

One day early in 1934, when her work was being featured in the *World-Telegram* and she was holding down what most newspaper women would consider a desirable job, she walked up to the city desk and handed in her resignation to B. O. McAnney, a city editor who has always backed up the girl reporter.

Miss Young left the Scripps-Howard service with a blast that might have jarred Mr. Howard at his dinner table, had he been the sort easily put out by the caperings of his staff. In the *Daily Worker* of January 6, 1934, she described the Scripps-Howard "editorial sweatshops" as the worst she had seen—in New Orleans, Chicago, Washington or New York. Explaining why she left she said:

> The few satisfying stories I could write were at the expense of writing uncounted reams of woman-story piffle which shamed me as a journalist as well as rendered me a tool in the Scripps-Howard process of deadening its vaunted labor readers

to important events affecting them by drowning them daily in sentimental pap.

Miss Young made the point that she was tired of all-night watches for a glimpse of the Mayor's wife, and of catching early coast guard cutters to go down the bay to greet "leisure class horsewomen." She was fed up with "indescribably tortuous and senseless assignments for a paper that seemed a nightmare of propaganda and distortion to the average balanced human being."

Miss Young's early training had been with the conservative A.P., and most of her work had been done in Washington. A stranger arriving on the same mission might have received a frosty reception, but she is personable, intelligent, and was known before for her good work. So her reappearance as a *Daily Worker* representative startled no one. It had been pretty well trumpeted. It was an experiment in journalism, and newspaper people are rarely narrow-minded. She was welcomed back into the Press Gallery, where there is more of the radical spirit now than there was a few years ago. She was not kept from anything she wanted. She had many personal associations that tended to offset political reactions.

Soon her bureau came to be accepted as a matter of course, although Department of Justice agents and the local police scan the paper regularly for dynamite. Eyebrows shoot up now and again when Miss Young asks pointed questions at a conference, but she does not believe in wasting any bolts. She rarely disturbs the calm of the White House press conference with a disturbing question, but when she does, she gets a candid and ready response from the President.

The labor leaders make no special efforts on her behalf. William Green has never acknowledged her existence in any shape or form. And Frances Perkins treats her as she does the other reporters. When the Secretary of Labor has anything to say, everyone gets it at once. When something special is wanted from her, she shuts up. Although Miss Young threw the searchlight somewhat devastatingly on her in an article in the *American Mercury*, Miss Perkins continued to beam on her without a flicker of the pain that she must have felt.

Miss Young has concentrated heavily on relief work and the parade of the labor forces. She has worked in Washington through a significant era in labor development and although she writes from an angle, she has tried to get away from the editorial writing that characterized her paper in the past and to cement her stories with a solid background of fact.

She was born in 1907 on a plantation in Louisiana. Her father was a planter originally, but Mississippi River floods, the boll weevil, the army worm and the bankers conspired to turn him into a contractor building roads and levees by the time Marguerite was growing up. And often the family was in financial straits. At the state university she joined all the societies but later became a typical undergraduate skeptic. She studied journalism, edited a campus paper, and plugged for scholastic honors. She was graduated at eighteen. Almost at once she got a job on the New Orleans *Item-Tribune*, starting out the first day looking a vision in a black satin dress and velvet hat. Her paper had a small staff. She got good breaks from the start, and did the general run of news.

Two years later she landed in New York with $40 and several letters of introduction. It was 1928, and it happened that she came from a paper that had already furnished the A.P. with two excellent women reporters—Ethel Halsey and Martha Dalrymple. She saw Kent Cooper. He engaged her at once and sent her to Washington to cover women's features. But Miss Young wanted to do more ambitious things. She volunteered to pinch-hit for men temporarily absent from their regular runs. In this way she soon got a steady beat of her own. Then she was shifted from one to another, until she had done virtually the whole round except the White House and Treasury Department. She was an idealist when she first arrived in Washington. She was barely twenty-one and was stuffed with school-of-journalism ethics, but she was totally ignorant of the processes of government. Disillusionment came when she covered the Federal Power Commission investigation. She watched the lobbyists and was shocked by the machinations of the politicians.

Miss Young took a leave of absence when she married Mr. Waldman and, when she returned, her job with the A.P. was gone. She was just beginning to study Marx, Engels and Lenin when she went to work for the Scripps-Howard organization. She was asked to submit suggestions for feature interviews. The first person picked' from her list was Rose Pastor Stokes. She went to see her, was stirred by her, began to move in radical circles and soon became a Communist herself.

Mr. Waldman was formerly on the staff of the *World*, and at one time was an instructor in the English Department of the College of the City of New York. He is the author of *Death and Profits*, published in 1932.

A realist who haunts the Press Gallery and is not fooled by mere oratory is Maxine Davis, a newspaper woman and magazine writer of perspicacity and experience. Miss Davis writes from behind the scenes with an initiated touch. She literally walked in on her first newspaper job. She had badgered most of the city editors in Chicago to take her on, with no results. Then one day she invaded the *Evening Journal*, now defunct. She learned the name of the managing editor, marched past all the copy boys, and approached his desk.

Richard Finnegan did not look up from the copy he was reading.

"Mr. Finnegan, I want a job," said Miss Davis.

His eyes were still invisible under his green shade but he shot at her, "What experience have you had?"

"None," said Miss Davis, "but I am a *very* bright girl."

He stopped writing, pushed back his eye-shade and regarded her with sympathy.

"Oh, are you?" he repeated. "Well, sit down."

Miss Davis got a job. Mr. Finnegan needed substitutes over the vacation period. This suited her, for she was in college at the time and wanted summer work. During her last year she did full time work on a morning paper. The most notable event of her early newspaper days was an assignment to cover an execution. She did not want the job. She has never been interested in crime. She begged to be excused. She even wept. But she had to go. She could scarcely have been more frightened had she been the criminal herself. At the last minute the governor ordered a reprieve. And Maxine promptly fainted.

She was determined to get to New York but whenever she mentioned her ambition her father announced oratorically that he would not "have his daughter in that cesspool of humanity." However, she got as far as Washington, landing there one hot day in July, at the beginning of the Harding administration. There were no jobs to be had, but Miss Davis decided she liked the city. She was nearly twenty and she saw that there was time to go home for a spell, save up some money, and return later on to launch a news service on women in Washington. After four months of diligent saving she toured the Middle West and signed up seventeen newspapers on a three months' contract for weekly letters at $5 each. At the end of that time only four of the papers were still on the string.

But Miss Davis landed a job on the old Washington *Herald* and kept her four papers, one of which was the Detroit *Free Press*. After she had had some more experience she tried the news service idea again on a daily wire and telegraph basis, and fed more than sixty papers for several years. Her associate in this venture was Dorothy Shumate, who worked for the *Evening World* for a time. The press services did not then have so many women as they do today. The United Press got all its Washington women's copy from Miss Davis's office. In the summer of 1929 she moved to New York and became editor of the women's pages of the *Telegram*. But this was not the ideal job for her. She wanted to put politics rather than beauty hints on the woman's page, and preferred a story on the Einstein theory to a good recipe.

Her news service suffered when she ran it by long distance telephone. In the autumn of 1930 she dropped it altogether, left the *Telegram* and went abroad to write about the Indian Round Table Conference. Her most dramatic memory of that period was the picture of Mahatma Gandhi as he sailed in to Marseilles on his way to the conference. His boat was to dock at six in the morning. Miss Davis was down at the pier before five. It was raining torrents. The P and O liner appeared like a gray cloud sailing past the Chateau d'If. Just as it slid into port, the clouds parted on an incredible sunrise. Gandhi stood at the bow, a minute figure in white, surrounded by a semicircle of Europeans and Indians. His hands were clasped in the ordinary Hindu salutation, but it seemed to the spectators on shore as if the gesture were one of prayer. And just then, as if it were stage-managed by some celestial Belasco, a great rainbow spread over the sky and the ship.

While she was in Europe Miss Davis acted as literary secretary to a Frenchwoman who was writing a book for an American publisher. It was a general survey of European politics. She went all over the continent with her, meeting the leading statesmen of the period. When she returned to America in the autumn of 1931 she decided to free-lance. Almost immediately she launched a magazine story of real news value. At the Children's Bureau she had stumbled on the preliminary report of a study on transient boys—a new problem that had not received any publicity up to that time. Again she predicted accurately that Frances Perkins was to be Secretary of Labor. She sprang the story on the best authority available but she worried considerably between the time her article was locked up and the Cabinet appointments were announced.

Miss Davis did a brilliant piece of reporting on the Economic Conference in London. She has taken the pulse of America a number of times. In the summer of 1935 she started out in a Ford—although she had never driven a car before in her life—and traveled 10,038 miles to write a series of articles on the youth of the country. En-route she did three pieces a week for the Washington *Post* and gathered material for a book, *The Lost Generation*. Miss Davis has not missed a presidential convention since she described what the wives of the delegates wore at the Harding convention in 1920. She is in and out of the Press Gallery and has a genuine flair for politics. She would rather do a political story than any other, and she writes with equal facility for a newspaper or a magazine.

One of the most energetic girls in the Gallery today is Lee Kreiselman, who scorns black sheets, works tirelessly and feeds her paper, the Wichita *Beacon*, with columns of sound copy. She keeps a sharp eye on agriculture and scored a clean beat with the McCarl report on the Farm Board in June, 1933. When she finally got hold of a copy through her good connections, she worked over it until 4.30 in the morning. She tore the report apart, had two stenographers copying it and had parts of it photostated.

Miss Kreiselman is a native of Pittsburgh and a graduate of a high school in Akron, Ohio. After she moved to Washington she did secretarial work for three years for Senator Henry Allen, former owner of the Wichita *Beacon*. When he retired, she was asked to become Washington correspondent for the paper. It was the time of the bonus march. She was one of the first reporters on the scene. She rescued two burning flags and was slightly gassed while the rumpus was going on. Along with Doris Fleeson, she accompanied the President to Annapolis when he reviewed the Fleet in 1935. She is one of the few women who attend his conferences regularly.

Miss Kreiselman sticks more closely to the Press Gallery than most of the women correspondents. She not only listens to speeches from the floor but she tests the sincerity of the congressmen later by interviewing them on the subjects that have inspired their oratory. She has never been refused an interview by anyone but Frances Perkins. For six weeks she tried to see the Secretary of Labor. She submitted a list of questions for her to answer, but they were ignored. The ladies of the press have had short shrift from the first woman Cabinet member.

Miss Kreiselman corresponds for the *North Western Miller*, the *Binghamton Press*, the *Five Star Weekly* and the *American Banker*, as well as the Wichita *Beacon*. She is married to Isadore Jaffe, a New York lawyer, and commutes back and forth between New York and Washington.

Another correspondent who landed in the Press Gallery through secretarial connections is Ned Brunson Harris, who heads the bureau of the Minneapolis *Star*. She had a brief whirl at newspaper work in Charleston, South Carolina, when she was a mere youngster. Early in life she devoted herself to the Congressional Record, making it her Bible. In 1918 she moved from Chattanooga to Washington to work in the office of Senator Kenneth D. McKellar of Tennessee. In the next few years she was secretary to a succession of legislators and got an excellent close-up view of national politics. James W. Gerard appointed her assistant treasurer of the Democratic National Committee. She went through two national campaigns in this capacity, functioning chiefly in New York. Then she went to work for John Edwin Nevin, of the Minneapolis *Star*. When he died in 1933 she was appointed head of the bureau.

While the Press Gallery was still practically bereft of women, Flora Orr, representing the St. Paul *Daily News*, the Omaha *News*, the Minneapolis *News* and two Scripps-Howard papers, became one of its habituées. This was in 1923. In the next few years she carried on many lively fights. She covered the Teapot Dome inquiry, took an active hand in starting the investigation on postal leases and pushed her paper's crusade to clean up St. Paul, which was described at the time by the Attorney-General as one of the worst places in the country. When three congressmen from Minnesota conspired against Miss Orr, because of her newspaper enterprise, her paper backed her up.

"There's no use your ever coming to us for news," they said.

"Always remember that you are first of all a newspaper reporter," her editor told her.

Miss Orr rounded up an unusual Sunday magazine story for her paper when she traced all the descendants of Abraham Lincoln now alive. She found six altogether, and it was a singularly difficult quest. The idea for the story came to her when she saw an item that Mary Lincoln Beckwith, great-granddaughter of Abraham Lincoln, was interested in aviation and was trying to get a pilot's license. She thought it would be a comparatively simple matter to trace the rest of the family.

But it was a task even to find out who they were or where they lived. And once that was done, no one would talk. All the members of the family shunned publicity and the lawyers were afraid to divulge anything that might offend them. Friends of the family were as inaccessible as the principals themselves. Robert Todd Lincoln, son of the emancipator, had resolutely shielded his children from publicity. It was a treasure hunt to find some family photographs and dig up details on the doings of the younger generation, but Miss Orr was successful and her story made absorbing reading.

She comes from a newspaper family. Two of her uncles published papers in their youth. Another uncle was a writer, an inventor and a linguist. A cousin was a city editor in Fond du Lac. Her mother was a typesetter for two years before her marriage and made an excellent salary for that period. Miss Orr is a graduate of the University of Wisconsin. She majored in science and food chemistry, a specialty which she has managed to combine with her literary work. She was with the Food Administration in its last year. Then she moved to New York and was home economics editor of the *Delineator* for two years, before taking her place in the Press Gallery. She resigned in the spring of 1935 to do publicity for the Resettlement Administration.

In addition to the regular habituées of the Press Gallery, a number of special writers drop in and out when things are stirring, or they are assembling material for articles. In this group are Anne O'Hare McCormick, Katherine Dayton, Mrs. Frances Parkinson Keyes, Ida M. Tarbell, Mrs. Emily Newell Blair, Anne Hard, Natalie Sumner Lincoln, Mildred Adams and Helen Essary, wife of J. Fred Essary, of the Baltimore *Sun*, who does a column for the Washington *Times*.

Chapter XXVIII

FOREIGN CORRESPONDENCE

I N THE FOREIGN FIELD THE LADIES OF THE PRESS HAVE MET ADVEN-
ture and a few of them have scaled the heights. Dorothy
Thompson and Anne O'Hare McCormick are two of the finest
products of journalism. They are internationally known and have
rolled up sound reputations unequaled by any other American
newspaper women.

Both have the gift for walking in where news is breaking and
getting into the heart of it. Both can write. Neither one ever worked
in a city room or had a day's newspaper experience before going to
Europe. But there the resemblance ends. They function with rare
independence but with dissimilar methods.

Mrs. McCormick is small, reddish-haired, quiet in her manner.
She sits back, observes, analyzes, never participates actively in what
is going on. She writes with the essayist's touch. Dorothy Thompson is tall, impressive and dominates any room she enters. Her copy
is packed with fact. It is alive, tight-knit, and is always expressive
of the vigorous character behind it. She cares less for writing than
for finding things out. The inquiring mind is carried into every
phase of her existence. Always an able speaker, lately she has developed a superb platform manner. The radio gives her another
medium of expression. She writes for the magazines and does a
column for the New York *Herald Tribune* called "On the Record."
It is typical of her intellectual force and is something new in the
way of a column done by a woman.

In private life Dorothy Thompson is the wife of Sinclair Lewis
and the mother of Michael Lewis, aged five and a half. She and her
husband met first at the Foreign Office in Berlin and Mr. Lewis
pursued her here and there on assignments until she said she would
marry him. He is proud of her as a newspaper woman but thinks
the oddest thing about her career is that she has scarcely ever seen
the inside of a city room. Mr. Lewis is an old newspaper man himself and understands all aspects of the craft. They spend part of the
year at their home in Bronxville, New York, part of it at their farm

in Vermont. They have hosts of friends and occasionally give parties which bring together the current celebrities, but they like a quiet evening together in their beamed living-room, or in their library, where Mr. Lewis, as inquiring as his wife, can dig in a reference book to settle some doubt that invades his nimble mind. He is a sociable creature until he starts on a book; then he shuts himself up, the air thickens with a spate of words and a novel gets born with dynamic propulsion.

But Dorothy Thompson works day in, day out. She has enormous vitality and moves with irresistible force—a "blue-eyed tornado," John Gunther has called her. She is preoccupied with the state of the world, the economic system, man's general indifference to his own development. She is less radical than she was fifteen years ago. She was never radical in the sense that she liked disorder. Miss Thompson has little tolerance for the muddle-headed. She is so clear-eyed, so capable herself, that she fails to see why things should get in a mess.

She has watched five revolutions, done dashing things as a correspondent and has stood unmoved on a balcony under fire, but the adventurous moments of her newspaper career seem to her only sparks in a great movement. They scarcely live in her memory. She is modest about her accomplishments as a foreign correspondent and believes that many of the men were better. She was always more concerned with the underlying motives and the march of history than the spot news of the day. And she never could give a story the half-romantic twist that some of her competitors achieved. Her dominating passion for facts made her realistic. She acknowledges that she made various mistakes in judgment, and that she was wrong in her estimate of Hitler as a man who could not lead Germany.

But irrespective of her own opinion of her newspaper work, her correspondence for the Philadelphia *Public Ledger* syndicate got the highest professional rating, and in eight years her name became well known in America. She had the knack of getting exclusive stuff—not that she cared about that aspect of it, except for her intense desire to be in the thick of things.

Every step of her career has been influenced by her personal life. She went to Europe, not to do newspaper work but to get away from an irksome situation. She landed in Vienna by chance, and suddenly her name was on the front page. She came home in 1928 as the wife of Sinclair Lewis and turned to magazine work. Again she was a success. Each time the wheel has turned, Miss Thompson has picked a winner.

She was born at Lancaster, New York, of mixed English, Scotch and Irish blood, the daughter of a Methodist minister. Her mother died while she was a child. She was graduated from Lewis Institute, Chicago, in 1911 and from Syracuse University in 1914. Almost at once she went on the stump for suffrage. For three years she worked as an organizer in upper New York State. When the suffrage amendment was carried, she looked around for something to do. She chose advertising, disliked it, then went to Cincinnati to do social work, a phase of her career which gave Mr. Lewis some of his ammunition on social workers for *Ann Vickers*.

When she sailed for Europe she had $150 in her pocket, and the idea that she would like to write. She canvassed the newspaper offices in London, wrote some pieces on space, got to know some members of the craft. One of them told her that things were happening in Ireland, so she crossed the Irish Channel and landed on the day that Hamar Greenwood became governor. She interviewed Terence MacSwiney just before he went to jail on his hunger strike —the last interview he ever gave. She returned to London with a series of stories, ignorant of how good they were. She told one of her colleagues about them and he snapped them up at once.

Then Miss Thompson went to Paris, and from there to Milan, where a metal workers' strike was in progress. She sopped up facts on this, and also so much rain that she fell ill with pneumonia. On her return to Paris she went to work for the Red Cross, and was soon assigned to go to Budapest to assist Captain James Pedlow, Commissioner for Hungary. Before leaving she arranged with Wythe Williams, of the Paris bureau of the Philadelphia *Public Ledger*, to act as Vienna correspondent for his paper at space rates.

Again she landed in the thick of things. The Karlist Putsch was on. Everything was fresh to her. She quickly learned the ropes and wrote vivid copy. In 1922 she had an interview with Dr. Eduard Beneš, which she considers the best piece of journalism she ever did. It was a six-hour talk at Prague just before the Genoa Conference, boiled down to a fifteen-hundred-word story of straight question and answer. The premier turned frank, disclosed the policies lurking in his mind, indicated that he favored recognition of Soviet Russia and a German moratorium. Miss Thompson's story was played up in the Manchester *Guardian*, and it affected the whole attitude of the British delegation at Genoa. But it attracted little attention in America, in spite of its significance. Generally speaking, Miss Thompson considers the interview the most futile phase of journalism. To her it has an artificial element that destroys its value as a source of news. She would much rather read Walter Duranty's impressions of Stalin than anything Stalin might say to Mr. Duranty.

The thing that first drew attention to Miss Thompson's work

was the way in which she stormed the castle of Count Johann Esterházy at Tata Varos and interviewed the Emperor Karl after his defeat and the collapse of the second Karlist Putsch in 1922. Instead of working through the usual official channels of the Foreign Office and being turned down like her colleagues, she went to Captain Pedlow.

"I want to get into that castle to see the King," she said.

"What do you think I am?" Captain Pedlow demanded.

"An Irishman with a sense of adventure," said the invincible Dorothy.

Her dismayed competitors saw her ride away with him and they knew what it meant. As a Red Cross official he would have entrée to the castle. They drove through cordons of troops and were admitted without trouble. Inside they were warmly received, for they were the first persons to bring news from the outside world. The entire cabinet was there. A small court had been set up, and royal etiquette was maintained. Miss Thompson talked to Zita, and found her superb in her attitude under stress. The deposed Empress was twenty-six at the time, and pregnant with her eighth child.

No one interviewed Karl again before his death. Zita entrusted Miss Thompson with a message to the Crown Prince Otto, then twelve years old. It read: "All well, don't be anxious. Mama."

When she got out she could not put it on the wire, nor could she give it to the Embassy. So she sent it by a sleeping car conductor to M. W. Fodor, of the Manchester *Guardian*, with whom she was in alliance. They had arranged that he should stay in the station at Vienna and meet every train coming in from Budapest, so that anything Miss Thompson got could be transmitted in this way. Mr. Fodor gave Zita's note to the British Embassy and it was delivered to the Crown Prince. Miss Thompson's own story made her rivals gnash their teeth.

By this time she had established something of a salon in Vienna. She believes that the woman correspondent in the foreign field has one advantage over a man—she can strengthen her news sources by using her home as a gathering place for the men and women who make news and write it. This was not difficult in her case, for she has the knack of attracting celebrities. Before long diplomats, artists, refugees, radicals, deposed grandees, spies, and writers of all kinds tramped in and out of her apartment, and news bloomed beside her typewriter. In 1923 she married Josef Bard, a Hungarian. Her divorce from him was made final on the day she met Sinclair Lewis.

She covered the Balkans, saw the King of Serbia married, was almost shot during the counter revolution in Bulgaria. A riot was in progress in front of the Palace Hotel. The mob thought that members of the government were in hiding inside. Miss Thompson stepped out on the balcony to see what was happening. The light shone behind her, outlining her clearly, making her a perfect target. Shots were fired at her. A waiter caught her and pulled her in. Several times in Europe she was in the thick of street warfare, but never had any sense of reality about it. She did not believe that she could be shot.

The correspondents used to gather every evening in the central telegraph bureau to study the ticker tape for news. When the story of the Pilsudski revolution broke, Miss Thompson heard of it when she went to the press room after the opera. Her friend, Mr. Fodor, showed up.

"There's a revolution in Poland," he announced. "Pilsudski is marching on Warsaw."

Miss Thompson was in her evening things. Without waiting to go home she went straight to the Polish consul, got a visa, borrowed $500 from Sigmund Freud, another of her friends, and rushed for a train. Her maid brought a bag and her typewriter to the station, but Miss Thompson did not have time to change her things.

Ninety kilometers out of Warsaw, she got off the train, still in her evening gown and satin slippers. The tracks had been mined and the train had come to a stop. All the correspondents haggled over cars. Karl Decker, Floyd Gibbons and some of the diplomatic representatives were with her. They gallantly said, pointing to a big Daimler, "You take that." They went off in whatever was left and Miss Thompson and an Italian diplomatic representative climbed into the Daimler. But they soon found that the fare would be $60, whereas everyone else was traveling free.

Miss Thompson wouldn't pay the price. So she picked up an ancient Ford and bumped over appalling roads toward Warsaw. It was a rainy spring day. At break of dawn they were still nine kilometers from Warsaw, but the driver was afraid to go farther. So Miss Thompson, still in her evening clothes, tramped the rest of the way with her companion.

She had arranged to meet her colleagues at the Europa Hotel, but it was opposite the Presidential Palace and was surrounded by a cordon of police. So she went to the Bristol instead. Floyd Gibbons' car had overturned by the wayside. While it was being righted, the Daimler flashed by, riddled with bullets. It had gone through machine-gun fire. Mr. Gibbons hailed the driver but he would not stop.

When Miss Thompson failed to show up at the Europa, Mr. Gibbons was sure she had been killed. But after a bath and a change of costume she went out to see what was doing and met him coming out of the Ambassador's office.

"My God!" said Mr. Gibbons. "Are you alive?"

"Yes," said Miss Thompson.

"I was sure you were killed. I just told the Minister to investigate." He told her about the car.

"Well, I took the cheap car and saved my life," said Miss Thompson.

The censorship at Warsaw was ironclad, but she circumvented it by driving out to a small village and filing her copy there. She guessed that the slow-moving bureaucracies of this region would not have blanketed the little places with the censorship ban, and her assumption was correct.

In 1925 she left Vienna to head the *Public Ledger* bureau in Berlin, one of the two women in Europe to hold down an important executive job of this sort. The other was Sigrid Schultz, who is still in charge of the Berlin bureau of the Chicago *Tribune*. Miss Thompson did not care for the executive detail of running a bureau, nor was she fundamentally interested in daily cables. She was more concerned with the evolution of ideas in practical politics. Her conception of good foreign correspondence is the type of dispatch that would give the complete social, diplomatic and economic history of a country, if assembled over a period of years. Spot news and the constant striving for scoops seem to her to create a false picture in the foreign field and nothing bores her more than the stunt journalist.

She was constantly amazed by the utter failure of the American diplomatic representatives to work with the press. On the other hand, she found Chancellor Gustave Streseman's Friday afternoon teas for the press, first suggested by Joseph E. Shaplen of the New York *Times*, a sound and genial way of cutting through red tape and establishing frank relations. She has never found the indirect approach a good journalistic device. Frankness is her natural habit.

It was in the summer of 1927 that Miss Thompson met Sinclair Lewis at the Foreign Office. Then H. R. Knickerbocker brought him to her flat for dinner. Edgar Ansel Mowrer was there and so was Michael Karolyi, former president of the Hungarian Republic. Mr. Lewis proposed as soon as the dessert and coffee were out of the way. Miss Thompson thought it was apt, as she had just got her divorce and it was also her birthday. She turned him down but he told her he would keep on proposing. After that he was constantly on her doorstep.

She flew to cover the riots in Vienna that summer and took Mr.

Lewis along, although he had never been in a plane and didn't like it. She got him to write some dispatches for her syndicate but not at regular Sinclair Lewis rates. Then he followed her to Russia. His own divorce complications were cleared up, and in the following spring they were married. On her return she wrote *The New Russia*. When Theodore Dreiser's book on Russia came out and she got it for review, she was struck by its similarity to her own work. They had been in Russia at the same time. She was amused. Mr. Lewis was furious. And before very long he delivered the famous Lewis slap on the equally famous Dreiser countenance at a dinner in New York.

In 1931 Miss Thompson interviewed Hitler. She said that he was a little man and could never become a dictator. She announced it quite publicly in her book, *I Met Hitler*. But she had to eat her words. When she went back to Nazi Germany three years later she was most unhappy. Her friends wanted to give her news and discuss what was going on, but every time she arranged a rendezvous she felt she might be imperiling them. It was no surprise to her when she was kicked out of the country. But she regretted her eviction, for she loves Germany and thinks the Germans the freshest and most dynamic people in Europe. It is her conviction that one day they will dominate Europe with some form of socialism.

Miss Thompson saw what she considered the most reasonable and least corrupt government in the world die when the Socialist régime fell in Austria. For eight years she watched the European struggle, and its drama changed the whole course of her life. She finds it impossible to believe in the New Deal, because she saw New Deals fail in Austria and Germany. She concedes that the world cannot yet be reformed by persuasion; that a war of rival powers is still inevitable.

Miss Thompson does not think that journalism demands a particularly high type of intelligence; but a good memory, an analytical gift and a knowledge of history and economics seem to her of the utmost importance. She has a thoroughly disciplined memory herself and rarely takes notes. She thinks that what one has to say is more important than how one says it. In spite of her own success Miss Thompson has never been persuaded that journalism is an ideal profession for women, or that they are particularly skilled at it. She believes that they are not sufficiently disinterested and that they need more solidarity. Her own pet admiration is Anne O'Hare McCormick.

Mrs. McCormick works so quietly that few people ever see her in action. She goes into a country, gets to the seat of government, interviews the most important figures, talks to the man in the street, catches the external drama; then if there is any question of censorship, she quietly crosses the border and sends her copy from another capital. Much of her work has been done in Italy.

Mussolini likes Mrs. McCormick. By chance she heard his first speech in the Chamber of Deputies in 1921. His name was still unknown to Italy and the world at large. She knew enough Italian to follow him but she was still a novice at journalism. However, she was struck by his oratory and the way in which he reduced a noisy gathering to dead silence. When she came out she said to a more experienced colleague, "Italy has heard its master's voice."

He laughed at her, but they were prophetic words. She has talked to Mussolini many times since then and has written illuminatingly about the Caesar of modern times. During an interview in the summer of 1935 she recalled his first speech to him.

"Was it a good speech?" he demanded.

She saw him soon after the Matteotti murder, when he was ill and shaken. She talked to him again when the Charter of Labor was promulgated. She found him jubilant on the night the Four-Power pact was signed. Mrs. McCormick is constantly baffled by his paradoxical nature; by his reasonableness when he sits behind his desk and gives an interview in a candid manner, and his arrogance in affairs of state. She has writted of him in the New York *Times*:

> Of all the public characters I have interviewed, Mussolini is the only one who seems interested not only in what he says himself but in what you have to say; he appears to weigh your suggestions, solicits your opinions.

He told Mrs. McCormick on one occasion that he detested society because it was dominated by women. In her early interviews with him he folded his arms, frowned at her and posed as the Iron Man. But as time went on he became simpler, more genial, more willing to discuss things in a friendly way. She can always reach him when she wants an interview.

Mrs. McCormick's newspaper career started almost by accident. She got little encouragement in the beginning to write for the *Times*. Like Dorothy Thompson, she set out for Europe without any newspaper connections. Her husband, Francis J. McCormick, of Dayton, Ohio, had to travel from country to country and she went with him. Her mother was a writer and she herself had written fiction before the war. She comes from Cleveland, was educated in private schools in America and abroad and is a graduate of St. Mary's College, Columbus.

When Mrs. McCormick found herself in the thick of European drama, she wrote to Mr. Van Anda asking him if she could do some correspondence for the *Times*. Mr. Van Anda, slightly myopic where newspaper women were concerned, responded on this occasion: "Try it." And thus one of the best foreign correspondents, men or women, got her start. Mrs. McCormick soon showed a real gift for newspaper writing and made a fixed arrangement with the *Times*. She can move about as she likes. Her footsteps are never tied. She is likely to turn up wherever an event of international importance is brewing. She is an interpretative reporter with an excellent sense of proportion and she has the knack of finding out what the average man is thinking of the political machinery that hedges him in. She browses among the book stalls of a street paved eighteen centuries ago, looking for copy, or drops in at a *trattoria* and subtly extracts from the padrone his views on taxes, government and war. She finds out what the shopkeepers as well as the diplomats think and synthesizes her impressions in lucid and readable terms.

Mrs. McCormick covers little spot news, although now and again her work appears in the daily paper. But she writes essentially in the magazine vein, and often quite poetically, as she did after listening to Beethoven and Respighi's "Pines of Rome" played in the Forum on a moonlit night:

> Softly, in the soft Roman night, the violins sang the loveliest phrases in the adagio movement of the Eroica symphony. It was full moon, and the sound was like the moonlight put to music, the silver voice of the silver light that flooded the vast arches overhead, poured down the deep hollow behind, swept the ancient terraces beyond so that each cypress and stone pine stood listening in a separate radiance.

Mrs. McCormick can pick up the theme in any capital in Europe. She writes of the Turk or the Frenchman with equal perspicacity and good sense. Her personal convictions do not drown her critical faculties. She is a roving correspondent of rare quality. She brings the same touch to bear on the American scene. In 1930 she wrote of the promise of the New South. Five years earlier she described the Florida boom. But she rarely goes outside of politics now. She has become a specialist in this field. In the summer of 1936 she became a regular contributor to the editorial page of the *Times*, another landmark for women in journalism.

Twenty years ago Alice Rohe, sister-in-law of Roy Howard, pioneered in Rome as correspondent and bureau manager for the United Press. At that time the reporters sat in the Sala della Stampa and waited for the Italian papers to inform them of what was going on. But she had had five years' training under Charles Chapin, of the *Evening World*, and had done newspaper work in the West, so she went out and hustled for news. She did not know a word of Italian, but coped successfully in her first year with the Avezzano earthquake, Italy's entrance into the war, and the Porter Charlton trial at Como in 1915. This was the case of the young American bank clerk who killed his wife and sank her body deep into Lake Como in a trunk.

Miss Rohe found it difficult to make the gallant Italians understand that she was more interested in getting the news than a compliment. It took persistence to break through the waves of *"bellas"* and *"simpaticas"* to find out what was going on. When she went to Como for the trial, a rival agency spread the report that she was German and that the United Press was subsidized by German money. She had to cross the Swiss border to file her telegrams and she was constantly being stopped on one pretext or another. On the day the verdict was due, she was held up at Chiasso and was refused permission to enter with her cable. She was told that the only employee who talked English was not there and that they feared her story might contain some anti-Italian news. She offered to translate it and an officer listened. But on her return she was seized again, searched and forced to strip. The idea was to keep her from getting to Como in time for the verdict. Miss Rohe caught the last electric car to Como. When the verdict of guilty came in, she had an automobile waiting and got to Chiasso so fast that she scooped her rivals. It created considerable stir in Italy that a woman should be covering a murder trial for an American news agency.

Miss Rohe returned to Italy in 1922 to pursue her hobby, which is Etruscology, and found as she moved around that Fascism was taking hold of the Italian people. She was one of the first to spot Mussolini as the future leader of Italy. The other correspondents scoffed at her belief in him, as they had in Mrs. McCormick's case. She did some interviews with him, which she had to submit for his approval. He expressed surprise at her knowledge of the political situation.

"But why shouldn't I understand?" Miss Rohe demanded.

"Oh, you're a woman," said Mussolini.

"I'm sorry you said that," Miss Rohe retorted. "Up to now I thought you the most intelligent person I had ever interviewed."

Miss Rohe's interviews appeared in the New York *Times* in the summer of 1922, before he was premier. They outlined his complete program of Fascism, a significant story to get at the time. In the same summer she got the last interview Sarah Bernhardt gave before her death. Three weeks later she persuaded Duse to break her long silence in an interview at Leghorn. Then she did some articles on

Pirandello and translated his *Man, Beast and Virtue*, which was produced in New York as *Say It With Flowers*.

Miss Rohe wandered all over Europe in quest of news. For a time she specialized in royalty. She interviewed Queen Marie in 1919 and was decorated by the Rumanian government. She talked to King Alexander of Greece and launched the story of his love for Ethel Kelly, an American girl. She smuggled the story through a secret channel to Floyd Gibbons, then manager of the Paris edition of the Chicago *Tribune*. He paid her $100 for it and after she had returned to America, he cabled offering her the post of correspondent at Rome for his paper. Miss Rohe was the first correspondent to reveal the liaison between Prince Carol of Rumania and Zizi Lambrino.

She interviewed Rodin, Maeterlinck, Cardinal Gasparri and scores of other celebrities during her years in Europe. In the war days she was stoned in Ravenna because of her passion for antiquities. She was examining an ancient tower when the cry was raised that she was a spy. Again she was imprisoned at Rimini en route to San Marino with her camera, when she was bent merely on the pacific mission of writing a piece for the *National Geographic Magazine*. Miss Rohe visited the Isle of Lesbos and wrote some articles on the attempts to whitewash Sappho. Her story on the now famous Venus of Cyrene was the first on the subject printed in America. It appeared in *Vanity Fair* and in fuller context in the Kansas City *Star*.

Miss Rohe is a native of Lawrence, Kansas, and a graduate of Kansas State University. She did her first newspaper work for the Kansas City *Star*. Then she moved East and was advertised by the New York *Evening World* as its woman humorist when she conducted a column called "The Girl From Kansas." After five years of strenuous effort she had to go to Denver for her health. There she worked on the *Post*, the *Times* and the *Rocky Mountain News*. She did drama, music, books and general news. Cured of tuberculosis she went to Rome in 1914, the first woman to head a bureau for one of the big news agencies. This also included being correspondent for the *Exchange Telegraph* of London, which demanded a different type of news.

Miss Rohe launched the dramatic, book and art departments of the United Press. She has worked for NEA, NANA and various American newspapers and magazines. She spends her time between Italy and America. In the autumn of 1935, when the Ethiopian situation was boiling, she had another talk with Mussolini, which made the front pages in New York. She still pursues her studies in Etruscology. Her sister, Margaret, wrote fashions before she married Roy Howard. She did weekly letters for the U.P., using the name Margaret Mason.

But the U.P. has always been slow to employ women for straight news coverage. Among the few who managed to batter their way into the foreign service was Mrs. Lucile Saunders McDonald, who got her newspaper training on small papers in Oregon and on the *Oregonian*. She went to South America in 1920 and was soon in the thick of news events. She became night editor of the U.P. in Buenos Aires at a time when there were no other women in newspaper work on the entire South American continent, except a few who contributed social notes to the Spanish papers. Mrs. McDonald's arrest on her way home from work at two o'clock one morning nearly provoked a diplomatic incident.

She rode nine days on horseback to the lost Inca city of Macchu Pichu in Peru, and did five Sunday features on what she saw. Again she investigated the authenticity of a Plesiosaurus which was said to inhabit an Andean lake on the western fringe of Patagonia. This story caused such a sensation that the U.P. was preparing to send her into the wilds with a museum expedition when the existence of the prehistoric monster was found to be purely mythical. Like the Loch Ness monster, it had had its day in the headlines.

She was trying to sell her press service in Asuncion, Paraguay, the day two of the local publishers decided to overthrow the prevailing government. Things were no less exciting when she went later to Turkey and sent back dispatches to the New York *Times*. There the only American correspondents in the field were women. Priscilla Ring, who spoke Turkish, took her under her wing. On one occasion she found herself in the Turkish ministry of public works at Angora without a Turkish dictionary or an interpreter, and with only half an hour to catch her train. But she got her story. She covered the Kurdish revolt in 1931, when no correspondents, Turkish or otherwise, were permitted in the disturbed sector. Reports had to be obtained from meager bulletins issued to the Istanbul morning papers. Mrs. McDonald lived on a hillside street in Istanbul overlooking a mosque which was no longer used as a place of worship, although the imam mounted the minaret daily and chanted the call to prayer. This was to camouflage the fact that small arms munitions were being unloaded at the mosque boat-landing on the Bosphorus, and were being stored in the church.

One afternoon she saw a puff of smoke go up through the roof of one of the buildings in the mosque courtyard, followed by a series of explosions that went on for half an hour. The hills along the Bosphorus were black with spectators. Street cars stopped running. The army was called out to extinguish the fire. Mrs. McDonald had a bird's-eye view of everything that went on. The minarets stood intact and the blaze finally was controlled. But when she tried to get statistics on the casualties, she was told coldly that there had not been a fire. She was headed off at every point. As military stores were involved, the hush policy was invoked. Although the local papers ignored this startling event, the New York *Times* ran Mrs. McDonald's dispatch detailing what she had seen.

When her husband's business took them to Alaska, she edited the Cordova *Daily Times* there and covered South Central Alaska for the Associated Press. She got a twenty-four hour scoop on the first expedition to scale Mount Logan successfully, although a chain of Canadian papers had backed the expedition and the story seemed sewed up. The leader of the adventure was on bad terms with his men, and they did not come out of the interior together. Mrs. McDonald got hold of one of the party in Cordova, while the head of the expedition stayed at Chitina, sending out a lengthy cable which did not arrive until twenty-four hours after her short takes had reached the A.P.

Mrs. McDonald has done newspaper work in New York, in addition to her foreign correspondence. She now lives in Wenatchee, Washington, still writes, and has a small son. Her foreign correspondence followed the trail of her husband's business connections in different parts of the world.

The stories carried by the New York *Herald Tribune* from Rome during the Ethiopian crisis were handled by Sonia Tomara, a slim Russian girl who speaks eight languages, can take a story over the telephone from any country in Europe, and has a shrewd grasp of international affairs.

Miss Tomara is a White Russian whose family owned large estates in the Caucasus before the revolution. She escaped with a sister and traveled by freight trains from St. Petersburg to the south. Once they were ordered shot by a nineteen-year-old Bolshevist general. Miss Tomara sailed from Batoum on a United States destroyer, after appealing to the captain for aid. Because she spoke Turkish she landed a job in Constantinople with the British High Commission. A year later she arrived in Paris with 150 francs and was taken on *Le Matin*. At first she was secretary to Jules Sauerwein, then his first assistant. After six years of this, Leland Stowe, head of the Paris bureau of the *Herald Tribune*, took her on his staff in 1928. When John T. Whitaker, the Rome correspondent, set out for Ethiopia, Mr. Stowe sent Miss Tomara to the Italian capital to substitute for him. She landed at a moment when news was breaking fast, and soon her stories were leading the paper, some days with three-column heads, a rare distinction for a woman in the foreign field.

When she first made her American connection Miss Tomara did

a weekly financial review for the *Herald Tribune* and other part time work, for she is an expert on financial and economic subjects as well as on art and music. But as time went on she became regularly attached to the staff. When President Doumer was assassinated she was one of the first reporters on the scene. She had only three blocks to go from her office. She got into Beaujon hospital, interviewed the doctors and rounded up the details with speed and thoroughness. By chance she was in Munich at the time of the Hitler revolution, telephoned out some stories, and on her return wrote some of the first uncensored accounts of the persecution of the Jews. Later she went to Frankfort and developed the return-to-the-ghetto theme.

When Yancey and Williams landed in Spain after their trans-Atlantic flight Miss Tomara took the story over the telephone from a Santander reporter because she could switch from French to Spanish without turning a hair. She does the same thing when a story is sought by telephone from Germany or Italy. This is invaluable in a foreign bureau. Miss Tomara is a hard worker and a shrewd political commentator. She knows how to assemble facts and she understands political trends. She responds quickly to a dramatic story, such as the riots in Paris during February, 1934, on which she did excellent work. She is now a naturalized Frenchwoman.

A number of women have functioned successfully in the foreign bureaus of the *Herald Tribune*. Elizabeth Keen, like her husband, Victor Keen, often makes the front page from Shanghai. Julie Rothschild does features from Berlin and Norah Thompson (now Mrs. Walter Millis) did similar work from London when Arthur S. Draper was head of the bureau.

Martha Dalrymple, wife of Joseph B. Phillips, Moscow correspondent of the *Herald Tribune*, has done excellent work on both sides of the Atlantic. She conquered opposition to women reporters in the London bureau of the Associated Press, and proved to the Italian gallants that an American girl could cover the collapse of the ceiling of the Vatican library or the visit of Secretary of State Stimson to Rome as well as the male of the species.

Miss Dalrymple broke into newspaper work when she was an undergraduate at the University of Wisconsin. She got a summer job on the Chicago *Journal* from the same Richard Finnegan who gave Maxine Davis her newspaper start. Her first assignment was to do some work on the Leopold-Loeb trial. She was nineteen years old and was much impressed that she should be permitted to telephone in the stories of the stars on her paper.

After her graduation in 1925 she was taken regularly on the staff. She began to meet movie stars as they changed trains in Chicago on their way from Hollywood to New York. When Charlie Chaplin asked her to dinner one night, she thought that life could hold no more.

The gangs were doing well at the time and Miss Dalrymple found herself covering the trial of Marty Durkin, the police killer. Once, when she was out on the North Side on a story and called her office for further instructions, the city editor grabbed the receiver from his assistant and yelled to her to go around the corner from her telephone booth to cover a shooting. He hung up without further ceremony. Miss Dalrymple arrived at the spot neck to neck with an ambulance. Something spattered on her stockings. She later found that it was the blood of the two men who had been killed by machine-gun fire from a second-story window. Her enthusiasm for life among the gangsters waned.

She wanted to work in New York and started out by the round-about route of New Orleans, where she landed on the *Item-Tribune*. The 1927 flood occurred almost at the moment of her arrival. During this period she got a stiff training in rewrite, which was useful later in her foreign correspondence. Then she was put on the dramatic desk, and learned to make up the Sunday dramatic page. But she didn't linger in New Orleans. She was on her way to New York. A letter of introduction landed her with the Associated Press. When the 1928 Presidential campaign got under way she was one of the girls who benefited by the A.P. decision to assign a woman to each candidate. She and June Rhodes, who was doing publicity for the Democrats, were the only unattached women on Al Smith's special train.

By the time President Hoover had been inaugurated Miss Dalrymple was working regularly in Washington. Again she was picked to pioneer. The A.P. had decided to try women in its foreign service. She was sent to the London bureau and Mary Bainbridge Hayden to Berlin. Her welcome in London was not cordial. Although the A.P. men themselves had no particular prejudice against women, the news sources all over Europe had. In England and France the antagonism is now moderating slightly, and here and there women cover big news stories, but they are not much in demand in the bureaus for diplomatic or political reporting. The British Foreign office is definitely averse to the indignity of imparting its secrets to a newspaper woman.

When she was coldly received in her new surroundings Miss Dalrymple felt like bursting into tears, but instead she smiled at the staff and went to work. Martha is one of the more irresistible members of the profession. For a week she crept mousily from desk to desk, from machine to machine, finding out how a foreign bureau worked, how it cleared the news of two continents and sent it to New York. At the end of a week she was taken for granted and got a few assignments, but mostly of the feminine type.

She was forced to concentrate on the women Members of Parliament. After she had dished them up in all variations and disguises, there was little left for her to do in this key, so she looked about for something more substantial and soon was taking her turn on the desk, like any of the men. She even braved the Foreign Office and covered international conferences. Bit by bit she edged her way into the confidence of the men with whom she worked.

After two years in London she got word that she was to be transferred to New York. In the meantime she had married Mr. Phillips, whom she had met at the Naval Conference. When he was transferred to Rome she became correspondent there for the New York *Evening Post*. She returned to Washington briefly during the first year of the Roosevelt administration and went to work in the political bureau of the Washington *Post*. After six months she returned to Rome and then went on to Moscow with her husband.

Another of the foreign stars of the Associated Press is Adelaide Kerr, who covered first string news as well as fashions in Paris from 1930 until 1936, when she returned to the New York office, where she had worked for three years before going abroad. The first story of any consequence that she did in Paris involved a brush with the French police. The body of Marshal Joffre was lying in state in the École Militaire. When she arrived early in the morning to cover the story, the police refused to admit her ahead of a great crowd already waiting. She had no police card to aid her. She argued as long as she could in her limited French, then broke away and ran, with the gendarme at her heels. She reached the door just as it was thrown open. She slipped inside and joined the queue beginning to file past the bier. To keep from being hurried along with the crowd, she kept untying and retying her shoe lace, thus getting time to look around. Then she slipped out through another door and went back to the office to write the story that got her her first European by-line.

One of her most dramatic stories was the arrival of the Spanish royal family in Paris when they fled to exile in 1931. A silent throng packed the station. Queen Victoria walked through it with a tragic face, treading on a long carpet of royal red velvet that the French had unrolled for her. Behind her came the children, her black robed ladies-in-waiting and a nun. Since then Miss Kerr has covered their activities in France. She had a beat when King Alfonso thwarted the attempt of his second son, Infante Jaime, to elope with a girl not of royal rank. Again she called on Infanta Eulalia, Alfonso's aunt, and got from her the exclusive story of her trunk of jewels which had been lost and had reappeared mysteriously in Madrid. She also broke the story when an amicable separation was arranged between Alfonso and his consort.

Miss Kerr covered the wedding of José Laval and Count René de Chambrun in the summer of 1935. She wrote columns on the troubled romance of the Count of Covadonga, eldest son of Alfonso, and Senorita Edelmira Sampedro; and of the Count of Paris, son of the pretender to the throne of France, and Princess Isabelle of Orleans-Braganza.

She was in the thick of the riot which broke up the International Peace Conference at the Trocadero in Paris in 1931. Four years later, when French *fonctionnaires* staged a demonstration over Premier Laval's decree cutting their salaries, she was one of the reporters covering the story in the avenue de l'Opéra. The crowd was marching in a mass, clenched fists raised in the Communist salute, shouting and singing the Marseillaise. The police charged, scattering them into side streets. Miss Kerr ran into a little shop to telephone. When she had finished, the proprietor, who had been hastily closing his shutters, insisted that she remain inside, since he was sure something would happen to her if she went out. It took several minutes of rapid French to convince him that she had to go. She was a *journaliste*.

The Associated Press has had women at the head of two of its European bureaus in recent years—Marylla Chrzanowska at Warsaw, working under the direction of the Berlin office, and Priscilla Ring, a fine correspondent who was chief of the bureau at Istanbul until her health gave out. She is the daughter of a naval officer and she first went to Turkey to work at Roberts College. She started as an assistant in the A.P. bureau but did excellent work and was soon in charge. She was sent to Greece when Samuel Insull was playing hide and seek with the law, and managed to get an exclusive interview with him. On one occasion she covered a mass hanging of nineteen persons in Turkey.

Mary Knight, an Atlanta girl, surprised even her own colleagues by dressing as a boy and getting in with the newspaper men to watch the execution of President Doumer's assassin. Not since the days when knitting needles clicked during the French Revolution had a woman gone out of her way to see a guillotining. Miss Knight wrote the story for the United Press. She is now doing feature stories on this side of the Atlantic.

There is no more capable newspaper woman in Europe today than Sigrid Schultz, who heads the Berlin bureau of the Chicago *Tribune*. She went through the difficult war days with independence of spirit and an infallible news sense. Her dispatches on the Kaiser were so fearless that she was called on to report twice a day to the police in Berlin. Miss Schultz, like Miss Tomara, is a linguist, speaking ten languages with ease. She has handled big news for so long that it is a commonplace for her to lead the paper. Her stories are copied, quoted and commented on by the European press. She has interviewed nearly every notable in Germany. She went through the hectic days of the revolution and watched the rise of Nazism. In 1926 she went to Warsaw to report the Polish-German trouble in upper Silesia.

Miss Schultz worked as George Seldes' secretary before becoming a foreign correspondent, so that she knew all the ins and outs of the profession when she inherited the job. She lives with her mother and, just as Dorothy Thompson used to do, she entertains a great deal in her home, thus keeping her news sources well built up. She handles her bureau admirably and men work for her without any friction. She is popular with all her colleagues and is the only American newspaper woman running a news bureau in Europe today.

The woman correspondent has not been encouraged at the battle front. Both Rheta Childe Dorr and Sophie Treadwell found themselves facing insurmountable difficulties in France. The only woman to get a properly accredited pass from the War Department was Peggy Hull. When America entered the war Miss Hull made up her mind that she would go to France. She had just completed an advertising stunt for the Cleveland *Plain Dealer* by having herself held up by a masked bandit to advertise a bank.

But she had trouble getting a paper to back her up on war correspondence. When she reached France she found allies in Floyd Gibbons, Ring W. Lardner, George Pattullo and Webb Miller. She saw the first American troops parade in Paris. She visited their camps and spent two months with an infantry brigade. In the summer of 1918 she had to rush back to America because her mother was ill. As soon as she was well again, Miss Hull made tracks for the War Department. She found that an expedition was going to Siberia. She queried fifty editors, offering them her services as correspondent. Finally NEA assigned her and she got her credentials through General Peyton March. A few days later she started off for Siberia, armed with the first war correspondent's pass granted to a woman by the War Department. She spent the next ten months with the American troops and learned something about war.

Russia has been the focusing point of a number of women correspondents—Anna Louise Strong, Rayna Prohme, Rheta Childe Dorr, Bessie Beatty, Clare Sheridan, Milly Bennett Mitchell and Louise

Bryant. Some of them have been more engrossed in the radical cause than in journalism but they have all had fiery careers.

Anna Louise Strong was persuaded by Lincoln Steffens in Blanc's café in Seattle to go to Russia. She had been writing for the Seattle *Daily Call* on the I.W.W. and other labor activities. Accepting his suggestion she sailed for Russia. In 1920 she was corresponding for the I.N.S. and was writing for the labor press as Anise. In 1929 she organized the Moscow *News*, asked Bill Prohme and Milly Mitchell to join her and fought many battles over the direction of the paper. Like Mary Heaton Vorse, who wrote for the *Globe* and *The Masses*, she backed the radical cause and turned out copy fluently in defense of her theories.

Louise Bryant was a native of San Francisco, a talented and fascinating girl who wrote for the Hearst services during the early days of the Russian revolution. She knew Lenin well and liked him. At one time or another she met all the dominant figures of the revolution. Her life was one of excitement and high journalistic fervor during the days that she was married to John Reed, whose ashes now lie beside the Kremlin. Two years after his death she met William C. Bullitt while he was engaged on a special mission to Russia for the American government. She married him in 1923 and they were divorced in 1930.

Miss Bryant was one of the ardent spirits of the revolution, like Rayna Prohme, the heroine of Vincent Sheean's *Personal History*. She was an enthusiast whose journalism was heavily tinctured by her personal convictions. She was well known in Greenwich Village, on the Left Bank and wherever radical thought foregathered, but little was heard of her in the few years preceding her death. Life flamed high for her, then burned low. She represented an era in journalism which seems to have come to an end.

Chapter XXIX

THE WOMAN COLUMNIST

"Beloved, question me not whence I have learned of men, his secrets. Have I not known one man well? And verily a woman need know but one man in order to understand all men; whereas a man may know women and understand not one of them."

HELEN ROWLAND WRITES HER COLUMN IN MODERN PARABLES. She is a columnist of wit and understanding. Three husbands have helped her to form her conclusions on men, but her style is distinctly her own.

When she took some of her earlier syndicated dialogue to a publisher, he glanced over the manuscript, looked disgusted and exclaimed, "My God! Another book on women! Isn't there anything funny about a man?"

Miss Rowland clutched the arm of her chair. She felt as if lightning had struck her. Here was something she could do. If there was one subject on which she felt well informed, it was man. Except for a few old jokes about drunks and hicks, they had simply been getting away with it, so far as the newspapers were concerned. The husband, the lover, the bachelor—a rich field for satire. Miss Rowland went out of the office with zip. Her mind was already at work. The bored editor had handed her a fresh idea. Next day "Reflections of a Bachelor Girl" was born. And for years thereafter she wrote about men. She thought they would hate her. They didn't. They ate it up and liked it. She got four times as many fan letters from men as from women. Few of them were protests. They came from lawyers, judges, doctors, actors, business men—all types. Miss Rowland's column has never been successfully copied, for she has an individual wit and an easy cynicism on men, marriage and love. Her aphorisms are usually as brilliant as they are bitter.

She was born in Washington of Virginia parents. She worried little about her education, which took her through public schools in Washington, private schools in Louisville, Kentucky, and Emerson College, Boston, where her instructor in English literature was Ralph Waldo Trine, author of *In Tune with the Infinite*. At different times

during her adolescence she had three burning ambitions. She wanted
to be an actress and play Hamlet. She wanted to be a nun. But most
of all she longed to be a circus rider and gallop in tarletan skirts on
a white horse. At no time did she think of writing. However, at
sixteen she was turning out verse and dialogue and selling it to the
Washington *Post*. The managing editor at the time was Scott Bone.
Her first professional effort was a satirical dialogue, inspired by a
vain young man. He had come to call on Miss Rowland, who already
had a devastating eye for life's absurdities. He spent the evening telling her what he would require of the girl he married. She would have
to have youth, beauty, a perfect disposition, domestic ability and
the brains to help him in his career. She would also have to be willing to live on his meager salary as a professor. Then he informed her
that she would do. In short, she was the lucky girl.

After he had gone and she had finished laughing, she went to her
room and jotted down her first satirical wisecracks. She got $3 for
the effort. When she proudly showed the check to her father, he
was furious and ordered her to return it at once to the editor with
the crushing information that Lee Rowland's daughter did not write
for money. That gave her the chance to meet Mr. Bone, who encouraged her to go on writing. His answer to her father's observation was: "What we consider worth printing, we consider worth
paying for. Do anything you please with the check—give it to
charity or go to a matinée, but don't leave it around here."

So big-hearted Helen went to the matinée.

After that she did interviews for the Washington *Post*, sold some
verse to Tom Masson, which was published in *Life*, and turned out
several short stories, which appeared in the lighter magazines. When
her father died she had to settle down seriously to work. So she
packed up and left for New York, determined not to be a newspaper
writer. She preferred the magazines. She went to the *Century* and
asked for a place on the editorial staff. She was courteously received
and sent on her way with a letter of introduction to the Sunday
editor of the *Press*.

She was young, southern, good-looking, romantic and in deep
mourning. The combination was irresistible. She got a job. Or, more
precisely, one was made for her. The editor was a brilliant young
man who taught her most of what she knows about writing. At first
he tried to make a straight newspaper woman of her but gave up in
despair. She wrote nearly everything that a Sunday paper runs—
fashions, features, editorials, verse, fillers and her own dialogue.

That went on for a year. Her next job was matrimony, but it had
a short run. However, it gave her enough material to start her on

her column of cynical reflections. Two succeeding husbands have helped to keep it going. When her first marriage began to waver, she launched a weekly dialogue for the Sunday papers and conceived the bright idea of syndicating it herself. S. S. McClure noticed it here and there throughout the country and offered to syndicate it for her. Since she hated work, she sank happily into the cushioned ease of the established syndicate. This was "Widow Wordalogues" which, like all of Miss Rowland's subsequent output, sold well. Then came "The Sayings of Mrs. Solomon," which was even more popular. At this time her work appeared in the *Evening World* in New York. After eleven years with McClure she moved over to the Wheeler syndicate. She changed the title of her column to "Meditations of a Married Woman" but it was essentially the same feature.

In 1924 she joined King Features. Her salary was trebled at the start. Her column soon became the "Marry-Go-Round." Her ingenuity is inexhaustible and her tabloid wisdom is read and quoted by thousands throughout the country. It isn't fare for romantics. Miss Rowland talks as well as she writes. She has had opportunities to do magazine and playwriting, but she prefers her daily column. She sticks to her satirical comment on men and believes in specialization for every newspaper writer. Her advice to beginners is:

Get a typewriter
Get a copy of Roget's *Thesaurus*
Get a specialty.

Miss Rowland has had eight books published—collections of her syndicated columns. They have sold well as gift books—dynamite for wives to try on their husbands in bitter moments.

When Heywood Broun left the *World* to work for the *Telegram*, Mr. Swope looked around the office and offered his column to Elsie McCormick, who had shown a witty touch in the Sunday department. No one was more surprised than Miss McCormick herself, although she knew quite well how to fill a column and had done it with success for the *China Press*.

It was not easy for anyone to follow Mr. Broun. His column was almost a religion to *World* readers, and the hard-to-please members of his own craft liked it. But Miss McCormick took hold. Three times a week her smooth prose flowed down the page, easy to read, enlivening to the intelligence. She had a graceful touch, a penetrating eye and a feministic turn of thought. Her favorite subject was China. It still is, for she spent the most exciting years of her life in the Orient.

Miss McCormick was born in San Francisco and began newspaper writing at the age of eleven when she ran a weekly column of school items in the *News*. The virus having thus entered her system, she continued to write for the *Bulletin* and other local papers during her years at the Convent of the Holy Name, Oakland High School and the University of California. After graduation she joined the staff of the Oakland *Post-Enquirer* and was the first woman to cover the local courthouse beat. Her amiable colleagues, who had nothing specific against her, said they would run her off the beat because women had a depressing effect on salaries. For weeks they traded news among themselves, leaving her to cover ten courts, the emergency hospital, the sheriff's office and a few other items, all by herself. However, gallant judges, prosecutors, and lawyers began to give her tips with instructions that she was not to tell the boys. One day when she had three exclusive stories on the front page, one of them carrying an eight-column head, she enjoyed hearing her competitors explaining simultaneously over the pressroom telephones just how they had come to be beaten. Next day the dean of the group announced that they had decided it was mean and unfair to work against a girl, and that thereafter she would be accepted into the combination. She never again encountered any serious sex discrimination in her newspaper work.

One of her oddest adventures dates back to this period, when she went into a court room while an insanity hearing was in progress. The man in question had acquitted himself well. He had answered all questions intelligently and was insisting that he had been brought up for commitment only because some of his relatives coveted his estate. The judge was about to release him and rebuke the family when Miss McCormick appeared, wearing a yellow georgette hat. The man under detention rose to his feet, exclaiming, "There is the Virgin Mary with a beautiful golden halo around her head."

It took two attendants to hold him down. The judge at once apologized to the relatives and made out the commitment papers, while Miss McCormick vanished with speed that would have done credit to Nurmi.

After a year of murders, accidents and alarms she went to New York and got a more soothing job doing publicity for the Methodist Centenary and the Interchurch World Movement. She was sent abroad a few weeks after the Armistice to write stories about their war work. She explored the devastated areas of France and Italy with eleven Methodist bishops and one bishop's daughter. She has never told the full story.

She managed to crash the Fourth Plenary Session of the Peace Conference, a feat which she undertook for a San Francisco paper.

It was done by such chicanery as the use of a vaccination certificate on a gendarme who was not bilingual, and several other impish measures known only to the ladies of the press. At last she reached the grand anteroom of the Quai d'Orsay, where a formidable major domo admitted those with proper passes and locked the door behind them, leaving Miss McCormick alone with the statuary. She finally got into the Chamber by ducking under the arm of the major domo when he opened the door for someone inside who wanted to get out.

Soon after this Miss McCormick went to China for the Interchurch Movement. She liked the country so well that she stayed on after the financial collapse of the organization. For more than a year she ran a column for the *China Press*. Much of it was compiled later in two books, *Audacious Angles on China* and *The Unexpurgated Diary of a Shanghai Baby*. Once she went off into the interior of Shantung to interview the seventy-seventh generation descendant of Confucius. She had heard of the Confucian Duke, and she thought that there might be a good story in his reactions to the perplexities of the modern world. Her editor quite agreed, so Miss McCormick started out on what proved to be a formidable journey. She traveled north from Shanghai for twenty-four hours on the famous "Blue Train," which turned out to be yellow inside and out from prairie dust. Then she changed to a local crowded with Chinese soldiers, their teapots and canaries.

The railroad avoids Chu'fu, the burial place of Confucius, because the Chinese officials fear that the noise of the trains might disturb his hallowed slumbers. So Miss McCormick had to engage a Peking cart and go jolting over the country on two iron-studded wheels. The trip was complicated by the fact that her coolie driver found hilarious entertainment in a copy of *Vogue* she had and failed to keep to the two ruts that were supposed to be the highway.

However, Miss McCormick scarcely noticed. She was lost in meditation, preparing lofty questions to put to the seventy-seventh descendant of Confucius. After many hours of travel she landed at last at Chu'fu. Not one white person lived anywhere about, but a Chinese, to whom she had a letter of introduction, invited her to spend the night with his family. Feeling somewhat overawed, and distinctly worried about the interview, Miss McCormick was taken next day to the ducal palace. She went through one stately anteroom after another, saw the great Confucian library and at last came to an inner courtyard of staggering beauty. There she met the Confucian Duke.

Her interview with him was never printed, for he turned out to be two years old.

Miss McCormick had a ringside seat at a number of local wars. She got used to pot shots, scampering Chinese and changing governments. She made many trips into the interior of China and visited Japan, Korea and the Philippines. When she returned to New York she got a job in the Sunday department of the *World* merely by walking in with her scrapbook under her arm. After a year of doing special features she went off to China again, where she married Marshall L. Dunn, who was then in the publishing business in Shanghai. They took a four months' honeymoon trip around the world, then settled in New York, and Miss McCormick resumed her work in the Sunday department of the *World* until she inherited Mr. Broun's column. She was one of the mourners the night the paper was sold.

In the summer of 1935 she flew more than 2,000 miles in Alaska and lived for a week in a homesteader's shack in the Matanuska Valley, doing magazine pieces on what she saw. She has traveled far and wide and has had many adventures. But like most of the newspaper women who have given up the arena for the calm of the fireside, she likes her home, her friends, books, her leisure and the theater. She has only to touch the keys of her typewriter and the words ripple forth. It's never a forgotten art.

"Listen, World!" cries Elsie Robinson, a columnist whose audience sits up and pays attention. She is not merely a writer but a dynamic personality, suggesting open spaces, mining camps, life in the raw. She has experienced them all, and still fills her copy with ozone. Miss Robinson is reputed to reach an audience of 20,000,000 persons. She is the most highly paid woman syndicate writer in the Hearst service. She is whole-hearted, original, intense. She deals in short words, short paragraphs, a punch in every line. Her copy is colloquial and pounds along with accelerated punctuation. Miss Robinson never tries to edify or make a sensitive approach to the intellectual. She pulls the heart strings. She is full of aphorisms—original ones—and eupeptic philosophy. Go dig the drain, she tells the depressed. That was what she did herself when she was practically down and out.

Miss Robinson has told her story in her own autobiography, *I Wanted Out*, one of the more naked confession books of the time. Her success has been dramatic. She skyrocketed in the Hearst organization in less than a decade. Now a single article will evoke a thousand letters, for she paints with broad strokes that attract the eye. She has lived like a man, worked like a man. After years in a mining camp she returned to civilization at the age of thirty-six— lean, bronzed, her face furrowed, her gait the slouching stride of one who had spent years behind a wheelbarrow. Her looks were odd. She wore miners' boots and a mackinaw. She was filled with terror, although she managed to mask her feelings.

Today Miss Robinson is handsome, self-contained, successful. She has mastered fate to an exhilarating degree. She lives on her California ranch, watches the shadows fall over her land and blot out the Sierra, has as companion her third husband, Benton Fremont, an engineer. Life at last has settled into comparative order for her tempestuous soul.

She was born in Benecia, California, in 1883. Her home was buried in roses and clematis. She ate polenta fresh from open braziers; waded for clams; talked to everyone who would listen to her. She was tall, rangy and eager. Then she married and spent ten unhappy years trying to adjust herself to a circumscribed life in New England. Her husband's family disapproved of her. She had a wild and alien strain that they did not understand. And she could not warm to them.

Her home was a prim house on a tidy street in Vermont. She couldn't bear it. She longed to be free. Her son was ailing, so she took him and fled to the West. The next three years were compounded of physical hardship, mental anxiety, and the odd stimulation of the atmosphere in which she lived. For she had found refuge in a mining camp, where bootleggers, bandits, trappers, sheep herders and miners of every breed foregathered. Miss Robinson toiled like a navvy. She worked with pick and axe. She wheeled her barrow and trundled heavy loads. In her cabin she cooked flapjacks, painted pictures and wrote when not too tired to use her right arm. She listened to the fantastic stories of men whose pasts bore little investigation. She watched her son gain health and strength in the good air.

Then in 1918 she returned to the world she had left. She walked through Market Street, San Francisco, in a daze, with $50 in her pocket, borrowed from her mining friends. She took her son to a basement apartment. His health failed in the grime of city life. She couldn't find a job. They both went hungry. September, October, November, December—not a door opened for her. She almost gave up. She looked at the river one night and thought it was one way out.

Miss Robinson had tried every newspaper office in San Francisco. But after touching bottom she decided to make one more effort. She crossed to Oakland. She interested the editor of the Oakland *Tribune* in her illustrated children's stories. He took her on to do a weekly column of animal stories at $12 a week. Fan mail poured in at once from children. Within two months the column had become two full-sized weekly pages covering all sorts of juvenile interests. Then it became an eight-page tabloid magazine on Sundays. There were Aunt Elsie picnics and parties. This went on for four years. In the second year the George Matthew Adams Service began syndicating her handicraft feature for children, and a cheer-up column for adults, which was called "Listen, World!" So her syndicate career began at $25 a week. She was thirty-eight years old at the time and celebrated by getting her first manicure and buying a pair of silk stockings.

She was forty when she left her paper and walked into Fremont Older's office. He was then editor of the *Call*. He and his wife were to help her over various crises in the years that followed. Soon she got a note from Arthur Brisbane, inviting her East. She went to the old Hearst building on William Street.

"What means most to you?" Mr. Brisbane demanded.

"Being a mother," said Miss Robinson.

"That's enough," he said.

She signed a fat contract and became a Hearst writer. Money flowed into the empty coffers. She and her son could live in luxury at last. But two years later he died. She had pulled him through serious lung trouble. A trivial operation for a lump on his foot was fatal. This wiped away the foundations of her life again. She remarried but the experiment was not a success. She packed up one day and went into the mountains at Mr. Older's suggestion. He thought that his favorite panacea of writing a serial might do her good.

So in 1929 she went to Sonora and found the Chinese lilies and daffodils in bloom. She studied the sky and the rolling land and decided that this was where she would like to settle. She built a summer camp. It is now an established ranch with twenty acres of vineyard, ten houses, and plenty of livestock. Miss Robinson does not cover spot news but occasionally she travels to keep in touch with what is going on. In 1932 she wrote about the Bonus March. Back in the nineties she had seen men marching to join Coxey's army.

Long before "Listen, World!" burst like a thunderclap on Hearst readers, Ruth Cameron's column was known throughout the country. Written by Persis Dwight Hannah, it has been going for twenty-seven years and is syndicated in hundreds of papers. It carries various heads but is most generally known as "The Woman Philosopher" or "Says She."

In 1907, when the Boston papers were just beginning to employ college girls, Miss Hannah, a graduate of Tufts, read a serial in the *Saturday Evening Post* called "The Autobiography of a Yellow Journalist." It was a gay narrative that rang bells in her head. Her family wanted her to teach Latin. But Miss Hannah was determined to be a girl reporter. The life of the yellow journalist seemed to be one round of giddy adventure. She lapped it up. This, she thought, was the career for her. So she threw her lexicon out of the window and began to pester city editors, in spite of her father's opposition. When friends asked him what his daughter was doing, he told them sadly that she had joined the circus.

But the joining was not easy. Editors rebuffed her. They told her she must have experience.

"But how did the men get started?" she asked, logically enough.

"Oh, sweeping out the office," she was told by one city editor.

"Well," said Miss Hannah. "I can do that, too."

Finally she had to use pull to get started, and at first she worked for nothing. Presently she was accepted at $10 a week on the Boston *Journal*, then owned by Mr. Munsey. She was one-quarter of the infinitesimal staff, and did straight news as well as occasional sob sister features—how it felt to live with a broken neck; how it felt to go through the Boston subway when it was a maze of mud and twisted wires.

Miss Hannah has an unforgettable mental picture of Julia Ward Howe, in lavender and old lace, sitting in a throne-like chair in her Beacon Street bay window. Her most exciting moment was when she was stoned out of a camp by gypsies who were furious because the camera man had taken their pictures, and they regarded this as bad luck. The photographer fled, having urged Miss Hannah to stay behind and keep the Romany troupe from breaking his camera.

After two years of active reporting on the *Journal* she moved over to the *Traveller*, where she was known as Phoebe Dwight. George Matthew Adams was just starting his syndicate and he asked her to write a daily talk for women. In this way the Ruth Cameron feature was born. The original idea was to make it a strictly feminine column, but Miss Hannah found that she could not keep within this limitation, so she turned out a column of general interest.

In 1912 she married Royal Brown, who was then executive editor of the Boston *Journal*, where he had started as a cub reporter. She reads every line of his fiction output, which is prolific, since he has more than three hundred short stories and novelettes to his credit. The Browns live for the greater part of the year at Humarock, Massachusetts, in a house which they built during the war, and to which they have added from time to time. It is a home of hard work, for husband and wife turn out a staggering number of words each year.

Another newspaper woman who has recently joined the syndicate ranks is Helen Worden, who knows New York as the historian, the antiquarian, the epicure, the genealogist might know it, all wrapped into one. She is familiar with the drawing-rooms of Park Avenue and the barge life of the East River. She knows who everybody's grandfather was and the recipe he used for his punch. Her curiosity is insatiable; the facts she collects are odd and absorbing. The result is a column of singular interest which appears in the *World-Telegram* in New York.

Miss Worden has silver hair and a youthful face, large brown eyes and a graceful manner. She runs her own column to suit herself. It has grown up spontaneously. One thing has led to another. She follows sports and social events. She goes wherever she thinks a story is forthcoming. She discovered early that newspaper readers like facts, so she gives them plenty. She runs short paragraphs, short sentences, with no essential continuity. But each paragraph carries the piquant answer to some minor matter that at one time or another has roused one's curiosity. It may be the old house at the corner, or the plane tree inside a railing, or the gas lamp over somebody's door, or the gargoyle in the eaves, or the old lady with antiquated habits who never leaves her house. She is an artist as well as a writer and does tiny humorous sketches to go with her column. The old lady with the lorgnette. The Peter Arno colonel. The galloping horse. The waving palms. Arnold, her cat. Henry Hawkins, her parrot. Each paragraph is a separate vignette.

Until she was twenty-eight Miss Worden was sure that her life work was art. She studied portraiture in schools in New York, Paris and Denver. She is a native of Denver, and was brought East when she was two years old. Her first observations of metropolitan life were gleaned in Rector's, where a special high chair was kept for her. Until 1906 she shuttled back and forth between Denver and New York, attending private schools and absorbing American history from her grandfather, Colonel Wilbert Barton Teters. Both he and his daughter, Mrs. Worden, were students of the dramatic and unusual in American history, so that Helen was more or less born with the inquiring mind. Her father, Charles George Worden, studied law and then turned to newspaper work. At the time of his death he was editing *Two Republics*, the first American newspaper in Mexico City.

Miss Worden's newspaper career started in Denver. She wandered into the *Community-Herald* one May day with a portfolio of her drawings. It was Denver's smallest newspaper, a weekly founded for the promotion of Music Week. She asked for the editor and was motioned to the rear of the office by the typesetter. The staff consisted of Michael Factorovitch, the publisher, whose name was Niehaus, and the editor, whose identity was soon made known to Miss Worden.

"He's a young fellow from New York," the typesetter explained. "We just got him. His name's Jed Harris."

Herbert Belford, who worked on the New York *Times*, had turned up in Denver to see his sister, "Pinky" Wayne, who is on the Denver *Post*. Jed Harris had gone West with him. He was on his way to Honolulu to conduct an orchestra. But he never reached Hawaii. Herbert got him a job on the *Community-Herald* the day before Miss Worden showed up with her drawings. The youth, who was later to become a successful producer on Broadway, was twenty-one and took himself seriously.

"I might use your drawings if you could write some stuff to go with them," he said. "But I can't pay much."

Jed, Helen and Factorovitch got out the paper. She made $12 a week. The office was so small that they couldn't all get in at once, so they met each noon in a fish house nearby to talk things over. Jed was hot-tempered then, as he still is. He wrote editorials that gave Mr. Niehaus the jitters because the advertisers did not care for them. Three months after Miss Worden had joined the staff, he stormed into the fish house one day, white with anger. He had had another battle with Mr. Niehaus.

"I'm through," he announced. "I'm going back to New York."

It was an exciting afternoon in the restaurant. The fish in the window tanks swished their tails as Jed roared and stalked about the room. He drew up a letter addressed to Mr. Niehaus. It was signed by Miss Worden, by Factorovitch and by Jed. It contained their resignations. They felt that Mr. Niehaus had not been loyal to principle. He was too much interested in advertising. The *Community-Herald* failed to appear on the newsstands that week. Mr. Niehaus could not make the grade without them.

In 1925 Miss Worden went to Paris to continue her art studies. She spent a year at André L'hote's Academy. She visited London, Florence, Rome, Venice, Milan. She returned to New York with samples of her work. She had several line drawings of people in the news. It occurred to her that some newspaper might buy them. She studied the classified telephone directory and made a list of all the New York papers. She decided to try the *World*.

Will ("Limpy") Johnston was then the feature editor. He looked at her drawings and was interested in them. "I think we can use some of your work if you write something to go with it," he told her. For the next six years she worked on the metropolitan section of the *Sunday World* with Louis Weitzenkorn. She did three features and illustrated them with her miniature sketches. The first, a cooking column, was called "Sally Lunn," the second was a strip known as "Fashions of the Theatre," and the third was "Belle Brummel," a style column which she still does for the *World-Telegram*. She also did special articles for Mr. Weitzenkorn.

The third week she was on the *World* she ran into Arthur Krock in the office one day.

"What are you getting a week?" he asked.

"Space rates," said Miss Worden. "I average $7.50."

"My God!" said Mr. Krock.

Next week her salary was doubled. At the end of two years she was working also for the *Evening World*. She started its society page and ran a feature called "What Society is Wearing." She did special interviews and got out the fashion section. Occasionally she did stories for James Robbins, who was then sports editor. By that time she was making so much that she was taken off space and was put on the regular staff.

Her most difficult assignments for the *World* were an interview with Colonel Charles A. Lindbergh, another with Mrs. Charles M. Schwab, and a contest she conducted on how to spend $10,000,000 for the good of humanity. The Lindbergh story was written just after the birth of the baby who later was kidnapped. The Colonel gave a revealing interview to Miss Worden. He talked to her for an hour and a half and told her how he would like to bring up his son, although it was not his habit to discuss his personal affairs. On the night the baby was kidnapped, George Lyon called her at her home and asked her to revise the interview for next day's paper. It was the most intimate story that had been written on the Colonel's own ambitions for his child.

Mrs. Schwab was another of the inaccessibles, put down in every newspaper office as hopeless for interviews. Miss Worden's story made the front page because it settled the recurrent rumors that the Schwab mansion on Riverside Drive would be sold. For two weeks Mrs. Schwab refused to see Miss Worden or to give her a message of any sort.

"Why don't you go to Mr. Schwab?" her friends asked. "He will give you the story."

But Miss Worden thought that the story did not lie in him. The house was Mrs. Schwab's home, so she stuck at it until she got what she wanted.

"Never, as long as I live, shall I sell the house," said Mrs. Schwab.

Through Josef Sigall, the artist, Miss Worden first met C. Harold Smith, the carbon king with a fortune of $30,000,000 which he planned to divide with his fellow men. He had written a biography, *The Bridge of Life*, and he wanted to put it across. It meant more to him than his millions. He planned a campaign on the provocative theme, "How Would You Spend $10,000,000 to Aid Humanity?" When he sat beside Miss Worden at dinner one night he proposed that the *Evening World* should run a contest with prizes for the best scheme submitted.

Miss Worden named a committee to run the campaign. On it were Mrs. Franklin D. Roosevelt, Emory Buckner, Dr. Alfred Adler, Frederic C. Coudert and the Rev. Dr. S. Parkes Cadman. The prize for the best plan offered was $1,000 and daily prizes of $10 were distributed for letters on how the money should be spent. All sorts of panaceas were submitted. A number of celebrities contributed their ideas. More than 100,000 letters were received, four-fifths of them of the begging order. The Associated Press carried the story all over the world. In India a poster advertised the campaign on the side of a caravan. Dr. Henry E. Garrett, professor of psychology at Columbia, won the $1,000 prize with his plan for an institute of mental hygiene, where research would be conducted into neuroses, and juvenile delinquents would be studied scientifically.

It was a stiff job for Miss Worden. Five readers helped her to weed out the letters. She submitted the best contributions to the committee. When it was over, Mr. Smith, a kindly philanthropist with a handle-bar mustache, gave a banquet, decked Mrs. Roosevelt and Miss Worden with corsages and gave Dr. Garrett his prize. But before anything could be done about the $10,000,000 the crash came. Mr. Smith's fortune shrank to $4,000,000. His wife became desperately ill. He took her to European watering places, hoping for her recovery. But he dropped dead by her bedside in 1931 as she lay in her own death coma.

Soon after this Miss Worden began to concentrate on her observations of New York. She makes a mental record of a street when she is out walking. Her mind is photographic and she has alert eyes for the odd and unusual. She knows all the little shopkeepers and most of the big ones. She follows the doings of the smart world but devotes most of her time to tracking down clues in out-of-the-way spots. She knows policemen, firemen, street-cleaners, newsboys, head waiters and politicians. At a moment's notice she can dig up peasant glassware from Majorca, sharp-bladed weapons from Arabia, gilded weathercocks for steeple vanes, or old Valentines. She can tell the born New Yorker where to find Alexandroff, the Russian letter writer of the East Side, or platinum-haired Maizie, Queen of the Venice on the Bowery. She knows the eating places of every race as well as the chefs of New York's smartest restaurants and hotels. Occasionally she gives her readers a choice recipe for food or drink. Her information is practical and specific.

On a waterfront tour of New York she and Mrs. Theodore Steinway skipped over crates and skirted dock diggings, made friends with rivermen, watchmen and innkeepers, were welcomed royally in some quarters and ordered out of others. They took ten different days to do their thirty-three mile trek around the island. They carried small cameras in their pockets. Miss Worden took few notes along the way. She believes that pad and pencil silence people more effectively than anything else. They lunched at hot dog stands and diners. They never carried more than a couple of dollars in their purses. Their discoveries were revelatory of the little known side of New York. They found a wooden Indian in front of a snuff shop at 396 Water Street. Lavender grew in Hannah Murray's yard on Front Street, surrounded by a picket fence and shaded by a plantain tree. A thundershower drove them into a stable, and they soon discovered that the owner and his secretary had been murdered there not long before. They found houses built before the Revolution standing along the waterfront beside soaring skyscrapers. They learned that New Yorkers fished from their back yards; they explored Patchtown, peopled by the unemployed; Itch Park, the rendezvous of the upper Bowery district, and River House, one of New York's most fashionable dwelling places—all strung along the waterfront. They looked over Al Smith's alma mater, the Fulton Fish Market, which he has described as the finest college in the world. They investigated St. Luke's Place, the home of James J. Walker and Starr Faithfull, both of whom captured their share of front-page space. They watched egg candlers juggling eggs in the West Washington Market and studied the haunts of the river pirates, who make off with monkey wrenches, life preservers, rope and odds and ends of river grist. They found the oldest apothecary in the city and the shop where one can buy an astrolabe. They talked to the descendants of the windjammers' captains who live now in the neighborhood of Corlear's Hook Park, and listening to them, saw the ghosts of white-sailed ships slip by.

Miss Worden has written two books about her favorite city. One is called *The Real New York*. The other is *Round Manhattan's Rim*, which is based chiefly on her walk around the waterfront. She is working now on a book on underground New York and another on the social circus. In the spring of 1935 she started a syndicated column called "Miss Manhattan" for the Scripps-Howard chain. Her mother shares her interest in historical research. She writes for the magazines and has done 350 articles of the Captain Kidd order—old bandit crimes and duels of river pirates. Her aunt, Lou Ellen Teters, was woman's editor of *Delineator* when it first appeared on the newsstands. Miss Worden lives with her mother on Park Avenue. They go wherever news is stirring. First nights. Cup races. Hunting. Polo. Racing. The spectacular parties. Smart weddings.

Her column runs alongside the regular social news and supplements it in a chatty and informative way.

What Miss Worden does for New York, the town, Alice Hughes does for its shops. Eight years ago she started a shopping column of such originality, profit and interest that it quickly became one of the valuable newspaper properties of metropolitan journalism. It first became known in the *World-Telegram*, then she went over to Hearst and it now appears in the *American*.

Miss Hughes is a power in the merchandising world. Her value is inseparable from her own personality. She started out with a smart idea, and put it across by skilled handling. She has many copyists now, some of them good, but hers is the name that tops the history of the shopping column. She is slim, dark, still in her manner. Her face is touched with melancholy. She parts her hair severely in the middle, speaks thoughtfully, surveys the world with slightly tilted eyes. But her somber air is deceptive. She is alert, ingratiating, vivid in her interests, optimistic in her outlook. She believes that good fortune comes to those who believe completely in what they are doing. She herself moves in the mystical aura of success.

By 9.30 every morning her car is parked in front of one of the big shops. She likes to watch the early shoppers flood the aisles, keen for bargains. She is curious to see what they are after. Some days she gets to a dozen stores, not making a cursory inspection of the counters but going behind the scenes and talking to the men and women who run the shop. She knows their trade secrets and has a shrewd idea of the value of their wares. She is not aggressive, but is smart at unearthing facts.

Miss Hughes grew up in New Hampshire. She attended the Columbia School of Journalism, then for six months she read manuscripts at $25 a week for *Detective Story Magazine*. She had a columnist's job on the *American* as far back as 1923, but it was not the hit it is today. It was called "Mary Jane's Household Guide." She made $45 a week but was lured into advertising for more money. She seemed to have special aptitude in this direction, in spite of her yearning to do some other kind of writing. It kept cropping out, no matter what she did. She studied typography, engraving, layouts. She associated with artists. She was appointed advertising manager of the shop where she had started.

She was married the day she left college, but the more her career advanced, the greater was her domestic unhappiness. She gave up her job and went to Europe, hoping that things would straighten out. They didn't. On her return she went to Columbus, Ohio, and did advertising there. But things went from bad to worse. Again she went to Europe. On her return she got a job in the advertising department of Macy's. She plunged with her usual enthusiasm into the study of promotion, exploitation, merchandising. She entertained her friends with stories of the life in the shop. One of the editors of the *World* who heard her said, "Why don't you write these stories? I'll print them. They're good."

So she began contributing features to the *Sunday World*. When the *Telegram* was bought by Mr. Howard, Macy's advertising was sought by the Scripps-Howard interests. It appeared in the other afternoon papers but not in the *Telegram*. Miss Hughes at the time was head of the apparel advertising group. On Fridays the afternoon papers were so glutted with advertising that no single display had any distinction. She saw that the *Telegram* had plenty of unspoiled white paper and she urged Macy's to try it. They did, to good effect. The Scripps-Howard organization was grateful to Miss Hughes. When she approached Mr. Howard with an idea for a supporting news column for shops, such as books and the theater had, she was taken on the staff. Almost immediately the column caught on. Before long she and Heywood Broun appeared on the same page. This was admirable for her. When surveys were made, their combined pull was found to be heavy.

Miss Hughes has been described in turn as a retailing reporter, a fashion columnist, a store scout, a style commentator. She prefers to be known simply as a reporter. She started out to give human interest sidelights on the stores. She delved into the history of merchandising and the involved processes that precede its appearance in purchasable form. She tried to divorce herself from the ordinary glamour words of advertising and fashion writing. She realized that an idea was always better than an adjective. Her advertising training had taught her to think in headline terms, which was useful for a column of this kind. It gave concentration to her style.

She had a hard time at first persuading the merchants of the merit of what she was doing. She had to sell herself as one who would be discreet. At first they were suspicious when she came to them with a thousand searching questions. Then her column began to get results. She would mention a shop and the next day crowds swarmed in. This was effective for Miss Hughes, as well as for the tradesman. It was hard work. It took four years to reach the point where they came to her. At first she had to do all the plugging. The shops were far apart. The advertising managers were always in remote corners on the top floor. She would come home exhausted from the day's round. But Miss Hughes herself has wrought a miraculous change in the publicity methods of the department stores. She is responsible for the creation of many jobs. Now every large shop has a regular publicity staff to feed the shoppers' columns which have sprung up everywhere. The columnists are swamped with releases. As soon as a new gadget reaches the market they get a full account of its merits.

Miss Hughes pioneered in rather dangerous territory, since the relation of the department store to the newspaper is one requiring tact. Some of the merchants liked the exploitation of store personalities at first; others detested it. But now they are all avid for the shopping columns and the newspapers have found them profitable features. They appear all over the country. Kay Austin does a good one for the *World-Telegram* and Cecile Gilmore for the *Post* in New York.

Miss Hughes was not the first person to do a strictly commercial shopping column. Jenny June originated the idea and Mrs. Edith Kibbe has conducted one in the Hartford *Courant* under the name "Deborah" since 1890. But Miss Hughes put the idea on a new basis and brought the academic touch to bear on the exploitation of bargains. Now she also conducts a weekly beauty page. She covers considerable territory both here and abroad, and has a special clause in her contract allowing for travel. For four consecutive years she went to Russia for the *World-Telegram*, writing stories on the changing phases of life there. In her first year with the Hearst service she went to Japan and Russia, and was on a train derailed by bandits in Manchuria.

Miss Hughes is generally recognized as one of the brightest girls in the newspaper profession. Her rise has been rapid. She is quoted and sought for speech-making. Her salary is something to make other newspaper women cheer. She goes everywhere, watches the passing show with an appraising eye. Her life is varied and fast-moving. She has an adopted son and is married now to Leonard Hall, having divorced her first husband. Mr. Hall is a writer who hates business as much as she loves it. He is contemplative; she is active. He is cautious; she is adventurous. The result of this divergence in interest is that they get along very well together.

Another newspaper column, unusual in character, is conducted by Alva Taylor, daughter of B. L. T., the famous Chicago columnist. She writes men's fashions for the Chicago *Tribune*-New York *Daily News* syndicate. Few of her readers ever suspect that Al Taylor is a girl, small and dark, with bangs and a sweet expression. Practically all of her letters come addressed to Mr. Taylor. She is unmasked most often on the telephone. "Yes, I am Al Taylor," she tells a surprised man over the wire. Sometimes the news is received calmly; at other times, it brings an astonished response. Only one man ever threatened to stop reading the column because it was written by a woman. He had seen an allusion to the fact that Miss

Taylor was the ex-wife of Paul Gallico in a tintype of the sports writer done by Sidney Skolsky. When Miss Taylor changed her column name from Al Gallico to Al Taylor, a correspondent wrote in to tell her how much better she was than the Gallico fellow. The feature has a large following. Miss Taylor gets letters from all parts of the country as well as from Canada, the Philippines, Panama and farther afield.

Her father had no thought of her ever becoming a newspaper woman. He expected her to be a singer. But after his death she had to earn her own living and the Chicago *Tribune* seemed the logical place for her to go. For years B. L. T.'s column had been one of the finest features of the paper. At first she worked in the Sunday department. Then, when she married Mr. Gallico, she moved East with him. She asked Mary King, of the *News*, to keep her in mind for any position that might be available. Almost immediately Miss King picked her to do men's fashions. The paper had just decided to launch this feature, and Miss King saw no reason why a woman should not make as good a job of it as a man. She gave Miss Taylor two weeks in which to study the situation and turn in her first piece. Until then Alva never had thought of men's clothes in any critical sense. She had merely registered the fact that a man was well turned-out or otherwise. Now she subscribed to trade journals, visited wholesale houses, looked things over in the best retail stores, and observed men in the smarter urban haunts.

Arthur Von Frankenberg was employed to illustrate the feature. The strange field she had invaded soon became familiar territory to Miss Taylor. She learned to stare discreetly at men in the street, in clubs and at the races. She interviewed well-known actors and the town's reputed Beau Brummels. When the Prince of Wales visited America in 1924 she followed him as closely as the reporters covering his movements for the city desk. The only difference was that she was not interested in what he did, but in what he wore. However, he launched nothing new on this occasion. He did not wear his boater with his dinner jacket or otherwise upset the conventions. But readers of the *News* got a precise account of the colors of his shirts and ties, the texture of his suits, the kind of hats and shoes he wore.

The problems put up to the column are often surprising. Many of Miss Taylor's correspondents send minute descriptions of themselves and even their photographs, so that she can give them precise advice for their types. She has leaflets that answer the stock questions propounded in the mail. Like Miss Worden and Miss Hughes, she gets about the town. She haunts night clubs, hotels, cocktail lounges, country clubs and the races. She keeps in touch with the better wholesale houses. She drops in at Tripler's, Brooks Brothers, Abercrombie and Fitch, looking for new tips for her devoted following. Motion picture celebrities give her the benefit of their advice from time to time. She will cheerfully work out a complete color scheme for any man who feels unable to do the job himself. The wholesalers and retailers react enthusiastically. It's good for their business. They are glad to give Miss Taylor all the advance information they can. She was the pioneer in this field. Now the *Herald Tribune* in New York and other newspapers throughout the country have taken up the idea and are giving serious attention to what the well-dressed man should wear, but Miss Taylor is still the only girl supplying the answers.

Walter Winchell has called June Provines, of the Chicago *Tribune*, the best woman columnist in the country. Her "Front Views and Profiles" are widely read and quoted. She thinks that the contemporary scene is often more accurately mirrored in a wisecrack than an editorial. She started her column because it seemed to her that many engaging items about celebrities were necessarily omitted from news stories—the details that would be included when the same tale was told to friends over the luncheon table. For instance, if a great mathematician is unable to make change, or Frank Lloyd Wright appears in blue corduroy evening trousers that gather in at the ankles, these manifestations give an accurate and human idea of their personalities. This sort of reporting seems to Miss Provines as valid as the scientist's conception of a prehistoric animal from a footprint on a rock. Nor does it do any harm. For she is scrupulous in her column. She makes it engaging, informative, but never to her knowledge harmful. She does not print all that she hears by any means, but she does give a sophisticated picture of the social scene and has all the curiosity of the good columnist about human motives and actions.

Miss Provines was a reporter before she became a columnist. For several years she did news and features for the Chicago *Daily News*. She went through the usual whirl—murder trials, interviews, conventions, visiting celebrities. She sat in court every day for six weeks during the Leopold-Loeb hearing, with a soundless typewriter before her and a telegraph operator behind her, banging out page one features. When it was over she escorted the two young murderers to Joliet. She covered Queen Marie's visit to the Middle West, trailing the indefatigable visitor from the Balkans through St. Louis, St. Paul and Chicago.

Shortly after Lindbergh's flight to Paris, Miss Provines discovered that he had a half-sister living in Red Lake Falls, Minnesota. She went there to see her. She was charmed to find that while papers everywhere were carrying interviews with aviators who had talked to the hero at some flying field, the Red Lake Falls *Gazette*, owned and edited by his brother-in-law, ran the story of his trans-Atlantic flight with the modest line appended: "Mr. Lindbergh is a brother of Mrs. George Christy, of Red Lake Falls."

She first did her column for the Chicago *Daily News* under another name. During this period she ran a paragraph telling how beer-runners bringing their booty into Chicago had to pass through a certain Wisconsin town. The bootleggers were so appreciative when the police made no move to molest them that they gave the town a new armored police car, a luxurious bit of equipment the local government had not been able to afford up to that time. It seemed to the columnist that no amount of oratory on the evils of prohibition could sum up conditions more conclusively than this.

Miss Provines had no special preparation for journalism. She moved to Chicago from Huntington, Indiana, after a finishing school education, and worked in succession on the *Evening Post*, the *Daily News* and the *Tribune*. In private life she is Mrs. Neil Cowham.

There have been few good creative women columnists and almost none of the F. P. A. and B. L. T. variety, except Clara Chaplin Thomas, now Mrs. Darragh Aldrich, who ran a column in the Minneapolis *Tribune* for ten years, doing special interviews and feature stories on the side. Her "Quentin's Column" was nationally known. She and McLandburgh Wilson, who wrote verse for the New York *Sun* at about the same time, were both admitted to the National Association of American Press Humorists on the assumption that they were men. Their names were noncommittal and their work had the satirical touch which did not suggest the feminine hand. Strickland Gillilan, a friend of Miss Thomas, put her over with his tongue in his cheek. When she attended the first convention, he introduced her as the wife of Quentin, to save his face.

When she broke into newspaper work in Minneapolis, she was almost alone in the field. Women had not yet come to roost in the city room. The first time she showed up in police court to write features, a well-meaning reporter, as young as she, led her firmly out of the place when a bawdy case was· called. She went back and got the necessary facts for her paper.

The most dramatic story she handled had its origin in her own office. It was the trial of a man who had murdered her city editor. It was a sex crime and sufficiently lurid. Up to that time Miss Thomas had never been present at a trial of any sort. The state's star witness was the girl around whom the case centered. When Miss Thomas interviewed her later, she said:

"Do you know why I looked at you when I told my story on the stand? Because you were the only person in that court room who understood how I could do what I did—and yet want to be good and fine."

They became friends after that. Miss Thomas saved her from suicide one night and then persuaded her to leave town and change her name. Later she married a man who knew her story and her life straightened itself out.

Miss Thomas did everything on her paper from a lovelorn column to being Sunday editor. She organized the woman's section, did society, criticism and straight news. She was as much at home in the composing room as in the editorial department. On her first appearance there the make-up men were flabbergasted and tempered their style for the time being. One young man who had come in with advertising copy thought he had gone balmy when he saw her. He wanted to know who the hell the fluff of a blonde was, rushing down the forms to press.

Mrs. Aldrich is now a successful novelist and magazine writer. She creates typical characters of the North Woods and the Minnesota logging camps. Her style is masculine and humorous. Reviewers frequently refer to her as Mr. Aldrich. She does much of her writing in a log cabin in the Minnesota woods. Her pet hobby is canoeing.

Chapter XXX

IN THE FIELD OF REVIEW

MARGARET FULLER WAS THE FIRST WOMAN OF GENUINE LIT-
erary attainments to write for an American newspaper.
She worked briefly and brilliantly for Horace Greeley
on the *Tribune* as critic and straight reporter. But she never settled
into the journalistic mold, for she hated the drudgery of a daily
paper and could not bring herself to write except when she felt so
inclined.

She was always late with her copy, suffered from violent headaches and was less adaptable than Mr. Greeley had hoped she would
be when he invited her to join his staff. However, she established a
new standard of literary criticism for the penny press and her vigorous mind struck flint on many of the issues of the day.

Merely to have her on the staff was a matter of talk in literary
circles. She was fresh from editing *The Dial* and was the friend of
Ralph Waldo Emerson and the other Transcendentalists. It was not
customary at the time to bring a literary figure into a newspaper
office, but Mr. Greeley had been much struck by one of her essays,
"The Great Lawsuit—Man versus Men, Woman versus Women."
It occurred to him that it would be an interesting experiment to get
her to write for his paper.

His wife suggested that she should live with them in their home
—a mellow old house on a lane off Harlem Road, with a brook and
pond, and a fine garden overlooking the East River. She accepted
the invitation without much persuasion and joined the staff in 1844.
Immediately a stream of thoughtful prose, signed only by an aster-
isk, began to appear on the front page, plainly the work of a scholar.
It was a period when there was room in the daily paper for a
leisurely essay on an abstract subject. The news of the world was
not tumultuous, nor did it arrive by the speedy means of to-day.
Mr. Greeley felt that his readers had time for an hour's lofty meditation over their coffee. And this they got from Miss Fuller's
writings.

An unusual upbringing had turned a bookish child into a pedantic woman. Her early days had been spent in Cambridgeport, Massachusetts, under the tutelage of her father, a lawyer and politician. She could read Latin at six and, indeed, was precocious from infancy. Her adolescence was tinged with strange fancies about the mythical characters she encountered in books. When she went to school she was desperately unhappy. The other girls found her awkward, sarcastic and lopsided in her development. She found them stupid and under-educated. After her school days she kept house for her father at Groton and then taught in Boston and Providence until she joined the staff of *The Dial*.

She was thirty-four when she first walked into the *Tribune* office, a short, ungainly figure with coarse fair hair, a nasal voice and a habit of blinking constantly. It was not until her superlative conversation absorbed the attention of a listener that her magnetism began to burn through the clumsiness of her manner. Emerson found that "she poured a stream of amber over the endless store of private anecdotes, of bosom histories, which her wonderful persuasion drew forth, and transfigured them into fine fables."

Her first article in the *Tribune* was an analysis of Emerson's essays, running two and one-half columns on the front page. Mr. Greeley gave her work a handsome play, but found it a problem to get her to turn it in on time. Most of her writing was done in his home. She disliked going to the office. Her room opened on the garden, and the shrubs and flowers continually distracted her attention.

For one so felicitous in conversation, she could be verbose and obscure on paper. Her articles often ran three or four columns long. She had rich material from which to draw among contemporary literary figures, and she wrote about them all with alternate praise and fury. She could be rude and brutal as well as charming. She cared nothing for the opinions or feelings of others and was dogmatic and exacting in her relations with people. Her judgments were often extreme. She liked to shy stones at the popular idol; to dig in the mud for an unseen jewel. She found Lowell exotic and despised Longfellow, setting him down as a commonplace jingler with the face of a "dandy Pindar." She refused even to review his poems until Mr. Greeley made an issue of it, and then she did it savagely and ungraciously. She was one of the first critics to recognize Robert Browning, giving him the leading place in contemporary British letters before his "Bells and Pomegranates" was finished. She did not really care for her newspaper work and on one occasion wrote in disgust: "What a vulgarity there seems in this writing for the multitudes! We have not yet made ourselves known to a single soul, and shall we address those still more unknown?"

Her headaches made her life wretched, and also had their effect on the Greeley household. Mr. Greeley shrewdly attributed her somnabulism and spectral illusions to the drinking of too much strong tea. He wrote of her:

> Though we were members of the same household, we scarcely met, save at breakfast, and my time and thoughts were absorbed in duties and cares which left me little leisure or inclination for the amenities of social intercourse. Fortune seemed to take delight in placing us two in relations of friendly antagonism, or rather to develop all possible contrasts in our ideas and social habits. She was naturally inclined to luxury and a good appearance before the world. My pride, if I had any, delighted in bare walls and rugged fare. She was addicted to strong tea and coffee, both of which I rejected and condemned, even in the most homeopathic dilutions; while, my general health being sound, and hers sadly impaired, I could not fail to find, in her dietetic habits, the causes of her almost habitual illness; and once, while we were barely acquainted, when she came to the breakfast table with a very severe headache, I was tempted to attribute it to her strong potations of the Chinese leaf the night before.
>
> She told me frankly that she declined being lectured on the food or beverage she saw fit to take; which was but reasonable in one who had arrived at her maturity of intellect and fixedness of habits. So the subject was henceforth tacitly avoided between us; but tho' words were suppressed, looks and involuntary gestures could not so well be; and an utter divergency of views on this and kindred themes created a perceptible distance between us.

Margaret Fuller was more generous in her estimate of Mr. Greeley, although her comments give little impression of their somewhat irascible relationship. With the exception of her mother, she rated him as the most disinterestedly generous person she had ever met. "He is, in his habits, a plebeian; in his heart a noble man," she said. "His abilities, in his own way, are great. He believes in mine to a surprising extent. We are true friends." She was devoted to his son, Pickie, who died later of cholera.

Miss Fuller's literary criticism was only one phase of her work for the *Tribune*. She did three general articles a week, and long before the day of the stunt writers, she visited Blackwell's Island and Sing Sing. But instead of writing personal stories exploiting herself, she turned out philosophical essays on the treatment of the prisoners. Her articles were choked with detail. They were editorial in tone and probably would seem out of place in the news columns today. But her point of view was advanced and her style was always

scholarly. She shocked the *Tribune* readers by writing sympa-
thetically of prostitutes. She believed in complete social and political
equality for women, at a time when such an attitude was revolutionary. She raised class issues and wrote on the poor man, the rich
man, politeness to the poor, the condition of the blind, and similar
subjects.

Mr. Greeley gave her a variety of assignments, but he did not
always get what he wanted, and on one occasion wrote of her:

> She could write only when in the vein, and this needed often
> to be waited for through several days while the occasion
> sometimes required an immediate utterance. . . . While I
> realized that her contributions evidenced rare intellectual
> wealth and force, I did not value them as I should have done
> had they been written more fluently and promptly. They often
> seemed to make their appearance "a day after the fair."

His annoyance probably would have been shared by any other
editor, since no paper can wait, even for the most brilliant composition. But Margaret Fuller was a personality. She could do what she
liked. And her literary criticism was a really distinguished contribution to his paper. In the summer of 1845 she went to Europe,
sending back travel correspondence and sketches of the men and
women she met abroad. Her best work was done on Goethe. She
visited England, Scotland, France and spent the winter in Rome,
where she met and married Giovanni, Marquis d'Ossoli, seven years
younger than herself. This plunged her into a new world, where
national feeling ran high. She and her husband took an active part
in the revolution of 1848. While he fought from the walls of Rome,
she nursed the wounded and dying. After the siege they went to
Florence, and from there to Leghorn to sail for America. It was an
unlucky journey. Angelo, their son, fell ill with smallpox. A terrific
storm caught them as they neared America. Their vessel, the *Elizabeth*, was wrecked off Fire Island in July, 1850. Margaret would
not leave her husband and son. The last recorded glimpse of her
showed her seated at the foot of the mast in her white nightdress,
her hair loose about her shoulders. The mast fell, carrying with it
the deck and all on board.

Three-quarters of a century later much of the literary criticism in
the leading papers of the country was being done by women, and
Irita Van Doren was directing the book review section of the paper
that employed Margaret Fuller. She joined the staff of the *Herald
Tribune* in 1924 to work with Stuart Sherman. She had been with
the *Nation*, she knew writers, critics and publishers, and had technical training which proved useful when she was assigned to work
out the format for the magazine. In a decade she has established

"Books" as a discriminating and ably edited medium of review. The guiding principle of her direction is her careful choice of critics. She gets the specialist whenever possible. Often the biggest literary names flash from her pages in judgment on their colleagues, with provocative results. When Stuart Sherman's scholarly essays disappeared from the book section with his death, Mrs. Van Doren got visiting critics to fill her front page. The result was a series of essays, of a type rarely seen in a newspaper setting, by such writers as Rebecca West, Virginia Woolf, Lytton Strachey, Hugh Walpole, James Branch Cabell, H. M. Tomlinson and others.

Mrs. Van Doren is a liberal in her outlook and is enthusiastic about the new writer of promise. There is nothing stuffy about the section she edits. The current trends are played hard and she believes in a tie-up between book reviewing and the news whenever possible. She has a theory that the first paragraph of a review should be informative, much like the news lead of a story for the front page, and wherever possible should provoke the reader's interest at once. She tries to strike the medium between the reportorial type of review and pure criticism. "Books" has forged steadily ahead in prestige, advertising and size under her handling. One-third of the books published get reviewed and an average of three hundred contributors submit their critical verdicts to her in a year. Periodically Mrs. Van Doren publishes readers' lists of books as a guide to the purchaser.

Although she has one of the top executive newspaper posts for women in the country, she is a retiring figure in her own office. Buried among books, her head a mass of dark curls, she functions quietly, without fuss or debate. Much of her time is taken up with executive detail, but she is always alert to the literary possibilities of her job. The distribution of the books as they pour in is no small task. They come in scores and hundreds. It takes judgment and knowledge to direct the incoming tide into sound channels and keep a weather eye for fresh talent. Women reviewers figure heavily in Mrs. Van Doren's columns. as they do in all the literary supplements. This is a branch of newspaper work from which women have never been barred and they flourish in it today. Nearly fifty per cent of the literary criticism in the New York newspapers is done by women. They practically monopolize the fiction field.

Mrs. Van Doren, who is capably assisted by Belle Rosenbaum, runs separate departments for special interests. The detective story fan gets guidance from Will Cuppy. Children's books are admirably handled by May Lamberton Becker. The bibliophiles have their own corner. The foreign field is covered. Mrs. Van Doren frequently runs original verse. Her best-seller list is one of the soundest of its kind. But the feature most eagerly looked for every Sunday by a large group of readers is "Turns with a Bookworm," by Mrs. Isabel M. Paterson, the pet and terror of the literary tea parties. Her initials suit her. There is something impish about her face, moon-pale, with dark eyes that glitter, black hair that crackles and an elfin twist to her delicate mouth.

Those who like her swear by her as a rare jewel; those who don't, think her a wasp. Her literary standards are high. She mentions only the books that meet them and usually ignores what she dislikes. She is at her best in the full-length review, at her most frivolous in her turns with a bookworm. Her styles are interchangeable but they always reflect an original turn of thought. Her word carries weight. Publishers kowtow to her; authors look at her wistfully, hoping for the best but fearing the worst. Visiting writers from abroad are always primed before the first handshake at a literary tea: "Now, her name is Isabel Paterson . . ."

Most of them know it by now. Some have purred under her velvet touch; others have felt her claws. Sooner or later, they all come face to face with her over the teacups. Occasionally she is interested; more often she ignores them, but her sudden disappearance to a corner to meditate or munch a sandwich is not an inevitable sign of her disapproval. She is simply a spontaneous child of nature who believes in doing as she likes. For Mrs. Paterson always has this elusive quality. Her attention wanders as one speaks to her; her eyes glow with images that have nothing to do with what is being said. She does not always answer. She may amble off, spring a devastating wisecrack, or turn sweet, gentle and kind in her unpredictable way.

Her fellow workers like her but never wholly understand her. Literary affectations bore her. She still prefers capital letters where they have always been, adequate punctuation and sound syntax. She thinks that sentences should parse. Dialect makes her weary. Unlike most of her masculine colleagues, she is not a pushover for the proletarian novel, unless it is superbly written. A trick style never makes any impression on her. Her enthusiasms are few and intense. She helped to start Robert Nathan on his way by praising *One More Spring* until the public had to listen, for this was a book in which she believed. She will keep pushing a book years after publication if she likes it enough and feels that it has not received the attention it deserves. But her taste is fastidious. She prefers a good piece of writing to raw meat, which means that many of the contemporary books leave her cold. She doesn't succumb to the popular crazes, although she admits merit when she sees it.

Mrs. Paterson has read with fury ever since she was an adolescent. She devours a book, hunched over it, the print jammed close to her eyes, scanning pages greedily. She likes good fiction and is in top form when reviewing memoirs. Ellen Glasgow is one of her literary idols. The best of the English women novelists get suave treatment at her hands. She likes Sheila Kaye-Smith and E. M. Delafield, and enjoys a good story as well as a smooth piece of writing. But she laps up history, economics, legend, romance and realism with avid interest. She rarely forgets what she reads, which makes her a formidable antagonist in debate. In spite of her erratic manifestations she is a thorough and scholarly workman, and her full-length reviews are usually models of mature judgment and choice diction. Her wit can be two-edged.

Mrs. Paterson lives at Stamford, Connecticut, in a house of her own design. It is only within recent years that she has settled in the country. Before then she made her home in Hell's Kitchen in New York, over a political club, and she dearly loved the noise. But the suburban life has beguiled her. She has acres of land and her leisure is now given over to contemplation of her trees. Her garden is a major interest in her life. She gets up at dawn to pull up poison ivy and see what the little plants are doing. She sets her friends to work on the weeds when they visit her. A boy helps her with the garden. Brainless, her cat, is always underfoot. Her books are scattered everywhere. She stops in the middle of anything to go on with her reading. She gets through hundreds of books in a year. She would read them even if she were not a critic.

Mrs. Paterson is shortsighted and types with her face close to the keys of her machine. Sometimes people make the mistake of thinking she is snubbing them, when the trouble is that she merely does not see them. She never misses a literary tea, if it can be helped—and the publishers arrange their dates so as not to conflict with one another. She likes simple food, prefers her cigarettes hand-rolled and her tea to be Chinese. She works at home in a kimono, for she cannot be bothered with clothes. In town she used to wear quaint bonnets and frocks, but lately has grown rather modish and has abandoned the scarlet, green and yellow stockings with which she used to startle the city room of the *Herald Tribune*. She can laugh at herself as well as at other people.

Mrs. Paterson spent her early days on farms here and there in the Canadian and American West. She still likes the West and goes rushing out when she gets the chance. She was born on Manitoulin Island, Lake Huron, and traveled to Alberta with her family by prairie schooner when she was a child. For the next few years she lived on a lonely cattle ranch, attended a log cabin school and learned what cold winters were. At the age of seventeen she set out to earn a living. She was a waitress first, then a bookkeeper for the

Canadian Pacific Railroad in Calgary. By chance she landed in the business office of a newspaper in Spokane, Washington, and soon got the idea that it was better to write than to add up figures. Her first sight of a library sent her wild. She became a glutton for books. She began to write them. The first dealt with the Canadian West, the next with medieval Spain. Then she went modern with *Never Ask the End* and *The Golden Vanity*. The critic became a successful author. Mrs. Paterson does her own fiction with boundless industry—polishing, destroying, discarding, slaving until all hours of the night. It took her three years to finish *Never Ask the End*, which was a success. Her earlier books had passed almost unnoticed.

Mrs. Paterson's name first appeared in the *Herald Tribune* in 1922, during Burton Rascoe's time. Her wit and sparkle were apparent almost at once. Her following grew. As a critic she is known as a holy terror, not without cause, for she flays the humbug and punctures the egotist. In herself she is a dark sprite, sometimes a little eerie.

As regular in their attendance at all the literary teas as Mrs. Paterson are Carolyn Marx of the *World-Telegram*, and May Cameron of the *Post*. Both girls do book notes for their papers, are substitute critics during vacation time, and assist the literary editors. Miss Marx was Harry Hansen's secretary on the *World*. She now writes an entertaining column which is closely followed by the book trade, and does a daily vignette of an author. Instead of depending wholly on publishers' publicity, she digs up exclusive items of news interest. Book shops, the small magazine, and the formation of any literary group get special attention in her column. Until recently Natalie Hankemeyer functioned in the same capacity for James C. Grey, literary editor of the *Sun*.

When Fanny Butcher says a book is good the Middle West reads it. She is one of the most powerful critics in the country, with her widely read column in the Chicago *Tribune*. She is both critic and book editor, and has functioned in several other capacities on the paper. She was born in Kansas, in a house on a hillside, overlooking a village. When she was nearly six years old her father moved to Chicago to attend the Art Institute, and they lived the erratic life of an artist's family. Illness impaired the family fortunes, but Miss Butcher went to grammar school, preparatory school and completed her education at Lewis Institute and the University of Chicago. Then she was appointed principal of a high school in Rolling Prairie, Indiana. For five months she battled with a mob of rural young that no teacher had been able to quell. She was glad to bid them good-by and seek other fields. The Little Theater had just been launched in

Chicago. Miss Butcher did publicity for it and performed all the secretarial functions for $10 a week, which she thought was too much, for the theater was poor.

By a roundabout way she landed on the Chicago *Tribune*. She had longed to be literary editor of a magazine now defunct. But the editor gave her features to do instead. Her name was signed to them but the pay envelope always seemed to get lost. However, this appearance in print enabled her to join the Women's Press Association. Eleanor Mary O'Donnell, then woman's editor of the *Tribune*, was president at the time, and she gave her a chance on the paper.

Miss Butcher ran a department called "How to Earn Money at Home." She did a little of everything—news, beauty, clubs, society, fashions and even an occasional murder. Then she was sent across the country on the Hughes train. This proved to be quite an experience, for she was cooped up in a compartment with a dipsomaniac. She was so young and innocent that she believed her traveling companion when she said she was taking medicine. The compartment reeked of whiskey and oranges, but the tippler was a lady from the old South and Miss Butcher did not suspect that she was just a Kentucky belle on the loose. Everyone else on the train knew it, however. The Pullman conductor fixed the lock on the door so that she could not shut Miss Butcher in. The carouser was thrown off after a day or two. In the meantime Miss Butcher had obligingly done all her work for her, as well as her own, because her companion had gray hair and seemed like a sick woman.

Finally Miss Butcher had a chance to work with books, which was what she had wanted to do from the beginning. She conducted the "Tabloid Book Review"—a Sunday column about books and authors. Soon she started her own book shop, which was a success. Not a day passed without a celebrity coming in. It got to be a friendly gathering place. She enjoyed her shop, and her acquaintance among authors widened. In 1922 she was appointed literary editor of her paper. This entailed added responsibilities. Ultimately the burden of work became too heavy, with all the reading that had to be done, so she sold her shop.

Miss Butcher is a level-headed critic who bears a charmed name in the book trade. She likes dogs and the country and she collects occasional modern first editions. She thinks that reading books for a living is one of the choicest jobs available to women.

For forty years Amy Leslie functioned as dramatic critic of the Chicago *Daily News*. She was the friend of scores of the stage celebrities of her day. Now she is more than seventy years old, and her memory is rich with echoes of an adventurous past. She was a comedienne and a light opera singer before she turned her critical attention to other artists. She appeared on Broadway in the early days of Gilbert and Sullivan and was the Princess in *The Mascot* during the flourishing days of the Wilbur Opera Company.

While she was on the stage she married Harry Brown, comedian and stage director. From him she learned much about the technical side of the theater. They had one son who died, and after that they drifted apart. Later she married Frank Buck, but that did not last either. When Miss Leslie found that her voice was impaired she thought of writing. At first she did hack work, then she began to concentrate on the theater. It seemed the natural thing for her to turn to, since it was one subject on which she was thoroughly informed. Her father had been a newspaper man and had founded various newspapers. Eugene Field, who was on the Chicago *Daily News* at the time, noticed her individual touch and took her on the staff, where she remained until 1930. In the intervening years Miss Leslie became one of the best known critics in the country. In her heyday she was a beauty and had great vitality and charm. She knew everyone in the theater and her approval was eagerly sought.

There have been few good women dramatic critics. Here and there they have functioned intermittently but have not built up the sustained reputation of a Percy Hammond or a Burns Mantle. Ada Patterson was excellent in this field as well as in general news. Wilella Waldorf does good work for the New York *Post* and Carol Frink is well known in Chicago for her dramatic and motion picture criticism. Miss Frink's newspaper career started in 1918 on the *Herald Examiner*. She made $12 a week for three months as a cub; then her salary jumped to $75 when she launched a column called "The Girl Reporter," for Walter Howey. It was during this period that her romance with Charles MacArthur bloomed beside the water cooler in the city room, before Helen Hayes entered his life.

One of the best of the women critics was Leone Cass Baer (now Mrs. H. W. Hicks), who was dramatic critic of the *Oregonian* in Portland. Her name was legendary on the coast. She wrote with finesse and was discriminating in her taste. All her copy was done in longhand, because of an accident to one of her arms. She would turn out a polished review like lightning while a copy boy stood at her desk, seizing it in quick takes as an edition went to press. She did interviewing as well as dramatic criticism and was widely known in the theatrical world. Some years ago she moved with her husband to Hollywood. She is now living in Portland again.

Although few women do dramatic criticism, the motion picture field is virtually their monopoly. All over the country feminine by-lines go with cinema reviews. It has opened up a new crop of jobs. Many of the girls who are doing it have had no general newspaper experience. The three pioneers were Mae Tinee, Louella Parsons and Harriette Underhill. Today Miss Parsons is the most widely known motion picture critic in the country—the czarina of Hollywood in actual fact. Producers and stars bow beneath her baton. Her word is law. She is consulted about many of the important moves made in the directorial field. She has swung a number of stars on their way. Her criticism is telling. She is often ahead with the news, for the notes in her column are not the usual canned publicity. She gets most of them at first hand. Her friends call her up and tip her off to their marriages and divorces. She goes to all the parties. Her ear is constantly to the ground. She is feared or liked, as the case may be.

Miss Parsons has rolled up her dictatorship under the Hearst auspices. She is now the motion picture expert on the air, which carries her voice still farther. Hers is one of the phenomenal success stories of Park Row. Her newspaper life began in Dixon, Illinois, at the age of sixteen, when she came home from college and covered everything from murders to social notes. She went around with a huge yellow notebook picking up items. When she was married a few years later she gave up her newspaper salary of $5 a week to become a wife.

But she had learned a lot about the craft in a short space of time. She had her first scoop when a young college boy walked into a saloon and shot a bartender who had refused to serve him with liquor because he was a minor. Before he was sent to Joliet for fifteen years he found time to get married. Miss Parsons' story of this strong-minded youth was carried in a Chicago paper. In 1915 she was assigned to an angle of the Eastland disaster, when a boat carrying 2,500 excursionists sank and 981 persons lost their lives. Her job was to interview some of the families and her story made the front page.

For a time she did straight news and interviewed the celebrities who passed through the city, but soon she concentrated exclusively on motion pictures. There was no thought of taking the subject seriously at the time. Her managing editor scoffed at the idea and wanted her column buried beside the obituaries. But Miss Parsons was sure she was on the right track, and later developments justified her confidence. When Mr. Hearst bought the Chicago *Herald* and combined it with the *Examiner*, the new management did not feel that there was enough interest in the films to make Miss Parsons' services necessary, so she was dropped. When she returned to the Hearst organization, it was at a salary that would have astounded her in those early days.

She started East with a baby under one arm and $200 in cash, her sole possessions. In New York she went to work for W. E. Lewis on the *Morning Telegraph*. She stayed there for five years, working with Theodora Bean and turning out reams of copy on the silent films. During its more progressive days the paper had thirty-two pages of motion picture news and advertising on Sundays. Miss Parsons slaved from eight o'clock in the morning until midnight, and wrote many editorials, alternately scolding and praising the industry. She watched it go through its puling stages and emerge a powerful monster. Then Mr. Hearst, attracted by something she wrote, made her an offer doubling her *Telegraph* salary. She signed the contract and has worked in his organization for fourteen years. At first she turned out her column in New York. Then she settled in Hollywood, and waxed powerful.

Miss Parsons has had more than her share of cinema scoops. She knows all the stars and is on intimate terms with many of them. They seek her advice about everything from contracts to husbands. She was first on the street with the story of Pola Negri's marriage to Prince Serge Mdivani. She had the first draft of Valentino's will and beat the field on the Mary Pickford-Douglas Fairbanks divorce. Her friends call her Love's Undertaker, so prompt is she when the inevitable at Hollywood comes to pass.

Miss Parsons is married to Dr. Harry W. Martin, chairman of the State Athletic Commission of California and head of the Civil Service Commission in Los Angeles. Harriet, the baby daughter she brought with her to New York two decades ago, when the films were still a matter of jest, is now busy writing for the screen and is standing on her own feet.

Mae Tinee, whose sprightly reviews have been appearing in the Chicago *Tribune* since pictures were in the kindergarten stage, is the daughter of a Denver evangelist. She is a free and independent critic who has never taken a cup of tea with a star. She looks at them on the screen but refuses to go to their parties. She dodges the private showing and prefers to see a new film with the regular audience. She makes her own rules and does not care too much what anyone thinks about them. Her reviews are straightforward, exclamatory, often sharp. They take the average point of view, and are never academic.

Miss Tinee was born in Longmont, Colorado, and spent her childhood in Colorado Springs and Denver. She started as a cub reporter on the Denver *Republican* at the age of seventeen. After a few months of this, she went over to the Denver *Times*, married an artist on the paper and soon afterwards moved to Chicago. Her marriage went on the rocks. So did her finances. She joined the staff of the Chicago *Tribune* a year or two later. At first she wrote Sunday specials, then did theatrical reviews and edited a page called "Right off the Reel."

She was not enthusiastic when she was assigned to do motion picture criticism. But her editor had seen ahead. "You must become an expert," he said. So she was sent to New York, which at that time was the center of the film industry. She visited studios, talked to stars and studied conditions. Then she went to California and looked over the field there. Every day she grew more interested in the subject. Today she cannot imagine anything she would rather do than see another picture, although she has watched thousands run off on the silver screen. In private life she is Mrs. David C. Kurner, the mother of a grown-up daughter who turned to nursing as a career. Miss Tinee likes to go horseback riding in the mountains, to read, to embroider, to walk, and even to make hook rugs.

A brilliant motion picture critic and gallant character was Harriette Underhill, who died in 1928, a few hours after her last interview had been sent by messenger to the New York *Herald Tribune*. She had had tuberculosis for years. In 1920 she was sent to the Adirondacks to rest, but could not bear the snowy wastes, far from Broadway. So back she came, knowing that she was doomed. For Miss Underhill was a child of Broadway. She hated being away from it for a day. To her it was truly the street of adventure. Until a month before her death she would saunter into the city room of the *Herald Tribune*, her hair a flaming orange, a large black picture hat framing features that still had traces of her early beauty, her manner gay and jesting. She was a matinée idol worshiper. All the stars knew her and appreciated her piquant quality, for she was a just and discerning critic. Her reviews were done in an intimate vein, using the editorial we. Often her Sunday interviews told more of Harriette than the star, but they were entertaining, and her judgment was highly regarded in the industry. She insisted on serious film criticism at a time when everyone thought the idea absurd.

Miss Underhill had sporting blood in her veins. Her father, Lorenzo Underhill, bred horses near Passaic, New Jersey. At sixteen, while she was still living at home, she made the first of several marriages, but it did not last. Then she went on the stage. She appeared in a company with the original Floradora sextet, a circumstance which surrounded her with the legend that she was one of the sextet. She toured the United States and Mexico with a Shakespearean company and in Mexico City she met and married an Englishman.

After his death she returned to the United States. At this time she was a rare beauty, with fine features and a graceful carriage. She went to all the races with her father, who wrote for the *Tribune* and the *Morning Telegraph*, and edited the *New York Sportsman*. Harriette used to go to the newspaper offices with him and when he died she took over his work and became permanently attached to the *Tribune*. This was in 1908, so that she was one of the first women sports writers as well as film critics. She did horses and dog shows. No one knew the points of a horse any better than Miss Underhill. Even after she gave up sports writing, she continued to do the Horse Show every year for her paper, almost up to the time of her death. She had many friends in the theater and was conscious of the dawning interest in the screen at its earliest stage. She begged to be allowed to try her hand at criticism and her work soon became a regular feature of the paper.

In 1919 she was knocked down by a car and was seriously crippled. Thereafter she wrote with difficulty. Every line was done in longhand with a stiff arm, but she turned out thousands of words every week for the Sunday and daily paper. She haunted Broadway at all hours of the day and night. Efforts to make her rest were futile. She wanted to die in harness. After writing for years about Hollywood she finally went West to the cinema capital. She was fêted extravagantly. She knew all the stars and was on friendly terms with many of them. They gave elaborate parties for her and treated her like a visiting queen. But Miss Underhill hated Hollywood. She abhorred the real estate signs, the hot dog stands, the open landscape. She rushed back thankfully to Broadway, where the lights twinkled and no one ever went to bed. She preferred the motion picture industry on the screen.

Miss Underhill wrote for the film magazines and turned out a number of scenarios. Producers considered her an authority and frequently consulted her on technical matters. She was cynical to the core, scorned sentiment, had a sophisticated wit, was generous and courageous. She was one of the rare personalities who appear in newspaper offices from time to time.

Kate Cameron, who runs the highly rated motion picture criticism of the New York *Daily News* by the star system, is a winner in all box office contests for her guesses are so often right. When she gives a picture four-star rating, the public takes heed, but she is careful with her stars—a criterion which her sister, Mary King, initiated. She sees from six to ten pictures a week and never tires of the round. She even goes on her days off to see films that she has not reviewed. Miss Cameron has always shared her sister's interest in motion pictures. For a time she was with Essanay. Then she was secretary to Henry Kitchell Webster. Her next step was to read manuscripts and do motion picture criticism for *Liberty*. When the magazine was sold in 1932, she was transferred to the *News* as assistant in the same department. Mabel McElliott and Mildred Spain, wife of Edward Doherty, another newspaper star, had preceded her. Within a year and a half she had full charge. Although known to the public as Kate Cameron, in private life she is Loretta King.

When the *News* was launched in 1919 Captain Patterson asked Miss McElliott to run the drama and screen news, which she did for more than three years. Miss McElliott had worked her way into the Sunday department of the Chicago *Tribune* in 1917, after following Mary King's advice to take a business course and try for a secretarial post as the best entering wedge for newspaper work.

Soon Miss King sent for her to take the place in the Sunday department of a secretary who had been promoted. For the next two years she got a thorough schooling in the practical aspects of newspaper work, while her sister, Martha, read copy on the editorial floor. During the summer of 1918 she substituted for Mae Tinee when she was on vacation. She was twenty-one at the time and the life of a motion picture critic seemed to her to be one long dream of ease and excitement. Moving East to New York she had a chance to sample it to the full. She ran a daily calendar of plays for the *News*, summing up in a sentence the faults or merits of a production. And she reviewed as many pictures as she could. In the summer of 1924 she joined the staff of *Liberty* as a reader. From then until June, 1931, she read more than fifteen thousand manuscripts. Many of them were bad, but occasionally she experienced the thrill of finding a new writer. She sold her first newspaper serial in the spring of 1931 and now does an average of two a year for NEA. Occasionally she sells a short story to the magazines. Her husband is Richard Clarke, of the *Daily News*.

Bland Johaneson, who looks after the screen interests of the *Daily Mirror*, cannot recall the time when she did not want to be a newspaper reporter. While the other little girls of Reading, Pennsylvania, haunted the stage door to watch the stock company actresses emerge, she stuck close to the family entrance of Johnny Garrett's saloon, waiting for the newspaper men to come out. She made herself such a pest that at last she was taken on the staff of the Reading *Telegram and News-Times* at $7 a week. The city editor manifested his disapproval of girls in the local room by assigning her to the tenderloin, in the naïve belief that she would mention her assignments at home and thus be withdrawn from a business suitable only for men.

She was sixteen when she came to New York, with a new hair ribbon and complete self-confidence. She enrolled at New York University, did night assignments for the Brooklyn *Times* and began to sell some of her copy. Then she got on the staff of the *Telegraph* and Miss Parsons borrowed her from the city room to review a picture starring Hope Hampton. This threw her into touch with the show business and she began to write for the fan magazines. Sime Silverman, of *Variety*, was engaged at the time in one of his battles with the big-time vaudeville trust. Bland's caustic reviews of vaudeville in one of the magazines attracted his attention. He gave her a place among his Variety Mugs, and in this way she learned some more about the show business. Walter Winchell recommended her to Victor Watson and she became motion picture critic of the *Mirror*—a job which she likes and does well. But she has other interests, too. She has written extensively on gastronomic entertainment and pursues cooking as a hobby.

Regina Crewe, a Viennese by birth, is motion picture editor of the New York *American*. She took special courses at Cornell and began her career as secretary to Richard Bennett. She has publicized and managed a number of stage and screen stars. She was motion picture editor of the *Morning Telegraph* and has been with the *Mirror*, International News and King Features.

Four other girls who have had wide experience in this field and whose criticism ranks high are Marguerite Tazelaar, of the *Herald Tribune*, Eileen Creelman of the *Sun*, Rose Pelswick of the *Journal*, and Irene Thirer of the *Post*. Miss Creelman did city staff work before switching her interests to the films. She is the sister of James Creelman, the cinema director.

Chapter XXXI

IN BLACK AND WHITE

IN 1907 A SHY GIRL WITH SKETCHING MATERIALS UNDER HER ARM walked timidly into the court room where Harry K. Thaw was on trial for his life. Her eyes were extravagantly blue; her blonde hair was fluffed in a halo around her face. She knew that she was supposed to sit in the press row, but beyond that her surroundings were a mystery to her. She had no idea where the jury box was. She did not know lawyers from reporters. But Dorothy Dix shepherded her about and showed her the ropes. She soon set to work on Evelyn Nesbit Thaw and turned out stunning sketches for the *Journal*.

This was Nell Brinkley, the creator of the Fluffy Ruffles girl, the artist whose pictures spread romance and glamour over the country like spun sugar. Her lovely girls, her dimpled babies, her fields of flowers, her floating bubbles, her young Adonis, became familiar wherever the Hearst syndicate features appeared. She took the town by storm. The Nell Brinkley girl succeeded the Gibson girl. She started an era of curls, dimples and cuteness. There were Nell Brinkley hats, blouses and perfumes. Mae Murray launched the Nell Brinkley girl in a *Follies* scene, with the chorus in white satin, their costumes outlined in black. The same idea was repeated in a Parisian revue. This was stimulating for the young artist from Denver.

The Nell Brinkley girl goes on, in spite of changing fashions. Today her creator lives in a quiet home behind a high garden hedge in New Rochelle with her twelve-year-old son, her husband, Bruce McRae, and her mother, Mrs. May French Brinkley. Marigolds grow at her front door. Her studio is lined with the Brinkley drawings assembled over the years. Her hair is blonde and fluffy and she bears a resemblance to the original Brinkley girl. She works night and day on the endless feathery detail of her sketches. The romantic fairy-tale touch of sleeping princesses and airy castles is ever present. Her technique is peculiarly her own. No one has been able to copy it successfully, although many have tried. It blossomed by itself. Her only training was a year in a Denver art school, which she at-

tended in the evenings after working during the day for the Denver
Post. Arthur Brisbane supplies the ideas for most of her drawings.
If he is in New York he gets her on the telephone when a new idea
strikes him. If he happens to be traveling he jots down suggestions
in blue pencil and sends them on to her.

The Nell Brinkley girl has changed slightly with the years. The
discerning eye can see that she has fewer ruffles now. Her curves
are less marked. Her lines have been simplified to accord more with
the new feminine ideal. But she is still the idealized creature of
thistledown and fluff. Twelve years ago the baby cupid shooting
darts over the idyllic fields turned into a more lifelike little boy.
This marked the birth of Miss Brinkley's own son, Bruce Robert
McRae. Up to that time mothers took her to task occasionally on
anatomical grounds.

"It's quite obvious that you don't know anything about babies,"
one of them wrote. "You put the wrinkles in the wrong places."

But from that time on Miss Brinkley drew from life. Every stage
of her son's development was reproduced in her pictures. The boy
grew older and older. Her favorite drawing is one that she has never
published. It is of herself and her son when he was two months old.
The young man who recurs in her sketches is modeled after her
husband, the son of Bruce McRae, the actor.

Miss Brinkley drew almost from infancy. She used to scribble over
her mother's cook book and she filled the backs of her schoolmates'
books with pictures. She sold her first drawing at thirteen. Three
years later she tucked a roll of her sketches under her arm and
walked into the office of the Denver *Post*, looking for a job. Alfred
Patek, who had worked on the *Journal* in New York before joining
the *Post* staff, turned over her sketches, spotted her unmistakable
talent and hired her. She illustrated editorials. She did portraits of
men and women in the news. She had not yet worked out her idealized technique but she was a great admirer of Howard Pyle and
followed his work closely.

These were the gaudy days on the *Post* when Bonfils and Tammen
raged about and Josiah M. Ward snapped his long scissors at quak-
ing reporters. Josiah wore plaid suspenders, his collar was always
wide open, a bottle of whisky was invariably at his elbow and he
made the staff jump like Mexican beans. Charlie Bonfils, Winifred
Black's husband, sat in the city room and sang songs by the hour.
Everything was very jolly, and more than a little mad.

S. S. Chamberlain drew Mr. Hearst's attention to Miss Brinkley's
work, which even at the beginning was highly individualized. She
was offered a job in New York. She traveled East, full of excitement,
and found her way to the old Hearst offices, where no one seemed

to expect her. She wandered about until at last Morrill Goddard, editor of the *Sunday American*, showed some interest in her work.

"I don't know who you are or why you're here, but you can work for me if you want to," he said, after looking at her sample sketches.

In three weeks' time Mr. Brisbane became aware of her presence.

"Oh, here you are," he said. "I've been searching everywhere for you."

The Thaw trial was about to begin. Miss Brinkley was assigned to it. From then on her success was assured. Her sketches from life were faintly idealized but also remarkably true. She went out on all the big news stories of the day. She did colored supplements for the *Sunday American*—the Summer Girl series, showing the swimming girl plowing through the waves with a bright red bandanna and extravagant eyelashes; the Girl in a Motor Boat, her long hair curling in the breeze, a young man with arresting profile at the wheel.

Women were getting realistic. They were after the vote. But the magazines were still glorifying the purely feminine type. A clever group of illustrators were turning out the glamour girls of the pre-war period. The Brinkley girl evolved into a definite type. Her vogue grew steadily. Business girls went curly-headed. Cuties began to swarm around the town.

The *Journal* gave Miss Brinkley's work a heavy play. Mr. Brisbane picked her news assignments carefully. He studied the types in each murder case, and if they seemed like Brinkley material he sent her out, usually with Dorothy Dix. Some of her finest work was done on the Marion Lambert case—the curious story of the youth accused in 1915 of feeding prussic acid to an eighteen-year-old girl in the woods of Waukegan. The boy, Will Orpet, was the son of the superintendent of Cyrus McCormick's Lake Forest estate. The girl was the daughter of the gardener on a neighboring estate. The McCormick lawyers defended Orpet. The townspeople brought bunches of lilac to court for him every day. Local sentiment was on his side. He was as cool as an effigy throughout the trial. His face was one of singular delicacy. Miss Brinkley caught its cameo-like repose from a dozen different angles. The subject suited her. The entire story had a Thomas Hardy touch. She dug up strange old quotations on murder to go with her sketches. The result was quite effective.

"This isn't your stuff," said Mr. Brisbane, when the Hall-Mills trial came along. The faces were heavy and saturnine. But she was in the press row with David Belasco, Maurine Watkins, Will Durant and the other headliners who watched the Snyder-Gray court drama —a more lurid show than Mr. Belasco ever staged. She did glorified drawings of Ruth Snyder. the ice-faced blonde. She found Peaches

Browning heavy and adenoidal, and Bruno R. Hauptmann a singularly engrossing study from the artist's point of view. Mr. Brisbane sent her to the Faber-Millen murder trial in Massachusetts. He saw in Norma Millen's young and still unmarred face good material for the Brinkley touch. But she had to use heavy crayons to get the sinister effect of Norma's gangster husband. She is not at her best when dealing with the gross or criminal face.

In her early days in the Hearst offices Miss Brinkley worked with Tad, Hype Igoe and Henry Davenport. For fifteen years she went to the office every day, going out on news stories and doing her three or four syndicate sketches a week in addition. She has always been one of the big earners in the syndicate field. For five years she did two dramatic criticisms a week as well as her other work. A *Follies* opening was never complete without a Nell Brinkley sketch next day, and Flo Ziegfeld was enthusiastic about her work. She added the halo to his already glorified girls. Billie Burke, a perfect Brinkley subject, is still her friend. Mary Pickford is another star whose curls and childlike quality supply the ideal material for her pen.

When Mrs. James Brown Potter, Fifi Stillman's mother, turned to vaudeville, Miss Brinkley went with Mary MacLane of *I, Mary MacLane* fame to interview and sketch her. Having written one of the early confession books, Miss MacLane was acutely conscious of her own notoriety at the moment and tossed a somewhat careless remark at the dazzling Mrs. Potter.

"Why, I thought you were beautiful and you aren't at all," she said, staring at the actress's red hair and large brown eyes.

Mrs. Potter leaped to her feet in fury. "If you don't get right out of here, there won't be any story," she stormed.

Miss Brinkley, who has a soft persuasive manner, calmed her down, and she and the press agent together got the story and drawing. Miss MacLane did not stay long on the *Journal*. From time to time Mr. Brisbane has drawn in celebrities and sent them out as working press. This sometimes leads to complications. They lack the reporter's knack of obliterating his own personality in order to bring out his subject.

Miss Brinkley has always done the Horse Show and anniversaries of all kinds. St. Valentine's Day was made to order for her style. Once, while she was in Canada on vacation, she got a message asking for a valentine sketch for the following day. She did it on the train traveling south. She sat up in her berth, propped her suitcase over her knees and drew the first rough outlines. But the train swayed so much that she could not go on until, by chance, it developed a hot box and stood for three hours among the snow-covered Canadian pines. Then she was able to finish her sketch down to the last tiny squiggle.

She went with Mr. Brisbane to the Bull Moose convention and did most of her work on the spot or in taxicabs that crawled through parades. Now and again she propped her paper on a policeman's broad back and swung her arm expertly. She has had to ransack the drug stores of country towns to get materials for her work when a hurry call has caught her on vacation. She has done her girls on counter perfume ads and on scraps of wrapping paper. In recent years most of her work has been turned out at home. Like most creative workers, she is usually in quest of ideas. Sometimes she sits and looks at her paper for hours, trying to conjure up a fresh theme. Early in her career Mr. Brisbane said to her, "You can *make* your brain work." She found that he was right.

The biggest response in letters always seems to come from the sketch expressing the most platitudinous sentiment. So she concentrates on homely everyday things. On one occasion she and Mr. Brisbane worked out a picture called "The Power of Prayer." It was the somewhat hackneyed idea of a child praying, but a flood of letters showed that it had reached the spot in many quarters. Miss Brinkley's mail is filled with the longings of plain girls for enchanting profiles. They used to sigh for curly hair and wistful eyelashes; but permanent waves and other beauty devices have changed their wish complexes. Now she is often asked: "How can one be romantic if one has to wear glasses?" Miss Brinkley's work is essentially romantic and has stirred the yearnings of countless girls at country crossroads whose own lives have been drab, ugly or uneventful. She has been a frivolous antidote to crime, politics, and the realism of the news column. Her own favorite published sketch is called "Spring." She did it long ago—a field of narcissi, a small nude figure lying on his back, a rabbit nibbling at grass. In short, a typical Brinkley effect.

Horace Greeley advised the young man to go West, but the newspaper girls have always insisted on moving East. Fay King is another graduate of the Denver *Post* who sought and found her fortune in New York. She worked in Denver during the dizzy days when Tammen and Bonfils were painting the town red. She got to know prize fighters, gamblers, celebrities and all the town characters. She rode as the queen of a float in a Denver carnival and was in bed for days afterwards, so rickety was the queen's throne. She had to sit like a statue and could not even wave to the boys in the *Post* windows.

Miss King is a remarkable newspaper woman with a wide acquaintance among persons of opposite interests. Like Miss Brinkley, she works under the Hearst auspices and her strip now runs in the

Mirror. In the corner there is usually a tiny figure with large shoes and bangs. This is her mascot and a burlesque of herself. None of her sketches would be complete without it. Miss King is small and animated. Her hair is dark and she has a straight heavy fringe. She is humorous, alert, kind and quick-witted. She reads newspapers from everywhere and believes whole-heartedly in the craft to which she belongs.

She was born in Seattle and had a roving childhood. Her family moved from place to place. Fay was delicate. Her mother had a talent for drawing and showed her how to make use of a lead pencil and a five-cent writing tablet. She drew anything from animals to bridges. She lived in a small world of her own, dreaming and sketching, and she hated school. During vacation she did cartoons for the theater and designs for postcards. She was not yet serious about her work. While she was sketching for a small weekly paper a colleague suggested that she should write text to go with her drawings, and so the idea of her present strip came into being.

She did a sketch of Battling Nelson at Hot Springs, Arkansas, that caught the pugilist's fancy. A romance later developed between them but their marriage did not last. When Nelson showed the sketch to Bonfils he sent for Miss King at once. She wrote telling him what she would look like when she arrived in Denver. She drew a sketch of herself with a bundle of papers under her arm. On the train Miss King told her fellow passengers that she was on her way to make her fortune. She said that Mr. Bonfils would be meeting her at the station. They were all sympathetic but slightly incredulous. However, when she got to Cheyenne she found that her letter and her sketch had been published in the *Post.* And when she got to Denver Mr. Bonfils actually was at the station to meet her.

For the first week or two she sat about in the local room, immensely impressed by the odd doings she saw in progress, but quite on the outskirts herself. No one gave her any work to do. She was disconsolate. So she went to Mr. Bonfils and asked him what was wrong.

"Honey," he said, "don't you know that the *Titanic* sank the other day and that we can't think about you now?"

Miss King had been so lost that she had not noticed the pounding march of history. She was never to ignore a big news story again. Soon she had plenty to do. Her first assignment was a baking strike. Josiah put her through the jumps. Since then she has never got over a weakness for tough city editors. She finds them too polite today and prefers the motion picture version. She liked Bonfils better than Tammen. She listened to Polly Pry spinning exciting yarns about her adventurous career from a gold chair that looked like a throne. She got steeped in newsprint. She went to prize fights and baseball games. She saw the hectic side of the town. Her employers also owned the Kansas City *Post* and Miss King went back and forth between the two cities. The high-hat reporters on the Kansas City *Star* were not allowed to speak to the riffraff on the *Post*.

One day in 1912, soon after she had joined the staff, Miss King ran into the society editor's office, which was so fancy that there was a mirror in it. She was drawing a powderpuff out of her bag when she noticed a stunning-looking woman sitting in a big chair.

"I beg your pardon," Miss King said. "I've come in here to powder my nose."

"Well, come in and powder your nose," said the occupant of the chair. "Do you write for the paper?"

"Yes."

"What do you do?"

Miss King told her.

"Well," she said, "I'm a newspaper woman, too. I'm Winifred Black."

This was a name greatly revered in newspaper circles at the time.

"You can't be," said Miss King.

"I am," retorted Mrs. Black.

A year later Miss King ran into her again, this time in the Baltimore Hotel in Kansas City. She saw her sitting at a table, walked over to her and recalled the Denver episode.

"I looked at your work after you told me who you were," said Mrs. Black. "How would you like to come into the Hearst service?"

"Work for Mr. Hearst!" screamed Miss King. "Merciful heavens, I would pack up and run to work for Mr. Hearst."

"Well, get twelve of your sketches and bring them to my hotel tonight and I will show them to him," said the practical Mrs. Black.

Miss King sent her the best samples of her work that she could assemble in a hurry, but years passed and she heard nothing. Then one night, when she was out dancing, she got word that the San Francisco *Examiner* wanted her on the telephone. She was offered a job. Mrs. Black had drawn Mr. Hearst's attention to her work and the summons had come at last. Mr. Bonfils made every effort to keep her on his paper, and after a break when she left him he continued to run her work until his death. He always felt that he had discovered Fay King.

She stayed on the *Examiner* for a year but did not like it. Then she wrote to Mr. Hearst telling him that she was unhappy in her job. His reply reached her on Armistice Day. "You can come to New York any time you want to," he wrote.

She traveled across the country in a cheerful state of mind. She had always longed to see New York and the Flatiron Building. She was also curious to see Mr. Hearst, Mr. Brisbane and Tad. It was a cold day in January, 1919, when she first found her way to Park Row. In the weeks that followed it baffled her that she could not catch a glimpse of Mr. Hearst. At no time had she worked for an editor who was never visible in his newspaper shop. She inquired around and found that people who had worked there for twenty years had never laid eyes on him.

She sat next to a financial writer. One day when he had a sore throat he asked her to make a financial report to Mr. Hearst over the telephone. She did this for him several days in succession. Then, when the invalid seemed about cured, she summoned up her courage and remarked, after finishing the report, "Oh Mr. Hearst, will you forgive me if I speak a word to you? This is Fay King."

"How are you, Miss King?" said Mr. Hearst.

"I didn't like to speak to you," Fay hurried on, "but I've been looking everywhere for you. I asked young and old around the office, and even some with side whiskers, about you, and none of them had ever seen you. And I don't want to work here for nineteen years and never see my boss."

"All right, come up and look at me," said Mr. Hearst.

An appointment was made. Miss King went up and was ushered into the library of his home. Mr. Hearst walked in laughing.

"Well, here I am," he said. "You wanted to look at me." He revolved like a teetotum. "Are you happy? Is everyone treating you right?"

"Everything is perfect," said Miss King. "I haven't a reason in the world for coming to see you except just to look at you."

They went over to a window with a view of the river and talked.

"I'm awfully glad you came," said Mr. Hearst at last. "If there is anything you really want some time, you get in touch with me and I will see you."

She ran into the diffident Tad quite unexpectedly when they were both getting their mail one day. In the meantime she had seen the Flatiron Building and so her immediate aspirations were realized.

Miss King follows the news closely and often builds her strip around the topical subject of the day or writes straight philosophical copy. When she draws from life she finds that women object less to cartooning than men who prefer not to appear bald and fat. She covers prize fights, the theater and current events. She is never ahead on her strip nor has she ever failed to deliver it on time. Her idea is always clear-cut; the verbal picture is sharply drawn.

She is so exact in preparing the 125-word text that the page can be locked and the make-up man can still be sure that it will fit.

Miss King lives in a busy mid-town hotel and does most of her work with a canary singing at her elbow. She likes to poke about the city room and to feel the excitement of the news coming in. But she finds it all quite tame when she remembers the Denver days. Among city editors she admires Stanley Walker but cannot forget dear old Josiah.

Few women have achieved success in the field of newspaper illustration. There have been no women political cartoonists. Kate Carew's caricatures, however, were famous in the early part of the century, and Jessie Wood, who was best known in the magazine world, worked for Hearst for a time. Women have had little success with the comic strip, although Mrs. Grace Gebbie Drayton, who died in 1936, was an exception. Her strip "Toodles and Pussy Pumpkins" appeared for several years in the Hearst newspapers. At the time of her death Mrs. Drayton was drawing "The Pussycat Princess" for King Features. She also did "Dolly Dimples and Bobby Bounce." She was the creator of the plump, red-cheeked Campbell's Soup Kids. Between 1900 and 1910 she illustrated verses and children's stories for newspapers. At various times she worked for the Philadelphia *Press*, the New York *Journal*, and the New York *Herald*.

Chapter XXXII

THE WOMAN'S PAGE

THE WOMAN'S PAGE HAS EVOLVED MORE SLOWLY THAN ANY other department of the modern newspaper. It was launched reluctantly as it dawned on editors here and there that the woman reader was a factor in circulation. In the beginning it dealt essentially with the same subjects as it does today—fashions, food, beauty, love, health, etiquette, home-making, interior decoration— but the treatment was different. It was florid and romantic. That nebulous creature known as Milady was inseparable from the fashion notes. Recipes were still full of starch. Often the page was garlanded with flowers, hearts and cupids. In the eighties women were noticed only in a single column, although as far back as 1880 the startling question was propounded in this department: "Ought Women to Vote?" By the nineties the woman's page was a definite feature in the larger papers. It took in clubs, which were just beginning to impinge on the social consciousness; society, which was riding high; and all subjects that were supposed to interest women.

Kate Masterson edited the woman's page of the New York *Herald* in the nineties—a good writer herself, although her executive duties irked her. She was followed by Mrs. Fannie E. Merrill, who made her girls hop, for she knew news and could handle any sort of story herself. When Nevada Victoria Davis arrived in New York, fresh from the West, where she had worked for the Salt Lake *Tribune* and the Cleveland *Leader*, she was so timid that she walked around the block three times before entering the portals of Charles A. Dana's dignified *Sun*. There was no place there for a woman, perish the thought! But next day she landed on the *Herald*, where Kate Masterson took her in hand. At that time women reporters occupied a great deal of space in their offices. Miss Davis' sleeves were like toy balloons. Her skirts were yards around. Her hatpins shone like daggers.

After a year she moved over to the *Press*, which had just been reorganized. Lemuel Eli Quigg was the new editor-in-chief; Emil

Wardman was managing editor; Curtis Brown was Sunday editor. Gertrude Eastman edited the Sunday woman's page and Miss Davis was taken on as her assistant. Grace Drew was a feature writer in the department. Frederick Palmer and Post Wheeler were both on Mr. Brown's staff. Miss Davis had to dig up news on the women's clubs. There were no press agents then. She had to find out what women were doing at home and abroad. Once in a while Mr. Quigg would call her in to give her advice on her work. The first time she appeared before him he said that her page was good but that it lacked sparkle.

"You must make it scintillate," he said. As she was about to go, he added, "There is one thing I like about you, Miss Davis. When I criticize your work you don't burst into tears. That's a great comfort."

There were faint glimmerings of interest in politics about this time. The State Republican Committee leaders were persuaded by Miss Davis to give her such crumbs of political wisdom as they felt her women readers could bear. The Women's Professional League, headed by Mrs. A. M. Palmer, had enterprisingly launched its own club house. The Health Protective Association was battling dirt and unhygienic conditions. Mrs. Josephine Shaw Lowell was making the Consumers' League a force in the community. Susan B. Anthony, Mrs. Elizabeth Cady Stanton and their associates gave Miss Davis plenty of material for her page. Once when Miss Davis was leaving Mrs. Stanton after an interview, she said, "There is a bit of advice I should like to give you and all women. Never leave your room in the morning before your hair is combed. It's a rule I've never broken myself." She was nearly eighty at the time. Her own silver locks were serene.

Like her predecessors, Miss Davis married and made room for another woman editor. But she could not forget the siren voices altogether. In 1916 she was again at work as home economics editor of the Philadelphia *Record*. Now, as Mrs. Nevada Davis Hitchcock, she edits a garden department for the Bridgeport *Post*.

But after the turn of the century syndicate names began to appear on the women's pages, giving them a certain uniform character— Dorothy Dix and Beatrice Fairfax on love, Marion Harland on cooking, Anne Rittenhouse on clothes. When Mrs. Harland recommended the use of liquor in some of her recipes considerable excitement was stirred up. The editor of a religious paper attacked her for making an assault on the American home and fostering the drunkard's cause. Mrs. Harland went calmly on her way, receiving more than twenty thousand letters a year on household matters.

Today food and fashions are still the chief drawing cards of the woman's page, but they are handled with a close tie-up to markets and shops, instead of the leisurely detachment of twenty years ago. Food leads in some cities, fashions in others. But a new note has been added. Intelligent editorial comment on current affairs spices the offering. It is considered bad journalism now to clog the woman's page with meaningless fillers or a surplus of canned copy. It is edited, controlled and made up apart from the rest of the paper. A city editor will see to it that little live news is allowed to settle into its somewhat static mold. But where a woman of wide newspaper experience takes hold, wonders can be done with the stepchild of the profession. With a little effort the page may become cerebral as well as decorative. Here and there throughout the country women with broad newspaper experience are now devoting themselves to a department which once merited the scorn it received.

A case in point is Mary King, who was Sunday editor of the Chicago *Tribune* from 1914 to 1926, and now edits the woman's section of the New York *Daily News*. She is also fiction editor of the combined syndicate. Miss King has done considerable pioneering for her sex in the newspaper field. She is a good executive and women like to work for her. She has developed talent in others and has started a number of newspaper women on their way. She thinks that women make excellent reporters and that they should be paid as well as men. She reached a high executive position herself with few stops by the way. Although she never worked on a city staff or went out on a news assignment, this in no way foreshortened her sight on news.

She is a native of Chicago, the daughter of a physician and one of a large family of girls and boys. She attended parochial and convent high schools and then took a business course. In 1907 she went to work on the *Tribune* as assistant secretary to Medill McCormick. Before long she became secretary to the Sunday editor. She was promoted again, this time to the post of assistant Sunday editor. In another year she was holding down one of the biggest newspaper executive posts in the country. Miss King had vision and was full of ideas. Her appointment as Sunday editor marked a great advance for women in journalism. She functioned ably for twelve years, with none of the friction that is supposed to surround a woman executive dealing with men on a paper. She had a staff of forty. She handled the comic strips, one of the best-selling features of the organization for which she works. She was in charge while the *Sunday Tribune* underwent its transformation from the traditional Sunday paper of the nineties to a publication making free use of service features, and particularly those of interest to women. In 1919, when her paper decided to buy first rights to long and short stories by the best authors at magazine prices, Miss King was put in charge of this department. She followed up authors, studied newspaper taste in fiction, and spent her paper's money with good judgment for the Blue Ribbon Syndicate. She is pursuing the same course in New York today.

She had a hand in the start of Fanny Butcher's column and was one of the first persons to draw attention to the possibilities of motion picture criticism. While she was still doing secretarial work in the Sunday department she observed the intense interest in the neighborhood cinemas. She wrote a two-page letter to her employers suggesting a motion picture department. A year later the question of establishing a department of this sort came up. Miss King was called into conference by the *Tribune* executives, for they remembered her letter. None of them had seen a future in the films. She got a raise that day. It was only a matter of weeks until she was appointed assistant Sunday editor.

Miss King is one of the personalities of the profession. She goes abroad frequently, keeps in touch with authors on both sides of the Atlantic, has a wide acquaintance among the town's celebrities, lives with her sister at Riverdale, and in her spare moments gives thought to her garden and rockery. She knows how to delegate authority— a gift in the newspaper executive. And she does not let herself be swamped by detail. Her theory is that all the features on a woman's page should be handled with absolute honesty. Everything must be tested. The patterns must work. The recipes must be sound. The beauty preparations must undergo chemical inspection. Health advice must come from physicians. There are no fillers of any sort. Every item used gives entertainment, information or service. The *News* dance contest of 1935 was Miss King's idea. More than 100,-000 spectators showed up for the finals in Central Park. The event had to be called off, because of crowding. Two weeks later it was held in Madison Square Garden with paid admission. The arena was packed with a crowd of 20,000, and 25,000 more were turned away.

In Antoinette Donnelly the combined Chicago *Tribune* and *Daily News* syndicate has one of the chief prizes in the woman's page field, for Miss Donnelly is the country's leading authority on beauty and charm. When she tells an ugly duckling how to turn into a swan her readers take heed. The professional beauties of two continents have confided their secrets to Miss Donnelly. In palaces and movie sets they have made her their confessor, for the good of their fellow women. But she is a realist, with a sense of humor. She knows that the secret elixir often has a soap and water base.

Miss Donnelly, as much as anyone, is responsible for the reducing craze. In 1917 Captain Patterson suggested that she take a fat woman and put her through a reducing process. The subject lost thirty pounds in six weeks with much attendant publicity. Then she engaged in a contest with Dr. John D. Robertson, Health Commissioner of Chicago, to see which could reduce twenty-five men and women most effectively. Miss Donnelly took the men and won with them. She repeated this stunt in New York later with Dr. Royal S. Copeland, when he was Health Commissioner. She won again. The men stuck to their regimen better than the women. Miss Donnelly has become an acknowledged expert on the subject. She has had 300,000 letters and telephone calls testifying to the interest in reducing. In a single day one of her columns on a new method to get rid of fat brought 9,800 telephone calls and letters. She finds that one-half of the reader interest in charm and beauty revolves around reducing—an astonishing change of taste from the gay but fattish nineties. Miss Donnelly admires Billie Burke, thinks Lady Diana Manners the perfect beauty and Katherine Hepburn a stunning type. She finds that men still prefer blondes and the fairy princess effect, but she does not think that the generation growing up will cherish this illusion. Cecile Sorel once confided to her that mystery, and mystery alone, was the secret of charm, but Miss Donnelly believes that a little practical aid is needed.

The beauty oracle no longer sits at a desk all day and turns out advice in the old-fashioned way. She goes out and about, and watches professional beauties in their favorite haunts. She has a comprehensive knowledge of the cosmetic market. She works with chemists and medical experts, and knows just what she is recommending from the scientific as well as the glamour point of view. Miss Donnelly has her own preparations on the market.

Once she went in quest of the twelve most beautiful women in America. Her search took her to Hollywood, where she lined up those she considered the loveliest of the stars. She then told why, and gave her readers the benefit of their beauty secrets. She took an ugly duckling and turned her into a passable beauty by diet, grooming, good clothes and lessons in speech and deportment. Soon the girl was married. Miss Donnelly's definition of a beauty is any woman who is well groomed, healthy and has a good smile. She thinks that the films have changed the shape of the American eyebrow, pointed up the profile, improved the feminine form, and totally altered the standards of pulchritude. There was little sound beauty advice in the papers before 1920. Now it is nearly always authoritative. The advertisements for false hair and bust development have been supplanted by a subtle mixture of aesthetic suggestion and commercial propaganda.

Miss Donnelly came originally from Mount Forest, Ontario, then moved to Buffalo, where she studied stenography. Her first job was not a success. She left it at once after stuffing her shirt-waist with the envelopes she had ruined. When she tried Chicago she had better luck. She landed on the *American Lumberman* and was soon allowed to write obits, wedding notices, incorporations, building permits and small fillers. She still did not know that her future lay in charm. After a year she landed on the Chicago *Tribune* as assistant to the woman's editor. It was 1913 and the two greatest causes known to women—beauty and love—were being handled in the *Tribune* columns by Lillian Russell and Laura Jean Libbey. Miss Donnelly read and answered letters addressed to them, edited contest features and made herself generally useful in both departments. She also did a bit of ghosting. Four years later she took Miss Russell's place as beauty editor under her own name and Mrs. Libbey's place as love expert, using the pseudonym Doris Blake. She conducts both columns today.

Miss Donnelly would still rather sing and play than write. Music was her earliest ambition. She likes the rural life and picture book farms, but she thrives in the metropolis, where she has a complete grasp of the beauty business and is in touch with every new development in her field. She has two adopted daughters and believes that any mother can make her children attractive by the right sort of haircut, healthy bodies, good teeth and fresh air.

Miss Donnelly's columns are models of concise and authoritative information. She frequently introduces a news note into them. In 1934 she got hold of the manual of West Point exercises, which she fed out gradually to her readers. She has a hundred pamphlets covering every possible beauty topic. She makes a point of answering all mail within two days. When she launched her shopping column, not using names, the response was overwhelming. She runs it twice a week and her office is then bombarded with calls. Miss Donnelly speaks over the air on charm.

Victorine Howard is another name known in the world of Rubinstein, Arden and Matchabelli. It appears in the *Sun*, on the paper trucks, and in out-of-town papers, and is always a slight surprise to its owner, whose real name is Marjorie Mears. She is never allowed to forget the ghost that walks by her side. She does features under her own name but is well aware that the chit Victorine outsmarts the parent and keeps her in silk stockings. When she goes to the beauty parties in the primrose salons she answers glibly to Miss Howard. She can't get away from it.

Miss Mears is a native of Elmhurst, Long Island, and got her first newspaper experience on the New York *Sunday World* under

Paul Palmer. From 1928 until the paper was sold she did features and interviews. Then she free-lanced, contributing often to the dramatic section of the *Herald Tribune*. She works now for Mary Watts, who edits the woman's page of the *Sun*, and has had wide experience as a reporter since the day she decided that newspaper work would be more romantic and exciting than teaching. Backed by her brother Miss Watts applied for a position on the *Herald*, where a friend of her father's was in power. Her parents were not anxious to have her work in the city, and a reporter seemed to them the lowest of God's creatures. When one of the neighbors in her native town—Burlington, New Jersey—asked her what she was doing in New York and Miss Watts said she was a reporter, her aunt poked her in the back and said in a crackling whisper, "Journalist."

Her family thought that she would soon tire of reporting but she clung to it with passionate determination. Editors came and went on the *Herald* with astonishing speed, but Miss Watts stayed on, covering women's clubs. From this she graduated to school news and suffrage activities. Then she became a sob-sister. She was put on a daily round which included Bellevue Hospital, the Tombs and the charity organizations. She was supposed to bring in a steady supply of pathetic stories. In time she began to do straight news. She had a smooth style, a sense of humor, and she knew how to get her facts. Later she was transferred to the Sunday department, where she did features and interviews. When Mr. Munsey bought the *Herald* Miss Watts went over to the *Sun*, to do straight reporting and features.

It was she who first sprang the story of J. P. Morgan's symbolic money bags carved above the choir stalls of St. Thomas's, an architect's jest in stone that the public had not yet discovered. The *World* had been working up a story on the carvings of this fashionable Fifth Avenue church, beginning with the dollar mark over the bride's door. They had published large lay-outs and stories about the gargoyles in the portico. A newly appointed managing editor on the *Sun* sent Miss Watts up to St. Thomas's with a microscope to see if she could find anything that the *World* had overlooked. She was dismayed, for she knew their round-up had been thorough. At the church offices she was severely snubbed. A crowd was standing outside, having read about the carvings. The church officials were much annoyed over all this vulgar publicity. Coming out of the office Miss Watts ran into an elderly woman who looked like a cleaner. She engaged her in conversation. She mentioned the vestrymen and asked if J. P. Morgan was one of them.

"No," said the woman, "but his money bags are up by the choir."

"What?" said Miss Watts. "Where?"

But the woman shut up like a clam. So Miss Watts went prowling along the choir stalls. It was not easy to trace the small carvings in the dim light of the church, but finally she found the three money bags with the initials J. P. M. This discovery made good copy and was a neat stroke of luck as an introduction to a new managing editor.

Another of Miss Watts' assignments was to interview Mrs. Nina Wilcox Putnam in 1924 when Mrs. Ellsworth Bassett threatened her with a suit for enlisting the affections of her handsome clam-digger husband. When the story broke Mrs. Putnam took to her bed in a New York hotel and the reporters swarmed around her, merciless and demanding. The author was in tears. She shed her pride and begged for mercy. "Girls, we're all writers," she implored the implacable group. "This is awful. You wouldn't hurt me, would you?"

There were twin beds in the room. A newspaper novice slid along the edge of the second bed and shouted into Mrs. Putnam's ear, "Where is your sense of humor now?"

The author uttered a wail and leaped with nervous shock. But she didn't get around the girls, in spite of her tears. They went back to their offices and did their worst to her. Afterwards the reporter who had startled Mrs. Putnam out of her wits explained that her city editor had told her to ask the horrid question and she was merely carrying out orders.

When the *Sun* got its Associated Press membership Miss Watts did more feature work and interviews for a time. Then she was put in charge of the woman's page, which is one of the most capably edited in the country. Mrs. Raleigh Hansl functioned in the same capacity on the old *Sun* for a number of years.

Few newspaper women have wider executive powers than Mary Dougherty, woman's editor of the New York *Journal*. She began her career in 1907, as a stenographer in the circulation department of the Chicago *American*. In the following year she became secretary to Charles Michelson, who was managing editor of the paper. As her work was not strenuous he encouraged her to write occasional news stories. Gradually she became more interested in writing than in stenography. Arthur Brisbane was in Chicago frequently during this period and Miss Dougherty worked for him in the same capacity. This kept her busy with office detail for two or three years. In 1912 she was appointed secretary to William C. Curley, who had come on from the Los Angeles *Herald* to edit the Chicago *American*. He encouraged Miss Dougherty to write. When Mabel De La Mater resigned as society editor to do other work on the paper, she inherited her job. She wrote as The Chaperon in the intimate, chatty vein characteristic of the Hearst papers. For several years she edited a Saturday page covering society, books, the arts and music.

Since 1927 she has been woman's editor of the *Journal*, doing a convincing job. During her first year the department received more than half a million letters from women readers. Miss Dougherty supervises all women's features, as well as society and music. She has conducted a number of forums that have attracted attention. Some years ago she did a series on Mrs. Edith Rockefeller McCormick, clarifying her obscure philosophy. Her own articles evoke quantities of mail. Often it overflows desks and tables and piles up on the floor in her office. When Mr. Curley goes to the coast for weeks or months at a time she is virtually acting managing editor of the paper in his absence. She is consulted both by the editorial and advertising departments on rapid-fire decisions and is often called at her home at night to pass on some policy. She has a key position on the paper. Miss Dougherty's family is well known in Chicago. Her sister is Patricia Dougherty, star on the *American*. Her brother is Charles S. Dougherty, assistant state's attorney who has figured in various notable trials.

The *World-Telegram*, under the Scripps-Howard régime, runs a progressive woman's page that goes further in its editorial comment than any similar page in the country. It's a long jump from the pink and lavender sentiments of the woman's page of the nineties to the forceful candor of Gretta Palmer and Dorothy Dunbar Bromley on social problems. Mrs. Bromley thinks nothing of tackling tabooed subjects in her column. She is a courageous writer and a deep thinker. Her point of view is often controversial and she puts it across without trimming her sails. Her column brings a big response. She is a native of Ottawa, Illinois, and a graduate of Northwestern University. She taught English for six months, then from 1919 to 1920 was secretary to the editor of the Detroit *Free Press*. She writes for the magazines, and her books on birth control are standard works.

Gretta Palmer, who preceded Mrs. Bromley as woman's page editor of the *World-Telegram*, also ran a smooth and enlightened column, which was read by men as well as women. She took a revolutionary stand on morals and behavior. There was nothing Victorian about the subjects she chose for discussion. Such unlikely woman's page topics as the increase in abortions, frigidity in American women and speakeasy etiquette were sprung quite casually on her readers. Mrs. Palmer did not cast the veil of illusion over her sex. Lee Wood, her managing editor, gave her a free hand in running the page. She was able to experiment with it in an interesting way. She could make it over three or four times a day in order to get in spot news. As a rule the woman's page goes through the day without variation, which is one reason why it has a frozen look to the professional eye. She was allowed to spend plenty of money on engravings, and used morticed combination cuts in the editorial columns.

Mrs. Palmer's aim was to keep canned copy out of her section and build up the woman's page standards to the same degree of excellence as those of the news department. She believed that there was at least one good story on fashions every day—a story that would have been acceptable on page two had the city editor got it first. She kept a sharp eye on the food markets, and recipes were gauged to coincide with the current shipments of meat and vegetables. She saw no reason why the woman's page should not be as productive of good news stories as the sports department.

Mrs. Palmer was graduated from Vassar in 1925, married Paul Palmer when he was Sunday editor of the St. Louis *Post Dispatch* and then came to New York with him, when he joined the staff of the *Sunday World*. Later they were divorced. She got her first news job by crashing Harold Ross's office at *The New Yorker* and telling him that his magazine did not give householders the lowdown on apartments for rent. So he hired her to launch a real estate department at a time when she still thought poets starved in Washington Mews. Later she initiated the "Out of Town" department for *The New Yorker*. In 1927 she left to do fashions for the *Sunday World*. Soon she started a column on collectors' items—intimate chit-chat on Ming vases, rare postage stamps, incunabula and other curiosa. She ran a department on contract bridge, which she could not play. With Evelyn Johnson she turned out a book of trick detective stories called *Murder*. It consisted of thirty-two stories with buried clues and the solutions in the back of the book.

In the autumn of 1931, the *Telegram* engaged her to run the woman's page. Six months later the *World* was absorbed and Mrs. Palmer continued her editorial functions under the Scripps-Howard banner. She now writes for the magazines.

For the last five years Sally MacDougall has been one of the mainstays of the woman's page of the *World-Telegram*, writing features and doing all sorts of odd jobs in this department. A lost handbag guided her to her first newspaper job in New York. She had arrived from Milwaukee with letters to Frank I. Cobb, of the *World*, and Sam Morse, of the *Times*. Mr. Morse told her at once that she was wasting her time interviewing editors. The thing to do, he said, was to study the newspapers and submit feature stories. He advised her to aim at the *Sunday World* magazine, then a colored supplement of tabloid size edited by John O'Hara Cosgrave. Next day she went to Police Headquarters in quest of a handbag she had left in a taxi. She failed to find the bag but she got a feature story on lost articles which interested Mr. Cosgrave and led him to offer her a job.

Soon her name was appearing regularly on feature stories. She was the only woman on the staff, working with eighteen writers and artists. Mr. Cosgrave gently scolded his staff if they failed to sell some of their work to the leading monthly magazines, and under this prodding Miss MacDougall had stories and articles accepted by *Harper's*, *Century* and other magazines. When the *World* was sold she went over to the *World-Telegram*, where she works with Elizabeth Clark, assistant editor of the woman's page, Gertrude Bailey, who does fashions, and Emily Genauer, an expert on interior decoration.

NEA, which is an offshoot of the Scripps-Howard organization, has employed a number of clever newspaper women at one time or another, including Helen Welshimer and the highly successful Mary Margaret McBride. One of the most popular was Julia Blanshard, who died in 1934. She came originally from Quincy, Illinois. Soon after her graduation from the University of Michigan in 1914 she became society editor of the Rochester *Democrat*. She was always a liberal in her sympathies, and in spite of the snobbish aspects of her job, she managed to pursue her own convictions by earnest advocacy of the cause of the garment makers. She lived among them in the industrial section of the city, marched in their parades, and shared in their defeats.

She worked on the *Sun* in San Diego, California, and the Newark *Ledger* before joining the staff of NEA. She was woman's page editor for seven years prior to her death and made trips to Russia and other European countries on behalf of her news service. She met her husband, Paul Blanshard, at the University of Michigan and was one of his closest advisers during the years that he was executive director of the City Affairs Committee. Mrs. Blanshard was a kind and charming member of her craft.

Hortense Saunders was another of the NEA girls. Her newspaper career began in Cleveland, where in 1916 she did an exposé for the *Press* of the exorbitant rates of interest charged by pawnbrokers. Miss Saunders pawned jewels to get her evidence on usury and then she exposed the pawnbrokers. After coming to New York she did woman's page work for NEA before succeeding Ruth Raphael, also a newspaper woman, as publicity representative of the Hearst magazines. Miss Saunders is the wife of George Britt, newspaper man and historian of Frank A. Munsey.

Both Mrs. Blanshard and Miss Saunders covered fashions as part of their regular work. Fashion writing for the woman's page today is practically a monopoly. A few headliners have the field sewn up. Their copy runs in scores of papers. It is no longer the haphazard matter it was when Jenny June wrote her first fashion notes, but is a highly specialized game. The outsider cannot hope to crash the openings in Paris. The woman reader is not easily fooled on fashions, for the papers are in competition with magazines that treat the subject in the smartest and most authoritative way. Any woman's editor must give careful attention to this department, and if she is wise she clears her page of all the old-fashioned clichés, such as "Dame Fashion decrees," and sees that the subject is handled much like news. Contemporary fashion writing is condensed, clear-cut and packed with information. The reportorial style is the best usage, with a dash of imagination added. The adjective continues to be more pervasive in fashion writing than in any other department of the modern newspaper. But the improvement in recent years has been striking.

Now and again the fashion writer pulls a scoop for her paper or syndicate. Through good connections she may get first access to details and photographs of a Princess' trousseau, for instance. Sometimes she plays a part in naming or launching a fashion. Adelaide Kerr, of the Associated Press, gave a novelty jeweler the suggestion which produced the earrings that hook around the ears like spectacle bows. And she named the Empress Eugénie hat that had a brief revival in 1931. Designers had been calling it "Second Empire." Miss Kerr thought that Empress Eugénie would mean more to the American public. So this was what it became.

There are four major style openings in Paris each year—the winter and summer shows, held in August and February, and the mid-season displays in April and October, which are less important. The dressmakers and modistes crowd the calendar to catch the American buyers, so that the fashion writer lives at high pressure over a fifteen-day period while the shows are on. Buyers, fabric manufacturers, a few private clients and the press crowd the salons where sables, velvets and wools are paraded in August, and summer attire is launched in February. Fans whir to cool the stifling air, the lights flash, a *vendeuse* calls the name of the first model, a mannequin glides out before the crowd and the show is on.

It is the business of the fashion writer to have a good seat in the front row with her back to the light, to catch everything from hem-lengths, waistlines, silhouettes, colors, fabrics and trends to the way the mannequin's hair is dressed. Her day begins officially with a show at 10:30 A.M. She gets a hasty lunch and dashes back to her office to check buyers and designers' activities by telephone, if she is a spot news writer. She is off to a new show at three and catches another at five. Somewhere in between she must write and file a night cable, concise as a stock market report, picturesque as a sports story, and clear enough to be understood by the man at the other end of the wire. By nine o'clock she is watching another mannequin parade, well turned out herself. Much is expected of the fashion reporter in Paris and she usually goes in for elegance. The show over, she files another cable. Next day the round begins all over again. When the openings are ended, she still has to turn out thousands of words to send by mail, to supplement her cable dispatches.

Her observations must be more than photographic. She needs the expert touch in this competitive field, for she has a trade following that can see right through the gloss of verbiage. She must not accept the freakish for the genuine as she watches the parade. When the buyers get back from the openings in Paris, the American shows begin. They are conducted on a larger and less exclusive scale. Again the fashion experts swarm together to get first-hand news for their public.

Most of the fashion writers live abroad, go scouting at the resorts, attend the races, haunt the fashionable beaches. They get to know the idiosyncracies of every designer, and to catch at a glance the infallible choice for American tastes. For years Anne Rittenhouse topped the fashion field. She was a reporter first and understood the newspaper game from all its angles. She worked for the Augusta *Chronicle*, then was woman's page editor of the Philadelphia *Public Ledger* and later became fashion editor of the New York *Times*. She went abroad to do fashions for the *Times* strictly on a news basis, and later did a daily feature for McClure's called "The Well Dressed Woman," which ran in more than one hundred newspapers, carrying her name to the most isolated homes in the country and bringing echoes of the giddy Continental world to the most drab housewife. She died in Philadelphia in 1932.

Corinne Lowe is a fashion writer who had a sound newspaper training before devoting herself to this specialty. She was born in Chicago, was taken at the age of two years to a small town in Pennsylvania, was graduated in due course from Swarthmore and then for two years covered straight news for the Philadelphia *Evening Bulletin*. Then she put in a year as editor of the woman's page before leaving to do advertising. In 1917 she joined the staff of the Chicago *Tribune* to write fashions and is still at it. She has two books to her credit and writes for the magazines. Miss Lowe is familiar with all the fashion shrines of Europe. She took a course in literature at the Sorbonne. She has studied Italian and done long walking trips in Switzerland and England.

Bettina Bedwell is another power in the fashion world. The dress-makers frequently ask her advice about American tastes. She is one of the best riders in Paris, for the simple reason that she learned to handle bronchos in Nebraska years ago—a long jump to the salons of Paris. Her childhood was spent on her father's cattle ranch in the West and the family home was in Denver. She attended a convent in Wisconsin. While still in school she appeared in a stock company with Douglas Fairbanks, Mrs. Minnie Maddern Fiske and other stars. She first did newspaper work in Denver, then went to Chicago, where she studied art. Toward the end of the war, she went abroad and studied costume design at the Ecole du Louvre, then did society for the Paris edition of the Chicago *Tribune*. Miss Bedwell has the knack of getting fashion scoops. She is chic herself, slim and dark. No one has any better standing with the designers. She is the expert in Paris for the Chicago *Tribune* and the New York *Daily News*. She was preceded by Mary Brush Williams, also a capable newspaper woman of wide experience.

Fanny Fern Fitzwater, who does fashions for the New York *Herald Tribune*, has the added advantage of being able to sketch as well as write. For years she lived in Paris, attended all the openings, was one of the best versed experts in the field. She now works on this side of the Atlantic and continues to write and sketch with a practiced hand, while Selina Yorke looks after the Paris end of the *Herald Tribune* fashions. Before Miss Fitzwater returned to America Sara Marshall Cook and Ruth Stuyvesant conducted the fashion department of the paper in New York. Miss Stuyvesant is the sister-in-law of Tess Slesinger.

Prunella Wood, who stars for King Features in the fashion field, learned to write for a newspaper by the old-fashioned swimming lesson method. Someone looking for a local correspondent for a paper in Florida offered her $15 a week to assemble news items, not knowing that she had stayed over an extra month after the close of the season in order to see the Royal Poinciana trees bloom. The real estate boom came along and things were lively. She got to know every man, child, cat, bootlegger, skeleton in the closet and social nuance of the locality. She had started out without knowing how to run a typewriter or an automobile. Soon she was adept at both and could operate a linotype, too. She saw a prison break and covered the last flare-up of the Ku Klux Klan. Then she blossomed out as art editor of her paper. Her father was a musician, so she already knew some of the visiting artists. She showed Zuloaga around and toured the state with the Cleveland orchestra in its heyday.

But Miss Wood could not get a raise, so she left her paper flat and made a year's salary in a real estate deal before nightfall the same day. However, her money soon vanished and she went to Cuba, where she landed a newspaper job at $15 a week. There she avoided Americans and lived grandly in a Cuban tenement, sharing rooms with a French milliner, a mad Spanish cobbler, a Puerto Rican Negro cook, and two Chinese importers of knick-knacks. When the place caught fire one day she carried thousands of dollars' worth of contraband Paradise plumes under her topcoat to safety at one of the big hotels, at the same time saving the $34 nest egg she had amassed after nine months of high living on her pittance. The tide turned and for a time she picked up as much as $200 a week on separate accounts.

When American interests bought her paper, she sold the idea to Conrado Massaguer, the Cuban cartoonist, of editing a smooth paper magazine in English. She worked at this for two years, which completed four years of association with interests distasteful to the government. When one editor took to a plane and another hid in an empty theater until he could escape next day, Miss Wood decided that flight was the better part of valor. She arrived in New York two weeks after the stock market crash and looked for a job. She got one on *Women's Wear* but that did not last. Later she went to the *World-Telegram*, where she worked first in the morgue, then for the woman's page, writing fashions. She was green at the subject, but she had the sensible notion of treating it as news. She understood magazine make-up and this made her valuable at once. Her salary was almost doubled and for two years she wrote ten interviews a week and learned about women's pages. Then she went to King Features, where she is the reigning fashion expert. She likes the composing room, type and make-up, and she firmly believes that women are only getting started in the newspaper world. Miss Wood is vivacious and handsome, a conspicuous figure in any newspaper group, like her colleague, Gloria Braggiotti, who does fashions for the *Post*.

The food features of the woman's page are usually in the hands of home economics experts. This department has improved vastly in recent years. It is conducted on scientific principles, often with model kitchens, as in the case of the New York *Herald Tribune*. Recipes are tested. The food market is studied. A housewife is not often led astray now in following food news in her daily paper. And it is still one of her chief interests there. Health and the care of children are in the hands of medical experts and psychologists. Some of the most moving mail that reaches the desk of a woman's page editor deals with the problems of childhood.

The active newspaper woman may sigh over the monotony of

club news, but it is still a heavy drawing card in any paper, large or small. Ever since the Sorosis Club brought a few women together to discuss the problems of the day, the American woman has been the most persistent club joiner of her sex. In the beginning the press was not welcomed at a club meeting. The members knew they were violating convention in meeting at all and they feared ridicule. Sometimes the subject under debate was nothing more than "Which is Preferable, Summer or Winter?" But they feared the scathing touch of the writer. Today publicity pours in a constant stream from clubs all over the country. Their leaders would feel aggrieved if their resolutions were ignored. The sage editor sees that club news is soundly and accurately handled. In 1935 the New York *Times* succumbed to the national custom and inaugurated a club page for women, proving that the branch of reporting that first gave women a foothold in the profession is still one of their mainstays.

Chapter XXXIII

THE SOCIETY PAGE

THE SOCIETY PAGE HAS BEEN THE OPPORTUNITY AND THE BUGABOO of newspaper women since the idea first was introduced in the New York *Herald* by James Gordon Bennett in 1840. The earliest society reporter in the country was William H. Attree, an ex-sports writer, who arrived in a suit of armor at the costume ball given by Mr. and Mrs. Henry Brevoort on February 25, 1840. Mr. Bennett had called on Mr. Brevoort to get permission for the vulgar person to attend. His presence was displeasing to his fellow guests, but Mr. Bennett's somewhat raffish circulation enjoyed Mr. Attree's account of the party next day, although it would seem quite tame to the punch-drunk tabloid readers of today.

As time went on and society news became part of any well-conducted newspaper, the job seemed to fall by divine right to the unwanted woman on the staff. It was not enough to say that Miss Cornelia Mapes was present. The question was—what did Cornelia Mapes wear? Only a woman could tell. But the elder Bennett, who put social news on the map in America, never succumbed to the idea that a woman was fit to chronicle the doings of society. Eventually they invaded the field everywhere but even today the society pages of some of the leading papers in New York are edited by men. Nowhere else is this true.

Publishers rarely underestimate the value of the society page. Their light-minded staffs often do. In any community, large or small, the names that appear in the social columns belong to the wives and daughters of the most important men in town. This tells the story in itself. It is an undoubted fact that the ambitious have been nursed to social security, or doomed to oblivion, by the reiterative paragraphs, dully arrayed, of the conservative society page. But the bars have fallen noticeably in the last few years. The commercial spirit has impinged on the Social Register. In some cities the inroads have been so heavy that the sacred blue book has been dropped altogether. Talent and charm have invaded the best parties. A newer and livelier social processional has taken hold, and the debbies would rather go to an Elsa Maxwell party than sit in state at the board of a social dowager. The tabloid readers are fully aware of this change of spirit. But the old guard stands its ground. The blithe spirit has not made a dent in the conservatism of the *Times* and the *Herald Tribune*. The outsiders are still more or less invisible to the social arbiters of these two papers.

Before the advent of the *Herald* the exclusive set would have suffered acutely had any mention of its parties appeared in the news sheets, which were then given over largely to political squabbles. This was before Ward McAllister had picked his Four Hundred. Henry Brevoort, Luther Bradish, William Aspinwall, William and Robert Bayard, Francis B. Cutting and Philip Hone were the social leaders. Most of the members of the exclusive set were merchants, and it was still undeniably a man's world. There were fifteen newspapers in Manhattan but the socially correct favored the *Courier* and the *Enquirer*. Mr. Bennett thumbed his nose at all the bigwigs. Philip Hone saw him as an "ill-looking squinting man whose penny paper was hawked about the street by a gang of troublesome ragged boys." Nevertheless, Mr. Bennett kept on prying into the affairs of those whom Mr. Hone considered his betters, until he pulled his coup and got his armored knight into one of the most exclusive parties. This was only the beginning. As long as he lived, he persisted in hounding the socially elect, but as time went on his wife was made to suffer for it by his powerful enemies. At last she gave up and went abroad, where her son, the younger James Gordon Bennett, was educated. Before his death the elder Bennett had become so rich and influential that he encountered less opposition, but during his lifetime the society page of the *Herald* never had the suavity that characterized the social news of the *Times*, *Tribune* and *Evening Post*. The jeering note was usually in the background.

But all doors opened to the younger Bennett, a sportsman and a character. The society page became sacrosanct as well as one of his chief interests in the paper. A whole stable of sacred cows was foisted on the society department. Nicholas Biddle became the social expert of the paper. In time Frank L. Baker came along. He pursued the same conservative tenor later with the *Times* until his death in 1936.

Nearly all society departments have their sacred cows and black lists. When Mrs. Stuyvesant Fish gave one of her most gorgeous balls on the same night as a prize fight and the make-up man got the two lists of names confused, she would not believe it was a mistake and raised bedlam about it. The managing editor was furious with Mrs. Fish. He decided that mishaps of this sort could best be avoided by omitting all reference to the Fish functions in future. The ban went into effect. Mrs. Fish appealed to Mr. Bennett, who always lent a listening ear to the complaints of his society friends. The order was promptly rescinded. Mrs. Fish filled many a column with her guest lists after that.

When Joseph Pulitzer took over the moribund *World* in the eighties and revived it with larger type and considerable noise, he still maintained a conservative society page. But, unlike Mr. Bennett, he thought a woman should cover society. By this time women were beginning to read the papers, chiefly for the social news. They wanted to know which of the dowagers sported emerald tiaras at the opera, what clothes they wore, how they did their hair.

This was the period when the girl assistants in the society department, making next to nothing, went dashing about from door to door by bicycle, trolley or hack, rounding up the sartorial details in advance. At night the society editor herself would burgeon forth, her pencil and copy paper nowhere in sight. If good at her job, she worked from memory and took accurate note of faces, clothes and jewels. She did not have the benefit of the telephone, or the lists of names and costumes that now flood her desk. There were no social secretaries or press agents to describe every detail, down to the flower decorations and the poundage of the wedding cake. It was all assembled at first hand. The effect was to make society reporting more picturesque but much less accurate.

The parties of the nineties were not touched again for spectacular effects. With the death of Mrs. Fish, competition languished, the blackbird pies disappeared, the prancing horses vanished from the banquet room, parties became somewhat standardized. Then the cinema took hold and the fans got all they wanted of sartorial flim-flam from the screen. By this time the papers were full of international news. The world had changed. There was no more space for columns describing the costumes worn at a party the night before. It is still done, but nowhere to the same degree, and practically not at all in the larger cities, except for a masquerade such as the Beaux Arts ball in New York.

But Mr. Hearst did more than anyone else to change the character of the society page, which was comparatively conservative after the death of the elder Bennett in 1874. When he invaded the New York field in 1895, society was still treated in a glamorous, touch-me-not way. The smart set was pictured as a group far removed from the orbit of those who read about them. The note of awe was ever present in the recital of their doings. They invariably got their full names, middle initials and titles, a convention which still seems to be the best usage. But they were also pictured as peo-

ple of magnificence, infinite leisure and enormous glitter. Mr.
Hearst introduced a new idea. He decided to show them as ordinary human beings with good clothes, plenty of money, yachts
and magnificent homes, but with nothing about them to inspire awe
in the heart of the little dressmaker. As time went on, his society
pages were to foster the note of familiarity. They were to give the
impression of being written from the inside. He began with the
Journal. Ivy Ross had been on the staff since 1890, during the ownership of Albert Pulitzer and John R. McLean. She stayed on when
Mr. Hearst bought the paper and in time became Cholly Knickerbocker. She covered the Bradley Martin ball and all the international
marriages of the period—Cornelia Bradley Martin and the Earl of
Craven, Consuelo Vanderbilt and the Duke of Marlborough, May
Goelet and the Duke of Roxburghe, Gladys Vanderbilt and Count
Szechenyi. She was the only reporter present when Benjamin Harrison married Mrs. Mary Lord Scott at St. Thomas's in 1896. She
got the first interview with Li Hung Chang when he arrived with
his Chinese retinue in 1895.

Miss Ross chronicled society for the Hearst interests for thirty-
two years. She retired shortly after the war and died in 1933. She
was not the first Cholly. A man initiated the feature. One of its
earliest incumbents was Isabel Fraser, who moved about from city
to city, wherever there was a Hearst paper, launching the column
under different names. The most outstanding characteristic of the
Cholly feature was the use of the first names of social leaders, to
imply familiarity. Mrs. Herman Oelrichs became Tessie and Mrs.
Stuyvesant Fish, Mayme, whenever their names were mentioned,
whether or not they liked it. Dowagers and that pompous creature
known to the press as the clubman (but probably a decent, quiet
fellow if one knew him) made a tremendous row over this assault
on their dignity. However, there was nothing they could do about
it. Mr. Hearst had the advantage of newsprint. At that, there was
none of the scandal freely spilled in gossip columns throughout the
country today.

The realistic note had its effect on papers everywhere. It is expertly pursued now by Maury Paul, who does not go so far as
some of his tabloid contemporaries in brashly spilling scandal but
conveys the idea by winks and nods; and by Molly Thayer, who is
Madame Flutterbye, of the *Journal*. All the large cities now get
their social news from two angles—the conservative and sensational,
in the court gazette manner and by way of the gossip column. And
somewhere in between are occasional columns which discuss society
in a chatty way, yet avoid scandal.

While it has flourished over the years, society as a newspaper department has come to be important only in so far as the paper that deals with it is important. On the smaller papers it is usually foisted on the novice—and preferably a woman—or on someone with social connections and no newspaper sense. But in metropolitan centers it gets high rating. No newspaper post is considered more difficult to fill, since it requires years of familiarity with consequential names and family lineage, absolute knowledge of the inflexible style rules of the society page, and good judgment.

The outstanding woman society editor in the country today is Ruth E. Jones, who functions for Mrs. Patterson on the Washington *Herald*. The capital, in some respects, is paradise for the society reporter. There is a constant influx of interesting figures from all parts of the world. The political aspects of the social scene add a measure of color and excitement to a job that, too often, is one of mere routine. When Joseph P. Tumulty was secretary to President Wilson he told Miss Jones that he read the social columns with close attention, since many a grouping gave him a clue to the development of political alliances. There is always a touch of fever behind the scenes in Washington. Publicity in the social columns is taken as part of the game. This means that it is less exclusive than it is in other metropolitan centers. The position is more important than the individual. A woman who could never hope to crash the social column in the town from which she springs, may rate the most conservative grouping in Washington because of her husband's political standing.

Chance dictated Miss Jones' choice of newspaper work as a career. Her father, John Paul Jones, was a well-known lawyer. He died just as she was leaving school. She had had a festive childhood but she and her mother faced poverty after her father's death. So she looked around for a job, and without any trouble became assistant to the society editor of the Washington *Times*. She had lived all her life in Washington and had gone to smart schools, so she knew the current crop of débutantes. This made her valuable for contacts. She started at $7.50 a week. Luck was with her. In six months' time the society editor married and she succeeded her at $15 a week. She has been successively with the *Times*, the *Post* and the *Herald*. On the *Times* she inherited an office name, Jean Eliot, which led to an amusing complication with Mr. Hearst. Her assistant, Gourley Edwards, used the name when Miss Jones was off duty. One day she wrote a story on the way the residents of Georgetown were snubbing Elinor Glyn. Mrs. Glyn had taken a house there, with the avowed intention of being let alone, and her neighbors were letting her alone quite handsomely. Miss Edwards' point was that they were missing something in not cultivating Mrs. Glyn. But the author didn't like it. She sent a two-page telegram of protest to Mr. Hearst. He promptly wired: "Fire Jean Eliot." So Jean Eliot was fired summarily but Miss Edwards, who actually had written the piece, stayed on. And so did Miss Jones. This ended the first chapter of the story.

The second began several years later when the Washington *Post* offered Miss Jones an advance in salary to join the staff. The publisher wanted the benefit of the name Jean Eliot, which had acquired value. The *Times* had dropped it after the Hearst order came through, and had no intention of reviving it. So Miss Jones took steps to have it registered and Jean Eliot was resurrected in the columns of the *Post*. Still later, when Mrs. Patterson took command of the *Herald* and sought Miss Jones' services, the society expert asked, not without cause, whether she wanted Ruth Jones or Jean Eliot. Mrs. Patterson wanted Jean Eliot. She consulted Mr. Hearst, got his approval, and soon both the *Herald* and the *Times* were advertising the fact that Jean Eliot would become society editor of the Washingon *Herald*.

Miss Jones has done a lot to humanize the Washington society pages; yet she is at heart a conservative and never deals in scandal. She has no objection to an action picture on the society page. She believes in attractive make-up, features of one sort or another, and the use of a daily news lead, with a political, personal or anecdotal angle. Quite often she gaily springs an item that would make good front-page reading and it is no novelty for her to land stories in the main news sheet. Miss Jones is handsome, sophisticated, smart. She knows the social life of the capital thoroughly, goes everywhere, and gets on equally well with the débutantes and their mothers. She likes human beings, so is never bored with her job.

Evelyn Peyton Gordon, daughter of the jurist who sentenced Harry Sinclair to jail, presides capably over the society columns of the Washington *Post*, a paper which has always maintained rigid standards on social news. Her work is sound and authoritative. Her assistant is Sydney Sullivan, daughter of Mark Sullivan, one of the solons of the capital. But the dowager empress is Mrs. Sallie V. H. Pickett, now society editor emeritus of the *Star*. She has seen Presidents come and go, administrations rise and fall, but has never missed a move in the social picture. Her record of functions exceeds all others in Washington and she has been indefatigable in her output of copy.

The only women society editors in New York today are Madeleine Riordan, who has done capable work for the *Post* through its conservative and radical phases, and Bessie I. Phillips, of the *Times*, one of the most experienced society reporters in the field.

Miss Phillips succeeded Mr. Baker in January, 1936. She was associated for years with Ivy Ross on the *American*, then worked for the pre-Munsey *Herald* and later for the *Sun*. She has covered every type of society assignment and is not easily fooled on matters affecting the Social Register.

For a number of years Mrs. Marie Louise Weldon was society editor of the *Times*. She joined the staff in 1901 and recorded the social doings of the era as an assistant in the society department. Later she assumed full charge and functioned in this capacity for many years. Mrs. Weldon was a retiring soul. Few of her colleagues knew anything of her private life or interests. She owned a choice collection of Japanese prints which she had assembled on a trip to the Orient. In her later years she inherited the estate of Prince Holm, a Danish explorer, whose portraits, emblems and personal property she distributed in her will. Pope Pius XI was among the beneficiaries, as were Edward G. Robinson, the cinema star; the Metropolitan Museum of Art, the British Museum and the United States National Museum.

The reigning social czars of the New York papers all have capable women assistants in their departments. Mrs. Helen Knapp is Howard White's chief aid on the *Herald Tribune*, which has the most exacting standards for its society page, and before her Deborah Corle and Mrs. Marshall Darrach filled the same post. Eve Brown is Cholly Knickerbocker's assistant and Dorothy Hall works with Paul Stewart on the *World-Telegram*.

At the beginning of the century the *World* sent for Josephine Robb and put her in charge of the society department. For the next thirty years she conducted a dignified department, which grew from one-half page in the Sunday edition to more than six pages, as club and resort news were added. And in time a daily column of social notes was instituted.

In 1912 Miss Robb was married to Frank Somes Ober. Her work with the *World* continued with scarcely a break, except for a short interval at the time of her husband's death, which occurred soon after their marriage. During all her years with the *World* Mrs. Ober's desk was in the Sunday department. Her early equipment was one table and a typewriter, but as time went on she superintended several desks and considerable paraphernalia in one corner of the big Sunday room. Working next door to her at various times were F.P.A., Alexander Woollcott, Deems Taylor, Samuel Chotzinoff, Heywood Broun and Laurence Stallings.

Mrs. Ober had the *World* instinct for an exclusive story. One of her best, obtained when she was on the Sunday staff, was with Helen Gould, now Mrs. Finley J. Shepard, who had never before, and has seldom since, given an interview. A little earlier Mrs. Ober had surprised George Bernard Shaw into a visit and an interview. She was in London and knew practically nothing about newspaper work at the time. Shaw's plays were just becoming the rage. Not knowing what she was up against, she wrote him a note, asking him to call on her and be interviewed for American publications. Mr. Shaw showed up, a favor which he never bestowed on a reporter again. Mrs. Ober got her interview. On her return she free-lanced and went out briefly with a road show in order to write a first-hand story from behind the scenes. She interviewed Sarah Bernhardt, Nordica, Calvé, Gadski, Schumann-Heink and other stars of the day, ghosting for some of them. She also did theatrical and operatic press work, representing James K. Hackett when he played his last New York engagement as star and manager. Soon afterwards she became society editor of the *World*.

Mrs. Ober is one of the few newspaper women who are native New Yorkers. Her father, Joseph Watkins Robb, was born in Spring Street when Greenwich Village was a fashionable section of the city. He was a member of New York's volunteer fire department. His grandfather, John Robb, came to New York from Scotland in 1835, and his father, Charles Robb, was an officer in the Veteran Corps of Heavy Artillery, the original National Guard. On the maternal side she is descended from James McBride, to whom William Penn gave a grant of land in Pennsylvania. She attended Montclair High School, spent two years in a private school in New York, then went abroad to study in London and Paris. She specialized in voice training and dramatic work. Since the sale of the *World* she has done magazine and radio work.

When Mrs. Ober first began covering society nearly all the débutantes were launched in their own homes. Now few girls make their débuts in private ballrooms. Everything has been transferred to hotels, restaurants and clubs. And the social secretaries have created a profession of their own. Another innovation designed to suit modern social needs is the publicity department of the large hotel. The society reporter who had much to do with the promotion of this idea was Caroline Harding. Her first newspaper work was to report for eight New York papers Harry Vardon's golf matches in Florida in the spring of 1900. In the same month she got an exclusive story on the meeting of Admiral Dewey and Prince Henry of Prussia at Palm Beach, when the Prince was on his way home from a two-year tour of the world.

Then James Gordon Bennett, who kept a wary eye on society news, suggested that Miss Harding should be sent to Hot Springs, Virginia, in the autumn to report the doings of Mrs. Fish, Mrs.

Oelrichs, Harry Lehr, the Langhorne sisters (including Lady Astor), Mr. and Mrs. Cornelius Vanderbilt, Mr. and Mrs. William B. Leeds and other social luminaries. After that she was sent by the *Herald* to cover Palm Beach in the winter season. She had no competition in this field for seven years and pioneered on resorts. Today a flock of society reporters parade the sands at Palm Beach during the season and observe everything from melting social alliances to the latest in bathing suits.

Henry Flagler was completing White Hall, his winter home, when Miss Harding first began to cover Palm Beach. William K. Vanderbilt, who had just been divorced from his wife, later Mrs. O. H. P. Belmont, showed up with a yachting party. Boni de Castellane was strutting about with Anna Gould. Frank Gould and his first wife, Helen Kelly, were on their wedding trip. Thomas F. Walsh, of fabulous gold mine wealth, was there. Emma Calvé, at the height of her fame as Carmen, was resting in the sunshine of the South.

In 1907 Miss Harding pioneered again, this time with a hotel column on the society page of the *Herald*. Up to that time a reporter had been as welcome in a hotel as a burglar. It was incredible that he should have any motive for being there except murder, suicide, robbery, fire or scandal. It took a year of hard work to persuade hotel owners and managers that her purpose was purely friendly. But since then it has been easy for the press to get news of a conventional sort at hotels. Miss Harding wrote the stories for the *Herald* when women embarked on smoking in fashionable hotels and restaurants. The first to be checked was Mrs. Patrick Campbell, who encountered opposition at the Plaza. The next was Baroness von Hengelmuller, wife of the Ambassador from Hungary. Another was Mrs. Frederick Lewisohn, who was told at Sherry's to throw away her cigarette. This was one of the social crises of the period. But the cigarette smokers survived it. Because of Mr. Bennett's interest in social news, many of Miss Harding's stories were run in the Paris edition of the *Herald*. A case in point was the opening of the first woman's bar in New York at the old Café des Beaux Arts. It was a logical step for Miss Harding to turn to hotel publicity. She functioned in this capacity for the Waldorf before the outbreak of the war, for the Ritz-Carlton from 1915 to 1921 and the Plaza from 1921 to 1933.

No society writer is more widely known on both sides of the Atlantic than May Birkhead, whose newspaper career began when the *Titanic* sank and she happened to be on the *Carpathia*, which rescued the survivors. She started for Europe in 1912 with no thought of a journalistic career and ran head on into one of the major stories of the decade. She talked to the survivors of the wreck, took photographs and gave the *Herald* a sensational clean-up. James Gordon Bennett's attention was focused on her at once. He took her on his staff. She stayed in France during the war and wrote feature stories. She won commendation from General John J. Pershing and did special work on the Peace Conference. When he bought the *Herald* Mr. Munsey recognized her value and kept her on the staff. She covered the wedding of Prince Christopher of Greece and Mrs. William B. Leeds. She was Mrs. Leeds' personal guest for a week before the wedding and did the publicity for this ornate event.

During the lush days when Americans overran Paris, Miss Birkhead recorded all their social activities. She came to be very well known. Late at night she would show up in her grubby newspaper office, handsomely gowned and jeweled, to bat out her story of the party she had just attended. She moved from the *Herald* to the Paris edition of the Chicago *Tribune* and in January, 1927, launched a front-page society column which ran until the paper was discontinued in 1934. Her society news from Paris now appears in the New York *Times* and the Chicago *Tribune*.

The best exponent of tabloid society reporting is Inez Callaway, who is Mrs. J. Addison Robb in private life and Nancy Randolph in the columns of the New York *Daily News*. She knows her onions, is never daunted by a lorgnette, is fearless, witty and bright. Her column is followed by the Four Hundred as well as the two million readers of the *News*. Her column has a gay, amusing tang. And her eyes are as perceptive as they are blue. In the South during the 1935 season she noticed that Doris Duke, sitting at a table nearby, was wearing a huge diamond on the third finger of her left hand. The rumor was in the air that she was going to marry James Cromwell. Miss Callaway did not wait for the formal announcement. She had received her news by the glitter route. Next morning her paper carried the story. Subsequent events justified her deduction.

She is not the sort of society reporter who likes to function from a desk. She goes where the smart foregather. She rolls up her sleeves and gets to work like a police reporter, when the occasion seems to demand tenacity. She stood on Miss Duke's doorstep for hours with the thermometer close to zero on the night of the richest girl's twenty-first birthday celebration. No guest list was available. She identified the arrivals as the photographers took their pictures. Again, when Percy Rockefeller's daughter, Winifred, was married at St. Bartholomew's, no one had thought of asking Miss Callaway to be present. But she was determined to be there. A column such as hers must be written from actual observation, not from vital statistics. It must reveal something more than the obvious facets of the Four Hundred.

An hour and a half before the ushers arrived, a woman in deep mourning stepped into the church and knelt in prayer. She seemed so devout that they hesitated to disturb her when they took up their posts. Finally the bridal party arrived, the wedding march was played, Miss Callaway saw quite clearly through her mourning veil and the *News* had an accurate picture next morning of the scene in the church. With equal presence of mind Miss Callaway crashed the wedding of Al Smith's daughter by persuading Justice John M. Tierney, of Brooklyn, that she had got separated from her parents, who had her invitation.

She had less success with the Edward F. Huttons, sparks always flying in any encounter with them. They disliked practically everything she wrote about them. They called up her managing editor repeatedly to tell him so. Then, in Palm Beach, after she made some merry quips when Hamilton Fish told the so-called idle rich that the veritable poor were ready to tear the pearls from their throats, Mrs. Hutton sent for Miss Callaway.

"So you are Nancy Randolph," she said, shaking a finger in Nancy's undaunted face. "Young woman, you should be more careful about the kind of jobs you take."

Mrs. Hutton recalled a story that had appeared about her in the *News* four years earlier. It happened that Miss Callaway had not written it. But she went at her hammer and tongs for an hour. Nancy gave soft answers, which is not her habit, for she has a witty tongue. But she refused to be drawn into a fight.

Next year Mr. Hutton sent for her. He wanted bygones to be bygones. But when the reporters had assembled, he began to berate her. The American press was turning people Bolshevist, he insisted. "I know the kind of stories you write," he said. "We took three thousand press clippings South with us to read. I forbid you to use our name in future."

"I have no power to keep your name out of my paper," said Miss Callaway. "As long as you make news, I shall use it."

In the spring of 1935 there was a rightabout face. Mrs. Hutton wrote that she was delighted with one of Nancy Randolph's stories. She was the only society reporter who showed any sense of humor, she said.

"Please put that letter in the files," said Miss Callaway cannily to her editor.

It always amuses her that she should be a society reporter. All she knew about society when she was growing up was culled from the Sunday magazines of the Hearst papers. She was born on a cattle ranch in California. Her grandfathers were forty-niners and Southerners. Her father was from Idaho and she spent her early days in Caldwell, Idaho, with a population of 4,000. The sagebrush grew right up to the window of her home. She got her first newspaper job when she was fifteen because she wanted silk stockings for school and her parents did not approve of such frivolity. She was high school correspondent for the *Capital News* in Boise, Idaho. Then she went to the University of Idaho on a scholarship and intermittently did social notes, which was a simple matter, for her Aunt Nell was social, and all she had to do was to record where she had gone and that was the news. Her next move was to take journalism at the University of Missouri, but she disliked the flat country. She happened to be in Tulsa, Oklahoma, during the race riots and the Ku Klux Klan upheaval. She stayed on and worked on the Tulsa *Daily World* for twenty-seven months. Then one day she walked into the Chicago *Tribune* with a scrapbook under her arm. Captain Patterson wrote to her later, offering her a job in New York.

She arrived in the metropolis in 1926 and went to work in the Sunday department of the *News* at double the salary she had been getting. One of her first assignments brought her face to face with the only living specimen of a butler she had ever seen and she mistook him for Hugh Walpole. Today she is on speaking terms with New York's best butlers. Her assignment was to interview Mr. Walpole, who was staying with a friend in the East Sixties. Miss Callaway had read his books and was thrilled to think that she was about to talk to a famous author. The door was opened by an impressive creature in a cutaway. His speech vaguely suggested Oxford. Miss Callaway started to interview him at once. But the butler was tactful. He led her gently upstairs and left her with the authentic Mr. Walpole. Then it was Mr. Walpole who interviewed her. The Hall-Mills trial was running at the time. He was intensely interested in it and asked her question after question. She enjoyed the interview. But she never misjudged a butler again.

In May, 1928, she was informed abruptly that she was to become society editor of the *News*. She felt chagrined. This seemed the last hope for a bright reporter from the West. An elegant young man had just been retired.

"How in the world could I be a society reporter?" Miss Callaway protested. "I don't even like champagne and I buy my hats in bargain basements."

"Well, try it for three weeks to tide us over," said an unsympathetic editor.

Nancy Randolph was a Chicago *Tribune* syndicate name. Miss Callaway's first story was written in a jesting vein. She went on in the same tempo. No one seemed to object. Soon she began to see that society reporting had its fascinations. She heard a rumor that she might even be sent to Palm Beach. She began to study the society pages and to explore the Social Register for names. She was appalled by the dullness of everything, since names in themselves held no charm for her. Only the Hearst society columns seemed to have any life. She decided to dig up a news angle every day. But she saw at once that she must get to know faces. The socially elect could not be recognized in a day. The photographers helped. By staying close to them she soon could spot the stars in the social firmament. She also learned about the small nucleus that never figured in the news, the set of which Mrs. Charles B. Alexander was typical.

In the intervening years she has mastered her subject remarkably well. She goes to the opera, races, polo matches, yacht races, night clubs, prize fights, the Horse Show, resorts—the entire social round. She looks for the bright bit of news but not the scandalous. What society editors need most, in Miss Callaway's opinion, is a sense of humor, a cast-iron constitution and plenty of clean white gloves. She has them all. And also a smart line of slang which she puts across in an individual manner in her column. She finds that the young would stand on their heads to make copy. The offspring of the publicity age think it amusing to have their antics show up in a tabloid. Miss Callaway watches them closely and often has beats on their doings. But in June she has bad dreams about strangling in tulle. The conservative papers send out questionnaires before an important wedding, and the details are filled in circumspectly. But any wedding covered in the *News* has to be watched at first hand. The Tucky French-John Jacob Astor nuptials were the tabloid sensation of the summer of 1934.

Mildred Lovell, Miss Callaway's assistant at that time, walked in boldly through the Chetwode gardens at Newport after a report had come through that Tucky and John Jacob Astor had had a row in Providence, Rhode Island. She met the hero among the shrubs.

"What are you doing on my property?" he demanded, with some degree of logic.

"Didn't you see the story in this morning's papers?"

"No, what was it?"

Miss Lovell told him.

"Well, what do you want to do about it?" he asked.

"I want you to tell your side."

"Aw, nuts!" said Mr. Astor and walked away.

Next morning the *News* showed that when an Astor says "Aw, nuts!" a society column of the new order hits the newsstands.

This is not how Olga E. Gellhaus directs her staid society department on the Philadelphia *Bulletin*. She rarely goes to parties. She hardly ever uses the telephone. She doesn't need to; for she is snowed under with items day after day. She is a tradition, so far as society is concerned. Nature gave her a deep-throated voice. People remember it, so that it almost passes as a trademark.

When Oscar Hammerstein opened his ill-fated opera house in Philadelphia, he wanted young music students to act as ushers. Miss Gellhaus was seventeen at the time and was studying singing. She and her sister were two of the group selected. They were assigned to the grand tier. There were twenty-eight boxes in the circle, preëmpted by Philadelphia's oldest families. The girl ushers were a novelty to the occupants of the circle. Gradually it dawned on Miss Gellhaus that the real show was not on the stage but in the grand tier. The ushers had to supply the society reporters with the names of those in the boxes. This was a simple matter, because all the important members of this compact group were confined in a circle. Miss Gellhaus got to know the reporters. She thought their work must be pleasant. Although she had no connection with the craft, she called on some of the occupants of the boxes to help her gather news. Alexander van Renssalaer was one of those who went from box to box, assembling notes for her which he handed over with a gallant bow.

Newspaper offers followed. She went to the Philadelphia *Press*. She still had no conception of how serious the social game could be. The boxholders continued to give her news, and liked it. The friendships she made at Hammerstein's leave their echoes today. The newer members of society are the children of her old friends. She never breaks a confidence. She does not believe in offending the people about whom she writes.

Miss Gellhaus remained with the *Press* until it was merged in 1919. Then she became society editor of the *Evening Bulletin*. She lives in the suburbs of Philadelphia and has a garden and three dogs. She never sang in opera, as she intended to do in the old Hammerstein days. Instead she became an expert society reporter and married Allen Davis, chief political writer for her paper.

Boston has its veterans, too. Mrs. Florence T. Hunt was society editor of the *Herald* for years. She was one of the first women to cover club activities and after a long and successful career she is now retired. A superb figure on the *Herald*, also, was Mrs. Carrie Washburn, member of an old Boston family. She went to Paris every year, and came back with gorgeous new attire. Her diamonds used to dazzle the men in the city room. A third who held the social fort for many years in Boston was Marion Howard Brazier, who wrote for the *Home Journal*.

Caroline Kirkland was the well-known Madame X of the Chicago *Tribune*, a column created in 1909. When Medill McCormick asked

Miss Kirkland to write a weekly lead for the society column, she was afraid she could not do it. But her anonymity saved her from self-consciousness and she let herself go in a sharp analysis of the current social scene. From then on she was the author of a column which she described as a pillar of polite piffle. During the next twenty years it became a well-known landmark in Chicago journalism. Her style was discursive, intimate, sometimes sharp.

The social czarina of Cincinnati is Marion Devereaux, who inherited from her mother the society desk of the *Enquirer*. She is a power in the city, is consulted about party dates, and can turn the straight story of a wedding into poetical parables. Her copy is sacred. No one would dream of curbing her style. The same is true of Anna Bolton Ellis, who has done society for the New Orleans *Times-Picayune* for the last thirty-four years.

At the turn of the century the social news of San Francisco had a distinctive touch, not matched anywhere else in the country. The old Spanish stock maintained its own etiquette, in spite of the invasion of a dozen different strains. In 1905 Mrs. Austin Walton, now Mrs. Marshall Darrach, began to record their social activities for the *Chronicle* as Lady Teazle. Married to an army captain, she had lived at an army post in Manila during the régime of Governor Taft, and had been left a widow with three sons to support. Since then she has traveled and turned out copy in all parts of the world. Before joining the *Chronicle* staff she attracted attention with a feature article she did from Hawaii on the removal of the bodies of the Hawaiian kings and queens from their historic burial place to a modern mausoleum in Nuano Cemetery.

When she became Lady Teazle, Mrs. Darrach did a daily column and filled two pages on Sunday with the activities of the smart set, then dominated by the sons and daughters of the old bonanza kings who lived in the architectural monstrosities on Nob Hill, soon to be destroyed by fire and the earthquake. She knew the city well and was a graduate of the University of California. She had a good memory for names and costumes. Soon she got a reputation for being able to return to the office at midnight from a ball and with absolute accuracy describe the costumes of most of the women present, without having made a single note. One of these stories, describing to the last diamond tiara what the women of San Francisco wore at the opera on the night of April 17, 1906, when Caruso and Fremstad sang in *Carmen*, got into print but never was read. Five hours later the city was in ruins in one of the disasters of the century, and no one gave a thought to the morning paper.

When Mrs. Smith Hollins McKim, now Mrs. Margaret Emerson, and other social leaders first made their appearance at prize fights, the *Chronicle* debated the advisability of sending Lady Teazle to the ringside. Would it lower the dignity of the society page if Lady Teazle went to the fight? Bill McGeehan, sitting in the sports department adjoining her desk, thought it would not.

Mrs. Darrach interviewed Tetrazzini on Christmas Eve, 1912, when she sang in the street to justify a remark she had made in New York that she would rather sing on a curbstone in San Francisco than in the finest opera house anywhere else. The *Chronicle* took her up on it and staged the performance in mid-winter as a testimonial to the Californian climate. It was a balmy night. Postcards showing women in evening gowns and hatless men listening to the diva on Market Street at midnight on December 24th were distributed by the Chamber of Commerce, to prove the superiority of San Francisco to snow-bound centers. During this period a new woman's page was made up on the *Chronicle*, featuring Helen Dare, Lady Teazle and Annie Wilde, who covered club news in an adroit and satirical vein. Mrs. Darrach, as Lady Teazle, turned out a free column of comment and observation, in the manner of some of the social gossip columns of today. She editorialized on any news items affecting the socially prominent.

In 1913, after her second marriage, she went with her husband to the Orient, where she free-lanced. She was widowed in 1917, returned to America and did newspaper work in Boston, Rochester and New York. For four years she wrote a daily article, "Keeping House with the Hoopers," syndicated by McClure. She was assistant society editor of the New York *Herald Tribune* while Mr. McGeehan was managing editor. One of her sons, Francis A. Walton, is a newspaper man and a novelist. He is on the staff of the New York *Times*.

Louise Weick, who conducted the Lady Teazle column for six years after Mrs. Darrach left, is one of the veterans of the San Francisco *News* today. She started her journalistic career doing police reporting and dramatic criticism in Denver. Then she fell heir to Kathleen Norris' post as society editor of the San Francisco *Examiner* and held it for eleven years. Mrs. Norris had been on the paper for several years in this capacity. When she asked for $50 a week she was told it was too much. So she announced that she would starve rather than stay on for what she was getting. She went to New York and soon she did not have to worry about starving.

Miss Weick was offered her job and took it eagerly. Soon she was doing features, too, and got the salary that Mrs. Norris had demanded. At one time or another she has done everything for a paper except set type and solicit ads. Now she scouts for women's news of a constructive sort. Her special interest in life lies in disseminating information about the menace of the munitions interests. She collects data on this subject and spreads it far and wide.

Ethel Whitmire, a relative of Mr. Hearst's, conducts the society department of the *Examiner*. Mrs. Oscar Sutro, Jr., functions on the *Chronicle* and Mrs. Marie Hicks Davidson on the *Call-Bulletin*. Eileen Jackson is the animated and capable society editor of the San Diego *Standard Union*.

The society editors are in a class by themselves among the ladies of the press. They operate with considerable authority. In many ways they are a remarkable group. Some have inherited their jobs. Some hold them by good social connections. Others are skilled reporters. The Social Register is their Bible. Where it doesn't exist, they try to please their public by quantity rather than quality. The society page is nearly always an accurate reflection of the community it represents. It may drivel or be discriminating, according to the intelligence of the woman directing it, the local sense of social values, or the policy of a paper. But it is rarely inconsequential, since it is a sound newspaper principle that names make news.

Chapter XXXIV

COUNTRY JOURNALISM

NOWHERE IS THE NEWSPAPER WOMAN MORE ACTIVE THAN IN country journalism. In plenty of small communities she practically raises her babies in the waste-paper basket, cooks rice pudding to the friendly thud of the linotype or chronicles the town doings from a cracker-box stance. Quite often she owns her own paper by inheritance from a husband or father. There are more than three hundred women editors and publishers in the country. This does not include the large group of women who help their husbands to get out papers. The jointly run newspaper is no phenomenon in the country town. The wife presides over the front office, often writes and edits much of the copy, is bookkeeper, proofreader and bill collector into the bargain. She can set heads, run the linotype, or make up the paper, and she frequently does.

In North Dakota several papers are owned and edited by sisters. In Kansas, where this type of journalism flourishes, seventy-five women are active on the joint husband and wife ownership basis, or on small dailies and weeklies of their own. As far back as 1894 *Jibber-Jab* was launched in Wichita by Minnie, Mabel and Flora Millison. It was the ancestor of today's paper, the *Democrat*, owned and edited by Mrs. Molly Warren Wilcox. The whist clubs that flourished then provided plenty of copy for the three enterprising women journalists. So did the churches. It was a time when the frivolous young brought whirring locusts into church and propelled them from row to row with their closed parasols. *Jibber-Jab* was described as a society journal. At the end of nine months the three sisters sold it to John Carter, who published it as the *Saturday Review*. Later it became the *Mirror*. For the last thirty-five years it has been known as the *Democrat*.

When Mrs. Ogden Reid received the award of the American Women's Association in the winter of 1935 for her distinguished work in journalism, she chose Mrs. Wilcox to speak for the press of America. "I feel like Cinderella," said Mrs. Wilcox modestly, standing on the same platform as Mrs. Franklin D. Roosevelt,

Anne Morgan, Mrs. Carrie Chapman Catt, Dorothy Thompson, Fannie Hurst, Mrs. Reid and others well known to the public. But Mrs. Wilcox, silver-haired and motherly, brought a fresh touch to the occasion. Her speech gave a vivid picture of the women who work on terms of absolute equality with newspaper men in small communities. There is never any question of sex discrimination in the field of country journalism.

Mrs. Wilcox runs her paper by inheritance. She owns it, edits it, writes for it. She engages in the amiable system of barter known as trade advertising that is characteristic of the small town paper. The *Democrat* has one exchange subscription for twenty cups of coffee and another for ten bowls of vegetable soup with two small restaurant owners who cannot afford the paper except on the barter system. Advertising is paid for frequently in the same way. The joint newspaper owners get their groceries, automobiles, gasoline, radios, shoes and other appurtenances through trade advertising. Rural editors with cows, hens or pigs may exchange subscriptions for feed for the livestock.

In the larger towns of Kansas there are a number of competent women editors, including one city editor. A few of them get out the paper themselves, while their husbands prospect for oil, run for public office, or hold civil service posts. In some cases the husbands are the local shopkeepers or postmasters and their capable wives look after the printing shop.

The newspaper tradition is strong in Mrs. Margie Tennal, of the Sabetha *Herald*, who has been a vivacious country newspaper woman for thirty-eight years and started with Ed Howe. Everyone in Kansas knows of Margie, who likes red velvet dresses and can turn out columns of chit-chat after a visit to the drug store. When she was asked to speak before a gathering of railroad officials at Topeka she took occasion to say that every woman should have three husbands—one to earn a living, one to beau her around, a third to do the housework. This was one of the remarks she dashes off without thought, but she was taken seriously. The item was flashed by the press services across the country. Arthur Brisbane took up the issue. He asked if the "learned Mrs. Tennal knew that in Darjeeling women had four husbands." She has not gone in for public speaking since. Now she puts everything she has to say in print.

Margie was one of a family of six girls and started her writing career by sending all the local gossip to her friends who had gone away to school. Her family lived near Ed Howe in Atchison and they were great friends. He read *The Story of a Country Town* aloud to her mother, chapter by chapter. After she had frivoled away several summers in the late nineties, Mr. Howe said to Margie,

"Why don't you try to work on the *Weekly Globe*, getting advertising?"

She jumped at the chance, worked all summer for $14 and in the autumn got her first job as society reporter for the *Globe*.

Again Mr. Howe interfered in her destiny.

"Margie," he said, "why do you frivol around with all these lads? Why don't you go after Doc? Now there's a man."

Doc was Ralph Tennal, the police-court reporter. Two years later he and Margie were married. They bought the Sabetha *Herald* in 1905. In a few months it was widely quoted. They wrote every line of the paper themselves. For a time Margie set type, but her husband did not approve, for he said that he never went into a country newspaper office that he did not find the editor's wife setting type, and the sight was abhorrent to him. However, she did make-up for years, splashed ink around with a careless hand and always gave her own copy the best play. She wrote a little of everything—advertisements, "sparklers," news items, society, books, drama, and vital statistics. She brought up her son William to be a newspaper man. She took in as many of the local whist parties as she could. She went scuttling to Kansas City for the new plays and found adventure at every street crossing.

Her husband sold the paper once and worked for four years on the Kansas City *Star*, where he edited the weekly edition. Then he resigned. His health was poor. He didn't like big city journalism. They went to California for a year, then bought their paper back at twice the price they got for it. Now their son runs it and they write whatever they like. It is intensely personal journalism. They live over the plant. Doc has a fine rocking-chair technique at mealtime and can eat and rock like no one else in Kansas. Margie does her housekeeping on original principles. She is much more interested in what goes in the paper. She does movie notes and book reviews, and when she goes junketing off in her car to Canada, or some distant part of the United States, she keeps her public posted on every move. Her readers like her to travel. When she does not seem to be getting around enough they write in and complain.

Mr. Tennal signs himself Number 1. Margie signs herself Number 2. When Bill, their son, writes for the paper, he is Number 3. Margie is witty, alert and imaginative—a good reporter. She has the proper spirit for small town journalism. Her sister, Nellie Webb, does society for the Atchison *Globe* and has a column called "Wreaths and Wallops for Women." She succeeded Margie when she married, and also had the benefit of Ed Howe's tutelage.

On a farm near Robinson, thirty miles from Sabetha, lives Hester Potter, a farm woman who contributes several times a week to the

Starbeams of the Kansas City *Star*. Her copy attracts attention. It has a homely flavor and often arouses a laugh. Her piece, "Now a Pumpkin Shortage?" is typical:

> Robinson, Kan. Sir: Just to let you know what is doing up here on the farm. The cows are still kicking the milk pails over. The mush season has arrived along with the spiders' spinning big webs between fence posts and trees. All late planting seems to be in a hurry to bloom. A kettle of soap was made last week. The old grand-daddy black tomcat was the center of the dog fight across the road and down aways; it took considerable in- terference to save his life. School kids are getting pretty well acquainted with their teachers. There seems to be a shortage of pumpkins for the county fairs.   Hester Potter.

One of the best jobs done by a Kansas newspaper woman is Marion Ellet's "Mugwump Musings" in the Concordia *Blade-Em- pire*, a column which is syndicated in some of the larger papers. She is considered a trifle highbrow by some of her colleagues in the state, for she never notices the cows, but writes mostly about poli- tics, music and books. She is small, dark and has a caustic wit. She is widely read and her newspaper copy has style.

Peggy of the Flint Hills lived on a farm until she and her hus- band were lured to Topeka to work for the Topeka *Capital*, Senator Arthur Capper's paper. Her column in the Cottonwood Falls *Leader* attracted the attention of the editors for whom she now works. The Flint Hills of Kansas are like the hills of Jerusalem—bare, rugged, beautiful, with brown and gray rocks. They are covered with blue stem grass which in winter turns wine-red. Cowboys still roam through this section of the state. Peggy, the product of the Flint Hills, goes in for homely philosophy and kindly comment. Her own name is Mrs. Zula Bennington Greene.

Mrs. Tom Thompson, of the Howard *Courant*, has been writing a column of women's observations for her husband's paper for half a century and her readers do not yet know her first name. She signs her work Mrs. Tom Thompson. While helping her husband to get out the paper she brought up her children, including Clad, who took over the difficult job of filling Charles Blakesley's shoes as the Starbeam of the Kansas City *Star*.

Anna Carlson is Lindsborg's prize newspaper woman. Lindsborg is the small country town in the dust storm region of Kansas where Handel's "Messiah" has been presented for the last fifty years. Anna once sang in the famous chorus. The "Messiah" is whistled there on the streets as familiarly as "The Music Goes Round and Around" on Broadway.

Kansas has always been advanced in matters affecting women's rights. It was Susan B. Anthony's state. And one of the women who helped to liberalize the laws of Kansas for women and children was an editor—Clarina Nichols, a friend of Horace Greeley, who ran a small paper in Vermont for ten years before she went to Lawrence in the fifties. Mrs. Carrie Chapman Catt also began her public life as a country newspaper woman. In 1885 she was joint proprietor and editor with her husband, Leo Chapman, of the Mason City *Republican* in Iowa. After a year she disposed of the paper and moved to California, where she continued newspaper work until 1888, when she began to lecture.

In the summer of 1935 Mrs. Mary Elizabeth Mahnkey arrived in New York, a living advertisement for the country newspaper woman. She had been awarded a magazine prize as the best country newspaper correspondent in America. Her work was weeded out from the entries of 1,581 contestants. Mrs. Mahnkey had been doing her gossip column for the *Taney County Republican* in Forsythe, Missouri, for forty-four years, but few persons outside her own community had heard of her until she invaded the front pages of papers all over the country. Immediately she became a refreshing personality to a public weary of synthetic celebrities. She was unmoved by the fast whirl to which she was subjected. She saw the things she wanted to see—Sherman's statue, because her father had served under him in the Civil War; Poe's cottage, the Fifth Avenue shops and Al Smith.

Mrs. Mahnkey did her first reporting at the age of fourteen. Her father corresponded for the Forsythe paper and when he went away on a business trip, his daughter carried on for him. On his return he found she had done such a good job that he let her continue. Since then she has written more than 2,200 weekly letters. All she got for her labor was stamps and stationery. She wrote for the love of it. She took down her notes on sugar sacks in her husband's store, then hung them up on a sticker until Monday morning, when she put her items together. She had a wise aversion to adjectives. Meanwhile she was her husband's active partner in running the country store, brought up three children and never let her newspaper work interfere with her skill at cooking dumplings.

Mrs. Mahnkey is small, plump and fifty-eight. She binds her white hair with a ribbon and has a benign air. Her three newspaper principles are: To tell the truth kindly, to remember that mankind's chief interest is man, and to read over one's copy and scratch out most of the adjectives. She believes in writing "simple and true" and putting plenty of names in the paper. She lives in Oasis, a village in the Ozark region of Missouri with twenty-seven inhabitants. The population of Forsythe is only 281, but her paper has a circu-

lation of 875 among the farmers of Taney County. Oasis has a
cinema theater but no library or bookshop. Mrs. Mahnkey has her
own conception of what makes news. It is more or less typical of
country correspondence. She sums it up like this:

> If any stranger came in or anybody moved or a baby was
> born or somebody got married or died, then that was news.
> And when kinsfolk come from a long way off I'd mention all
> their names and brighten up the columns or make someone
> laugh or please some little child or some old person. If any ex-
> citing crime or anything not exactly right happened in Oasis,
> I just let it go and didn't write it up, because those sort of things
> happen in any place.

Mrs. Mahnkey would pass up a first-class murder any day for a
report on the huckleberry crop around Oasis. She left Charles Preston Mahnkey, proprietor of the Oasis general store, to his har-
monica playing when she traveled East, getting her first experience
of a Pullman car, the subway and skyscraper architecture. She could
not understand why she should win the award or be the object of
so much fuss. "Land's sake," she observed, "out our way women do
everything." When the news is meager she fills out space with her
own verse. Her Ozark lyrics have been published in book form. Her
father was a political figure in the Ozarks. Her son, Douglas, is in
the state legislature. Another Missouri newspaper woman is Mrs.
A. L. Preston, who publishes the *Liberty Tribune and Advance* and
is the mother of the state's largest newspaper family. Seven children
help her manage her plant.

Mrs. Zell Hart Deming, president of the Warren *Tribune Chronicle* in Ohio, was one of the best known of the women publishers
up to the time of her death in 1936. She knew all the mechanical
problems of the plant as well as the pressmen and stereotypers, and
she directed her paper as capably as any man. She pioneered in gaining admission to the conclaves of the Associated Press at its annual
convention and was elected to membership. In 1917 she staged a
fight from the floor to obtain an A.P. franchise for her paper and
won by a vote of 214 to 19, notwithstanding the protests of a
powerful publisher from Youngstown. Mrs. Deming started as a
feature writer, then bought stock in the *Tribune Chronicle* until
finally the editor discovered that she owned the paper, which is the
second oldest in Ohio. It scored a beat in 1812 on Perry's victory on
Lake Erie, the messenger bringing the news on horseback.

Nebraska has a fighting woman publisher, too, in Mrs. Marie
Weekes, who has put over many a campaign in the quarter of a
century that she has been a successful country editor in Norfolk,
Nebraska. She was born on a farm in a tiny box of a house and

taught for four years before going to work on the local newspaper. She started as a reporter and hand compositor. When two of her colleagues went off on a jamboree she had to get out the paper. Thus having learned the business, she mortgaged her home, bought printing equipment and started a fourth weekly in a town of 1,500 persons.

She married a newspaper man and they moved from place to place, launching papers and running them. At last they pulled up in Norfolk and built a newspaper out of a weekly that was practically defunct. They had less than $100 capital to start with, a family to support, and the competition of three other weeklies in a town of about 7,000 population. Everyone predicted they would fail, but eventually they bought the plant, added to it, and prospered. Mrs. Weekes sold the paper in 1931, four years after her husband's death.

It was she who drafted its policy—that it should be readable, truthful, clean and courageous. It was independent politically and she made many friends and enemies. In 1920 she was a farmer-labor candidate for Congress. In the same year she was William Jennings Bryan's candidate as a delegate to the National Democratic Convention. She made a picturesque campaign and although the Harding landslide swept the Republican candidate to victory, she carried several counties without the aid of a party label.

In 1924 she was president of the Nebraska State Press Association, the first woman to act in this capacity. In the same year she organized the Nebraska Writers Guild with Willa Cather and Bess Streeter Aldrich among its members. She is now postmaster at Norfolk, after having put up a stiff fight for the appointment. She was opposed by the local daily, which has frequently engaged her in journalistic combat while she has held state and political offices. Her newspaper column, "A Woman's Viewpoint," has always been widely quoted in her native state.

The country newspaper woman has a freedom of expression denied the metropolitan reporter. She can push a local cause, mix freely in political fights, write what she likes and continue at her job until she is eighty years of age, if her eyesight is good and she so desires.

Chapter XXXV

THE FIELD WIDENS

THE NEWSPAPER SERIAL WRITER RARELY SEES THE INSIDE OF A newspaper office. She is of the profession, yet apart from it. If she is successful she makes a princely salary and pours out volumes of words that go on, day after day, ringing the changes on a single theme. Every syndicate has its pet serials. The public eats them up. The troubles of the married have most pull in this field. Their problems become extraordinarily real to their scattered audience. Sometimes when an author tries to bring a popular serial to an end, the clamor keeps it going, as in the case of "Helen and Warren," written by Mabel Herbert Urner for the McClure syndicate, and "Chickie," written by Elenore Meherin, who was one of Fremont Older's pupils until Mr. Hearst lured her away to do six serials at $15,000 each. She started on "Chickie" purely by chance, never dreaming that it would turn into a gold mine.

When she was fifteen years old Miss Meherin made a tour of the newspaper offices of San Francisco, but failed to impress any of the editors. On her last call she alarmed a youthful city editor by telling him she could not go home without a job. He handed her a clipping about some evictions that had taken place. "Get the dope on some of these," he said. "Maybe there's a story."

Miss Meherin did enough research for a master's thesis. No one was slighted—the sheriff, the landlords or the wretches whose goods were dumped in the street. Next day she turned in a column story and got a by-line.

"Now," said the editor. "Show me what initiative you have. Go out and get a story on your own."

At the moment she could scarcely remember what initiative meant, but by morning her confidence had returned. It was a Saturday. Her father, a great adventurer, gave her his horse and buggy. She took her young sister and together they trundled six miles to the poorhouse. Her object was to find out what had become of the people thrown out of their homes. She did character studies of some of them. Again she got a by-line.

Miss Meherin worked for the rest of her vacation on this paper, receiving twenty cents an inch for her copy. When a ghost story, sent to the Sunday magazine section and garishly illustrated, brought in $7.50, she felt that her career had started. But it was a long time before she landed a regular job and a real salary. Her luck turned in 1915, when she got on the staff of the Oakland *Post-Inquirer* at $15 a week. Two years later she finished her course at the University of California. At about the same time she wrote two stories that attracted the attention of Annie Laurie and Emil Gough, managing editor of the *Call-Bulletin*. One of these was a signed interview with one of the girls involved in the Diggs-Caminetti Mann Act test case in 1913. The story attracted national attention because one of the men involved was the son of a United States Commissioner of Immigration. The other was an architect who belonged to a well-known family. Miss Meherin's interview was the first statement from any of the principals. The paper played it for a full page. She was offered a job on the *Call-Bulletin* as special writer at $30 a week and continued to do feature work during the war.

Her serial career began when Al Jennings, famous bandit of the Southwest who was familiar with the prison in which O. Henry served his term, walked into the office one day. He was a picturesque little dynamo—not at all the traditional bad man. He was undersized and magnetic, standing about four feet eleven inches, with brick-red curly hair, wild gray eyes and a juvenile grin. He had a remarkable gift for anecdote and began quite casually to tell the inside story of O. Henry's Jimmy Valentine. Mr. Older, a good story-teller himself, saw possibilities for a serial. He called Miss Meherin into the office to hear Jennings talk. Jennings differed from Oliver Goldsmith in being an inspired angel when he talked, a dullard when he wrote. After two hours of graphic narrative he left. Mr. Older, greatly stimulated, asked Miss Meherin to write a foreword for a serial. She was dismayed. She had enough material for three good features and that was all.

Jennings was in San Francisco making a personal appearance while his cowboy film was being run off. He was as hard to catch as mercury. For three days she chased him through speakeasies, dressing-rooms and into churches, where he liked to sit on a Sunday night. Then he bolted to Los Angeles. The story was already running. Miss Meherin had to keep it going, so she pursued him there and dragged all she could out of him in six hours. Having read most of O. Henry she drew her own conclusions.

The serial ran for sixty chapters. It was later published by Jennings under the title *Through the Shadows with O. Henry*, and it was Miss Meherin's first plunge into this field. Mr. Older wanted her to start immediately on another, since he regarded a good serial as the best of all circulation bait. She suggested writing the romance of a San Francisco girl, bringing in as much local color as possible. She knew nothing of fiction writing, but she embarked on "Ann." She would do a chapter and get it finished only a few minutes before the deadline. It was no sooner set up than another idea always came to her—the right one. She harassed the men in the composing room. Often she sneaked down at midnight and cajoled them into setting whole galleys.

When the shop girls began ringing up to say they would cancel their subscriptions if the villain were not punished, the circulation department asked that the story be continued indefinitely. The result was a sequel, "Ann and Phil," which ran 134 chapters. After this Miss Meherin had no chance to do anything but write serials. She had one under way in 1923 when she happened to visit the San Francisco General Hospital. A young girl was brought into the emergency ward who had just attempted suicide in the waters of the bay. She was a handsome Norwegian, well-educated, unmarried and about to have a baby. Her case was a little different from the usual one of its kind. It affected Miss Meherin profoundly. From it she wove her synopsis for "Chickie." When Mr. Older read it over he ran his hand in a characteristic gesture over his face and remarked, "If you live to be a hundred years, you will never get a better plot than this. When will you have the first chapters?" "Chickie" ran 113 chapters and was followed by a sequel of 90 chapters. She was making $75 a week at the completion of her fourth serial, so with the new one pending she left her job and announced that she would not work again unless she were paid $125 a week. The paper thought it a hold-up, but agreed, and gave her the salary she wanted at the start of "Chickie." The story went over with a bang. The circulation made a record gain. The story was syndicated in hundreds of papers and was later screened. It was published in book form and, along with its sequel, sold 300,000 copies. At about this time she signed her contract with the Hearst organization to write serials, which she has been doing on and off ever since.

Dicky and Madge Graham, another pair of serial ghosts, are as real to their followers as two flesh and blood persons. Their matrimonial ups and downs have been chronicled by Adele Garrison for the last twenty years in "The Revelations of a Wife" and its sequels. She has written 6,000,000 words about the Graham family, their relatives and friends—more than twice the wordage of the Bible, the Arabian Nights and the works of Shakespeare combined. Dicky and Madge have lived through many hair-raising adventures. There has never been a day when the last line of one instalment has not left the fans in suspense and ready to walk through snowdrifts for next day's paper.

Miss Garrison is the wife of Martin A. White, commonly known as "Matty" White. She was born in Clinton Junction, Wisconsin, and taught school in isolated Wisconsin villages and in Milwaukee. Then she turned to newspaper work, first on the Milwaukee *Sentinel*, where she was assistant Sunday editor, then for the Hearst papers in Chicago. She could write straight news and turn around and do a woman's angle with equal facility. She wrote as Evelyn Campbell and her signed stories dealt with murders, fires, trials, political scandals or whatever came along. She retired from active newspaper work when she married Mr. White.

For the next eight years she devoted herself to her husband, her home and her small son and daughter. Then, in 1915, she embarked on "The Revelations of a Wife," turning out daily instalments of 1,000 words. There have been fifteen phases in the lives of the Grahams but no let-up in the excitement. Miss Garrison's ingenuity is boundless. She weaves a plot, unravels it and gets a fresh start now and again. She can turn out her copy in intervals between entertaining friends, seeing that her household is running smoothly, and carrying on her club work. She goes for days on end with little sleep, sits up half the night with guests, and when the last one has started for home, continues her revelations, due in the office next morning. A few hours of sleep and she starts off on a 350 mile drive into northern New Hampshire for a week-end at a lakeside cabin. She now writes in her automobile to save time. She plants her portable on a suitcase on her knees and turns out copy, or else she takes the wheel herself and dictates to a secretary or to one of her children. Reading and gardening are her two recreations.

Another of the more talented serial writers was Mrs. Idah McGlone Gibson, author of the popular "Confessions of a Wife," who died recently at the age of seventy-three. She was born in Toledo, Ohio, and worked for years on the Toledo *Blade*. Later she was on the Chicago *Tribune* and the Los Angeles *Herald*, ultimately going over to NEA.

The woman sports writer is a comparatively new factor in the newspaper world. Here and there one of the earlier women reporters may have turned her hand to an occasional sports story, but only in an emergency or for a novelty. Now the larger papers are definitely featuring their women sports writers. It is no longer a trial for the hard-boiled experts of the sports department to find a young girl underfoot when they launch their choicest expletives.

When Margaret Goss, sister of Eleanor Goss, the tennis champion, joined the staff of the New York *Herald Tribune*, the question arose whether to let her loose in the jungle inhabited by Grantland Rice, Bill McGeehan, Bill Hanna, and some equally courteous associates, or plant her safely beside the two women reporters on the city staff. Miss Goss was fresh from college, young, eager, thrilled to have a place anywhere on the editorial floor. She was put at a desk beside the two reporters and pioneered so successfully that most of the New York papers soon followed suit.

Miss Goss is one of the six Goss sisters, all fine athletes. Late one summer night, soon after her graduation, she was sitting in the living-room of Ogden Reid's camp in the Adirondacks when suddenly Mrs. Reid asked her about her plans for the future. As a strong feminist it was unthinkable to Mrs. Reid that a girl of twenty-three should not want to take up some work. "Marry if you must," she advised her, "but keep your own identity and be able to stand shoulder to shoulder with any man. How splendid to hold your own place in the world, in spite of home, husband and babies! Have you ever thought what you would like to do? Would you care to try a job on the *Herald Tribune*?"

Julian S. Mason, managing editor of the paper at the time and an executive who always was friendly to newspaper women, proposed to Miss Goss that she should try the kind of column on women in sports that Grantland Rice did on men—a blend of criticism, comment and verse. Her department was launched with a series of articles on sports at the women's colleges. She toured them all, talked to the students, took careful stock of what she saw. Although it was her first newspaper work, the series was done in a professional and entertaining manner. It began on the front page in the spring of 1924 and carried Miss Goss's by-line.

Next, her column "Women in Sports" appeared in the regular sports section. She had to dig up her own ideas. She interviewed the women athletes who figured in the news at the time. Helen Wills, Glenna Collett, Mary K. Brown, Gertrude Ederle, all passed in review. As time went on she got assignments and went out on sports events. She did an exceptionally fine story when Mary Brown defeated Glenna Collett in the golf national at Shenecossett.

When tennis, golf and swimming petered out, Miss Goss still had basketball, field hockey and track events on which to fall back. Her own sound background in sports gave her column authority. She did not have to grope for technical knowledge. She already had it. In addition, she had a neat turn of phrase and wrote good verse. The innovation was a success. Letters of commendation came in. The idea was taken up elsewhere. She started a vogue for women sports writers. Grantland Rice was enthusiastic about the column and offered suggestions from time to time. And Bill McGeehan, shyest and most silent of men, stopped Miss Goss one day and observed in his absent-minded manner: "Your stuff is good. Keep it up." This was all he ever said to her in the two years that she worked in his department, but it was volumes, coming from Mr. McGeehan. But her big moment came one day on the top deck of a Sandy Hook steamer, which was jammed with brokers reading their papers. She watched with interest as one man turned to the sports page which featured her own column. She held her breath. Could it be possible? He folded the paper in half, then again in quarters. At last, with great care, he narrowed it down to a single column and settled back to read. The column was "Women in Sports."

After two years Miss Goss left the *Herald Tribune* to marry Walter Huber. She is now the mother of four sons, including twins, and lives in Locust, New Jersey. She still wields a competent tennis racquet, rides, swims, skis and goes in for the athletic life. She was followed some time later on the paper by Janet Owen, who does sports for George Daley. Years earlier Harriette Underhill also turned in sports copy to Mr. Daley, for she was really the pioneer woman sports writer in New York. Miss Owen is a graduate of Barnard. In 1928 she went into the *Evening World* office one day and proposed that she should do a sports column. Gertrude Lynahan and Nan O'Reilly had both done good work in this field for the Pulitzer papers.

Miss Owen's column pleased Jack Rainey and she was taken on the staff. At first she did women's hockey games and basketball. Then her activities widened. Sometimes she had to talk herself into exclusive clubs. They were not all prepared for the advent of the woman sports writer. She went about her job seriously and studied the technical side of sports. When the *World* was sold, her by-line began to appear in the *Herald Tribune*. She occupies a desk in the sports department now and comes and goes, as matter of factly as if she had never worked anywhere else. She gets assignments, like the men on the staff, and covers them capably, with no fuss.

Nan O'Reilly, who does sports for the New York *Evening Journal*, was put through a rough apprenticeship before she made a place for herself with her brightly written copy. She was the oldest of eight children and started out at fourteen to earn a living. She worked for Earl Hathaway, who did a real estate column for the *Tribune*. When he died, she inherited his job. Her next venture was working for Percy Pulver, the golf expert, and when he found that he could not cope with all his orders, he asked her to do a column for the *Post*. She signed it Jean Sanderson, and the general assumption was that it was written by a man. Under the same name she did jobs for the Associated Press. Joe McGinnis sent her all her checks, so that she need not put in an appearance and disclose the fact to the staid A.P. that she was a baby-faced girl with rather long curls.

Miss O'Reilly and Mr. Pulver got out a magazine together—*The Professional Golfer.* She solicited ads, wrote much of the copy, signed all sorts of names, took pictures, got to know the golfers. Then one day she walked out on Mr. Pulver, who had his crabbed moments. After that she sold sports stories to most of the New York papers, and finally settled on the *World*, when Mr. Swope had been converted to the idea by a story she had written for the Sunday paper

In time Bill Farnsworth invited her to join the *Journal* staff as a golf expert. She has covered tournaments all over the world and knows what she is writing about. She does a daily golf column, summer and winter, covers horse and dog shows, interviews the wives of pugilists, but refuses to turn sob sister under any circumstances. She gets on well with her colleagues, although she had some heavy pioneering to do in the closed corporation of sports writers.

While working overtime for Mr. Pulver, Miss O'Reilly wrote insurance policies on Maiden Lane and typed for the Authors' Service Bureau. She got a job with the telephone company so that she could write an authentic story about the life of an operator, but she never found time to do it. She worked for Rex Beach in her spare moments, and for Willard Mack when he was writing *Tiger Rose*. She had a play *Four O'Clock* produced on Broadway.

For two years Miss O'Reilly concealed the fact at her office that she had married a man of wealth. She loved her job, but feared it might fade from her life if the news got around that a car with chauffeur was waiting for her down the block, that she had a sixteen-roomed house in the fashionable Sixties, and five maids to get her started for the day. However, the depression made all things equal, and now she cherishes her pay check.

The conservative *Times* has also opened the door to a woman sports writer—Maribel Vinson, the skating champion, who shows up regularly in the office and is nimble on a typewriter when not cutting figures on the ice. Miss Vinson, a Radcliffe graduate, comes from Boston, the child of professional skaters. She learned to perform on double runners at the age of three. Her progress was rapid. She became national champion at sixteen, and has won many titles since then. She writes about baseball, basketball or anything that comes along, but she avoids any comment on skating, lest she run into a snag on her amateur standing.

Frances Turner has done sports for the Baltimore *Sun* for the last six years. But it took two years of constant badgering to persuade an editor that it would be a good idea to have her on his staff. She is a graduate of Goucher College, where she took a short course in journalism. She did some writing on space, worked in the Enoch Pratt Free Library and after much persistence at last got on the *Sun*. In three months' time she had a by-line and a cut of herself at the head of her column. At first it made her shudder to see people walking on it in the gutter, and to catch her own face grinning at her from several morning papers in the street. She felt as if she were a public exhibit. But she soon got over this. She accompanied the United States Women's Lacrosse team on its four weeks' tour of Great Britain in the summer of 1935. She belongs to a number of clubs and writes on sports for the magazines. Miss Turner got her start in athletics at Camp Ken-Jockette in Vermont. She won her first spurs there, making teams, winning swimming emblems and cups. She is a cousin of Lida Larrimore, the author.

Here and there throughout the country women city editors and copy readers compete with men, but they are the rare exceptions, although on a small paper a woman may fill all the functions of newspaper editing without carrying the title. Ruth Finney, Helen Havener, Virginia Brastow and Laura Vitray all were city editors at one time or another. Today one of the few working anywhere in the country is Lucille Norton, who is city editor of the *Daily Record* in Canon City, Colorado. She has held down the job for eight years. On the night of the riot at Canon City state penitentiary, she and her staff of men were on the spot and worked all night rounding up the story. Miss Norton writes her own heads, does make-up, handles the United Press reports, edits copy, reads proof and directs her staff. By way of diversion she writes a human interest column called "Fancy That."

But Portland, Oregon, boasts two first-rate women copy readers. One of them is Jessie Goulds Olds of the *News-Telegram*; the other is Elinor Pillsbury of the *Oregon Journal*. Miss Olds started life in Wenatchee, Washington, and in her adolescence worked in a printing shop. She attended the University of Oregon for three years but found that she learned a good deal more while she worked as a waitress in a down town restaurant to help pay for her college tuition. In 1926 she occupied a desk outside the editorial rooms of the *Telegram*, an office where Rudyard Kipling once applied for a job as a reporter and was turned down. She answered telephone calls and dealt with the curious procession that invades the outer offices of most newspapers—the woman who has crocheted a crossword puzzle for the paper, the taxpayer, the crank, the fanatic and the publicity man.

She handed in stories now and again and finally produced one that caught the fancy of the news editor. With a flourish he marched out into the hall, picked up her typewriter and deposited it inside the charmed door of the news room. Because his domain was the copy desk, Miss Olds became the special pet of this department. It was an old-time copy desk, with ancients sitting around the rim who had seen life here and there and were so hard-boiled that they were petrified.

Miss Olds did courts, crime or any news that broke in the city. She watched Schumann-Heink being squeezed into her corsets, heckled Aimee McPherson, carried a spear in Pavlowa's ballet and stood five feet from her while she did the swan dance. She got to her first murder so fast that she stepped right into a pool of blood. She exposed a tuberculosis cure sponsored by a rival paper and was such an eager little worker that she was kept around the office waiting for anything that came up. So she took to writing heads in her spare time, and soon landed on the desk opposite the city editor. In 1931 the *Telegram* was bought by the *News*, a Scripps paper, and she went on the copy desk.

She now takes stories over the telephone, writes heads on local and wire copy, does captions for pictures, edits some of the syndicate features, and dashes to the composing room with copy in an emergency. Having tasted the excitement of trying to get the sense of the gold-clause decision into a banner line, or having the Wiley Post-Will Rogers crash break exactly on the deadline for the morning bulldog edition, society news and Cynthia Gray seem tame to Miss Olds. But she still winces when she thinks of the head she wrote on a second-day story from Chicago about the deluded crowds that thronged to see a vision of the Virgin Mary in a lighted window. The gist of the story was that the vision was just an odd shadow on the window curtain in a flat occupied by a gangster. Her head ran:

VISION OF VIRGIN
IN GANGSTER'S FLAT
HELD NO MIRACLE

The *News-Telegram* also has a clever girl reporter who covers the waterfront—Katherine Watson Anderson. She has found plenty of excitement at the docks, but little time for gentle contemplation in the Max Miller manner. During the longshoreman's strike of 1934 she was sent to the scene to get sidelights. She managed to get farther than anyone else because she was a girl. The men on the story were forever explaining that they were not strike-breakers, whereas Kitty could walk for miles unmolested. She got the best stories of the strike. She camped with the pickets and the police force at the terminal where the major battles were staged. She was tear-gassed at the height of the excitement.

Miss Anderson was sent to one of the docks with a photographer while the strike was at its worst. Press passes were of no use, since the pickets had issued an ultimatum that morning that no one was to be admitted to the dock where a ship was trying to load up with the help of a scab crew. By this time it was the custom to admit Miss Anderson when the men were barred. But when she got to the gate a striker from out of town was in charge. He failed to recognize her and he held her back. He told the men to slash the tires of the car and smash the photographer's camera, if any attempt was made to enter. Miss Anderson told the photographer to wait for her. She walked through the picket lines and kept on going in spite of threats and longshore curses. She is only five feet tall and even the enraged strikers could see that it was as well to let her alone. The picket who turned her back was almost tossed out of the union when word of the incident spread. After that Miss Anderson had a special escort from her longshoremen friends. The head of the beat-up gang was assigned to take her to any place at any time, proving that the girl reporter may have her uses in the roughest spots.

Miss Pillsbury, who has put in ten years of work on the copy desk and another five on general work, is rated one of the most capable newspaper women of the West. She is calm, expert and fast. She thinks the copy desk the most fascinating spot on a paper, but believes that it will never be an open field for women. She started newspaper work when she was twenty, after a year's teaching in the country and a summer job in a railroad office, filing freight bills of lading and watching the trains going by. It was war-time and she landed without much difficulty on the Portland *News*. At first she did general work, but because the staff was small, she was often called on to help out for an hour or two on the copy desk. In a short time she learned what to do and could write heads, cover the court-house beat and do woman's page stuff all on the same day.

By 1921 she was working full time on the copy desk. For the next seven years she was the stand-by of the paper in this capacity, proving her capability time and again. Then she went to San Francisco and worked briefly on the *Bulletin*. She returned to Portland and her old paper. She now edits the club department, does general news, and assists on the city desk.

The newspaper morgue welcomes women, although in New York men direct the most important libraries. But there is an even division of the sexes among the reference workers throughout the country and women run three of the best newspaper libraries—Mildred

Burke of the Chicago *Tribune*, Agnes J. Petersen of the Milwaukee *Journal*, and Blanche Davenport of the *Christian Science Monitor*.

The old-time morgue where clippings and cuts were haphazardly filed away is passing out. The up-to-date newspaper prides itself on its orderly, complete and usable reference department. When news breaks close to the deadline and a fifteen-year-old clipping sometimes holds the vital clue to a story, the morgue becomes the indispensable stand-by for reporter and editor.

The improvement in the newspaper library has been effected largely since the war. The calls at that time were unprecedented, and the stupidity of archaic filing methods became apparent. The war itself added its most fascinating page of live history to the newspaper library. Today the morgue librarian must be a college graduate, preferably from a school of journalism where library courses are given. She must have some special training for her work, and she is not a complete success unless she has as keen a news sense as a reporter.

Miss Burke attended the University of Chicago and Columbia University, and took special training in library work at Western Reserve University. She managed a bookshop and had business training, so that she has thorough equipment for her post. Under her direction more than 100,000 clippings are filed in a year and 2,500 subjects are listed. There are 15,000 books on the library shelves, including all the standard reference works, for the calls made on a newspaper library cover much ground and range from Egyptian dynasties to Huey Long.

The real excitement lies in the constant calls from reporters who hurry in as news is breaking. Old crimes are dug out of the files. Forgotten catastrophes are rehashed. The moldering clippings come into the open, with romantic echoes from the past. They make an authentic historical record available nowhere else. But the calls from inside the office are only part of the story. Thousands of demands come from all parts of the world—from scientists, research workers, students and the man in the street. Their requests are often fantastic, obscure or difficult.

The Milwaukee *Journal* has built up one of the best libraries in the country from small beginnings. It was started a quarter of a century ago with a few cuts and mats, some clippings, a copy of Webster's dictionary, half a dozen annuals and the Wisconsin Blue Book, all within reach of the city editor's desk. After the war Miss Petersen took charge. At that time the calls averaged 504 a month. Today they run up to 4,000 a month. The files contain more than 550,000 photographs, 100,000 cuts and mats and 750,000 clippings. The library has been enlarged and modernized. There is a special section for the exclusive use of the public. Miss Petersen directs a staff of eight. Like Miss Burke, she had special library training. She is a native of Manitowoc, Wisconsin, took a library course at Wisconsin Library School, and worked in various public libraries before joining the staff of the Milwaukee *Journal* in 1919.

A number of school of journalism graduates have found their way into newspaper libraries throughout the country. It gets them at least next door to the excitement they seek. For by now the student of journalism knows when she embarks on her course that girl reporters are not strewn as thickly as daisies through the profession. Today the schools emphasize the opportunities on the small daily or weekly. They do not harp unduly on the chances in the metropolitan field, for they know that this is futile. But there is no stemming the tide that pours forth hopefully every year, some to marry, some to drift into other occupations, the lucky few to invade the city room. More than 1,900 daily newspapers are published in America and 10,200 weeklies and semi-weeklies. The number of school of journalism graduates who get a foothold is increasing every year. Some of the best newspaper women in the country have arrived by this conventional route, in spite of the openly expressed skepticism of city editors.

As far back as 1903 Joseph Pulitzer talked of endowing a school of journalism. In 1908 the first department of this sort was established by the University of Missouri, and four-year courses in journalism were launched in other state universities. The first school of journalism in the East was started at Columbia in 1912 with Mr. Pulitzer's $2,000,000 bequest. By 1925 more than two hundred American colleges were offering instruction in journalism and twenty universities had fully organized departments.

In 1926 Professor Charles P. Cooper set up a separate women's copy desk table at Columbia. The make-up used was that of an afternoon paper with a four o'clock deadline. The students had to write heads, edit copy, go through the entire routine of the newspaper day. His idea was to test the skill of the girl students against that of the men. He found that they were equally competent. The finished papers were as good as those of their rivals, sometimes better.

Theta Sigma Phi, the national professional fraternity for women in journalism, has a membership of 4,600 women all over the country, with nearly 3,000 engaged in some form of writing. It has chapters in forty colleges and alumnae chapters of active workers in twenty-one cities. It was founded twenty-five years ago with two professed purposes: to improve the status of women in journalism and to aid in raising the standards of journalism itself. It publishes *The Matrix* regularly—a magazine which follows the activities of newspaper women throughout the country and records the progress of the graduates of the schools of journalism.

Thousands of girls have taken the journalism course; thousands more are taking it now, dazzled by the legends of the profession. More and more of them are likely to crash the pearly gates, for the young college girl is undoubtedly making headway against the faded veteran in the city room.

PART FOUR

Chapter XXXVI

BOSTON

IN 1842 CORNELIA WELLS WALTER WAS STEALTHILY APPOINTED
editor of the Boston *Transcript*, to succeed her brother, Lynde
M. Walter. She was twenty-seven at the time and the paper tried
to keep the dreadful secret that a woman was at the helm. However,
the news got out and the other papers patronizingly applauded the
Transcript's enterprise in trying petticoat rule.

Miss Walter believed in editing the paper from her drawing-room.
She visited the office only now and again, and did most of her work
at her home in Belknap Street. But she gingered things up all around.
More attention was paid to literary, social, dramatic and musical
matters. Boston was in its heyday of concerts and lectures. The lively
doings of a single evening were summed up by Miss Walter in an
editorial which appeared on November 7, 1842:

> Boston is a great city. There was, last evening, a lecture and
> a tea party at the Odeon—a concert at the Melodeon—a fair and
> tea party at Amory Hall—*something* at Ritchie Hall—a temper-
> ance meeting at Faneuil Hall—preaching in Park Street Church
> —dramatics at the Museum and at the National—a fair at Tre-
> mont Temple—a lecture at the Masonic—a concert at Washing-
> tonian Hall, besides a meeting of the Common Council, and
> probably more religious meetings than we have time or room
> to name.

Miss Walter was a conservative, and deeply religious. She opposed the preaching of Theodore Parker and found his views "vitally
dangerous." She nailed all scientific theories that seemed to conflict
with the Old Testament. "Science is emphatically carried *too far*,
when its far-pushed results become after all only *vain speculation*,"
she pointed out. She was opposed to women's rights but went so far
as to advocate "colleges for females" in the year 1843. She was scornful of the literary efforts of such upstarts as Emerson and Lowell,
and was constantly digging pits for the writers of the day. Looking
over Lowell's first book of poems she found that "a wilderness of

mingled thorns, brambles, shrubs, flowers and trees scattered over with rocks and brawling streams, rather than an exquisitely arranged and beautiful garden, represents the poetry of the new school." She thought that he poured out his rhymes too fast; that he did not condense enough; or file, polish and perfect each piece before writing another.

Miss Walter was harsh with Emerson when he lectured on "Young America" in 1844, but it was her attack on Edgar Allan Poe that set the town talking. Poe visited Boston to speak at the Lyceum on October 16, 1845. Next day Miss Walter delivered an editorial broadside, proclaiming him a washout. The audience had fled from the "singularly didactic excordium" of Mr. Poe reciting "The Raven," she said. She continued her attack day after day until the poet got angry and replied in the *Broadway Journal*. He lampooned Boston and Frogpondians and said he was ashamed of having been born in such a city. Boston didn't like it. Neither did Miss Walter. At last she dropped Poe altogether and turned her attention to other matters. She cared little for politics or national news, but concentrated on Boston, its people, its traditions and its civic customs. There were two reporters on the *Transcript* at the time, and they made $11 a week each. Miss Walter made $500 a year, which was neither more nor less than her brother had made.

The *Transcript* was still in its infancy. Its one woman editor retired in 1847 to marry William B. Richards, and papers in different parts of the country made editorial comment on the end of the venture. Henry Worthington Dutton and James Wentworth, the owners of her own paper, gave her a complimentary send-off:

> It was a great experiment to place a lady as the responsible editor of a daily paper. She made the trial with fear and trembling, and her success has been triumphant. She was quick to conceive an idea; her first thought was always the best; and consequently what flowed from her pen needed little or no alteration. As an editor, she was a woman of great resolution and high determination, and when she took ground, no flattering tongue could dissuade her from her purpose.

Miss Walter died in 1898. The next woman to show up in the *Transcript* offices was Mrs. A. Lincoln Bowles, known professionally as Nancy Hanks. When she went out on an assignment in the nineties, she returned to the office post haste in a horse car, rolled back her veil, dug her notebook out of her reticule and busied herself with a pen. Pursuing her duty one day, Mrs. Bowles heard a tremendous crash and in the ambiguous language of the day "knew no more." There had been an explosion in the subway, which was then in process of construction, Boston beating the field in this respect.

She was badly hurt, but recovered and returned to the paper to work for another forty years. In the city room of the *Transcript* there is still a picture of her, taken thirty years ago, showing her with plumed hat, pompadour, voluminous skirt and shirt-waist with watch pinned to it. She is still alive, a dignified old lady with rich newspaper memories.

Mrs. Bowles is a link between the old and the new. She saw Sally Joy's generation die out and Mary Elizabeth Prim's take over. Although the Boston papers have come around slowly to the idea of using women for general work, they have had a number of enterprising girl reporters, dating back to the day when Sally Joy stormed the city room of the *Post* and had a path of newsprint laid for her. In the late eighties and the early nineties all the girls who worked for the papers in Boston were literary in their tastes. They made no attempt to go in for stunts like their contemporaries in New York, and although they read of Nellie Bly's doings with interest they did not envy her. Things were done on the dignified scale.

There were no balloon flights or deep-sea diving for Lilian Whiting, a native of Niagara Falls, who was literary editor of the Boston *Traveller* from 1885 to 1890 and was leading a sheltered life while Nellie Bly was unmasking the mashers in Central Park and invading institutions in disguise. Just about the time Nellie completed her dash around the world Miss Whiting became editor-in-chief of the Boston *Budget*. She wrote editorials, literary reviews and a Beau Monde column that was popular. She contributed to various papers throughout the country and wrote essays and verse.

Miss Whiting is a descendant of Cotton Mather. Her father, L. O. Whiting, helped to frame the constitution of Illinois. Her first journalistic work was done in 1879 for the Cincinnati *Commercial*, Murat Halstead's paper. Her literary and art criticism was popular in Boston during the eighties and nineties. Miss Whiting still lives in Boston.

All the advances made by women in journalism during this era were chronicled with spirit by Helen M. Winslow, a Vermont girl who wrote for the *Transcript*, the *Beacon*, the *Herald*, the *Globe* and several other papers. She was one of the six women who founded the New England Woman's Press Association in 1885. Sally Joy was president, Estelle Hatch was secretary and Miss Winslow was treasurer.

She began on space rates, nosing out things not regularly covered, and finally was engaged at $15 a week to edit a woman's page. She grew familiar with all the columns that represented the feminine interests of the period. No one seriously believed that women read papers for the news. She looked after the bicycle craze, fancy work, palmistry, fashions, health, the drama, hotels, books, cooking, clubs, and the correspondence department. It saddened her to see how little welcome women were in newspaper offices. She was consumed with a realization of their wrongs and frequently vented her emotions on this subject in print. When she started a Saturday department that proved popular, her editor announced that he was going to drop her by-line.

"You are getting a great deal of glory out of it," he said, "and some of the men upstairs who do good work but are not allowed to sign their stuff are jealous. You can't blame them."

Miss Winslow was also a feminist. In 1895 she launched the *Club Woman* as the organ of the recently formed General Federation of Women's Club. She published it for seven years. Then she sold it, and it soon died. She wrote her first book in 1899 and her last in 1923. There were twenty-one altogether. Her health gave way in 1930. She is now eighty-four and lives in Shirley, Massachusetts. Her interest in newspaper women and their work is still alive. She was one of the best known members of her craft in the early days.

Another familiar figure in Boston journalism was Mrs. Margaret J. Magennis, who joined the staff of the *Traveller* in 1874 and kept on writing until the time of her death in 1918. She was an ardent temperance and reform worker. For years she not only edited the weekly religious review but did all kinds of reporting, even covering municipal courts for a period of twenty years. Her first important assignment was the Jesse Pomeroy case. She served as probation officer long before women were employed in this capacity in Boston. In her later days she was known affectionately on the *Herald* and *Traveller* as "Old Lady Magennis."

During the years that Miss Winslow was championing the woman reporter and Mrs. Magennis was covering religious news, Mildred Aldrich was active in a parallel field. She put in twenty years of writing for the Boston papers before she went abroad in 1898 to live in France. She started as a clerk on the *Home Journal*, then assumed editorial duties on the same paper. And long before she gave up her desk in 1892 she was the moving spirit of the paper, although her name never appeared in its pages. For the next few years she published *The Mahogany Tree*, but it was not a success. At the same time she wrote for the Boston *Journal* and Boston *Herald*, mostly on the theater.

She was forty-five years old when she went to Paris, where eventually she became a member of the Gertrude Stein group. She took a quiet little gray stone house in the country in 1914 and suddenly found herself a fascinated witness of the Battle of the Marne, which raged right on her own hilltop. She had retired to the country for peace, but found herself in the spotlight. Miss Aldrich and her house escaped miraculously. She stood by her lilac bushes and knew that history was in the making right under her eyes. The bombs passed her by, but later on she found one or two in the fields. The Germans had swung about at a cleft in the hills within view of her house. Her book, *A Hill Top on the Marne*, brought tourists swarming to her door. Miss Aldrich died in 1928.

When Marguerite Mooers Marshall was starting her newspaper career in Boston in 1908 the papers were just beginning to take on college girls. Eleanor Ladd, the widow of Earl Derr Biggers, was one of them. When Miss Ladd left the *Traveller*, her place was taken by Foster Gilman, who is now a literary agent in New York in partnership with Page Cooper. Gertrude Bell Dunn, a Chicago girl, and Jane Pride were two of the brightest newspaper girls of the period. Miss Pride was city editor for a time. She is the ex-wife of Ralph Frye, long a Hearst employee. Jessie E. Henderson, a Radcliffe graduate and afterwards a foreign correspondent for the Consolidated Press, worked on the *Herald* beside Harriet Houghton, a Wellesley girl. Alveda Greenwood, a graduate of Tufts, was on the *Journal*. Solita Solano and Katherine Wright, both of whom later landed on the *Tribune* in New York, started on the Boston *Herald*. Miss Solano, a Spanish girl of talent and temperament, was the first woman dramatic critic in Boston. She stayed briefly in New York, then went abroad to live and to write books. Miss Wright did music criticism for the New York *Herald Tribune* and was Chaliapin's publicity representative at the time of her death.

Even today, some of the Boston newspaper girls have worked their way into the city room through reviewing or criticism. Miss Prim, the ranking woman star on the *Transcript*, is a case in point. She was H. T. Parker's "young woman," just as Brooks Atkinson, Kenneth MacGowan and Hiram Moderwell were his young men. He used to say to her, "Go do the St. James Stock Company. You can get sunshine out of cabbages."

Miss Prim has a delicate wit and a sensitive touch on life and the news. She makes the front page of the *Transcript* constantly with the feature story that runs under a two-column head and is often picked up and commented on by other papers throughout the country. They are known as the Baby Claus stories, named after Henry Claus, the managing editor. More often they are called simply Miss Prim's Babies, so that no one was astonished to hear the make-up man shout to the city desk on one occasion: "Hey, Charlie, we're tight. Can you hold Miss Prim's baby until to-morrow?"

Miss Prim's name is a source of constant jest to her colleagues.

When she was assigned to do antiques, she was sure it was only because she was born Mary Elizabeth Prim. She knew nothing about furniture and never got to like it, or the dealers. But she has made a substantial reputation for herself on the paper and has a sprightly touch for features. Her favorite reading when she was growing up was Elizabeth Jordan's *Tales of the City Room*. Inspired by these, she wrote a series of newspaper stories while still in high school. She had never seen the inside of a city room at the time. They were evolved out of her inner consciousness and her admiration for Miss Jordan. But she sold them to the *Woman's Magazine*, and when the second serial rights were sold to the Boston *Post*, they fooled even a hardened compositor, who said it was easy to see that they had been written by a reporter. Since then she has added real city room tales to those of her imagination. They have been more dramatic than anything she dreamed of when she first broke into newspaper work in the spring of 1929. Miss Prim belongs to the new school of woman reporter. She is scholarly and unobtrusive, applying a humorous, intelligent touch to her work.

Few newspaper women in the country have seen, heard or recorded as much as Mary Mahoney, who starred on the Boston *Traveller* and then the *Globe*, over a period of thirty years. Her scoops are legendary in Boston. She is rarely in competition with women, but works most often with the star men, and they worry until they know that Mary Mahoney is safe in bed for the night. Otherwise, she is likely to be putting something over on them. She had a regiment paged for her once, in order to find one man. She put on a diver's suit and went down to the bottom of the Bay of Biscayne when the bodies which were swept out to sea from Miami in the disaster of 1926 were being raised. She worked with the medical unit doing rescue work, as well as covering the story for her paper. She went through the Gulf of Mexico in a submarine while giant torpedoes were set off and conversation was sustained with other submarines forty feet below the surface of the water.

Some of Miss Mahoney's best work was done on Charles Ponzi, the swindler who caught the country napping. She broke the first Ponzi story on July 3, 1920. She trailed him to Florida when the police were looking for him and was a step ahead of them all the time. Later she had an exclusive interview with him in jail but she could not use it because of court orders. She even dug up angles of the story in Rome and did smart sleuthing on the whole case.

Miss Mahoney is a dauntless character. She has gray eyes, a vivacious manner, a humorous approach to life. Her results are often obtained by her persuasive tongue. She can thaw the stiffest functionary with her Irish wit. When the aggressive manner is needed she can apply it, but usually she wins her way with personality and blarney, for she gets an instant reaction from all social strata. People who never heard of her paper know Mary Mahoney. She is charitable, takes part in the official life of Boston, is a rare soul.

When the war was over, she was assigned repeatedly to cover the incoming ships. She boarded more than a hundred altogether and worked up a record number of human interest stories on the soldiers. When General Charles H. Cole returned, she got in through one of the coal ports of the ship to extend the greetings of her state and city to the hero. Her competitors were always baffled by Miss Mahoney's success at getting on troop ships. There was no stopping her. General Pershing got to know her well, for he heard so many complaints about her. When a ship bringing home 4,500 men cast anchor beyond Ambrose Channel she got aboard and stayed there all night. A rival Boston newspaper man reported the General who permitted her to board the troop ship, and there was an investigation. But a friendly congressman went to the hearing and straightened things out for Miss Mahoney. She gets out of jams as easily as she gets in through locked doors.

She was more amused than anything else when she was arrested in New York with two assistant district attorneys in connection with a jewel robbery. She was taken for the diamond queen and they for the jewel thieves. But she was soon freed when a policeman recognized her as the ubiquitous Mary Mahoney. She has helped the police on a number of stories, and has dug up angles for them when their own ingenuity has given out. Once she trailed a young girl who had been kidnapped, found her, brought her home and had the man in the case arrested and convicted. He served three years for the crime and Miss Mahoney had a clean beat on the story. It took her months to find the girl and push the case through to a finish.

Miss Mahoney went abroad with the Knights of Columbus pilgrimage in 1920. She and her sister, Gertrude, who does society for the *Globe*, were the only women allowed on the trip. She received holy communion from Pope Benedict in the Vatican gardens at a mass celebrated in the open. On this trip Queen Sophia of Greece invited the Mahoney sisters to tea at the palace because, she said, she was interested in American women and thought she could learn something about them from two reporters.

At one time Miss Mahoney was engaged on a series of Black Hand stories that brought strange repercussions. She received a letter saying that if she did not drop them at once she would be found hanging from the cross tracks over Dewey Square. Her paper wanted to turn over the letter to the postal authorities but she would not hear of it, as she thought she knew who had written it. She didn't give the man away and he is now a friend of hers.

When three of the Black Hand murderers went to the chair and a fourth, who had turned state's evidence, was freed, Miss Mahoney was assigned to find him and get a human interest story on how his family welcomed him and what he intended to do. She went to his home in the North End. The woman who opened the door refused any information. The man's two sisters were equally tongue-tied. It was the feast day of the patron saint of Messina and the Italians were celebrating. Flags hung from every window. Colored lights arched the streets. Bands played. Young girls laid bouquets at the foot of the shrine on Hanover Street where the Prado now stands. When the statue of the Virgin was lifted from its shrine and carried on a float through the streets, a procession fell in behind. Miss Mahoney noticed a strange figure, marching triumphantly along— an old woman, barefoot, her skirts full at the waist, short to her knees, the wind blowing her gray hair back from her face. Her lips moved in prayer.

"Who is she?" Miss Mahoney demanded.

"Oh, she's giving thanks. Her boy Tony is just out of jail."

Here was Miss Mahoney's story waiting for her. She followed the woman. Hurrying along beside her, she heard someone call out to a young man holding a child on his shoulder: "Tony, here comes your mother."

She stopped. This was her man.

"Your mother must be glad to have you home," she said.

"Yah?" He glared at her.

She chatted along until she had thawed him. She got him to promise that he would let her photographer take his picture. But the photographer had disappeared. She finally persuaded him to go with her to her office to pose for a picture. Jim Reardon, her city editor, looked astounded when she walked in and announced that she had brought Tony with her.

"Mary, that man is as guilty as hell of four murders and you walked along with him," said Mr. Reardon. "Mary, I never intended you to do that."

"And what would be happening to me?" said Mary lightly.

As Tony was leaving the office, she asked him what he was going to do.

"Oh, some of the fellows are throwing a party at Orient Heights for me tonight," he said.

They did. They took him for a ride. He was driven to Orient Heights and in the morning his body was found in a field with his heart carved out and laid beside him. He paid the price of one day of freedom with his life. His party friends had avenged the death of his three pals.

Miss Mahoney was born in Boston, went to a convent and then attended Simmons College. She was catapulted into newspaper work when a train was wrecked at Sharon, twenty miles from Boston. The Mahoney home was nearby. Mary's father was asked by the Associated Press to assemble facts as fast as he could. He had one of the few telephones in the neighborhood. Soon the Mahoney house was full of reporters, writing bulletins and telephoning to their papers. After that the A.P. asked her father to cover any big news that broke in the vicinity. The whole family pitched in and helped when anything happened. Then the Boston *Globe* asked for the same sort of service, and Mary went into town and said she would like the job.

"No, we can't have you," said A. A. Fowle, the editor. "I have two big objections—one is, you are a woman and I don't want women falling on my neck and weeping; and the other is, I like to use pretty plain language to my boys and it would never do with a woman around."

Miss Mahoney promised never to weep. She said she would ignore the bad language. She got the job and soon became a star. She never heard Mr. Fowle say a harsh word to any of his boys and when he was past ninety she reminded him that she had not yet wept on his shoulder.

For a time she owned and edited a weekly of her own—the Sharon *News*—but when the war tightened her resources she wrote its swan song and bade farewell to her subscribers. Miss Mahoney is married, has a son and three daughters. She lives on Beacon Street, but still rushes out with dash and enthusiasm when the fire engines shriek. She lectures on journalism every year at Emerson College. No one has a better right to say how a story should be covered, but few could ever pick up the knack that Mary Mahoney possesses. It isn't to be found in textbooks. It lies within herself.

Two other Boston newspaper women who know how to crash jails, be on the spot for every emergency, and turn in lucid action copy are Katherine Donovan who has been on the *Daily Record* since 1921 and understands the art of writing for a tabloid, and Peggy Doyle, of the *Boston American*, who took the transition from Chicago to New England without a flicker of concern. After a long siege covering gangster life in Chicago, she landed smack in the middle of the Millen-Faber crime in New England. It was not quite what she had expected of New England.

Miss Doyle started work on the Chicago *Herald-Examiner* in 1917 because her brother Tom, who was on the staff, was about to leave for camp and no one else could decipher the penciled notes of Boersianer, the Hearst financial expert. Peggy substituted for her brother and for two years she typed Boersianer's notes. She got a few financial assignments to cover and then did general work under Frank W. Carson, now with the *Daily News* in New York. Before long she was forced to the conclusion that none of the subjects she interviewed was more agreeable or obliging than the lords of the underworld. The discreet Al Capone once parted with a statement to Miss Doyle that was hot news in Chicago at the time.

"I didn't kill McSwiggin," he told her, when she asked him if he was responsible for the machine-gun death of the young assistant state's attorney on a spring night in 1926. "Quite the reverse. I paid him and I paid him well."

Another of the baddies Miss Doyle covered was Marty Durkin, who was responsible for some of the most spectacular shooting in Chicago's gang history. But Big Tim Murphy was the prize of the lot. He was most considerate always of the girl reporter and often telephoned to Miss Doyle to let her know what was going on in the explosive domains of the underworld. His predictions were invariably correct, except that he didn't see his own doom coming. He was full of jests and inventions. One of his favorite observations was that Smith and Wesson made all men equal.

One rainy day Miss Doyle was assigned to interview Lois Booth, the Canadian heiress who married Prince Erik of Denmark, a match which ended in divorce.

Miss Doyle got on the running-board of the car. The Princess was in a bad humor. She spoke to her chauffeur through the tube, asking him to call a policeman.

"Officer," said the chauffeur. "Look into this, will you? This person is intruding."

Miss Doyle merely wanted to be sure that she really had the Princess in her grip, and that it was not a case of mistaken identity.

"Who are you?" the policeman demanded.

"I'm a *Herald-Examiner* reporter," said Miss Doyle. "But the question is, who is she? Are you afraid to ask her?"

"And who are you?" barked the policeman, sticking his face inside the car.

"I am Princess Lois of Denmark," was the icy retort.

When Miss Doyle moved from Chicago to Boston she thought that the news would be different. But it was essentially the same. She wrote the life story of young John Jacob Astor for her paper, and with equal facility ground out the somewhat tarnished epic of

Norma Millen's life and that of her mother, Mrs. Margaret Smith Brighton.

When Ruth Mugglebee, also of the Boston *American*, was covering the trial of Jessie Costello in Salem, she met Dr. Harry Freedberg, clinical pathologist of the J. B. Thomas Hospital. She was in the press row. He was a witness. They fell in love and were married, in another fast-moving newspaper romance. Only this time the bridegroom was not a member of the press.

Miss Mugglebee broke into newspaper work as a student correspondent at Boston University. Her first assignment was a smoker. She was shy and she suffered. But nothing seemed difficult after that. For the last ten years she has done every type of editorial job for her paper, from society to the lead story of the day. When three car-barn bandits were about to be executed for the murder of a watchman, a Hearst order came through for a drive against capital punishment, to be based on the execution of this trio. Mr. Hearst is opposed to capital punishment and has used his papers repeatedly to foster this opposition, as in the case of Nellie Bly and Gordon Hamby.

Miss Mugglebee was assigned to go out through the community and inspire a sympathy wave against the death penalty, the main idea being that only one of the three had fired the fatal shot. Why, then, should all three die, Magna Charta notwithstanding? One member of the trio was a boy named Eddie Heinlein, who came from a good family. Miss Mugglebee cultivated his mother while the campaign was on. She was assigned to devise some way of getting into the death house to do a story on Eddie. No writer is allowed in Cherry Hill, murderers' row at the Massachusetts State Prison. But Eddie's family coöperated with her and helped her to pose as his cousin, recently returned from a trip and anxious to say good-by to the condemned boy. The family visit to the death house was arranged. A colleague on her paper was assigned to clear the coast of other reporters, so that the warden would not be informed of what was happening.

Eddie's parents and Miss Mugglebee arrived at the prison, laden down with fruits and sweets. The warden was fooled. A guard was assigned to escort her to where Eddie waited for his final summons. But as she was about to enter Cherry Hill door, a reporter from the Boston *Post* spied her and worked like lightning. She was snatched from the death house by the warden, just when the plan seemed airtight. She stayed with the Heinlein family on the night of the execution. Eddie's parrot shrieked. His mother screamed with hysteria. To make things easier for her, the clock was put back an hour, so that she would not know the exact moment of the execution.

Miss Mugglebee worked on the Starr Faithfull case, which was followed with interest in Boston for the good reason that a former mayor of the city was implicated. She ghosted a series of articles for Mary Pickford. She sat with Rudy Vallee most of one night at the Hollywood Restaurant, preparing an answer to Fay Webb's charges, only to have Rudy's attorney destroy the copy. But Miss Mugglebee had a carbon tucked away. She kept a forty-eight-hour vigil outside his Maine house at the time of his mother's death. She is the author of *Father Coughlin of The Shrine of the Little Flower*.

It was another world that Sally Joy invaded—a leisurely world where the essay was good journalism. But today the newspaper women of Boston move fast, do not blink at crime, and are just as aggressive as their sisters in any part of the country.

Chapter XXXVII

BALTIMORE

THE NEWSPAPER WOMEN OF BALTIMORE STARTED EARLY IN THE day to make themselves felt. Mary Katharine Goddard founded the *Maryland Journal* with her brother in 1773 and when he was busy elsewhere she published the paper by herself. It was a big day in her life when she printed the Declaration of Independence. All through the war she got out "extraordinaries," notably one on July 12, 1775, with a three-column account of the Battle of Bunker Hill. She had a hard time keeping the paper going when newsprint got scarce and rags were not forthcoming. But it came out without intermission. She had only one carrier and when he fell ill, customers were asked to call for the paper. Miss Goddard published it in her own name from 1775 to 1784. Then her brother returned and took up the duties of publisher again. The *Maryland Journal* was the ancestor of the present Baltimore *American*, one of the oldest papers in the country.

The conservative city room of the Baltimore *Sun* first harbored a woman in 1888 when May Garrettson Evans went out on night assignments, chaperoned by her mother. The city room was four flights up, so her mother always waited downstairs in the business office until May finished her piece. Finally the girl reporter shook off the maternal shackles and got a stiletto instead. Her colleagues thought she might find it more useful than her bonnet pin.

Returning from an assignment one night along a dark and lonely street she bumped into a man who wouldn't let her pass. When she went to the right, so did he. When she darted to the left, there he was. At first she thought it a ludicrous impasse. Then she saw that he meant it. "What shall I do? What shall I do?" Miss Evans mumbled to herself with Victorian desperation.

With a sudden impulse she jerked out her bonnet pin and decided to go for his eyes. Just as she was about to lunge, the villain retreated and besought her to hold off. His voice was strangely familiar. It soon developed that he was a relative trying to tease her from the depths of his high coat collar. He escorted her home.

When she reached the front steps she sank to the ground and burst into tears. He was dismayed and repentant. The story reached her office. Her chivalrous editors and fellow reporters were appalled at such rude treatment of their Miss Evans. Two days later she found a slim stiletto on her desk, the blade in a leather case. From then on she carried it at night, ready for instant use, partly in her glove, partly up her sleeve. But she never had occasion to draw it. She uses it now as a paper cutter.

Inside, as well as outside the office, her venture into newspaper work caused a stir. To be the first woman reporter on the leading paper in a city with Southern traditions was a radical step. To have left the shelter of the home was a matter of some concern in itself. At that time the editors frowned if anyone in the office dared to speak of the *Sunpaper*, as it is now affectionately known. The *Evening Sun* and the *Sunday Sun* had not come into being. There were only a few telephones in the city. Copy was written in long hand. The reporters toiled up four flights of stairs to the editorial room. The last horse car left downtown before midnight. After that it was either a long walk home or else the shocking expense of a hack. And long skirts gathered dust.

Miss Evans was so much of a novelty that she had to explain herself everywhere. She was always being interviewed on her own emotions, and what her family thought of her hazardous undertaking. The general opinion was that it was a shame to expose a girl to such fearful pitfalls. One warm evening she arrived in the office unexpectedly. She saw that something was wrong. The city editor was overcome with amusement. No one would tell her what was up. So she lingered about and finally went out on an assignment. Later she learned that the assistant city editor had been caught in his shirt sleeves and suspenders. On seeing her coming, he had dived quickly under the city desk to conceal this disgraceful disarray from the *Sun's* Miss Evans. He had stayed doubled up in great discomfort until she went on her way.

"Now look here," she announced to the city room at large after hearing this story. "This will never do. You simply must treat me like one of the boys."

They got over their painful formality but never relaxed on points of courtesy and thoughtfulness.

The round was much the same in the eighties and nineties as it is now. Miss Evans interviewed musicians, lecturers, actors, churchmen, social leaders and strivers, artists, educators, merchants, inventors, fashion experts, prodigies, criminals, reformers, philanthropists, politicians, revivalists, craftsmen and the creature who was just beginning to get herself talked about as the "new woman." Susan B.

Anthony is one of her early memories. Mark Twain told her that he liked the knack his good friend Evangelist Moody had of pronouncing Jerusalem in one syllable. Rhéa, the French actress, drew her young leading man into the interview she was having with Miss Evans and said, "His middle name is Shakespeare—William Shakespeare Hart." Today he is better known to a larger audience as Bill Hart, of cinema fame.

More and more Miss Evans did drama and music. Richard Mansfield told her, "No, I'm not giving Shakespeare this time—it might make the débutantes think a bit, and that would never do." And Nat Goodwin said, "The true comedian acts as if the whole thing were desperately serious to him—there is seldom enough laughter to spare for both sides of the footlights." Joe Jefferson, waiting for his next entrance, slipped into her box unobserved by the audience and concealed himself behind the draperies to admire Mrs. John Drew as Mrs. Malaprop. "Ah," he whispered ecstatically, "what a combination of the unctuous and the intellectual!"

Paderewski, young, with a halo of glinting hair, moved through delirious mobs in Baltimore, did memorable Chopin interpretations, wrote his autograph for Miss Evans on the only white spot, except the face, that he could find on a dark-tinted photograph—the collar. Then one night she listened to Phillips Brooks. At first disappointment engulfed the audience. No one could follow him. But gradually they caught the tide, rose with it. And, again, she saw an audience drunk with delight at the first hearing of the Intermezzo in *Cavalleria Rusticana*. Wagner had just become the subject of violent debate.

Miss Evans heard and talked to all the musical celebrities of the day—the De Reszkes, Plancon, Sembrich, Eames, Calvé—young and at their peak; and Adelina Patti, no longer young, not at her best, but still hailed as the "divine" and making farewell tours; and Campanini, the tenor; and Emma Abbott, keeping her own grand opera company going against odds. Light and comic opera was in high favor. Large-toned singers and choruses in sacred music were popular, as well as oratorio and music festivals. The phantom host of celebrities Miss Evans has interviewed lives in her memory now, in the days of her retirement. In 1929 she ended thirty-five years of active work with the Peabody Conservatory.

One day in the nineties she saw on the *Sun* assignment book opposite her name the note: "Hustle for news." She decided to work up a story on a subject that had long occupied her thoughts—the development of a preparatory music course that would be to a conservatory what elementary and high schools are to college. She got Asger Hamerik, the Danish director of the Peabody Conservatory, to propose the idea to the board of trustees. The story was played up in the *Sun*. It was merely an effort to foster news on a dull day, but it had far-reaching effects. Miss Evans afterwards mapped out a plan for the Conservatory but nothing was done about it until she and her sister, Marion Dorsey Evans, opened a school of their own in 1894. She continued her newspaper work at first, but eventually the school took all her time. Pupils poured in from distant points. In the fifth year it was merged with the Peabody Conservatory and became its preparatory department.

Another of the pioneer newspaper women of Baltimore is Louise Malloy, who started on the editorial staff of the Baltimore *American* under General Felix Agnus. She had a free hand and launched various departments. She did women's clubs, school announcements, dramatic work and editorial paragraphing, which was a feature of the paper. She launched a humorous column under the name Josh Wink, which she kept up for years and which was widely quoted.

Miss Malloy crusaded against the committal of delinquent children to jail for petty offenses, and backed the establishment of the Juvenile Court. She became interested in the Fire Department through a family friend who was a Fire Commissioner. The department had been neglected by the city and the papers, and she practically constituted herself press agent for its expansion and betterment. The resources of her paper were behind her. The high pressure system, at the time of its installation the best in the country, was the result of her enterprise. Conditions in general were improved. Because of her work the Fire Commission suspended its rules and gave her the badge of a registered voter. Besides her newspaper work, Miss Malloy has written plays and operettas.

The fragile and charming sketches which appeared for thirty years in the *Sun*, written by Emily Emerson Lantz, were the output of a newspaper woman who braved the early prejudice and took her place in the city room of the Baltimore *Evening News* in 1894. At the same time she conducted the woman's club page in *Time*, a Baltimore weekly edited by George V. Hobart. From the *News* she moved to the Baltimore *Herald*, then to the *Sun* in 1901. She was an expert on genealogy but, like most of the early newspaper women, she did a little of everything. She was literary editor and dramatic critic at different times and sandwiched in some general reporting. She ran a department known as "Frocks and Frills," wrote a series on Chesapeake steamboat companies and another on the streets of Baltimore. The history of the twenty-three counties of Maryland, published in the *Sunday Sun*, was her last piece of work before her death in the spring of 1931. She was engaged continuously in newspaper work in Baltimore for more than three decades. She was of

Swiss lineage, a native of Lancaster City, Pennsylvania, and was educated at Augusta Female Seminary, Staunton, Virginia.

At the turn of the century baseball stories appearing in the Baltimore papers signed by S. K. M. were written by a woman, although the public did not suspect it until Mrs. Sadie Kneller Miller was unmasked when she went on a tour of the country with the Oriole team. Mrs. Miller not only wrote newspaper and magazine articles but illustrated them herself and came to be one of the crack photographers of the country. She went all over the world, covered national conventions, and was made a sergeant-at-arms to facilitate her activities. President Theodore Roosevelt liked a picture she made of him as well as any ever taken of him.

Mrs. Miller wrote vivid copy, and knew how to hold her tongue when she stumbled on official secrets. She was the only photographer allowed at Indian Head proving grounds. Again she went to the leper colony at Molokai and was allowed to take photographs, under the supervision of Father Damien. When she was sent to the concentration camps near the Mexican border, she conceived the bold idea of crossing the border and interviewing Villa. He received her with civility; sent her with an armed escort to photograph his armored car; showed her his wife's magnificent jewels—looted in a raid on a jewelry store in El Paso.

She went to Hayti to cover a revolution and sent back a series of articles on what she saw. She was at the scene when the wreck of the *Maine* was raised. She made several visits to Panama while the canal was being built and climbed a hundred feet up an iron girder to take pictures, although warned by the officers not to attempt it. But her most venturesome feat was her photography on the firing line at the battlefield of Melilla, when the Spaniards were fighting the Riffs. Her camera was literally under the guns. She was always on the spot for military maneuvers and never missed the annual events at Annapolis or West Point.

After the Germans had taken Heligoland from the English, Mrs. Miller, accompanied by her husband, undertook to photograph the fortifications and war vessels. She had taken several pictures when she was interrupted by a German sentry, who told her that she and her husband were under arrest. They were taken before the commander, who thought they were English spies. They protested that they were merely American tourists taking harmless pictures. Mr. Miller established their nationality with official documents but the commander confiscated Mrs. Miller's films. However, she had substituted blank films for the real ones. She walked off with the authentic pictures and afterwards made duplicates for the government. When Mrs. Miller was taking photographs of the Indian tribes in various states she was cursed by the native priests for photographing their snake dances. They thought that this irreverence would entail bad luck.

Much of her work appeared in *Leslie's Weekly*. She was one of the few newspaper women who could write a good news story and do first-rate photography too. This made her a unique figure in the profession. She became interested in baseball while she was attending Western Maryland College. There she met Charles R. Miller, president of the Fidelity and Deposit Company of Baltimore, whom she later married. She was a descendant of Sir Godfrey Kneller, the English artist. Mrs. Miller died in 1920.

The two Baltimore newspaper women whose names are most widely known today are Sara Haardt, who died in the summer of 1935, and Marguerite Harrison, who left newspaper work to travel and write for the magazines. Miss Haardt, who married H. L. Mencken in 1930, was graduated from Goucher College ten years earlier and then engaged in post-graduate work at Johns Hopkins University. While at college she began writing verse and essays. This led to short stories and novels. She did book reviewing, and from 1925 on was a frequent contributor to the editorial page of the *Sun*, writing sparkling essays once a week in the space usually occupied by her husband.

Mrs. Harrison is a newspaper woman who has sought adventure abroad, done war correspondence, traveled all over the world and written as the spirit moved her. She began her writing career in 1916 as a reporter on the Baltimore *Sun*. Two years later she was a correspondent with the A.E.F. in France, at the same time working as a government agent. She was in Germany for eight months after the armistice, and then went on to Soviet Russia, where she was thrown into jail under suspicion of being a spy, although she was merely looking for local color for her stories. She has traveled through Persia, Turkey, Arabia and the Far East, going into the homes and marketplaces of the natives, to find what women were thinking, doing, saying. She is a journalist in the larger sense of the foot-loose traveler who writes as she wanders. She has found copy wherever she has gone.

In spite of all the enterprising women who have worked in the editorial rooms of the *Sun*, from the days of Miss Evans to May Irene Copinger, Katherine Scarborough found that there still was pioneering to be done as recently as 1918, when she was offered a job on the copy desk. The staff was much depleted because of the war. She was the first and—up to now—the last woman to read copy for the *Sun*. She handled war news, politics, financial copy and local news and she became proficient at the job.

At the start she was not received with enthusiasm by her colleagues. This was an invasion of a strictly masculine domain. They feared it might mean disorganization and cream puff heads, not to mention a cut in pay. So they did not spare her feelings. For a week they gave her rough treatment. But she was so busy trying to master heads that she did not even notice. Then they took her into the brotherhood and accepted her as a capable initiate. She worked side by side with them for three years with no favors asked or given on the score of sex. It was only when they all knocked off work at 2 A.M. that they remembered she was a woman, and one or another of them insisted on escorting her home, because they thought it wouldn't do for a girl to be out on the streets alone at that time of night. But at the end of three years she felt the limitations of her hours and work. After a trip to Europe and a brief period on her return as society editor of the *Sun*, a post which she disliked, she was transferred to the reportorial staff to do politics and general assignments. This was what she wanted.

One night, when Marshal Foch was paying his post-war visit to America, she was assigned to interview him if she could as he whizzed through Baltimore on his way to Washington. But his train was not scheduled to stop en route. Miss Scarborough realized that her city editor could have little hope of her reaching Marshal Foch, but she decided to get the interview at all costs. She trailed the division manager of the railroad to the Rennert Hotel, where he was booked to speak at a banquet. He denied her request and said that only the station master could help her. She asked him for a chit to back her up. He had no paper. Neither had she. So she tore a leaf from a book of powder papers that she carried in her purse. He wrote a note to the station master, as though indulging a child. She rushed out of the Rennert, jumped into a taxi and speeded for the station. Her time was short.

The station master said no. Nothing could be done. The train could not be stopped, not even for a second, not even to oblige the Baltimore *Sun*. It had already left Havre de Grace and would go through Baltimore without a halt. She left his office, feeling that the game was up. But a youth of sixteen who had overheard her request followed her out.

"Lady, do you really want to get on that train?" he asked.

"Do I?" echoed Miss Scarborough. "I can't think of anything in the world I want to do more. Is there any way it can be done?"

"There is," he said. "If you don't mind running over a lot of railroad tracks with me down in the yard. One of the company officials is on that train and I'm to carry his overcoat to him. The train isn't going to stop, but it will slow up long enough for you to climb on board."

Off they went. They scuttled through the yards and reached the strategic spot just as the engine came through the tunnel. The official appeared on the platform. Miss Scarborough gasped out her errand as the train slowed down.

"Sure, hop on," he said, seizing her and his coat at the same moment. The train picked up speed again without having stopped. Luck was with Miss Scarborough all the way, for Marshal Foch had just begun his interview with the reporters who had come with him from New York. She was ushered in just as he was warming up to his subject. Next morning her story appeared on the front page of the *Sun*. Simultaneously the *American*, the rival paper, announced that Marshal Foch had passed through Baltimore the night before on a train which had not stopped, and that he had been invisible to newspaper men who had gone to Union Station to see him.

After the death ten years ago of Katherine McKinsey, who was a mainstay of the *Sunday Sun* for many years, Miss Scarborough was transferred to the Sunday staff. For a time she edited the music, dramatic and art pages of the paper, but recently she has devoted all her time to feature writing on a variety of subjects. She is an expert on Colonial furniture and architecture, and is the author of *Homes of the Cavaliers*.

Miss Scarborough comes of newspaper stock. She is the daughter of Harold Scarborough, who was a political writer on the Baltimore *News* before the Hearst ownership, and has been on the *Sun* since then, in addition to owning and editing two county weeklies. Her brother, Harold E. Scarborough, was head of the New York *Herald Tribune* bureau in London and was one of the best known American correspondents in Europe until his death in 1935. Miss Scarborough studied piano at the Peabody Conservatory of Music and is a graduate of Goucher College.

Chapter XXXVIII

WASHINGTON

WHEN MRS. ELEANOR MEDILL PATTERSON WALKS INTO THE city room of the Washington *Herald*, gorgeous, casual and possessive, the air becomes electric. She is not only the editor-in-chief of the paper, but a woman of dynamic propensities. The drab grow more faded in her presence. She radiates the quality which she defines as flash. She thinks that too many papers are run on fuddy-duddy principles. Hers isn't. It would not be hers if it were.

She was forty-six when she entered active newspaper work, but the transition was simple, for journalism was a family tradition with her. When she started on August 1, 1930, her ideas about newspaper work were already well defined. "Newspaper people," she said, "must have flash, intelligence and a certain amount of ruthlessness. Their work must come first, always first, before everything else."

Mrs. Patterson has worked hard at her editorial job. She is generally credited with having made a success of it. Her first move was to give dash to the columns of the *Herald*. She wanted to make her paper smart. She bothered little with the news, which is more or less standardized in the Hearst papers. All her energies were focused on the departments. She catered quite frankly to women. She began by applying a diagnostic touch to the women's pages, society and clubs—the old stand-bys that have kept newspaper women in jobs since they first got a foothold in the profession.

Like all good executives, she scouted for talent to support her. She got Ruth Jones back from the *Post* to run the society page, a priceless catch for any Washington editor, since Miss Jones is worth every cent of the high newspaper salary she gets. Then Mrs. Patterson embarked on stunning experiments with photography. Her débutantes, brides and patronesses fill practically the entire length of the society page. From this point she went on to dramatizing still life, so that farther back in the paper the housewife finds arresting effects, even with spinach and carrots. She gave emphasis to club news, a department run by Lillian Cutlip. Her dramatic critic is a woman, Mabelle Jennings. Beauty and fashions get a heavy play. She gave the sports section more prominence and instituted a page of pictures. She made Cecilia Barber ("Jackie") Martin her picture editor, an enterprising photographer who has eight men working for her.

Mrs. Patterson likes handsome effects and good-looking girls on the staff—girls who know their way about the capital. She favors social gossip columns such as "Peter Carter Says" or "These Charming People," done by the decorative Martha Blair. The result of all this has been to give the *Herald* a class circulation that it did not have before. It has gained prestige, circulation, advertising, and Mrs. Patterson continues to be one of the most discussed women in Washington. She likes to see the paper come out, and to be within reach of the city room. The first time she ever walked into it she looked around and remarked: "I think that I am going to like this." And she has. She is in and out of the office at all hours of the day. Sometimes she appears in riding breeches, swinging a crop or a sombrero. Often she shows up in her evening things, ready to cast a critical eye over the first edition.

Mrs. Patterson manages to combine her editorial duties with a full social life. She gives elaborate parties at her Dupont Circle home, once occupied by President and Mrs. Coolidge, and at Dower House, in Maryland. Celebrities circle around her. She is picturesque in her habits and appearance. She is tall, has reddish hair, a bored voice and a vivid expression. Causes interest her momentarily, but her paper interests her all the time. She thinks that more girls should take up journalism and begin at an early age. "Start young," is her advice. "Get the technique, the flash, the bloodhound news-nose, the quick pencil, the true judgment, the intuitive sense of mass psychology, while you are still young. And you won't have to fall back on the record of your family as I do."

Mrs. Patterson is the granddaughter of Joseph Medill, founder of the Chicago *Tribune*, the cousin of Colonel Robert R. McCormick, its present publisher, and the sister of Captain Patterson, of the New York *Daily News*, so that she is not lacking in newspaper tradition.

"Mrs. Patterson got in on the roof; most women get in on the ground floor," said Arthur Brisbane, shortly after she started her editorial duties on the *Herald*. Four years earlier Mrs. Patterson had tried to buy the paper but Mr. Hearst would not sell it. Then she proposed that she should take it over and run it, but he turned her down again. Some time later Mr. Brisbane told her there was a chance that she might edit it. She put out feelers and Mr. Hearst made her a flat offer to act as editor-in-chief. Mrs. Patterson leaped at the chance. She wanted to run a paper.

There was considerable apprehension on the staff when she took over. They feared a clean sweep. But although she changed the paper almost overnight, she caused no upheaval in the city room. In time even the cynical copy desk came to approve of her. Except for an influx of social orchids, things went on in a normal manner. She did over the office of the editor-in-chief, but in a less boudoir-ish way than legend had it. She had her walls tinted, had draperies hung at the wide windows, brought a bookcase and some rugs from her father's home, installed a businesslike looking desk and put a portrait of her grandfather on the walls for inspiration. She sought advice from men who knew their business, but if she did not care for their suggestions, she went ahead on her own initiative. She fought bitterly with Eugene Meyer of the *Post*, over the right to run Andy Gump, and continued to address sharp paragraphs to him on the front page of her paper, but Mr. Meyer politely ignored her gibes and bowed to her at parties.

She introduced a personal note into journalism not much prac-tised nowadays and entertained the capital with her open attack on Alice Longworth five days after she took hold of the paper. The editorial was prominently displayed at the bottom of the first page on August 5, 1930:

Interesting But Not True

The news is that Mrs. Alice Longworth will be not only con-fidential adviser to Mrs. Ruth Hanna McCormick, but that she will campaign publicly for her life-long friend. Interesting but not true.

Mrs. McCormick takes no advice publicly or otherwise, from Mrs. Longworth.

Mrs. Longworth gives no interviews to the press.

Mrs. Longworth cannot utter in public.

Her assistance will, therefore, resolve itself, as usual, into posing for photographs.

(Signed) Eleanor Patterson.

This was hitting without gloves. Washington gasped, then laughed. The tea tables buzzed with excitement. Would Alice reply? Alice didn't. She continued not to utter in public. It was an old antago-nism between two women of strong personality. They had once been friends, which gave their enmity a deadly zest. Each knew the other's possibilities. They had furnished gossip before. They did it again. Mrs. Patterson has frequently said that she would rather raise hell than raise vegetables. And hell she raised for the time being. Her gesture promised sensational things to follow. But she soon settled down to the business of improving the paper, with only an occasional signed editorial on the front page—the privilege of any editor-in-chief.

In the winter of 1931 she made a first-hand study of unemployment conditions in Washington. She abandoned her elegant attire, got into frayed clothing and spent a night on a Salvation Army cot. For a week she explored the flop houses and then wrote up her experiences. This, also, was piquant breakfast fare for her smart Washington friends. In the following spring she had an oxygen chamber brought from New York to save the life of N'Gi, the gorilla in the National Zoological Park who was desperately ill with pneumonia.

Like so many newspaper women who spring from Chicago, Mrs. Patterson has interviewed Al Capone. She got him at Miami Beach when, as usual, he was ducking the press. He talked quite frankly to the vivacious "Cissie," as she is generally known in Washington. Mrs. Patterson has a thoroughly feminine outlook on newspaper work. She believes that a good-looking woman can get news where a man cannot. It is a point her brother has proved repeatedly with the *Daily News* in New York. She has not fostered the business-like woman in the city room. She would rather see a débutante go out representing the *Herald*. "I cannot believe that women have caught up with men yet," she commented on one occasion. "Perhaps the best of them are those who are smart enough to gold-dig men's ideas."

Mrs. Patterson's own life has been one of excitement, glamour and conflict. She was born in Chicago in 1884 and was educated in Boston. In 1904 she married Count Joseph Gizycka, a handsome Polish nobleman. Her wedding was one of the social events of the year, although her family had done all they could to break up the match. For four years they lived together and had a daughter, Felicia, who was born in Hungary in 1906. Her father snatched her away from her mother in London and a long contest followed. For two years Mrs. Patterson fought to get her daughter back. Then Medill McCormick went to Russia to lay the facts before the Czar, who brought pressure to bear on the court. Felicia was restored to her mother. In 1925 Mrs. Patterson married again. Her second husband was Elmer Schlesinger, who has since died. In 1926 she published *Glass Houses*, a novel which Washington enjoyed. It held some surprises for Senator William Borah, Alice Longworth and other celebrities who floated in the Patterson orbit. Her next book, *Fall Flight*, was published in 1928. She has written hunting stories and serials as well as books.

Mrs. Patterson is one of the potent newspaper executives of the country today. She puts vitality into what she does. She has shown that a woman editor-in-chief can command her staff, keep things running smoothly, experiment with ideas and yet not gum up the works for men who have coped for years with the technical problems of getting out a paper.

The newspaper instinct in Mrs. Patterson's family seems to be irresistible. Her cousin, Katrina McCormick (Mrs. Courtlandt D. Barnes, Jr.) writes a column for the Rockford Consolidated Newspapers, Inc., owned by her mother, Mrs. Ruth Hanna McCormick Simms, daughter of Mark Hanna and widow of Medill McCormick. And two of Captain Patterson's daughters have made places for themselves on merit. Alicia Patterson got her initiation in newspaper work on the city staff and in the advertising department, and is now literary editor of the New York *Daily News.* Her sister, Josephine, chose to work on the Chicago *Daily News* rather than on one of the papers with which her family is identified. She sailed along successfully under her own steam, in spite of the professional handicap of being born into a noted newspaper family. In the summer of 1936 she was married to Jay Frederick Reeve, a Chicago lawyer whom she had encountered on many of the court cases she covered, including the Insull trial.

While Mrs. Patterson has been livening things up on the *Herald,* women have been having their innings on the Washington *Post,* too, since Mr. Meyer took it over. Long ago Mrs. Meyer worked for a year on the *Sun* in New York. Just out of Barnard, she stormed the gates and was one of the first women to invade that conservative city room, so that she is completely sympathetic to the idea of a large staff of women on the *Post.* This attitude has been reflected in the number hired. The woman's page editor, Malvina Lindsay, is one of the best newspaper women in the country, with an enviable career behind her in Kansas City. During her exciting days working for Tammen and Bonfils on the Kansas City *Post,* Miss Lindsay would have been astonished had anyone suggested that one day she would settle down to editing a woman's page in Washington. But having taken all the hurdles, from fires to politics, she has come to the conclusion that no job is more desirable than the woman's page, provided the editor is allowed freedom to pick her own features and does not have synthetic material thrust at her.

Miss Lindsay's first newspaper assignment was to write a humorous story on a baseball game. Her second was to get the picture of a woman whose husband had knocked her down for flirting with the iceman. She landed on the Kansas City *Post* while she was still attending the School of Journalism at the University of Missouri. She worked for nothing during vacation and got a job at $10 a week after graduation. She chased pictures ardently, and most of the time had to think up her own assignments. Her city editor would greet her with: "Go out and get a feature story," or "Well, what have you up your sleeve?" Miss Lindsay finds that the newspaper woman today invariably wants a ready-made assignment.

Once she was launched, every day was jammed with excitement. She interviewed politicians, opera stars, murderers, freaks and celebrities of all sorts. She conducted baby and beauty shows, bicycle marathons, perfect foot contests and anything that an ingenious editor could think up for her. She did straight crime and politics. Often she edited the church, motion picture and women's pages. And day in, day out, for fifteen years, she wrote the weather story. For the first five years she tried to give it a whimsical twist, but finally gave up and merely recorded the facts.

When the Kansas City *Post* was bought by the Kansas City *Journal* in 1921, life grew a little quieter. Miss Lindsay had time to breathe in this more conservative atmosphere. She became a rewrite expert. She did excellent political work and soon was known throughout the country as a newspaper woman of the first rank. She was well equipped to cover politics, for she had a good background in economics and history, but she found that the human element was the important thing, and that contacts were the most valuable stock in trade of the political writer. By the time the Democratic convention had dragged to a slow finish in Madison Square Garden in 1924, she was anxious to leave the city room forever. She had had all she wanted of the nerve-racking grind of doing front-page news. Escape came in January, 1934, when she was asked to edit the woman's page of the Washington *Post*. She moved East with the idea that most women's pages were still antiquated and wooden; that they had progressed less than any other branch of newspaper work. She knew that they had to carry a certain amount of claptrap, but she saw no reason why women in the news should not supply realistic copy in place of some of the stereotyped features that usually swamp the woman's page. The *Post* gave her a free hand to carry out her ideas.

Miss Lindsay's daily association with job seekers and free-lance writers has persuaded her that what newspaper women need most is to learn how to write. She maintains that real enlightenment came to her ten years after she started newspaper work, when she woke up one day to a realization that she knew nothing about writing. She decided that her work was sloppy and shoddy. So she bought Genung's primary rhetoric and went through it in her spare time, doing all the exercises. She followed this with Genung's two advanced rhetorics. This slowed her up in her rewrite but it tightened and clarified her style.

In June, 1933, Miss Lindsay was awarded a medal for distinguished service in journalism by the University of Missouri, the first woman graduate to receive this award. She got honorable mention in an essay contest on journalism conducted by H. L. Mencken for her article, "Jackdaw in Peacock's Feathers," published in the *American Mercury* in 1929.

Two stand-bys of the *Post*, who have carried over from the McLean régime and are well known to official Washington, are the Poe sisters—Miss Elisabeth Ellicott Poe and Mrs. Vylla Poe Wilson. They have done newspaper work from various angles but specialize in historical subjects. Before Mr. Meyer took over the paper they covered the White House, art, books, woman's page work and a little of everything. Few writers know as much about the capital and its residents as the Poe sisters, who are descended from Edgar Allan Poe. They are an indefatigable and interesting pair, an essential part of the newspaper life of the capital. They know what is happening behind the scenes and enjoy the confidence of many of the old guard. Miss Poe figured as a witness when Gaston B. Means and Norman T. Whitaker, alias "The Fox," were charged with conspiring to swindle Mrs. Evalyn Walsh McLean out of $100,000 so-called ransom money for the Lindbergh baby. Miss Poe gave valuable information which helped to convict the two men.

The Sunday editor of the *Post* is Laura Vitray, a versatile girl who has worked at many things and was broken in on Park Row with the short-lived *Graphic*. Louis Weitzenkorn hired her as city editor. The appointment was made haphazardly. She crashed in on him past a row of applicants. He looked at her clippings, then said,

"Yes, I'll hire you, but I don't know what I'll do with you. Let me see. I have a contract for the woman's page."

"Oh, I should hate anything like that," said Miss Vitray.

Just then Paul Sifton, the night editor, stepped into the room. Mr. Weitzenkorn whirled around and said to him, "I want you to meet Laura Vitray. I have just hired her as city editor."

Mr. Sifton eyed her suspiciously. He went out and slammed the door.

"What do you know about the city desk?" Mr. Weitzenkorn then demanded.

"Oh, absolutely nothing," she gasped.

"Well, you can learn, can't you?" he asked. "Come in at six tomorrow night and sit on the copy desk. When you've learned about that, I'll make Sifton teach you the rest."

Miss Vitray was thoroughly alarmed. She had no idea what a copy desk was. Next night she was painfully initiated into the various types of heads that could be used to express the single thought, "Dope Queen of Chinatown." After she had been on the copy desk for four months, Mr. Weitzenkorn was out in one of the upheavals that shake newspaper offices from time to time. Howard Swain, the new managing editor, switched her to the city staff. It was the period when Ciro Terranova, the artichoke king, was in the headlines. Miss Vitray went out to find him. She got as far as the door of his Pelham home and came face to face with Mrs. Terranova.

"The police are looking for your husband, for murder," she said. "I thought perhaps he might like to tell me his side . . ."

As she was being pushed out, Terranova himself appeared. "Come in," he said.

Miss Vitray went in and planted herself on a red plush sofa.

"What did you come here for?" he demanded.

"Terranova," said Miss Vitray hardily, "I am a reporter. If I come here at two in the morning, it isn't to ask after your health. What I want to know is—did you murder Yale and Marlow?"

Terranova roared with laughter.

"I like you," he said. "I'm going to play your game. But you mustn't doublecross me. I'm going to tell you a lot of things. Some of them you can write and some you can't. And you can tell Grover Whalen to come and get me. He's more afraid than I am."

Miss Vitray went back to her office with a good story and the elusive Terranova's address and private telephone number. She came to know a number of gangsters and murderers during her lively *Graphic* days. One of them got in touch with her after reading a story she had written, accusing him of the murder of a girl whose body had been taken out of the East River. He said he had not killed the girl but he thanked her for the publicity. He met her on Broadway in front of the Paramount that afternoon, and suggested that she might like some ice cream and strawberry shortcake. So she went into a restaurant with him and questioned him about his crimes.

Shortly afterwards Mr. Swain appointed her city editor, without having any inkling that this was the job for which she had first been slated. She had been in newspaper work for less than eight months. The staff worked for her without a trace of resentment and she was a success as city editor. During this period on the *Graphic* she mastered the technical side of newspaper work, a chance which few metropolitan newspaper women ever get. She struggled with dummies and make-up, handled hundreds of pictures, read telegraph copy, made up the first edition and staggered home at night, exhausted to the last degree. After this she did a year's reporting on the New York *Journal*, wrote fiction for the Scripps-Howard papers, and then landed on the Washington *Post*. She started the special article section, took on the Sunday magazine and the rotogravure, and finally assumed charge of all the Sunday sections.

Miss Vitray spent most of her early years in France, where she was the protégée of the French tragédienne, Madame Aimée Tessandier, of the Comédie Française. The actress made her spend three or four hours every day reciting Racine. When she failed to make Agrippine sufficiently blood-thirsty, the old lady would stalk up and down the room, finally snatching off her wig and hurling it to the ground as she screamed, "*Ah, tu me fais perdre les cheveux!*"

Miss Vitray married a young French actor of the modern art theater group and for a time her life was centered on their little theater in Paris—the Vieux Colombier. She started writing before her baby was born, and continued working from five to eight hours a day on an old Corona after the child's arrival. She returned to America in 1927 with a three-year-old son, $50 and a few letters of introduction. She had bitter days of hardship. Then she worked for *Time* for nine months, writing science, and then for William Grady, doing publicity at Columbia University. Her next move was to the *Graphic*.

In the summer of 1935, when she was on vacation from the Washington *Post*, Miss Vitray found herself at the scene of the *Morro Castle* disaster. She rounded up the stories of the survivors as they were brought ashore. She is a dyed-in-the-wool newspaper woman who likes to run around in all weathers, with the wind in her face, and humanity at the mercy of her reportorial instincts.

Another woman holding down a stiff job on the *Post* is Anna Youngman, who writes on finance and economics. The women's features of the *Post* are promoted by Alice Fox Pitts, who was previously on the Buffalo *Evening News* for eight years. She married a newspaper man when she was twenty and fresh from the Columbia School of Journalism. In the early days of her marriage she and her husband both wrote for the New Bedford *Standard* in Massachusetts, and she wheeled the baby carriage around on her first assignments. She wrote the life story of a New Bedford labor leader, interviewing him in his parlor with one eye on the baby parked in a carriage on the front lawn. After a few months George A. Hough, managing editor of the paper, offered her a regular job.

"But don't think you can make a day nursery out of this city room," he said, eying her severely.

When the Buffalo *Evening News* needed a picture page and feature editor, Mrs. Pitts got the job. She joined the staff of the Washington *Post* along with her husband, Frederic C. Pitts. She has edited the bulletin of the American Society of Newspaper Editors for the last three years.

Lora Kelly, club editor of the *Post*, did newspaper work in Cleveland for two decades before moving East. In the interests of journalism she was hoisted to the top of a 250-foot smokestack; shuttled on a Lake Shore passenger engine at 100 miles an hour on a wild winter night; bought a corpse for $10; hunted for an armadillo in the suburbs of Cleveland; made skirts in a garment factory during a strike; went on picket duty a week later and was mobbed; spent a night at the mouth of a coal mine waiting for rescuers to bring up the victims of an explosion; rode on a fire truck being tested simultaneously for speed and endurance; and spent Christmas day with eighty sandhogs who were boring a waterworks tunnel under Lake Erie.

Miss Kelly saw Amelia Earhart, tousled-haired and tired, tumble out of the skies after her Atlantic flight, to be greeted by the mayoress of Southampton and the American consul. Again she spent a week-end with John Drinkwater and his wife at their summer home—Samuel Pepys' cottage at Frampton. She had a chat with Commander Balbo in Reykjavik, Iceland, as he waited for the fog to lift to enable him to continue his flight to the Chicago Fair. She had tea with Ruth Bryan Owen at the American Legation in Copenhagen. She has listened to Lincoln Ellsworth's thrilling tales of polar dashes, twirled spaghetti with Rosa Ponselle, and tried to make sense out of a tariff debate in the Senate.

One of the better known newspaper women of Washington is Martha Strayer, who works for the Washington *Daily News*, a tabloid. Her work is thirty per cent national and seventy per cent local. She comes from Ohio, where she did secretarial work until she gravitated to the society page of a small-town paper. She met the trains—the traditional small-town initiation—and filled two columns a day with the doings of the townspeople. Miss Strayer moved to Washington because two of her sisters were there. Lowell Mellett gave her a chance to combine secretarial work with reporting when the *Daily News* was getting under way. She soon worked herself into good standing on the city staff.

The women writing for the Washington papers live separate lives from those who cover Capitol Hill. They meet frequently on the same stories, but their interests are far apart. The local girls cover the news of the capital for Washingtonians, while their colleagues are preoccupied with the political scene and are virtually unaware of the lost babies, the murders, the fires and everyday happenings of the city itself. The political writers see Washington solely in terms of Capitol Hill, the White House, and the complex machinery of government. They work in an exhilarating atmosphere of national drama. Once bitten with it, they rarely want to do anything else.

Chapter XXXIX

PHILADELPHIA

WHEN EVELYN SHULER OF THE PHILADELPHIA *Ledger* POSED as a member of the bar, she was sent to jail, but not until she had her story, and so she did not mind. It was all in the day's work. Miss Shuler looks like a modern Portia—tailored clothes, a severe haircut, a judicial manner.

Once at a Methodist Conference a frock-coated deacon put his arm around her competent shoulder and hissed in her ear, "Sister, are you saved?"

"I'm the press," said Miss Shuler indignantly.

"Beg pardon, Miss," he said, moving away with haste.

When the number racketeers were mulcting citizens of Philadelphia, she worked night and day rounding up evidence that the police maintained they could not get. So convincing was her exposé in the columns of the *Ledger* that the police were forced to act. More than three hundred of the racketeers were arrested and the number game was checked for the time being. They had been taking $100,000 a day from people of small means. Again, when she made a crime survey of the underworld the stories she turned up were so full of dynamite that they never were printed. There are times when caution keeps a newspaper from spreading everything on the record.

She wrote the news lead for her paper on the Hauptmann trial— the only girl in the country to do the main story, except Dixie Tighe, who was cabling hers to the *Daily Express* in London. She covered the kidnaping of the Lindbergh child from the beginning, directing a staff of men. She stayed up for eighty-seven hours without a bath or sleep in the early days of the quest. Through an ingenious arrangement which she never has divulged she got two exclusive stories from inside the Lindbergh home at that time in spite of the cordon of state troopers assigned to keep the press away from the house.

Miss Shuler has often been ahead of the police in rounding up facts, for she is fast, accurate and resourceful. After the riot in the Philadelphia County Prison at Holmesburg, in which six hundred prisoners kept up a twenty-four-hour mutiny in face of tear gas bombs, Miss Shuler found the wife and daughter of the disappearing warden when subpoena servers were looking for them. On another story she turned up a woman formerly tried for murder and acquitted. Two subpoena servers had been trying unsuccessfully for a week to reach her. The woman was living under an assumed name.

Nothing stops Miss Shuler when she is out to get a story. She is the reporter of legend, the unbeatable girl of the films. But although nimble on a fire escape and quite capable of wearing a disguise, her work shows balance and capacity that the monkeyshine reporters frequently lack. Her stories are objective and businesslike, and she is not afraid to meet danger halfway. She climbed in the fire-escape window of a hospital once to get an interview with a cabaret dancer who was shot and who died a few hours afterwards. Another time she got an exclusive story from a girl who had taken poison and refused to reveal her identity. From the initials on her vanity case and a chance remark she dropped, Miss Shuler picked up a clue and trailed her sister to a neighboring city. The two women were reunited after a separation of ten years, and Miss Shuler kept the story sewn up tight until the moment came to beat the town with it.

Again she was first on the spot when the demented Gladys Mae Parkes, the baby killer, tried suicide after her conviction at Camden. Gladys took an electric light bulb from its socket, broke it and tried to slash her wrists. Miss Shuler has talked to scores of would-be suicides. She finds that usually they do it for love, but that they are glad to live after they have tried to die.

On one murder case to which she was assigned, she stayed up for three nights keeping a cemetery vigil. She had a feeling that the bodies would be exhumed. She was right. Just before dawn on the third night, a party arrived with lanterns and the digging began. Miss Shuler dashed in her car to Mount Holly, eight miles away, and roused the other reporters and the photographers.

Miss Shuler was at Lakehurst when the Graf Zeppelin circled thrillingly like a silver pencil over the field and came to rest after its first Atlantic flight. This was one of the most harassing newspaper assignments of the decade. The reporters worked in the huge hangar under difficult conditions. For three days they had little to eat but hot dogs. At night many of them slept spread out on tables and they did most of their stories sitting on drawers pulled out of desks, for there were few chairs. There was great uncertainty as to the hour the Zeppelin would arrive. The Hearst papers had the story sewn up, with Karl Von Wiegand and Lady Drummond Hay on board. The dirigible landed after dusk, in a scene of wild excitement, flares burning, crowds swarming around the exhausted passengers. There was wire trouble and copy piled up while the frantic reporters of the morning papers yelped over a hopeless mechanical snag. In the end most of them got on telephones and dictated their stories direct to their offices.

A group of newspaper women swarmed around the hangar. Miss Shuler did her usual calm and thorough job. Later she worked on the Akron crash, the only woman to cover the naval inquiry that followed, along with a group of thirty-five men. She flew in a Goodyear blimp from Aberdeen, Maryland, to Central Airport as a stunt, and also tried an autogyro with Jimmy Ray, the crack pilot. At different times she has sampled the hydroplane, the open cockpit plane and practically everything else that takes off the ground. There is no phase of newspaper work that she has not tackled. She has covered women in politics for the last ten years, more or less on the side, and has gone to scores of state conventions. Once she crashed a Shriners' convention. She was on hand for the Coolidge and Hoover inaugurations. She takes in the beauty pageants at Atlantic City and writes two pages of copy annually on the Mummers' parade, Philadelphia's own festival.

Miss Shuler never studied journalism, had little academic education. She left high school after a year and a half, and deserted Temple University by request of the officials, for a series of pranks. Later she went back, completed her credits and took entrance examinations for Goucher College. She was admitted as a probational student but never attended. She was bitten with the newspaper bug at sixteen. For two years she solicited ads for the *Evening Telegraph* of Philadelphia, now defunct. In 1918 she landed on the *Ledger* as editorial auditor. She devised a system for paying out-of-town and state correspondents and for two years did editorial paragraphs and fillers under John J. Spurgeon, then editor-in-chief. When she told him that she wanted to be a reporter, he insisted she was too young. So she left the paper in 1921, went to work in a mail order house, but was back as a staff reporter in 1922, at a time when women were still barely tolerated in the city room. The *Evening Ledger* now gives its women excellent opportunities.

In the first two months of newspaper work she learned what it was to get exclusive stories. She landed an interview with Pauline Frederick in which she admitted that she was separated from her third husband. The actress had been ducking reporters all the way across the country, but Miss Shuler got her to talk. Her second scoop concerned a quarter-million-dollar jewel robbery in the Van Rensselaer family. This time she had to match wits with a Pinkerton man.

In 1924 Miss Shuler moved over to the *Evening Ledger* for better hours. Her city editor never thinks of assigning her to do an angle on a big news story. She writes the lead on anything that comes along. She is one of the most competent front-page girls in the country. A predecessor, widely known through her syndicate work, was Constance Drexel, who traveled here and there and wrote for the *Ledger* syndicate for years. Her interview with Madame Poincaré, appraising the American soldiers in France, caused a stir. She did stories on the Peace Conference for the Chicago *Tribune* and was the only woman member of the International Association of Journalists accredited to the League of Nations.

There are few types of assignments that Elizabeth K. Read has not covered in her eleven years on the *Evening Bulletin*. Fresh from Wellesley, she started by giving Jovian advice on the ethical questions propounded to the paper. From this she moved into the sports' department to do girls' sports and men's golf; then she gravitated to the city staff to do general assignments. She now does straight politics on a thoroughly masculine basis. Working for a conservative paper with a circulation of more than 500,000, Miss Read has found absolute equality of treatment for men and women on the city staff. When she first set out to do straight politics the party leaders were more amused than concerned; then, when they learned that she could be trusted, they treated her with the confidence they would repose in any sound political writer. For eight years she has done both the presidential and gubernatorial inaugurations and has made a point of writing the swan songs of those going out of office.

When she interviewed Crown Prince Adolphus Augustus of Sweden on his visit to America, he turned the tables on her. He has always been interested in newspapers and he subjected her to a thorough examination on how the newspaper women of America did their work. Miss Read followed the entire Lindbergh story for her paper, from the day of the kidnaping until Bruno Hauptmann almost fell into her lap as he stumbled out of the court room at Flemington, convicted of the crime. Watching the Graf Zeppelin come over the horizon toward Lakehurst she had the feeling that the wheels of a century were turning before her eyes. Now and again the reporter is visited by flashes of insight in witnessing historical events. But more often she is dulled to the implications of a story by the immediate need for speed, action, concentration.

Miss Read has done special articles for papers in England, Germany and Sweden. While abroad she did features for her own paper but was dismayed by the solemnity and red tape that tie the reporter's footsteps on the other side of the Atlantic. There was no question of walking in on a subject with an animated spray of questions, as even the cub reporter can do in America. Miss Read has broadcast and lectured. She is the author of a mystery story, *Death in the State House,* written with Charles E. Fisher, a newspaper colleague, under the pseudonym Timothy Knox.

When Dorothy D. Bartlett, now a star on the Philadelphia *Inquirer*, started newspaper work, she was told that she was utterly miscast. Men assured her she was the domestic type and would never be able to stand the newspaper grind. The more experienced newspaper women thought her gullible and snubbed her as a hopeless cub. She was shy and easily intimidated. In 1924 she landed a job on the *North American*, doing part-time work while she attended the University of Pennsylvania. The assistant city editor tried three times to have her fired. She arrived at the office every day in fear and trembling. Then her paper was sold in the spring of 1925 and she was out of a job, until by luck she landed on the *Inquirer*.

She earned her first by-line when President and Mrs. Coolidge attended the opening of the Sesqui-Centennial Exposition, but she had a less fortunate experience with Mrs. Herbert Hoover when the President's wife visited Philadelphia and found that no one was on hand to receive her. There had been confusion over train schedules. The reception committee had met an earlier train, then had left when Mrs. Hoover did not show up. Miss Bartlett was still hanging around the station when she saw a figure that was unmistakably Mrs. Hoover's walking along the platform. A later train had just pulled in from Washington. She rushed forward.

"Oh, Mrs. Hoover, there has been a mix up," she said. "I happen to be a reporter, but if you'll wait right here I'll try to round up the members of the committee for you. They understood you were taking an earlier train."

Miss Bartlett found the committee. But Mrs. Hoover was not appreciative.

"I won't talk to the reporters," she told the committee at once. "Let's get away from this annoying press following." Miss Bartlett was left flat.

She continued to do women's clubs and school conventions until she overheard a new city editor say of her, "Oh, that shrinking violet would be too scared to cover this story." That hurt. She made up her mind that she was going to be a good reporter or get fired trying. She marched up to the city desk and demanded men's assignments. She didn't get them right away. But her chance came in 1931, when Mrs. Clara Grace Prophet was held for the murder of her husband. Just as she was leaving the office one Saturday night

Miss Bartlett was assigned to find Mrs. Prophet and get an interview with her. From six o'clock until midnight she and a group of reporters and photographers toured the police stations within a radius of sixty-five miles, trying to find the woman prisoner. They reached the right station at last and the men got all they wanted from the police. Miss Bartlett, bedraggled and tired, made an impassioned plea to the detective in charge to let her have an interview with the woman alone. He did. And he took her to the cell of the woman's brother, Harold Williams, who had plotted the murder with her for the sake of her husband's insurance.

Reporters are rarely permitted to talk to prisoners held on a capital charge while the police are still trying to break them down. But Mrs. Prophet discussed her guilt with Miss Bartlett freely. However, when the pair went on trial, she was not assigned to write the lead, but merely the features on the story. The woman was convicted. When Williams was retried she was trusted with the lead story. At last she felt she was beating the sweet, simple and girlish handicap that had dogged her early days.

When Virginia Penfield, a Columbus girl, disappeared from a finishing school at Swarthmore ten days before Christmas, 1931, and turned up later in Providence, Rhode Island, Miss Bartlett was rushed to the scene to interview her. She managed to gain the confidence of the girl's father on the trip to Providence and was taken in for an exclusive interview half an hour after their arrival. This made no hit with her competitors. They tried to get her to share what she had. But the shrinking violet held out. She hung over the telegraph operator as he sent her story, and then took the copy to her hotel and slept on it, since importunate reporters have been known to swipe their rivals' copy from the telegraph hooks in time of need. It's an old trick that the scoop artist must circumvent.

Next day Mr. Penfield was severely lectured by the craft. But while he was sitting in one room assuring them that Miss Bartlett would have no further talk with his daughter unless they were in on it, too, Dorothy was on her way into Virginia's room in pursuit of a messenger boy carrying a box of flowers. She talked to the girl for thirty minutes and got a better story than she had had the night before. It was so good, in fact, that her paper copyrighted it.

She did bold work on the *Morro Castle* disaster, going heavily after the bad discipline angle. She went to the bedsides of dozens of the survivors and corroborated the details given her by a sailor on the demoralization of the crew. A week later she married Carl W. McCardle of the *Bulletin*, with whom she had worked on the Lindbergh kidnaping and other stories. They have a typical newspaper ménage and are often separated in the pursuit of professional duty. While she was in Flemington for six weeks on the Hauptmann case, he was covering a murder trial in Pennsylvania.

Shortly after Geane Geddes joined the staff of the *Ledger*, a woman who was in the news at the time called the city desk to say that if a reporter were sent out to see her, she would tell exactly how her husband had shot her and tried to cut her throat. She maintained that the details in the paper were all wrong. She was just out of the hospital and was convalescing from her injuries.

Miss Geddes was sent to see her. The woman lived in a large house in West Philadelphia. A Negro butler ushered her into a room furnished with heavy Victorian pieces, all covered with dust. She appeared like an apparition from the dusky end of the room. She was slight and middle-aged. Her faded blonde hair hung in two long braids over her shoulders. Her eyes had a bright glitter. But her voice was soft and charming as she rattled off the names of well-known Philadelphians. She took Miss Geddes into the bathroom and proudly showed her a dark brown stain on the marble basin and another on the floor. Then she got out a razor and demonstrated how her husband had tried to cut her throat. Next she brought out a black lace negligee and showed the bullet holes where she had been shot in the back. Finally she produced an automatic, meanwhile rambling along with the incoherence of mania. By this time Miss Geddes was getting alarmed. She persuaded her to put the automatic out of sight, after she had demonstrated how close her husband had stood to her when he fired. At last Miss Geddes managed to get out of the house, although the raving woman did her best to keep her talking.

Five years later she came into the *Ledger* office and had a long conversation with the managing editor. Miss Geddes spotted her at once and telephoned across the editorial floor to warn him that he was dealing with a paranoiac. The husband in this case disappeared and never was convicted, but he actually had tried to kill the woman.

Once Miss Geddes broke through a guard of two policemen and several hospital officials to interview a woman who had tried to commit suicide, but instead had killed one of her two sons with gas fumes. She walked two and a half miles on a pipe line to get a story about Hog Island, where black widow spiders are now being gathered to make anti-venom serum.

A number of the former newspaper women of Philadelphia have gone into publicity. Olive Cranston, who once did excellent work for the *Inquirer*, is a case in point. Dorothy Bauer, who was broken in by William B. Craig on the *Bulletin* in 1910, and during the war worked for the *North American*, publicizes the Philadelphia Orchestra. And May Schupack, who worked on the *Inquirer*, the

North American and the *Evening Bulletin*, does publicity in New York.

Miss Schupack took journalism at the University of Pennsylvania, but soon learned on the *Inquirer* how to puff a two-stick story into a streamer head, which was what her paper required at the time. She had every kind of story to do that a man would get from the city desk. On the *North American* conditions were different. Girls were treated like flowers who might wilt easily if exposed to cold. There were no night assignments for the women of the staff and working hours were from one to six. On the *Evening Bulletin* she found things correct, conservative and noncommittal. Often a newspaper woman becomes what her paper makes her. Newspaper style is a variable quantity. But the fundamentals of good reporting remain the same. She may go from the most conservative paper to a lively rag and fit into the new frame without trouble. Or she may move from a tabloid to a staid journal and temper her stories to suit her audience.

A girl who rarely writes a line of copy, yet continually supplies her paper with exclusive tips on crime, is Dorothy Ann Harrison, who was on the *Ledger* for six years and is now on the Philadelphia *Record*. She has an extraordinary connection with the underworld and is known personally to most of the gangsters in town. Pius Lanzetti, one of the more notorious, once sent word by the grapevine route: "If ever you meet Miss Harrison, treat her like one of the boys."

Two years ago she was tipped off that two well-known underworld characters were missing from home. She was told: "Keep your eyes open. If two guys are found dead somewhere in the next couple of days, it will be Willie Schwalbe and Tony Massino." She turned in this information to her city desk, and all the district men were told to be on the lookout for unidentified dead men. Forty-eight hours later, Massino and Schwalbe were found tied together by the necks, in a shallow creek near Wilmington, Delaware. Clutched in the hand of each was a penny, the underworld's sign of a pay-off to chiselers.

In November, 1934, when William Weiss, one of the bootleg kings, was secretly kidnaped, Miss Harrison was informed that he had disappeared, that the ransom figure was $100,000, that Weiss's partner was having trouble raising it, and that the snatchers were Robert Mais and Walter Legenza, leaders of the Tri-State gang who had shot their way out of jail in Richmond, Virginia, while awaiting electrocution for murder. It was impossible to verify Miss Harrison's tip. A week went by, then two weeks. Finally Jean Barrett, the only other woman on the *Record*, got complete verification from Sue

Weiss, sister of the kidnaped man, whom she had known years earlier. Members of the family were taken to the Department of Justice offices by *Record* reporters, and the paper broke the story on the front page. Weiss was found dead weeks later. Mais and Legenza and five others were arrested and later electrocuted.

Once Miss Harrison was a witness in a murder trial which resulted in a notorious gunman going free. He was Frank Ripka, known in the old Tenderloin as "Lefty," a sleek young man who had been tried and convicted of the murder of another racketeer. His attorney was C. Stuart Patterson, Jr., a friend of William Fallon, and in his time one of the smartest criminal lawyers of Pennsylvania. Ripka, in the golden days of prohibition, was bodyguard to Mike Duffy. He was a crack shot, with the left hand. The testimony which convicted him came from a girl named Bertha Ginsberg. She said she was in a restaurant in the heart of the Tenderloin when Ripka came in with two other men and, standing in the doorway, fired at a man inside. On this testimony Ripka was sentenced to death.

After the trial Bertha walked into the *Record* office one night and asked Miss Harrison to help her. She said she had lied about Ripka and that she was sending an innocent man to his death. She had been held under surveillance for 125 days after the crime and had been intimidated, she maintained. This was during the period that the Wickersham Crime Commission visited Philadelphia, made a survey of police methods and criticized the police habit of keeping witnesses "on ice."

Miss Harrison wrote the story of Bertha's harsh treatment by the police and ran into it the girl's retraction of the testimony against Ripka. Next day Mr. Patterson called Miss Harrison on the telephone to verify the fact that she had talked to Bertha. She was served immediately with two subpoenas, one by the defense, the other by the Commonwealth. Forty-eight hours before the time set for Ripka to go to the chair, Mr. Patterson argued his appeal before a court en banc. Miss Harrison was called as a witness. She reported what Bertha had told her—that a detective had beaten her to make her admit she saw Ripka do the shooting. She explained that she had warned the girl about perjury, but Bertha had said she did not care, and had glibly named the detective who had beaten her. On the strength of Miss Harrison's information, the detective was held for subornation of perjury, Bertha was held for perjury and the court granted Ripka a new trial without leaving the bench. Ripka was retried and acquitted. When the verdict came in he turned to Miss Harrison and said, "I owe you my life."

"You owe me nothing," she told him, "except the promise to behave yourself. The day you go bad I'm going to take a first-class razzing from everybody. They all expect you to go out and raise Cain. I want you to promise me that you won't carry a gun and that you won't shoot anybody."

He promised Miss Harrison he would behave. Any time she has heard of him since, he has been carrying a revolver.

Three years ago Miss Harrison was saved from being shot because the men who were about to wipe out the gangster with whom she was walking, recognized her as the girl from the *Record*. There had been a bad shooting in town, and she had arranged to meet a gunman of her acquaintance to see if he could give her any leads on it. They met in an outlying part of town and were walking along the street when a car crept up on them. Miss Harrison's escort suddenly shoved her into a taxi, told the driver to take her back to her office, and disappeared like magic. A week later she got a message from the underworld to stay away from the man she was with that day, for he was on the spot.

An agent of the Department of Justice took occasion to tell her city editor that she would undoubtedly be killed, because of the gangsters with whom she associated. Some time later she was asked by another federal agent to approach Mary McKeever, gang moll of the Mais-Legenza mob, and ask her if she would be willing to turn informer for the G-men. But Miss Harrison drew the line at this. Her name never appears on a story. This is a protective measure. She comes and goes as she likes, for her work is unique among newspaper women. Few of them ever have any sustained contact with the underworld, although occasionally they may interview gangsters.

Miss Harrison never divulges her sources of information, nor does she let one mob leader know what a rival thinks of him, although she could sear their vanity without stretching her fancy. The police keep in close touch with her and often she is wakened out of her sleep to hear weird whispers from the underworld reaching her over the wire.

Chapter XL

BUFFALO AND POINTS NORTH

A T NINETY-TWO MRS. ESTHER DAVENPORT STILL WALKS UP-
rightly to her desk in the office of the Buffalo *Evening
News* and wonders why it takes six women to handle the
woman's department, a job that she once did single-handed.

She is the grand old lady of the profession in Buffalo today. She
started as society editor when the paper was founded more than fifty
years ago and she stood over the forms day after day until she was
eighty years old, making up her page. Old-timers in the composing
room miss her now that she does not travel far beyond her desk. She
was a stickler for form and was as exacting about make-up as a
writer is over the sequence of his paragraphs. But she turned her
copy in punctually, if she had to stay up all night after a charity ball
to write her story in longhand.

She was forty-eight years old when she entered newspaper work.
She began on the Buffalo *Times*, then moved to the *Evening News*
in 1893. She knew Jenny June and all the newspaper women of her
period, and was active in launching the New York State Federation
of Women's Clubs, along with Mrs. Simon Baruch, mother of
Bernard Baruch, Mary Garrett Hay, Madame Doré Lyon, Mrs.
Donald McLean and Mrs. William Cummings Story.

Every year she attended the D.A.R. conventions in Washington.
On one of these occasions D. S. Alexander took her to call on Theodore Roosevelt. Anna Katherine Green was in the visiting group.
When Miss Green was presented to the President, he reached out
both hands and embraced her, saying he was overjoyed to meet the
author of *The Leavenworth Case*. He told her he thought it the
greatest detective story ever written by an American.

Mrs. Davenport had an earlier presidential encounter with Ruther-
ford B. Hayes, after he left the White House. She was sent to
Chautauqua, where Mr. Hayes was to speak before the State
Grangers Society and the Veterans of the Civil War. The Chautauqua idea was still new and all the large Eastern papers were

represented. After Mr. Hayes had delivered his speech to the Grand Army, the reporters followed him to his hotel, then disappeared one by one, leaving Mrs. Davenport with the uneasy feeling that they were upstairs interviewing the visiting celebrity. So she sent up her card and Mr. Hayes announced that he would receive her in his room. She found him alone.

"It was raining when I came in from speaking," said Mr. Hayes. "As I was overheated and the hotel was cold I thought it better to rest in bed. And if you will draw up that rocking chair, we will be able to talk in comfort."

He asked Mrs. Davenport to dig out the proofs of his speech from his coat pocket. They talked about his wife, who had died recently, and the memory book he was preparing. On his return to his home in Ohio he sent her an autographed copy of the book and a letter telling her he liked the humorous story she made of her bedside interview with him.

Mrs. Davenport has always been a gorgeous figure sartorially. For years she dazzled her colleagues with her heavy brocaded silks and velvets, and the glitter of her jewels. Red, lavender and green are her favorite colors. Because of her social engagements she often showed up in the morning in full fig. But her trains never kept her from swishing into the composing room or lifting out a form in an emergency with the aid of a make-up man, burning her fingertips as she did so, but determined to insert a story that she thought should run.

Fifteen years ago Mrs. Davenport sold her home in Buffalo and bought Casa Comellas in Hamburg, New York, where she now lives and keeps open house. She is an expert cook. Her sight is failing and a companion reads to her, but she keeps in close touch with everything that goes on in her profession. She still turns out her weekly column, "As I Went Home Last Night," which has an amazing following, for she is known to nearly everyone in Buffalo.

So was Marion de Forest, who died in the spring of 1935. For many years she was one of the personalities of the profession. She was society editor and dramatic critic of the *Express* and until 1924 conducted a column of criticism called "As I Go To The Play." She knew Sarah Bernhardt, Caruso, Lily Langtry, Mrs. Minnie Maddern Fiske and many another star. It was Mrs. Fiske who urged her to undertake the dramatization of *Little Women*. Later she wrote *Erstwhile Susan* for her. After leaving newspaper work Miss de Forest was manager of the Buffalo Musical Foundation, Inc., for several years. In 1933 she collaborated with Zona Gale in a series of radio dramalogues.

One of the few women reporters in the country doing politics today is Mary F. Nash of the Buffalo *Evening News*, who has handled straight news on the most capable plane for the last fourteen years. She was graduated from the State Normal School but had no taste for teaching. So she went to a business school and then managed to get on the *Courier*, where she was soon substituting as society editor. With Marion de Forest filling the same post on the *Express*, the competition was stiff.

When the regular society editor returned, Miss Nash was switched from one job to another for training and experience. She edited copy, wrote feature stories, assisted the financial editor, did editorials, and was secretary to the managing editor. When the rotogravure editor left she inherited his job. Sunday tabloid sections were flooding the country at the time. The *Courier* decided to launch one, so Miss Nash was assigned to make a special study of this new development. Soon she was appointed Sunday editor, handling the tabloid and a full-sized section in color, filled with syndicated material. She bought all the special Sunday material, edited the sections, made up the pages, wrote bookstrap publicity and covered the theaters. She inaugurated two pages for children in the tabloid section and started a club for them. This went over so well that soon a separate eight-page tabloid called the *Junior Courier* was launched. All sorts of contests were promoted. Shows were put on for the children. The section was so well handled that it served as a model for other papers which later adopted the same idea. After the *Courier* and the *Express* were merged, the club was kept up and is still thriving. Most of the policies, heads and stunts initiated in the five years that Miss Nash had charge were continued.

She resigned shortly before the merger, expecting to take a syndicate job which had been offered her in New York. But it fell through and she went to work on the Buffalo *Evening News*. There she found that Alfred H. Kirchhofer, who believes thoroughly in the value of newspaper women to a paper, wanted to build up women's political news, which had been neglected. So Miss Nash was assigned to work up political stories. But when she found that women were getting their cues from men, she became interested in general politics. Charles H. Armitage, political editor of the paper, coached her and she took his place while he was in Albany, covering the Legislature. Next she took on the State Building beat. This, too, was strictly masculine territory but she showed that a woman could do as capable a job as any man on such subjects as the Public Service Commission, the Tax Department, the Labor Department, or any of the other offices coming within the purview of the state. Miss Nash has been fortunate in working for editors who have not discriminated against women. Her own capacity has beaten down any lingering suspicions they might have had about the functions of a good woman reporter on a daily paper.

Kate Burr, of the Buffalo *Times*, is as widely known to the public as any newspaper woman in Buffalo today. She broadcasts and does a column, which is a mixture of philosophy, anecdotes and items of old Buffalo. It has a wide following. In private life she is Mrs. Louis B. Lane.

"No woman is worth it," said Neil McDonald of the Albany *Argus*, when Pauline Mandigo told him that the editors of the *Knickerbocker Press* wanted her to run their woman's page at a salary of $22 a week, an advance of $10 over the salary the *Argus* was paying her. Miss Mandigo made the change, worked on the staff for four years, took special courses at the State College along with her work and got good assignments. This was the period when the suffrage campaign was at its height in New York State. When General Jones and her army advanced on Albany Miss Mandigo crossed the snowy hills to Greenbush and wrote the finale of their dramatic appeal to the Legislature. Like most of the newspaper women of that era she was a suffrage advocate. When the anti-suffrage leaders advertised a newspaper woman from the West as among their speakers, Dr. Anna Howard Shaw disposed of her opponent by calling her the only newspaper woman on the anti-suffrage side, which was scarcely an exaggeration.

In November, 1917, Judge Lynn J. Arnold, publisher of the *Knickerbocker Press*, started Miss Mandigo off on a survey from town to town, interviewing political leaders, analyzing what they told her and writing what she saw and heard. "Women are voters now," said Judge Arnold. "I want you to write political stories that will interest them."

"But I don't know a thing about politics," Miss Mandigo protested.

"You will learn," he told her. "Better read Bryce's *American Commonwealth* and Thurlow Weed Barnes' *History of the State of New York*."

In this way Miss Mandigo became a political reporter. In January, 1918, she was assigned to the State Capitol as a legislative correspondent, arriving there almost simultaneously with Elizabeth King of the New York *Evening Post*. She covered the State Senate for a year, then went into publicity and launched the Phoenix News Publicity Bureau with Ruth Byers and Rosepha Chisholm. She now runs the bureau, using the political background she gained in her newspaper days, and specializing in public affairs, education, art and music.

Working with Miss Mandigo was Anne Wheaton, who started

on the *Knickerbocker Press* twenty years ago. At first she was dramatic and music critic and on occasions covered police. She followed the "water run" and wrote innumerable stories about deepening the Hudson River to make Albany a fine port, a project in which her editors were interested. When she switched to politics and was assigned to the Capitol she was quite at home. Her father had been a public official for more than twenty years. She covered both Senate and Assembly and all the government departments, including the executive chamber, during the administrations of Al Smith and Nathan L. Miller. When she left Albany she did syndicate work. From 1924 to 1930 she directed publicity for the National League of Women Voters from its Washington headquarters. Since 1930 she has publicized all manner of public events, from the women's anti-prohibition campaign to horse shows. Her husband, Warren Wheaton, was formerly with the Philadelphia *Ledger* and is now a propagandist for the Republican Party.

Another of the former Albany newspaper women who has turned to publicity is Mollie E. Sullivan, who directs this department for the Y.W.C.A. Through Miss Mandigo she obtained a post as editor of the woman's page of the *Argus*, which is now defunct. Later she did politics, covering state departments and hearings on special legislation for women. In 1919 she left Albany and newspaper work behind her.

Dorothy Craigie was one of the ablest women reporters to work at Albany. Her first reporting was done for the Catskill *Examiner*, published by her father, Frederick E. Craigie. Then she joined the staff of the *Knickerbocker Press* as a feature writer, and soon began to do political correspondence and features for the *Mail* in New York. Miss Craigie was the first woman to make a non-stop air flight across New York State. She died in 1924 at the age of thirty. She was the wife of George Morris, political writer of the *World-Telegram*.

A pioneer up-state newspaper woman was Mrs. Mary L. Parsons, known as Edith Cornwall to her readers. She was on the Syracuse *Herald* for twenty-five years, a Vassar graduate who did not have a penny when she first walked into a newspaper office. She offered to go down to Water Street, accompanied by her brother, and visit some of the houses of ill fame for newspaper copy. The *Herald* played up her story and gave her a job. As the years went on, she became a prolific writer. Her copy was always readable, although sometimes embroidered. She covered the American Tragedy case and William Barnes' suit for libel against Colonel Roosevelt. The colonel had classed Mr. Barnes with Charles Murphy, Tammany leader. The case was tried in Syracuse in 1915 and the jury found for the colonel.

Mrs. Parsons was a character. She cared little about her attire. Her skirt might trail and her shirt-waist escape from her belt, but she knew how to turn out diverting newspaper copy. As the years went on she amassed piles of newspaper clippings which she kept in bureau drawers. In her old age she would dig down among the yellowing papers and pull out her account of a murder that had been the talk of the state a decade earlier.

Her junior on the paper was Ramona Herdman, who was on the *Herald* from 1921 to 1927, with a brief interlude on the Rochester *Post-Express*. Miss Herdman was born in Greenwich, New York, went to Syracuse University, and landed in newspaper work by winning a $150 prize for the best news story written by a student. It was a simple narrative, done in five short paragraphs, of an Oxford graduate who had besought aid at the Salvation Army, down and out. It quite outclassed the more florid efforts of her competitors.

Her first assignment for the *Herald* was the story of a girl who had been killed by a truck. She was too timid to ring the bell at the home, so she went next door. The neighbor turned out to be the little girl's aunt, who told her that the child had been confirmed the Sunday before and, strangely, had prophesied her own death. She handed her the child's picture. The *Herald* gave the story a heavy play.

Miss Herdman did station news, domestic relations court, City Hall, anything that came along. She interviewed Queen Marie in the railroad station and talked to Annie Besant and her protégé, Krishnamurti, in their private car. She took in a number of state political conventions. Along with her general work she edited the woman's page. She traveled to New York to escort Celia Cooney, the bobbed-hair bandit, back to Auburn Prison. Celia was one of the front-page characters of the period—a product of the prohibition era. Miss Herdman sat with her in the train on her way to prison and listened to the story of her life. One of Ramona's first assignments had been to spend a day in Auburn Prison to study conditions there, so she knew just what the bobbed-haired bandit was facing. From time to time Celia reappeared in the news columns.

In 1927 Miss Herdman took six months' leave of absence, moved to New York, did publicity and enrolled at Columbia. But she never attended classes, for she began to sell stories to the editor of the metropolitan section of the *World*. Although she returned to Syracuse at the end of six months to work as director of health education for the Milbank Foundation, she soon returned, for New York had got into her blood. Since 1930 she has done publicity for Harper and Brothers and is the author of a novel, *A Time for Love*.

For twenty-three years Mrs. A. M. York covered society for the Syracuse *Herald* and only recently retired. Her husband edited the *Standard* until the time of his death. Her first newspaper work was done for his paper. When she moved over to the *Herald* she did news as well as society. At first her department was small, but it soon was expanded. Photographs were added to the society columns. She made up rotogravure pages and did a series of travel stories. The money she made bought party frocks and slippers for her daughters.

Syracuse's best known newspaper graduate was Mrs. Mabel Potter Daggett, author, reporter and suffragist, who died in the winter of 1927. Soon after her graduation from Syracuse University in 1895 she became editor of the woman's page of the Syracuse *Post-Standard*. From there she went to the Philadelphia *North American*. During 1902 and 1903 she contributed to the Sunday edition of the New York *World*. She was later an associate editor of *Hampton's Magazine* and *Delineator*. Mrs. Daggett used to tell her newspaper colleagues that there was a story in everything, if only the writer could see it. She went to Rumania to visit Queen Marie and wrote a book about her which was published in 1926. William Jennings Bryan also furnished her with a rich store of copy.

When President Taft, golfing at Poland Spring, was asked to speak at a state convention of teachers, a girl reporter walked away with the honors and saved her paper from the hideous mistake of attributing a speech made by a woman on household arts to the President of the United States. The girl was Helen Havener, who later became city editor of the Portland *Press* in Maine. On this occasion it was assumed that the President would have the usual advance manuscript. Miss Havener was told she could ignore the speech itself and concentrate on color. But because she was young and naïve she took voluminous notes on the speech. A rival paper had made arrangements to get out an extra edition, running the text in full. Two or three moments before the President appeared on the platform, an excited youth dashed into the convention hall and handed a manuscript to the press section. One of the reporters assumed it to be the President's speech. Nothing less would justify the breathless state of the bearer. So he tossed it over to the stenographers who were to take down the President's address verbatim, and said, "You don't need to wait; here's the speech."

The stenographers went back to their roost. The convention continued. Miss Havener went home for dinner before writing her story. When she picked up the extra of the rival paper she was astounded to see that the text printed in full and attributed to the President was the speech made by Mary Snow, of Chicago, on household arts. Miss Havener realized that she was the only person in the country with any notes on what the President actually had said. Rival reporters had to come to her office and beg for help.

Miss Havener followed every step of Henry Hummel's contest over the estate of Abraham H. Hummel, who dazzled juries until he was sent to Blackwell's Island for subornation of perjury. Later he retired to England, a disappointed man, a brilliant lawyer disgraced.

Leila Farrell, the opera singer whom he was reported to have married and then deserted, settled in Portland with her parents and her small son, Henry. Years later, when Henry was in his early thirties, Abe died in England and Miss Havener was assigned to ask the youth if he intended to contest the estate. At the time he was driving his own bakery cart and Mr. Hummel was reputed to have had millions. But Henry turned up his nose at the idea of bringing suit. "Bake Cart Driver Sneers At Millions," written by Miss Havener, made a good news story which went over the Associated Press wires and brought a denial from Abe's sister in London that he had ever married or had a son.

Henry read the denial and called on Miss Havener. He was not interested in the money, he said, but he wanted to clear his mother's name. He had made up his mind to enter a claim for part of the estate. He asked Miss Havener how he should proceed. Her paper told her to get counsel for him and handle the matter as her judgment dictated. So she took young Hummel to New York for a week when the lawyer's body was brought home from England. He attended the funeral and the New York papers took note of his presence. The resulting publicity evoked a great many clues which Miss Havener had to sift to their sources.

The first time she saw Henry she asked him to show her anything he had that might support his story that his mother had married Mr. Hummel. He brought out some silver, initialed L.F.H., inscribed stationery, and empty envelopes which he said had contained checks for him, and which unquestionably bore the firm name of Howe and Hummel in the left-hand corner. He also produced photographs of Miss Farrell, taken with Mr. Hummel, together with clothes from an old trunk which had obviously been worn when the pictures were made. He showed her a tiny dress suit which he said his father had ordered for him when he was a small boy. He insisted that Abe had shown him off to his friends in this outfit and had called him his son.

When this story was published a woman, claiming to be the

daughter of Mr. Hummel's tailor, wrote to say that her father had made the miniature dress suit; that Mr. Hummel had brought the boy to the shop, had lifted him up on a table and said, "Now, Henry, make your speech to the jury." The woman added, "If you are the same boy you should remember." Then she quoted the rest of the speech.

Miss Havener read the letter to Henry and stopped when she reached the quotation. Without a moment's hesitation he repeated the speech, word for word. The tailor's daughter also said that if the coat lining of the tiny suit were ripped her father's label would show up. They did this, found it, and the coat became evidence in the case. Subsequently it developed that Mr. Hummel had transferred nearly all his property before his death, so that the estate did not warrant any sort of contest. The case was settled out of court, Henry getting a small sum of money. The story absorbed Portland for months.

When the Halifax disaster occurred in 1917, with 2,000 persons killed, 6,000 injured and $40,000,000 worth of property destroyed, the first train-load of survivors passed through Portland. The city editor assigned all the men on the staff to go out and interview them. Just before they left, the managing editor appeared and asked who were assigned. The city editor told him.

"Isn't Helen going?" he demanded.

"No," said the city editor.

"You're mistaken," said the managing editor. "A woman is likely to dig up something that a man wouldn't see. Take her along too."

The reporters had to do a quick clean-up at the station. They had only five minutes in which to get their eye-witness stories from the survivors. They dashed about, rounding up passengers with bandages or scars. Just before the train pulled out, Miss Havener stumbled on a young British officer who seemed unscathed but who had a different slant on the story. No one up to that time had intimated that the collision of the French munitions ship *Mont Blanc* with the Belgian relief ship in Halifax harbor might be anything more than an accident. The British officer said that it was a German plot.

Miss Havener scented a story at once. She had left her office with nothing but carfare. She jumped off the train as it was pulling out, borrowed a dollar from one of her competitors and scrambled on board again. She rode to Biddeford, the next station along the line, and got all the details she could from the British officer. But when they reached the station she was in the last Pullman of a long train. The conductor had forgotten that she wanted to get off. No one was allowed to leave the Pullman cars, so she found herself traveling toward Boston with what she felt must be the story of the day. She dashed to the coaches, jumped off the moving train into a high snow bank, went back to town with her story and got an eight-column streamer, "Halifax Horror Plotted"—a signed story leading the paper.

Miss Havener was always in the thick of things. She had the lucky knack of catching news in bud. She was the first woman to cover criminal courts in Portland and while listening to a minor case one day she was impressed by the imposing defendant. He was held for forging a small check in Brunswick, Maine, where he had been managing a motion picture theater. His name was James D. Hallen. When he rose to plead not guilty she noticed his accent, his bearing, his good clothes. He pled his own case in a convincing way and apparently with full knowledge of the law.

Miss Havener followed up the case next day. He turned out to be an international forger. Her stories brought reporters to court from all parts of New England. For the next ten days Hallen staged a fine drama in the little court room. The leading lawyers of the Portland bar flocked to hear him. He knew half a dozen languages. He out-witted the handwriting experts. One of them, with a national repu-tation, denied his own testimony on the stand under Hallen's skil-ful cross examination. He disqualified two others. Finally he was freed by a directed verdict because the case had not been proved against him.

Hallen cleared himself of two other charges, lived luxuriously in Portland for five years and married a Maine woman. But fate over-took him at last. He had fleeced Benjamin H. Turner, whom he had pretended to defend on a murder charge in Mexico. When Turner was released he trailed Hallen for three years, found him at his home on the Falmouth shore and ended his suave career with five con-clusive bullets.

Hallen had studied law at Heidelberg, had lectured on interna-tional law and the drama, was an authority on Italian art and litera-ture and had done some newspaper work. But for Miss Havener, the chances are that no one would have paid any attention to the smooth rogue whose international record was dug up only after she had fastened attention on him.

Miss Havener was in her early twenties and looked extremely young when she was appointed city editor of her paper. After she had held down the post for a short time a strange man ambled into the local room and sat around all day without apparent purpose. When she came back from dinner, he was still there, reading the evening paper. At last he walked over to her.

"They tell me you have a woman city editor on this paper," he said.

"Yes," said Miss Havener.

"Well, doesn't she ever do any work around here?"

"Yes, quite a bit of it," Miss Havener retorted.

"But she never seems to come in. I've been around here nearly all day waiting to get a look at her and she hasn't been in yet."

His astonishment was profound when Miss Havener told him, "Yes, she has. You're looking at her now."

He stood with his hat in his hand, studying her from head to foot.

"Good God!" he said and went out. She never saw him again.

But Miss Havener was accepted by her staff without question. She is one of the extremely small group of women in the country who have held down the post of city editor. For a time she edited *The Independent Woman*. She is now in the Will Hays' organization.

Chapter XLI

DETROIT

ONE OF THE NEWSPAPER PHENOMENA OF THE COUNTRY IS
Nancy Brown's "Experience" column in the Detroit *News*.
In 1919 Nancy wandered into the city room, the widow
of a newspaper man, seeking a job. She had no newspaper experience. She was tiny and looked benevolent, with brown eyes and
snow-white curls. Mac Bingay, then city editor of the paper, had
always wanted a confession column. He had assigned various girls
to the task, but they had failed to show enthusiasm for it. He made
one more try with Nancy Brown—a lucky shot, for she proved to
be the perfect person for the job. Her fame grew until it became
apparent that she could roll up enough votes to get herself elected
mayor of Detroit, should this rash ambition settle beneath her silver
curls.

Her paper guards the secret of her identity, and she functions in
a dual rôle. She gave Detroit the largest party in its history but
she did not appear among the crowd of 100,000 that gathered for
the occasion. She counsels and aids multitudes of the harassed. She
calls her column a forum of public opinion, and this is what it actually is, for it evokes extraordinary letters, some of them good,
some of them goofy. They come from every type of person. Occasionally they are gems. She lets no one call "Experience" a lovelorn
column, although it has been more candid on moral questions than
any similar newspaper column in the country. Nancy calmly prints
letters that a preacher could never get past the city desk.

She is absolutely sincere. She suffers and prays over her letters.
Every year she selects the best of those that have appeared in the
intervening months and the *News* publishes them in book form. Like
everything she has a hand in, the demand is at once terrific. She
has reached her public as none of the front-page girls ever could
hope to do. She can settle civic problems faster than any board of
investigation. In a week she can marshal the sentiment of an army
of average readers.

When her column became a battleground between teachers and parents on the subject of heavy homework for high school students, the Board of Education sent a committee to Nancy Brown to discuss a compromise on the allotment of so much work. This crowded out a still more spirited period in the life of the column occasioned by the publication of two letters signed "Fallen Leaves." They were the frank confessions of two girls who had deserted the straight and narrow path and wanted Nancy to tell them if they were evil. Letters poured in from girls who had shared their experience and others who had not; those who had married subsequently and those who had not. Husbands and wives wrote. Doctors wrote. Lawyers wrote. Ministers took up the discussion in their pulpits. All Detroit seemed to concern itself with the problem of the fallen leaves.

Nancy had hesitated to launch the subject, but finally went full sail ahead on the theory that this was a moral problem confronting many of the younger generation. Nearly all the letters that came in applauded the discussion. No one wrote facetiously. The subject was treated with due solemnity. But Nancy found she had started something she could not stop. She was swamped with letters. It was some time before she could take up another subject. Her discussions are public irritants and the forum gives readers with the urge to appear in print a platform for their views. When one of her correspondents asked why anyone should go to church, doctors, lawyers, ministers, professors, students, business men and women supplied hundreds of answers.

Books, art and music are all discussed in Nancy's column. Subjects spring up by chance and instantly the deluge starts. It may be world peace, or the dateless girl, or homesteading in the north, or the difficulties of finding work, or economics, but whatever it is, the column has the knack of attracting responses. It was started on April 19, 1919. At first it appeared only once a week and was not signed. In less than two months, it was running every day. Then, because there was speculation as to the sex of the editor, Nancy picked her pen name and called the column "Experience." In the first year she received 30,000 letters. But their character changed as time went on. They became more scholarly, as a new type of correspondent entered the field. Many of them bear little resemblance to the letters that usually swamp a department of this sort.

When the column had been going for three or four years it got a sound foothold with the social service and educational departments of the city. Nancy can call on any civic agency for aid and she gets it promptly. She could fill her columns every day with the letters of the adolescent but she restricts their contributions to

Wednesdays. Teachers and parents follow this weekly column with attention. It gives them insight into their young.

Her own comments are brief. She lets her correspondents have the forum. Obviously, this is a popular idea. Between Christmas and New Year columns of space are devoted to the reunion letters. They are published without answers and are illustrated with drawings. The subject for discussion is decided on beforehand. Nancy is a stickler for giving her column cumulative effect. This keeps it from having the muddled effect of most confession columns. One theme is pursued until it burns itself out.

Her contributors have planted fourteen forty-acre tracts of land in various counties of Michigan in her honor. In 1934 they held a Sunrise Service on Belle Isle. Forty thousand of her fans gathered in the Shell for a religious service. The Detroit Street Railway doubled its service on all lines to carry the worshippers to their destination. Then the *News* sent her to California to attend the Easter service at Mount Rubidoux. Her second sunrise service brought out 70,000 worshippers. By this time Dr. Edgar De Witt Jones was chaplain of the column. But her biggest triumph was the party at the Art Institute in 1930, when the crowd was estimated at 100,000 and traffic was blocked for miles. It was by all odds Detroit's gala party. Thousands of letters poured in afterwards. Four years later a painting was given to the Art Institute by the column contributors as a memento of this occasion. Again the crowds turned out for the unveiling. And in 1935 this gesture was repeated.

Nancy concerns herself with good deeds. She has built up the Goodfellow Fund for social service work at Christmas time. When the Detroit Symphony Orchestra asked her to sponsor a series of six concerts, they were an overwhelming success. She uses the proceeds from the sale of her books for the benevolent causes backed by the column. Some of the money goes to help students. She lends them small sums, taking their promissory notes to pay it back when they can. Nancy was one of the early broadcasters and is still on the air.

Long before her day Ellen Browning Scripps worked as a proofreader on the Detroit *News*, which had just been founded by her brother, James E. Scripps. She was born in London and took forty-four days to cross the Atlantic in a sailing ship. It was not yet the time when women went to college, but Ellen insisted on attending Knox College in Galesburg, Illinois. She was graduated in 1858. At first she taught. Then in 1873, when the panic was on, she took her savings with her to Detroit instead of hiding them under the mattress as so many people were doing. She went to work on the *News*, and put her money into the papers founded by her brothers—the Detroit

News, the Cleveland *Press*, the St. Louis *Chronicle* and the Cincinnati *Post*. She was an ardent suffragist and spent money lavishly on this and the temperance cause.

Since Miss Scripps' times the *News* has produced a number of talented newspaper women. Miriam Teichner got her early training there, along with Sara Moore, a brilliant girl who can write straight news stories, features or verse, and also knows how to sketch. Miss Moore was born in Detroit. Her father died when she was three. Her early years were spent trailing a nomadic step-parent about the world. Her education was diverse, and ranged from convent to public school. At sixteen she settled down in Detroit. A long skirt and some carefully adjusted hairpins helped to fool E. G. Pipp, of the *News*, so that he was persuaded to give her a trial.

She wrote obits and sermons and then graduated to state legislative sessions, Supreme Court and the Press Gallery at Washington. She interviewed Carrie Nation, Anthony Comstock and President Taft, among others. Her paper sent her to England to cover Mrs. Pankhurst's hussies. She lingered to make a study of the Englishwoman in industrial life. Then she went to Paris, where she changed her tack and turned to fashions. About that time her paper let her do a series called "Cartoonettes," which was syndicated.

Then she moved to New York, where she free-lanced. Her sketches appeared constantly in the *Mail*. She was sent to Europe on the Peace Ship. On her return she was about to accept an assignment to travel through Canada, and beyond the Arctic Circle, when Frank G. Eastman, to whom she was engaged, objected. So she changed her plans and married him in the Little Church Around the Corner. He was formerly a newspaper man and now does advertising. They live in Winnetka, Illinois. After the birth of three children Miss Moore took up her newspaper career again with a feature called "Maiden Meditations," which appeared in the Chicago *Tribune*.

Today the Detroit *News* has one of the expert newspaper women of the country in Florence Davies, a seasoned member of the craft who started her newspaper career in Cleveland, then moved to the Detroit *Journal*. When it was merged with the *News* she edited the woman's page, also writing a daily column of comment. In recent years she has written and edited all the art news of the paper, at the same time supervising the woman's department.

Few newspaper women can match Mary Humphrey's record. For years she was Sunday editor of the Detroit *Free Press*, doing a difficult job with skill. Not more than half a dozen important papers throughout the country have tried women Sunday editors and Miss Humphrey is one of the most distinguished examples. She inherited the job when her editor died. At first it involved looking after the color feature magazine, the rotogravure section, the girls' and boys' page, two women's pages and two columns of book reviews. But during her term of office, everything was expanded. The book reviews were published in a twelve-page tabloid. The children had their own tabloid magazine in color. One page was devoted regularly to reviews of the new juvenile books and another to verse from young contributors, which was criticized by the editor. This feature became popular with the young. It put them on the adult plane. The verse writers had a club of their own and met regularly.

Miss Humphrey ran a number of contests and started a column called "Your Problems" under the name Ruth Alden. She conducted it for twelve years and it is still a popular feature in the *Free Press*. Her duties were legion. She also ran the Fresh Air Camp sponsored by her paper. When she published a series of quilt patterns and got a quick reaction from women readers she began having quilt shows. But these were given up in favor of spring and fall fashion shows, in which all the advertisers participated. They were staged in a theater and were good bait for women readers.

During her last five years on the *Free Press*, before she became a publicity expert, Miss Humphrey supervised the daily as well as the Sunday women's pages. Besides conducting her problems department, she turned out a column of gossip. Her Sunday staff, except for the artists, was composed entirely of women, and she took on the first trained home economics expert to work for a Detroit paper. During her régime the complete novel, run in tabloid form, was launched in the Sunday edition. Her work, in many respects, paralleled Mary King's. Miss Humphrey brought zest and judgment to her job and worked indefatigably at it, for the woman Sunday editor must cope with composing-room problems as well as the ordinary complications of the editorial department.

The *Free Press* has not been one of the closed shops to newspaper women by any means. It has given them excellent opportunities. As far back at 1878 Jennie O. Starkey was taken on the staff to run a department known as "The Puzzler." She was a high school girl at the time. Later she ran other departments variously called "The Household," "Fair Woman's World," "The Letter Box" and "The Sunday Breakfast Table." For years she was society editor of the paper. Another of the early woman columnists on the *Free Press* was Elizabeth Johnstone, whose pen name was Beatrix. Jennette McColl, a graduate of the University of Michigan, today edits the woman's club page of the *Free Press* and writes a daily column called "Silhouettes"—humorous incidents about well-known residents of Detroit. Marjorie Avery functions capably as society editor. Detroit is going in more and more for the chatty, intimate method of covering society news, which is gaining ground all over the country. One of the best exponents of this style, Monica Weadock Porter, recently left newspaper work to do publicity. She was originally The Passerby for the *Free Press*, then Judy O'Grady for the *News*.

Vera Brown, who works for the Detroit *Times*, is the one newspaper girl in the country who pilots her own plane when she goes on assignments. She does not worry about trains or motor cars. She puts on her helmet and sprints into the clouds to cover a murder, with all the nonchalance of a good Hearst reporter. Once she cracked up, spinning, and landed in Lake St. Clair with a land plane. She could not walk away because she had to be rowed ashore. But Vera was only mildly injured and the experience did not shake her nerve. She had another smash in northern Michigan but it was all in the day's work. In her spare moments she writes lively newspaper serials about a girl pilot.

She knows as many policemen as any reporter in Detroit. Her hobbies are flying and books, and she collects modern plays. She is quite a picturesque reporter. Nothing frightens her in the way of an assignment, although she has worked at all hours, in all sorts of places. Once, when she visited the home of a Detroit hold-up man, his pals threatened to shoot her if she did not leave at once. She left, so she still does not know if they meant it. Miss Brown found a baby contest much worse. The mothers wanted to tear her limb from limb. She has covered prize fights, women's conventions, murder trials, divorce trials and the saga of the Dodge family. She has interviewed the usual crop of celebrities who make life diverting for the girl reporter, and has made a specialty of looking up all the noted aviators, men and women. They have been equally interested in her. She has covered a bullfight in Madrid, the Paris aviation show, and every aircraft show Detroit has had, as well as the Cleveland races and the Thompson Trophy Race. She has traveled around the world, her eyes always open for newspaper copy.

When Merton W. Goodrich, the trap drummer who murdered a ten-year-old girl in Detroit, was picked up as a vagrant in New York, Miss Brown flew on to accompany him back to his retribution. Again she was on the spot soon after Howard Carter Dickinson, nephew of Chief Justice Charles Evans Hughes, was found shot to death in a Detroit park in the summer of 1935. She covered the subsequent trial, and was also one of the many newspaper women to see Hauptmann take the stand and deny the murder of the Lindbergh baby. She saw three men acquitted of the murder of Gerald E. O. Buckley, political commentator on the radio.

Miss Brown's license number is 10591. She learned to fly in 1929, in order to write a series of six Sunday articles on the subject. But the idea of being a pilot fascinated her. She finds her hours in the air exhilarating and she uses her plane for nearly all out-of-town assignments. She has ghosted for cinema stars, dope fiends, a beauty contest winner and a woman rescued on the *Lusitania*. In 1934 she covered the World Series and interviewed the Dean family, mother and sons. She took the winner of a spelling contest to the White House while President Coolidge was in office. She covered Mrs. Franklin D. Roosevelt on her visit to Detroit with her husband during his first campaign. She accompanied the Detroit bonus army to Washington and stayed with them in Camp Anacostia for three days.

Miss Brown was born in Lansing, Michigan, and is a graduate of the University of Michigan. While at college she got her first reportorial experience on the *Michigan Daily*. She has never forgotten her first assignment. It was September, 1918, and the casualty lists were coming in. She was sent to the suburbs to see a Scotswoman whose son had been killed. As she boarded the street car she held in her hand the slip of paper announcing his death. Then she began to wonder how she should break the news to his mother.

When she arrived, the woman was scrubbing her porch. Miss Brown decided hastily that she would say the boy was wounded. He had been a football star at one of the local high schools. She sat down on the front steps with her and got up enough courage to tell her story.

"You wouldn't lie to me?" the woman asked, looking her straight in the eye.

"No," gasped Miss Brown, and because the mother wanted to believe her, she did.

But she made one mistake. She stayed too long. Before she left the telegram arrived with government notification of the death of her son. Miss Brown will never forget the next few minutes. Since then she has heard a boy confess to murder, watched a man sentenced to be lashed, informed people of all kinds of calamities, but nothing has ever moved her like this first assignment. She went back to her office crying. Her nerves are now like steel. They need to be, when she starts off on an assignment by the aerial route.

Chapter XLII

CHICAGO

A MONG THE HORDES OF IMMIGRANTS WHO WALKED ASHORE AT
Ellis Island in October, 1921, was a slim girl who moved
freely among them, with none of the baffled air of the arrivals from Europe. She had crossed from Ireland in the steerage,
eaten the unsavory food, gone through the mad huddle that was
characteristic at the time of America's welcome to the foreigner.
Her experience bore out all the charges against Ellis Island.

This was Genevieve Forbes, just beginning her newspaper career,
and soon to achieve top standing for her complete competence
under all conditions, her personal charm and integrity. Unlike most
women reporters, she started with a spectacular assignment. Her
talent was evident at once. She skyrocketed to fame in journalistic
circles because of her clear and sparkling style, her vivid way of
nailing the right phrase, her instinct for handling news. For a decade
her by-line, which became Genevieve Forbes Herrick after her
marriage in 1924, was constantly on the front page of the Chicago
Tribune, a guarantee of good writing and sound reporting.

Her trip to Ireland was a brisk initiation. It was not the sort of
assignment that the girl reporter usually draws out of the hat when
she is still a novice. Her stories were so potent that she was called to
Washington in the following November to testify ·before the Congressional Committee on Immigration. The tide of immigration was
at its height and the complaints were deafening. Mrs. Herrick's articles crystallized the general situation. As a result of the committee's
investigation the laws were amended and things were made better for
the immigrant.

Almost overnight she had become a front-page girl. But she had
been on the paper for three years already, looking longingly toward
the city room while she clipped papers and used her paste pot as
assistant exchange editor. A brief period as assistant literary editor
had not eased the pain. Before joining the staff of the *Tribune* in
1918 she had taught in Waterloo. She is a native of Chicago, attended
the McPherson grammar and Lake View high schools and was

graduated from Northwestern University in 1916. The following year she took her master's degree in English at the University of Chicago.

Her first newspaper assignment was to interview a man in a hotel. She was not sure whether she should ask him to come down to the lobby or go up to his room. He solved the problem by appearing in the lobby. She wrote the story and told her family to watch for it. Next day they hunted all through the paper. It failed to appear. She thought her newspaper career had ended. Soon after that she went to Ireland and she never had to worry about her assignments again. They came thick and fast. She covered princes, prelates and pugilists; was scorned by butlers; was royally received by Al Capone; did a brilliant job on the grim Leopold-Loeb case; was on the spot for every spectacle of consequence; and proved her superiority a thousand times by her smooth work on the typewriter. Her subject often was crime, which she covered with the literary skill of an essayist and the hard punches of a sports writer. She learned to get about the town, to talk to gangsters and their wives, to write about them in the vernacular, but she always sharpened the sordid with humor and a crisp approach.

When Nathan F. Leopold, Jr. and Richard Loeb confessed the so-called thrill murder of Robert Franks in the summer of 1924, Mrs. Herrick was assigned to the case. The hearing that followed before Judge John Caverly was one of the most extraordinary in the annals of crime. She followed every turn of the dramatic case as the various phases of the youths' dementia were exploited in court. Her stories were scholarly, vivid and revealing. She had to fashion her wedding plans to the assignment, for when it was over she and John Herrick, a colleague on the Chicago *Tribune*, were married. Judge Caverly timed his verdict to make things simpler for them.

For the next six years crime raged in Chicago on an unprecedented scale. On a spring day in 1930 Al Capone, fresh from ten months in the Eastern Pennsylvania Penitentiary at Philadelphia, received Mrs. Herrick in his hotel suite, with pictures of George Washington and Big Bill Thompson smiling down on his gold-encrusted inkstand. The interview led her paper next day and carried a streamer. It was a rare piece of reporting. Mrs. Herrick found Capone casual, affable, wary. He was annoyed because he had been picked up in the City of Brotherly Love on the insignificant charge of carrying a gun, mere common sense in the life of a Capone. He brought in his wife and his sister, Mafalda. It was clear that he wanted to impress Mrs. Herrick. The women chatted in a noncommittal way and retired in swirls of chiffon. He drew attention to the fact that his wife had gray hair at thirty-eight. Worrying over him.

Like Jack Diamond, he detests publicity. He has given few interviews. Mrs. Herrick's was a *tour de force*. Looking at her across
his desk Capone said:

> You know, lady, I'd rather the newspapers wouldn't print a
> line about me. That's the way I feel. No brass band for me.
> There's a lot of grief attached to the limelight. Say, if I was
> just plain Izzy Polatski, living in Chicago, I'd not stand out
> in the gutter trying to get a peek at Capone. I'd attend to my
> business and let him attend to his; no use making a laughing
> stock of the city. . . . All I ever did was supply a demand
> that was pretty popular. Why, the very guys that make my
> trade good are the ones that yell the loudest about me. . . .
> They talk about me not being on the legitimate. Why, lady,
> nobody's on the legit, when it comes down to cases; you know
> that.

Chicago enjoyed this intimate picture of its pet villain the following morning. Next Mrs. Herrick went out to explore the lives of
the women of gangland. She fastened on Florence Diggs Murphy,
who had buried two notorious husbands—Big Tim Murphy and
Dingbat Oberta. She got under Florence's skin and gave a rip-roaring
picture of her gangland codes. Her story was a curious study in
human nature. Florence made up her own epitaph for her husbands
when she was interviewed. "I've had more love and better husbands
than most women," she announced proudly.

This was only one phase of Mrs. Herrick's work for the *Tribune*.
She handled science, politics, the arts, all the news of the day. She
covered visiting celebrities, among them Queen Marie, Lady Astor
and Lloyd George. She followed Lindbergh through the gala day of
his return to Washington after his trans-Atlantic flight, and later
rode up Broadway after him, ducking the blinding mass of ticker
tape.

She could turn her hand to anything. Her fashion stories were
models of grace and brevity. Although she worked in a highly competitive field, Mrs. Herrick never favored the indirect approach
or dare-devil doings to get her story. She collected her facts by
sensible means, weighed them shrewdly, then put the utmost emphasis on good writing. In talking to the women of her craft, she has
summed up her point of view:

> Let us first of all be good writers and men and women after-
> wards. Tradition may be stacked against women but there are
> many stories that a woman reporter can get more readily than
> a man. Women should concentrate on being good general re-
> porters first. . . . The woman's angle in journalism has become
> hopelessly enmeshed in silk and chiffon. An editor may give a

woman her assignment but she gives herself her style. She should strive to write all the news she can better than as many men as she can.

In 1930 Mrs. Herrick left newspaper work for a year and she and her husband retired to Vermont. Then they returned, this time to the Washington bureau of the Chicago *Tribune*, where they worked together on politics and life at the capital. Soon after the Roosevelts entered the White House, Mrs. Herrick left the Chicago *Tribune*. She now does features for NANA and magazine work. She is one of the newspaper women closest to Mrs. Roosevelt.

The Herricks live in an old Colonial house in Alexandria. Like most of the members of her craft who have coped with high adventure at one time or another, Geno, as she is known to her intimates, has a strong domestic sense. She likes the fireside and her dogs, and a quiet moment to pursue her interests, after her breathless days of city staff work. She is active in the Women's National Press Club and is an able platform speaker. She lectures with authority on a profession to which she herself has added real distinction.

Mrs. Herrick was seriously injured in 1935 in the motor accident which resulted in the death of Mrs. Harold Ickes. She was a close friend of Mrs. Ickes and was staying with her at Santa Fe when they started out on their disastrous motor trip.

The Chicago *Tribune* has been the training ground of many fine newspaper women. Mary King and Antoinette Donnelly are two of its most noted products. It has given its women broad executive powers. During the years that Miss King was Sunday editor she backed newspaper women consistently, gave them opportunities wherever there were openings and steered some into original channels. From 1920 to 1925 Martha McElliott read copy on the *Tribune*. This was an innovation and when she spoke about her work at the Medill School of Journalism, she was bombarded for months with letters from ambitious girls who wanted to be copy readers and thought she could show them the way.

Captain Patterson decided one day out of a clear sky to put her on the night desk. Her father objected. He knew that it would mean coming home at three or four o'clock in the morning, and with gunmen running loose in the streets of Chicago! But she edited all kinds of copy for the Sunday edition, prowled around the composing room, did make-up and won prizes for her headlines. Then she married Sheppard Butler and moved to New York with him when he was appointed editor of *Liberty*. Since then she has read thousands of manuscripts, dabbled in the literary agency business and raised delphiniums.

Both Kathleen McLaughlin, who is now on the New York *Times*, and Maureen McKernan worked on the Chicago *Tribune* at the same time as Mrs. Herrick and Miss McElliott. One hot Sunday morning the city desk assigned Miss McKernan to do a feature on a Maharajah and Maharanee who were staying at a local hotel with a large native staff, most of whom sat cross-legged on guard outside the suite assigned to the party. The Princess wore a diamond in her nose. The *Tribune* wanted a picture of this phenomenon. But the Maharanee scuttled through the lobby like an animated cocoon and refused to pose for pictures. The other reporters left but Miss McKernan returned, and persuaded the management to let the housekeeper take her on her staff as an impoverished gentlewoman. She wore a uniform, cleaned and dusted, tried to make beds but did a bad job of it. She mended a stocking for the blonde wife of a race-track man and turned down a chance to become her maid. Waiters came and went through the doors of the sacred suite all day, but they were barred from the Maharanee's rooms by an English-speaking Hindu coiled in blue Indian silk.

At six o'clock Miss McKernan, large and commanding, took a pail of water and marched boldly into the drawing-room of the suite. On the floor was a tablecloth, heaped with fruits, vegetables and cheeses. The Maharajah and his retinue were sitting cross-legged, enjoying their evening meal. The staff was thrown into a panic at the sight of the white-faced invader. The Maharajah, in brown tweeds, merely glared at her. She was rushed from the room but she maneuvered things so that her retreat led her straight into the bedroom of the Maharanee. She found her sitting on the floor with her maid, her face uncovered, the diamond visible in her nose. They were sorting out laundry.

Miss McKernan stood her ground for five minutes while the Hindus did their best to rush her out. When she seemed as immovable as a marble column, they tried another tack and bustled the Maharanee into the bathroom, locking the door. The man from Cook's and the hotel manager arrived simultaneously. Maureen was fired and she went out in tears. But downstairs she and the manager enjoyed the joke. No one else was in on the secret.

Miss McKernan attended the University of Kansas and started her newspaper career on the Topeka *Daily Capital*. Most of the men had gone to war. She edited the woman's page but varied the monotony by doing night police news. When her city editor moved to the Kansas City *Journal* she went with him. She covered the federal beat for two and a half years and learned about dope peddlers, automobile thieves, and the operation of the Department of Justice.

Robert Lee, city editor of the Chicago *Tribune*, took her on his staff in 1923 when she was down to $1.15. She got a by-line soon afterwards by doing a solo act on the fire escape while the other reporters tried to get into the home of Wanda Stopa. Wanda was the Polish immigrant girl who studied law, went demented, and shot at Mrs. Y. Kenley Smith, whose husband she loved. Five bullets went wild but with her final shot she killed a caretaker who had come to Mrs. Smith's rescue. Wanda disappeared and poisoned herself in a Detroit hotel without delay. Miss McKernan also worked on the mysterious death of William Nelson McClintock and the subsequent trial of William D. Shepherd, who was accused of feeding him typhoid germs, the crime sensation of 1925. Shepherd was acquitted.

She left the *Tribune* to go to the *Herald Examiner*, where she stayed for six months before she tried press-agenting. She married John Cooper Ross in 1930 and moved to New York. When she went to Westchester County to do special work for the Macy papers in a hot county election, she intended to stay for a month, but she is still there after four years. She does straight women's stuff and after her exciting Chicago days she no longer runs a temperature over her assignments. She works in the county news bureau in White Plains which serves all the dailies and some of the weeklies of Westchester.

Just before Kathleen McLaughlin landed on the *Tribune* Maurine Watkins had worked briefly but to good effect on the city staff. During her eight months on the paper she had absorbed enough to write the play *Chicago*, startling in its tough momentum. She was twenty-six at the time. The Beulah Annan trial was running. It was the heyday of the murderess. Juries wept over the dear little things, usually weighing two hundred pounds. Miss Watkins, fair, fastidious and surprised, patterned her Roxie Hart after Beulah. Sam Harris read her play and liked it. Looking at her, he could not imagine how she had come to write it. Her newspaper experience was limited, but her fame spread far beyond that of her colleagues. Her play was a hit. She moved to New York. She did special stories on the Snyder-Gray trial for the Scripps-Howard chain. Her next move was to Hollywood, where she became one of the most industrious women writers in the film capital.

Today Kay Hall, Ruth de Young, Marcia Winn, Betty Browning, Irene Steyskal and Virginia Gardner are all contributing to the columns of the Chicago *Tribune*. Under the pseudonym Barbara Adams, Miss Gardner did an exposé in 1935 of fake psychologists, quacks and healers. She visited thirty of these "specialists" and worked for six weeks on her series, which ended in court action against the most flagrant offenders. She listened to the drivelings of yogis and the complacent revelations of greasy mediums. One woman, her vast bulk swathed in white robes, emerged from a cabinet in a room that was pitch-black except for a tiny red light bulb, while her husband assured Miss Gardner that this was her mother come to see her.

One of the most bizarre of the healers took her to an ornate chapel in an old frame house in the Negro district and practised a silent laying-on of hands to drive away her mythical neuritis. But her prize subject was a professor who specialized in mesmerism and guaranteed to cure epilepsy, blindness, paralysis, anemia or practically anything else, under the influence of hypnosis. He wore resplendent clothes, had a tattooed wrist and a scarred left cheek. He had had his face lifted, too. The effect was magnificent. His efforts to hypnotize Miss Gardner led to his arrest, after a special woman investigator had gone over the same ground and fortified the reporter's evidence.

The arrests were effected before the Barbara Adams stories ran. They were handled as spot news by the *Tribune*. Next day the first of the series appeared. Miss Gardner's stories brought a heavy reaction. The other papers were forced to carry the straight news developments, which had been precipitated by her investigation. Two of the healers were convicted. A third, a goateed "doctor" who read palms and horoscopes and was an unlicensed chiropractor, was acquitted. He claimed to be the former pal of Sitting Bull. He had been a radio lecturer and circus performer. His specialty was the odic force, magnetic waves to stir up humanity.

Miss Gardner comes from Fort Smith, Arkansas, and was graduated in journalism from the University of Missouri in 1924. She studied advertising, then did newspaper work in Pawhuska, Ponca City, Fort Smith and Kansas City. A letter of introduction to Kate S. Webber landed her on the *Tribune* in 1929.

Miss Webber is another Fort Smith girl. In 1918 she joined the *Tribune* staff as assistant society editor. Then she became club and exchange editor. She left the paper to get married, and returned later to newspaper work. She now does a shopping column for the Chicago *American*. Miss Webber started her newspaper career in Fort Smith as society editor of the *Southwest American*, where Thyra Samter Winslow got her early training under the editorial direction of Colonel W. E. Decker. Miss Winslow is one of the newspaper women who have gone on to fame in fiction, but she still thinks there is nothing like the city staff. When she did some stories for King Features in 1935 and Jack Lait said to her, "You're a good newspaper woman," she thought it the best compliment she had ever received.

Miss Winslow saw her first contribution in print at the age of seven. Her mother sent it in to the children's page of the St. Louis *Globe Democrat* and it took the prize of the week. It was only a matter of a few years until Thyra became society editor and dramatic critic of the paper in Fort Smith. She made $7 a week. After two years at a state university she tried unsuccessfully to get on the Chicago *Tribune*. So she went into the chorus instead. Now and again she drifted in to the paper, to make sure that she was not forgotten. And at last Burns Mantle, who was then Sunday editor, told her to write about the chorus. She winced when her story, which she had thought most sophisticated, appeared with the head: "Mother's Darling Goes In The Chorus." She was eighteen at the time. Her next assignment was to interview a girl who was about to marry an Indian. Having come from the Oklahoma border she had vigorous ideas on the subject. Miss Winslow wrote the story and Mr. Mantle took her on the staff at $15 a week. Mary King was Mr. Mantle's assistant at the time. It was just before she became Sunday editor. Courtney Ryley Cooper was on the staff. Some of her other colleagues were Burton Rascoe, Charles MacArthur and John V. A. Weaver. Percy Hammond was dramatic critic and now and again he let Miss Winslow cover a show, just as Walter Howey, who was city editor, sent her out on an occasional assignment.

One was to track down some odd marriage rules a bartender and his bride had framed up. It was a wet day and the other reporters sent out on the story gathered comfortably in a nearby saloon to await the homecoming of the bride and groom. For hours Miss Winslow sat miserably on the front stoop in the rain, so that when the principals came home they felt sorry for her and gave her the story. No one else got a look in. She was the one girl who worked for Mr. Howey in a sensational exposé of fortune tellers. Nearly five hundred were shown up altogether. She went to at least a hundred of them, had her palm read, her horoscope studied and listened to the hoarse whispers of the synthetic spirits.

When the New York *Mirror* was first launched and Mr. Howey was put in charge, he called her up one day and said, "Thyra, you're the best newspaper woman in New York. I want you to work on a new paper with me."

She rushed down to the *Mirror* office. Mr. Howey looked apologetic and said, "Thyra, you're the *only* newspaper woman I know in New York. Won't you help me out with some stuff?"

So for a month she did a daily true story, the women's features, the voice of the people and a few other odds and ends until things got under way. Then she thankfully went home and settled down at her typewriter to more free-lance fiction.

A more recent newspaper graduate from Arkansas is Marcia Winn, of the *Tribune* staff, who stayed with Dillinger's father and brother for fifteen hours the day the gangster was killed. Another time she was assigned by her city editor to catch a tiny monkey which had escaped from a Frank Buck shipment and gone on a tour of the rafters in a train shed. Armed with a paper sack of ripe bananas she and a photographer climbed to the roof and stayed there for hours, trying to frighten the monkey with screams, seduce him with bananas, or cajole him with prayers. But he refused to budge. At nightfall Miss Winn climbed down, black, disheveled, blistered, her nails broken and her face sooty. But that night, before she had a chance to change, she had to cover an exclusive dinner on the Gold Coast given for a Japanese Prince and Princess.

One bitter day shortly after Christmas she was sent to eight homes to tell the inmates that their mothers, husbands and sons had been killed in an accident. In each case she followed up her announcement by asking for pictures. A Jewish mother rushed at her insanely, tore her hat, scratched her face and finally sank moaning to a low stool.

Miss Winn is a graduate of the Mississippi State College for Women. She edited her college paper and corresponded for the Memphis *Commercial Appeal* before getting a job on the Arkansas *Gazette* the day after she returned from college. Kathleen McLaughlin, whom she met at a woman's convention in Hot Springs, brought her on to Chicago in 1934.

When Kay Hall, of the *Tribune*, caught a stink bomb at a Red meeting, her office bought her a new fur coat and paid damages to her cab driver, who said that his taxi was ruined for good. This was only one of many adventures experienced by Miss Hall, who comes from Bluffdale, Texas, and broke into newspaper work modestly as campus correspondent for the Dallas *Dispatch*, while she was attending Southern Methodist University. Soon after she got to Chicago she drove a yellow cab for a week to record her experiences. She was shot at once by a demented woman. On another occasion she and a photographer walked out fast when an angry husband cocked a long blue rifle in their direction. Her first airplane ride was with Eddie Stinson in Texas. Next time she saw him was on an undertaker's slab in Chicago.

She worked on the Chicago *Times* for five years before joining the staff of the *Tribune*. For one period she was assistant city editor but she cringed every time she asked the ace rewrite man to take a story over the telephone. Experience hardened her, however, and she had assurance by the time she sat in at the Wynekoop and Insull trials and did feature stories on the political conventions.

A dominating newspaper personality in Chicago today is Leola

Allard, who has held down several newspaper jobs, put over an uncanny number of exclusive stories and is a formidable member of her craft. She does not believe in working with her colleagues when she scents a story around the corner. Consequently, she is known as one of the genuine scoop artists of the profession. The Chicago *Daily News* has always prided itself on its woman's section and Miss Allard now edits it skilfully. She insists on sparkling copy and prefers the unconventional approach to a story. She is not afraid to run caricatures instead of photographs and she maintains a high standard of excellence in her fashion, food and beauty departments.

Miss Allard comes from Pueblo, Colorado. She started her newspaper career in 1907 as a society reporter on the Pueblo *Chieftain*. A year later she went to the Denver *Post*. After two weeks her job came to an end, but she stayed on, working for nothing. She covered a murder so well that she was put back on the payroll. She did all sorts of jobs around the office and finally gravitated to the society desk. In 1911 she moved to Chicago and worked in turn for the *Herald Examiner* and the *Tribune*, where she soon showed her enterprise. Her colleagues worried considerably when she was around. Miss Allard was not a rival who could be overlooked. She unearthed Mrs. Dion O'Bannion when the ex-choir boy who became known in Chicago as King of the Beer Runners was shot in his flower shop in a death-dealing handshake.

Miss Allard worked on the Billy McClintock case and was in the thick of things during gangland's wildest days. Like all the Chicago newspaper women of this period most of her stories dealt with crime. In 1926 she moved to Pittsburgh to launch a new woman's page on the *Post Gazette*. Then she did a daily column for King Features. In 1931 she joined the staff of the Chicago *Daily News*.

Another Chicago veteran skilled in the craft who has put over many a scoop is Patricia Dougherty, sister of Mary Dougherty of the New York *Journal*. She was the original Princess Pat of the Chicago *American*. Several smart pieces of newspaper strategy have been chalked up to her credit. She had the story of Pola Negri's love for Valentino so securely sewn up at the time of the actor's death that no other reporter could get a look in. In September, 1926, Pola, who had announced that she was engaged to Valentino, accompanied his body back to California, after the New York public had smashed the plate-glass windows of the funeral parlors in their anxiety to pass the bier of the screen idol. Miss Dougherty practically kidnapped Miss Negri until she had dragged her whole story from her. She boarded the train and saw to it that her competitors did not get near the actress. Miss Negri had refused to talk to reporters, but she spilled the story of her love for Valentino with fluency into Miss Dougherty's receptive ears, and at the time it made good reading for the fans.

Another of the *American* stars today is Hazel Macdonald, who has done newspaper work in different parts of the country, and always with marked capacity. She wrote the straight news lead on the Samuel Insull trial, a story of prime importance in Chicago. Again she did admirable work on the trial of the aged Dr. Alice Lindsay Wynekoop, who killed her daughter-in-law, Rheta, for no discernible motive.

Miss Macdonald did her first newspaper work for the Salt Lake *Telegram*. Then she shuttled back and forth between Los Angeles, Chicago and Seattle, where she worked briefly on the *Post-Intelligencer*. She spent a year and a half on the Lasky lot in Hollywood and did the continuity for a silent picture called "After the Snow." But she left the movies without a qualm to join the staff of the Los Angeles *Herald*. She got her first taste of the front page on the coast when Mrs. Clara Phillips introduced the ten-cent hammer technique in polishing off a rival in love. It was one of the flashy cases of the era. The hammer murderess was convicted.

In the Pacific northwest Miss Macdonald was thrown off Queen Marie's train oftener than anybody else. The dog fight that had been raging more or less all the way across the country had reached a hectic stage as the Queen neared the coast. Loie Fuller had been left by the wayside. So had a number of newspaper people. Again Miss Macdonald applied her penetrating touch to regal doings when she went abroad in 1931 and rounded up stories for the New York *Sun* on the Spanish royal family, who were living in retirement at Fontainebleau after the revolution in Madrid. She worked for the Paris edition of the Chicago *Tribune*, now defunct, then returned to Chicago and the *American*.

Miss Macdonald is always ready for adventure. In the autumn of 1935 she was in southern Utah and Arizona, wrangling horses from the national parks to their winter pasturage on the rim of the Grand Canyon, 120 miles away. This meant being in the saddle while she rode forty miles a day. It was not an assignment but voluntary punishment. She goes where the spirit moves her.

When Roger Touhy and his cohorts were tried for the kidnapping of Jake Factor, Ruth Cowan, of the Associated Press, was present for the verdict. The court room had been closely guarded throughout the trial. The night of the verdict it was like an armed camp. Officers with drawn revolvers stood posted around the court room. The verdict was guilty. Next morning Miss Cowan was assigned to cover the formal sentencing of the prisoners. They were to be rushed to Joliet at once and she was assigned to go along. She was admitted to the high walled courtyard behind the Criminal Courts Building. Captain John Stege, a veteran in Chicago crime, snapped an order to her: "Stay close to the wall."

Looking around she saw machine gunners standing at strategic points. She backed up against the wall. The prisoners were brought out under heavy guard. It was a swift ride to Joliet. Driving at top speed, a squad car raced ahead, stopping all traffic at crossroads to let the police procession speed by. The sirens whined. Passing motorists gaped at the strange parade escorting Roger Touhy to Joliet.

Miss Cowan saw Dr. Wynekoop take her life sentence stoically, her eyes glued to the clock above the bench, no clue to her feelings apparent except her ashen color. She watched Capone accept his irksome fate with comparative good humor when the government finally got him. She had been writing features about him throughout the trial; had noticed his gay attire, and the new tan shoes that pinched his feet and made him wince.

He has a good memory for faces. He had seen her about the court, had talked to her twice.

"Hi, sister," he grinned, on his way in to court one day.

But he was grave when the jury filed in with its verdict. He took out his handkerchief and mopped his brow. Suddenly he looked toward Miss Cowan, saw her watching earnestly for some sign of emotion. He smiled, a quick flash, just as the verdict was announced. In a moment the smile was gone. His face became a mask before the last word was spoken. The law had caught him at last.

When not engaged on crime, fashions or women's stories of one sort or another, Miss Cowan covers markets, a meticulous job where an eighth of a cent has meaning. She fell heir to the assistant market editor's job during his vacation. After that she was called on frequently for market reports. Now she can read the market page and ticker tape with perfect understanding. She is one of the few newspaper women in the country who have followed in Midy Morgan's footsteps.

Miss Cowan was born in Salt Lake City, attended the University of Texas, worked in the book department of an Austin store, then in the Texas State Library, then as secretary in the engineering department of the university. She returned to San Antonio to teach. She was still quite young. Her roommate, Mary Carter, was a feature writer on the San Antonio *Evening News*, and she envied her the excitement of her job. She substituted for her at vacation time. Her first interview was with Stark Young, who was then dramatic critic of the New York *Times*, and was visiting his sister in San Antonio.

In 1927 she deserted the schoolroom for a desk in the local room.

She soon found that men got most of the breaks in the newspaper world, so she decided to sign herself R. Baldwin Cowan when she corresponded for papers out of town. The U.P. got hold of her name after she covered an American Legion national convention and, assuming her to be a man, asked her to do special assignments in her territory. When Ralph Turner, Southwest division manager, showed up and saw that Baldwin Cowan was a girl, the arrangement was almost off. The U.P. frowns on women reporters. But she won him over and was assigned temporarily to the legislature at Austin. When it adjourned she was notified that she could no longer be retained on the U.P. payroll, although her work was good. So she wrote to Kent Cooper of the A.P. and in this way landed her Chicago job.

While the newspaper women in Chicago today are preoccupied chiefly with crime and the fast action story, forty years ago their predecessors were writing editorials, doing criticism or stunting in the Nellie Bly manner. Nora Marx aped Nellie with an exposé of asylum abuses. She got inside and made first-hand observations. At the turn of the century Mary Abbott and Margaret Sullivan were writing editorials. Mrs. Amber Holden, who founded the Bohemian Club, was doing dramatic criticism. Mrs. Elia Wilkinson Peattie, mother of Donald Culross Peattie, worked on the staff of the Chicago *Tribune* side by side with the men reporters in the late eighties, after her marriage to Robert Burns Peattie, also a newspaper man. Later she went to the Chicago *Daily News* and then was chief editorial writer for the Omaha *World Herald*. She did historical sketches, literary criticism, politics and dramatic reviewing.

Marion Bowlan contributed to the Chicago *Journal* and sent a series of sketches from the Ford Peace Ship. Ethel M. Colson Brazelton wrote editorials for the Chicago *Tribune* at one time, and Alice Johnstone did occasional political editorials for the Chicago *Inter-Ocean*. Mary O'Connor Newell made her start in the journalistic world with an editorial study of the big business trusts. Dorothy Richardson, now with Paramount, did first-hand studies of the women in shops, laundries and factories, first in Chicago, then in New York, where she worked for the *Herald*.

Earliest of all was Minnie Roswell Langstadter, who appeared in the local room of the Chicago *Record* in 1878, at the age of fifteen. She interviewed John D. Rockefeller, J. Pierpont Morgan, and the other financiers of the period. William H. Vanderbilt's historic exclamation "The public be damned" was first made in Mrs. Langstadter's presence. She died in the summer of 1936. Her last years were devoted to writing metaphysical articles for religious publications.

Chapter XLIII

THE MIDDLE WEST

WHEN A GIRL FIRST APPEARED IN A ONE-PIECE BATHING SUIT on a Lake Erie beach in the gay nineties one of the early newspaper women was on hand to chronicle this innovation. She was Marguerite Birdelle Switzer, of the Cleveland *Plain Dealer*, and her account of the event follows:

> A strange object is seen approaching, tripping nimbly down the bath house stairs and proceeding leisurely across the sands. Is it—it is a woman, clad in tights, sans skirt, sans blush, sans self-consciousness, even. The scandalized matrons in the water turn their backs hastily, casting furtive glances over their shoulders as they quickly move away from the spot. At a little distance they gather in an excited bunch and proceed to limber their paralyzed tongues.

"Birdie," as she was known in the profession, was one of the group of Cleveland women who called on William McKinley at Canton after his nomination for the Presidency. She presented a basket of flowers to his wife. This was in the summer of 1896. Again, when William Jennings Bryan was campaigning, she boarded his train just as the press service girl of today accompanies a candidate across the country. "Richly dressed ladies with plumed hats and bouffant sleeves" surrounded Mr. Bryan, who was still young and popular. Miss Switzer found Mrs. Bryan "sensible, observant, calm and sincere, with a grasp of American politics that is astonishing to the ordinary woman."

They chatted for hours. Miss Switzer thought her a shrewd campaigner. It was a dramatic moment when Mr. Bryan entered the McKinley stronghold and the home of Mark Hanna. Crowds swarmed to hear him speak. When the meeting was over he put his arm around his wife, staved off the crowd, lifted her into the carriage and they made their escape from the mobs which were even more insistent in 1896 than a political crowd today.

Miss Switzer also went in for the personal experience stories popularized by Nellie Bly. She visited a gypsy camp. She spent a day in the Cleveland telephone exchange. The hello girls were still a novelty to the public. She went with Salvation Army workers into Cleveland's "hovels of sin." She toured the police stations for copy. She saw Santanelli hypnotize a sleeping boy while the youth and beauty of Cleveland watched this Svengali with fascinated eyes. But Miss Switzer plainly was a skeptic. Her copy is as plausible today as when it was written.

In addition to covering news, she wrote fiction for her paper, conducted a woman's column signed "Eve" and ran the woman's department. There was nothing Victorian about her work. In 1899 she resigned to marry David B. Carse, the eldest son of Mrs. Matilda B. Carse, philanthropist, writer and temperance worker. Their son is Robert Carse, the fiction writer. Mrs. Matilda Carse, with Frances Willard, was one of the temperance pioneers who launched the W.C.T.U. and built the Woman's Temple in Chicago.

Early in the century Winona Wilcox Payne caused a stir in Cleveland with the progressive ideas she launched in the woman's page of the *Press*. The page was largely her own creation and had little relation to the accepted model of the era. Her questions and answers column was marked by sound thought, good writing and a definitely feministic point of view.

A year ago Mrs. Payne, now living in retirement in Cleveland, went through her scrapbooks and burned every trace of her work, thereby closing the record on a singularly rich and enlightened newspaper career, for she put punch and irony into the woman's page at a time when it was still smothered in lavender and old lace. She was one of the early feminists who scorned the sentimentality of the period and ran a Beatrice Fairfax column as Dorothy Thompson might conceivably do it today. Mrs. Payne's work showed the influence of her father, John Wilcox, a political leader in Cleveland and the first editorial writer for the *Press*, the earliest paper launched by E. W. Scripps. It was called the *Penny Press* and was the first one-cent newspaper in the country. It advocated advanced economic theories, fought the single tax and championed as mayor Tom Johnson, who took over the street railways of Cleveland and ran them as a municipal project, cutting the fare to three cents.

Many of the liberals of the day, including Henry George and Lincoln Steffens, gathered at the Wilcox home and it was in this environment that Winona Wilcox developed the interpretative and logical qualities which later characterized her work. It was not, however, until she had married Seymour C. Payne and brought up two boys to adolescence that she turned definitely to newspaper work. The year was 1905. Woman suffrage was still an unpopular cause. The Pankhursts were raising a stir in England. Mrs. O. H. P. Belmont and her associates were soon to muster their backing in America. Only the most advanced thinkers accepted the implications of the movement. Mrs. Payne wrote editorials setting forth the feminist viewpoint. In these and in her column, "Answers by Mrs. Maxwell," she was a decade ahead of her time. Her stuff was radical, brilliant, penetrating. It was discussed by men as well as women. Her mail ran to two full pages on Saturdays and sometimes filled a section. She did interviews for NEA with Mrs. Pankhurst, Emma Goldman, Sarah Bernhardt, Clarence Darrow, Eugene Debs and other headliners of the period. Soon after Harry Payne Burton became editor of *McCall's* in 1922 he engaged her to run a question and answer page for him. By this time she had given up newspaper work, but once again she brought a sparkling touch and good reasoning to bear on current problems.

Her son, Kenneth Wilcox Payne, is managing editor of *The Reader's Digest*, and her sister's son is John McClain, the popular ship news reporter of the New York *American*.

In the early part of the century Edna K. Wooley arrived in town to launch a woman's department for the Cleveland *News*. She is still in harness on the same paper. Miss Wooley began her newspaper career with the Chicago *Journal* shortly after the Spanish-American War. In those days the paper was familiarly known as Grandma. But it was so blatant during the war that it earned the title of The War-Cry. Miss Wooley did book reviews and editorials. She was the youngest woman editorial writer in Chicago at the time. Mrs. Margaret Sullivan, writing for the *Chronicle*, was the oldest. Miss Wooley's contributions were more or less sub rosa until the publisher's eye lit with approval on one entitled "Home." He sent for her and she expected to be fired. Instead he told her it was good and that he wanted her to turn out a column.

Peter Finley Dunne, James O'Donnell Bennett, Edward Mott Woolley, Bert L. Taylor and F.P.A. were all on the *Journal* at the time. F. P. A. was just starting out. It was a brilliant assemblage of talent. But women reporters were reluctantly accepted on a newspaper staff. City editors regarded them with horror. When Miss Wooley was assigned to interview a man of shady reputation she followed him through street after street, unable to catch up with him. At last he disappeared in a saloon. She gave a newsboy a nickel to ask the man to come out. He sent back word that if she wanted to see him she would have to go in where he was. So she walked up and down, waiting for him to emerge. He failed to show up. She gave the newsboy another nickel to see if he was still in the saloon. The boy came back with word that he had left long ago by the back door. When Miss Wooley got back to her office and reported the bad news, her city editor slammed his hand on the desk, swore violently and shouted, "That's what comes of hiring a woman to work on a newspaper."

But she soon lived it down. She wrote some of the earliest stories about Schumann-Heink and her babies, borrowing all the pictures the diva had of her family, which was later to undergo tragic disruption. The singer was appearing in opera at the old Chicago auditorium. At that time Chicago had only two weeks of grand opera, imported from New York. Miss Wooley met all the singers and attended the premières. She witnessed the furore over the first American production of La Tosca with Scotti and Ternina. Feeling ran high over Wagner. Nobody slept the night Tristan and Isolde was sung for the first time. Her own family stayed up all night to discuss it.

Her saddest experience was when she was sent to write a feature story about the hundreds of children burned to death in the Collinwood school fire in 1908. She walked among their charred bodies laid out in orderly rows in the New York Central shops, watched parents bending over, trying to identify their children, listened to their sobbing, smelled burned flesh and staggered out through a door to be ill. This was after she had moved from Chicago to Cleveland.

Miss Wooley did newspaper work in Chicago from 1902 to 1906. When her editor took charge of the Cleveland *News* she went with him to a new post. She was told to start a woman's department. She took a domestic science course and attended a cooking school so that she could cope with a subject quite alien to her previous experience. She ran the department until 1933, when she went back to a column of general comment. She has interviewed all manner of celebrities and particularly remembers the time that Theodore Roosevelt patted her on the shoulder during his first campaign for the Presidency, and asked her if she were not too young to be doing newspaper work. She was, but she would not admit it. Miss Wooley was born in Chicago of pioneer parents. Her grandfather first moved there in 1838 when it was Fort Dearborn and he was a young army man. She attended the public schools of Chicago and started newspaper work when most girls are still in school.

Early in Marguerite Martyn's career on the St. Louis *Post-Dispatch* she was told by Oliver K. Bovard, her managing editor: "Always remember, your work is not important. It is merely interesting." For thirty years Miss Martyn has kept it interesting. She has held the fort practically alone until recent years, for the *Post-Dispatch*, a liberal paper in all other respects, has shared the attitude of the New York *Times* toward the woman reporter. Most of her copy appears in the daily magazine, where the paper segregates and confines its women's interests.

Miss Martyn's whole life has been identified with the paper. Her husband, Clair Kenamore, has held down various desks on the *Post-Dispatch* and has done war correspondence. She joined the staff at the age of twenty as an illustrator, straight from the St. Louis School of Fine Arts. In those days there was a demand for line drawings, so she both sketched and wrote for the paper. This was a popular novelty. But as photographs came into more general use she found herself devoting more of her time to writing. Now she draws only when a subject lends itself to imaginative illustration or when a photograph is not available.

Her work is widely known throughout the Middle West. She is still an enthusiast about her job and goes from one story to another with an unjaded sense of expectation. She does three or four features a week and has traveled over the country in quest of news. She has followed women's activities from fashions to politics, has interviewed celebrities, and done the woman's angle on innumerable big stories. She knows exactly what her paper wants and is a skilled and enlightened craftsman.

Another of the scintillant names of the Middle West is Frances Boardman, of the St. Paul *Dispatch*, who has experienced the newspaper game from all angles and has achieved distinction as a music critic. She is a native of St. Paul, the granddaughter of a Democratic politician who became mayor and congressman in turn. Her other grandfather was a Presbyterian minister in Philadelphia. Miss Boardman's first ambition was to be a nurse. She had no desire to go to college, so she tagged along after an older sister, took a year's kindergarten training and taught for a while in a state hospital for crippled children. As soon as possible she entered Presbyterian Hospital in New York and completed her training before collapsing so completely that there never was any question of her going on. She felt that her life was ruined. For months she could not look at a hot water bottle without bursting into nostalgic tears.

An aunt with a Western newspaper background persuaded the contemporary owner of the *Dispatch*, an old friend, that he needed her niece on his staff. Frances had never touched a typewriter. She did not have the vaguest idea how news was gathered or written. But she landed on the paper, and through a variety of circumstances, soon drew small parts in the music and drama departments. In this way she became identified chiefly with criticism and interviews, although she has done plenty of straight reporting, features and editorial writing.

Like Miss McDowell of the New York *Times*, Miss Boardman,

in spite of a Presbyterian background, is one of the best and most experienced reporters of Catholic news in the country. Her apprenticeship coincided with the last years of Archbishop Ireland, who was an important figure in the Middle West but a great annoyance to editors, since he resolutely refused to give interviews. Miss Boardman got beyond the archepiscopal door—something none of her colleagues had been able to do—because the Archbishop and her grandfather had been old friends. When he died she had full responsibility for everything that was printed about him—his obituary, the funeral story and the installation of his successor. Working for a Catholic paper, Miss Boardman has covered many assignments involving the church in one way or another. Because she was not of the faith she investigated every step with the patience of a Scotland Yard detective and so became an expert on ritualistic detail.

Miss Boardman is the possessor of singularly beautiful hands. Sarah Bernhardt admired them in the course of an interview she had with her on one occasion. Paderewski kissed her wildly when he heard her say *"boze shaw Polske,"* which she had memorized off the wall of a local Polish church. Another time, a woman, seeing her in Ossip Gabrilowitsch's dressing-room, took her for Mark Twain's daughter and was indignant when she found she had been fooled. Years ago Miss Boardman lunched every day for a week with Lily Langtry. The beauty was elderly at the time but was infinitely entertaining as she kept dragging up Edwardian anecdotes from the grave.

For two years Miss Boardman worked in Winnipeg, doing theatrical publicity and free-lance work. She spent a year in Denver, where she organized the music, drama and motion picture departments of the *Express*, now defunct. She is a real power in music circles in the Middle West. Her sparkling wit can be sharp, if the occasion seems to demand it, but her work is essentially mellow and sophisticated.

Until ill health drove her out of newspaper work, Clare Shipman did good work for the St. Paul *Pioneer Press*. She began as woman's page editor, established a school page, and at the same time did general news and feature work. She found that the schools yielded plenty of good news stories—one of them being the case of the mother who was quarantined in her house with an alligator for three weeks. Her son had agreed to take care of it for a few days; then he came down with scarlet fever and it was too cold to put the alligator outdoors.

When Queen Marie passed through the Twin Cities on her way West, Miss Shipman had to shepherd three children who had received autographed photographs from the Queen after they had written her admiring letters about her fairy tales. Miss Shipman was to stay with the youngsters until the Mayor presented them to the

Queen, who was speaking from a broadcasting station. Then she was to sink into the background and chronicle what happened. But the Mayor forgot about the children. The Queen came sweeping in on his arm, made her speech and saw that the Mayor had missed his cue, so she stepped over casually to the waiting group. Miss Shipman introduced her charges; the Queen chatted amiably but the children were stricken dumb.

Before settling in St. Paul Miss Shipman did newspaper work in Canada, getting her early training under the gifted Nell Dyas, woman's page editor of the Toronto *Daily News*. One of her ablest colleagues in St. Paul was Elizabeth Forman, now Mrs. Kent B. Stiles.

Two of the early newspaper women were identified with the Twin Cities, although neither one was a native of Minnesota. Mrs. Jane Swisshelm, pioneer of the Press Gallery, published her paper at St. Cloud while Minnie Lee Wood was editing the Sauk Rapids *Frontiersman* with her husband. In 1868 Mrs. Wood helped to found the Sauk Rapids *Sentinel*. She was born of New Hampshire parents and her own name was Julia Amanda Sargent. She married a newspaper man from Kentucky and while she lived in the South she wrote for Boston and Philadelphia papers. They moved to Sauk Rapids in 1849, when it was nothing but a trading post of the American Fur Company. Minnie Lee Wood wrote sentimental fiction as well as news. She helped her son, Delacey Wood, to establish several of the thirty-three papers which he launched in Minnesota, Dakota, Michigan and Wisconsin. She ended her days with the Benedictine Sisters in St. Cloud.

St. Paul and Minneapolis have a number of women active in the newspaper field today. None is better known than Mrs. Bess M. Wilson, woman's editor of the Minneapolis *Journal*. She was trained for teaching and then found herself, almost overnight, the owner of a debt-burdened weekly in Redwood Falls, Minnesota. With two children dependent on her she knew that she had to make it pay. For fifteen years she ran the weekly. Born and bred in Minnesota, her childhood spent on a farm, she had the background which enabled her to meet farmers and rural business men on their own ground. She ran two full pages of personal items and wrote short editorials in the same simple vein as the personals.

Mrs. Wilson took an active part in local, state and national politics. For nine years she was a member of the board of regents of the University of Minnesota. When she sold her paper in 1927 she joined the staff of the Minneapolis *Journal*, specializing in school news, a subject which has always interested her deeply. Now she does features, interviews and book reviews, in addition to directing the women's pages. She writes a weekly column of chatter, not unlike the one she did for her paper in Redwood Falls. She believes that people like best to read about themselves; and, after that, about their neighbors.

Club women all through the Northwest know the Taaffe sisters and their good newspaper work. Agnes Taaffe is club editor of the Minneapolis *Star* and used to be on the *News*. Lillian Taaffe functions in the same capacity for the *Tribune*.

May Stanley, who now does book reviews with Max Miller on the San Diego *Standard-Union*, was the first woman Sunday editor in this region. She was born in northern Washington, started newspaper work early, and after an apprenticeship on country papers and in Spokane, she moved east of the Rockies, settled in Duluth, did dramatic and musical criticism and finally was made Sunday editor of the *Herald Tribune* there. In 1914 she left Duluth for New York and joined the staff of *Musical America*. After the war she and her husband lived for five years in a tiny fishing village on the coast of Maine. In 1925 they returned to New York, where she did short stories about fishing people and wrote *Blue Meadows*, a story of the Maine coast. She now lives in La Jolla, California, and continues to write.

Adventure has come the way of Esther Hamilton, of the Youngstown *Telegram*, who nearly lost her life on a trestle one February night while walking along the railroad tracks to a farmhouse where an old woman had been murdered in the last of a series of maniacal crimes. She hung onto the rain barrels while a train went by. Next day she learned that the murderer had seen her pass his hiding place. But she got an exclusive story and pictures.

Miss Hamilton is the daughter of Scott B. Hamilton, newspaper cartoonist and the brother of Grant E. Hamilton, originator of the "Full Dinner Pail" cartoon. She comes from a line of teachers, newspaper men and iron manufacturers. While she was in high school at New Castle, Pennsylvania, she wrote a daily column of chatter for the New Castle *Herald*, chiefly because the editor was a friend of her mother's. She went to work on the paper as a staff reporter after attending the University of Chicago. Soon she became a columnist, doing "The Dormer Window" by Ann Onymous, when the regular columnist got drunk and disappeared for several days. At the same time she covered the court-house beat and Ellwood City. The *Herald* carried a daily page of news about this nearby town, and when she went to cover a speech delivered there by William Howard Taft, she found after she had boarded the train that she had no money. So she borrowed enough from him to take her back to New Castle.

Late in 1921 she turned up the information that resulted in the arrest of A. T. (Bluebeard) White at New Castle for the murder of his wife on Christmas Eve. She covered the subsequent trial and was offered a job with the Youngstown *Telegram* as a result of the scoops she had. During the same period she handled a number of murder trials involving a black hand ring. Ever since, she has been with the *Telegram* and does a daily column. She won first place three times as the best woman columnist in the state—the choice of the Ohio Newspaper Women's Association. In 1935 she got top ranking for the best feature story written by a member of the association. This was for her work on the Hauptmann trial.

In 1929 she took Youngstown's "best girl" to Hollywood as the guest of Mary Pickford, and did a series of stories on the film capital. A year later she went to Arizona and traveled back with Irene Schroeder, known as the "Blonde Gungirl," and Glenn Dague, convicted at New Castle of the murder of Brady Paul, a state policeman. Later she did feature stories on the trial. On one occasion Miss Hamilton got into a powder factory where there had been an explosion. No one was being admitted, but she rode in the hearse carrying the priest, who was an old friend of hers. She posed as a nurse, copied the list of dead and injured and did a thorough clean-up on the story.

For ten years she ran the marble tournament for her paper and took a contestant to Atlantic City. She wrote the life story of Rae Samuels, vaudeville star who hails from Youngstown. She is a close friend of Sally Rand and thinks her a clever girl. Once she went to jail in Cleveland to get information from a murderess and break a story there. In 1935 she caused a stir when she went to Washington to see what was being done about the canal Youngstown has been trying to get for the last fifty years. Her story, "Washington Never Heard of Our Canal," swept the valley and reopened the fight. A bill to start the canal is now pending.

Lola Bullard, of the *Wisconsin News*, in Milwaukee, is one of the ranking stars of the region. She handles the stiffest assignments with ease and competence. Sophie Kerr Underwood and Katherine Brush, two of the more successful novelists and magazine writers, got their early newspaper training in Pittsburgh, the city which also launched Nellie Bly on an astonished public. Mrs. Underwood was woman's editor, music critic and Sunday editor of the Pittsburgh *Gazette* at a time when executive newspaper posts for women were rare. Miss Brush did not linger long in the city room but gained enough experience to write her veracious *Young Man of Manhattan*.

For thirteen years Gertrude G. Gordon, known to the police and the newsboys as "Our Gertie," contributed to the columns of the Pittsburgh *Press*. She worked in a biscuit factory, in a glass house, in a tin factory and a laundry before trying newspaper work. She also tried domestic service and stenography. Miss Gordon went up in a balloon for a story; walked into a cage with seven lions; helped the police to raid a Chinese gambling den; covered the Billy Whitla kidnaping and a mine disaster; was kissed by Sarah Bernhardt and interviewed all kinds of celebrities. She moved to New York in 1928 and since then has lectured on her high-powered newspaper experiences, which have the Nellie Bly touch.

Farther West, Omaha has produced a number of talented newspaper women. It was there that Mrs. Anna Steese Richardson began her literary career after she was thirty years of age, working for the Iowa *Nonpareil* at $5 a week. She moved on to the Omaha *Daily News*, the New York *World* and the McClure Syndicate. When she reached New York every newspaper staff was filled. Her reserve funds dwindled. She moved from an airy front room in her boarding house to a hall bedroom, thence into a skylight closet where she could scarcely turn around.

She went into the Criminal Courts Building one day, chiefly to escape from the heat, and found a young girl on trial for attempted suicide. She talked to the probation officer, to the girl, to her employers, and wrote the story. It was full of heart throbs. A Sunday editor paid her $50 for it and offered her a guarantee of $30 a week for more stories of the same sort. Mrs. Richardson now directs the Good Citizenship Bureau of the *Woman's Home Companion* and handles a correspondence of 36,000 letters a year.

Rose Henderson began on the Des Moines *Register* in 1909. Four years later she became associate editor of the paper, doing editorials, features and dramatic criticism. Before taking up newspaper work she was an instructor in English at Washington University. From Des Moines she moved East to New York and joined the editorial staff of the *Evening Post*. After leaving newspaper work she devoted herself to reviewing and to writing books and verse.

Sue McNamara, for several years dramatic editor and special feature writer of the Des Moines *Daily News*, was sent to Panama in the autumn of 1911 by NEA to get a series of human interest stories. While there she interviewed General Goethals and rode through the Culebra Cut. In 1908 she covered the opening of the Rosebud reservation in South Dakota for a number of papers. Miss McNamara made a specialty of the interview. She was working for the Associated Press in Washington at the time of her death in 1932.

Chapter XLIV

DENVER AND KANSAS CITY

A GENTLE OLD LADY OCCASIONALLY WANDERS INTO THE DENVER
Public Library nowadays and digs about among the books
in the Western History collection. Her eyes have a mournful beauty, for they have seen uncanny things. It is difficult for a
younger generation to believe that this is the Polly Pry of legend—
wild, beautiful, fearless.

She and "Pinky" Wayne, who is still on the Denver *Post*, are
writing Polly's memoirs. Both women have known journalism at its
most sensational. At the turn of the century Polly Pry fought the
Western Federation of Miners single-handed. She launched her own
weekly to back up her stand on organized labor. She has ducked
bullets, lived in mining camps, traveled far afield, been received by
brigands and statesmen, crusaded passionately.

She still has the remnants of her good looks. In her youth she was
a blonde of the statuesque type. She, "Pinky" Wayne and Winifred
Black were three of the early beauties of the profession. Polly Pry
was as impressive in the rough togs she wore in a verminous troop
train on her way to see Villa as in a Worth gown. She was always
adventurous and had a vivid temper. She could scream at Frederick
G. Bonfils with as much fervor as he at times applied to her when
she worked on the Denver *Post*.

Winifred Black, Julian Hawthorne and Polly Pry were all brought
to the *Post* by Bonfils and Harry H. Tammen in the early days of
their joint publishing venture. Polly's real name was Leonel Campbell. She was born in Mississippi, one of a large family brought to
the verge of destitution by the Civil War. At the age of fifteen she
married George Anthony, well known throughout Kansas, and went
with him to Mexico. But the fetters of marriage did not suit Leonel's
proud spirit. She walked out on her husband and landed in New
York at the age of seventeen. By this time she had developed into a
dazzling beauty. She fastened her attention on the gold dome of the
World building and got in to see Mr. Cockerill.

"Give you a job?" he exclaimed. "I ought to spank you and send you home to your husband."

But he took her on the staff at $6 a week, and soon sent her to South America. Her career as a newspaper woman had begun. Life now became a succession of adventures for Polly. All doors opened for the lovely blonde from the West. She sent back vivid stories and in time returned to New York. When she left the *World* she did some pulp fiction, then went back West with her mother. On the train she met Mr. Bonfils. He was proud of the blazing headlines that spanned a copy of the Denver *Post* lying on the seat beside him. They horrified Leonel. But when he asked her if she would like a job on his paper she said yes.

Soon she became adept at writing stories that justified the most bizarre banners that the combined wits of Bonfils and Tammen could launch on the street. When the paper campaigned for prison reform Polly Pry toured the jails, talked to the prisoners and conceived deep sympathy for Alfred Packer, who was in for life on the quaint charge of having killed and eaten five prospectors in the wintry days of 1873.

Polly Pry thought Packer innocent. She persuaded the *Post* to launch a campaign to have him pardoned. W. W. Anderson, a local attorney, was employed to represent the American cannibal. But Mr. Anderson proved to be more of a problem than the man-eater. Packer was paroled and showed his gratitude by hanging around the office in all his spare moments. But the $1,500 he had earned from his handiwork in prison went into Mr. Anderson's pocket, and the lawyer also looked forward hopefully to the $1,000 that the *Post* had promised him if he got Packer out of jail.

This annoyed Polly Pry. It also aroused the fury of Bonfils and Tammen. Polly went to his office to tell him he was fired. But Mr. Anderson insisted on making a personal call on the owners of the *Post*. Polly rushed back with the news but he arrived at the same moment, a revolver in the pocket of his coat. When he seemed about to use it, Polly screamed, Bonfils knocked him down and Anderson took his departure. But only for a moment. He merely went through the door to get an advantage with his revolver. He was back in an instant, firing at Bonfils and Tammen. He hit both. Polly Pry jumped at him like a wild cat. She got hold of the pistol, and hung on to it.

"I'll kill you," said Anderson.

"Go ahead," said Polly defiantly. "Then hang for it."

Her blue eyes blazed into his. He didn't shoot again. The news room was a shambles. Bonfils was unconscious and Polly Pry was shielding the moaning Tammen. Anderson left them all. He walked out and gave himself up to the police. He felt that he had dealt justly with two villains.

Polly was never so friendly with her employers again. Trouble grew up between them, chiefly over her attitude on labor. This had been brewing for some time. One of her early assignments had been to clear up the murder mysteries in the Western Federation of Miners. In this she matched wits with Big Bill Haywood, Charles H. Moyer and other labor leaders. In 1902 she went to Telluride, the stronghold of the Federation, where Arthur J. Collins, of the Smuggler Union Mine, had been killed. She visited the mine, talked to the mine owners and the men. She interviewed Vincent St. John, president of the Federation, and then wrote a story for the *Post*, quoting him in defense of the murder. He repudiated Polly's interview. The union boycotted the *Post*. Finally her own paper turned on her. She always believed that Haywood, Moyer and the others had convinced Mr. Bonfils that it was in his business interests to make some sort of reparation to St. John.

When the *Post* refused to back her up, there was nothing for her to do but leave. For the next two years she published her own paper, which she called *Polly Pry*. In it she fought the Western Federation of Miners. It was described as a journal of comment and criticism, but was chiefly a platform for the exploitation of its editor's social theories. It was too sensational to last for long. In the issue of January 16, 1904, she announced that an attempt had been made to assassinate her in her home. The public was skeptical, but Polly Pry insisted that she had opened the door when the bell rang, two shots had been fired, she had seen a long red flame, and caught a glimpse of a tall man in dark clothes and a derby, with a dark mustache and a scarred face.

She gave up her paper at the end of two years. Later she went to work for the *Rocky Mountain News*, under the ownership of John C. Shaffer. During this period she went to Mexico to interview Villa and got into revolutionary territory under a flag of truce, an arrangement made possible by the American naval forces. During the war she went abroad as publicity chairman of the American Red Cross Commission to Greece. Her second marriage was to H. J. O'Bryan, an attorney who died some years ago. Few American newspaper women have lived more vivid lives than Polly Pry. Her work was always militant. She scorned the conventional sob story and could out-match most of her masculine competitors in getting what she was after.

Her close friend, Frances Wayne, more widely known as "Pinky" because of her red hair, has had a long and illustrious career on the *Post*. Her father was James B. Belford, Colorado's first member of

Congress, known as the "Red-headed Rooster of the Rockies" because of his effective eloquence. He was good for copy on any subject from the redemption of arid lands to the Greek classics. Her
mother was a social power in the state.

Mrs. Wayne's parents settled in Colorado in the pioneer days.
Her father rose to the Supreme Court bench; her mother shared in
all the activities that went with the foundation of the state. As a
bride moving from Missouri to Indiana on order of the Secessionists,
she and her young husband had stopped in Springfield and called
on Abraham Lincoln, who had just been elected President. This visit
and the spell he cast over Mrs. Belford resulted many years later in
her proposal that the only adequate monument to his memory would
be the Lincoln Highway. With the aid of Congressman Rainey of
Illinois, she instigated the resolution passed in Congress, providing
for the highway which now crosses the continent.

Mrs. Wayne got her first impressions of newspaper work and the
gentlemen of the press when she stowed away in her father's office
as a child and listened to the Washington correspondents questioning
him. It seemed to her that they asked a great many questions. This
memory was tucked away in her subconscious mind along with
another one of the miners who dug gold in old Central City, where
they lived during one period. The thought of a career never entered
her head. Her education had been frivolous. But after being married
and widowed, she was asked to become society editor of a Denver
paper.

For five months she coped with the social aspirations of her contemporaries and then went to a hospital, a trifle disillusioned about
her own sex. She had failed to enjoy this taste of newspaper work.
Recovered, she returned for more punishment and some real work.
She became an excellent newspaper woman. She did criminal courts,
the legislature, interviewed senators, Cabinet members, candidates
for President, criminals, actresses—the whole throng that passes before the reflector. She had many tingling moments. She was in the
thick of the "massacre at Ludlow" which sent Upton Sinclair picket-
ing the offices of John D. Rockefeller on Wall Street. She covered
the strike, counted the dead lying between the railroad tracks,
dodged the bullets of striking miners sniping from the hills, and
forgot there was such a thing as time. One of the newspaper men
working with her on this occasion was John Reed. It was she who
broke the news to the mother of Chester Gillette, the original of
Theodore Dreiser's *American Tragedy*, that her son was to hang.
Mrs. Gillette was a Holy Roller and she gave a startling revelation
of the sustaining power of religion.

Mrs. Wayne did book reviews and became dramatic editor of the

Post, and later of the *Examiner* in Chicago. On both papers she was barred from theaters for her frank criticism and her complete disregard for the advertiser. The *Post* backed her in her stand. After that she became a campaigner, and a good one. When the state treasury professed itself in the red, she organized public sentiment to force large appropriations for the insane, to match a $750,000 gift promised by John D. Rockefeller for a hospital. She campaigned for funds to build and operate a state psychopathic hospital, to clean up a rotten reformatory, and to put through other humanitarian measures at the expense of the taxpayer. Mrs. Wayne became a power in the state. Her campaigns met with success. The University of Colorado awarded her a gold medal inscribed "For service in behalf of the common good," and on the reverse, "From the State she merits well."

In spite of her experiences as a society editor she pushed the suffrage cause through the columns of the Kansas City *Post.* Mad as the Denver *Post* and its foster sister in Kansas City may have been under the Bonfils and Tammen regime, Mrs. Wayne always loved them and she found her publishers open to any ideas that were workable. As a reporter, feature writer and campaigner she has had fun, influence and success. Hers has been one of the more effective newspaper careers.

Elizabeth Kelly had never known a newspaper man or woman when she wandered into the office of the Denver *Times* early in the century, looking for a job. The paper was failing and so she concluded it might be less discriminating than its more prosperous competitors. She was disillusioned with teaching after six weeks of it. Tall and unfashionably thin, she selected an austere black gown for her meeting with the managing editor. He took her on without salary, feeling it was a good turn that would do no harm, since the sale of the paper was then being negotiated. By the time the deal went through, she was put on the payroll at $5 a week, chiefly to impress the new owner.

In return, she was supposed to perform the duties of society reporter. Soon she was doing dramatic reviews and covering criminal courts, an innovation at the time. But Miss Kelly almost lost her job as dramatic critic in the first week, for telling Mrs. Patrick Campbell how far short she came of being a good actress. Mrs. Campbell at once addressed a complaint to the business office. The managing editor did not fire Miss Kelly, however, for he needed her to cover an important trial that was pending in the criminal court. It became the turning point in her career and established her as a first-rate reporter, with standing equal to the best of the men. A soldier had killed a local restaurant keeper and escaped. The case had baffled the police for several years. A suspect had been held in solitary confinement for two months in a Denver jail and was about to be tried. The *Post* had turned out its best talent to make a big splash. Winifred Black was already there, a host in herself, and several men from her paper. Miss Kelly was terrified by the Bonfils and Tammen array. They filled nearly all the seats at the press table. They were on intimate terms with the court attachés. They exuded assurance.

Miss Kelly was working alone. She did the running story of the testimony in court and a feature lead at the office between morning and afternoon sessions. The case moved smoothly for the first two days. Everyone in the Rocky Mountain region was watching it. On the third day the district attorney stopped her as she was hurrying out at the noon recess. He said he was sorry for her because of her youth and inexperience, and the competition facing her across the table. Her accounts of the trial had seemed to him to be fair, he said, and he wanted to give her a break. Then he told her that the murder suspect lacked an essential scar and the trial was about to blow up.

"We'll nol-pros as soon as this witness finishes," he said. "Write your story and you can release it by telephone from the clerk's office if you stand out there and listen to me make the motion."

She gave her word to protect him and the arrangement went through like clockwork. An extra edition of the *Times* was on the street before the competition realized what was happening. She got credit for being an ace reporter and a few weeks later she moved over to the *Post* as an expert on trials. When she was making $5 a week on the *Times* she had asked Josiah Ward for a place on his staff at $10. His reply was characteristic: "Hell, no. A *good* woman isn't worth $10 a week." He was on leave of absence, writing a book on archaeology, when she made the change, and he returned to find her on his payroll at $35 a week. But she never had a more stanch supporter. He advanced her steadily and gave her the best assignments.

She was trained by Thomas H. A. McGill, a New York newspaper man who was in Denver for his health. His methods and Josiah's were in tune. Soon she could pinch-hit for any man on the staff. She read every line in the paper, even the sports section. Her chance to show her versatility came one day five minutes before the deadline. The sports writers had gone for the day and the city editor was in a rush. The Ministerial Alliance had obtained an injunction to stop a boxing bout which was to pack the athletic stadium that night.

"Quick, Miss Kelly," he said. "A paragraph for the first page saying that Jack 'Twin' Sullivan will not be allowed to fight to-night."

"It's Mike 'Twin' Sullivan," she said, as she ran her fingers nimbly over the typewriter keys. "Jack 'Twin' is fighting in Waco to-night."

He took her word for it and this story became part of the training of all cubs on the Denver *Post*. It taught them to read the papers.

Miss Kelly was sent into some of the Western states on murder trials, while the labor troubles in the mining region were at their height. While used to hearing herself referred to as a sob sister, she never realized how convincing her copy was until she got a proposal of marriage from a murderer whose trial she had covered. He had killed his wife with the frying pan that he thought she should have been using to prepare the evening meal. She had been playing euchre instead. That was why she was now dead.

Miss Kelly's picture of the neglected home and the faithful father was so graphic that when she stood on the station platform, home-ward bound, a few hours after the man had been acquitted, he walked up to her and said, "I never knew what a lovely little family I had until I read what you wrote, and I want to ask you to come and take up her work and help us to forget."

Miss Kelly covered the trial of Dr. Bennett Clark Hyde for the murder of Colonel Thomas H. Swope, the sensation of the decade in Kansas City. The Colonel died under mysterious circumstances, then the death rate became high among his beneficiaries. His friend, J. Moss Hunton, and his nephew, Chrisman Swope, expired in con-vulsions, as the Colonel had done. Dr. Hyde's wife was young Swope's sister and a $3,000,000 estate was involved. Suspicion fas-tened on Dr. Hyde. He was tried three times and was acquitted finally in 1909. He retired to Lexington, Missouri, and continued to practise medicine until 1934, when he dropped dead of heart disease as he listened to election returns in a newspaper office. By that time nearly everyone had forgotten about the sensational trial. Frank P. Walsh and James A. Reed, both of whom later achieved national prominence, were the counsel on opposite sides of the fence. Mr. Walsh defended Dr. Hyde. Mr. Reed was the special prosecutor.

Miss Kelly was sent to Kansas City to cover the trial for the Kan-sas City *Post*, which Bonfils and Tammen had just taken over. Six weeks of running copy on this important case would have finished a reporter with less vitality. But Miss Kelly survived and did a bril-liant job. A. B. McDonald, later a Pulitzer prize winner, was city editor of the paper, and Raymond H. McCaw, now night managing editor of the New York *Times*, headed the copy desk. Mr. McDon-ald was new on the paper and at first he was dubious over the wisdom of letting a mere woman write the lead on such an important story. He knew nothing about Miss Kelly except that Mr. Bonfils had described her as the "wheel horse of the Denver *Post*."

"The wheel horse," he said when it was over. "I'll say you're the team of horses and the little dog that runs under the wagon, too."

It was during the Hyde trial that she met Arthur La Hines, whom she afterwards married, and who is now on the copy desk of the New York *Times*. In addition to writing the heads for her copy, he kept her pencils sharpened, a great indulgence from the hard-boiled copy desk, where the girl reporter's severest critics usually sit. When Miss Kelly left the Denver *Post* a year later to be married, Mr. Bonfils wanted to know what paper she would work for in New York. In her best sob squad manner, she said, "I am to make a home."

"What a waste!" mourned Mr. Bonfils. "You can have your home made for $6 a week."

Mrs. La Hines is now active in club work. She has a daughter in college and a son just graduated.

The pioneer among the Denver newspaper women was Jenny Lind Hopkins, who later married Louis Seibold. She was born on a farm when Jenny Lind was at the height of her popularity, and her parents, Martin and Phidelia Hopkins, decided to name her after the Swedish singer. Her newspaper career began at eighteen with the Denver *Tribune*, then edited by Eugene Field. She was assigned to society, but the mere presence of a girl on a paper at that time was a sensation. The year was 1880. When she asked Mr. Field if she might do the same work as a man, he exclaimed: "Well, by the left leg of the prophet, who ever heard of such a thing? What next? You're crazy, Miss Hopkins. Absurd, preposterous, impossible! Be satisfied with what you've got and don't let me hear any more about it."

On one occasion Mr. Field remarked that he did not care for a woman in the office, because he liked to take off his shoes and unbutton his outer shirt. But when the *Tribune* became the Denver *Republican* under new ownership, Miss Hopkins got her chance. The new editor was more tolerant than Mr. Field. He gave her a reporter's job and a man's pay. She did everything from a dog fight to an interview with Madame Modjeska.

In court one day the clerk gave her such a rapid-fire summary of one of the cases that she could not follow him. She looked bewildered. A young man, standing nearby, volunteered to help. He was from the *Rocky Mountain News*, he said, and his name was Louis Seibold. He had just come on from Washington. This was the start of one of the early newspaper romances. Many another newspaper marriage has had its beginnings in court-room competition. The Seibolds were married in New York in 1890. Mr. Seibold worked at first for the Associated Press, then moved to the *World*, where he remained for thirty years, building up one of the finest newspaper reputations.

Mrs. Seibold continued to write. She worked for *Cosmopolitan* and *Harper's Weekly* and for a time edited the *Jenness-Miller Magazine*, which advocated dress reform for women. She wrote a play, *Girl from Somewhere*, which was produced in New York. Her only son, Martin, who was an actor, died soon after coming of age. Her own death occurred in 1925, while she was at Asbury Park with her sister, Mrs. Marian Leland, the dramatic reader.

Denver and Kansas City have produced a fine crop of newspaper women. Some have traveled East; others have stayed in the home territory and made big reputations for themselves. Nell Brinkley, Fay King and Mildred Morris all started in Denver. Malvina Lindsay and Frances Davis starred together in Kansas City before moving East. They were both employees of the dashing Bonfils-Tammen combination. When things grew dull they built up a stooge whom they could quote at will. The acquiescent creature was known as Nan O'Neill and she became more or less of a town character. They dressed her in their own clothes, added hornrimmed glasses and gave her a strong slant on property rights, woman's suffrage, love or any burning issue of the day.

When Miss Davis was assigned to an Oklahoma murder she got hold of the intimate diary of the woman prisoner, who happened to have shot a Senator. The press services all tried to crib it, so the city editor stayed around to see that there was no interference with the girl reporter. A Universal Service man marched up and said, "Let me look at that." He made a grab for the diary. After that Miss Davis was secreted away in a quiet room with two armed bruisers, ready to protect her with their revolvers while she wrote the story and dug the best bits from the diary. Her copy was sent to the composing room under guard.

Just before she took her first flight another plane crashed within full view and the pilot was burned to death. She ran across the field with the gruesome details, telephoned them in, and while her office tried frantically to stop her, went ahead with her assignment. She stepped calmly into the waiting plane and flew all over Kansas City.

During the war days she often had to break the news to mothers that their sons had been killed. One in particular was airing snowy pillows in the sunshine on her porch when Miss Davis arrived and looked apprehensively at the serene figure in a pink-checked apron.

When she told the mother that her son was dead, the woman said nothing, but her shoulders sagged and she stared in a hurt way until Miss Davis felt as if she had shot the boy herself.

Her first assignment was a fire in a large mercantile house and the cinders burned a hole in the top of her new hat. She spent a night in jail with a woman who had killed her husband, a church organist. The murderess was in a curious state. She seemed comatose and could not concentrate on anything. "I killed him because I loved him. I wanted to kill him," she kept repeating all night long.

Miss Davis accompanied federal agents on several raids into Little Italy and watched them padlock cellars containing barrels of wine. She covered the Rose Pastor Stokes case, one of the sensations of the period. It was she who first announced the arrival of the Peruvian mummy which R. Bryson Jones brought home for the Kansas City Institute of Art. She stumbled on the story by accident and scooped the town with it. The *Post* was something of a madhouse and its girl reporters were frequently called on to perform impossible feats. The city room was full of freaks. A dope fiend who had been freed from the penitentiary was assistant managing editor for a time.

Miss Davis is now the wife of Richard Lockridge, dramatic critic of the New York *Sun* and an old newspaper colleague from Kansas City. With Miss Lindsay and Miss Davis both in the East, there are still two nationally known newspaper women in Kansas City—Nell Snead and Mrs. Minna K. Powell.

Miss Snead edits the woman's page of the Kansas City *Star* and also lands on the front page of her paper with astonishing frequency. She is preeminently a reporter. For the first four years that she was on the *Star* she did straight reporting and helped to cover the Legislature. She does her editing with a sophisticated touch and refuses to allow the woman's section to grow stodgy. She is witty, traveled, original. She journeys East and goes down the Bay to interview celebrities. She goes abroad and writes about resorts, museums, clothes, food and her fellow travelers. Her pages are run on magazine principles with a staff of contributors and artists. Anything that would make good general reading is apt to appear in her department. She cannot see why there should be any distinction between men's and women's interests. So book reviews, politics, dramatic criticism, or spot news frequently run along with recipes. Miss Snead gets a free hand and does as she likes.

On one of her periodical trips abroad she cracked up in a plane near Boulogne. She was knocked unconscious and her arm was injured. As she came to, she heard a voice say, "That woman's dead."

"I'm not," protested Miss Snead.

"Lord, I'd give anything for a camera now to get a picture of this," the same voice insisted.

Miss Snead pointed to hers. The voice belonged to an English newspaper man. The pictures were taken and appeared in the London *Daily Mail*.

Miss Snead put in some time at the University of Nebraska and the University of Chicago but was not graduated from either institution. For a period she taught English in a high school in Tekamah, Nebraska. When she joined the staff of the *Star* in war-time she did not even know the terminology of the profession. She thought that copy in this connection meant a duplicate. But she soon became a crack newspaper woman, one of the naturally gifted types. She is tall, rather graceful, has gray eyes. She will not be badgered into doing anything she doesn't like. Miss Snead is equally at home in the Middle West, New York, London or Paris.

Her colleague, Mrs. Powell, is an institution in the Middle West, known far and wide for her music and art criticism. She is generally credited with having discovered Marion Talley. Friends who had heard Marion sing at school and church entertainments asked Mrs. Powell to give an opinion on her voice. She went to hear her one snowy January night at a piano recital given by one of her classmates. There were about sixty persons in the hall. Marion was only the assisting artist. She was fifteen at the time but looked about twelve when she walked on to the stage in a brown wool school dress, knee-length, her stiff dark curls dangling over her shoulders. Her face was that of a child. But Mrs. Powell sat up in amazement when she heard her sing "Jubal's Lyre" in tones that were astonishingly full, round and tender. Returning to the *Star*, she told the night editor of the child's incredible voice. She wrote a short piece, saying that it was the most promising within her memory. That was in January, 1922, the second year of radio broadcasting at the *Star*. Marion was invited to the studio to sing, and a number of prominent persons were rounded up to listen to the prodigy. There was talk of financing her training but nothing came of it, because Mrs. Powell could not give the desired guarantee of future success. But the following May, Galli-Curci visited Kansas City and Marion sang for her. Later Schumann-Heink came and heard her. Both singers were amazed. All that they said was reported on the front page of the *Star* by Mrs. Powell, who continued to urge proper training for Marion.

In autumn she got the cooperation of the local Masonic Lodge and the use of its new auditorium for a benefit concert for the young songbird, whose fame was beginning to spread. The concert became a municipal affair. Seats were bought for as much as $25 and even

$100. The benefit netted $10,000 for Marion's training and 1,800 people were swept off their feet by her voice. A week earlier she had sung at a revivalist's tent meeting. She was a religious girl with lofty thoughts of singing for God, an ambition that almost nipped her career in the bud.

Before the echoes of her concert had died down Marion was on her way to New York. After her audition at the Metropolitan, Mrs. Powell took her to Mme. Sembrich, on the advice of Gatti-Casazza and Otto Kahn. The fiasco of the Sembrich lessons was a great disappointment to her, the first of many she had in connection with Marion Talley. At about this time Mrs. Powell retired with her husband to their Puget Sound home in the Northwest, and was still in her forest retreat forty miles from Seattle when Marion made her début at the Metropolitan three years later. When Mrs. Powell returned to the *Star* in 1928, her protégée was talking of retiring. She had been industrious and frugal, and had received $3,000 for each of her concert appearances, most of which she had saved. In 1929 she retired at the age of twenty-two, only to reappear a few years later before the Kleig lights in Hollywood.

Mrs. Powell was born on a farm near Red Wing, Minnesota, of Scottish parentage. She spent much of her early life on a ranch in western Minnesota, where the cattle were herded on a range. When she was not riding the range, she was sketching prairie life, which fascinates her to this day. She studied music and art while she was a student at Carleton College in Northfield, Minnesota, and later she attended an art school. Her first newspaper work was done for the St. Paul *Dispatch*. Soon she was covering art and music regularly, and for a number of years she continued her study of these two subjects with Dr. W. Rhys-Herbert, the Welsh composer.

As a young reporter in St. Paul, she trembled before the cross looks of James Whitcomb Riley, who was annoyed when she turned up instead of the dramatic critic he expected. She heard F. Hopkinson Smith and was repelled by the overhanging mustache which veiled his words. She was enchanted by Yeats and his fairy lore. Sometime later she had a violent tilt with Margot Asquith. She saw the violin bow spring from Kreisler's hand on his first American tour, sail in an arc over the heads of the audience and land at the feet of a young girl, so animated was his playing. He was flushed and embarrassed when the girl walked down the aisle and handed back the acrobatic bow.

When Cardinal Gibbons visited St. Paul during Mrs. Powell's first year as a cub reporter, she was suddenly called on to help in an emergency. The three star men on the paper had been assigned to follow the Cardinal. But the guest of honor had slipped away from the reception committee and driven to St. Paul's Seminary, halfway between St. Paul and Minneapolis.

Her city editor summoned Mrs. Powell. "You'll have to go," he said. "There's no one else—not a man in the office."

It was obvious he thought it a pity. An inexperienced girl to interview the Cardinal! No taxicabs were available in those days, so she hurried to her destination by street car. A young seminarian opened the door and told her that Cardinal Gibbons was at his devotions and was not to be disturbed. She saw him through the window. He was walking up and down alone beside a stream, a slim ascetic in purple and black, his breviary in his hand. She watched him closely, wondering what she should do. The spectacle overawed her. But soon she heard a commotion at the door and saw three of her colleagues from Minneapolis. They were less reverential and more practical.

"He wouldn't see you?" asked one.

Mrs. Powell shook her head. The leader of the group was Arthur James Pegler, the father of Westbrook Pegler. She knew his reputation as a reporter of force and vigor, and he justified it at once by getting his man. As the Cardinal approached the seminary and the reporters were about to be ushered in, Mr. Pegler asked Mrs. Powell how he should address a Cardinal. She couldn't remember at the moment.

"How would 'Your Excellency' do?" he speculated.

The reporters did not think it sounded right but no one could recall "Your Eminence." However, the Cardinal neither smiled nor winced when he was addressed as "Your Excellency." He affably answered all the questions put to him about the Boxer uprisings, the troubles of the Catholic Church in China, and other problems of the day. Mrs. Powell was not well posted on the subjects under discussion. She didn't dare take notes. All the reporters present represented afternoon papers, and noon was approaching. When her three colleagues left for Minneapolis, she boarded a street car for St. Paul. All the way back to her office she kept jotting down as much as she could remember of the interview. It was a stiff baptism. But when she compared her piece later with Mr. Pegler's, she seemed to have everything. Her editor was pleased. He complimented the girl reporter on a good job.

In 1911 she married George Edmond Powell, a newspaper man. They went to live in a national forest near Sante Fe. They built a house of adobe bricks and there she learned to cook. When they came out of retirement again they moved to Kansas City, because her husband had worked for the *Journal* there. In 1915 she joined the staff of the *Star* as successor to Karl Walter, an Englishman who had returned to his country with the outbreak of hostilities. During the war she was Sunday editor. Little art or music was running in the paper at the time. She has been with the *Star* continuously since then, except for the years she spent in the Puget Sound country.

When Sir Joseph Duveen was put through the most embarrassing moments of his career in the art suit brought against him in 1929 by Mme. Andrée Hahn over her alleged Leonardo, Mrs. Powell not only reported the trial for her paper but figured as a witness. She testified that she had doubted the authenticity of the picture from the start. The officials of the Kansas City Institute of Art were about to buy La Belle Ferronière for $250,000, believing it to be a genuine Leonardo, when Sir Joseph flatly pronounced it a fake. The sale was off. Mme. Hahn was aggrieved. She sued for libel and $500,000 damages. The suit was something new in court trials. Art experts were brought in. The pigments used by Leonardo were analyzed. For days Sir Joseph was kept squirming on the witness stand, while his knowledge of art was thoroughly explored. Although the leading art dealer in the world, he was forced to admit that his knowledge was instinctive rather than technical. But he took it with good grace. The jury disagreed. The case was settled out of court.

It was a suit of absorbing interest to Kansas City, which is proud of William Rockhill Nelson's contribution to its art possessions. Mrs. Powell has fostered this interest over the years and her word is accepted as law in her own sphere. Mme. Hahn consulted her about the painting long before Sir Joseph condemned it, and Mrs. Powell told her she did not see how a Leonardo could be at large and available for Kansas City.

One of the first women to work on a newspaper in Kansas City was Mary Paxton Keeley, now teaching journalism at Christian College, Columbia, Missouri. She was a member of the first graduating class of the School of Journalism at the University of Missouri. She worked for two years on the Kansas City *Post* prior to 1910.

Chapter XLV

CALIFORNIA

WHEN MR. HEARST WAS ENCOURAGING HIS WOMEN RE-porters to do dare-devil stunts in California at the turn of the century, Helen Dare rode down a lumber flume in the Sierras tied to a log, her hair waving wildly, the spray pounding her face. Adventure was her daily fare. Once she accompanied a posse of sheriffs through the wilds of Calaveras County in pursuit of a stage-robbing bandit. Another time she sat up all night in a haunted house.

The public demand for this type of sensation persisted in San Francisco until the first motion picture melodramas arrived by way of the nickelodeons. These episodic thrillers, running for weeks, provided the sort of excitement that Helen Dare had been dishing up for years as a Hearst reporter. When the public transferred its attention to Pearl White and the Perils of Pauline, Miss Dare abandoned her hair-raising technique and settled down to good human interest reporting. She still turns out newspaper copy—one of the Californian women who can look back on a life packed with excitement. The assignments handed out to the girls on the *Examiner* in those days were guaranteed to lead them into any sort of adventure. They loved it and became gluttons for thrills. Nothing was too dangerous for them to tackle. It was not enough to report the acts of God. They had to make things happen—and the more startling the better.

Fremont Older believed in manufacturing news too. He started a flock of girls doing unheard of things for newspaper copy, but all his ideas had the social service slant and he made crusaders of his reporters. With Mr. Hearst it was a case of entertaining the public and launching a lively story. His girls excelled at this. Helen Dare was the most fearless of the lot. Her pen name was apt. By birth she was Elizabeth Brough, a small, dark, vivid figure with an invincible spirit. She had done some newspaper work in New York before going to California. She was one of the first women to cover races. She did the woman's angle on a number of big racing events, and took in the English Derby.

Miss Dare was well established as a stunt reporter at the time of the earthquake, but she put across a neat piece of work on this occasion by sending through the first detailed story of the disaster. She started out for San Jose, looking for a telegraph office that was still intact. But the wires were down there, just as they were in San Francisco and Oakland. So she detoured through the San Joaquin Valley to Stockton, knowing that she had the story of a century, desperate to get it on the wire. At Stockton the telegraph office was about to close. But she happened to know the operator. She had once done him a service, so she dragooned him into action. The office stayed open. She managed to file 4,000 words of graphic copy before this wire petered out, too. It was the first coherent eye-witness story of the earthquake to reach the outside world.

Miss Dare worked for the *Call*, the *Examiner* and the *Chronicle* in turn. For more than ten years after the earthquake she did a daily feature story for the *Chronicle*. These human interest pieces usually ran about a thousand words. San Franciscans looked for them. Often they espoused a cause, for this was an era when propaganda of one sort or another constantly tinged the news columns. She wrote about dispossessed widows, tubercular factory girls, crippled children and the prostitute, who was an object of public concern during the period when the churches were trying to shut up the red light district and Fremont Older was skirmishing on behalf of the fallen woman. Helen Dare was particularly interested in the prisoners of San Quentin. She made heroic efforts on their behalf whenever she got the idea that there had been a miscarriage of justice.

In 1924 she decided to take a five-year leave of absence and make a leisurely tour of the world. At a time when most women would be ready to settle down at the fireside, she started off on an old sailing ship—an adventurer still—and wandered about for two years, finally settling in Rome and corresponding for the *Chronicle* for the next five years, thereby rounding out a spectacular newspaper career with foreign service. Since her return to San Francisco she has run the annual Christmas party for the *Chronicle*. Her human interest stories still bring in checks, toys and comforts for the poor. Her newspaper career has been almost continuous for forty-five years.

The first newspaper woman on the *Chronicle* to become well known was Mabel Craft, who would have emerged as a superior reporter in any era, for she wrote well, had legal training, a good approach, and knew how to dig up facts. She had the added advantage of being striking looking. She and Winifred Black worked in competition on many stories in the nineties. They covered the Durrant trial together.

Miss Craft joined the *Chronicle* staff in 1898. She was the first woman to invade this sanctified city room and her coming caused a sensation. She was not allowed to roam at large in the early days, but was cooped up, first with the commercial editor, then with the dramatic critic, then with another woman. She wrote longhand but in time learned to use a typewriter, although never nimbly. Typewriters were just coming in, but they were not yet popular for reportorial purposes. The telephone was almost unknown. Competition was terrific, even on the most minor police detail. The reporters traveled hot-foot in street cars and only something phenomenal justified the expense of a hack.

But Miss Craft was skilled at her work. Because she was a law graduate of the University of California she got complicated legal cases to cover. And she interviewed all the visiting celebrities. One Sunday she was assigned to meet Paderewski. He arrived by special car and practised for two hours on the spot, as was his custom. She sat reading, entranced and alert. It did not bore her to hear Paderewski go over the same phrase a hundred times. Miss Craft had met him on the Oakland side of the Bay, so she was the only reporter to cross on the ferry with him. It was his first trip to America and she got an excellent interview with him. Their friendship continues to this day.

In November, 1899, Miss Craft was appointed Sunday editor—an important post then, as it would be today. It was so cold and wet in the composing room when she made up the Sunday edition that she wore rubber-soled shoes because her parents were sure she would take pneumonia. She thought up all her own features. There was little syndicated material at the time. These were the Gold Rush days and she went in heavily for history. She formed her own syndicate on amateur principles. She sent out photographs, and stories on proof sheets, making from $70 to $150 a week.

In the same year she and Alice Rix went to Honolulu for the annexation of Hawaii. She covered the Hawaiian Nei for the *Chronicle*, the *Oakland Tribune*, the New York *Sun*, the New York *Tribune* and a paper in Los Angeles. It was a barbaric and memorable spectacle. It had been her own idea to make the trip, for she thought she saw history in the making. The return of the dethroned Queen Liliuokalani to Honolulu was more of a funeral than a fête. The *Gaelic*, bearing her, was sighted off Koko Head at midnight. Her people waited for her at the wharf. It was a perfect night. The sky was a deep purple studded with stars and rimmed with clouds.

The full moon silvered the green water and the distant hills. Prince David and some of the royalists walked up the gangplank and greeted the Queen, who had been pacing the deck for hours as she neared her lost domain. She was dressed in black. Her face was melancholy under its shelter of black plumes. She walked ashore in dead silence. "Aloha, aloha," she greeted her people in soft Hawaiian tones. A storm of alohas broke loose. An old woman chanted weirdly. The Queen and Prince David drove off behind white horses, alohas and sobs echoing in their ears.

Miss Craft followed them to the Queen's residence and watched a dynasty in its dying ceremonial that night. The House of Keawe-a-heulu went out with primitive savagery. She stood hour after hour in the gardens watching the flames rise from the *kukuinuts* bound in ti leaves. The burning of these nuts was the prerogative of the royal house. Chamberlains in black broadcloth and white rosettes held them, standing stiff and watchful. The house was garlanded in green. The fragrance of jasmine and the pungency of spider-lilies filled the air. The priestesses kept up their melancholy *oliolis* all night—weird chants set to music. The fruits of the island were brought to the Queen by young girls waving white feather *kahilis*. Her people passed her in a long processional. An old couple did the hula-hula as it is never done today. At last the sun rose, the waters of Waikiki sparkled, an historic Hawaiian night had ended and the day grew rosy behind the banana leaves that fringed the Queen's gardens.

The *Chronicle* was in favor of annexation. In order to get at the news, Miss Craft had to win the sympathy of the royalists. The Queen gave her an interview, which rounded out her successful trip to Hawaii. She sent her copy back by mail and it made picturesque reading in New York and San Francisco.

In 1902 Miss Craft resigned to marry Frank P. Deering, a well-known San Francisco lawyer. She was one of the most accomplished newspaper pioneers. Her career was exciting and filled with honors while it lasted.

When Fremont Older walked into the local room of his paper, his manner was magnetic. He was unlike any other editor before or since. He charmed those who were prepared to hate him. Even when he said nothing, his influence was felt. He was six feet two, moved with curious light-footed grace and used his expressive hands like a mesmerist. His eyes glowed constantly with the unquenchable enthusiasm of the crusader and his staff was always at the mercy of his whims. He would get a reporter out of bed in the middle of the night in order to read him Montaigne. But he never countenanced news that did not interest him. He ignored the arrival of the fleet, for instance. When his imagination was aflame, however, the atmosphere around him crackled. He liked vivid narrative and short sentences. He always felt the drama behind the news and frequently anticipated what was going to happen.

Mr. Older believed in women reporters to the last ditch. He thought they had more facility of expression than men, were diligent workers, could get anything they wanted. He deplored only one thing about them—that love sooner or later messed up their careers.

When Evelyn Wells walked in one day with a letter from the divorced wife of Thorstein Veblen, he shot at her, "How old are you?"

"Nineteen," said Miss Wells.

"Write me the story of the first nineteen years of your life," he told her.

Then he forgot all about her. But she returned with the story. He gave her a job. She went to the Older home to stay overnight and remained for six years, until her marriage. This was typical of Fremont Older. He and his wife, Cora, took a persona' interest in the talented group of girls who worked for him like charmed beings. Bessie Beatty, Rose Wilder Lane, Caroline Singer, Sophie Treadwell, Pauline Jacobson, Elenore Meherin, Josephine Bartlett, Ernestine Ball, Virginia Brastow—he put them all through their paces. The best known of his graduates today is Mrs. Lane, who did newspaper work with the same skill that she has applied to all her other activities. She was more the pictorial writer than the crusader. Bessie Beatty and Pauline Jacobson were the two he fostered for radical thought and social reform.

Mr. Older believed that a serial was the best feature a paper could have. Wherever possible, he took a news story and had it treated in this form. He started Mrs. Lane off on a tour of the farming district for a serial called "Soldiers of the Soil." She had the soil in her blood. She was born in Dakota territory, she traveled West in a covered wagon during the panic of 1893, her family settled in a log cabin in the Ozark hills, and she learned what it meant to pioneer. She moved from point to point with amazing rapidity. She was office clerk, telegrapher, reporter, feature writer, advertising writer, farmland salesman and successful author in turn.

She began writing first when she worked as a telegraph operator in a Western Union branch in San Francisco. She had watched reporters file their stories and had been interested in their activities. Then Miss Beatty asked Mr. Older if she could have Rose Wilder do some work for the feature page she was running called "On the Margin." So Rose joined the staff, wrote thousands of words for the paper and she and Mr. Older became excellent friends. She did several Sunday stories for him on the life of the girl telegrapher, a subject on which she had accurate data. And she tramped the countryside with the energy and perceptions of a pioneer. Since then Mrs. Lane has traveled far, worked hard, and become well known for her fiction.

Miss Beatty, a reporter after Mr. Older's heart, worked with him from 1907 to 1917. She was his chief ally in his campaign for Tom Mooney, shared in the Abe Ruef fight, did vivid work both in California and Russia. She had the social conscience and was a fearless and intelligent reporter. Mr. Older never bullied her, as he did some of his women reporters.

At twelve years of age Miss Beatty decided she was going to be a writer. At eighteen, while she was still attending Occidental College, she got her start on the Los Angeles *Herald*. In her third year of journalism she was dramatic critic and had charge of the women's pages. Then she went to the Nevada mining country, where there was labor trouble. She was fascinated by the region and gave up her newspaper job to live in a cabin near the gold mines for six months while she wrote a book. A strike was in progress at the time and the San Francisco papers all sent reporters to cover it. She gave the press a gala dinner and decorated her cabin with sagebrush.

"You should be doing newspaper work in San Francisco," they insisted. "Why don't you try it?"

So she went on a three weeks' visit and landed on Mr. Older's paper. She refused to run a woman's page for him and compromised with her feature page "On the Margin." Elsie McCormick, Josephine Bartlett and Ernestine Ball, who married Orlow Black, Winifred Black's first husband, all worked for this page, as well as Mrs. Lane. Miss Beatty went in for series and social work. She launched the Christmas exchange, the Red Stocking campaign, one of the first outdoor Christmas trees, and a summer camp for children.

She ran Mr. Older's campaign on behalf of the prostitutes when the red light district was closed. She was in one of the larger houses of ill fame shortly after word arrived that they were to close up. The girls were sitting about, feeling sorry for poor Miss Fanny, the fat, blondined madame, who soon showed up in person. It was St. Valentine's Day and Miss Fanny had little hearts for everyone and a big one for the house. So Miss Beatty ate a heart-shaped cake with a dove on the icing and listened to the girls as they chatted about their futures. Later she tried to get jobs for them, and she and Lucy White, another of Mr. Older's reporters, helped to organize the prostitutes' union and march them to church to protest against the action of the preachers in trying to close their houses.

"You have taken our jobs away," the girls argued from the church pews. "Now what are you going to do?"

The church did not know the answer. But the columns of the *Bulletin* kept the issue alive until things went back to normal in the red light district. Mr. Older had one of the prostitutes tell her story serially in "A Voice from the Underworld."

The day she read of the Russian Revolution Miss Beatty decided that somehow she must make her way there. Her decision was made as quickly as Rheta Childe Dorr's. S. S. McClure happened to be in Mr. Older's office that day on his way to Japan. Miss Beatty volunteered to go if the paper would continue to pay her salary. Her idea was to do a series called "Around the World in War-Time."

She sailed two weeks later on the same ship as Mr. McClure. Four days out, the ship's wireless brought the news that the United States had declared war on Germany. She visited Japan and China, then proceeded to Petrograd and the heart of the revolution. For nine months she followed the dramatic sequence of events, conscious every moment of the march of history. She saw bloodshed, famine, and the new Russia emerging. She believed in the experiment she was watching. She traveled by car to the Russian front through miles of lavender poppies, green oats and cornfields. She saw the trenches zigzagging back and forth and got to within 160 feet of the enemy's front-line trenches. She sat in a bomb-proof observation station and looked through a peep hole across a narrow strip of sand dunes to a tangle of barbed wire—no man's land. Once she was permitted to put her head over the trench to see the remains of a Russian village. She went into barracks with the Battalion of Death along with Mrs. Dorr, slept on wooden boards, shared the soup and kasha of Bochkareva's regiment. She saw them trudge away to battle through the rain and mud, singing a Cossack marching song.

When she got back she was knocked down in the street in the first uprising of the Bolsheviki. She saw every phase of the revolution. She spent hours in the Soviet, weighing developments from day to day. She talked to soldiers and working men. She interviewed Catherine Breshkovskaya, the Little Grandmother of Russia, in the Winter Palace where the quarters of the Emperor had been. She watched at close range the meteoric rise and fall of Miliukoff and Kerensky in 1917. She and Mrs. Dorr saw the revolution from different points of view. In *The Red Heart of Russia* Miss Beatty summed up her experiences and her conclusions. On her return she lectured on what she had seen. When she spoke in Boston before an audience of radicals, a stiff police guard surrounded the hall in anticipation of a riot. Her life has been full of such moments.

Miss Beatty returned to Russia in 1921. It took her nine weeks to get into the country this time but she finally managed it, although there was a ban on American correspondents at the time. She and Louis Levine got permits to enter for two weeks but they missed connections at the train. He had the passports, money and luggage checks. She was thrown off the train at the border and was contemplating life in a peasant's hut when the news that her visa had gone through came by telephone. She hopped back on the train just as it was leaving. The guard gave her enough money to get her to the Foreign Office at Moscow and she took up residence in the verminous Savoy Hotel. She stayed there for nine months. Before long Walter Duranty and Herbert Pulitzer arrived on the scene. They took a flat and Miss Beatty often joined them for meals. She had met Lenin briefly in 1917. Now she wanted to get an interview with him. Gregory Weinstein helped arrange it. She went in with the idea that she would remember everything in the room. Later she remembered nothing except the man before her. She found him more humorous than Trotzky, whom she also interviewed. Trotzky was on the defensive.

When she talked to Tchicherin, she found him curious about America. "Why is your Mr. Hughes so bitter against us?" he asked. "He comes from a dissenting tradition and I cannot understand it." Later, when Miss Beatty called on Charles Evans Hughes with a delegation, she repeated this remark to him. He dropped his eyes and made no comment.

Miss Beatty made a month's trip down the Volga with Mikhail Kalinin through the famine region, seeing unforgettable sights. Her stories were featured in the *Bulletin* but on her return she did not go back to newspaper work. She became editor of *McCall's*. She lives in New York now and does publicity.

Before Bessie Beatty's day Mr. Older appointed a delicate girl named Virginia Brastow to the post of city editor. It was quite an experiment, for the *Bulletin* was in the thick of every fight and these were by no means peaceful days in San Francisco. He had collected some quixotic characters on the staff and they were not too easy to handle. But such was their passion for Mr. Older that they were completely loyal to him on every point, even to accepting a woman city editor. However, her health gave out from the strain.

When Sophie Treadwell came along, there was no place for her on the staff. She was a graduate of the University of California and had played stock in Los Angeles. There she had attracted the attention of Mme. Modjeska and had become her protégée. When the actress died she gave up her plans for a stage career and decided to try newspaper work. Mr. Older took her on as his secretary at $10 a week. She could answer the telephone and type a little. This was just after Miss Brastow's era. From her cubby hole outside Mr. Older's office Miss Treadwell could see the magic realm of the local room. It was not like the metropolitan news rooms of today. The desks were battered, the typewriters were rickety, the floor was strewn with copy paper. Sitting about on the desks was a choice collection of wits, poets and gallants who worried little about their attire.

One Saturday afternoon when Ralph E. Renaud, the young dramatic critic fresh from Leland Stanford University (now on the New York *Times*), left some pink pasteboard tickets on the city desk for the Sunday matinée of the new stock company that had opened on Valencia Street, Miss Treadwell was assigned to review the show. This small circumstance changed the course of her life. Next day at the theater she met W. O. McGeehan, whom she later married. The show was *Graustark*. Her review made a hit. Her pay went up. She got news assignments. Soon she was doing the federal beat, then police. When she got a confession from a suspected murderer, she was offered $25 a week to work on the *News*.

In 1911 she married Mr. McGeehan. He was then on the *Chronicle*, but later was to become one of the best known writers in the country. For years his suave philosophical style illumined the sports pages of the New York *Herald Tribune*. After her marriage Miss Treadwell stayed at home, but kept up her newspaper connection to the extent of doing a weekly page of book reviews for two years. Then she returned to the *Bulletin* and Mr. Older started her off on serials. The first was called "An Outcast at the Christian Door." She dressed as a down-and-outer and invaded the leading churches to see what sort of reception she would get. It was not cordial. The series was a great success. Mr. Older considered it one of his best ideas. She did several other series and then the war began. She was sent to France but got strangled in red tape. She couldn't get anywhere near the front. Why? she asked the authorities day after day. The answer was always the same: "Because you are a woman." It was an answer that never satisfied Miss Treadwell. Later she was to become one of the founders of the Lucy Stone League. But finally she got the point. She saw that she was in the way. So she went into a hospital to nurse. It was not what she had gone abroad to do, but no choice had been left her.

On her return she went to work for the New York *American*, which was different from the gay, good-natured, dait old *Bulletin*.

She did signed human interest stories and at the end of the first year was offered a five-year contract. The vista alarmed her. Five years was a long tie-up. She wanted to write plays. So she left and after that she did not work regularly in a newspaper office, but took occasional.assignments, some of them highly spectacular. When Carranza was overthrown, she was in Mexico for the New York *Tribune*. She covered his flight from the capital, his murder, and the entry of General Obregon into the city. She got a number of exclusive interviews. Obregon would see her when he refused to see anyone else. He was suspicious of the newspaper men but felt that she was harmless. Or it may have been his Mexican courtesy. At any rate, he outlined for Miss Treadwell his policy toward the United States. It was a fine newspaper coup.

Next year the *Tribune* sent her to Mexico to try to get to Villa. He had just retired with his men to a huge ranch in Chihauhau and was in an evil humor. Orders had been given to chase off every interviewer who tried to approach the place. Cameras were broken and further violence was threatened. But on her previous trip Miss Treadwell had rolled up that priceless newspaper asset, good-will, and so she was able to arrange an interview with the bold bad man of Mexico. He sent out some of his caballeros to bring her to his headquarters in northern Mexico. They made the trip as far as they could by train, then went the rest of the way by Ford and horseback. He received her courteously and devoted most of his time to her for the few days she was there. However, she was never allowed to forget that he was Villa the terrible. They rode over his ranch together and she got good newspaper copy out of him. Later she patterned the leading character in her play *Gringo* after him.

Several years later, when Felipe Carillo was murdered in Yucatan, she returned to Mexico and did a series for the *Tribune* on the country in general. This was her last newspaper assignment. Since then she has been writing plays. She made her greatest success with *Machinal*, which was produced in various European countries as well as in America.

Miss Treadwell speaks perfect Spanish and French, which has helped her in her foreign correspondence. She is of Spanish ancestry. Her great-grandmother was Dona Viviana de la Barra. Her great-grandfather was an American from Tennessee who led a filibustering expedition into Mexico that captured the state of Sonora. Her father was sent to the City of Mexico at the age of four. He spent his boyhood there, was educated in a Catholic college and afterwards fought with the army of General Diaz.

Caroline Singer, now Mrs. C. LeRoy Baldridge, followed Miss Treadwell on the *Bulletin* but was not one of Mr. Older's worshipers. She worked for next to nothing in a dirty office, poorly lighted, poorly ventilated, meanwhile drawing attention to the bad working conditions of girls in shops and factories. She investigated restaurant kitchens and was sent to a fake agency to be recruited for a dance hall. When a half-breed Indian reported that he and his gang had been deserted by their employers at a lumber mill and were starving to death, Mr. Older, the humanitarian, rushed Miss Singer out of the office to look over the scene at first hand and bring food from the *Bulletin*.

The train crew were so concerned over her fate, knowing conditions at the camp, that they wanted to get up a purse to send her home. Two lumbermen from Pennsylvania, sharing a stage coach with her and the half-breed, insisted on taking her to a country hotel for the night for her protection. When she finally reached the lumber mill she found the gang dead drunk and living on the fat of the land. Money which the *Bulletin* had sent them had been spent on liquor. Miss Singer telephoned a realistic account of conditions to her office, but when she got back to San Francisco her paper was already on the street with a fantastically distorted story. "Girl reporter rescues starving men" was the general theme. She was furious over such hokum.

Miss Singer worked for two years for the *News*, doing features, book reviews, theaters and music, all for $7 a week. For a time she was on the staff of the *Examiner*, then returned to the *Call*. From newspaper work she went on to the Creel bureau, and then to the War Department to do publicity. She arrived in France a week after the Armistice and wrote for the American Red Cross. Then she met Mr. Baldridge, who was official artist for the *Stars and Stripes*. They were married in 1921. Next year they bicycled through Italy and France. Miss Singer wrote travel articles which her husband illustrated. Since then they have traveled extensively and have three joint books to their credit, stunningly illustrated by Mr. Baldridge: *Turn to the East*, *White Africans*, and *Black Boomba*. They were in Peking through the military occupation, and in India when Gandhi returned from the Round Table Conference and was thrown into jail.

A good letter could always engage the attention of Mr. Older. When Pauline Jacobson wrote to him, describing a prize fighter, he was interested and sent for her. When she walked into his office he took her on the staff at once. She was an unusual character and unlike any of the other girls who worked from time to time on the *Bulletin*. She was the daughter of a Cantor and the sister of a Rabbi and she was immensely proud of her race. She had majored in philosophy, but she could not write for anybody except Mr. Older, although her work for him was brilliant.

He was Svengali to her in actual fact. He knew when to praise her, when to bully her, and they got on well together. He would come to the door of his office, a long black cigar in his eloquent fingers, and Pauline would jump to do his bidding. Her hair was dyed a bright red and she usually wore orange. She wanted to look a siren and this was her conception of the rôle. She visited New York once, was frightened to death, hated it and hurried back to San Francisco. Without Mr. Older's direction she was completely lost. She wrote articles about old California, did clever character sketches and interviews. One of her best was about Wilson Mizner. She and Frances Joliffe, another of the *Bulletin* graduates, are both dead now.

Betsy Strong, now Mrs. Waldemar Young, also worked for Mr. Older. Her first husband was Joe Strong, stepson of Robert Louis Stevenson. Austin Strong, the playwright, is her stepson. Her present husband is the continuity writer responsible for *Tales of a Bengal Lancer*. She was educated in a young ladies' seminary and turned to newspaper work through Ambrose Bierce. She had been to the Hawaiian Islands and on her return he asked her to write something and let him read it. She did. He gave her a letter to the Sunday editor of the *Examiner*.

"You are just back from Honolulu?" the editor asked her.

"Yes."

"Then I think you're the person we want."

The season's bathing suits had scandalized San Francisco. Women bathers were going into the water without skirts or stockings. Indignant letters were pouring in to the editor. What was the younger generation coming to? The Sunday editor thought it would be a good idea to have Mrs. Strong compare the bathing costumes of California with those worn on Waikiki Beach. Sitting near her when she went to work was Harrison Fisher, bending over a drawing board, less well known that he is today, but even then doing dazzling girls.

Mrs. Strong's story appeared the following Sunday. Her next assignment was to interview a woman and two men who headed a free-love cult. When the Hearst magazine became a syndicated section, she moved into the local room and did general reporting. Then she began selling features to the magazine sections of the *Chronicle* and *Call*.

The writers of San Francisco all knew one another in those days. They met often for good conversation in Sanguinetti's, Coppa's or the old Mint Restaurant, famous for its Pisco Punch. Among those who foregathered were Will and Wallace Irwin, George Sterling,

Kathleen Norris, Gelett Burgess, Sophie Treadwell, Marie L. Walton, Annie Wilde, Helen Dare, Pauline Jacobson, Betsy Strong, Ralph Renaud, Isabel Fraser, Charles Norris, James Hopper, Harvey Wickham and Charles Remington.

Eleanor Gates, now Mrs. Fred Moore, was on the *Examiner* at the turn of the century. She was married first to Richard Walton Tully and collaborated with him on *Rose of the Rancho* and the *Bird of Paradise*. Miss Gates imported Arabian horses and bred blooded steeds on a Western ranch. After her divorce from Mr. Tully, she wrote several novels and plays, including *The Poor Little Rich Girl*.

Genevieve Parkhurst, who has since become well known in the magazine field, worked on the *Call* and the *Chronicle*, after being left with two children to support. She was society editor of the *Chronicle* for a time. Then she did an interview with Mary Garden for the city editor. After that she was assigned regularly to news features. She was on the *Call* for two years and did practically everything but work for the financial page. She covered the waterfront, wrote sports and did strenuous work on the Mooney trial. During the San Francisco Exposition she was in charge of women's features and the general publicity.

A later generation included Milly Bennett Mitchell, who worked on the San Francisco *News*, covered all types of stories and was one of the numerous Cynthia Grays of the Scripps-Howard chain. She moved on to the Honolulu *Advertiser*, then went to China, joining Rayna Prohme who had gone to the Orient in 1922 with her husband, William F. Prohme, a San Francisco editor. They worked for the Kuomintang in Peking, then assumed editorship of the *People's Tribune*. In 1926 they took over the Canton *Gazette*, the official paper of the Cantonese Nationalist Government. When the government moved to Hankow Mrs. Prohme went with it and founded the *People's Tribune*. Meanwhile she and her husband ran the Nationalist News Agency. They remained faithful to the revolutionary section of the government and accompanied the leaders through the disaster of July, 1927. They moved to Moscow with Eugene Chen and other Chinese and Russian revolutionaries, and there Mrs. Prohme died in 1927. While the trouble was at its height, Miss Mitchell, who had worked with them in Canton and Peking, was thrown into jail by the Peking authorities and was only freed after Randall Gould, of the United Press, raised a dust about her plight.

Of the contemporary generation of newspaper women on the coast one of the best known is Alma Whitaker, for the last twenty-five years a columnist on the Los Angeles *Times*. Katherine Beebe does capable work for the Associated Press in San Francisco. She is a graduate of the University of Wisconsin, was club editor of the

Kansas City *Journal*, hitch-hiked her way through the West, worked on the Salt Lake City *Telegram* and taught in the wilds of Wyoming. In the autumn of 1922 she returned to newspaper work in Madison, then joined the publicity staff of Leland Stanford University. Her next move was to the Oakland *Tribune*; then, in 1926, to the Kansas City *Star*. For a time she worked for the A.P. in New York, then trekked across the country again to the coast.

One of the finest and most experienced newspaper women in the country today is Marjorie Driscoll, of the Los Angeles *Examiner*. Few can touch her in handling a big news story, directing a staff of men, and turning out a top-notch job under difficult conditions. She is modest, retiring, and rarely talks about herself or her work. She directed the *Chronicle* staff on the Argonaut mine disaster. She stuck by her typewriter for forty hours, waiting for the rescuers to break through. Again she ran things for the *Chronicle* while President Harding lay dying in San Francisco. Her funeral story was so impressive that she was invited next day to join the Hearst organization at her own figure. The sum she named was double what she was getting on the *Chronicle* but it was still a modest salary for a newspaper woman of her capabilities. She moved to the *Examiner* in 1923. She has avoided the woman's angle at all costs and will not write a sob story. Her work is all on the masculine plane. She often shows up on stories, the only woman with a score of men. She has specialized in aviation, the sea and other subjects not usually covered by women reporters. She is happy covering an air meet or a fleet review, and completely lost at a woman's club meeting.

She has been in newspaper work for twenty-two years. She covered the St. Francis dam flood, any number of airplane crashes, and the Griffith Park fire in Los Angeles. She has worked on all the big crime stories of recent years on the coast—the Ruth Judd case, the Father Heslin murder in San Francisco, Fatty Arbuckle's trial and scores of others. She has done a number of stories from the air —the return of the Army world flight, forest fires, floods and spectacles—and has interviewed the usual collection of celebrities.

Miss Driscoll broke into newspaper work on the Pasadena *Star* in 1913 after some preliminary work on the same paper during summer vacations while she attended Leland Stanford. This paper, under the ownership of Charles H. Prisk, was an excellent training ground. She did a little of everything, which is what makes the good woman reporter. She was city editor, telegraph editor, city room supervisor, copy reader and general factotum. In 1919 she moved to the *Chronicle* and put in six months on the society desk, the one newspaper job she detested. She was transferred to general reporting and did some dramatic criticism. Before long she had made a fine reputation for herself. On the *Examiner* she does general work and rewrite. Her mind works with precision. She can handle squads of men. She is fast, capable, accurate and writes effective copy without slopping over. Miss Driscoll is one of the exceptional women of the profession.

Chapter XLVI

THE SOUTH

WHEN A TIMID GIRL NAMED ELIZA JANE POITEVANT SUB-
mitted some of her verse to Nathaniel Willis in the sixties
and had it printed in the New York *Journal* her brothers
stamped on the paper instead of reading it when it reached New
Orleans.

She signed herself Pearl Rivers but this in no way appeased her
snobbish family, who thought that Pearl should bloom beside the
magnolias until a good man arrived to take her into his home. They
had no means of foreseeing that Eliza would own and run the New
Orleans *Picayune*, turning it from a bankrupt property into a fine
political daily with real power in the South. They would have been
filled with horror at the thought of such enterprise on the part of
a woman.

Eliza was born in 1849 in Pearlington, Mississippi, on the banks
of the Pearl River, from which she later took her pen name. Her
aunt brought her up on a huge plantation, the only white child in
sight. She was taught at home by governesses, then went to a seminary designed to equip her for a life in which social functions,
fashions, housekeeping and children would be the dominating factors.
She was an imaginative child who had roamed about the woods
and was filled with nature lore. Her début in print was a blow to her
family. It was bad enough to have a sister who wrote verses about
the birds, but to have them appear in a newspaper was a social error
of the worst order.

At that time the *Picayune* was owned by Colonel Alva Morris
Holbrook, who liked her verse and asked her to become literary
editor of his paper at a salary of $25 a week. It was practically un-
heard of for a woman to work for a paper in the South. The Poitevant family objected strenuously but Eliza defied the whole clan and
took the job. Her work was good. In course of time she established
another bond with the paper by marrying Colonel Holbrook. A few
years later he sold the *Picayune* to a group of merchants who tried
to run it on a coöperative basis. But the paper went downhill until

Colonel Holbrook bought it back. Before he had time to rehabilitate it, he died, leaving the property heavily mortgaged, and with so little credit that no one would deliver a barrel of ink at the plant.

Eliza was invited to return to her home, but she had other plans. She was still young, frail and totally inexperienced in the management of a paper, but she slipped into her husband's editorial chair one day and assembled the staff. She told them that she was going to manage the paper. She invited the resignation of any man present who did not want to work for a woman. Several got out. She dismissed one or two more, just to prove that she was hard-boiled enough to do it. Then she made another bold move by giving important executive posts to two newspaper men who had been Yankee officers, at a time when sectional prejudice was still strong. She gathered about her a talented staff and was most successful, anticipating by years some of the features that are now a part of every daily paper. She helped to develop the Sunday newspaper as a medium of entertainment for the entire family. She opened the journalistic field to women in the South and started Dorothy Dix on her extraordinarily successful career.

When she died in 1896 she left the *Picayune* a prosperous and sound paper. Her second husband was E. J. Nicholson. Some years after her death the *Picayune* and *Times-Democrat* were merged, her son, Leonard Nicholson, becoming manager of the *Times-Picayune*. When Mrs. Nicholson first took over the paper a clever girl named Martha Field was writing for it under the pen name Catherine Cole. Her father was one of the editors and she was taken on the staff to cover all kinds of assignments. In 1890 she left America and went to live in England.

Although somewhat obscured by the fuss over Nellie Bly's success, Elizabeth Bisland, who got her early training on the *Times-Democrat*, raced her around the world and lost by four days. She made the race for *Cosmopolitan*, traveling west as Nellie traveled east. However, she made better time than Phileas Fogg, completing the trip in seventy-six days. She was less fortunate than her rival in making her connections. She expected to catch a North German Lloyd steamer at Southampton but found it had been withdrawn. She missed a French ship at Havre. Miss Bisland worked side by side with Lafcadio Hearn on the *Times-Democrat* and some time after her dash around the world she wrote a book about him. She became Mrs. Charles W. Wetmore and settled in Washington. Her sister, Mollie Bisland, also started her newspaper career in New Orleans, then moved to New York and became associated with Mr. McClure in his early syndicate work.

In 1913 a handsome seventeen-year-old girl invaded the local room of the New Orleans *Item*. She had promised her mother that she would stick to clubs and society, but she soon persuaded Marshall Ballard, her managing editor, that police news was more her style. This was Bessie James, the wife of Marquis James, whom she met six months after she joined the staff of the *Item*.

James E. Crown, the best known city editor of the Southwest, had arrived from the Chicago *Inter-Ocean* to take over the city desk of the *Item*, with two promising young reporters in tow—Sam Blair and Marquis James. Drifting reporters traveled hundreds of miles to work for a spell under Jim Crown, who drove his staff hard, but filled them with a frenzy of accomplishment. After a year he gave Mrs. James a court run. In the first week she was sadly beaten and melted into tears, which thawed the political opponents of her paper, so that the error never was repeated.

Her prize scoop concerned the Mrs. Cook whose husband owned the yellow taxi service in New Orleans, but who preferred a Mississippi River steamboat captain and eloped with him on her yacht. The story did not break for several days. Then it appeared with the twist that Mrs. Cook was holding the captain a "love prisoner" on the yacht. The runaways cruised around the Gulf for two weeks, and then the papers were tipped off that the boat had entered Lake Ponchartrain and was heading for its anchorage.

Mrs. James was the one woman assigned to the story. The yacht tied up with Mrs. Cook pointing a gun from behind a curtained porthole, and threatening to shoot any reporter who stepped on her property. The men took her threats seriously but Mrs. James kept walking nearer and nearer the barrel of the gun. Mrs. Cook was so surprised that she did not shoot. Neither would she give an interview.

But next morning, after she had gone ashore, she admitted the reporter to her house. Mrs. Cook became Mrs. James's exclusive property for twenty-four hours—a severe blow to 'her competitors, who scattered right and left on the lawn when the brigand again thrust her gun through a window, this time firing it into the air, on the advice of Mrs. James and her photographer, who then breakfasted heartily with the obliging Mrs. Cook. The steamboat captain was missing. He had gone home to patch things up with his wife.

After fifteen months of stunting and appropriating news and pictures for her paper, Mrs. James concluded that she was ready to work for Mr. Hearst. So she went to Chicago and got on the staff of the *Examiner*, where things were tougher, for the men were hard-boiled and did not respond so easily to tear-filled Southern eyes.

In 1916 Mr. and Mrs. James arrived in New York, by way of Niagara Falls, carrying a heavy old-time Remington, which was all the property they owned. Marquis went to work on the *Tribune* and for two months his wife swam in the ocean, explored Coney Island and absorbed some of the fascinations of New York. Then she went job-hunting. She landed on the Brooklyn *Times*, but was fired in two weeks because she got lost and couldn't find her way back to the office in time for the home edition. Then she changed her course and embarked on a highly successful publicity career with the National League for Woman's Service, organized by Anne Morgan and Maude Wetmore. The only stunt she ever had vetoed was her suggestion that a chorus girl step out on the hands of the Metropolitan Tower clock at a quarter to three and paste a Liberty Loan poster on the clock's face. It was Mrs. James who first proposed that society women should serve as referees at a prize fight exhibition—a stunt she suggested to Scotty Monteith when he had just lost his job as Johnny Dundee's manager and was anxious to get it back.

Since then Mrs. James has helped her husband with his research and has written a number of books herself, including some popular juveniles. She is now working on a biography of Anne Royall, one of her journalistic predecessors.

At about the same time that Mrs. Nicholson functioned boldly in New Orleans, Maude Annulet Andrews started the woman's department of the Atlanta *Constitution*, a radical departure for the South. She worked with Henry Grady and Joel Chandler Harris. Soon after marrying her city editor, Josiah K. Ohl, she went to live in Washington. On her staff was a young girl of charm named Ismay Dooly, who had been allowed to write for the *Constitution* after promising her mother that she would do all her work at home. But when her family was finally persuaded that her activities were harmless and Mrs. Ohl gave up her post, Miss Dooly succeeded her. In the next twenty-eight years she became one of the well-known women of the South and a notable figure in journalism. At a time when women's clubs were ridiculed she championed their interests, took up causes and forced through public measures. She developed a sound woman's page and backed every measure involving the welfare and advancement of women and children.

Miss Dooly worked strenuously on welfare projects for tne Negro and for the mountain children of North Georgia. The Ismay Dooly auditorium at Tallulah Falls Industrial School, owned and conducted by the Georgia Federation of Women's Clubs, is a memorial to her work for this institution. Another of her pet causes was the admission of women to the University of Georgia and a tablet in the first woman's dormitory commemorates her efforts. Her name is listed in the State Capitol as one of the benefactors who did most for their state.

Much of her work was done through the columns of the *Constitution*. She was allowed freedom of expression to back her various interests. She ran one of the first club pages in the country and helped to found the Atlanta Woman's Club, the Atlanta City Federation of Woman's Clubs and the Georgia Federation of Women's Clubs. But Miss Dooly would never speak in public, although an engaging conversationalist in private life. She died in 1921, soon after collapsing in her office with an attack of angina pectoris. Her sister, Louise, did newspaper work also until her health gave out.

One of the active newspaper women of Atlanta today is Mrs. Medora Field Perkerson, who helps her husband, Angus Perkerson, edit the Sunday magazine section of the *Journal*. She entered newspaper work by way of an original idea. Seeing a fashion show on the screen she decided that a shopping column, with space paid for by the merchants, would be a good newspaper feature. She launched the column and deducted her own commission. One Christmas Eve, dressed as a beggar woman, she canvassed the downtown section for alms and wrote a newspaper story about it. She was assistant to Mr. Perkerson on the Sunday paper for two years before she married him.

Another wife who has worked with her husband in an editorial capacity in the South is Mrs. Julia Collier Harris, who wrote many of the editorials which drew attention to the Columbus *Enquirer-Sun* and won for it the Pulitzer prize one year. Her husband is Julian Harris, editor of the Chattanooga *Times* and former Sunday editor of the New York *Herald*. Mrs. Harris has written a biography of her father-in-law, Joel Chandler Harris.

A Southern newspaper woman who achieved a national reputation with her books and short stories was Corra Harris, who died in 1935. For the last three years of her life she wrote a column for the Atlanta *Journal* called "Candlelit." Mrs. Harris was the wife of a Methodist circuit rider and in her nomadic years she gathered the material which she used later in her fiction, particularly in *The Circuit Rider's Wife*. Born in 1869 at Farm Hill, Georgia, she was educated at home by her parents in the ways of the old South. Her first published story appeared in the Atlanta *Constitution* and in 1899 she began writing for the magazines. Thereafter her life became more complex. She was a war correspondent, political commentator and practical philosopher. Essentially she remained a good reporter to the day of her death.

Mildred Seydell, traveler, lecturer and newspaperwoman, is known as the Nellie Bly of the South—largely because she is such a persistent globe trotter. She entered the journalistic field in 1922 with a column in the Charleston *Gazette,* and since 1924 she has been with the *Georgian-American* in Atlanta. Her column carries the head "Mildred Seydell" and in it she editorializes with complete freedom. In 1925 Mrs. Seydell wrote special features for the Universal News Service on the Scopes trial in Dayton, Tennessee. Since then she has made annual trips to various parts of Europe, Asia, Africa, Central and South America, interviewing celebrities, and studying the social and political reforms of the countries visited.

Mrs. Seydell is chairman of the publicity committee of the National Woman's Party. She married Paul Seydel, a scientist, soon after completing a course at the Sorbonne, but she expresses her individuality by spelling her name with two "l's". She has two sons, is the author of a novel *Secret Fathers* and writes for the magazines.

A newspaper woman well known in Georgia for her public works as well as for her journalism is Emily Woodward, who edited the Vienna *News* for many years. She entered newspaper work by chance. The paper was to be sold. Its owner had been appointed postmaster. He walked into the office of Miss Woodward's brother to discuss probable buyers. She happened to be sitting reading a magazine when he arrived. There were no women editors at that time in Southern villages but Miss Woodward announced at once that she would like to tackle the job. The day she first filled the editorial chair she was innocent of journalistic training.

She was the youngest member of a family of eight, born near Vienna. She had lived the first ten years of her life on a big plantation with a horde of Negro servants on the place. She had received a good education but none of it included any training that would help her to edit a paper. She wrote her copy in longhand. The one linotype operator who could decipher it with ease, or even at all, kept his job in spite of an occasional jag and various detours from the path of rectitude. Her backbone stiffened as she saw the disapproving looks of her fellow townsmen, who could not understand why a woman should want to edit a paper. However, she ran it with a professional touch and never asked for any favors. The experiment was successful.

Soon after she embarked on her newspaper career Miss Woodward joined the Georgia Press Association and in time became president. It was she who first proposed the school for editors which broadened into the Georgia Press Institute held annually at the University of Georgia. For years she was a member of the State Democratic executive committee, and twice she was a delegate to the national conventions. The first note sounded against prohibition in Georgia came from her in a speech she made at the state university. The state registrar, a friend of hers but an ardent dry, tried to have her removed from the building, but she stood her ground. Later she received an honorary degree from the University and made the baccalaureate address there. She has done a great deal of public speaking and has interested herself in various projects.

For a long time Miss Woodward was the only woman in the state to own, edit and manage a paper. With her profits she paid off all the original costs, equipped the plant with modern machinery and came through the depression with her titles clear. In 1932 she sold her paper and since then has been free-lancing. Her work frequently appears in the Atlanta *Journal*. She lives much of the time in a cabin which she designed herself. She made her garden out of the wild plants and flowers that grow around her door—a paradise where the thump of the linotype no longer sounds in her ears.

As far back as 1888 Ellen J. Dortch owned and edited the *Tribune* in Carnesville, Georgia. The plant consisted of 150 pounds of long primer type, a few cases of worn advertising type and a subscription book with a credit column that had long been neglected. Miss Dortch was only seventeen when she started. She installed new presses, fought the boycotters and ignored the Southern prejudice against women working. The circulation of the paper increased by thousands.

During the eighties Mrs. Elia Goode Byington, another native of Georgia, was joint proprietor with her husband, Edward Telfair Byington, of the Columbus *Evening Ledger*, a successful Southern daily. With the exception of the carrier boys and four men for outdoor work, all the employees of the paper were women—the foreman, artist, proof reader, reporter, mailing clerk and typesetter. Mrs. Byington saw to it that they received men's pay.

Today good newspaper women abound in the South. Savannah has its Jane Judge, on the *News*, a reporter who also does a weekly book page for her paper. Memphis has Mary Raymond, on the *Press-Scimitar*, to whom Schumann-Heink exclaimed on one occasion: "My God! Do I have to be interviewed before I take my hat off?" Miss Raymond writes serials for NEA, in addition to covering news. One of the best known Southern newspaper women was Grace Boylan Geldert, also of Memphis, who died in 1935. And Ida Clyde Clarke, later associate editor of *Pictorial Review*, pioneered for the Nashville *Tennesseean*.

Texas has sent a number of excellent newspaper women north and still has good ones within its borders. Mary Caroline Holmes covers every sort of story, even City Hall, for the Dallas *Journal*. Allena Duff James does society and fashions for the Dallas *Times*

Herald. Bess Stephenson is a feature veteran on the *Star Telegram* of Fort Worth. Clara Ogden held her own with the men on the staff of the Houston *Chronicle* until she moved north. She is now married to Burton Davis, the novelist.

Any novice could get lessons in the technique of bucking hostile desks and sex discrimination from Margaret Shuttee Hester, who has worked for the last seven years as telegraph, city and day news editor for the *Times Record* of Fort Smith, Arkansas. She is also an expert at copy reading, a branch of the profession almost unknown to women. Mrs. Hester subdued the composing room foreman on one occasion by brandishing a copy hook at him when he launched into his choicest invective over a last minute make-over. She swore at him in his own terms; after that she had his respect. When a metropolitan copy reader got a job on her paper he was filled with contempt for her executive powers. "It'll be a hell of a long time before I get used to a city editor who uses a powder puff," he declared.

Mrs. Hester was born and educated in Missouri. While attending the University of Missouri she was head copy reader with Frank L. Martin, now dean of the school of journalism, on the exciting day that the U.P. sent out its false armistice story. She worked for the Springfield *Republican*, and was with the *Southwest American* when it was consolidated with the *Times Record*. She was head of the telegraph desk during the Leopold-Loeb hearing. On the night before the decision was due she found she had to do the page one make-up. She had had no experience along this line. The wire was hot with news, all on the one story. Frantic, she sought the advice of Presley E. Bryant, now of the Fort Worth *Star Telegram*.

"That's your problem," he told her. "You're head of the desk. Get over there and sink or swim."

She swam but didn't sink. Somehow she put the front page together and got all the Loeb and Leopold copy in. It was an exhilarating night. Later, when she went on the city staff, her work seemed much less complex than it was when she headed a desk.

Now and again a newspaper woman does a typical cinema act, but not always so conclusively as Nellie Kenyon, of the Chattanooga *News*, who caught a bandit as well as writing the story of his capture. Miss Kenyon started her newspaper career working for nothing on the society page. Then she went on to special interviews and features. She talked to Presidents and gangsters. Warren Harding told her when she saw him in Chattanooga that a job would always be waiting for her on the Marion *Star*. Al Capone, en route to the Atlanta Penitentiary, called her a cutie and asked her to take charge of his affairs until he got out of jail. John McCormack once gave a concert for her in his private railway car. She covered the Scopes trial and was warned by Daytonians not to go into the court house while Clarence Darrow was speaking, for the whole building would be destroyed by God in his vengeance.

But it was Miss Kenyon's bandit who brought her her newspaper reputation. In the summer of 1931 a $6,617 hold-up was staged in the local bank. At about the same time a nurse who was looking after Miss Kenyon's mother happened to mention the odd ways of a boarder living in her house. His room was filled with crime magazines. He was usually out all night. On the day of the robbery he made a nervous departure.

Putting two and two together Miss Kenyon became suspicious. She asked the nurse to let her know if she heard from the youth, who had left most of his clothes behind him. Meanwhile, she drew the attention of the police to his behavior, but they thought it a reporter's pipe dream. However, a letter soon arrived from Detroit with a mailing address. The young man wanted his clothes sent on, and particularly two keys which he had left behind him. Miss Kenyon led the police to the nurse's home. They found that the keys fitted the handcuffs used to imprison the bank employees. They also discovered that one of the magazines featured a story which duplicated the hold-up in the bank. The robber had climbed the water pipes to the roof, sawed out a panel of the skylight and climbed down into the bank. In each case the victims were bound in the same manner.

The police, convinced at last, made an easy arrest in Detroit. The bandit was Robert Walton, alias Joe Martin. He was brought back to Chattanooga and was sentenced to twenty years' imprisonment. His arrest was a scoop to which Miss Kenyon was fully entitled. But hers was an afternoon paper and she feared that her morning competitor might get wind of the story. She stayed up all night, waiting for the opposition paper to be delivered at her door. When it came she saw at once that she had a clean beat. Her paper gave the story an eight-column streamer. She got full credit for the capture. The front-page lay-out included pictures of the magazines found in the bandit's room and also the nurse's story. Miss Kenyon's copy was introduced as evidence at the trial. George Fort Milton, publisher of her paper, gave her a wrist watch for distinguished service. She wrote a magazine story, "The Girl Reporter Gets Her Man," for which she won a $1,000 prize. She also received part of the reward offered for the arrest of the bandit. Months later he wrote to her from the state penitentiary and asked her to help get him out—a typically absurd touch in the life of a girl reporter.

This was a case where the newspaper woman had a hand in making news. More often she is a spectator, calmly taking notes.

By slow degrees she has moved out of the false framework of legend and prejudice that has surrounded her for the last fifty years, although there is no denying that she is still a negligible factor in the newspaper office, and is there only because of her own insistence, not because anyone has wanted her. She has her compensations, however. Invariably she likes her work beyond all telling. Adventure, excitement, romance, danger, praise and blame, glamour and drudgery, keep her spinning self-forgetfully day after day in the dizzy world inhabited by the ladies of the press.

INDEX

Abbott, Emma, 495
Abbott, Mabel, 176
Abbott, Mary, 20, 551
Abrams, Norma, 297-298
Acosta, Mrs. Bert, 126
Acton, Harry, 103
Adams, Mrs. Annie, 71
Adams, Barbara, see Virginia Gardner
Adams, Franklin P., 91, 139, 152, 398, 447, 554
Adams, George Matthew, 386, 387
Adams, John Quincy, 27, 28, 30
Adams, Maude, 71
Adams, Mildred, 163-164, 359
Addington, Sarah, 120, 125
Ade, George, 258
Adler, Dr. Alfred, 391
Adler, Felix, 83
Adolphus Augustus, Crown Prince of Sweden, 514
Agnus, General Felix, 496
Albany Argus, 524, 525
Albany Evening News, 175, 189
Albuquerque Journal, 331
Alden, Ruth, see Mary Humphrey
Aldrich, Bess Streeter, 464
Aldrich, Mrs. Darragh, see Clara Chaplin Thomas
Aldrich, Mildred, 484-485
Alexander, Mrs. Charles B., 453
Alexander, D. S., 512
Alexander, King, of Greece, 370
Alfonso, King, of Spain, 130, 375, 376
Allard, Leola, 548
Allen, C. B., 175, 225
Allen, Edward H. B., 211
Allen, Senator Henry, 357
Allen, Maud, 65
Allen, Robert S., 340
American Banker, 357
Ames, Mary Clemmer, 326, 327
Anastasia, Princess of Greece, 159, 160
Anastasia, Princess (Russia), 176
Anderson, Dutch, 267
Anderson, "Gil," 181
Anderson, Katherine Watson, 473-474
Anderson, W. W., 563
Andrews, Maude Annulet, 594
Andrews, Stephen Pearl, 31
Annan, Beulah, 544

Annis, W. E., 72
Anthony, George, 562
Anthony, Susan B., 112, 116, 426, 462, 495
Antonio, Mrs. Anna, 237
Arbuckle, Fatty, 221, 589
Archambeau, Gaston, 223
Arden, Elizabeth, 235
Arkansas Gazette, 547
Arlen, Michael, 200
Armitage, Charles H., 523
Armstrong, Robert A., Jr., 346
Arno, Peter, 388
Arnold, Judge Lynn J., 524
Ashley, Lady Sylvia, 291
Ashmead, Ruth (Ruth Ashmore), 21
Aspinwall, William, 442
Asquith, Margot, 94, 573
Astor, John Jacob, 209, 453, 490
Astor, John Jacob (senior), 86
Astor, Mrs. John Jacob, 86, 87
Astor, Lady, 95, 103, 104, 126, 449, 541
Atchison Daily Globe, 161, 460
Atchison Weekly Globe, 460
Atkinson, Brooks, 485
Atlanta Constitution, 594, 595
Atlanta Georgian-American, 596
Atlanta Journal, 595, 597
Attree, William H., 441
Augusta Chronicle, 437
Augusta Victoria, Empress, 102
Austin, James, 192
Austin, Kay, 395
Avery, Marjorie, 537
Ayer, Harriet Hubbard, 88
Ayres, Ann Grosvenor, 260

Baer, Leone Cass, 409
Bailey, Edward, 292
Bailey, Dr. Gamaliel, 327, 329
Bailey, Gertrude, 435
Baker, Frank L., 276, 442, 447
Baker, Professor Henry, 472
Baker, Ray Stannard, 135
Balbo, Commander, 510
Baldridge, Cyrus LeRoy, 586
Baldridge, Mrs. C. LeRoy, see Caroline Singer
Ball, Ernestine, 580, 581
Ball, Mrs. Isabel Worrell, 331-332
Ballard, Marshall, 593

Baltimore *American,* 493, 496, 500
Baltimore *Evening News,* 496
Baltimore *Evening Sun,* 494
Baltimore *Herald,* 496
Baltimore *News,* 500
Baltimore *Sun,* 359, 471, 472, 493, 494, 495, 496, 498, 499, 500
Baltimore *Sunday Sun,* 494, 496, 500
Banks, Elizabeth L., 17, 18
Bara, Theda, 92
Bard, Josef, 363
Bargeron, Carlyle, 319
Barker, Ama, 291, 292
Barnard, Mrs. H. M., 326
Barnes, Mrs. Courtlandt D., Jr., *see* Katrina McCormick
Barnes, William, 525
Barrett, Jean, 518
Barrymore, Lionel, 304
Bartlett, Dorothy D., 515-517
Bartlett, Josephine, 580, 581
Bartnett, Edmond P., 227, 228
Baruch, Bernard, 176, 521
Baruch, Mrs. Simon, 521
Bassett, Mrs. Ellsworth, 432
Battle Creek *Evening News,* 205
Battle Creek *Journal,* 205
Bauer, Dorothy, 517
Baumhart, Carl, 224
Bayard, Robert, 442
Bayard, William, 442
Bayes, Norah, 257
Beach, Rex, 471
Bean, Edgar R., 235
Bean, Theodora, 89, 257-259, 411
Beatty, Bessie, 377, 580, 581-583
Beck, Teddy, 206
Becker, Charles, 69, 70, 182
Becker, Mrs. Charles, 69, 70, 182
Becker, May Lamberton, 404
Beckley, Zoë, 93, 97-105, 124, 256
Beckwith, Mary Lincoln, 358
Bedwell, Bettina, 438
Beebe, Katherine, 588
Beecher, Catherine, 46
Beecher, Henry Ward, 31, 32, 33, 34, 35, 41, 326
Belasco, David, 418
Belford, Herbert, 389
Belford, James B., 564
Belford, Mrs. James B., 565
Bell, Alexander Graham, 332
Belmont, Mrs. Oliver H. P., 92, 123, 127, 128, 258, 449, 554
Benedict, Pope, 170, 487
Beneš, Dr. Eduard, 362
Benét, Stephen Vincent, 230
Benét, William Rose, 164
Bennett, Arnold, 11, 141
Bennett, James Gordon, 15, 16, 23, 24, 83, 128, 153, 156, 235, 258, 312, 334, 441, 442
Bennett, James Gordon (younger), 442, 443, 448, 449, 450
Bennett, James O'Donnell, 554
Bennett, Richard, 415

Bergdoll, Grover, 230
Bergen *Evening Record,* 212
Bergeron, Marion, 299
Berlin, Mrs. Irving, 276
Bernays, Edward L., 125
Bernhardt, Sarah, 64, 88, 93, 369, 448, 522, 554, 557, 561
Bernstein, Hillel, 223
Besant, Annie, 526
Biddle, Nicholas, 442
Bierce, Ambrose, 587
Bigelow, John, 145, 147
Bigelow, William F., 114
Biggers, Earl Derr, 485
Bingay, Mae, 532
Binghamton Press, 357
Birkhead, May, 449-450
Birmingham *Ledger,* 185
Birmingham *News,* 185
Bishop, Courtland, 223
Bisland, Elizabeth, 61, 592
Bisland, Mollie, 592
Black, Orlow, 581
Black, Ruby, 317, 319, 320, 336, 347-349
Black, Winifred, 20, 22, 59, 60-67, 417, 422, 562, 567, 576, 578, 581
Blaine, James G., 329, 330
Blaine, Mrs. James G., 329
Blair, Mrs. Emily Newell, 359
Blair, Martha, 502
Blair, Tom, 593
Blake, Doris, *see* Antoinette Donnelly
Blakesley, Charles, 461
Blanshard, Julia, 435, 436
Blanshard, Paul, 435
Block, Paul, 245
Blood, Colonel James H., 31, 34
Bloomer, Mrs., 2
Bly, Nellie (Elizabeth Cochrane), 14, 17, 24, 48-59, 60, 66, 176, 237, 241, 251, 483, 491, 551, 553, 560, 561, 592, 595
Boag, Gil, 302
Boardman, Frances, 556-557
Bochkareva, 582
Bodine, Tom, 255
Boehm, Sid, 245
Boersianer, 490
Boettiger, John, 319
Bohnsack, Christie R., 220
Boise Capital *News,* 452
Bok, Edward W., 20, 21, 22, 241
Bok, William J., 21
Bolton, Whitney, 212
Bone, Scott, 142, 380
Bonfils, Mrs. Charles A., *see* Winifred Black
Bonfils, Charlie, 417, 420, 421, 422
Bonfils, Frederick A., 562, 563, 564, 566, 567, 568, 569, 570
Boone, Evelyn, 232
Booth, Lois, 490
Borah, Senator William, 504
Boston *American,* 235, 489, 491
Boston *Beacon,* 483

Boston *Budget*, 483
Boston *Daily Record*, 489
Boston *Globe*, 483, 486, 487, 489
Boston *Herald*, 2, 95, 454, 483, 484, 485
Boston *Home Journal*, 454, 484
Boston *Journal*, 387, 484, 485
Boston *Olive Branch*, 41
Boston *Post*, 1, 2, 483, 486, 491
Boston *Sunday American*, 235
Boston *Transcript*, 481, 482, 483, 485
Boston *Traveller*, 175, 387, 483, 484, 485, 486
Boston *True Flag*, 41
Botchkereva, 110
Bovard, Oliver K., 555
Bowlan, Marion, 551
Bowles, Mrs. A. Lincoln, 482-483
Boyd, Isabel, 175
Boyle, Mrs. H., 37
Brace, Blanche, 125
Brackett, Charles, 236
Braddock, James J., 209
Bradish, Luther, 442
Bradley, Mrs. Annie M., 71, 72
Braggiotti, Gloria, 439
Brastow, Virginia, 472, 580, 583, 584
Brazelton, Ethel M. Colson, 551
Brazier, Marion Howard, 454
Breitigan, Gerald, 233
Breshkovskaya, Catherine, 582
Breuer, Bessie, 125
Brevoort, Henry, 441, 442
Brevoort, Mrs. Henry, 441
Bridgeport *Post*, 426
Briggs, Mrs. Emily Edson, 326
Bright, John, 46
Brighton, Mrs. Margaret Smith, 491
Brinkley, Mrs. May French, 416
Brinkley, Nell, 22, 416-420, 570
Brisbane, Arthur, 17, 24, 58, 73, 78, 79, 80, 83, 177, 179, 300, 301, 386, 417, 418, 419, 420, 423, 432, 459, 502
Britt, George, 436
Broadway Journal, 482
Brodsky, Magistrate Louis B., 351
Brody, Catherine, 116-117, 168
Bromley, Dorothy Dunbar, 433
Brooklyn *Eagle*, 236, 237, 238, 259
Brooklyn *Times*, 214, 238, 259, 415, 593
Brooklyn *Times Union*, 238
Brooks, Phillips, 495
Brough, Elizabeth, 576. *See also* Helen Dare
Broun, Heywood, 121, 167, 259, 381, 384, 394, 447
Brown, Senator Arthur, 71, 72
Brown, Curtis, 426
Brown, Eve, 447
Brown, Harry, 409
Brown, Mrs. John Nicholas, *see* Anne S. Kinsolving
Brown, Mrs. Josephine, 288, 289
Brown, Mary K., 469
Brown, Nancy, 84, 532-534

Brown, Royal, 387
Brown, Vera, 537-538
Browning, Betty, 544
Browning, Edward W., 201
Browning, Peaches, 304, 418
Browning, Robert, 36, 328, 401
Bruna, Jan, 102
Brunen, "Honest John," 184
Brunen, Mrs., 184
Brush, Katherine, 560
Bryan, William Jennings, 464, 527, 552
Bryan, Mrs. William Jennings, 552
Bryant, Louise, 111, 377, 378
Bryant, Presley E., 598
Buck, Frank, 409
Buckley, Gerald E. O., 538
Buckner, Emory, 391
Buffalo *Courier*, 131, 523
Buffalo *Enquirer*, 304
Buffalo *Evening News*, 335, 509, 521, 523
Buffalo *Express*, 131, 522, 523
Buffalo *Junior Courier*, 523
Buffalo *Sunday Express*, 304
Buffalo *Times*, 220, 521, 524
Bugbee, Emma, 122-126, 315, 316, 317, 320, 321
Bullard, Lola, 560
Bullard, General Robert Lee, 276
Bullitt, William C., 378
Burdick, George, 122, 123
Burgess, Gelett, 588
Burke, Billie, 419, 429
Burke, Mildred, 475, 476
Burns, Rev. Vincent G., 209
Burr, Kate, 524
Burstall, Phyllis, 284
Burt, 274, 276
Burton, Harry Payne, 91, 92, 554
Bushel, Hyman, 190
Bushel, Mignon, 190
Butcher, Fanny, 128, 407-408, 428
Butler, Sheppard, 542
Butt, Dame Clara, 103
Byers, Ruth, 180-182, 524
Byers, Vincent G., 213
Byington, Edward Telfair, 597
Byington, Mrs. Elia Goode, 597
Byrd, Commander Richard E., 126

Cabell, James Branch, 404
Cadman, Rev. Dr. S. Parkes, 391
Caldwell, Mrs. Louis, *see* Clemens, Mazie
Callaway, Inez, 450-453
Calvé, Emma, 448, 449, 495
Cameron, Kate, 413-414
Cameron, May, 407
Cameron, Ruth, *see* Persis Dwight Hannah
Campanini, 495
Campbell, Colin, 167, 246. *See also* Colin Close
Campbell, Evelyn, *see* Adele Garrison
Campbell, Leonel, *see* Polly Pry
Campbell, Mrs. Patrick, 257, 449, 566

Campbell, Phil, 350
Canon City *Daily Record*, 472
Canterbury, Archbishop of, 170
Canton *Gazette*, 588
Capone, Al, 162, 490, 504, 540, 550, 599
Capone, Mafalda, 540
Capper, Senator Arthur, 461
Caraway, Senator Thaddeus H., 344
Carew, Kate, 88, 424
Carillo, Felipe, 585
Carlson, Anna, 461
Carnesville (Ga.) *Tribune*, 597
Carol, Prince of Rumania, 370
Carpender, Henry, 170, 277
Carpenter, Mary Osborne, 335
Carr, Ann, 190
Carr, Rosemary, 230
Carranza, 585
Carse, David B., 553
Carse, Mrs. Matilda B., 553
Carse, Robert, 553
Carson, Frank W., 490
Carter, John, 458
Carter, Marion, 248
Carter, Mary, 550
Caruso, Enrico, 106, 226, 455, 522
Caruso, Gloria, 173
Cary, Alice, 41, 45
Cathcart, Lady, 303
Cather, Willa, 464
Catledge, Turner, 341
Catskill *Examiner*, 525
Catt, Mrs. C. C., 123, 140, 458, 462
Cattell, Hettie, 301-302
Caverly, Judge John, 540
Cerretti, Bonaventura, Cardinal, 170
Chaliapin, 485
Chamberlain, John, 173
Chamberlain, S. S., 61, 417
Chang, Li Hung, 444
Chapin, Charles E., 263, 300, 368
Chaplin, Charlie, 373
Chapman, Gerald, 266, 267, 288
Chapman, Leo, 462
Charleston *Gazette*, 596
Charlestown *Daily Mail*, 169
Charlton, Porter, 368
Chattanooga *News*, 598
Chattanooga *Times*, 595
Chatzinoff, Samuel, 447
Chen, Eugene, 588
Chesterton, G. K., 141
Chicago *American*, 432, 433, 545, 548, 549
Chicago *American Lumberman*, 430
Chicago *Chronicle*, 257, 554
Chicago *Daily News*, 258, 397, 398, 408, 409, 505, 548, 551
Chicago *Evening Journal*, 355
Chicago *Evening Post*, 398
Chicago *Examiner*, 566, 593
Chicago *Herald Examiner*, 214, 291, 409, 410, 489, 490, 544, 548
Chicago *Inter-Ocean*, 551, 593
Chicago *Journal*, 373, 551, 554

Chicago *Post*, 301, 566
Chicago *Record*, 551
Chicago *Sunday Tribune*, 427
Chicago *Times*, 257, 547
Chicago *Tribune*, 7, 20, 36, 61, 161, 162, 163, 177, 206, 230, 269, 292, 317, 342, 343, 365, 376, 395, 396, 397, 398, 407, 408, 411, 412, 414, 427, 428, 430, 437, 438, 450, 452, 454, 468, 475, 502, 514, 535, 539, 540, 541, 542, 543, 544, 545, 546, 547, 548, 551; Paris Edition, 259, 272, 370, 450, 549
Chisholm, Rosepha, 524
Christian Science Monitor, 130, 131, 314, 332, 333, 334, 475
Christian Union, The, 32
Christopher, Prince, of Greece, 160, 254, 450
Christy, Mrs. George, 398
Chrzanowska, Marylla, 376
Cincinnati *Commercial*, 483
Cincinnati *Enquirer*, 169, 455
Cincinnati *Post*, 291, 535
Claflin, Tennessee, 27, 31-35
Clark, Elizabeth, 435
Clarke, George, 300
Clarke, Ida, Clyde, 597
Clarke, Richard, 291, 414
Clarke, Sara Jane, *see* Grace Greenwood
Claus, Henry, 485
Clemenceau, Georges, 170
Clemens, Mazie, 169-171
Clements, W. Wallace, 186
Cleveland, Grover, 82
Cleveland, Mrs. Grover, 311
Cleveland *Leader*, 425
Cleveland *News*, 554, 555
Cleveland *Plain Dealer*, 377, 552
Cleveland *Press*, 255, 435, 535, 553
Cleveland *Times*, 85
Cline, Leonard, 232
Close, Colin, 246
Close, Mrs. Colin, 246, 247
Coates, Foster, 78
Cobb, Frank I., 91, 434
Cobb, Irvin, 65
Cockerill, John A., 50, 177, 562
Cody, Mrs. Elizabeth, 155
Cogan, Alice, 238
Cogan, Constance, 238
Cogan, Joseph, 238
Cogswell, Mrs. E. S., 327
Cohen, Bella, 176
Cole, Catherine, *see* Martha Field
Cole, General, Charles H., 487
Cole, Evangeline, 123
Collett, Glenna, 469
Collings, Mrs. Lillian, 243
Collins, Arthur J., 564
Columbus *Enquirer-Sun*, 595
Columbus *Evening Ledger*, 597
Coman, Martha, 124, 126, 127-129
Comstock, Anthony, 31, 34, 535
Concordia *Blade-Empire*, 461
Connolly, Joseph V., 240

Conway, Robert, 277
Cook, Sara Marshall, 438
Cook, Mrs., 593
Coolidge, Calvin, 105, 164, 211, 313, 336, 346, 502, 513, 515, 538
Coolidge, Mrs. Calvin, 309, 313, 314, 333, 502, 515
Cooney, Celia, 526
Cooper, Professor Charles P., 476
Cooper, Courtney Reilly, 546
Cooper, Kent, 354, 551
Cooper, Page, 485
Copeland, Dr. Royal S., 429
Copinger, May Irene, 498
Coquelin, 88
Cordova *Daily Times*, 372
Corelli, Marie, 88
Corle, Deborah, 447
Cormack, Shannon, 275, 276
Cornwall, Edith, 525. *See also* Mrs. Mary L. Parsons
Corrigan, Chief Magistrate, 351
Cosgrave, John O'Hara, 435
Costello, Jessie, 244, 252, 491
Cottonwood Falls *Leader*, 461
Coudert, Frederic C., 391
Coué, Emile, 98, 103
Cov, Eva, 244
Covadonga, Count of, 376
Cowan, R. Baldwin, *see* Ruth Cowan
Cowan, Ruth, 549-551
Cowham, Mrs. Neil, *see* June Provines
Craft, Mabel, 6, 65, 577-579
Craig, B., 255
Craig, Donald, 336
Craig, Mrs. Elizabeth May, 335-336
Craig, William B., 517
Craigie, Dorothy, 525
Craigie, Frederick E., 525
Crane, Nathalia, 236
Cranston, Olive, 517
Crater, Justice Joseph F., 189
Crater, Mrs. Joseph F., 190
Craven, Earl of, 444
Crawford, Arthur, 292
Crawford, Emily, 88
Crawford, Remsen, 294
Creelman, Eileen, 415
Creelman, James, 415
Crewe, Regina, 415
Crockett, Albert, 228
Croker, Mrs. Richard, 87
Cromwell, James, 450
Cross, Harry, 305
Crouch, Mary, 37
Crown, James E., 593
Cuppy, Will, 404
Curie, Madame, 126, 141, 345
Curley, William C., 432, 433
Curran, Commissioner Henry, 302, 303
Curry, Anne Hirst, *see* Anne Hirst
Curry, John F., 352
Cushman, Howard, 250
Custer, Elizabeth, 236
Cutler, Ann, 169
Cutler, Grace, 236

Cutlip, Lillian, 502
Cutting, Francis B., 442
Czar of Russia, 109, 111, 176, 257, 272, 504
Czarina, 110, 111

Dafoe, Dr. Allan Roy, 96
Daggett, Mrs. Mabel Potter, 527
Dague, Glenn, 560
Dahl, Anna, 318
Daily Graphic, 44, 45
Daily Investment News, 214
Daily Iowan, 177
Daily Oklahoman, 226, 227
Daily Worker, 352, 353
Dallas *Dispatch*, 547
Dallas *Journal*, 597
Dallas *Times Herald*, 597
Dalrymple, Martha, 354, 373-375
Damien, Father, 62, 497
Dana, Charles A., 425
Danbury (Nebraska) *News*, 345
d'Annunzio, 170
Dare, Helen, 456, 576-577, 588
Darrach, Mrs. Marshall, 447, 455-456
Darrow, Clarence, 251, 554, 599
Davenport, Blanche, 475
Davenport, Mrs. Esther, 521-522
Davenport, Henry, 419
David, Prince, 579
Davidson, Mrs. Marie Hicks, 457
Davies, Florence, 235, 535
Davila, Carlos, 232
Davis, Allen, 454
Davis, Burton, 598
Davis, Charles H., 258
Davis, Frances, 570-571
Davis, Maxine, 354-356, 373
Davis, Nevada Victoria, 425, 426
Davis, Richard Harding, 181
Davison, Henry P., 201
Dawson, Thomas F., 366
Dayton, Dorothy, 225-228
Dayton, Katherine, 359
Dayton, Ruth, 186
Dean, Sidney Walter, 96
Deane, Martha, *see* Margaret Mary McBride
Debs, Eugene, 554
de Castellane, Boni, 449
de Chambrun, Count René, 376
Decker, Karl, 364
Decker, Colonel W. E., 545
de Coppet, Theodosia, *see* Theda Bara
Deering, Frank P., 579
de Forest, Marion, 522
de Graff, June, 300, 301
de la Barra, Dona Viviani, 585
Delafield, E. M., 406
De La Mater, Mabel, 433
Delany, Dr. Selden P., 159
Delmar, Viña, 303
Delmas, Delphin, 90
Deming, Mrs. Zell Hart, 463
Dempsey, Jack, 175, 189, 193, 268, 289

Denby, Secretary of the Navy Edwin, 343
Denver *Community-Herald*, 388, 389
Denver *Express*, 557
Denver *News*, 301
Denver *Post*, 63, 67, 143, 301, 370, 389, 417, 420, 421, 548, 562, 563, 564, 566, 567, 568, 569
Denver *Republican*, 214, 411, 569
Denver *Rocky Mountain News*, 301, 370, 564, 569
Denver *Times*, 301, 370, 411, 566, 567
Denver *Tribune*, 569
Depew, Chauncey M., 86, 146
De Reszke, 495
Des Moines *Daily News*, 561
Des Moines *Register*, 561
Des Moines *Tribune*, 177
Detroit *Free Press*, 355, 433, 535, 536, 537
Detroit *Journal*, 535
Detroit *Mirror*, 235
Detroit *News*, 84, 105, 107, 108, 235, 532, 534, 535
Detroit *Times*, 537
Deuell, Harvey, 230
Devereaux, Marion, 455
Dewey, Admiral, 19, 20, 142, 448
de Wolfe, Elsie, 259
de Young, Ruth, 544
de Zouche, Emma, 171
Diamond, Jack, 190, 270, 297, 298, 304, 541
Diamond, Mrs. Jack, 270, 297
Diaz, General, 585
Dibble, Tom, 199
Dickens, Charles, 45, 327, 328
Dickinson, Howard Carter, 537
Dillon, Thomas J., 207, 208
Disraeli, 46
Ditmars, Dr. Raymond L., 187
Dix, Dorothy, 20, 22, 65, 74-79, 84, 124, 426, 416, 418, 592
Dixon, Jane, 191-194, 236, 312
Dodge, Mary Abigail, *see* Gail Hamilton
Doheny, Edward L., 340
Doherty, Edward, 414
Doherty, Rosaleen, 296
Dollar, Robert, 223
Donahue, Jack, 187
Donaldson, Francis A., 211
Donnelly, Antoinette, 428-430, 542
Donnelly, Norah, 19, 20
Donovan, Katherine, 489
Dooly, Ismay, 594-595
Dooly, Louise, 595
Dorman, Marjorie, 236
Dorr, John Pixley, 112
Dorr, Julian, 111, 112
Dorr, Rheta Childe, 9, 109-116, 128, 246, 377, 582
Dortch, Ellen J., 597
Dougherty, Charles S., 433
Dougherty, Mary, 432-433, 548

Dougherty, Patricia, 433, 548-549
Doumer, President, of France, 373, 376
Dowie, Alexander, 143
Doyle, Arthur Conan, 199
Doyle, Lucy, 275
Doyle, Peggy, 489-491
Doyle, Tom, 489
Draper, Arthur S., 373
Drayton, Mrs. Grace Gebbie, 424
Dreiser, Theodore, 244, 366, 565
Drew, Grace, 426
Drew, Mrs. John, 495
Drexel, Constance, 514
Drinkwater, John, 510
Driscoll, Marjorie, 7, 221, 589-590
Drucker, Rebecca, 125
Ducas, Dorothy, 210-213, 246, 316, 320
Duestrow, Dr. Arthur, 67, 68
Duffy, Mike, 519
Duke, Doris, 450
Duluth *Herald Tribune*, 559
Duncan, Isadora, 200
Dundee, Johnny, 594
Dunlap, Anne, 183-186
Dunn, Gertrude Bell, 485
Dunn, Marshall L., 384
Dunn, Martin, 187
Dunne, Peter Finley, 554
Durant, Will, 418
Duranty, Walter, 362, 582
Durkin, Marty, 374, 490
Durrant, William Henry Theodore, 64, 65
Duse, Eleanora, 369
Dutton, Henry Worthington, 482
Duveen, Sir Joseph, 575
Dwight, Phoebe, *see* Persis Dwight Hannah
Dyas, Nell, 558

Eames, Madame, 495
Earhart, Amelia, 220, 510
Early, Stephen, 277, 319
Eastman, Frank G., 535
Eastman, Gertrude, 426
Eddy, Mary Baker, 87
Ederle, Gertrude, 262, 269, 469
Edinburgh, Duke of, 414
Edison, Thomas A., 214
Edward VII, King, 88, 276
Edward VIII, King, 80, 140, 273, 274, 275. *See also* Prince of Wales
Edwards, Elvin I., 243
Edwards, Gourley, 445, 446
Einstein, Dr. Albert, 216, 220
El Dorado *Daily News*, 214
Eliel, Minnie, 83
Eliot, George, 36
Eliot, Jean, *see* Ruth E. Jones
Elizabeth, Queen, of Belgium, 170
Ellet, Marion, 461
Ellis, Anna Bolton, 455
Ellsworth, Lincoln, 510
El Paso *Times*, 218
Elwell, Joseph Bowne, 261, 270

Emerson, Mrs. Margaret, *see* Mrs. Smith Hollins McKim
Emerson, Ralph Waldo, 400, 401, 481, 482
Empire News, 296
Erik, Prince, of Denmark, 490
Eskey, Elizabeth, 97, 174
Essary, Helen, 359
Essary, J. Fred, 359
Esterházy, Count Johann, 362
Eugénie, Empress, 46, 86
Eulalia, Infanta, 375
Evans, Ernestine, 125, 128
Evans, Marion Dorsey, 496
Evans, May Garrettson, 493-496
Evanston *News-Index*, 351
Everett, Ethel Walton, 149

Faber, Abe, 240
Factor, Jake, 549
Factorovitch, Michael, 388, 389
Fairbanks, Charles W., 154
Fairbanks, Douglas, 291, 411, 438
Fairfax, Beatrice, 20, 79-81, 83, 84, 176, 426, 553
Faithfull, Starr, 208, 235, 243, 392, 492
Fall, Albert B., 218
Fallon, William, 519
Farley, Cardinal, 154, 155
Farnol, Lynn, 305
Farnsworth, Bill, 471
Farrar, Geraldine, 205, 206
Farrell, Leila, 528
Farry, Bridget, 351
Fay, Larry, 294
Fellows, Dexter, 107, 126, 173, 257
Ferber, Edna, 205
Ferdinand, of Bulgaria, 256
Ferguson, Edna, 293-296
Ferguson, Harry, 192
Ferguson, Jim, 348
Fern, Fanny, 16, 39-43, 45, 329, 332
Field, Eugene, 409, 569
Field, Kate, 20, 27, 28, 36-37, 38, 39, 44, 45, 336
Field, Martha, 592
Finley, Dr. John H., 158
Finnegan, Richard, 355, 373
Finney, Ruth, 4, 7, 336, 339-342, 472
Firpo, Luis, 175, 193, 268, 289, 303
Fish, Hamilton, 451
Fish, Mrs. Stuyvesant, 87, 442, 443, 444, 448
Fisher, Charles E., 515
Fisher, Harrison, 587
Fiske, Jim, 31
Fiske, Mrs. Minnie Maddern, 438, 522
Fitch, Geraldine, 186-189
Fitzwater, Fanny Fern, 438
Five Star Weekly, 357
Flagler, Henry, 449
Fleeson, Doris, 350-352, 357
Fleischman, Doris E., 125
Floyd, "Pretty Boy," 215
Foch, Marshal, 111, 170, 499, 500
Fodor, M. W., 363, 364

Foldes, Peggy, 238-239
Foley, Surrogate James J., 165
Forbes, Genevieve, *see* Genevieve Forbes Herrick
Ford, Andrew W., 91, 192, 236
Ford, Ford Madox, 209
Ford, Henry, 105, 106, 172
Forman, Elizabeth, 558
Forrest, Wilbur, 172
Forsythe *Taney County Republican*, 462
Fort Smith (Ark.) *Times Record*, 598
Fort Worth *Record*, 301
Fort Worth *Star Telegram*, 597, 598
Fosdick, Dr. Harry Emerson, 157, 158
Foster, Stephen C., 49
Fowle, A. A., 489
Fowler, Gene, 183, 304
Fox, Helena, 190
Franklin, Anna, 37
Franklin, Ben A., 165
Franklin, Jane, 299-301
Franks, Robert, 540
Fraser, Isabel, 444, 588
Frazier, Corinne R., 347
Frederick, Pauline, 513
Freedberg, Dr. Harry, 491
Fremont, Benton, 385
Fremstad, Madame, 455
French, Tucky, 453
Freud, Sigmund, 364
Friedman, Benny, 207
Frink, Carol, 409
Frye, Ralph, 485
Fuller, Loie, 549
Fuller, Margaret, 16, 39, 327, 400-403
Fuller, Mrs. Mary, 327
Furman, Bess, 317, 319, 320, 321, 345
Furness, Lady, 196

Gabrilowitsch, Ossip, 557
Gadski, Madame, 448
Gailor, Bishop Thomas F., 263
Gale, Zona, 20, 176, 522
Gallico, Paul, 194, 252, 395, 396
Galli-Curci, Madame, 572
Galsworthy, John, 97
Galveston *News*, 63
Gandhi, Mahatma, 356, 586
Gann, Dolly, 232, 345
Gannett, Lewis, 171
Garbo, Greta, 271, 272
Garden, Mary, 187, 588
Gardner, Virginia, 544
Garrett, Garet, 206
Garrett, Dr. Henry E., 391
Garrett, Oliver H. P., 197, 274
Garrison, Adele, 467-468
Gasch, Herman, 81
Gasch, Mrs. Marie Manning, 319. *See also* Marie Manning
Gasparri, Cardinal, 370
Gates, Eleanor, 588
Gatti-Casazza, 573
Gauvreau, Emile, 296, 303

Gebhart, Paul, 192
Geddes, Geane, 517
Geissler, Mrs. Louis F., 93
Geldert, Grace Boylan, 597
Gellhaus, Olga E., 453-454
Genauer, Emily, 435
George, of Greece, 256
George, Henry, 553
George, Lloyd, 541
Gerard, James W., 358
Gertrude, Sister Rose, 62
Giannini, Amadeo Peter, 218
Gibbons, Cardinal, 573, 574
Gibbons, Floyd, 193, 230, 364, 370, 377
Gibbs, Sir Philip, 95
Giberson, Mrs. Ivy, 288
Gibson, Mrs. Idah McGlone, 468
Gibson, Jane, 75, 265, 278
Gilbert, John, 252
Gillette, Chester, 292, 565
Gillette, Mrs., 565
Gillilan, Strickland, 398
Gilman, Foster, 485
Gilman, James, 251
Gilman, Mildred, 246-251
Gilmer, George O., 77
Gilmer, Mrs. Elizabeth Meriwether, 76. *See also* Dorothy Dix
Gilmore, Cecile, 395
Ginsberg, Bertha, 519
Giovanni, Marquis d'Ossoli, 403
Gizycka, Count Joseph, 504
Glasgow, Ellen, 406
Glass, Franklin P., 185
Glickstein, Dr. Abraham, 200
Glyn, Elinor, 445
Glyndon, Howard, *see* Laura Catherine Redden
Glynn, Governor Martin H., 123, 124
Goddard, Mary Katherine, 493
Goddard, Morrill, 418
Goddard, Sarah, 38
Goebel, Senator William, 64
Goelet, May, 444
Goering, General, 250
Goethals, General, 561
Goldman, Emma, 554
Gollomb, Joseph, 99
Goodman, Dora, *see* Theda Bara
Goodrich, Merton W., 537
Goodwin, Nat, 495
Gordon, Evelyn Peyton, 446
Gordon, Gertrude B., 560-561
Gordon, Mrs. Leon, *see* Natalie Mc-Closkey
Gordon, Vivian, 165, 351
Goss, Eleanor, 468
Goss, Margaret, 468-470
Gough, Emil, 466
Gould, Anna, 440
Gould, Beatrice Blackmar, 177
Gould, Bruce, 177
Gould, Frank, 449
Gould, Helen, *see* Mrs. Finley Shepard
Gould, Jay, 31

Gould, Randall, 588
Grady, Henry, 594
Grady, William, 509
Grange, Red, 207
Grant, Jane, 149, 150, 151-152
Grant, Dr. Percy Stickney, 157, 264
Grant, Ulysses S., 33, 145
Graves, Ralph, 151
Gray, Judd, 278
Gray, Mrs. Judd, 197
Great Neck *News*, 351
Greeley, Horace, 16, 33, 86, 87, 147, 323, 324, 330, 400, 401, 402, 403, 420, 462
Greeley, Ida, 93
Greeley-Smith, Nixola, 22, 65, 86-94, 95, 101, 176, 205
Green, Anna Katherine, 521
Green, Hetty, 57, 73
Green, Martin, 183
Green, William, 353
Greene, Elinor, 235
Greene, Mabel, 233-235
Greene, Mrs. Zula Bennington, 461. *See also* Peggy of the Flint Hills
Greenwood, Alveda, 485
Greenwood, Grace, 16, 39, 327-329, 332
Greenwood, Hamar, 362
Greer, Bishop David H., 154
Grey, James C., 407
Griffin, Bulkley S., 349
Gross, Pearl, 190
Guard, Bill, 106
Guinan, Texas, 167, 245
Gunther, John, 361

Haardt, Sara, 498
Hackett, James K., 448
Hadakin, Helen, 302-303
Hager, Read, 174
Haggard, William, 214
Hahn, Madame Andrée, 575
Hains, Claudia Libbey, 72
Hains, Major Peter C., 72
Hains, Thornton Jenkins, 72
Hale, Annie Riley, 259
Hale, Nancy, 150
Hale, Nathan, 150
Hale, Ruth, 259
Hall, Dorothy, 447
Hall, Dr. Edward, 170, 277, 278
Hall, Mrs. Frances Noel, 74, 75, 232, 265, 277, 278
Hall, Kay, 544, 547
Hall, Leonard, 395
Hallen, James D., 530
Halsey, Ethel, 354
Halstead, Murat, 483
Hambidge, Charles G., 245
Hamby, Gordon, 491
Hamerick, Asger, 495
Hamilton, Esther, 559
Hamilton, Gail, 16, 39, 327, 329-331
Hamilton, Grant E., 559
Hamilton, Scott B., 559
Hamm, Margherita Arlina, 88

Hammerstein, Oscar, 454
Hammond, Percy, 409, 546
Hampton, Hope, 415
Hankemeyer, Natalie, 407
Hanks, Nancy, *see* Mrs. A. Lincoln Bowles
Hanna, Bill, 469
Hanna, Mark, 505, 552
Hannah, Persis Dwight, 386-387
Hansen, Harry, 407
Hansl, Mrs. Raleigh, 432
Hard, Anne, 359
Harding, Caroline, 448-449
Harding, Warren G., 194, 207, 221, 336, 343, 356, 464, 589, 598
Harding, Mrs. Warren G., 194, 312, 313
Harland, Marion, 238, 426
Harpman, Julia, 184, 261-270, 277, 291
Harrington, John Walker, 279
Harris, Carlyle, 178
Harris, Corra, 595
Harris, Jed, 388, 389
Harris, Joel Chandler, 594, 595
Harris, Mrs. Julia Collier, 595
Harris, Julian, 595
Harris, Ned Brunson, 357-358
Harrison, Dorothy Ann, 518-520
Harrison, Marguerite, 498
Harrison, Walter, 227
Hart, Lavinia, 88
Hart, William Shakespeare ("Bill"), 495
Hartford *Courant*, 395
Hatch, Estelle, 483
Hathaway, Earl, 470
Hauptmann, Bruno R., 192, 200, 203, 209, 235, 241, 419, 514, 537
Hauptmann, Mrs. Bruno R., 209
Hause, Frank, 272, 289
Havana *Telegram*, 218
Havener, Helen, 472, 527, 531
Hawkins, William W., 91
Haworth, Mary, *see* Elizabeth Reardon Young
Hawthorn, Julian, 562
Hawthorne, Nathaniel, 329
Hay, Lady Drummond, 212, 245, 512
Hay, Mary Garrett, 521
Hayden, Mary Bainbridge, 374
Hayes, Cardinal, 155
Hayes, Helen, 252, 409
Haywood, Big Bill, 564
Hearn, Lafcadio, 592
Hearst, Mrs. Phoebe Apperson, 66
Hearst, William Randolph, 9, 17, 18, 20, 24, 25, 61, 62, 63, 66, 78, 79, 80, 82, 83, 92, 95, 160, 181, 182, 186, 188, 190, 213, 241, 245, 251, 252, 259, 262, 305, 339, 378, 384, 386, 393, 395, 410, 411, 416, 417, 419, 420, 422, 423, 424, 433, 436, 443, 445, 446, 451, 453, 457, 465, 467, 468, 485, 490, 491, 500, 501, 502, 512, 537, 576, 587, 589, 593
Heaton, Mrs. Eliza Putnam, 238
Heaton, John L., 238

Heed, Mrs. Thomas D., *see* Ruth Byers
Heinlein, Eddie, 491
Hemingway, Mrs. Ernest, 255
Henderson, Jessie E., 485
Henderson, Rose, 561
Henning, Arthur Sears, 342, 343, 344
Henry, Prince, of Prussia, 448
Henry, O., 466
Hepburn, Katherine, 429
Herdman, Ramona, 526-527
Herrick, Mrs. Christine Terhune, 238
Herrick, Genevieve Forbes, 7, 238, 292, 317, 539-542, 543
Herrick, John, 540
Herzog, James, 210
Heslin, Father, 589
Hester, Margaret Shuttee, 598
Hickok, Lorena, 7, 161, 166, 203-209, 317, 320
Hicks, Mrs. H. W., *see* Leone Cass Baer
Higgins, Josephine, 187
Hirst, Anne, 84-85
Hitchcock, Mrs. Nevada Davis, *see* Nevada Victoria Davis
Hitler, Adolf, 361, 366, 373
Hobart, George V., 496
Hobby, Lieutenant Governor William P., 348
Hobson, Thayer, 246
Hoershgen, Ruth, 300
Hogan, Frank J., 340
Holbrook, Colonel Alva Morris, 591, 592
Holden, Mrs. Amber, 551
Holden, Ed, 224
Holm, Prince, 447
Holmes, Mary Caroline, 597
Hone, Philip, 442
Honolulu *Advertiser*, 588
Honolulu *Star-Bulletin*, 221, 231, 232
Hoover, Herbert, 142, 143, 165, 314, 333, 344, 374, 513
Hoover, Mrs. Herbert, 309, 314, 346, 515
Hope, Anthony, 222
Hopkins, Harry L., 209
Hopkins, Jenny Lind, 569-570
Hopkins, Martin, 569
Hopkins, Phidelia, 569
Hopper, James, 588
Hornaday, Hilton, P., 335
Hornaday, James P., 335
Hornaday, Mary F., 334-335
Hornaday, William D., 335
Hough, George A., 509
Houghton, Elizabeth, 174
Houghton, Harriet, 485
House, Colonel E. M., 135
Houston *Chronicle*, 598
Howard *Courant*, 461
Howard, Roy W., 25, 91, 352, 368, 370, 394

Howard Victorine, *see* Marjorie Mears
Howe, Ed, 459, 460
Howe, Eugene, 161
Howe, Henry, 102
Howe, Julia Ward, 1, 387
Howe, Louis McHenry, 315
Howey, Walter, 263, 302, 303, 304, 546
Hubbard, Mrs. Worthington, 221
Huber, Walter, 470
Hudson, Virginia, 124
Hughes, Alice, 393-395, 396
Hughes, Charles Evans, 128, 129, 345, 408, 537, 583
Hughes, George T., 116
Hughes, Sam, 92
Hull, Peggy, 230, 377
Hummel, Abraham H., 528, 529
Hummel, Henry, 528, 529
Humphrey, Mary, 535-536
Hunt, Mrs. Florence T., 454
Hunton, J. Moss, 568
Hurst, Fannie, 459
Hutton, Barbara, 252
Hutton, Edward F., 451
Hutton, Mrs. Edward F., 451
Hyde, Dr. Bennett Clark, 568
Hyland, Dick, 252

Ibañez, 200
Ickes, Mrs. Harold, 542
Igoe, Hype, 419
Illustrated News, The, 263
Independent, 326
Indianapolis *News,* 335
Insull, Samuel, 376, 549
Iowa *Nonpareil,* 561
Ireland Archbishop, 557
Irvin, Warren, 259
Irving, Henry, 64
Irwin, Wallace, 587
Irwin, Will, 587
Isabelle, Princess, of Orleans-Braganza, 376

Jackson, Eileen, 457
Jackson, Hilda, 125
Jacobson, Pauline, 580, 586-587, 588
Jaffe, Isadore, 357
Jaime, Infante, of Spain, 375
James, Allena Duff, 597
James, Bessie, 593-594
James, Marquis, 593
Janis, Elsie, 257
Jefferson, Joe, 495
Jennings, Al, 466
Jennings, Mabelle, 502
Jerome, Leonard, 147
Jerome, William Travers, 90
Jewett, Helen, 15
Jimerson, Lila M., 95
Joffe, Lou, 239
Joffre, Marshal, 88, 375
Johaneson, Bland, 414-415
Johansen, Louise, 222

Johnson, Charles B., 67, 68
Johnson, Earle, 192
Johnson, Evelyn, 434
Johnson, Senator Hiram, 341
Johnson, Mr. and Mrs. Martin, 234
Johnson, Nancy (Minnie Myrtle), 46-47
Johnson, Tom, 553
Johnston, Isabel, 247
Johnston, Will ("Limpy"), 389
Johnstone, Alice, 551
Johnstone, Elizabeth, 536
Joliffe, Frances, 587
Jolson, Al, 257
Jones, Dr. Edgar De Witt, 534
Jones, John Paul, 445
Jones, R. Bryson, 571
Jones, General Rosalie, 123, 124, 524
Jones, Ruth E., 445-446, 501
Jordan, Elizabeth, 9, 20, 24, 176, 177-179, 486
Josephy, Helen, 256
Joy, Sally, 1, 2, 483, 492
Joyce, Peggy Hopkins, 163, 186, 232
Juarez, Ray, 247
Judd, Ruth, 589
Judge, Jane, 597
June, Jenny, 16, 21, 39, 43-46, 332, 395, 436, 521

Kahn, Otto, 573
Kalinin, Mikhail, 583
Kane, Dr. Elisha Kent, 210, 211
Kansas *Chronoscope,* 331
Kansas City *Journal,* 506, 543, 574, 589
Kansas City *Post,* 422, 505, 506, 566, 568, 571
Kansas City *Star,* 255, 332, 370, 422, 460, 461, 571, 572, 574, 575, 589
Kansas City *Times,* 332
Kanter, Belle, 190
Karl, Emperor, 362
Karolyi, Michael, 365
Kate Field's Washington, 27, 37
Kaye-Smith, Sheila, 406
Kearney *Daily Hub,* 346
Keating, Isabelle, 236-237
Keating, Micheline, 304-305
Keating, Mrs. Pearl, 304
Keeley, Mary Paxton, 575
Keen, Elizabeth, 373
Keen, Victor, 373
Keislich, Emma S., 195
Keller, Helen, 237
Kellogg, Elenore, 7, 24, 165-169
Kelly, Elizabeth, 566-569
Kelly, Ethel, 370
Kelly, Helen, 449
Kelly, Lora, 510
Kenamore, Clair, 556
Kenyon, Nellie, 598
Keppel, Mrs. George, 87
Kerensky, 582
Kerr, Adelaide, 375-376, 436
Key, Ellen, 114

Keyes, Mrs. Frances Parkinson, 47, 359
Kibbe, Mrs. Edith, 395
Kilgallen, Dorothy, 240-245
Kilgallen, James, 240, 241, 242, 243
King, Dot, 267
King, Elizabeth, 524
King, Fay, 420-424, 570
King, Harold, 243
King, Loretta, *see* Kate Cameron
King, Mary, 396, 413, 414, 427-428, 536, 542, 546
Kingsford-Smith, Charles, 220
Kinkead, Ellis Guy, 200
Kinnear, Isabel, 349
Kinsolving, Anne S., 190
Kirchhofer, Alfred H., 523
Kirkland, Caroline, 454-455
Kirkwood, Frances, 298
Kluxen, Francis, 174, 175
Knapp, Mrs. Helen, 447
Kneller, Sir Godfrey, 498
Knickerbocker, H. R., 365
Knickerbocker Press, 524, 525
Knight, Mary, 376
Knopf, Alfred A., 218
Knowles, Fred, 100
Knox, Timothy, *see* Elizabeth K. Read
Knoxville *Sentinel,* 291
Kollontai, Alexandra, 130
Koss, Isabel, 223
Kreiselman, Lee, 357
Kreisler, Fritz, 573
Kresel, Isadore, 167
Krishnamurti, 526
Krock, Arthur, 390
Krum, Morrow, 268, 269
Kuhn, Bert L., 231
Kuhn, Irene Corbally, 197, 228-233
Kuhn, Rene Leilani, 231
Kurner, Mrs. David C., *see* Mae Tinee

Ladd, Eleanor, 485
Ladies Morning Star, 15
La Guardia, Fiorello, 351
La Hines, Arthur, 569
Lait, Jack, 545
Lake, Captain Simon, 181
Lambert, Marion, 418
Lambrino, Zizi, 370
Lamont, Hammond, 113
Landor, Walter Savage, 36
Lane, Mrs. Louis B., *see* Kate Burr
Lane, Margaret, 213
Lane, Rose Wilder, 580, 581
Lang, Anton, 107
Lang, Elsa, 139
Langstadter, Minnie Roswell, 551
Langtry, Lily, 257, 522, 557
Lantz, Emily Emerson, 496-497
Lanzetti, Pius, 518
La Prensa, 335
Lardner, Ring, 304, 377
Larrimore, Lida, 472
Lauferty, Lilian, 83-84
Laurie, Annie, 60, 65, 66, 67, 466

Laval, Charles, 222
Laval, José, 345, 376
Laval, Premier, 376
Lavelle, Monsignor Michael J., 153
Lawes, Warden, 237, 278
Lawrence, Jack, 193
Lawrence, Janette, 174
Lawson, Louise, 268
Leary, Annie, 87
Leavitt, Mrs. Helen, 138
Leavitt, Martha, 139
Lebaudy, Jacqueline, 182
Lebaudy, Jacques, 182, 183
Lebaudy, Mrs. Jacques, 182, 183
Lee, Gertrude, 348
Lee, Ivy, 173
Lee, Mary, 246
Lee, Robert, 543
Leeds, Flo, 201
Leeds, William B., 160, 449
Leeds, Mrs. William B., 449, 450
Legenza, Walter, 518, 519
Lehman, Herbert, 352
Lehr, Harry, 87, 449
Leiter, Margaret H., 70
Leland, Mrs. Marian, 570
Le Matin, 372
Lenin, 354, 378, 583
Leopold, Nathan F., Jr., 540
Leslie, Amy, 408-409
Leslie, Mrs. Frank, 332
Levine, Louis, 583
Lewis, Dorothea, 348
Lewis, Mrs. Liston L., *see* Ethel Lloyd Patterson
Lewis, Sinclair, 360, 361, 362, 363, 365, 366
Lewis, Ted, 285
Lewis, W. E., 411
Lewisohn, Mrs. Frederick, 449
Libbey, Laura Jean, 430
Liberty Tribune and Advance, 463
Liliuokalani, Queen, 578, 579
Lincoln, Abraham, 326, 328, 344, 358, 565
Lincoln, Natalie Sumner, 359
Lincoln, Robert Todd, 358
Lind, Jenny, 569
Lindbergh, Colonel Charles A., 190, 191, 203, 220, 228, 245, 269, 298, 304, 390, 397, 398, 541
Lindbergh, Mrs. Charles A., 131, 210
Lindsay, Malvina, 84, 505-507, 570, 571
Lindsey, Judge Ben B., 159, 166
Lingle, Jake, 161
Lippincott, Leander K., 328
Lippmann, Walter, 91, 139
Lipton, Sir Thomas, 193, 200
Little, Herbert, 348, 349
Littledale, Mrs. Walter, *see* Clara Savage
Littleton, Martin, 100
Littleton, Mrs. Martin, 100
Lochner, Louis, 106
Lockridge, Richard, 571
Lodge, Sir Oliver, 101

Loeb, Richard, 540
Loeb, Sophie Irene, 117-118, 176, 205
Logue, Cardinal, 170
Lombardo, Tony, 162
London *Daily Express*, 212, 246, 511
London *Daily Mail*, 213, 572
Long, Huey, 164, 293, 352, 475
Long, Lois, 304
Longfellow, Henry Wadsworth, 401
Longworth, Alice, 232, 330, 345, 503, 504
Longworth, Nicholas, 259, 311
Lord, Kenneth, 120
Los Angeles *Examiner*, 7, 214, 252, 589, 590
Los Angeles *Herald*, 251, 252, 433, 468, 549, 581
Los Angeles *Illustrated Daily News*, 216
Los Angeles *Times*, 588
Louisville *Courier-Journal*, 209, 210, 327
Lovell, Mildred, 453
Lowe, Corinne, 437-438
Lowell, James Russell, 401, 481
Lowell, Mrs. Josephine Shaw, 426
Lowrie, Governor, of Minnesota, 323, 325
Lunn, Rev. George R., 91
Luxton, Anne, 238
Lydig, Mrs. Rita de Acosta, 264
Lynahan, Gertrude, 175-176, 470
Lyon, Madame Doré, 521
Lyon, George F., 220, 390

MacAlarney, Robert E., 100, 126
MacArthur, Charles, 409, 546
MacCarroll, Marion Clyde, 167
MacDonald, Hazel, 549
MacDonald, Ishbel, 212, 213, 314, 345
MacDonald, Ramsay, 314
MacDougall, Sally, 434-435
Macfadden, Bernarr, 262
MacGowan, Kenneth, 485
Mack, John E., 185
Mack, Willard, 471
Mackay, Clarence H., 275
Mackay, Mrs. Clarence H., 127, 128
Mackay, Ellin, 276. *See also* Mrs. Irving Berlin
Mackay, Mrs. John W., 276
MacLane, Mary, 419
MacMurphy, Harriett Sherrill, 561
MacSwiney, Terence, 362
MacSwiney, Mrs. Terence, 343
Macy, Anne Sullivan, 237
Madden, George A., 49
Maeterlinck, 370
Magennis, Mrs. Margaret J., 484
Mahnkey, Charles Preston, 463
Mahnkey, Douglas, 463
Mahnkey, Mrs. Mary Elizabeth, 462-463
Mahoney, Gertrude, 487
Mahoney, Mary, 486-489

Mais, Robert, 518, 519
Mallon, Mrs. Isabel A., 21
Mallon, Winifred, 342-345
Malloy, Louise, 496
Man, 14
Manchester Guardian, 362, 363
Mandigo, Pauline, 524, 525
Manila *Bulletin*, 231
Mann, Colonel William Dalton, 235
Manning, Bishop, 157, 159, 166, 264
Manning, Daniel, 82
Manning, George H., 348
Manning, Marie, 80-83, 176
Manners, Lady Diana, 163, 429
Mansfield, Richard, 495
Mantle, Burns, 409, 546
Manuel, King, of Portugal, 256
Mapes, Cornelia, 441
Marble, Anna, 259
Marble, Manton, 147
March, General Peyton, 377
Marcosson, Isaac, 217
Marie, Queen, of Rumania, 98, 104, 105, 130, 228, 283, 290, 304, 369, 397, 526, 527, 541, 549, 557, 558
Marion *Daily Star*, 194, 599
Markel, Lester, 239
Markey, George W., 239
Marlborough, Duke of, 444
Marlowe, Frankie, 299
Marquis, Dean S. S., 106
Marshall, Marguerite Mooers, 94-96, 176, 205, 485
Martin, Bradley, 444
Martin, Cecilia Barber ("Jackie"), 502
Martin, Cornelia Bradley, 444
Martin, Frank L., 598
Martin, Dr. Harry W., 411
Martin, Joe, 599
Martin, John Biddulph, 35
Martyn, Marguerite, 555-556
Marx, Carolyn, 407
Marx, Karl, 354
Marx, Nora, 551
Maryland Journal, 493
Mason City *Republican*, 462
Mason, Julian S., 469
Mason, Margaret, *see* Margaret Rohe
Mason, Walt, 112
Massaguer, Conrado, 439
Masses, The, 378
Massino, Tony, 518
Masson, Tom, 380
Masterson, Kate, 425
Mather, Cotton, 483
Matteotti, 367
Mattingly, Marie, 142, 143, 332. *See also* Mrs. William Brown Meloney
Maxwell, Elsa, 442
Maybrick, Mrs., 330
McAllister, Ward, 442
McAnney, B. O., 352
McBride, James, 448
McBride, Mary Margaret, 254-256, 435

McCabe, Robert, 183
McCardle, Carl W., 516
McCarthy, Florence, 279
McCarthy, Julia, 194-202
McCaw, Raymond H., 568
McClain, John, 554
McClintock, William Nelson, 544, 548
McCloskey, Natalie, 125
McClure, S. S., 20, 381, 582, 592
McColl, Jennette, 536
McCutcheon, John T., 258
McCormack, John, 223, 599
McCormick, Anne O'Hare, 4, 25, 150,
  163, 359, 360, 366-368, 369
McCormick, Cyrus, 418
McCormick, Mrs. Edith Rockefeller,
  433
McCormick, Elsie, 222, 381-384, 581
McCormick, Fowler, 201
McCormick, Francis J., 367
McCormick, Katrina, 505
McCormick, Medill, 427, 454, 504, 505
McCormick, Colonel Robert R., 502
McCormick, Mrs. Ruth Hanna, 503,
  505
McDonald, A. B., 568
McDonald, George, 299
McDonald, Mrs. Lucile Saunders, 370-
  372
McDonald, Neil, 524
McDowell, Rachel K., 149, 150, 152-
  161, 169, 557
McDowell, Rev. Dr. William Ander-
  son, 161
McDowell, Dr. William O., 160
McElliott, Mabel, 414
McElliott, Martha, 414, 542, 543
McGeehan, W. O., 456, 469, 470, 584
McGill, Thomas H. A., 567
McGinnis, Joe, 471
McKee, Joseph V., 352
McKeever, Mary, 520
McKeller, Senator Kenneth D., 357
McKenna, Edmond, 183
McKenney, Ruth, 246
McKernan, Maureen, 543-544
McKim, Mrs. Smith Hollins, 455
McKinley, William, 345, 552
McKinsey, Katherine, 500
McLaughlin, Kathleen, 150, 161-163,
  543, 544, 547
McLaughlin, Tex, 229
McLean, Mrs. Donald, 521
McLean, Mrs. Evalyn Walsh, 507
McLean, John R., 444
McMahon, Edward J., 244
McManus, George A., 351
McNamara, Sue, 561
McNitt, V. V., 101
McPherson, Aimee, 473
McRae, Bruce, 416, 417
Mdivani, Prince Serge, 411
Means, Gaston B., 507
Mears, Marjorie, 430-431
Medill, Joseph, 502
Meherin, Elenore, 465-467, 580

Melhuish, Edwin J., 249, 250
Mellett, Lowell, 287, 288, 510
Meloney, William Brown, 143
Meloney, Mrs. William Brown, 139,
  141-144
Memphis *Commercial Appeal*, 547
Memphis *Press-Scimitar*, 597
Mencken, H. L., 498, 507
Menuhin, Yehudi, 223
Mercier, Cardinal, 159, 170
Merian, Matthew, 235
Merrill, Bradford, 68
Merrill, Mrs. Fannie E., 425
Merrill, Dr. William P., 156
Merrill, Mrs. William P., 156
Mexico City *Two Republics*, 388
Meyer, Eugene, 503, 505, 507
Michelson, Charles, 172, 432
Michigan Daily, 538
Milanoff, Olgivanna, 161
Miley, Jack, 297
Milholland, Inez, 122
Milukoff, 582
Millard, Ruth, 176
Millen, Irving, 240, 241
Millen, Murton, 240, 241
Millen, Norma, 419, 491
Miller, Charles R., 498
Miller, Max, 473, 559
Miller, Nathan L., 229, 525
Miller, Mrs. Sadie Kneller, 497-498
Miller, Webb, 377
Millis, Mrs. Walter, *see* Norah
  Thompson
Millison, Flora, 458
Millison, Mabel, 458
Millison, Minnie, 458
Mills, Mrs. Eleanor, 74, 75, 170
Milton, George Fort, 599
Milwaukee *Journal*, 475, 476
Milwaukee *Sentinel*, 205, 468
Minneapolis *Journal*, 558
Minneapolis *News*, 358, 559
Minneapolis *Star*, 357, 358, 559
Minneapolis *Tribune*, 206, 207, 398,
  559
Mitchel, John Purray, 115
Mitchell, Charles E., 209, 352
Mitchell, Hannah, 125
Mitchell, Milly Bennett, 217, 377, 378,
  588
Mitchell, Brigadier General William,
  245
Mizner, Wilson, 587
Mockler, Helen, 174
Moderwell, Hiram, 485
Modjeska, Madame, 569, 584
Mohr, Harry C., 184
Montague, Richard, 213
Montalvo, Marie, 125
Monteith, Scotty, 594
Mooney, Tom, 581
Moore, Mrs. Fred, *see* Eleanor Gates
Moore, Sara, 535
Moran, Eugene, 188
Morehauser, Justice Joseph L., 279

Morgan, Anne, 98, 254, 458, 594
Morgan, Anthony, 146
Morgan, Helen, 167, 190
Morgan, J. Pierpont, 431, 551
Morgan, June, 148
Morgan, Mrs. Laura K., 196
Morgan, Midy (Marie), 145-149, 550
Morgan, Victor, 255
Morner, Count Gösta, 186
Morner, Countess, *see* Geraldine Fitch
Morning Star, The, 16
Morris, George, 525
Morris, Mildred, 214, 570
Morrow, Dwight W., 166, 298
Morse, Sam, 434
Moscow *News,* 378
Mother's Assistant, 40
Mount, Laura, 246
Mowrer, Edgar Ansel, 365
Mowry, Elizabeth, 246
Moyer, Charles H., 564
Mugglebee Ruth, 491-492
Muir, Florabel, 224
Muir, Raymond, 319
Mulvaney, Joe, 186, 187
Munsey, Frank A., 23, 24, 127, 138, 139, 153, 156, 168, 235, 256, 334, 387, 431, 436, 450
Murphy, Big Tim, 161, 162, 490, 541
Murphy, Charles. 525
Murphy, Florence, 161, 162, 541
Murray, Mae, 416
Mussolini, Benito, 111, 115, 116, 141, 367, 369, 370

Nangle, Eleanor, 163
Nash, Mary F., 523
Nashville *Tennesseean,* 597
Nathan, Robert, 405
Nation, Carrie, 78, 258, 535
Nazimova, 259
Nealy, Mrs. Mary E., 327
Nearing, Scott,
Nebraska State Journal, 112
Negri, Pola, 411, 548
Neil. Edward J., 189
Nellist, George, 221
Nelson, Battling, 421
Nelson, William Rockhill, 575
Nevin, John Edwin, 358
Newark *Ledger,* 279, 435
Newark *News,* 160
New Bedford *Standard,* 509
New Castle *Herald,* 559
Newell. Mary O'Connor, 551
Newell. William, 15. 16
New Mexico *State Tribune,* 218
New Orleans *Item,* 593
New Orleans *Item Tribune,* 354, 374
New Orleans *Picayune,* 36, 77, 78, 332, 591, 592
New Orleans *Times-Picayune,* 455, 592
New York *American,* 68, 69, 70, 124, 180, 181, 182, 183, 185, 186, 187, 188, 189, 225, 232, 238. 250, 252, 277, 270. 298, 302, 393, 415, 433, 447, 554, 584

New York *Call,* 168, 176
New York *Courier,* 442
New York *Daily Mirror,* 189, 195, 208, 230, 232, 252, 262, 263, 277, 278, 296, 299, 300, 301, 302, 303, 304, 305, 414, 415, 421, 546
New York *Daily News,* 7, 23, 24, 194, 196, 224, 230, 232, 235, 236, 262, 263, 264, 266, 267, 269, 270, 271, 272, 274, 278, 279, 282, 288, 290, 291, 292, 293, 294, 295, 296, 297, 298, 300, 350, 351, 395, 396, 413, 414, 427, 428, 438, 450, 451, 452, 453, 490, 502, 504, 505
New York *Enquirer,* 442
New York *Evening Graphic,* 247, 262, 507, 508, 509
New York *Evening Journal,* 17, 470
New York *Evening Post,* 177, 210, 375, 442, 524, 561
New York *Evening World,* 20, 22, 92, 93, 95, 101, 107, 117, 176, 227, 355, 368, 370, 381, 390, 391, 470
New York *Globe,* 105, 107, 108, 116, 168, 187, 229, 256, 259, 378
New York *Graphic,* 327
New York *Herald,* 15, 17, 23, 44, 63, 83, 127, 128, 129, 137, 138, 143, 153, 154, 155, 156, 157, 160, 184, 218, 260, 263, 334, 336, 424, 425, 431, 441, 442, 447, 449, 450, 551, 595; Paris Edition, 372, 450
New York *Herald Tribune,* 25, 26, 115, 116, 122, 135, 137, 138, 139, 140, 141, 142, 163, 167, 172, 175, 186, 210, 212, 305, 315, 320, 335, 360, 372, 373, 397, 403, 406, 407, 412, 415, 431, 438, 439, 442, 447, 456, 469, 470, 485, 500, 584
New York *Home Journal,* 327
New York *Journal,* 17, 20, 58, 59, 75, 78, 79, 80, 83, 95, 194, 196, 198, 199, 202, 209, 236, 240, 242, 244, 245, 246, 247, 248, 249, 250, 251, 305, 415, 416, 417, 418, 419, 424, 432, 433, 444, 471, 508, 548, 591
New York *Ledger,* 41, 42, 43
New York *Mail,* 256, 263, 279, 332, 334, 525, 535
New York *Mail and Express,* 100, 101, 103, 104, 105, 109, 111, 115
New York *Mirror,* 327
New York *Morning Telegraph,* 258, 259, 411, 413, 415
New York *North Side News,* 238, 239
New York *Post,* 75, 78, 84, 109, 113, 114, 167, 189, 210, 212, 224, 246, 395, 407, 409, 415, 439, 446, 470
New York *Press,* 99, 380, 425
New York *Recorder,* 238
New York *Sun,* 15, 91, 109, 112, 114, 119, 120, 121, 143, 153, 157, 225, 227, 228, 233, 234, 235, 263, 279, 398, 415, 425, 430, 431, 432, 447, 505, 549, 571, 578
New York *Sunday American,* 169, 418
New York *Sunday News,* 291

New York *Sunday World*, 17, 20, 57,
86, 87, 88, 93, 95, 175, 177, 178, 202,
223, 336, 389, 393, 430, 434, 435
New York *Telegram*, 91, 104, 167,
192, 194, 219, 235, 236, 256, 259, 312,
355, 356, 381, 394, 434
New York *Telegraph*, 227, 304
New York *Times*, 25, 35, 44, 46, 47,
70, 129, 136, 145, 147, 149, 150, 151,
152, 153, 154, 157, 159, 160, 161, 163,
164, 168, 176, 239, 245, 259, 275, 276,
277, 279, 327, 329, 332, 341, 342, 344,
365, 367, 368, 369, 371, 372, 389, 434,
437, 440, 442, 446, 447, 450, 456, 471,
543, 550, 555, 557, 568, 569, 584
New York *Tribune*, 15, 16, 36, 44,
86, 113, 120, 121, 122, 123, 124, 125,
126, 129, 136, 137, 138, 147, 150, 206,
265, 324, 325, 328, 330, 400, 401, 402,
403, 413, 442, 470, 485, 578, 585, 593
New York *World*, 7, 17, 24, 43, 44,
48, 50, 51, 52, 53, 54, 55, 56, 57, 59,
68, 69, 81, 82, 83, 87, 88, 91, 92, 93,
97, 117, 136, 143, 147, 165, 166, 167,
168, 169, 170, 171, 172, 173, 174, 175,
176, 177, 178, 179, 202, 206, 214, 222,
223, 225, 274, 330, 336, 354, 381, 384,
389, 390, 407, 431, 432, 434, 435, 443,
447, 448, 470, 471, 526, 527, 561, 562,
563, 570
New York *World-Telegram*, 174, 216,
217, 220, 223, 228, 232, 233, 352, 388,
389, 393, 395, 407, 433, 434, 435, 439,
447, 525
Niehaus, Mr., 388, 389
Nieuwe Courant, 102
Nicholas, Prince, of Rumania, 163, 228
Nicholl, Louise T., 246
Nichols, Clarina, 462
Nicholson, E. J., 592
Nicholson, Mrs. E. J., 77
Nicholson, Leonard, 592
Nicoll, De Lancy, 178
Niemeyer, Harry, 233
Niles, T. E., 100, 103
Noah's *Sunday Times*, 44
Nolan, Helen, 189-190, 298
Nordica, Madame, 448
Norris, Charles, 588
Norris, Magistrate, Jean, 351
Norris, Kathleen, 456, 588
North Carolina *New Era*, 327
Northcliffe, Lord, 88, 111
North Western Miller, 357
Norton, Allen, 165
Norton, Lucille, 472
Nyack *Evening Journal*, 236, 237

Oakland *Post-Enquirer*, 382, 466
Oakland *Tribune*, 385, 578, 589
O'Bannion, Mrs. Dion, 548
Ober, Frank Somes, 447
Ober, Mrs. Frank Somes, 447-448. *See also* Josephine Robb
Oberta, John ("Dingbat"), 162, 541
Obregon, General, 585

O'Brien, John, 191
O'Brien, J. P., 352
O'Bryan, H. J., 564
Ochs, Adolph S., 25, 149, 152, 158
O'Connor, T, P., 180
Oddbody, Ann, 14
O'Donnell, Eleanor Mary, 408
O'Donnell, John, 350
Oelrichs, Mrs. Herman, 444, 448
Ogden, Clara, 597
O'Grady, Judy *see* Monica Weadock Porter
O'Hagan, Anne, 176
O'Hare, Edward, 203
Ohl, Josiah K., 594
Older, Cora, 580
Older, Fremont, 26, 386, 465, 466, 467,
576, 577, 579, 580, 581, 582, 583, 584,
585, 586, 587
Olds, Jessie Goulds, 472-473
Omaha *Bee*, 279
Omaha *Daily News*, 346, 561
Omaha *News*, 358
Omaha *World-Herald*, 233, 551, 561
O'Malley, Frank Ward, 119, 236
O'Reilly, Nan, 470-471
Orpet, Will, 418
Orr, Flora, 358-359
Otto, Crown Prince, 363
O'Toole, Francis T., 252
O'Toole, John L., 160
Oulahan, Richard V., 344
Owen, Janet, 470
Owen, Russell, 119
Owen, Ruth Bryan, 510

Packer, Alfred, 563
Paderewski, 495, 557, 578
Palm Beach *Post*, 245
Palmer, Mrs. A. M., 426
Palmer, Frederick, 426
Palmer, Gretta, 177, 433-434
Palmer, Paul, 431, 434
Pankhurst, Christabel, 115, 554
Pankhurst, Mrs. Emmeline, 114, 115,
123, 535, 554
Paris, Count of, 376
Paris *Herald*, 256
Paris (Missouri) *Mercury*, 255
Paris *Times*, 223
Parker, Dan, 304
Parker, Sir Gilbert, 95
Parker, Gilman, 302
Parker, H. T., 485
Parker, Theodore, 481
Parkes, Gladys Mae, 248, 249, 512
Parkhurst, Dr. Charles H., 51, 153
Parkhurst, Mrs. Charles H., 87
Parkhurst, Genevieve, 588
Parrott, Lindsay, 165
Parrott, Ursula, 303
Parsons, Louella, 258, 410-411, 415
Parsons, Mrs. Mary L., 525-526
Pasadena *Star*, 589
Patek, Alfred, 417
Paterson, Mrs. Isabel M., 405-407

Patterson, Ada, 22, 65, 66, 67-73, 124, 409
Patterson, Alicia, 505
Patterson, C. Stuart, Jr., 519
Patterson, Mrs. Eleanor Medill, 5, 445, 446, 501-505
Patterson, Ethel Lloyd, 124
Patterson, Captain Joseph M., 24, 271, 276, 414, 428, 452, 502, 505, 542
Patterson, Josephine, 505
Patterson, Nan, 70, 74
Patterson, Raymond A., 342
Patti, Adelina, 495
Pattullo, George, 377
Paul, Alice, 115, 124, 236
Paul, Brady, 560
Paul, Maury, 444
Paul Pry, 27, 29, 30, 37
Payne, George Henry, 101
Payne, Kenneth Wilcox, 554
Payne, Philip A., 208, 230, 232, 262, 263, 264, 265, 266, 277, 278, 282, 284, 286, 287, 303, 304
Payne, Seymour C., 553
Payne, Winona Wilcox, 553-554
Peacox, Dolly, 247
Peacox, Earle, 167, 247, 248
Peat, Leslie, 85
Peattie, Donald Culross, 551
Peattie, Mrs. Elia Wilkinson, 551
Peattie, Ralph Burns, 551
Peck, Robert B., 186
Pedlow, Captain James, 362, 363
Peggy of the Klint Hills, 461
Pegler, Arthur James, 574
Pegler, Westbrook, 261, 270, 574
Pelswick, Rose, 415
Penfield, Virginia, 516
Penny Press, 553
People's Tribune (Hankow), 588
Perkerson, Angus, 595
Perkerson, Mrs. Medora Field, 595
Perkins, Frances, 219, 318, 353, 356, 357
Perrin, Dwight S., 212
Pershing, General John J., 111, 170, 450, 487
Petersen, Agnes J., 475-476
Peyser, Ethel, 123
Phelps, Edward R., 51
Phelps, Grace, 182-183
Philadelphia *Bulletin*, 453, 516, 517
Philadelphia *Evening Bulletin*, 437, 454, 514, 518
Philadelphia *Evening Ledger*, 513
Philadelphia *Evening Telegraph*, 327, 513
Philadelphia *Inquirer*, 515, 517, 518
Philadelphia *Ledger*, 78, 246, 259, 511, 513, 514, 517, 518, 525
Philadelphia *North American*, 183, 515, 517, 518, 527
Philadelphia *Press*, 183, 326, 424, 454
Philadelphia *Public Ledger*, 361, 362, 365, 437

Philadelphia *Record*, 85, 426, 518, 519, 520
Phillips, Bessie I., 446-447
Phillips, Clara, 252, 549
Phillips, Joseph B., 373, 375
Phillips, Osmond, 157
Phillips, Ruth, 304
Pickett, Mrs. Sallie V. H., 446
Pickford, Mary, 174, 190, 252, 411, 419, 492, 560
Pierce, Madeline, 122
Pillsbury, Elinor, 472, 474
Pilsudski, 364
Pipp, E. G., 108, 535
Pirandello, 369
Pitts, Alice Fox, 509
Pitts, Frederic C., 509
Pittsburg (Kansas) *Sun*, 350
Pittsburgh *Commercial Journal*, 324
Pittsburgh *Dispatch*, 49
Pittsburgh *Gazette*, 560
Pittsburgh *Post Gazette*, 548
Pittsburgh *Press*, 561
Pittsburgh *Saturday Visiter*, 324
Pius XI, Pope, 153, 447
Place, Martha, 72
Plancon, 495
Plummer, Mary Elizabeth, 209-210
Poe, Edgar Allan, 482, 507
Poe, Elizabeth Ellicott, 507
Poincaré, Madame, 514
Poitevant, Eliza Jane, 591
Pollock, Mrs. Channing, *see* Anna Marble
Polly Pry, 564
Pomeroy, Jessie, 484
Ponselle, Rosa, 510
Ponzi, Charles, 486
Porter, Monica Weadock, 537
Portland *Evening News*, 348
Portland *News*, 474
Portland *News-Telegram*, 472, 473
Portland *Oregonian*, 371, 409
Portland *Oregon Journal*, 472
Portland *Press*, 95, 527
Portland *Press-Herald*, 335
Portland *Telegram*, 472
Post, C. W., 205
Post, Emily, 81
Post, Governor Regis, 335
Post, Wiley, 293, 473
Potter, Bishop Henry Cadman, 155
Potter, Hester, 460, 461
Potter, Mrs. James Brown, 419
Potts, Helen, 178
Poughkeepsie *Star*, 194
Powell, George Edmond, 574
Powell, Mrs. Minna K., 517, 572-575
Pratt, Margaret, 175
Preston, Mrs. A. L., 463
Pride, Jane, 485
Prim, Mary Elizabeth, 483, 485-486
Prince, Dr. Walter, 200
Pringle, Henry, 168
Prisk, Charles H., 589
Prohme, Rayna, 377, 378, 588

Prohme, William F., 378, 588
Prophet, Mrs. Clara Grace, 515, 516
Providence *News*, 238
Provines, June, 397-398
Pry, Polly, 59, 421, 562-564
Pueblo Chieftain, 548
Puerto Rico *La Democracia*, 320
Pulitzer, Albert, 444
Pulitzer, Herbert, 583
Pulitzer, Joseph, 9, 14, 17, 24, 48, 50, 52, 82, 88, 107, 165, 443, 470, 476
Pulitzer, Joseph, Jr., 233
Pulver, Percy, 470, 471
Puritan Recorder, 40
Putnam, Mrs. Nina Wilcox, 432
Pyle, Howard, 417

Quigg, Lemuel Eli, 425, 426

Raft, George, 299
Rainey, Congressman, 565
Rainey, Jack, 470
Raizen, Mrs. Lillian S., 200
Rand, Sally, 560
Randolph, Nancy, *see* Inez Callaway
Raphael, Ruth, 435
Rappe, Virginia, 221
Rascoe, Burton, 407, 546
Raskob, John J., 176, 202, 208
Rasputin, 111
Ray, Jimmy, 513
Raymond, Henry J., 46, 47, 147
Raymond, Mary, 597
Read, Elizabeth K., 514-515
Reading *Telegram and News-Times*, 414
Reardon, Jim, 488
Recorder, 17
Red Lake Falls *Gazette*, 398
Redden, Laura Catherine, 332
Reed, James A., 568
Reed, John, 378, 565
Reeve, Jay Frederick, 505
Reick, William C., 157
Reid, Clementine, 37
Reid, Mayne, 343
Reid, Ogden, 25, 123, 135, 136, 138, 139, 140, 469
Reid, Mrs. Ogden, 25, 135-141, 458, 459, 469
Reid, Wallace, 252
Reid, Whitelaw, 140, 330
Reid, Mrs. Whitelaw, 136, 138, 140
Reilly, Edward G., 200
Remington, Charles, 588
Renaud, Ralph E., 584, 588
Renfrew, Baron, 281, 284. *See also* Prince of Wales
Revell, Nellie, 256-257
Rex, Margery, 198, 199. *See also* Julia McCarthy
Reynolds, Ruth, 291-292
Rhéa, 495
Rhinelander, Alice, 279
Rhinelander, Kipp, 279
Rhodes, June, 374

Rhys-Herbert, Dr. W., 573
Ricasoli, Baron, 146
Rice, Grantland, 469
Rich, Corinne, 213
Richards, Mrs. George, 309
Richards, William B., 482
Richardson, Mrs. Anna Steese, 561
Richardson, Dorothy, 260, 551
Rickenbacker, Eddie, 199
Rigby, Cora, 314, 332-334, 335
Rigby, Judge William L., 333
Riley, James Whitcomb, 573
Rinehart, Mary Roberts, 194
Ring, Priscilla, 371, 376
Riordan, Madeleine, 446
Ripka, Frank, 519
Rittenhouse, Anne, 426, 437
Rix, Alice, 578
Robb, Charles, 448
Robb, Mrs. J. Addison, *see* Inez Callaway
Robb, John, 448
Robb, Joseph Watkins, 448
Robb, Josephine, 176, 447
Robbins, Dean Howard Chandler, 159
Robbins, James, 390
Robertson, Dr. John D., 429
Robinson, Edward G., 447
Robinson, Elsie, 384-386
Robinson, Grace, 7, 270-280, 291
Robinson, Richard P., 15
Robinson, Selma, 125
Rochester *Democrat*, 435
Rochester *Post-Express*, 526
Rockefeller, John D., 214, 565, 566
Rockefeller, John D., Jr., 157, 551
Rockefeller, John D., 3d, 173
Rockefeller, Percy, 450
Rockefeller, Winifred, 450
Rockne, Knute, 207
Rodgers, Viola, 124
Rodin, 370
Roe, Dorothy, 214-215
Rogers, Earl, 251
Rogers, Will, 257, 293, 473
Rohe, Alice, 368-370
Rohe, Margaret, 370
Roosevelt Alice, 259, 311. *See also* Mrs. Nicholas Longworth
Roosevelt, Franklin D., 157, 194, 208, 276, 277, 316, 317, 318, 319, 350, 352, 357, 375
Roosevelt, Mrs. Franklin D., 9, 81, 122, 125, 142, 208, 209, 277, 309, 310, 311, 312, 313, 314, 315, 316, 317, 318, 319, 320, 321, 322, 337, 343, 347, 350, 353, 391, 458, 538, 542
Roosevelt, Theodore, 113, 143, 311, 497, 521, 525, 555
Roosevelt, Mrs. Theodore, 311
Rosenbaum, Belle, 404
Rosenthal, Herman, 69
Rosenthal, Mrs. Lillian, 69, 70
Ross, Harold, 152, 434
Ross, Ivy, 444, 447
Ross, John Cooper, 544

Ross, Mary, 128, 171
Rothschild, Julie, 373
Rothstein, Arnold, 188, 351
Rowland, Helen, 99, 104, 379-381
Rowland, Lee, 380
Roxburghe, Duke of, 444
Royall, Anne, 27, 28-30, 38, 324, 594
Ruef, Abe, 581
Rumely, Dr. Edward A., 101, 115
Runyon, Damon, 270
Russell, Lillian, 257, 430

Sabetha, *Herald*, 459, 460
Sabin, Mrs. Charles A., 252
Sacramento *Bee*, 340
Sacramento *Star*, 339, 340
St. Cloud *Visiter*, 325
St. John, Vincent, 563
St. Johns, Adela Rogers, 251-253
St. Johns, "Ike," 252
St. Louis *Chronicle*, 535
St. Louis *Globe*, 332
St. Louis *Globe Democrat*, 546
St. Louis *Post-Dispatch*, 212, 233, 234, 434, 555, 556
St. Louis *Republic*, 68
St. Louis *Republican*, 332
St. Louis *Times*, 327, 348
St. Paul *Daily News*, 358
St. Paul *Dispatch*, 556, 573
St. Paul *Globe*, 327
St. Paul *Pioneer Press*, 557
Salt Lake City *Telegram*, 589
Salt Lake *Telegram*, 549
Salt Lake *Tribune*, 224, 425
Saltis, Polack Joe, 162
Sampedro, Senorita Edelmire, 376
Samuels, Rae, 560
San Antonio *Evening News*, 550
San Antonio *Express*, 226, 227
Sanderson, Jean, *see* Nan O'Reilly
San Diego *Standard Union*, 457, 559
San Diego *Sun*, 435
San Francisco *Bulletin*, 26, 382, 474, 582-587
San Francisco *Call*, 26, 386, 577, 586, 587, 588
San Francisco *Call-Bulletin*, 457, 466
San Francisco *Chronicle*, 6, 65, 221, 224, 297, 346, 455, 456, 457, 577, 578, 579, 584, 587, 589
San Francisco *Examiner*, 6, 7, 61, 62, 190, 422, 456, 457, 576, 577, 586, 587, 588
San Francisco *News*, 217, 340, 382, 456, 584, 586, 588
Sanger, Margaret, 171
Santanelli, 553
Sargent, Julia Amanda, *see* Mrs. Minnie Lee Wood
Sarnoff, David, 254
Sartain, Geraldine, 220-224
Sauerwein, Jules, 372
Sauk Rapids *Frontiersman*, 558
Sauk Rapids *Sentinel*, 558
Saunders, Hortense, 435-436

Savage, Clara, 245
Savannah *News*, 597
Savell, Morton, 237
Sayre, Joel, 176
Scarborough, Harold E., 500
Scarborough, Katherine, 498-500
Scheide, Mrs. Malvina, 317, 319, 322
Schiff, Frances, 212
Schlesinger, Elmer, 504
Schoemmell, Lottie, 189
Schroeder, Irene, 560
Schultz, Sigrid, 365, 376-377
Schumann-Heink, Madame, 448, 473, 555, 572, 597
Schupack, May, 517-518
Schwab, Mrs. Charles M., 390
Schwalbe, Willie, 518
Schwartzkoff, Colonel Norman H., 203
Schwimmer, Rosika, 105, 106
Scott, Mrs. Mary Lord, 444
Scotti, 555
Scripps, E. W., 553
Scripps, Ellen Browning, 534-535
Scripps, James E., 534
Seaman, Robert L., 57
Searing, Edward W., 332
Seattle *Daily Call*, 378
Seattle *Post-Intelligencer*, 549
Seeley, Evelyn, 216-220
Seibold, Louis, 569, 570
Seibold, Martin, 570
Seldes, George, 377
Sembrich, Madame, 495, 573
Serge, Grand Duchess, 110, 111
Seydell, Mildred, 595-596
Seydell, Paul, 596
Shaffer, John C., 564, 301, 302
Shanghai *China Press*, 222, 230, 231, 381, 383
Shanghai *Evening Star*, 230
Shanghai *North China Daily News*, 223
Shaplen, Joseph E., 365
Shaw, Dr. Anna Howard, 122, 123, 524
Shaw, George Bernard, 97, 448
Sheean, Vincent, 223, 378
Sheffield, James R., 99
Shek, Madame Chiang Kai, 174
Shepherd, William D., 544
Sheridan, Clare, 377
Sherman, Stuart, 403, 404
Shipman, Clare, 557-558
Shuler, Evelyn, 246, 511-514
Shuler, Marjorie, 130-131
Shumate, Dorothy, 355
Siam, King of, 140, 228, 314, 345
Sifton, Paul, 177, 507
Sigall, Josef, 390
Sigourney, Mrs., 15
Silbermann, Magistrate Jesse, 351
Silverman, Sime, 415
Simmons, Eleanor Booth, 119-122, 123, 124

Simms, Mrs. Ruth Hanna McCormick, 505. *See also* Mrs. Ruth Hanna Mc-Cormick
Simpson, Senator Alexander, 170
Sims, Admiral, 343
Sinclair, Harry, 446
Sinclair, May, 98
Sinclair, Upton, 565
Singer, Caroline, 580, 585-586
Skolsky, Sidney, 395
Skridlova, Marie, 110
Slesinger, Tess, 438
Slott, Molly, 292-293
Smith, Alfred E., 125, 166, 194, 202, 208, 213, 344, 374, 392, 451, 462, 525
Smith, Mrs. Alfred E., 125, 172
Smith, Ballard, 178, 179
Smith, Mrs. Beverly, *see* Grace Cutler
Smith, C. Harold, 390, 391
Smith, Elisabeth, 235-236
Smith, F. Hopkinson, 573
Smith, Frances St. John, 189
Smith, Helena Huntington, 168
Smith, Colonel Nicholas, 93
Smith, Mrs. Y. Kenley, 544
Smits, Janette, 247
Snead, Austine, 327
Snead, Mrs. F. C., 327
Snead, Nell, 571-572
Snow, Mary, 528
Snyder, Milton, 123
Snyder, Ruth, 72, 193, 198, 232, 267, 278, 288, 418
Solano, Solita, 125, 485
Sopher brothers, 222
Sophia, Queen, of Greece, 487
Sorel, Cecile, 429
Southwest American, 545, 598
Spain, Mildred, 414
Sparkes, Boyden, 265
Spencer, Dr. M. L., 205
Spewack, Sam, 176
Spillane, Richard J., 63, 99, 100
Spiro, Amster, 242
Spitzer, Antoinette, 190
Spitzer, Marian, 259-260
Splivaloo, Rheba Crawford, 216
Springfield *Journal*, 257
Springfield *Republican*, 598
Springfield *Union*, 175
Spurgeon, John J., 513
Stalin, 362
Stallings, Laurence, 447
Standard, 326
Stanley, Henry, 64
Stanley, Imogene, 281, 282-290
Stanley, May, 559
Stanton, Eleanor, 227
Stanton, Elizabeth Cady, 112, 426
Star, 21
Starkey, Jennie O., 536
Stars and Stripes, 152, 586
Stearns, Mrs. Frank, 313
Steffens, Lincoln, 209, 378, 553
Stege, Captain John, 550
Stein, Gertrude, 22, 484

Steinway, Mrs. Theodore, 391
Stephens, James, 200
Stephenson, Bess, 597
Sterling, George, 587
Stern, J. David, 78
Steuer, Max, 167
Stevens, Willie, 265, 277, 278
Stevenson, Fay, 176
Stevenson, Robert Louis, 587
Stevenson, Mrs. Robert Louis, 82
Stewart, Kenneth, 217
Stewart, Paul, 447
Steyskal, Irene, 544
Stiles, Mrs. Kent B., *see* Elizabeth Forman
Stillman, Anne, 201
Stillman, Bud, 218
Stillman, James, 201
Stillman, Mrs. James A., 184, 185, 201, 218, 219, 419
Stimson, Secretary Henry L., 373
Stinson, Eddie, 547
Stires, Dr. Ernest M., 159, 160, 195
Stoddard, Henry L., 100, 101, 103
Stokes, Rose Pastor, 354, 571
Stone, Fred, 257
Stone, Lucy, 1
Stone, Olivia, 186, 200
Stong, Phil, 177
Stopa, Wanda, 544
Story, Mrs. William Cummings, 521
Stowe, Harriet Beecher, 32, 329
Stowe, Leland, 372
Strachey, Lytton, 404
Straton, Dr. John Roach, 213
Straton, Mrs. John Roach, 213
Straus, Nathan. 83
Strayer, Martha, 510
Streseman, Chancellor Gustave, 365
Stretz, Vera, 252
Strong, Anna Louise, 377, 378
Strong, Austin, 587
Strong, Betsy, 587, 588
Strong, Joe, 587
Stuyvesant, Ruth, 438
Suffolk, Earl of, 70
Sullivan, Frank, 235
Sullivan, Jack "Twin," 568
Sullivan, Margaret, 20, 551, 554
Sullivan, Mark, 446
Sullivan, Mike "Twin," 568
Sullivan, Mollie E., 525
Sullivan, Sydney, 446
Sullivan, Vinnie, 169
Sulzer, Governor, 264, 265
Sutro, Mrs. Oscar, Jr., 457
Svasti, Princess, 314
Swain, Howard, 508
Sweet, Ada C., 61
Sweet, Colonel B. J., 61
Swiney, Colonel William S., 296
Swisshelm, Mrs. Jane, 16, 323-326, 336, 558
Switzer, Marguerite Birdelle, 552-553
Swope, Chrisman, 568

Swope, Herbert Bayard, 171, 175, 176, 177, 202, 381, 471
Swope, Colonel Thomas H., 568
Syracuse *Herald*, 229, 525, 526, 527
Syracuse *Post-Standard*, 527
Syracuse *Standard*, 527
Szechenyi, Count, 444
Szold, Bernadine, 265, 266

Taaffe, Agnes, 559
Taaffe, Lillian, 559
Tad, 419, 423
Taft, Mary, 149, 150-151, 152
Taft, William Howard, 279, 343, 455, 527, 528, 535, 559
Taft, Mrs. William Howard, 88, 312
Talley, Marion, 219, 220, 254, 572, 573
Talmey, Allene, 176-177
Tammen, Harry T., 417, 420, 421, 505, 562, 563, 566, 567, 568, 570
Tanguay, Eva, 257
Tarbell, Ida M., 98, 359
Taylor, Alva, 395-397
Taylor, Bert L., 395, 398, 554
Taylor, Davidson, 210
Taylor, Deems, 447
Taylor, Governor William S., 64
Tazelaar, Marguerite, 415
Tchicherin, 583
Teazle, Lady, *see* Mrs. Marshall Darrach
Teichner, Miriam, 105-108, 128, 535
Tennal, Mrs. Margie, 459
Tennal, Ralph, 460
Tennal, William, 460
Ternani, 555
Terranova, Ciro, 508
Terranova, Mrs. Ciro, 508
Terrett, Brick, 198
Terrington, Lady, 195, 296
Terrington, Lord, 296
Tessandier, Madame Aimée, 509
Teters, Lou Ellen, 392
Teters, Colonel Wilbert Barton, 388
Tetrazzini, Madame, 456
Thackeray, William Makepeace, 93, 329
Thaw, Evelyn Nesbit, 22, 65, 74, 89, 90, 91, 416
Thaw, Harry K., 65, 74, 268, 416
Thayer, Molly, 444
Thirer, Irene, 415
This Week, 141
Thomas, Clara Chaplin, 398-399
Thomas, Sir Godfrey, 285
Thompson, Clad, 461
Thompson, C. V. R., 246
Thompson, Dorothy, 4, 130, 360-366, 367, 377, 458, 553
Thompson, Harlan, 260
Thompson, Norah, 373
Thompson, Mrs. Tom, 461
Thomson, "Wild Bill," 205
Thornton *Hustler*, 348
Tierney, Justice John M., 451
Tighe, Dixie, 245-246, 511

Tighe, Josephine, 245
Tighe, Colonel Matthew F., 245
Tilton, Theodore, 32, 33, 34
Timothy, Elizabeth, 37
Tinee, Mae, 410, 411-412, 414
Tinney, Frank, 257
Toledo *Blade*, 468
Tomara, Sonia, 372-373, 377
Tomlinson, H. M., 404
Topeka, *Capital*, 461
Topeka *Daily Capital*, 543
Topeka *Daily Commonwealth*, 331
Toronto *Daily News*, 558
Toronto *Telegram*, 275
Touhy, Roger, 549, 550
Townsend, Mrs. Rosina, 15
Tracy, Morris, 218
Trans, Peter, 248
Treadwell, Sophie, 124, 377, 580, 583-585, 588
Trine, Ralph Waldo, 379
Trollope, Anthony, 36
Trotter, General Gerald F., 284, 285, 286
Trotzky, 583
Tully, Richard Walton, 588
Tulsa *Daily World*, 452
Tumulty, Joseph P., 445
Tunney, Gene, 193
Turner, Benjamin H., 530
Turner, Frances, 471-472
Turner, Ralph, 551
Twain, Mark, 88, 143, 254, 495, 557

Underhill, Harriette, 410, 412-413, 470
Underhill, Lorenzo, 412
Underwood, Sophie Kerr, 560
Urbas, Anna, 188
Urner, Mabel Herbert, 465
Utley, Uldine, 213

Valentino, Rudolph, 304, 411, 548
Valesh, Eva McDonald, 327, 332
Valleau, Christine, 123
Vallee, Rudy, 492
Van Anda, Carr V., 25, 149, 151, 279, 367
Van Clief, Eugene, 298
Vanderbilt, Mrs. Alice Gwynne, 195
Vanderbilt, Commodore, 31, 145, 148
Vanderbilt, Consuelo, 444
Vanderbilt, Cornelius, 449
Vanderbilt, Mrs. Cornelius, 449
Vanderbilt, Cornelius, Jr., 235
Vanderbilt, Gladys, 444
Vanderbilt, Gloria Morgan, 195, 196
Vanderbilt, William H., 551
Vanderbilt, William K., 449
Van Doren, Irita, 139, 403-404
Van Duzer, Winifred, 213, 214
Van Loan, Charles E., 251
van Rensselaer, Alexander, 454
Van Zetten, Vrouw, 102
Vardon, Harry, 448
Verne, Jules, 54, 56
Vernon, Jean, 247

Victor Emmanuel, King, of Italy, 145, 146, 147, 149
Victoria, Queen, 36, 46, 86, 160, 257
Victoria, Queen, of Spain, 375
Vienna *News*, 596
Villa, Pancho, 193, 497, 564, 585
Villard, Mrs. Henry, 122
Villard, Oswald Garrison, 113
Vinson, Maribel, 471
Virubova, Anna Alexandrovna, 111
Visconti, 211
Vitray, Laura, 472, 507-509
Von Frankenberg, Arthur, 396
von Hengelmuller, Baroness, 449
von Luckner, Count Felix, 186
Von Weigand, Karl, 205, 512
Voorhees, John R., 208
Vorse, Mary Heaton, 89, 378

Wald, Lillian D., 121
Waldman, Seymour, 352, 354
Waldorf, Wilella, 409
Wales, Prince of, 199, 281, 282, 283, 284, 286, 287, 290, 345, 396
Walker, James J., 208, 243, 245, 269, 272, 273, 351, 392
Walker, Stanley, 424
Wallace, Mrs. E. D., 327
Walpole, Hugh, 404, 452
Walsh, Frank P., 568
Walsh, Monica, 142
Walsh, Thomas F., 449
Walter, Cornelia Wells, 481
Walter, Karl, 574
Walter, Lynde M., 481-482
Walton, Mrs. Austin, *see* Mrs. Marshall Darrach
Walton, Francis A., 456
Walton, Marie L., 588
Walton, Robert, 599
Ward, Fanny B., 332
Ward, Josiah, 301, 417, 421, 424, 567
Wardman, Emil, 425
Warren, Carl, 295
Warren *Tribune Chronicle*, 463
Washburn, Mrs. Carrie, 454
Washington *Chronicle*, 326
Washington *Daily News*, 287, 288, 510
Washington *Herald*, 5, 245, 319, 355, 445, 446, 501, 502, 504, 505
Washington *National Era*, 327
Washington *News*, 336
Washington *Post*, 84, 142, 356, 375, 380, 445, 446, 501, 503, 505, 506, 507, 508, 509, 510
Washington *Star*, 446
Washington *Times*, 245, 359, 445, 446
Watkins, Maurine, 161, 418, 544
Watson, Victor, 184, 187, 415
Watts, Mary, 431-432
Wayne, "Pinky," 59, 389, 562, 564-566
Weaver, John V. A., 546
Webb, Fay, 492
Webb, Herbert, 230, 231
Webb, Nellie, 460
Webber, Kate S., 545

Webster, Daniel, 323, 324
Webster, Henry Kitchell, 414
Weekes, Mrs. Marie, 463-464
Wehncke, Mrs. Martin H., *see* Evangeline Cole
Weick, Louise, 456-457
Weinstein, Gregory, 583
Weiss, Sue, 518
Weiss, William, 518, 519
Weitzenkorn, Louis, 177, 223, 389, 507, 508
Welch, Mrs. Philip, 150
Welch, Robert, 151
Weldon, Mrs. Marie Louise, 447
Wells, Evelyn, 580
Wells, H. G., 95, 97, 98
Wells, Major W. H., 191, 192, 193
Welshimer, Helen, 435
Wendel, Ella, 220, 223, 293, 294
Wentworth, James, 482
Wessels, Florence, 190
West, Clyde, 189
West, Julia, *see* Julia McCarthy
West, Mae, 245
West, Rebecca, 120, 121, 404
Wetmore, Mrs. Charles W., 592. *See also* Elizabeth Bisland
Wetmore, Maude, 594
Whalen, Grover A., 166, 245, 508
Wheaton, Anne, 524-525
Wheaton, Warren, 525
Wheeler, Post, 426
Whipple, Sydney, 192
Whitaker, Alma, 588
Whitaker, John T., 372
Whitaker, Norman T., 507
White, A. T. (Bluebeard), 560
White, Howard, 447
White, Lucy, 581
White, Martin A., 208, 468
White, Pearl, 576
White, Stamford, 90
Whiteman, Paul, 254, 256, 285
Whiting, Lilian, 483
Whiting, L. O., 483
Whitla, Billy, 561
Whitman, Charles S., 69, 70, 183
Whitmire, Ethel, 457
Whittier, John Greenleaf, 329
Wichita *Beacon*, 357
Wichita *Democrat*, 458, 459
Wichita *Jibber-Jab*, 458
Wichita *Mirror*, 458
Wichita *Saturday Review*, 458
Wickham, Harvey, 588
Wiese, Otto, 213
Wilcox, Ella Wheeler, 21, 88
Wilcox, Grafton, 342
Wilcox, John, 553
Wilcox, Mrs. Molly Warren, 458, 459
Wilde, Annie, 456, 588
Wilhelm, Kaiser, 102, 103, 376
Wilhelmina, Queen, of Holland, 88
Willard, Frances, 553
Willard, Jess, 181, 193
Williams, Florence, 151

Williams, Fred V., 217
Williams, Harold, 516
Williams, Mary Brush, 438
Williams, T. Walter, 159
Williams, Talcott, 181
Williams, Dean Walter, 214
Williams, Wythe, 362
Williamson, Margaret. 334
Willis, N. P., 324, 591
Willis, Sara Payson, *see* Fanny Fern
Wills, Helen, 469
Wilson, Mrs. Bess M., 558-559
Wilson, Lena Viola, 218
Wilson, Louisa, 171-174
Wilson, McLandburgh, 398
Wilson, Woodrow, 115, 120, 124, 156, 211, 312, 445
Wilson, Mrs. Woodrow, 88
Wilson, Vylla Poe, 507
Winchell, Walter, 397, 415
Windle, Mary J., 326
Wink, Josh, *see* Louise Malloy
Winkler, John K., 183
Winn, Marcia, 544, 546-547
Winn, Mary Day, 141
Winslow, Helen M., 483-484
Winslow, Henry Field, 329
Winslow, Thyra Samter, 545-546
Winterich, John T., 152
Winthrop, Patience, 20
Wisconsin *News*, 292, 560
Wodehouse, P. G., 141
Woelfkin, Dr. Cornelius, 157
Wohlforth, Robert, 248, 249, 251
Wolfe, James, 83
Woman, 14
Woman's Home Journal, 17
Women's Wear, 439
Wood, Delacey, 558
Wood, Jessie, 424
Wood, Lee, 434
Wood, Minnie Lee, 558

Wood, Prunella, 438-439
Woodford, William, 172
Woodhull, Dr. Canning, 31
Woodhull, Victoria, 27, 28, 30-36, 38
Woodhull and Claflin's Weekly, 27, 31, 37
Woods, Mrs. William, 255
Woodward, Emily, 596-597
Wooley, Edna K., 554-555
Woolf, Virginia, 404
Woollcott, Alexander, 121, 152, 447
Woolley, Edward Mott, 554
Worden, Charles George, 388
Worden, Helen, 177, 387-393, 396
Wright, Frank Lloyd, 161, 397
Wright, Katherine, 485
Wynekoop, Dr. Alice Lindsay, 549, 550
Wynne, Dr. Shirley, 295

Xenia, Princess, 160

Yale, Frankie, 202
Yates, Mary, 249, 250
Yates, Roberta, 291
Yeats, William Butler, 573
York, Mrs. A. M., 527
Yorke, Selina, 438
Young, Caesar, 70
Young, Mrs. Elizabeth Reardon, 84
Young, Marguerite, 332, 352-354
Young, Owen D., 141, 254
Young, Stark, 550
Young, Mrs. Waldemar, *see* Betsy Strong
Youngman, Anna, 509
Youngstown *Telegram*, 559 560

Zander, Harry Richard, 292
Ziegfeld, Flo, 419
Zita, Princess, 256, 363
Zuloaga, 439

Women in America

FROM COLONIAL TIMES TO THE 20TH CENTURY

An Arno Press Collection

Andrews, John B. and W. D. P. Bliss. **History of Women in Trade Unions** (*Report on Conditions of Woman and Child Wage-Earners in the United States,* Vol. X; 61st Congress, 2nd Session, Senate Document No. 645). 1911

Anthony, Susan B. **An Account of the Proceedings on the Trial of Susan B. Anthony, on the Charge of Illegal Voting at the Presidential Election in November, 1872,** and on the Trial of Beverly W. Jones, Edwin T. Marsh and William B. Hall, the Inspectors of Election by Whom her Vote was Received. 1874

The Autobiography of a Happy Woman. 1915

Ayer, Harriet Hubbard. **Harriet Hubbard Ayer's Book:** A Complete and Authentic Treatise on the Laws of Health and Beauty. 1902

Barrett, Kate Waller. **Some Practical Suggestions on the Conduct of a Rescue Home.** *Including* **Life of Dr. Kate Waller Barrett** (Reprinted from *Fifty Years' Work With Girls* by Otto Wilson). [1903]

Bates, Mrs. D. B. **Incidents on Land and Water;** Or, Four Years on the Pacific Coast. 1858

Blumenthal, Walter Hart. **Women Camp Followers of the American Revolution.** 1952

Boothe, Viva B., editor. **Women in the Modern World** (*The Annals of the American Academy of Political and Social Science,* Vol. CXLIII, May 1929). 1929

Bowne, Eliza Southgate. **A Girl's Life Eighty Years Ago:** Selections from the Letters of Eliza Southgate Bowne. 1888

Brooks, Geraldine. **Dames and Daughters of Colonial Days.** 1900

Carola Woerishoffer: Her Life and Work. 1912

Clement, J[esse], editor. **Noble Deeds of American Women;** With Biographical Sketches of Some of the More Prominent. 1851

Crow, Martha Foote. **The American Country Girl.** 1915

De Leon, T[homas] C. **Belles, Beaux and Brains of the 60's.** 1909

de Wolfe, Elsie (Lady Mendl). **After All.** 1935

Dix, Dorothy (Elizabeth Meriwether Gilmer). **How to Win and Hold a Husband.** 1939

Donovan, Frances R. **The Saleslady.** 1929

Donovan, Frances R. **The Schoolma'am.** 1938

Donovan, Frances R. **The Woman Who Waits.** 1920

Eagle, Mary Kavanaugh Oldham, editor. **The Congress of Women,** Held in the Woman's Building, World's Columbian Exposition, Chicago, U.S.A., 1893. 1894

Ellet, Elizabeth F. **The Eminent and Heroic Women of America.** 1873

Ellis, Anne. **The Life of an Ordinary Woman.** 1929

[Farrar, Eliza W. R.] **The Young Lady's Friend.** By a Lady. 1836

Filene, Catherine, editor. **Careers for Women.** 1920

Finley, Ruth E. **The Lady of Godey's:** Sarah Josepha Hale. 1931 **Fragments of Autobiography.** 1974

Frost, John. **Pioneer Mothers of the West;** Or, Daring and Heroic Deeds of American Women. 1869

[Gilman], Charlotte Perkins Stetson. **In This Our World.** 1899

Goldberg, Jacob A. and Rosamond W. Goldberg. **Girls on the City Streets:** A Study of 1400 Cases of Rape. 1935

Grace H. Dodge: Her Life and Work. 1974

Greenbie, Marjorie Barstow. **My Dear Lady:** The Story of Anna Ella Carroll, the "Great Unrecognized Member of Lincoln's Cabinet." 1940

Hourwich, Andria Taylor and Gladys L. Palmer, editors. **I Am a Woman Worker:** A Scrapbook of Autobiographies. 1936

Howe, M[ark] A. De Wolfe. **Memories of a Hostess:** A Chronicle of Friendships Drawn Chiefly from the Diaries of Mrs. James T. Fields. 1922

Irwin, Inez Haynes. **Angels and Amazons:** A Hundred Years of American Women. 1934

Laughlin, Clara E. **The Work-a-Day Girl:** A Study of Some Present-Day Conditions. 1913

Lewis, Dio. **Our Girls.** 1871

Liberating the Home. 1974

Livermore, Mary A. **The Story of My Life;** Or, The Sunshine and Shadow of Seventy Years . . . To Which is Added Six of Her Most Popular Lectures. 1899

Lives to Remember. 1974

Lobsenz, Johanna. **The Older Woman in Industry.** 1929

MacLean, Annie Marion. **Wage-Earning Women.** 1910

Meginness, John F. **Biography of Frances Slocum, the Lost Sister of Wyoming:** A Complete Narrative of her Captivity of Wanderings Among the Indians. 1891

Nathan, Maud. **Once Upon a Time and Today.** 1933

[Packard, Elizabeth Parsons Ware]. **Great Disclosure of Spiritual Wickedness!!** In High Places. With an Appeal to the Government to Protect the Inalienable Rights of Married Women. 1865

Parsons, Alice Beal. **Woman's Dilemma.** 1926

Parton, James, et al. **Eminent Women of the Age:** Being Narratives of the Lives and Deeds of the Most Prominent Women of the Present Generation. 1869

Paton, Lucy Allen. **Elizabeth Cary Agassiz:** A Biography. 1919

Rayne, M[artha] L[ouise]. **What Can a Woman Do;** Or, Her Position in the Business and Literary World. 1893

Richmond, Mary E. and Fred S. Hall. **A Study of Nine Hundred and Eighty-Five Widows Known to Certain Charity Organization Societies in 1910.** 1913

Ross, Ishbel. **Ladies of the Press:** The Story of Women in Journalism by an Insider. 1936

Sex and Equality. 1974

Snyder, Charles McCool. **Dr. Mary Walker:** The Little Lady in Pants. 1962

Stow, Mrs. J. W. **Probate Confiscation:** Unjust Laws Which Govern Woman. 1878

Sumner, Helen L. **History of Women in Industry in the United**

States (*Report on Conditions of Woman and Child Wage-Earners in the United States,* Vol. IX; 61st Congress, 2nd Session, Senate Document No. 645). 1910

[Vorse, Mary H.] **Autobiography of an Elderly Woman.** 1911

Washburn, Charles. **Come into My Parlor:** A Biography of the Aristocratic Everleigh Sisters of Chicago. 1936

Women of Lowell. 1974

Woolson, Abba Gould. **Dress-Reform:** A Series of Lectures Delivered in Boston on Dress as it Affects the Health of Women. 1874

Working Girls of Cincinnati. 1974